THE BLOOMSBURY GROUP

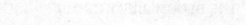

THE BLOOMSBURY GROUP

A Collection of Memoirs, Commentary and Criticism

Edited by

S. P. Rosenbaum

University of Toronto Press
Toronto and Buffalo

First published in Canada and the
United States by University of Toronto
Press, Toronto and Buffalo.

©University of Toronto Press 1975

ISBN: 0–8020–2182–4 (cloth)
       0–8020–6268–7 (paper)

Printed in Great Britain
by Redwood Burn, Trowbridge and Esher

CONTENTS

PLATES   Between pages 288–289

FOREWORD

This collection of memoirs, commentary, and criticism written by and about the members of the Bloomsbury Group is based on two assumptions, both of which have been questioned. The first assumption is that the Bloomsbury Group existed. The second is that the Group is worth studying seriously. The justification for the second assumption will be found in the essays and excerpts that follow, but before explaining their purpose and scope, it is necessary to confront the problems in definition that the existence of the Bloomsbury Group poses.

Bloomsbury, wrote E.M. Forster in 1929, 'is the only genuine *movement* in English civilization. . .'. By then its influence had been extended from fiction, biography, economics, and painting through literary, social, and art criticism to publishing and journalism. Partly as a result of its influence, Bloomsbury has been widely misunderstood as a cultural, social, and even sexual phenomenon by its friends and its enemies. The term 'Bloomsbury' has been applied in the loosest possible way to people and events that had nothing whatsoever to do with the Bloomsbury Group. The pejorative connotations of Bloomsbury (it has been described not merely as a group, set or circle, but as a clique, coterie, gang, clan, commune, and mafia – and its members have been called everything from Bloomsberries to Bloomsbuggers) have led a number of the Bloomsbury Group to deny the very existence of their Group. 'Once more I cry aloud: Who were the members of Bloomsbury? For what did they stand?' Clive Bell's challenge at the end of his 1954 essay on Bloomsbury may be unanswerable but it cannot be avoided by anyone proposing the scholarly study of the Bloomsbury Group.

The 1972 supplement to the *Oxford English Dictionary* – the most authoritative dictionary of the language – defines Bloomsbury as 'A school of writers and aesthetes living in or associated with Bloomsbury, that flourished in the early twentieth century; a member of this school.' The inadequacy of this definition illustrates nicely the problems of identifying Bloomsbury. 'Aesthetes' is a grotesquely understated classification in which to fit a renowned painter or a great art critic, and 'writers' is hardly a precise description of an economist or a political theorist. Nor was Bloomsbury ever a school. It had no body of doctrine, no code of conduct, no masters. The original and enduring basis of the Group was friendship. Because Bloomsbury cannot be said to have held any distinguishing principles in common, some critics have argued that one cannot talk of Bloomsbury's ideas, beliefs, or tastes. But this is not so. The ideas, beliefs, and tastes of the various original members of Bloomsbury, though they were not held in common, nevertheless display that overlapping and criss-crossing similarity that Wittgenstein has called a family resemblance. In art and literature, in aesthetics, epistemology and ethics, in economics and politics, in love and friendship, in celebrations and denigrations, the Bloomsbury Group displays a unique complex resemblance that cannot be reduced to a platform or creed, nor argued away because of its intricacy. What they stood for is what they were and what they did. That is why a collection of descriptions of the Bloomsbury Group's lives and works may be the only wholly satisfactory way of defining what Bloomsbury means.

The answer to Clive Bell's first question is a little easier, though not exactly straightforward. Because Bloomsbury was a circle of friends who came and went over the thirty or forty years or so that Bloomsbury flourished, it is difficult to determine just who were members and who were not. About midway in its history, however, thirteen members of what might be called the immediate family of Bloomsbury met together in 1920 to found the Memoir Club. They were to meet periodically, dine together, and read their memoirs to one another. The members of Bloomsbury were, at one time or another, involved in various clubs or societies; at Cambridge there were the Apostles, the Midnight Society, and the X Society, and later in London there were the Play-reading Society, the Friday Club, the Novel Club, and others. The importance of the Memoir Club is to be seen not only in its longevity — its last meeting was held in 1956 — but also in its purpose, which appears to confirm the shared experience of a group of old friends that was the original basis of the Bloomsbury Group. The least that can be said of the original thirteen members of the Memoir Club is that no roster of Bloomsbury ought to leave them out. According to Leonard Woolf these thirteen were identical with the thirteen members of what came to be called Old Bloomsbury. The thirteen were Virginia and Leonard Woolf, Vanessa and Clive Bell, Molly and Desmond MacCarthy, Adrian Stephen, Lytton Strachey, J.M. Keynes, Duncan Grant, E.M. Forster, Saxon Sydney-Turner, and Roger Fry. In all lists of Bloomsbury there is room for disagreement and need for qualification, however. Quentin Bell states that Adrian Stephen, the brother of Vanessa and Virginia, was not in fact a member of the Memoir Club and that Sydney Waterlow was, though he would probably not be considered a member of Old Bloomsbury. Leonard Woolf's list is, nevertheless, as reasonable a one as any that has been made of Bloomsbury's core, and I have accepted it for the purposes of this collection.

It must be emphasized that this is a minimum list of a changing group and that there are many other names that could plausibly be added to it. Edwardian Bloomsbury appears to have included, in addition to the original thirteen, H.T.J. Norton, Gerald Shove, Sydney Waterlow, and innumerable Stracheys, expecially James and Marjorie. War-time Bloomsbury saw the advent of a second generation, chief of whom was David Garnett; but also closely associated with the Group were Francis Birrell, Mary St John Hutchinson, Karin Costelloe, Barbara Hiles, Arthur Waley, Alix Sargant-Florence, Dora Carrington, and Ralph Partridge. Raymond Mortimer, George Rylands, Angus Davidson, Stephen Tomlin, Frances Marshall, Roger Senhouse, and Lydia Lopokova, among others, were all involved with Bloomsbury in one way or another during the twenties, and by the thirties the Bell children Julian, Quentin, and Angelica were active in the Group along with friends such as John Lehmann and Jane Bussy. But Bloomsbury cannot be stretched to include all the well-known contemporaries of the Group. Despite claims to the contrary, Lady Ottoline Morrell, T.S. Eliot, Bertrand Russell, Vita Sackville-West, Harold Nicolson, and the three Sitwell siblings, to take just these few, were never considered to be part of Bloomsbury, either by members of the Group or by themselves.

Death changed Bloomsbury as much as new friends did. Thoby Stephen died in 1906, Lytton Strachey in 1932, Roger Fry in 1934, and Virginia Woolf in 1941. Late in 1917 Roger Fry wrote to Vanessa Bell that Clive had proposed 'a great historical group portrait of Bloomsbury'. Fry thought he would like to try it, though perhaps Vanessa could do it better. It was left to Vanessa to paint Bloomsbury's portrait in the form of an oil sketch of the Memoir Club as it existed around 1943. The sketch is reproduced as the first plate to this collection. Seated together from left to right are Duncan Grant, Leonard Woolf, Vanessa Bell, Clive Bell, David Garnett, J.M. Keynes, Lydia Keynes, Desmond MacCarthy, Molly MacCarthy, Quentin Bell, and E.M. Forster. MacCarthy is reading a paper while the others listen. On the walls are Bloomsbury portraits of the three deceased members, Virginia Woolf, Lytton Strachey, and Roger Fry. Vaness's sketch depicts the changing nature of the Bloomsbury Group and also serves — as do the portraits of thirteen of the members of Bloomsbury by its three painters that illustrate this collection — to remind readers that in Bloomsbury the art of painting was at least as important as the art of writing.

The justification for the second basic assumption of this collection — that the Bloomsbury Group is worth studying seriously — is to be found in the memoirs, commentary, and criticism themselves. In gathering together the most important recollections of Bloomsbury and combining them with various observations, discussions, and critiques of the Group, I have tried to provide a scholarly sourcebook for a collectivity of writers, artists, critics, and political economists who have been the object of two generations of widespread interest, admiration, and abuse. Much of the contents of this collection comes from books now out of print or from the back files of periodicals. Vanessa Bell's 'Notes on Bloomsbury' and the excerpt from Saxon Sydney-Turner's letter to Virginia Woolf are published here for the first time.

The pieces of this collection are arranged under four headings. This arrangement is not rigidly exclusive, however, and there are several pieces that could easily fit in more than one section. The first section, *Bloomsbury on Bloomsbury*, contains the basic memoirs and discussions of the Group itself by twelve of its original members. These recollections range from private correspondence and journals to formal autobiographies, and they were written over a period of nearly sixty years. Here as in the sections that follow there has inevitably been a certain amount of repetition, but sometimes what appears to be merely repetitious actually reveals an interesting difference among the points of view that are to be found even at the centre of Bloomsbury. The second section is entitled *Bloomsberries*; this term of Molly MacCarthy's provides a heading under which to present a series of essays on ten members of Bloomsbury and their importance in the Group. Many of the pieces here, though not all, were also written by Bloomsberries. The third section, *Bloomsbury Observed*, contains mainly reminiscences of the Group by their contemporaries, some of whom are often considered to be members of Bloomsbury. As in the first section, these observations are arranged chronologically to suggest the growing sense of the Group's significance. Finally, some of the disputes that have surrounded Bloomsbury almost from its inception are brought together in the fourth section, which is entitled *Bloomsbury Criticisms and Controversies*. Here are selections from the most influential, articulate, or representative critics of Bloomsbury, along with some rejoinders from the Group.

The four sections are preceded by a chronological table recording the principal events in the careers of the original members of the Bloomsbury Group and followed by bibliographies of the principal works by and about individual members. After the bibliographies is a series of identifications that briefly describe the more important people and places mentioned in the text. Within each section I have tried to introduce the separate pieces in such a way as to make them as clear as possible to the reader. The particular occasions for which the pieces were written have been explained, and names alluded to have been identified when necessary. These headnotes — which are enclosed in square brackets — sometimes contain additional information and commentary on the Group by its members, observers, or critics that is not listed in the Contents; notes at the end of the volume identify the sources of this material. (A footnote number in the text refers to a note of an author or editor given at the end of the selection.) The titles of excerpts from books or essays have in most cases been supplied by the editor.

The Bloomsbury Group. A Collection of Memoirs, Commentary, and Criticism was originally begun in preparation for the writing of a literary history of the Bloomsbury Group. Though its scope now extends considerably beyond this, one of the purposes of the collection is to provide the background for such a history.

Unitersity of Toronto   SPR

v

ACKNOWLEDGEMENTS

In addition to the authors, executors, and publishers cited in the text, acknowledgement is gratefully made to the following for permission and assistance in reproducing portraits of the Bloomsbury Group: Mrs Barbara Bagenal, Mr Evert Barger, Professor Quentin Bell, His Grace the Duke of Devonshire, Mr Duncan Grant, Gallery Edward Harvane, King's College, Cambridge, The National Portrait Gallery, Mr Anthony d'Offay, Mrs Ian Parsons, and Mrs Ann Synge. I also wish to thank Dr A.N.L. Munby and the staff of the library of King's College, Cambridge, and the staff of the library of the University of Sussex.

To Mrs Bagenal and Mrs Parsons I am further indebted for permission to reproduce excerpts from unpublished writings by Saxon Sydney-Turner and Leonard Woolf. Finally, I am deeply grateful to Mrs Angelica Garnett for allowing me to print her mother's unpublished essay on Bloomsbury, and to Professor Bell, whom I have bothered in innumerable ways.

A BLOOMSBURY CHRONOLOGY

1866
Roger Fry born

1877
Desmond MacCarthy born

1879
E.M. Forster born
Vanessa Stephen born

1880
Lytton Strachey born
Thoby Stephen born
Saxon Sydney-Turner born
Leonard Woolf born

1881
Clive Bell born

1882
Virginia Stephen born
Mary Warre-Cornish born

1883
J.M. Keynes born
Adrian Stephen born

1885
Duncan Grant born
Roger Fry enters King's College, Cambridge

1888
Roger Fry obtains a First Class honours in natural sciences and decides
    to study painting

1892
Roger Fry studies painting in Paris

1893
Roger Fry's first writings on art

1894

Roger Fry gives university extension lectures at Cambridge mainly on Italian art

Desmond MacCarthy enters Trinity College, Cambridge

1895

Death of Mrs Leslie Stephen

Virginia Stephen's first breakdown

1896

Roger Fry and Helen Coombe married

1897

E.M. Forster enters King's College, Cambridge

Desmond MacCarthy leaves Trinity College

Virginia Stephen attends Greek and history classes at King's College, London

1899

Roger Fry: *Giovanni Bellini*

Clive Bell, Thoby Stephen, Lytton Strachey, Saxon Sydney-Turner, Leonard Woolf all enter Trinity College, Cambridge.

The Midnight Society — a 'reading society' — founded at Trinity by Bell, Sydney-Turner, Stephen, and Woolf

1900

Roger Fry gives university extension lectures on art at Cambridge

1901

Roger Fry becomes art critic for *The Atheneum*

Vanessa Stephen enters the Royal Academy Schools

E.M. Forster leaves Cambridge, travels in Greece and Italy, begins *A Room with a View*

1902

Duncan Grant attends the Westminster Art School

Leonard Woolf, Saxon Sydney-Turner, and Lytton Strachey elected to 'The Apostles' (older members include Roger Fry, Desmond MacCarthy, E.M. Forster)

Clive Bell does historical research in London after leaving Cambridge

Adrian Stephen enters Trinity College, Cambridge

J.M. Keynes enters King's College, Cambridge

Virginia Stephen starts private Greek lessons

1903
G.E. Moore: *Principia Ethica*

Roger Fry's first exhibition of paintings and drawings
Desmond MacCarthy writes criticism for *The Speaker*
J.M. Keynes elected to 'The Apostles'
E.M. Forster's first short story published

1904
Virginia Stephen publishes her first review
Leslie Stephen dies, and the Stephen children move to 46 Gordon
    Square, Bloomsbury
E.M. Forster acts as tutor to Countess von Arnim's children in Germany
Clive Bell lives in Paris and does historical research
Leonard Woolf leaves Cambridge, takes the Civil Service examination
    and sails for Ceylon as a cadet in the Ceylon Civil Service
Saxon Sydney-Turner leaves Cambridge and becomes a clerk in the
    Estate Duty Office
Lytton Strachey works on a fellowship dissertation
Virginia Stephen's second breakdown

1905
Euphrosyne: A Collection of Verse, with anonymous contributions by
    Clive Bell, Saxon Sydney-Turner, Leonard Woolf, and Lytton
    Strachey
Roger Fry edits *The Discourses of Sir Joshua Reynolds*
E.M. Forster: *Where Angels Fear to Tread*
Adrian Stephen leaves Trinity College
Virginia Stephen teaching at Morley College, London
Thoby Stephen begins the Thursday evenings at Gordon Square for his
    friends
Vanessa Stephen organizes The Friday Club, which is concerned with
    the arts
Lytton Strachey leaves Cambridge
J.M. Keynes bracketed Twelfth Wrangler

1906
Clive Bell reads for the bar
Desmond MacCarthy and Mary Warre-Cornish married
Roger Fry accepts curatorship of the Department of Painting, Metro-
    politan Museum of New York, and subsequently declines the
    directorship of the National Gallery in London
Duncan Grant studies art in Paris

J.M. Keynes joins the India Office
The Stephens tour Greece
Thoby Stephen dies of typhoid fever

1907
E.M. Forster: *The Longest Journey*
Desmond MacCarthy: *The Court Theatre: A Commentary and Criticism*
Vanessa Stephen and Clive Bell married
Adrian Stephen called to the bar
Duncan Grant lives in Paris after studying a term at the Slade School
Virginia and Adrian Stephen move to 29 Fitzroy Square (Thursday evenings begin again)
Virginia Stephen works on her first novel
Roger Fry in Italy with J.P. Morgan; resigns curatorship and becomes European advisor to the Metropolitan Museum
Desmond MacCarthy edits *The New Quarterly* (until 1910)
Lytton Strachey begins weekly reviews for *The Spectator* (until 1909)
Play-reading Society begun at 46 Gordon Square with the Bells, Adrian and Virginia Stephen, Strachey and Sydney-Turner; meets intermittently until 1914

1908
E.M. Forster: *A Room with a View*
Julian Bell born
Leonard Woolf becomes Assistant Government Agent, Hambantota, Ceylon
J.M. Keynes leaves the Civil Service

1909
Roger Fry: 'An Essay in Aesthetics'
Lytton Strachey proposes to Virginia Stephen
Duncan Grant moves to 21 Fitzroy Square
Roger Fry becomes editor of *The Burlington Magazine*
Lady Ottoline Morrell comes to Thursday evenings in Fitzroy Square
J.M. Keynes elected to a fellowship at King's
Saxon Sydney-Turner and Virginia and Adrian Stephen go to Bayreuth for the Wagner Festival

1910
E.M. Forster: *Howards End*
The *Dreadnought* hoax takes place
Roger Fry meets Duncan Grant, the Bells; talks to the Friday Club; is

dismissed from the Metropolitan Museum by J.P. Morgan

Helen Fry confined to a mental institution as incurably insane (dies in 1937)

Virginia Stephen doing volunteer work for women's suffrage

Lytton Strachey and Lady Ottoline Morrell meet

Quentin Bell born

First Post-Impressionist Exhibition at the Grafton Galleries organized by Roger Fry, with Desmond MacCarthy as secretary (from October to January 1911)

1911

E.M. Forster: *The Celestial Omnibus and Other Stories*; also writes 'The Heart of Bosnia', an unpublished play

Virginia Stephen leases a house at Firle, Sussex

Roger Fry declines the directorship of the Tate Gallery; starts lecturing at the Slade School.

The Bells, Fry, and later Virginia Stephen travelling in Turkey

Leonard Woolf returns from Ceylon

J.M. Keynes becomes a lecturer in economics at Cambridge

Virginia and Adrian Stephen move to 38 Brunswick Square where they share a house with Woolf, Keynes, and Grant

1912

Lytton Strachey: *Landmarks in French Literature*

E.M. Forster travels in India

J.M. Keynes becomes editor of *The Economic Journal* (until 1945)

Leonard Woolf resigns from the Colonial Service

Virginia Stephen and Leonard Woolf married; they live in Clifford's Inn, London, and at Asham House, Sussex, after travelling in France, Spain, and Italy

Second Post-Impressionist Exhibition organized by Roger Fry with Leonard Woolf as secretary (from November to February 1913)

1913

Leonard Woolf: *The Village and the Jungle*

J.M. Keynes: *Indian Currency and Finance*

E.M. Forster returns from India, begins *A Passage to India* and writes *Maurice*

Lytton Strachey finishes writing *Ermyntrude and Esmeralda*

Saxon Sydney-Turner joins the Treasury

Leonard Woolf begins reviewing for *The New Statesman* and studying the Co-operative Movement

Desmond MacCarthy becomes drama critic for *The New Statesman*
Omega workshops founded by Roger Fry with Duncan Grant as co-director
Virginia Woolf suffers another breakdown and attempts suicide
Novel Club exists for about a year

1913

Clive Bell: *Art*
Leonard Woolf: *The Wise Virgins*
Adrian Stephen and Karin Costelloe married
Desmond MacCarthy joins the Red Cross and serves in France (until 1915)
J.M. Keynes joins the Treasury
The Woolfs move to Richmond, Surrey, from Clifford's Inn

1915

Clive Bell: *Peace at Once* (ordered destroyed by the Lord Mayor of London)
Virginia Woolf: *The Voyage Out*
E.M. Forster in Alexandria with the Red Cross (until 1918)
The Woolfs move to Hogarth House, Richmond

1916

Leonard Woolf: *International Government: Two Reports*
Lytton Strachey's claim of conscientious objection to conscription is denied but he is granted exemption for medical reasons
Leonard Woolf is exempted from conscription for medical reasons
Clive Bell does alternative service on the Morrells' farm at Garsington
Vanessa Bell, her children, Duncan Grant, and David Garnett move to Wissett in Suffolk so that Garnett and Grant can do alternative service on a farm; later in the year they move to Charleston, Firle, Sussex where the Bells and Duncan Grant live permanently
J.M. Keynes and friends take over 46 Gordon Square, which remains Keynes's London home

1917

Leonard Woolf: *The Future of Constantinople*
Clive Bell: *Ad Familiares*
The Woolfs buy a printing press: *Two Stories Written and Printed by Virginia Woolf and L.S. Woolf* is publication #1 of the Hogarth Press
Leonard Woolf edits *The Framework for a Lasting Peace*; founds The 1917 Club; and becomes secretary to the Labour party advisory

committee on imperial and international questions for more than twenty years

Virginia Woolf begins keeping a regular diary

Lytton Strachey and Carrington set up housekeeping at the Mill House, Tidmarsh, Berkshire.

1918

Lytton Strachey: *Eminent Victorians*

Clive Bell: *Pot-Boilers*

Mary MacCarthy: *A Pier and a Band*

Desmond MacCarthy: *Remnants*

Leonard Woolf: *Co-operation and the Future of Industry*

Omega workshops: *Original Woodcuts by Various Artists*

Leonard Woolf becomes editor of *The International Review*

Katherine Mansfield's *The Prelude* published by the Hogarth Press

At the suggestion of Roger Fry and Duncan Grant, J.M. Keynes persuades the Treasury to purchase works of art from the Degas sale in Paris

Angelica Bell born

1919

Virginia Woolf: *Night and Day*

The Hogarth Press publishes Virginia Woolf's *Kew Gardens* and T.S. Eliot's *Poems*, but are unable to publish James Joyce's *Ulysses*, offered to them the year before

J.M. Keynes in Paris as the principal representative of the Treasury at the Peace Conference; he resigns in June and writes *The Economic Consequences of Peace* at Charleston, which is published at the end of the year

The Bells, Woolfs, Keynes, Fry, Grant *et al.* meet Diaghileff's troupe in London, including Picasso, Derain, Stravinsky, Massine, Ansermet, Nijinski, and Lydia Lopokova

Woolfs move from Asham to Monk's House, Rodmell, Sussex

Clive Bell in Paris; friendship with Derain, Braque, Dunoyer de Segonzac, Cocteau, *et al.*

Lady Strachey and daughters move to 51 Gordon Square

1920

Roger Fry: *Vision and Design*

Leonard Woolf: *Economic Imperialism* and *Empire and Commerce in Africa*

The Hogarth Press publishes Maxim Gorky's *Reminiscences of Tolstoy*,

translated by S.S. Koteliansky and Leonard Woolf, and E.M.
Forster's *The Story of the Siren*
Leonard Woolf writes leaders on foreign affairs for *The Nation* for three
months
Omega workshops close
First Meeting of the Memoir Club
Duncan Grant has his first one-man show in London
Desmond MacCarthy becomes literary editor of *The New Statesman*
(until 1927), reviews under the pen name 'Affable Hawk'
E.M. Forster becomes literary editor of the London *Daily Herald* for a
year

1921
Clive Bell: *Poems*
Virginia Woolf: *Monday or Tuesday*
Lytton Strachey: *Queen Victoria*
Roger Fry: *Twelve Original Woodcuts*
Leonard Woolf: *Stories from the East* and *Socialism and Co-operation*
J.M. Keynes: *A Treatise on Probability*
E.M. Forster in India as temporary secretary to the Maharajah of Dewas
State Senior
Virginia Woolf is ill and inactive for four months
Ralph Partridge and Carrington married

1922
Clive Bell: *Since Cézanne*
Lytton Strachey: *Books and Characters: French and English*
E.M. Forster: *Alexandria: A History and a Guide*
Virginia Woolf: *Jacob's Room*
J.M. Keynes: *A Revision of the Treaty*
Vanessa Bell and Duncan Grant decorate Keynes's rooms at King's
Leonard Woolf defeated as the Labour candidate for the Combined
University constituency

1923
Clive Bell: *On British Freedom* and *The Legend of Monte della Sibilla
or Le Paradis de la Reine Sibille*, with illustrations by Vanessa Bell
and Duncan Grant
Roger Fry: *Duncan Grant* and *A Sampler of Castile*
E.M. Forster: *Pharos and Pharillon*
J.M. Keynes: *A Tract on Monetary Reform*
The Hogarth Press publishes T.S. Eliot's *The Waste Land*

Leonard Woolf edits *Fabian Essays on Co-operation*

J.M. Keynes becomes chairman of the board of *The Nation and Atheneum*; Leonard Woolf becomes the literary editor (until 1930)

1924

E.M. Forster: *A Passage to India*

Mary MacCarthy: *A Nineteenth-Century Childhood*

Virginia Woolf: *Mr Bennett and Mrs Brown*

Roger Fry: *The Artist and Psycho-analysis*

The Hogarth Press publishes Freud's *Collected Papers* and begins the Psycho-Analytic Library; 'The Hogarth Essays' also begun

Lytton Strachey, Carrington, and Ralph Partridge move to Ham Spray House, Berkshire.

The Woolfs (and the Hogarth Press) move to 52 Tavistock Square in Bloomsbury

1925

Virginia Woolf: *The Common Reader* and *Mrs Dalloway*

Leonard Woolf: *Fear and Politics: A Debate at the Zoo*

Maynard Keynes: *The Economic Consequences of Mr Churchill* and *A Short View of Russia*

E.M. Forster: *Anonymity*

Lytton Strachey's play *The Son of Heaven* performed and he lectures on Pope at Cambridge

J.M. Keynes and Lydia Lopokova married; Keynes visits Russia; then takes a lease on Tilton, near Charleston, which remains his country home

Virginia Woolf ill for three months

1926

Roger Fry: *Transformations* and *Art and Commerce*

Julia M. Cameron, Victorian Photographer, with introductions by Roger Fry and Virginia Woolf

Vanessa Bell and Duncan Grant decorate the house of Mr and Mrs St John Hutchinson

Adrian and Karin Stephen obtain bachelor of medicine degrees to become psycho-analysts

1927

Virginia Woolf: *To the Lighthouse*

Clive Bell: *Landmarks in Nineteenth Century Painting*

Leonard Woolf: *Essays on Literature, History, Politics, etc.* and *Hunting the Highbrow*

E.M. Forster gives the Clark lectures at Cambridge, which are published
as *Aspects of the Novel*; becomes a Supernumerary Fellow of King's
College
Roger Fry: *Flemish Art* and *Cézanne*; translates Charles Mauron's *The
Nature of Beauty in Art and Literature*; lectures on Flemish Art at
the Queen's Hall, becomes an honorary fellow of King's
The 'Hogarth Lectures on Literature' started
Julian Bell enters King's College, Cambridge.

1928
Clive Bell: *Civilization* and *Proust*
Leonard Woolf: *Imperialism and Civilization*
E.M. Forster: *The Eternal Moment and Other Stories*
Virginia Woolf: *Orlando: A Biography*
Lytton Strachey: *Elizabeth and Essex: A Tragic History*
Desmond MacCarthy succeeds Edmund Gosse as senior literary critic
for the *Sunday Times*; also edits *Life and Letters* (until 1933)
The Bells, Duncan Grant, occasionally the Woolfs and Roger Fry, stay
at 'La Bergere,' Cassis, near Marseille, regularly until 1938
Lady Strachey dies

1929
Virginia Woolf: *A Room of One's Own*
Duncan Grant: a retrospective exhibition (1910-29)
Roger Fry lectures at the Royal Academy

1930
Mary MacCarthy: *Fighting Fitzgerald and Other Papers*
Roger Fry: *Henri Matisse*
J.M. Keynes: *A Treatise on Money*, 2 vols
Vanessa Bell: exhibition of her paintings in London
Leonard Woolf helps to found *The Political Quarterly* and becomes an
editor next year (until 1959)
The 'Hogarth Day to Day Pamphlets' started

1931
Virginia Woolf: *The Waves*
Clive Bell: *An Account of French Painting*
Desmond MacCarthy: *Portraits*
Leonard Woolf: *After the Deluge*, vol. I
Lytton Strachey: *Portraits in Miniature*
J.M. Keynes: *Essays in Persuasion*
E.M. Forster: *A Letter to Madan Blanchard* (first of the Hogarth

letters)
Roger Fry: retrospective exhibition of paintings
John Lehman joins the Hogarth Press (leaves in 1932)

1932
Virginia Woolf: *The Common Reader* Second Series and *A Letter to a Young Poet*
Desmond MacCarthy: *Criticism*
Roger Fry: *Characteristics of French Art* and *The Arts of Painting and Sculpture*
Lytton Strachey dies; Carrington commits suicide
Roger Fry lectures at the Queen's Hall
Exhibition of recent paintings by Vanessa Bell and Duncan Grant in London
New Signatures begun by the Hogarth Press

1933
Roger Fry: *Art-History as an Academic Study*
J.M. Keynes: *Essays in Biography*
Leonard Woolf edits *The Intelligent Man's Way to Prevent War*
Virginia Woolf: *Flush: A Biography*
Lytton Strachey: *Characters and Commentaries*
Roger Fry appointed Slade Professor at Cambridge
Clive Bell becomes art critic of *The New Statesman and Nation* (until 1943)

1934
Clive Bell: *Enjoying Pictures: Meditations in the National Gallery and Elsewhere*
E.M. Forster: *Goldsworthy Lowes Dickinson*
Roger Fry: *Reflections on British Painting*
Virginia Woolf: *Walter Sickert: A Conversation*
Roger Fry dies
Exhibition of Vanessa Bell's paintings

1935
Desmond MacCarthy: *Experience*
Leonard Woolf: *Quack, Quack!*
Vanessa Bell and Duncan Grant execute decorations for the *Queen Mary* which are never used
Virginia Woolf's unpublished play 'Freshwater, A Comedy in Three Acts' privately acted
J.M. Keynes helps to build the Arts Theatre in Cambridge

1936

J.M. Keynes: *The General Theory of Employment, Interest and Money*
E.M. Forster: *Abinger Harvest*
Mary MacCarthy: *Handicaps: Six Studies*
Leonard Woolf: *The League and Abyssinia*
Adrian Stephen: *The 'Dreadnought' Hoax*
Stephane Mallarmé's *Poems*, translated by Roger Fry with
    commentaries by Charles Mauron
Virginia Woolf ill for two months

1937

Virginia Woolf: *The Years*
Mary MacCarthy: *The Festival, Etc.*
Desmond MacCarthy lectures on Leslie Stephen at Cambridge
Vanessa Bell: exhibition of paintings
Duncan Grant: exhibition of paintings
Julian Bell killed in Spain
J.M. Keynes seriously ill

1938

Virginia Woolf: *Three Guineas*
Clive Bell: *Warmongers*
E.M. Forster: *England's Pleasant Land: A Pageant Play* produced
Julian Bell: *Essays, Poems and Letters*, ed. Quentin Bell
The Greville Memoirs, ed. Lytton Strachey and Roger Fulford, 8 vols
John Lehmann rejoins the Hogarth Press as general manager and
    partner, buying Virginia Woolf's interest in the Press
Leonard Woolf appointed a member of the Civil Service Arbitration
    Tribunal (for seventeen years)
J.M. Keynes reads 'My Early Beliefs' to the Memoir Club

1939

Leonard Woolf: *After the Deluge*, vol. II, *The Barbarians at the Gate*,
    and *The Hotel*
E.M. Forster: *What I Believe*
Roger Fry: *Last Lectures*
Woolfs and the Hogarth Press move to 37 Mecklenburgh Square

1940

Virginia Woolf: *Roger Fry: A Biography*
Desmond MacCarthy: *Drama*
Leonard Woolf: *The War for Peace*
Angelica Bell's 21st birthday: 'the last Bloomsbury party'

Hogarth Press bombed in Mecklenburgh Square; moved to Hertfordshire

E.M. Forster broadcasts regularly throughout the war to India

1941

Virginia Woolf: *Between the Acts*

Virginia Woolf commits suicide

Vanessa Bell: exhibition of paintings

1942

E.M. Forster: *Virginia Woolf*

Virginia Woolf: *The Death of the Moth and Other Essays*

Angelica Bell and David Garnett married

J.M. Keynes becomes chairman of the Committee for the Encouragement of Music and the Arts (which becomes the Arts Council in 1945); awarded a peerage

1943

Virginia Woolf: *A Haunted House and Other Short Stories*

Vanessa Bell, Duncan Grant, and Quentin Bell complete paintings for the parish church at Berwick near Firle, Sussex

1944

J.M. Keynes at the Bretton Woods International Conference

1945

E.M. Forster elected honorary fellow of King's College and takes up residence there after his mother's death

J.M. Keynes: 'The Arts Council: Its Policy and Hopes,' BBC broadcast

Duncan Grant: one-man exhibition

J.M. Keynes goes to America to negotiate a loan for Britain

1946

J.M. Keynes dies

Leonard Woolf sells John Lehmann's interest in the Hogarth Press to Chatto and Windus

1947

E.M. Forster: *Collected Tales*

Virginia Woolf: *The Moment and Other Essays*

1948

Adrian Stephen dies

1949

J.M. Keynes: *Two Memoirs*

1950
Virginia Woolf: *The Captain's Death Bed and Other Essays*

1951
Desmond MacCarthy: *Shaw*
E.M. Forster: *Two Cheers for Democracy*; writes the libretto for Benjamin Britten's opera *Billy Budd*
Desmond MacCarthy knighted

1952
Desmond MacCarthy dies

1953
Desmond MacCarthy: *Humanities* and *Memories*
Leonard Woolf: *Principia Politica* (vol. III of *After the Deluge*)
Virginia Woolf: *A Writer's Diary*, ed. Leonard Woolf
E.M. Forster: *The Hill of Devi*
Mary MacCarthy dies

1954
Desmond MacCarthy: *Theatre*

1956
Clive Bell: *Old Friends: Personal Recollections*
E.M. Forster: *Marianne Thornton: A Domestic Biography*
Virginia Woolf and Lytton Strachey: *Letters*
Vanessa Bell: exhibition of paintings
Last meeting of the Memoir Club

1957
Duncan Grant: exhibition of paintings

1958
Virginia Woolf: *Granite and Rainbow: Essays*
Duncan Grant decorates Russell Chantry, Lincoln Cathedral

1959
Duncan Grant: retrospective exhibition at the Tate Gallery

1960
Leonard Woolf: *Sowing: An Autobiography of the Years 1880–1904*; revisits Ceylon

1961
Leonard Woolf: *Growing: An Autobiography of The Years 1904–1911*
Vanessa Bell dies; memorial exhibition of her paintings

1962
Leonard Woolf: *Diaries in Ceylon: 1908–1911*
Saxon Sydney-Turner dies

1964
Leonard Woolf: *Beginning Again: An Autobiography of the Years 1911-1918*
Lytton Strachey: *Spectatorial Essays*
Duncan Grant and His World: An Exhibition
Vanessa Bell: A Memorial Exhibition of her Paintings by the Arts Council
Clive Bell dies

1965
Virginia Woolf: *Contemporary Writers*

1967
Leonard Woolf: *Downhill All the Way: 1919–1939*

1969
Leonard Woolf: *The Journey Not the Arrival Matters: An Autobiography of the Years 1939–1969*
Lytton Strachey: *Ermyntrude and Esmeralda*
Portraits by Duncan Grant: an Arts Council exhibition
E.M. Forster awarded the Order of Merit
Leonard Woolf dies

1970
E.M. Forster dies

1971
E.M. Forster: *Maurice* and *Albergo Empedocle and Other Writings*
Lytton Strachey by Himself: A Self Portrait

1972
Roger Fry: *Letters*, 2 vols
E.M. Forster: *The Life to Come and Other Stories*
Lytton Strachey: *The Really Interesting Question and Other Papers*
Duncan Grant: exhibition of watercolours and drawings

1973
Virginia Woolf: *Mrs Dalloway's Party: A Short Story Sequence*
Vanessa Bell: Paintings and Drawings, An Exhibition

BLOOMSBURY ON BLOOMSBURY

INTRODUCTION

The Memoir Club first met on 4th March 1920, but long before then Bloomsbury had been discussing itself in letters, journals, and essays written for friends. The portrait, in words or paint, was a preferred mode of expression for the members of Bloomsbury. Biography was their favourite form of history; along with fiction it was the genre in which their most important literary writing was done. Philosophically, Bloomsbury's high valuation of personal relations came from G.E. Moore's conclusion in *Principia Ethica* that 'personal affections and aesthetic enjoyments include *all* the greatest, and *by far* the greatest, goods that we can imagine. . .'. The aesthetic treatment of personal affections was thus a natural way of approaching these ideal goods.

The pieces collected in this section range from private correspondence and diaries to public memoirs. All are accounts — sometimes almost immediate and other times quite remote — of Bloomsbury and its various activities and relations by those individuals who made up the immediate family of Bloomsbury. The selections have been arranged in the approximate chronological order of their writing so that they convey the developing awareness of Bloomsbury among its members. The disadvantage of this arrangement is that the history of Bloomsbury does not unfold very clearly. The reader who wishes to start with general views of Bloomsbury before disappearing into the thickets of letters and diaries should begin with the excerpts from Leonard Woolf's autobiographies and then proceed to the essays of Keynes and the Bells.

Adrian Stephen: A Bloomsbury Party in 1909

Reprinted from Quentin Bell, Virginia Woolf: A Biography *(London: The Hogarth Press 1972), I 146—7, by permission of the author and The Hogarth Press;* © *1972 by Quentin Bell and reprinted by permission of Harcourt Brace Jovanovich, Inc.*

[After the death of Leslie Stephen in 1904 his four children moved from Hyde Park Gate near Kensington Gardens to 46 Gordon Square, Bloomsbury. Then after Thoby Stephen's death in 1906 and Vanessa's marriage to Clive Bell in 1907, the two remaining Stephens, Virginia and Adrian, moved to Fitzroy Square in Bloomsbury and continued the Thursday evening gatherings that Thoby had begun for his Cambridge friends in London. 'It was there,' wrote Duncan Grant, 'that what has since been called "Bloomsbury" for good or ill came into being' (see p.66).

A contemporary account of what one of those Thursday evenings was like is to be found in a 1909 diary entry of Adrian's. 'The Goat' was a pet name for Virginia. The precise identity of Miss Cole has not been preserved.]

Thursday July 1st

On my way home I went to Gordon Square where I found the Goat and walked home with her. We dined alone together and after dinner waited a long time before anybody appeared. Saxon as usual came in first but was quickly followed by Norton and he by James and Lytton Strachey. We were very silent at first, Virginia and Lytton and I doing all the talking, Saxon being in his usual state of torpor and Norton and James occasionally exchanging a whisper. Later on Vanessa and Clive came in bringing with them Duncan Grant. After this the conversation became more lively. Vanessa sat with Lytton on the sofa and from half heard snatches I gathered they were talking about his and James's obscene loves. Whatever it was they were discussing they were brought to an abrupt stop by a sudden silence, this pleased them very much, especially Vanessa, and I kindly added to their joy by asking why they stopped. Soon afterwards Henry Lamb came in having returned from doing some portraits at Oxford. The conversation kept up a good flow, though it was not very interesting, until at about half past eleven Miss Cole arrived.

She went and sat in the long wicker chair with Virginia and Clive on the floor beside her. Virginia began in her usual tone of frank admiration to compliment her on her appearance. 'Of course, you Miss Cole are always dressed so exquisitely. You look so original, so like a sea shell. There is something so refined about you coming in among our muddy boots and pipe smoke, dressed in your exquisite creations.' Clive chimed in with more heavy compliments and then began asking her why she disliked him so much, saying how any other young lady would have been much pleased with all the nice things he had been saying but that she treated him so sharply. At this Virginia interrupted with 'I think Miss Cole has a very strong character' and so on and and so on. Altogether Miss Cole was as unhappy and uncomfortable as she could be; it was impossible not to help laughing at the extravagance of Virginia and Clive and all conversation was stopped by their noisy choruses, so the poor woman was the centre of all our gaze, and did not know what to do with herself. At last, a merciful diversion was made and Virginia took my seat and I hers and with, I may say, some skill I managed to keep Clive under control.

James and Lytton Strachey left and we played an absurd game which Vanessa and Clive had learnt at the Freshfields. The principle of the game was as follows: that person won who in half a minute could say the most words beginning with any given letter. Clive held the watch and gave us each a turn. Norton being given G started off with Jerusalem and Jesus, which I am afraid must have added another pain to poor Miss Cole's already lengthy list. We all had our turns, Vanessa trying to sail as near to the wind as she could, she is always trying to bring out some bawdy remark and is as pleased when she has done it as a spoilt child. Miss Cole went at one and Duncan Grant at about the same time, when a great discussion was started, I know not by whom, about vice. Very soon Virginia with exquisite art made herself the centre of the argument making the vaguest statements with the intensest feeling and ready to snap up anybody who laughed. Her method is ingenious and at first is rather disconcerting for when someone has carefully examined her argument and certainly refuted it she at once agrees with him enthusiastically saying that he has put her point exactly.

The argument such as it was degenerated into mere phrase-making and so regarded was quite amusing; this gave way in its turn to the game of bantering Saxon. He was chaffed and laughed at for all his little peculiarities and all the time he kept his silence, only giving an occasional smile. He could not be provoked into saying anything even by Virginia's most daring sallies which never fail of their guffaw when Clive is present. At last everybody went except Saxon. Saxon went on to discuss different ways to Germany having obtained further information from Cooks. Virginia and I were however so sleepy that we managed by sheer indifference to oust him. We got to bed as the dawn was coming up about 5.

Lytton Strachey: Monday June 26th 1916

Reprinted from Lytton Strachey by Himself: A Self-Portrait, *edited by Michael Holroyd (London: Heinemann 1971), 139–56, by permission of the Society of Authors, and Mr Michael Holroyd on behalf of the estate of Lytton Strachey:* © *1971 by Alix Strachey and reprinted with permission of Holt, Rinehart & Winston, Inc.*

[Lytton Strachey never wrote an account of Bloomsbury, though his letters, diaries, and Memoir Club papers contain pictures of Bloomsbury life. As early as 1906 he described, in a letter to Maynard Keynes (see pp.182–83), a vision of life with friends that – apart from the conspicuous absence of women – depicted life as at least some of the members of Bloomsbury thought it might be lived. In 1910 Strachey noted in a diary that he went to a gathering at Lady Ottoline Morrell's but found 'no Bloomby' there. This is, I believe, the first recorded use of the word 'Bloomsbury' to stand for the Bloomsbury Group. Two days later Strachey dined with the Bells at Gordon Square and wrote in his diary: 'Complaints of Clive as to collective affectation and dullness of set. "Everyone tries to make his individuality tell" I couldn't believe it. He refused to go to Fitzroy. I went with Vanessa.' Thus the internal criticism of Bloomsbury, of which there was to be a considerable amount throughout the history of Bloomsbury, appears almost at the same time as the word that identified the Group.

Lytton Strachey's most important description of Bloomsbury life is contained in a paper that he read to the Memoir Club. The idea occurred to him, he says, towards the end of the essay, of writing a 'microscopic description of a day'. The purpose of such a description is given in the opening words of the essay and bears a striking family resemblance to Virginia Woolf's famous manifesto in the essay 'Modern Fiction', where she urged writers to give us 'the life of Monday or Tuesday' by recording 'the atoms as they fall upon the mind in the order in which they fall . . . however disconnected and incoherent in appearance. . .'. Virginia Woolf practised what she preached in a brief prose sketch entitled 'Monday or Tuesday'. The 'luminous halo' she evokes there shows how different were the atoms that fell on her consciousness from those that fell on Lytton Strachey's.

The life of Monday or Tuesday that Strachey chose to describe took place during the First World War at Wissett Lodge, a farmhouse in Suffolk that David 'Bunny' Garnett and Duncan Grant had rented in order to do fruit farming and thus avoid conscription. Wissett was presided over by Vanessa Bell and her young children Julian and

Quentin. For Strachey it was one of the places, like Lady Ottoline's at Garsington, where he could stay with his friends. On this particular visit he was accompanied by Harry Norton, a Cambridge friend and mathematician, who helped Strachey out financially; *Eminent Victorians*, which Strachey was in the midst of writing, is dedicated to him.

In order to understand the particular tone of Strachey's account, it is important to remember that this essay was read to and perhaps even written for very close friends who could be expected to respond to the ironic nuances of Strachey's self-portrait. ('L' probably refers to Lytton's friend Henry Lamb.)]

To come close to life! To look at it, not through the eyes of Poets and Novelists, with their beautifying arrangements or their selected realisms, but simply as one actually *does* look at it, when it happens, with its minuteness and its multiplicity and its intensity, vivid and complete! To do that! To do that even with a bit of it – with no more than a single day – to realize absolutely the events of a single and not extraordinary day – surely that might be no less marvellous than a novel or even a poem, and still more illuminating, perhaps! If one *could* do it! But one can't, of course. One has neither the power nor the mere physical possibility for enchaining that almost infinite succession; one's memory is baffled; and then – the things one remembers most one cannot, one dares not – no! one can only come close to *them* in a very peculiar secrecy; and yet . . . there remains a good deal that one can and may even perhaps positively *ought* to give a fixity to, after all!

I had already had some vague, half-dreaming thoughts about the Piero della Francesca portrait downstairs, and whether what Duncan had said about the goodness of the composition was really true, and whether Norton's exclamation about both his and Nessa's self-delusion . . . when I was woken up properly by Blanche putting my breakfast-tray down on the table beside me, and pulling the curtains. It was eight o'clock. I was happy – as usual – to find food before me, all ready to be eaten; I certainly wanted nothing else in the world just then; but, having put on my eye-glasses, I saw two letters crouching under a plate, and realized that I was very glad to have letters too. One was some damned bill, and the other was a huge affair from Ottoline; I opened it, and saw that it covered sheets and that it had enclosures, so I thought that before reading it I'll have my breakfast. And then, as I ate my boiled egg and drank my rather thick tea – but the toast was on its accustomed royal scale – I suddenly remembered the dubiousness of my position, and all that I had decided the night before. Nessa's – yes, one could only call it sulkiness – that oppressed silence all the evening after our late return – how could I doubt its meaning? – 'For heaven's sake – *can't* you leave me with Duncan for a moment? Is it *never* to be?' How her dumb animality – like some creature *aux abois*, as I've often thought – came out more unmistakably than I'd ever known! And yet, perhaps it *was* a mistake! How can one tell, I reflected, what that woman's thinking, with her extraordinary simplicities? But I was as certain as ever that I must do something to settle it one way or the other, that I should have to suggest my going, which meant of course Norton's too, I'd no doubt, and then – I could judge from how she took it what I was to do next. I did not like the thought of going away, though why I didn't I could not be sure. Certainly it might have been a much happier visit; somehow, I had been lonely – and why? There was Norton to talk to about the war and mathematics – wasn't that enough to satisfy me? – And they were all very kind; but had they been kind enough? Was it their married state that oppressed me? But then – were *they* married? – Perhaps it was their *un*married state. Perhaps if I could have lain with Bunny – and then I smiled to think of my romantic visions before coming – of a recrudescence of that affair, under Duncan's nose – and of his dimness on my arrival, and of how very very little I wanted to lie with him now! – Only, all the same, the thought of going away depressed me. Perhaps it was simply because of the easy-goingness of the place and the quantities of food, or was it because . . . and then the vision of that young postman with the fair hair and lovely country complexion who had smiled at me and said 'Good evening, sir', as he passed on his bicycle, flashed upon me, and that other unexpected meeting – but I felt that *that* train of thought was too exciting to be hurried over, and decided, as I'd finished my breakfast, to get through Ott's letter before anything else.

I enjoyed reading it; for it was one of her tremendously expansive and affectionate letters, which invariably carry me off my feet. And it showed me *(apparently)* that she was not annoyed with me (though why one should care whether she was annoyed or not . . .) and that she was ready to have me back again at Garsington, which was a relief, because, if I *had* to go away, it was as well to have somewhere to go to. As for the enclosure, it was an appalling coloured photograph of a young man by Titian, all vague and turd-tinted, and incredibly sentimental, which I was to give to Duncan with her love.

It took a long time getting all the writing clear, but I did it at last;

and then, feeling considerably more cheerful, I fished my manuscripts out of the big envelope which I'd put the night before on the lower shelf of the table and began brooding over my poem on Kisses, but I added nothing, and my digestion beginning to work, I fell back drowsily on the pillow, and for a moment there was L. before my eyes. But only for a moment; it was the post-youth who fascinated me now. My scheme of meeting him in the long lane past the village recurred to me, and then I began embroidering romantic and only *just* possible adventures which might follow — the bedroom in the inn at Norwich, and all the rest; but there was the necessity of talking to him first; and I went once more through the calculations of time and place, and saw that my plan really might, if I had the nerve, come off. The down on his cheek, the delicious down on his cheek! It was true that his nose had looked stupid, but perhaps not *too* stupid. Oh! there was no doubt that he was nice. Why, why, had Norton been with me at that second meeting? And he had not even looked in his direction! He had not even been aware that a bicycle had passed!

It was about eleven by the time I was dressed, and when I came down I found Norton and Duncan in the drawing-room. I had hardly finished reading them Ott's letter when Vanessa came in. I gave it to her to read to herself, and of course she could hardly spell out a word of it, and thought a good deal of it dull. I was slightly annoyed, and went off to the dreadful E.C., where I could only just scrape together enough earth out of the tin coalscuttle to cover my addition to the mountain, which, even before my addition, had been far too high.

The sun was shining, and there was my chair in the little arbour at the corner of the lawn. And Blanche came with my midday cocoa, and after that I studied the Bishop of Oxford's book on the Sermon on the Mount. It was a foolish book, but I found in it a charming little poem by an old lady in Torquay to Florrie Ewbank about the coal-strike and the neighbours and 'Sweep' who turned out to be a new dog — 'such a companion'. It was as good as anything in Samuel Butler. Then I saw that the time had come to face Vanessa. I went upstairs, and knocked at the door of her studioroom, which I'd never been in before, and went in, and there she was in front of me in the white room, on a dilapidated basket chair, and in one of her most collapsed and dreamy attitudes.

Was she plain or beautiful? I could not decide. I talked vaguely — about the room, about Ottoline — and she was very nice. I suddenly wondered why I had knocked at the door; was it idiotic? How well I know her! — And how little — how very little! Even her face, which seemed now almost chocolate-coloured, was strangely unfamiliar. If I could only have flung myself into her arms! – But I knew so well what would happen – her smile – her half-bewilderment, half infinitely sensible acceptance – and her odd relapse. As it was, I walked about uncomfortably, looking at moments vaguely out of the window; and I was decidedly uneasy when I said at last 'I think I shall have to drift off'. Of course she simply answered 'Shall you really?' I said, 'Yes – I think so – I think tomorrow.' She said 'Will you go to Garsington?' And I saw then, in the same moment, both that I couldn't bear the thought of going, and that I should have to go. I thought that perhaps she would have liked me to stay if that hadn't involved Norton's also staying; but I felt unable to disentangle that – and I got no atom of encouragement. When I had got out of the room, I entirely failed to shut the door, after repeated efforts; there was something wrong with the lock. She called out, still in her chair, that she would shut it. Before going, I had wildly glanced at a picture half-painted on an easel, representing a group of people, with what was apparently a saint in a halo in mid-air. It looked very niggly, and the colours were extremely garish – altogether it alarmed me. In the drawing-room I found the Daily News and the Daily Mirror, and went out with them into the garden again.

Norton had vanished; his chair in the sun was empty. There were only the children playing by the pond. I was terrified of their coming and pulling me to pieces, but for some reason or other they didn't, and I could read my newspapers in peace. I read the Daily News, but there was nothing to interest me. As for the Daily Mirror, what *could* there be to interest me in that? A face perhaps . . . but for weeks past I had never found a single one that wasn't disgusting; and I thought of that time at the Lacket, when every day I had found some living creature in it – usually killed. And then I *did* come on a face – a charming one – of a young boxer – 'Jimmy Wilde, the famous flyweight', whom I'd never heard of before. I longed to go and see him boxing: I have never seen a boxing-match. What would happen? I wondered. Would the blood pour down over his eyes? But the match he was to box was to be that very night, so that was impossible – though for a second I actually envisaged going up to London on some excuse that afternoon. But then – the post-boy? No! It was all ridiculous: the boxing match would come and go without me; and after that what chance would I have of ever seeing Jimmy Wilde again? At that moment I looked up, and saw, slowly pounding along the farm-road on the other side of the house, a waggon and horses, driven by a youth. It was too far off to be sure, but he seemed handsome, I was feeling *désoeuvré* and distracted, and so I thought I'll go and see what he was like. But then I thought after all I wouldn't, and remained sitting there — undecided, vague and miserable. I was in my slippers, I reflected: and how could I go through the dirt? The cart and horses and young man had vanished; but they might still be in the farm-yard: should I go after all? I still waited. I begun to think that I should have to tell Norton that I was going next day, and that he would certainly then say that he was going too, so that we should have to travel together to London; oh! was there no way out of that? Or should I rather like it, really? He was so amusing, and so agreeable, and I liked talking to him; but how could one have adventures when he was there? Suddenly, for no apparent reason, I got up, went in, went up to my room, put on my boots, and came down again, and walked by the back way into the farm-yard.

There was no sign of a waggon; but I noticed, what I'd never noticed before, that the farm-road did not end in the farm-yard, but continued past some indefinite pig-styes, through a field, and then turned round a corner out of sight. So after all the waggon — and the waggonner — might be further on — not very far away — engaged in some promiscuous occupation. I began to walk through the farm-yard, when Bunny appeared, at the door of a barn.

He was in his shirt, with the sleeves rolled up, engaged also, apparently, in some extremely promiscuous occupation. What *was* he always doing in those odd purlieus? Something with the rabbits I suppose.

I talked with him — vaguely; and felt once more the pleasure of being able to do that. And the happier I felt, the more my heart sank at the thought of going away. It sank down and down, and I kept chattering with him about the hens, and wanted to take hold of his large brown bare arm. *That* I knew was beautiful; and then my heart sank so very low that I conceived the possibility of *his* asking me to stay on, if I could suggest adroitly enough that I should like to. But who can be adroit with his heart in his boots? My attempt was really feeble; and when I blurted out, apropos of nothing, that I was going tomorrow, he said, in his charming way 'Oh, I *am* sorry', and I saw that I was dished again.

Then, after a little more talking — about the new Dostoievsky — I went on along the path, and he disappeared into the recesses of the barn. I passed the indeterminate pig-styes, went through a gate, turned the corner, and found myself in a field. No waggon was anywhere in view, but, as I crossed the field, I forgot all about it — I could think of

nothing but the mere pleasure and beauty of the summer day. I came
into a second field, and then, to one side of me, the country dipped
down at a little distance, rising again in a lovely little landscape – lovely
and yet perfectly ordinary – of fields and trees and hedges and blue
sky. And the field I was in was full of splendid grasses, and there were
wild flowers scattered all about, and wild roses in the hedge at my left
hand. I walked entranced; that feeling of a sudden explanation came
upon me – a sudden easy mysterious explanation of all the long
difficult mysterious embroilments of the world. 'Est-ce que j'ai trouvé
le grand Peut-être?' I thought. 'Am I luckier even than Rabelais? – How
miraculously lucky I am!' And I sat down, absolutely comfortable, with
a little bank of earth under the hedge for my back to lean against, and
the charming English prospect before my eyes. I thought of my friends,
and my extraordinary happiness. I thought of Death, of Keats and the
Ode to the Nightingale, of 'easeful Death' – 'half in love with easeful
Death' – and I was convinced, as I'd been convinced in the train coming
down from London that if Death would only come to one in a mood of
serene happiness, he would be very welcome. I thought of suddenly
dying, painlessly, where I lay. I wondered whether that was morbid;
and then I imagined them finding my dead body – so singularly
thin – and what their thoughts would be. All the time the sun warmed
me deliciously, and the landscape beamed in front of me, and visions of
Jimmy Wilde, half naked, with bruised ears, floated in my
imagination – or dressed, in a fascinating tweed suit, rather too big for
him, staying with me for a week-end at my cottage at Garsington,
coming out through the door onto the lawn . . . And L? . . . The
dazzling happiness, coming, in flood after flood, over my soul, was so
intense that it was like a religious conversion. And through it all there
was an odd waft of melancholy – a kind of vibration of regret. A
strange importance seemed to invest and involve into a unity the scene,
the moment, and my state of feeling. But at last I knew it was time to
go back to the house. As I walked back, I felt as if I had made an
advance – as if I had got somewhere new. But it seemed far shorter
going back than going, and very soon I was through the back premises,
and, coming onto the lawn through the gap in the bushes, found them
all quite close to me sitting in the verandah, having lunch. I was
late – they had almost finished their meat – and it occurred to me that
all the time I had been there I had never been late for lunch before.
Nessa seemed slightly surprised, and asked me whether I'd been for a
long walk. My plate was filled with food, and as I ate I began to ask
Duncan about the National Sporting Club – whether he had ever been

there, and what boxing was like. The wretch saw at once what I was up to and said 'You've been looking at the Daily Mirror'; I didn't attempt to deny it, and went on with my questions; but his answers were unsatisfactory. He said that I would certainly enjoy the National Sporting Club very much, because one had to go there in evening dress, and that I might get Lord Henry Bentinck to take me; but he admitted that he'd never been there himself; and Nessa said that he didn't understand me at all. Bunny advised me to go to some boxing haunt in the East End that he knew of, where he said the blood flowed by the bucket-full. Norton pursed himself up, and said that all this was very disgusting, and said that I was like Nero at a gladiatorial show. I rather testily replied that he was an 'anachoret', and Nessa again took my side. Then the conversation somehow got on to George, and my relations with him, and Duncan's relations with him; and Duncan was very amusing, confessing that he still sometimes thought of him sentimentally, and that at one time he would have been willing to give him a hundred a year, to have him as his mistress. We asked him where he would have got a hundred a year from, to give to George. He said he would have borrowed it. We asked 'Who from?' And Norton and I at once saw that of course it would have been from Maynard, and everybody laughed. After that Ottoline loomed up in her accustomed style, and there was a long and rather fierce argument as to whether she had any artistic capacity, and whether she was 'creative'; I said that she was, and that Garsington proved it; but all the others were against me. Norton declared that Garsington was the work of a bower-bird, and that to talk of its showing 'creativeness' was absurd. I answered in a voice more contemptuous than my feeling but gradually I felt my feeling growing as contemptuous as my voice. Then Nessa began on the 'artistic' tack, and for a moment I almost became better; all that violent discussion of my second evening shimmered in the background, and I got as far as saying that I didn't think I agreed with her notion of art. But it passed off, and the children appeared, and we all got up from the table. I found myself standing next to Duncan on the lawn, and he was holding the Daily Mirror open at the picture of Jimmy Wilde. I said 'Don't you think he's beautiful?' And he said 'Yes'; but added almost immediately, 'I expect it's only because he hasn't got a collar on. If his neck was covered he'd probably look like anyone else.' I didn't believe it, and I was slightly annoyed.

Then I went upstairs, heavy with all that eating, and lay down on my bed, where I began again thinking out my plan of campaign with the postboy, until I fell asleep; and I slept solidly for over an hour. I was woken up by the piercing screams of the children, as they played on the little piece of grass outside my window. The noise gradually penetrated my sleep, and reached a climax with Quentin bursting into sobs. I head Julian's cockney voice, full of guilt and self-justification, calling out to Flossie ('Flossay') that Quentin was very naughty and would *not* play with him. After a confused interval, Nessa's voice emerged – low and plaintive – 'I've *told* you, Julian, that you must *not* . . . You're much stronger than Quentin, and he can't defend himself . . . I've *told* you . . .' And then utter silence on the part of Julian. Irritation came upon me at the woman's weakness. – Or *was* it weakness? Wasn't it perhaps simply common sense? Did she see that no amount of punishment would ever prevent Julian from being cruel? That it would only make him dislike her to no purpose? Perhaps; but still I was angry with her for her lack of indignation; and my hatred of Julian was intense.

However, silence was re-established, and I picked up the copy of Temple Bar on the bed-table, to see if there was anything in it that I hadn't already read. I struck at once upon an article by some woman or other on political parties in Bohemia. It was all entirely new to me, and most interesting; I had never before seen the names of Rieger or Gregr; I knew nothing whatever of the history of those movements. The article was not very profound, but it was not badly done either. I was amazed and appalled by my ignorance – that at the age of 36 it should only be by a chance article in a back number of a second-rate magazine, written by an unknown woman, that I should have become acquainted with facts of that magnitude, with names as important in Austrian history as those of O'Connell and Parnell in ours. And I, and my likes, are supposed to be well educated persons! I then skimmed an article on Thurlow, which was slightly interesting too; by that time it was four o'clock, and I got up and went downstairs for my afternoon stroll.

On the lawn I saw Norton reading mathematics so I took the opportunity of telling him that I had decided to go away next day; and he immediately announced that he would go with me. I assented, and drifted off, leaving him with his mathematics.

I drifted down the dreary road that goes in the opposite direction to the village. My mind, which (with exception of the interval of sleep) had been in a state of constant activity since 8 o'clock in the morning, now relapsed into dreaminess. The expectation of tea was one of the few things definitely present to it, as I walked along between the hedges on the empty road. – That, and the feeling that it was only *after* tea that anything exciting could happen – that *then* something exciting would happen — that *then* there would be the crisis of the meeting with the bicycle, and the conversation, and all the possibilities involved — so that *until* then I had nothing to do but to meander about and fill up the interval as best I could. I fancy I thought a little about Sarah Bernhardt, and, after I'd turned back, the puzzle of my relations with women flickered before me. Carrington occurred to me, and then, for some odd reason, Maria. Why on earth had I been so chaste during those Latin lessons? I saw how easily I could have been otherwise — how I might have put my hand on her bare neck, and even up her legs, with considerable enjoyment; and probably she would have been on the whole rather pleased. I became certain that the solution was that I was restrained by my knowledge that she would certainly inform 'Auntie' of every detail of what had happened, at the earliest possible opportunity. It would be practically copulating with Ott looking through the keyhole — which I was by no means prepared to do. There are limits in these matters, I reflected; strange that it should be so, but there are. I turned in at the gate, passed the angle of the house, and saw to my delight that tea was ready and Vanessa actually pouring it out.

Norton appeared immediately, and Duncan and Bunny a little later. There was not very much conversation; what there was chiefly circled round the question of the train that Norton and I should go by. He wanted to go after lunch, and I wanted to go after tea. As he had no motive to produce and I had — viz that dinner in a train was so amusing — it was eventually settled that I should have my way. I ate my frugal spongefingers contentedly, listening to their gibes. Duncan at last got up and went into the drawing-room, where he began to play his Bach composition. I followed him, with what I hoped was an air of detachment, pretended to look for a book, went out through the drawing-room door into the passage, and so through the front door out of the house.

My fear had been that Norton would want to walk out with me, but I seemed to have escaped him successfully. He would hardly follow me now. The time, too, was exactly right, so far as I could judge. I had nothing to do now but to walk forward, and I was bound to meet . . . the bicycle, either before I got to the pillar-box at the crossroads, or, if necessary, *at* it. I walked down the road towards the village, wondering how it would turn out. I felt to see that I had my letter to Ottoline in my pocket, and rehearsed the meeting — my stopping him, my asking him if he would mind taking the letter, and then, somehow, my offering him a cigarette. It was fairly clear, although I foresaw that the actual stopping of the bicycle might be difficult — especially if he was coming down hill — so far it was fairly clear; but after the opening — *after* the preliminary conversation and the cigarette — then everything was a blank, to be filled in at the moment according to his amiability, and as my presence of mind would suggest. But both his amiability and my presence of mind were highly dubious entities. I had the wildest, and the bleakest, visions — of amusement and charm and successes culminating in Norwich, and of crushing failure — sheer stupidity, or undisguised annoyance — or perhaps of missing him altogether by some unforeseen mischance. It was a preposterous errand! I laughed, and imagined myself reading about myself in a novel by Tolstoy — reading quickly, and turning over the pages as fast as I could, in my excitement to know what would happen in the end. What *would* happen? I took the shortcut by the field with the poppies, emerged onto the high road, turned to the left, away from the village, and then off to the right, up the long narrow lane, at the end of which was the pillar-box. It was half-past five; the collection at the pillar-box was due at five minutes to six; the lane was probably about two miles long; therefore, if he was punctual, it seemed certain that I should meet him in it, as there was no other way from the pillar-box to the village, and he had to be in the village at half-past six. I had remembered the lane as being fairly level, but now it seemed to go up and down in the most alarming manner. If I were to come upon him as he was on a downward dip — should I have the nerve — or even the strength of voice — to stop him? And wouldn't he be furious if I did? Perhaps he would be mollified if he saw that my letter was to a Ladyship. Or perhaps . . . my mind lost itself in speculations. I imagined his nose, his cheek, and his complexion with a tantalizing mixture of indistinctness and intensity. His cap, too, and his yellow hair, lighter than his skin — and that odd armlet . . . and why, to be sure, *wasn't* he in the army? Surely he wasn't under age? . . . A woman in a drab mackintosh appeared on the road in front of me, going in the same direction. I passed her easily, and sped on. It seemed almost probably that I should reach the pillar-box before he did, in which case I should have to linger about; and then — if there were other people there? — old gaffers posting letters to their sons at the front? I might be done for in that case. I had passed the turning down which Norton and I had gone after meeting him the time before, so that, supposing the time to have been the same on that occasion, he might appear at any moment now. But he didn't appear: the lane went on and on indefinitely, its only merit being that it kept more or less straight, so that one could see people approaching from a good distance, and prepare accordingly. But no one did approach. Meanwhile the sky had been growing darker and darker, and I expected it to rain at any moment; that would be an additional complication. Then I saw that the pillar-box could not be far off; it was almost in sight, in a group of trees in front of me, I had no doubt; I recognized the place from some cottages on the right hand, so I *should* have to wait there, after all. Suddenly I heard a whistle – and an immediate reminiscence flashed upon me: it was of 'Signor Grasso', the postman on the Loch-an-Eilan road, when he came on his bicycle with the letters in the morning. My mind shot back for an instant to Milton Cottage – how many years ago? – with Pippa and Pernel in the garden, and Sharp Cottage, too, and its dreariness, and James of course – it all came and went in a moment; was it possible that *he* too – ? That he was whistling to warn those cottages that he was coming? Oh no! Such things weren't done out of the Highlands . . . and then his bicycle appeared, slowly advancing: it *was* he, there could be no doubt. But he did not stop at the cottage, he came on, and we should meet almost at once. He looked rather bigger than I had remembered him, and he had something in his mouth – a cigarette? Then *that* plan was shattered. But I saw at once that it was the whistle, and as I took the letter out of my pocket he actually began slowing down, almost as if he was expecting me to give it him. 'This is a very favourable beginning', I thought. And on the very heels of that, came the perception that something was all wrong, hopelessly wrong, that he wasn't – that he couldn't be – that it was somebody else. Yes, it was another postman, with black hair, and a red Presbyterian face, and a most unattractive briskness about him altogether, stopping with an *écoeurant* politeness to take my letter, as I handed it to him, saying 'Would you mind taking this?' with the most natural air in the world. 'So *that's* all over,' I said to myself, as he vanished, and I turned automatically on my tracks, for obviously there was now nothing to be done but to trudge back home. I nearly burst out laughing aloud at the farcicality of my proceedings, but was restrained by the re-appearance of the woman in the mackintosh, whom I now saw, as I passed her, looked like a lower-class Vernon Lee. I began to wonder what had happened – why he had failed me – whether it was only a temporary change, or whether . . . Perhaps he'd joined the army, perhaps that armlet meant that he was going to be called up, and very likely, as today was Monday . . . anyhow it was just like my luck. There was a servant-maid waiting at the corner of the branch road – waiting rather mysteriously; she was pretty, and sad. Could she have been waiting for . . . ? I passed on, and by this time the clouds had disappeared from the sky and the sun was out again. I thought of the youth at Lockeridge who had been obliterated in the same silent way: but, after all, I considered, some remain. There are so many possibilities in this world, and I shouldn't have been much surprised if something extraordinary had happened almost at once. But nothing happened, except that, quite suddenly and apparently irrelevantly, a phrase from Handel sounded in my mind – a phrase that I don't believe I'd thought of for years. – 'Rejoice! Rejoice! Rejoi-oi-oi-oi-oice greatly!' And then the thought occurred to me of writing this microscopic description of a day. I was delighted with the idea and went on elaborating it for a long time, until at last I drifted into the plan of a satirical poem on Winston in the style of the chorusses in Samson Agonistes, which should begin

> Strange are the ways of men;
> And the ways of God are still more curious;

and I was still murmuring these lines when I reached the house; and as I went upstairs to my room I saw that they would have to end the poem too.

In my room, I fell with extraordinary energy on my Arabian story, which I had a wild notion that I might finish before dinner. It was obvious, really, that I couldn't, yet I wrote on at top speed for more than an hour, covering the pages in a most unusual manner. I heard them calling to me to come to dinner, but still wrote. They called again, and then I realized that it was useless going on – the wretched thing wasn't nearly finished; so I went down into the kitchen and had dinner with them – rather silent, while they discussed the superfetation of rabbits, and whether wildflowers might be legitimately classified as yellow, blue and red.

I went out of the room before anyone else, and walked through the drawing-room out onto the lawn. It was still quite light, though it must have been past nine o'clock. I paced once or twice up and down the lawn, when Bunny appeared and immediately joined me. I had a sharp and most queer feeling that it was somehow done by arrangement – though of course we had arranged nothing of the sort. We went at once through the pergola into the strip of kitchen garden, and began walking up and down the path. I felt nervous, almost neurasthenic – what used to be called 'unstrung'. He was so calm and gentle, and his body was so large, with his shirt (with nothing under it) open all the way down – that I longed to throw myself onto him as if he were a feather-bed, to tell him everything – everything, and to sob myself asleep. And yet, at the same time, the more I longed to expand, the more I hated the thought of it. It would be disgusting and ridiculous — it was out of the question. And I became astringent, and would talk of nothing but the vegetables as we walked up and down. The vegetables, and still the vegetables — it almost seemed at last that there was nothing else that one could possibly talk about; and, as the subject was not very interesting, why not give it up and go in? I was in terror that this would happen, and yet my congealment was such that when, at the end of one of our turns, we got to the pergola, I made as if to go through it, back on to the lawn. At that, he came out in that lovely firm way that he sometimes so unexpectedly has, and turned right off through an asparagus bed into that other more remote part of the garden, where the grass is so thick and lush, and everything is tangled and overgrown with weeds and roses — a place that trembles on the edge of sentimentality, but is saved by being so small and unkempt and tumbledown. We went and sat on a dirty wooden seat at the farthest end of it, and I thought that if it had been a clean stone seat, and if he had been dressed in white knee-breeches and a blue coat with brass buttons, and if I had been a young lady in a high waist — or should it have been the other way round? — the scene would have done very well for an Academy picture by Marcus Stone.

And so we did talk at last — about other things than vegetables — about Barbara, and that fandango of the letter; and he made me realize what a charming creature she was. And he chaffed me about my 'affair with Carrington'[1]; and I explained in great detail that it couldn't be called that; and as we talked I grew comfortable, and in fact happy; and then, when the conversation touched upon the changeability of moods, I said that I had been in a wretched mood all day, that I had felt everything with an unnatural acuteness, as if I had had no skin. It wasn't at all an accurate statement, and his sympathy — 'Oh Lytton, how dreadful!' — made me feel myself a silly beast, and I quickly covered my tracks by bringing up the subject of his life at Wissett, and his prospects, and his general state. He talked for a long time about these things — about his settled happiness and the problems of his future — and I felt very sympathetic, and wished I had several thousand a year. He was amusing, too, very amusing, and I saw how shy and distrustful of himself he was in company. It grew darker and colder, but we stayed on. At last it seemed quite natural to ask him whether he thought they really liked me. 'Who, Lytton?' — 'Duncan and Vanessa — no, not really; but sometimes they seem very severe. Perhaps I'm too uppish.' 'Oh Lytton, how absurd you are. They call you "the

old gentleman". I heard them saying that they hoped the old gentleman
was happy.' — The darling! How beautifully he had smoothed me
down! So that everything was now calm and good — so that that was
the ordinary state of the world — and all those doubts and itches — how
futile and preposterous! I laughed, and said 'Do *you* call me "the old
gentleman?" ' He answered, flirting, 'The Prince of Darkness is a
gentleman.' Without any difficulty I stretched out my hand and put it
into his breast, which was glowing a warm pink in the twilight. I said
'An *old* gentleman?' and he answered 'No; that's just the difference.'
'Have I more experience than the Devil?' I murmured as we laughed. We
came nearer to one another, and, with a divine vigour, embraced. I was
amused to notice, just before it happened, that he looked very
nervously in the direction of the house. We kissed a great deal, and I
was happy. Physically, as well as mentally, he had assuaged me. That
was what was so wonderful about him — he gave neither too little nor
too much. I felt neither the disillusionment of having gone too far, nor
any of the impatience of desire. I knew that we loved each other, and I
was unaware that my cock had moved.

It was too cold to stay out any longer, and we came in to find the
room in almost pitch darkness, with three figures over the fire. He went
out with Duncan; left alone with Norton and Nessa, I instantly realized
that we must have been out rather a long time. Norton said something
which I took for an indecent joke, and I answered with unnecessary
self-conscousness; then, of course, he said that he had meant nothing at
all. There was a long pause, during which I imagined Duncan furious in
the kitchen, and Bunny pacifying him. But when they appeared at last
with the lamp, Duncan seemed perfectly cheerful, and the evening at
once became very gay. We ranged over Ka and her complicated history,
we discussed our private weaknesses, and ended in a fantastic [blank in
MS] of idiotic rhymes.

> Ka is my Ma,
> But who is my Pa?

was Norton's first inspiration, which set us all off in a string. How
adorable was Nessa, as she sat, rocking with laughter at the bawdiness
of the jokes! We got up from our chairs somehow, at about one o'clock.
Duncan and Bunny disappeared as usual, to lock up. Nessa went off,
and Norton briskly mounted his attic-ladder. I tore off my clothes in
my bedroom, with only one desire — to sleep. In bed, I thought of
Bunny, and then, as I was dozing off, something strange happened. I

suddenly found myself with Duncan under the bushes in the drizzle on that first afternoon on Hampstead Heath. The vividness of it was so great that I woke up with a start. Then that too melted in oblivion; and it was L. who was with me when I finally fell asleep.

Note

1. 'What I remember must have been the next day – the day he apparently left', David Garnett told the editor. 'We went for a walk along the edge of a cornfield and he told me that he was in love, or more than a little in love with Carrington and made me promise not to tell Vanessa or Duncan or anyone. He was afraid of Ottoline finding out – and I think of Virginia also. I kept my promise . . . I suppose it was the reassurance I had given him which led him to confide in me and he was also perhaps more ready to confide a hetero-sexual attachment to me than a daydream about the postman which would have strained my powers of sympathy!' [Holroyd's note]

Roger Fry: A Great Historical Portrait Group of Bloomsbury

Reprinted from Letters of Roger Fry, *edited by Denys Sutton (London: Chatto & Windus 1972), II 423, © Mrs Pamela Diamand, with permission of Mrs Diamand, Chatto & Windus, and Random House, Inc.*

[Roger Fry was the oldest member of the Bloomsbury Group and the last one to join 'Old Bloomsbury'. He did not meet the Bells and Duncan Grant until 1910, the year of his first Post-Impressionist Exhibition, which was so important for Bloomsbury and English art. Fry wrote nothing about Bloomsbury, but the following extract of a letter to Vanessa Bell, dated 12th December 1917, confirms his awareness of the Group, though his list leaves out such members as Leonard Woolf and E.M. Forster. Mary St John Hutchinson was at this time, according to Quentin Bell, 'the most important woman in Clive's life . . . and this of course meant that she became, if not a "member", at least a very frequent visitor in Bloomsbury.' The painter Walter Sickert, though by no means a member of Bloomsbury, was highly regarded by them; Clive Bell considered him 'the greatest British painter since Constable', and Virginia Woolf even wrote a conversation about him.

For the oil sketch that Vanessa Bell finally did of the Group, see the first plate and the Foreword.]

... Clive and Mary came for Sunday and as it was wet and cold we
never stirred from the fire all day long, and talked incessantly. Clive
was in great form; Mary, sympathetic and discreet. I enjoyed it very
much. Clive is amazing in the quantity and flow of his mind, and the
quality gets better, I think. I expect it's good for him being a good
deal alone in the country and doing a lot of reading.

He suggested a great historical portrait group of Bloomsbury. I
think I shall have a shot at it − it would be rather fun. Lytton,
Maynard, Clive, Duncan, me, you, Virginia, Mary, Molly, Desmond.
Is there anyone else that ought to be in? P'raps Walter Sickert
coming in at the door and looking at us all with a kind of benevolent
cynicism.

But p'raps its too hideously difficult and p'raps you ought to do
it, as being so brilliant at likeness, though I seem to be getting rather
better ...

Saxon Sydney-Turner: Notes Toward a Descriptive Definition of Bloomsbury

Quoted by permission of Mrs Barbara Bagenal.

[The most obscure member of the Bloomsbury Group was Saxon
Sydney-Turner. A close friend of Leonard Woolf's at Cambridge and
a member of the Apostles, he spent most of his life in the Treasury. 'He
was an eccentric in the best English tradition,' Woolf wrote of him in
the *Times* after his death; he possessed 'an extraordinarily supple,
subtle, and enigmatic mind,' and 'wrote elegant verse and music, but
published nothing' (see also Woolf's description on pp.92−94).

The following unpublished extract from a letter written to Virginia
Woolf on 9th February 1919, while Sydney-Turner was staying with
Lytton Strachey at Tidmarsh, was found among the papers of Leonard
Woolf, who had labelled it 'Description of Bloomsbury'. (Woolf's
papers are now in the library at the University of Sussex.) It is not clear
what the pages of Virginia Woolf's were that Sydney-Turner refers to
(they may have had something to do with her second novel, *Night and
Day*, which was about to be published), but the interest of his letter lies
in his attempt to suggest how Bloomsbury came about and what it was

in 1919. The influence of G.E. Moore and his 'black box' analytic method receives an early stress here, and the question of just who the members of Bloomsbury were – in this instance whether Oliver Strachey and Barbara Hiles Bagenal should be included or not – was already a question in 1919].

. . . I must try – to show myself not ungrateful for your three large pages to induce you to send some more.

So far you certainly avoid the dangers you foresaw: I should like that chapter (?with illustrations) on the difficulty of getting into touch. But I don't really remember in my own case any acute discomfort in the process of getting intimate. Perhaps this is entirely due to chance. Partly the fact that some of them started at Cambridge accounts for the ease of the early stages of the intimacies. One was the right age and the conditions were right. Looking back it seems as if there were no early stages in some cases, as if one just fell in. Then if you take Clive and Adrian there was the fairly long period there of, at any rate, getting accustomed, which laid a foundation against the time when we came together again in London. Perhaps also it's easier between man and man. I remember that at one time I thought you rather difficult, which was at least as reasonable as you thinking me shocked[?]. One may have been the result of the other.

I agree though – and I think that if I were a quite dispassionate outsider I should still agree – that our friends do come out of it rather well. Whether this is because of Gordon Square and Fitzroy Square I don't know: I'm not clear whether you think so. But I fancy there was something there first that made those aggregations natural, and this suggests that our distinctive characteristic isn't simply middle age. Is there really any except that we are all rather nice and that about certain things we have much the same point of view derived by some of us from Moore's black box? And won't a descriptive definition like this include, say, Oliver and Barbara? Of course the black box influenced Oliver too, . . . [sic].

But perhaps this is all beside the real point, and that is what has come of it not how it came. And this is very complicated. I see in the collection each of us connected up with each of the others by particular peculiar links: some are more and some less important but they all have some meaning . . . [sic].

Virginia Woolf: Sex Talk in Bloomsbury

Reprinted from Quentin Bell, Virginia Woolf: A Biography *(The Hogarth Press, London 1972), I, 124, by permission of the author and The Hogarth Press;* © *1972 by Quentin Bell and reprinted by permission of Harcourt Brace Jovanovich, Inc.*

[Although complete candour was one of the aims of the Cambridge Apostles, it was some time before this ideal was interpreted in such a way as to dissipate the Victorian reticence that was to be found even in Bloomsbury drawing rooms. Virginia Woolf's account of how Bloomsbury came to plain speaking is, according to her biographer, from a paper read to the Memoir Club around 1922; the event she describes took place about 1908.]

It was a spring evening. Vanessa and I were sitting in the drawing room. The drawing room had greatly changed its character since 1904. The Sargent-Furse age was over. The age of Augustus John was dawning. His Pyramus filled one entire wall. The Watts portrait of my father and my mother were hung downstairs if they were hung at all. Clive had hidden all the match boxes because their blue and yellow swore with the prevailing colour scheme. At any moment Clive might come in and he and I should begin to argue — amicably, impersonally at first; soon we should be hurling abuse at each other and pacing up and down the room. Vanessa sat silent and did something mysterious with her needle or her scissors. I talked egotistically, excitedly, about my own affairs no doubt. Suddenly the door opened and the long and sinister figure of Mr Lytton Strachey stood on the threshold. He pointed his finger at a stain on Vanessa's white dress. 'Semen?' he said.

Can one really say it? I thought and we burst out laughing. With that one word all barriers of reticence and reserve went down. A flood of the sacred fluid seemed to overwhelm us. Sex permeated our conversation. The word bugger was never far from our lips. We discussed copulation with the same excitement and openness that we had discussed the nature of good. It is strange to think how reticent, how reserved we had been and for how long.

Virginia Woolf: A Bloomsbury Party

Reprinted from Leonard Woolf Downhill All the Way: An Autobiography of the Years 1919–1939 *(London, The Hogarth Press, 1967),
115–6, by permission of the author's literary estate and the Hogarth
Press;* © *1967 by Leonard Woolf and reprinted by permission of
Harcourt Brace Jovanovich, Inc.*

[Bloomsbury's parties attracted a considerable amount of interest from
inside and outside Bloomsbury. A diary entry of Virginia Woolf's in
January 1923, is quoted by Leonard Woolf in his autobiography as an
illustration of Bloomsbury's festivities and the social excitement they
could generate in Virginia.]

Let the scene open on the doorstep of number 50 Gordon Square. We
went up last night, carrying our bags and a Cingalese sword. There was
Mary H[utchinson] in lemon coloured trousers with green ribbons, and
so we sat down to dinner; off cold chicken. In came Roger and Adrian
and Karin [Stephen]; and very slowly we coloured our faces and made
ready for number 46. It was the proudest moment of Clive's life when
he led Mary on one arm and Virginia on the other into the
drawingroom, which was full, miscellaneous, and oriental for the most
part. Suppose one's normal pulse to be 70: in five minutes it was 120:
and the blood, not the sticky whitish fluid of daytime but brilliant and
prickly like champagne. This was my state and most people's. We
collided, when we met; went pop, used Christian names, flattered,
praised, and thought (or I did) of Shakespeare. At any rate I thought of
him when the singing was doing. Shakespeare I thought would have
liked us all tonight . . . My luck was in though and I found good
quarters with Frankie [Francis Birrell] and Sheppard and Bunny
[David Garnett] and Lydia [Lopokova] – all my friends in short. But
what we talked about I hardly know. Bunny asked me to be his child's
godmother. And a Belgian wants to translate me. Arnold Bennett thinks
me wonderful and . . . and . . . (these, no doubt, were elements in my
hilarity). Jumbo [Marjorie Strachey] distorted nursery rhymes: Lydia
danced: there were charades: Sickert acted Hamlet. We were all easy
and gifted and friendly and like good children rewarded by having the
capacity for enjoying ourselves thus. Could our fathers? I wearing my
mother's laces, looked at X's Jerboa face in the old looking glass – and
wondered, I daresay no one said anything very brilliant. I sat by Sickert
and liked him, talking, in his very workmanlike but not at all society

manner, of printing and Whistler; of an operation he saw at Dieppe. But can life be worth so much pain, he asked. 'Pour respirer,' said the doctor. 'That is everything'. 'But for two years "after my wife's death" I did not wish to live,' said Sickert. There is something indescribably congenial to me in this easy artists' talk: the values the same as my own and therefore right: no impediments: life charming, good and interesting: no effort: art brooding calmly over it all: and none of this attachment to mundane things, which I find in Chelsea. For Sickert said, why should one be attached to one's body and breakfast? Why not be satisfied to let others have the use of one's life and live it over again, being dead oneself? No mysticism, and therefore a great relish for the actual things – whatever they may be – old plays, girls, boys, Proust, Handel sung by Oliver [Strachey], the turn of a head and so on. As parties do, this one began to dwindle, until a few persistent talkers were left by themselves sitting in such odd positions. . . And so, at 3, I suppose, back to No 50 to which Clive had gone previously.

E.M. Forster: Bloomsbury, An Early Note (February 1929)

Reprinted from Pawn, *a magazine produced in King's College, Cambridge, November 1956.* © *The Provost and Scholars of King's College Cambridge.*

[Although E.M. Forster was a Cambridge Apostle at the turn of the century, a founding member of the Memoir Club, and close friend for many years of Leonard and Virginia Woolf, of Lytton Strachey, and of Roger Fry, he stated in his old age that he did not regard himself as having belonged to Bloomsbury. There is certainly a critical detachment in his 1929 'note' on Bloomsbury which he allowed to be published in an undergraduate magazine at King's in 1956. But as various other selections in this collection reveal, there was a considerable amount of critical detachment from Bloomsbury among its members. Forster's comments on Bloomsbury's intellectuality in his note do define some of his differences from several other members of Bloomsbury, yet in essays such as the famous *What I Believe* or his tribute to Virginia Woolf (see pp.207–128), there is a distinct resemblance between Forster's convictions and those of most of his Bloomsbury friends.

If further evidence were needed of Forster's involvement in Bloomsbury, it could be found in an undated rough draft of a paper possibly intended for the Memoir Club and now preserved with

Forster's papers at King's. The subject of this fragmentary essay is Forster's introduction to Bloomsbury through early encounters with Lytton Strachey, Duncan Grant, Clive Bell (they quarrelled over Bell's praise of the Second Empire), and Roger Fry, whose lectures Forster attended in the late Nineties – lectures in which Forster says he detected the essential Bloomsbury undertone that maintained it was not the subject but the treatment that mattered in art. Forster's own tone in this draft is much more affectionate than in his 1929 note. It suggests how suitable he was to do the comic guide to Bloomsbury that the Woolfs suggested he write in 1935. 'He nibbles', Virginia Woolf noted in her diary, but that was apparently all, and what might have been a Bloomsbury masterpiece remained unwritten.

In 'Bloomsbury, An Early Note' Forster refers not only to Virginia Woolf's *Orlando*, published the previous year, but also to the death of Lytton's mother, Lady Strachey, whose obituary Virginia Woolf had written for the *Times*. The identity of 'M' is uncertain. Gerald Heard's *The Ascent of Humanity* (published in 1929 and dedicated to 'E.M.F.' and 'K.W.') is subtitled *The Evolution of Civilization from Group Consciousness Through Individuality to Super-Consciousness*. In the fifth chapter Heard explains how the divergence of thought and feeling in 'upper individuals' needs to be reconciled though a new super-individuality. Intellectuals must face the choice between this new consciousness and destruction; they must recognize 'that the heart is as valid a detector of reality as the head', even though it 'challenges intelligence's position as the only way of advance and individuality as the final aim of civilization. . .' 'We can only understand the intellectuals' intellectualization of their own emotion when we realize that what they sense and dread is their individuality's destruction . . . ']

Bloomsbury, hopes W.J. Turner, will not enjoy Schnabel, a pianist whom he enjoys himself. Why drag the place in, I wonder? I suppose because it is the only genuine *movement* in English civilization, though that civilization contains far better and more genuine individuals. The other movements are anti-Bloomsbury, and cheap, envious and self-conscious, which Bloomsbury as a movement is not, being composed of people who hold similar opinions and like being with one another. But unkind, despite irritable protests to the contrary: Orlando regards centuries of flesh and spirit as fresh fuel for her bonfire, and death can only be laughed at (can't forget their laughter at M's) or adorned with a tasteful garland like Lady S's – Contempt for the outsider plays a very small part in Bloomsbury's activity and rests on inattention rather than arrogance. Once convinced that he is not a figure of fun, it welcomes and studies him, but the rest of humanity remains in a background of screaming farce as before.

Meanwhile the intellect – thinking and talking things out – goes steadily ahead, 'things' looking rather like small Xmas trees when they come into the room and trees minus their leaves and decorations when they are carried out. The final bareness isn't tragic, the horrors of the universe being surveyed in physical comfort and suffering only apprehended intellectually.

Essentially *gentlefolks*. Might occasionally open other people's letters, but wouldn't steal, bully, slander, blackmail, or resent generosity as some of their critics would, and have required a culture in harmony with their social position. Hence their stability. Contrast them with *(a)* gamindom – Joyce, D.H. Lawrence *(b)* aristocracy, who regard culture as an adventure and may at any moment burn their tapering fingers and drop it. Academic background, independent income. Continental enthusiasms, sex-talk and all. They are in the English tradition.

Gerald Heard, *The Ascent of Humanity*, Chapter V, though dealing with the wider subject of intellectualism, explains Bloomsbury without denouncing it – never done before I think. ('Why are intellectuals so irritated by emotionalism? Because they are not wholly intellectual'.)

Desmond MacCarthy: Bloomsbury, An Unfinished Memoir (1933)

Reprinted from Memories *(London, MacGibbon & Kee, 1953), 172–5, by permission of Granada Publishing Ltd.*

[Desmond MacCarthy appears to have been the most genial member of Bloomsbury. He was a little older than most of the others, and although his career was a disappointment to himself and his friends, he did become the most influential English newspaper critic of his time and gave wide currency to certain Bloomsbury values. It is completely characteristic of him that his memoir of Bloomsbury should be unfinished.

MacCarthy's summary of the hostility that the Bloomsbury Group had provoked by the early thirties is accurate as far as it goes, but in denying that Bloomsbury was a movement, he presents a much more

limited conception of the Group than E.M. Forster. MacCarthy
indentifies Bloomsbury with what came to be called 'Old Bloomsbury',
as did various other members; his disclaimer that Bloomsbury was not
his spiritual home is one that perhaps all the members of the Group
could have made.]

'Bloomsbury' is a regional adjective which has been used as a label for a
few writers and painters who dwell, or have some time or other dwelt,
in that part of London; and who used to, or do, see a good deal of each
other. It is chiefly used as a term of abuse in reviews. In the shortahnd
of colloquial criticism and gossip it connotes, vaguely, a certain
arrogant exclusiveness, anti-herd intellectualism, and a superior moral-
frivolity. 'Bloomsbury', as a word, has also found its way into the
jargon of French and German criticism of contemporary English
literature, where it takes on the significance of a literary movement.
But in England, where spectators see, at any rate, that there is little in
common between the work of Lytton Strachey, Virginia Woolf, Clive
Bell, David Garnett, Roger Fry, Maynard Keynes, Leonard Woolf,
Vanessa Bell, Duncan Grant, E.M. Forster, it does not suggest so much
a movement as a 'push'; a mutual-admiration society, to which some,
suffering from suspicion-mania, have attributed a sinister power over
the Press. Writers and painters who are indignant, sometimes rightly,
sometimes wrongly, at their works not meeting with universal praise,
and looking about for an explanation of the inexplicable, have been
known to mutter darkly 'Bloomsbury' and find relief.

> Of all the clever people round me here
> I most delight in Me —
> Mine is the only voice I hear,
> And mine the only face I see.

Roy Campbell's epigram, which he calls *Home Thoughts in
Bloomsbury*, expresses a conception of it which is only an exaggeration
of one that is fairly common. But, in fact, 'Bloomsbury' is neither a
movement, nor a push, but only a group of old friends; whose affection
and respect for each other has stood the test of nearly thirty years and
who intellectual candour makes their company agreeable to each other.
It never was a movement. In taste and judgment 'Bloomsbury' from the
start has been at variance with itself. Indeed, here lay its charm as a
social circle. There was enough mutual respect and affection, well

tested by time, to supply cement; enough difference of temperament
and opinion to stimulate talk; enough intellectual honesty to enable
them to learn from each other. Their association began when they were
far too young (with the exception of Roger Fry) to have achieved
anything; and by the time the world heard of 'Bloomsbury',
'Bloomsbury' as a group had ceased to exist. Though old ties remained,
friends were scattered; and most of them were seeing much more of
new friends than of each other: 'Marriage and death and division make
barren our lives.'

And so far from being a mutual admiration society, 'Bloomsbury' is
the last place where a Bloomsburian, who has just written a book,
would look for that enthusiastic amazement at his achievement which
authors enjoy most. A considerate silence, a carefully measured
commendation veering at once into a discussion of generalities, is the
most he, or she, ever hopes to get *there*. In early days, before they had
done anything, they did believe in one another — perhaps more than
each believed in himself or herself.

'Bloomsbury' has never been a spiritual home to me; but let me add
that I have not got one, although at Cambridge for a few years I fancied
that I had. 'Bloomsbury' had been to me, rather, what those who cater
for sailors (like theirs, my home is a floating one) call 'a home from
home'. Looking back I see that I converged upon 'Bloomsbury' by
three ways: through making friends with Clive Bell, through getting to
know some Cambridge 'Apostles' junior to me, and through my
introduction into the home-life of Miss Vanessa and Miss Virginia
Stephen. Although the second of these approaches was prior in time I
will begin with my first encounter (it was strikingly accidental) with
Clive Bell.

My undergraduate days were over, and I was going down to
Cambridge one November afternoon in 1901 to visit George Moore, the
philosopher, who still had rooms in Neville's Court. It must have been
that train which gets us up to Cambridge in time for dinner. My mood
was one of dejection; and when such moods come upon me I take any
modest steps handy to relieve them. If I happen, for instance, to be
travelling, and to have money in my pocket, I will travel first-class. It
does me hardly any perceptible good, but still perhaps — a little. There
was on this occasion one other occupant of the carriage that I entered
that afternoon. He was a youth with a noticeable head of wavy auburn
hair, and that milk-white skin which often goes with it. I cannot
visualise him completely, but I think I am safe in saying that he was
dressed with careless opulence, and that he wore, flung open, a dark fur

coat with a deep astrakhan collar. I thought his appearance distinctly enviable, and I was prepared by my melancholy to take a pathetically unselfish interest in the good fortune of others. It was not his aspect which struck me as proclaiming him to be one of the fortunate; not even his youth, a quality, which, at the age of twenty-four, I thought even more enviable than I think it now, but his eager and enjoying temperament, with which in the first ten minutes of conversation I came in contact. I forgot in talk with him the weight of troubles, cosmic and private, which were oppressing me; and I fancied myself to be enjoying, vicariously at any rate, through him, the prospect of helping myself in a generous manner to the pleasures of life. My attitude towards this young man (it was inevitable in one so rent and bruised by experience as myself) was distinctly avuncular. Happily either he did not perceive this or he did not resent it. I delighted in him because I could see in imagination the enormous rich hunk he was about to cut from the cake of life. What we talked about I cannot remember, but that was the residual impression. I must, of course, have asked him if he did not know 'So-and-So, and So-and-So', mentioning those younger Cambridge 'Apostles' who, as I said, also proved to be roads leading to 'Bloomsbury' — Lytton Strachey certainly was one of them. Anyhow we got on so well together that he asked me to lunch with him the next day. One other thing interested me in him, the orientation of his life at the moment seemed to resemble what my own had been when I first went up to Cambridge.

He appeared to have a foot in two communities which, in the University, and indeed in the world itself, are separated from each other by as deep a trench as divides, say, Roman Catholics from the rest of mankind. He seemed to live, half with the rich sporting-set, and half with the intellectuals; and sure enough next day I found my host in a white hunting-stock and a dressing gown. His aspect was reminiscent of a sporting young man in a Leech picture at that delicious moment when he has pulled off his top-boots and is about to take his hot shower-bath. That it was a Sunday and he could not have thrown a leg over a horse that morning, added to his character a touch of fantasy, which was in harmony with my first impression of him.

Desmond MacCarthy: The Influence of Henry James and Lytton Strachey's Cambridge

Reprinted from Portraits I *(London, Putnam, 1931), 164–6, by permission of the publishers, and from* Memories *(London, MacGibbon and Kee, 1953), 39–41, by permission of Granada Publishing Ltd.*

[Desmond MacCarthy was closer to G.E. Moore than anyone else in Bloomsbury. His autobiographical digressions in essays on Henry James and on Lytton Strachey supplement MacCarthy's incomplete memoir with brief views of the academic origins of what MacCarthy calls a 'colony of Cambridge'. MacCarthy's conclusions about the influence of Henry James's philosophy on himself and his friends are quite similar to his later remarks on Moore's influence – and they anticipate Keynes's celebrated interpretation of Moore's influence in *My Early Beliefs* (pp.48–64).]

. . . Nevertheless my own generation, when we discovered Henry James, read him on the whole for his substance, for precisely that side of his work which appears now to be wearing thin. Our generation, at least that part of it with which I was best acquainted and most at home, was interested in those parts of experience which could be regarded as ends in themselves. Morality was either a means to attaining these goods of the soul, or it was nothing – just as the railway system existed to bring people together and to feed them, or the social order that as many 'ends' as possible should be achieved. These ends naturally fined themselves down to personal relations, aesthetic emotions and the pursuit of truth. We were perpetually in search of distinctions; our most ardent discussions were attempts to fix some sort of a scale of values for experience. The tendency was for the stress to fall on feeling rightly rather than upon action. It would be an exaggeration to say we cared not a sprat either for causes or for our own careers (appetite in both directions comes with eating, and we had barely begun to nibble); but those interests were subordinate. Henry James was above all a novelist of distinctions; he was, indeed, the master in fiction of the art of distinguishing. His philosophy amounted to this: to appreciate exquisitely was to live intensely. We suspected, I remember, that he over-valued subtlety as an ingredient in character, and was perhaps too 'social' in his standards, employing, for instance, 'charm' too often as the last test of character. But whether or not we always agreed with his estimate of values, he was pre-eminently interested in what interested us; that is to say, in disentangling emotions, in describing their appropriate objects and in showing in what subtle ways friendships might be exquisite, base, exciting, dull or droll. That his characters were detached from the big common struggling world, that its vague murmur floated in so faintly through their windows, that they moved and had their being in an environment entirely composed of personal relations, aesthetic emotions, and historic associations, seemed to us unimportant limitations to his art. Nor were we particularly interested in the instincts or the will compared with the play of the intelligence. What was the will but a means, a servant? Or what were the instincts but the raw stuff out of which the imagination moulded a life worth contemplating?

It still seems to me, on the whole, a sound philosophy; only the fiction which reflects these things to exclusion of all else now appears to me to shut out much which is both more absorbing and more important than I once supposed – even also to falsify the flavour of those very experiences on which it exclusively dwells. . . . It was a letter from Walter Raleigh announcing that a distinctly remarkable undergraduate was about to join us, which largely determined Lytton Strachey's circle of friends at the university.

As he kept those friends all his life; as that London set of writers and artists, known afterwards as 'Bloomsbury', in which he was the most prominent figure, was really an off-shoot or colony of Cambridge at the beginning of the century (with Leslie Stephen's two daughters, Virginia Woolf and Vanessa Bell, added), I shall try to indicate the spirit of that Cambridge generation to which I also belonged.

We were not much interested in politics. Abstract speculation was much more absorbing. Philosophy was much more interesting to us than public causes. The wave of Fabian socialism, which affected some of Lytton Strachey's younger contemporaries like Rubert Brooke, had not reached Cambridge in my time. What we chiefly discussed were those 'goods' which were ends in themselves; and these ends, for which the rest of life was only a scaffolding, could be subsumed under three heads: the search for truth, aesthetic emotions and personal relations — love and friendship.

Those who have been to a university will remember how each decade, as far as the intellectual life of the young is concerned, tends to be dominated by some unusually gifted man. The dominating influence when Lytton Strachey came up was metaphysical, embodied in G.E. Moore and Bertrand Russell who had shaken confidence in the Idealism of McTaggart. Thus Amurath to Amurath succeeds. Lytton Strachey himself was the next influence. He remained at Cambridge after he had taken his degree, a second in History, sitting for a Fellowship at Trinity till 1905 and writing a dissertation on Warren Hastings. The curious can read that essay in his posthumous volume *Characters and Comment-aries*. It is an elegant and surprisingly mature piece of work. No doubt he was attracted to the subject through the connection of his family with India, but it was not a subject particularly suited to his hand, and it failed to win him a Fellowship. Meanwhile, as I said, he had become a leader among the young, not only through his culture, his wit and the discrimination of his taste, but thanks above all to the vehement and passionate nature of his judgments upon character. The drift of his influence was away from metaphysical speculation, for though he had a clear head in argument he was not particularly fitted to follow complicated trains of abstract reasoning. His days and nights were spent in reading and in long, leisurely, laughing, intimate talks. It has been said of Edward Fitzgerald that his friendships were more like loves, and that might also be said of Lytton Strachey.

His influence, especially upon his younger contemporaries, was to fix their attention on emotions and relations between human beings. He was a master of what may be called psychological gossip, the kind which treats friends as diagrams of the human species and ranges over the past and fiction as well as history, in search of whatever illustrates this or that side of human nature . . .

Adrian Stephen: The *Dreadnought* Hoax

Reprinted from Adrian Stephen, The 'Dreadnought' Hoax *(London, The Hogarth Press, 1936), 16–47, by permission of the author's literary estate and The Hogarth Press.*

[Two famous events in the early history of Bloomsbury occurred in 1910. Roger Fry's first Post-Impressionist Exhibition opened in October and stunned the established English art world, and the previous January Adrian Stephen, his sister Virginia, and Duncan Grant joined three friends to hoax the Royal Navy so successfully that newspaper headlines and questions in Parliament resulted. The celebrated *Dreadnought* Hoax was organized by Horace Cole, a wealthy practical joker and college friend of Adrian's, and participated in by two other friends, Anthony Buxton and Guy Ridley. In his account of the hoax, which was written a quarter of a century later, Adrian tells how Cole and his friends at Cambridge had hoaxed the mayor several years before by disguising themselves as the Sultan of Zanzibar and his suite. For Adrian at least these hoaxes had a purpose beyond that of simply having fun at other people's expense: 'It had seemed to me ever since I was very young, just as I imagine it had seemed to Cole, that anyone who took up an attitude of authority over anyone else was necessarily also someone who offered a leg for everyone else to pull . .'. Adrian had hopes, in that far off world before the war, of pulling the legs of the German army and the French government by marching a detachment of German troops into France, but he settled finally for hoaxing the English senior service.

Virginia Woolf also left a fragmentary account of this hoax. After mentioning that one result was the tightening up of regulations concerning official visitors, she observes, 'I am glad to think that I too have been of help to my country'. When Admiral Sir William Wordsworth Fisher, the Stephens' first cousin who had been chief of the Admiral's staff on the *Dreadnought*, died the year after Adrian's account was published, Virginia wrote in a letter, 'Yes I'm sorry about William – our last meeting was on the deck of the Dreadnought in 1910, I think; but I wore a beard. And I'm afraid he took it to heart a good deal . . .']

. . .The *Dreadnought* Hoax took place a few years later. The 'Channel Fleet' (I believe it was called this) was then lying at Weymouth under the command of Admiral X, whose flagship was the *Dreadnought*, and, in short, we proposed to visit it in the characters of the Emperor of Abyssinia and his suite. The idea was suggested to Cole by a naval officer as a matter of fact, and those who made a to-do about the honour of the Navy would have been interested to hear this. I am afraid I may be letting something out of the bag, too, if I say that one of his first aims was to pull the leg of another naval officer, a cousin of my own. My cousin was chief of the Admiral's staff at that time and so might be considered to be involved.

Cole asked me to meet his friend at luncheon, and he and I took to the plan at once, and the next thing was to collect our troupe of hoaxers. Cole got hold of two friends, Mr Anthony Buxton and Mr Guy Ridley, and I got hold of my sister Virginia, now Mrs Woolf, and Mr Duncan Grant.

The plan which had worked so well at Cambridge was to be repeated as nearly as possible, but this time Cole was to be a young gentleman from the Foreign Office, Buxton was to be the Emperor of Abyssinia, Virginia, Guy Ridley and Duncan Grant were to form the suite, and I was to be the interpreter.

Virginia and I lived in Fitzroy Square in those days, and it was arranged that the whole troupe should meet in our house early one morning to be made up for their parts. Clarksons undertook to dress us up, and I believe the great Mr Willy Clarkson himself came to superintend, though, of course, we let no one into our plot. Horace Cole just had to wear a top-hat and tail coat, but the Emperor and his suite, including Virginia, had to have their faces blackened, to wear false beards and moustaches and elaborate Eastern robes. I was merely disguised with a false beard, a moustache and a little sunburn powder. I wore a bowler hat and a great coat and looked, I am afraid, like a seedy commercial traveller.

When all was ready we took taxis to Paddington Station and got into a train with a luncheon car bound for Weymouth. The telegram, warning the Admiral to expect us, was to be sent off after we started, and it was to be signed 'Hardinge', though the friend who sent it was named in sober fact Tudor Castle. Hardinge, however, was the name of the permanent head of the Foreign Office.

There is little to tell of the journey down. Cole and I insisted that the others should not go with us into the luncheon car, as we were afraid of accidents to their make-up. He and I went and lunched together, however, and spent our time largely in the attempt to teach me the Swahili language. Swahili is, I believe, spoken in some parts of East Africa. Whether it is spoken in Abyssinia or not I don't know, but we thought it might be as well for me to know a few phrases, and to that end we had bought a grammar from the Society for the Propagation of the Gospel. Of course, when the time came, I could hardly remember two words, though some newspapers later described us as having talked 'fluent Abyssinian'. However, if it did nothing else, the study of Swahili helped Cole and me, at any rate, to pass the time, for to tell the truth we were feeling rather nervous. Something might so easily go wrong. It might be that the telegram ought to have been written in some special code, or it might be that the Admiral would send a message by wireless to get it confirmed, or perhaps my cousin might recognize me (he would hardly recognize Virginia) and then we should get into trouble.

I think that perhaps the most exciting moment for me that day was first the arrival at Weymouth — that was the plunge into the cold bath. As the train slowed down for the station we were all agog. I think I half expected that no notice would be taken of us at all, and we should just have to slink back to London but no, there on the platform stood a naval officer in full uniform, and the hoax had begun.

As we got out of the train the officer stepped smartly up and saluted the Emperor formally, and Cole and I made whatever introductions seemed necessary.

In spite of the short notice we had given, everything was ready for our reception. Inside the station a red carpet was laid down for us to walk on, and there was a barrier in position to keep sightseers at a proper distance. Outside we were conducted to cabs which took us down to the harbour and there, again, was the smart little steam launch which was to take us out to the Fleet.

By the time we reached the *Dreadnought* the expedition had become for me at any rate almost an affair of every day. It was hardly a question any longer of a hoax. We were almost acting the truth. Everyone was expecting us to act as the Emperor and his suite, and it would have been extremely difficult not to.

It may have seemed to some an odd introduction to the story of a hoax in which I took part to say that I am incapable of deception. Of course, I did not mean the words to be taken too pedantically. Suppose someone sent word to an unwelcome visitor that he was not at home you could hardly on that ground describe him as a liar without being so misleading as to be guilty of falsehood yourself. Pedantically speaking, he would, of course, be a liar, and, pedantically speaking, I must admit myself capable of deception when I took part in the hoax. But once the telegram had been sent off, and we had arrived and been received, it would not have been an easy matter to tell the truth, and we almost, I think, believed in the hoax ourselves.

We steamed out then in our little brass-funnelled launch into the bay where we saw the *Dreadnought* lying among the Fleet, with lines of marines drawn up on her deck and flags flying from her mast. Then, as we came alongside and approached the ship's gangway, the band struck up its music.

As a matter of fact, the ship was smaller than I expected, I remember, and uglier, with its funnels and its great tripod mast and its gun turrets and what not, stuck all about. However, I had not much time for criticism. When we arrived the Admiral and his staff and the captain of the ship, all in their gold-laced uniforms, were ready to receive us.

Cole went on board first, I think, and then the Emperor and his suite, and I was last. I had one or two surprises at this point. Cole was performing the introductions, and I was a little taken aback to hear myself introduced as Kauffmann. We had all chosen our own names coming down in the train and Cole, who was rather deaf, had misheard me. I had chosen an English name that sounded a little like Kauffmann and Kauffmann with a German name I was to be. I was a little alarmed at this, because German spy scares were for ever being started in those days, and I was afraid of an extra close scrutiny. At the same time I was conscious of looking the most awful 'outsider' and of not knowing in what form to return the Admiral's welcome, whether to take my hat off or shake hands or what. On the top of this I saw my cousin standing staring at me from a few yards off, and since I stood 6 ft 5 in. in my socks I was afraid he might observe me. Then I became aware of another source of danger, too, that was quite unexpected, for the captain of the ship also turned out to be a man with whom I was personally acquainted. I belonged at that time to a small club which took long country walks on Sundays, and the captain had several times joined in and spent whole days in our company. I knew, of course, that he was a Captain in the Navy, but did not know his ship.

The situation, then, was becoming very embarrassing, but I was saved by the naval officers' proverbial tact. Their cordiality was such that it put me at my ease at once and the inspection of the ship began.

I am afraid that my memory of the visit must necessarily refer mainly to my own experience, and it is rather scrappy, but a few moments seem to stand out specially. The first thing to do was to inspect the Guard of Honour, and this put the first strain on my powers of interpretation. There were two kinds of marines in the guard, and some of them had blue uniforms and some red, some were, I think, artillery and some infantry. The Admiral explained this to me and told me to pass it on to the Emperor. For a moment I boggled at this, I could not think what to say. 'I am afraid it will be rather hard to put that into Abyssinian, sir,' I said. 'However, I'll try.' 'Entaqui, mahai, kustufani,' I started, addressing Anthony Buxton, and whether those were real Swahili words learnt from the grammar, or whether they were invented on the spur of the moment, I don't remember, but they have stuck in my memory ever since. If they were real Swahili they were the only native African words that any of us used, and I could get no further. I don't find it easy to speak fluent gibberish impromptu, and I was again in something of a difficulty. I must somehow produce something that would not be too jerky, and too unplausible. After a pause I began again as follows: 'Tahli bussor ahbat tahl æsque miss. Erraema, fleet use . . .' and so on. My language may have sounded a bit

odd, but at any rate I could be fluent enough. When I was a boy I had
spent years on what is called a classical education, and now I found a
use for it. It was the habit in the middle forms of my school to learn by
heart the fourth book of Virgil's *Æneid* as 'repetition'. I was able,
therefore, to repeat whole stretches of it, and I knew a good deal of
Homer in the same way. I was provided by my education, then, with a
fine repertory of nonsense and did not have to fall back entirely on my
own invention. I had to take care that neither the Latin nor the Greek
should be recognized, of course, but I felt that probably few naval
officers had suffered an education like mine and, in any case, I so broke
up the words and so mispronounced them that probably they would
have escaped notice even of the best scholar. The quotation that I
started with by the way is from the *Æneid* Book IV, line 437.

I found that my plan worked excellently, and even began to improve
on it as in some emergencies that occurred more than once such as
telling the Emperor to mind his head in a doorway, I would remember
what I had said last time and use the same phrase again. This may have
given us a little plausibility, especially as Anthony Buxton was very
quick in picking up some of my words, and using them in his replies. I
remember, though, hearing two officers who were eavesdropping
behind some corner remark on the oddness of our lingo.

There was only one further precaution that I had to take about our
speech. Since there were two men on board, with one of whom, indeed,
I had to converse a great deal, who might be expected to know my
voice, some disguise was clearly necessary. Instead of my usual rather
high register and Cambridge accent, therefore, I used a most unnatural
deep bass, and an accent that was meant to be German. With that our
disguise was as good as I could make it, but there was one other
moment of suspense in connection with our speech, though I don't
remember exactly when it occurred. Someone told me that there was
one man in the Fleet who could speak to the Abyssinians in their own
tongue, but mercifully added that he was away on leave.

The Admiral received us then and inspected the Guard of Honour
with us, and then handed us over to Captain Y (my acquaintance) to be
taken over the ship. I cannot remember now all that we saw, but I
remember going down long corridors, looking at the wireless room, the
sick bay if that is what it is called, and the Mess, having the big guns
turned and aimed in different directions and so forth and so on. All
these things I duly described in a mixture of Homer and Virgil.

As one might have expected the officers were almost too hospitable,
and pressed us hard to eat and drink, but I was too afraid of the effect

on our make-up. I excused us on the grounds that the religious beliefs of Abyssinia made it impossible for the Royal family to touch food unless it was prepared in quite special ways. The feeding problem was easily dealt with, but a worse moment was when I saw that Duncan's moustache was beginning to peel off. A slight breeze had got up, and a little rain began to fall, so that I was terrified what might happen next. I did what I could with an umbrella, but there were five people to cover, and then I saw the obvious solution. I spoke to the captain of the heat of the Abyssinian climate and the chill of England, and he saw my point at once and took us below. For a moment or two I had to separate Duncan from the rest and dab hastily at his upper lip, but I was able to be quick enough to escape notice.

Another problem arose about a salute. The Emperor of Abyssinia might expect to be saluted by the firing of guns, and I was consulted as to whether this should be done. I took the course which I think at any rate most of us approved of and said that it was not necessary at all. The French Fleet had not saluted us at Toulon, why should the English? The real fact was that I understood that firing salutes meant cleaning guns afterwards, and it seemed too much of a shame to cause such unnecessary trouble — besides, it was almost as grand to refuse a salute as to accept one.

After going all over the ship, there was nothing left but to return home. Cole who had been enjoying himself in the ward room rejoined the party, and we embarked again on our little steam launch.

We were accompanied again by a young officer, and I remember his pleasure at the astonishment of the simple natives when he switched on the electric light. I think it was this young man, too, who spoke to me about the tune with which the band had welcomed us. The band-master had been unable to get a copy of the Abyssinian National Anthem, but had played, as the next best thing, the Anthem of Zanzibar. I said I thought it did excellently, and considering Cole's and my history, I thought it did.

Another incident happened, I believe, during this short passage to the shore, but I did not notice it — another vessel crossed our bows. But our launch contained Royalty and it is, apparently, a great breach of etiquette to cross the bows of Royalty, so the young officer who was responsible was had up by his Captain and reprimanded. Now the officer who was reprimanded was the young Prince of A. I had this story from another naval officer, and whether it is true or not I feel it ought to be.

When we reached the shore Cole tipped the sailors who came with us royally, and tried to pin a fancy-dress order on the breast of our young officer. He refused it rather shyly, saying he could not accept it without permission from his superiors. He was a nice young man, I thought, and I was really saddened a few years later when I saw what I believed to be his name in the list of those killed in some battle.

We drove to the station, then, and I think when we got into the train we were all except, perhaps, Cole, thoroughly exhausted. The only thing we could think of was our dinner, and luckily we were able to have it in our own compartment, so we ate it in comfort. We only kept up the hoax so far as to insist on the waiters wearing white gloves to serve us. I believe they had to dash out and buy them.

I suppose that most of us imagined that with our arrival home the whole incident was finished. We had decided not to tell the newspapers and, though something was bound to leak out, we did not expect what happened. We had had a photograph taken of ourselves in our fancy dress as a memento, and one day walking in the street I saw this reproduced on the poster of (I think) the *Mirror*. I believe that was how I first realized that someone had given the story away, and I have never felt the slightest doubt that it was Cole who did it, and he would certainly never contradict it.

After this we heard nothing more for some time, till one day walking with Cole near the top of Sloane Street, I saw Captain Y and his wife. He saw us, too, and recognized us and pretended at first to be horrified and then to call a policeman. After a second or two, though, he began to laugh and, in fact, took the whole affair in the best of good humours. There were certain other officers, however, who took it in a different spirit.

It was several weeks after the hoax was over when I was called down early one Sunday morning to see my cousin Z and found him waiting for me in the hall with an expression that I felt to be grim. He told me that he had come to find out just who had taken part in the hoax and that he wanted us all to apologize. He said that he already knew Cole's name, and that Virginia was involved, but he did not know who the others were. For my own part, I said, I did not mind apologizing in the least if it would make things easier for the Admiral. There had been questions asked in Parliament, and we had never meant to cause serious trouble, so if trouble could be avoided by an apology I should be quite ready to make one; though, of course, the others would have to be asked what they felt. My cousin asked me who the others were and, innocent as a lamb, I gave him their names. I, of course, had been hoaxed in my own turn, for the names were needed for another purpose.

My cousin almost snorted with contempt when I suggested that an apology might make things easier for the Admiral — as though such miserable creatures as the hoaxers could possibly make things easier or harder for such an exalted being as an Admiral. I gathered, though, what he minded even more than the questions of the gentlemen in Parliament was the behaviour of the little boys in the streets of Weymouth. When the hoax became so widely known as it did through the *Daily Mirror*, one of the newspapers published an interview. I think it was supposed to be with one of the assistants at Clarksons, who professed to know a great deal more than he did, and in particular stated that we had used the expression 'Bunga-Bunga'. Anyhow, the words 'Bunga-Bunga' became public catchwords for a time, and were introduced as tags into music-hall songs and so forth. Apparently the Admiral was unable to go on shore without having them shouted after him in the streets, and I suppose that other officers suffered in the same way. Naturally, I was very sorry about this — we had no wish to make anyone really uncomfortable — and I expressed my sympathy to my cousin. He left me, then, but as he went he asked me whether I knew what the officers were saying about Virginia in the Mess. 'They are saying that she is a commom woman of the town — and *I* have to sit and hear this in silence.' With this, holding his right hand in a marked way aloof from mine, he closed the door.

Of course, I got into touch at once with Cole, and then I heard his story. Things had gone very differently with him. The evening before my cousin and another naval officer had arrived at his house and asked to see him. Cole received them in his sitting-room, and they announced that they had come to avenge the honour of the Navy. They proposed to achieve this by beating him with a cane. In ordinary circumstances there would probably have been a free fight, and as Cole was pretty formidable, and as his manservant had scented trouble and was waiting outside the door in case he was needed, there is no telling who would have won. There was one thing which complicated matters, though. Cole was only just recovering from an illness which would have made violent exercise rather a serious danger. This was pointed out to the officers, and it put them in a dilemma. This was the third week-end, they said, that they had journeyed up to London to avenge the Navy, and they could not be foiled again. Eventually Cole made a proposal: he would agree to be beaten if he was allowed to reply in kind. This was agreed to, and the whole party adjourned to a quiet back street. Here they were safe from interruption, either from Cole's manservant or from the public, and here six ceremonial taps were administered to Cole's hindquarters, and six ceremonial taps were administered by him in return.

After this the Navy's honour was at least partly cleared, and the two sides shook hands and parted.

The only other adventure of this kind that I heard of was Duncan's. Whether Buxton or Ridley received visits from the Navy I never heard, and I have scarcely seen either of them since, but Duncan certainly did. He was sitting at breakfast with his father and mother one Sunday morning when a maid announced that some gentlemen had called to see him. It must have been the same morning that my cousin called on me, because Duncan had no warning, and went to see his friends who were waiting outside. Looking out of the window, Mrs Grant saw her son tripped up and pushed into a taxi, the door slammed and the taxi driven off. She was naturally alarmed, and appealed to her husband to know what they should do. 'I expect it's his friends from the *Dreadnought*,' said Major Grant, with his usual beaming smile, and so, of course, it was. When he looked about him in the taxi Duncan found himself seated on the floor at the feet of three large men who were carrying a bundle of canes. They drove on for a bit in silence and Duncan asked where they were going. 'You'll see plenty of *Dreadnoughts* where you are going,' answered my cousin in an ominous voice. Then they asked Duncan whether he was ill, fearing, I suppose, a repetition of the night before.

At last they arrived somewhere in the region of Hendon, and here they stopped, and Duncan was told to get out and go into a field. There was no use in fighting against overwhelming odds, as Duncan said, and out he got and did as he was told.

'I can't make this chap out,' said one of the officers, 'he does not put up any fight. You can't cane a chap like that.' In the end it proved that they could cane a chap like that, but only with some difficulty. My cousin was unable to do it himself, but he could order his inferior officer to do so and the inferior officer could carry out his orders. Duncan, then, received two ceremonial taps, also, and the little party broke up. It so happened, though, that Duncan had only his bedroom slippers on, and no hat, and this so distressed the officers that they pressed him to accept a lift home. 'You can't go home like that,' they said, but Duncan felt it less embarrassing to travel home by tube.

And now I come to what was, so far as I know, the last episode. A great many people – even those who had been thoroughly amused at the Cambridge joke – were profoundly shocked at the idea of hoaxing the Navy. I had an elderly relation, for instance, who had been delighted with the first hoax, and who kindly wrote offering his help in case there were legal proceedings in connection with the second. In his letter, however, he implored me 'for God's sake' to 'keep Virginia's name out of it,' and felt bound to state his opinion that 'His Majesty's ships are not suitable objects for practical jokes'. Other people, and especially a certain military gentleman, began to ask questions in Parliament, and word came round to me that some form of reprimand was going to be administered to the Admiral. Whether the rumour was true I don't know, but it reached me apparently very directly from Mrs McKenna, who was the wife of the First Lord of the Admiralty. It was suggested again that an apology might make things easier. If the hoaxers were to apologize that might appease those who wanted the Admiral punished. When I heard this, there was no time to waste. Cole was either ill or away, and I could not get hold of either Ridley or Buxton, but I did get hold of Duncan, and together we went down to Whitehall. The door-keeper at the Admiralty seemed a little surprised to see us, but when we told him that we wished to see the First Lord about the *Dreadnought* hoax he gave us an interested look and went to make inquiries. We did not have to wait long, but were taken upstairs to what I suppose was Mr McKenna's private room. Mr McKenna took it for granted at once that we had come to beg for mercy. He told us that at least one of us had committed a forgery under the Post Office Acts, and was liable to go to gaol and he at any rate had better lie low, while the position of the rest of us was doubtful. We tried to get him to see that we were not in the least concerned with what the Government proposed to do to us and were, indeed, extremely sceptical as to whether they could do anything at all. We were only offering, if he wanted it, an easy way of smoothing things over, but he would have none of it, and bundled us out. I think I really felt quite ill-used about this. We had come absolutely gratuitously to make what seemed a generous offer, and I did not see why this politician should treat us *de haut en bas*, not even if he had rowed in the Cambridge boat before he was First Lord of the Admiralty. Perhaps, really, we had put him in an awkward position, and he did not know quite what to say; perhaps, indeed, he was laughing up his sleeve.

This was the end of the whole affair. I waited expecting to receive some sort of visitation from the Navy, but none came. Just why they beat Cole and Duncan, and not me, I have never understood. Anyone who does not know me may possibly think that it was because I was 6ft 5 in. high, and might have been a formidable customer. That is not so, however; if matters had come to a trial of strength I should have fallen a much easier victim than Cole. In any case, had I been a Goliath I am sure the Navy's gallantry would have risen to the occasion. I should be sorry, indeed, if anything I wrote were taken as intended to cast doubts on the bravery of naval officers. These men have very particular feelings on this point. Bravery is as much a matter of professional pride to them as is the quality of his potatoes to a greengrocer. I should be sorry without the strongest reasons to cast doubts on either.

Personally, I have always felt, as I expect most of those concerned did, that the officers' wisest course would have been that which the Vice-Chancellor recommended to the Mayor of Cambridge — to take no notice of us. As for 'revenge', if they wanted any they had already had plenty before the hoax was over. They treated us so delightfully while we were on board that I, for one, felt very uncomfortable at mocking, even in the friendliest spirit, such charming people.

Virginia Woolf: Julian Bell

Reprinted from Quentin Bell, Virginia Woolf: A Biography *(London, The Hogarth Press, 1972), II, 255–9, by permission of the author and The Hogarth Press;* © *1972 by Quentin Bell and reprinted by permission of Harcourt Brace Jovanovich, Inc.*

[Vanessa and Clive Bell's son Julian was killed while serving as an ambulance driver for the Loyalists in the Spanish Civil War. It has been said that after the death of Thoby Stephen in 1906 Bloomsbury was refounded by his relatives and friends who were brought close together in their grief. But the death of Julian Bell a generation later effectively shattered Bloomsbury. Thoby's death from typhoid fever was a private tragedy, but Julian's death belonged to the public events that overwhelmed Bloomsbury and the world. 'In those twilight days,' Julian's brother wrote later, 'it was bloody to be alive and to be young was very hell.'

Several weeks after his death in July 1937, Virginia Woolf set down her immediate recollections of her nephew. The abridged version of her memoir given here was first published in Quentin Bell's biography of her. It is not a Memoir Club paper; the tone is too painfully serious, the shock of events too close for detached reminiscence. Virginia's memoir is important not only for what it reveals about Bloomsbury's life in the twilight of the thirties but also for the tensions that it reveals at the very centre of Bloomsbury between the Bells and the Woolfs — tensions that had been part of Bloomsbury in one way or another at least since Leonard Woolf's return from Ceylon in 1911.

Virginia Woolf's recollections contain allusions to the deaths of Thoby Stephen and Roger Fry, to Lottie Hope, a servant of the Woolfs and Bells, to Clive's brother Cory Bell, to Desmond MacCarthy's Leslie Stephen Lecture at Cambridge, to Virginia's obituary of her Greek teacher Janet Case, to Labour MP Hugh Dalton, to the poet Stephen Spender, to the editor of *The New Statesman*, Kingsley Martin, and to Julian's essay 'On Roger Fry — A Letter to A', which was published the next year in Julian's *Essays, Poems and Letters*. (The arrangement of the text in Quentin Bell's biography has been slightly altered.)]

I am going to set down very quickly what I remember about Julian, — partly because I am too dazed to write what I was writing: and then I am so composed that nothing is real unless I write it. And again, I know by this time what an odd effect Time has: it does not destroy people — for instance, I still think perhaps more truly than I did, of Roger, of Thoby: but it brushes away the actual personal presence.

The last time I saw Julian was at Clive's, two days before he went to Spain. It was a Sunday night, the beginning of June — a hot night. He was in his shirtsleeves. Lottie was out, and we cooked dinner. He had a peculiar way of standing: his gestures were, as they say, characteristic. He made sharp quick movements, very sudden, considering how large and big he was, and oddly graceful. (They reminded one of a sharp winged bird — one of the snipe here in the marsh.) I remember his intent expression; seriously looking, I suppose at toast or eggs, through his spectacles. He had a very serious look: indeed he had grown much sterner, since he came back from China. But of the talk I remember very little; except that by degrees it turned to politics, and Clive and Julian began to talk about Fascism, I dare say: and I remember thinking, now Clive is reining himself in with L[eonard]: being self-restrained: which means there's trouble brewing. (I was wrong, as L. told me afterwards.) Julian was now a grown man: I mean, he held his own with Clive and L.: and was cool and independent. I felt he had met many different kinds of people in China. Anyhow, as it was hot, and they talked politics, V[anessa] and A[ngelica] and I went out into the Square, and then the others came, and we sat and talked. I remember saying something about Roger's papers, and telling Julian I should leave them to him in my will. He said in his quick way, Better leave them to the British Museum, and I thought, That's because he thinks he may be killed. Of course we all knew that this was our last meeting — all together — before he went. But I had made up my mind to plunge into work, and seeing people, that summer. I had determined not to think about the risks, because, subconsciously I was sure he would be killed; that is I had a couchant unexpressed certainty, from Thoby's death I think; a legacy of pessimism, which I have decided never to analyse. Then, as we walked towards the gate together, I went with Julian, and said, 'Won't you have time to write something in Spain? Won't you send it us?' (This referred of course to my feeling, a very painful one, that I had treated his essay on Roger too lightly.) And he said, very quickly — he spoke quickly with a suddenness like his movements — 'Yes, I'll write something about Spain. And send it you if you like.' 'Do,' I said, and touched his hand. Then we went up to Clive's room: and then they went: we stood at the door to watch them. Julian was driving Nessa's car. At first it wouldn't start. He sat there at the wheel frowning, looking very magnificent, in his shirt sleeves; with an expression as if he had made up his mind and were determined, though there was this obstacle — the car wouldn't start. Then suddenly it jerked off — and he had his head thrown slightly back, as he drove up the Square with Nessa beside him. Of course I noted it, as it might be our last meeting. What he said was, 'Goodbye until this time next year.'

We went in with Clive and drank. And talked about Julian. Clive and L. said that there was no more risk in going to Spain than in driving up and down to Charleston. Clive said that only one man had been hurt by a bomb. And he added, But Julian is very cool, like Cory and myself. It's spirited of him to go, he added. I think I said, But it's a worry for Nessa. Then we discussed professions: Clive told us how Picasso had said, As a father, I'm so glad my son does not have one. And he said, he was glad Julian should be a 'character'; he would always have enough money to get bread and butter: it was a good thing he had no profession. He was a person who had no one gift in particular. He did not think he was born to be a writer — No he was a character, like Thoby. For some reason I did not answer, that he was like Thoby. I have always been foolish about that. I did not like any Bell to be like Thoby, partly through snobbishness I suppose; nor do I think that Julian was like Thoby, except in the obvious way that he was young and very fine to look at. I said that Thoby had a natural style, and Julian had not.

There was also the damned literary question. I was always critical of his writing, partly I suspect from the usual generation jealousy; partly from my own enviousness of anyone who can do in writing what I can't do: and again (for I can't analyse out the other strains in a very complex feeling, roused partly by L.; for we envied Nessa I suspect for such a son; and there was L.'s family complex which made him eager, no, on the alert, to criticize her children because he thought I admired them more than his family) I thought him very careless, not 'an artist', too personal in what he wrote, and 'all over the place'. This is the one thing I regret in our relationship: that I might have encouraged him more as a writer. But again, that's my character: and I'm always forced, in spite of jealousy, to be honest in the end. Still this is my one regret; and I shall always have it; seeing how immensely generous he was to me about what I did — touchingly proud sometimes of my writings. But then I came to the stage two years ago of hating 'personality'; desiring anonymity; a complex state which I would one day have discussed with him. Then, I could not sympathise with wishing to be published. I thought it wrong from my new standpoint — a piece of the egomaniac, egocentric mania of the time. (For that reason I would not sign my Janet article.) But how could he know why I was so cool about publishing his things? Happily I made L. reconsider his poems, and we published them.

I could be hurt sometimes by his rather caustic teasing, something like Clive's, and I felt it more because I have suffered from Clive's caustic and rather cruel teasing in the past. — Julian had something of the same way of 'seeing through one'; but it was less personal, and stronger. That last supper party at Clive's I remember beginning a story about Desmond. It was about the L.S. lecture. I said 'Desmond took it very seriously as a compliment.' And I could not remember who had had the L.S. lectureship and said 'Didn't David [Cecil] do it?' and then Julian gave his flash of mockery and severity and said 'Ah, how like you. That's what you said' — looking at Clive as though they both joined in suspecting my malice: in which he was that time wrong. But not always. I mean he had claws and could use them. He had feelings about the Bells. He thought I wanted to give pain. He thought me cruel, as Clive thinks me; but he told me, the night I talked to him before he went to China, that he never doubted the warmth of my feelings: that I suffered a great deal: that I had very strong affections.

But our relationship was perfectly secure because it was founded on our passion — not too strong a word for either of us — for Nessa. And it was this passion that made us both reserved when we met this summer.

I was so anxious to do everything to stop him from going that I got him to meet Kingsley Martin once at dinner, and then Stephen Spender, and so never saw him alone — except once, and then only for a short time. I had just come in with the *Evening Standard* in which *The Years* was extravagantly praised, much to my surprise. I felt very happy. It was a great relief. And I stood with the paper, hoping L. would come and I could tell him when the bell rang. I went to the top of the stairs, looked down, and saw Julian's great sun hat (he was amazingly careless of dress always — would come here with a tear in his trousers) and I called out in a sepulchral voice, 'Who is that?' Whereupon he started, and laughed and I let him in. And he said, 'What a voice to hear,' or something light: then he came up; it was to ask for Dalton's telephone number. He stood there; I asked him to stay and see Leonard. He hesitated, but seemed to make up his mind that he must get on with the business of seeing Dalton. So I went and looked for the number. When I came back he was reading the *Standard*. I had left it with the review open. But he had turned, I think to the politics. I had half a mind to say, Look how I'm praised. And then thought No, I'm on the top of the wave: and it's not kind to thrust that sort of thing upon people who aren't yet recognised. So I said nothing about it. But I wanted him to stay. And then again I felt, he's afraid I shall try to persuade him not to go. So all I said was, Look here Julian, if you ever want a meal, you've only to ring us up. Yes he said rather doubtingly, as if we might be too busy. So I insisted. 'We can't see too much of you.' And followed him into the hall, and put my arm round him and said, 'You can't think how nice it is having you back.' And we half kissed; and he looked pleased and said 'Do you feel that?' And I said yes, and it was as if he asked me to forgive him for all the worry; and then off he stumped, in his great hat and thick coat.

When I was in that horrid state of misery last summer with the proofs of *The Years*, in such misery that I could only work for ten minutes and then go and lie down, I wrote him my casual letter about his Roger paper, and he only answered many weeks later to say he had been hurt; so hadn't written: and then another letter of mine brought back the old family feeling. I was shocked at this, and wrote at once, in time to catch him before he started home, to say don't let us ever quarrel about writing, and I explained and apologized. All the same, for this reason, and because of his summer journey, and also because one always stops

writing letters unless one has a regular day, we had one of those lapses
in communication which are bound to happen. I thought, when he
comes back there'll be time to begin again. I thought he would get some
political job and we should see a lot of him.

This lapse perhaps explains why I go on asking myself, without
finding an answer, what did he feel about Spain? What made him feel it
necessary, knowing as he did how it must torture Nessa, to go? He
knew her feeling. We discussed it before he went to China in the most
intimate talk I ever had with him. I remember then he said how hard it
was for her, now that Roger was dead; and that he was sorry that
Quentin was so much at Charleston. He knew that: and yet deliberately
inflicted this fearful anxiety on her. What made him do it? I suppose its
a fever in the blood of the younger generation which we can't possibly
understand. I have never known anyone of my generation have that
feeling about a war. We were all CO's in the Great war. And though I
understand that this is a 'cause', can be called the cause of liberty and
so on, still my natural reaction is to fight intellectually: if I were any
use, I should write against it: I should evolve some plan for fighting
English tyranny. The moment force is used, it becomes meaningless and
unreal to me. And I daresay he would soon have lived through the
active stage, and have found some other, administrative, work. But that
does not explain his determination. . .

John Maynard Keynes: My Early Beliefs

Reprinted from John Maynard Keynes, Two Memoirs *(Rupert Hart-
Davis, London, 1949), 78–106, by permission of Granada Publishing
Ltd.*

[Of all the memoirs of Bloomsbury, J.M. Keynes's *My Early Beliefs* is
the most widely known. Since its publication in 1949 Keynes's brilliant
description of how Moore converted him and his friends to a limited
yet pure religion of love, beauty, and truth has been taken by
Bloomsbury friends and foes alike as the definitive account of the
Group's origins. (See, for example, F.R. Leavis's review, pp.387–95.) It
was only later that such authorities as Leonard Woolf qualified in
important ways the accuracy of Keynes's interpretation (see
pp.101–109).

My Early Beliefs was published with an introduction by David
Garnett who explained that Keynes's memoir was written as a result of

a paper by Garnett recalling D.H. Lawrence. (Garnett later included the substance of his paper in his autobiography *The Flowers of the Forest*; see pp.361–70 of this collection.) Lawrence had written to Garnett after visiting Cambridge as the guest of Bertrand Russell; '. . . You must leave these friends, these beetles, Birrell and Duncan Grant are done for forever. Keynes I am not sure – when I saw Keynes that morning in Cambridge it was one of the crises of my life. It sent me mad with misery and hostility and rage.' Recently published letters from Russell and Lawrence to Lady Ottoline Morrell indicate that homosexuality was one of the reasons why Lawrence disliked Garnett's Bloomsbury friends. Russell wrote of Lawrence's and his discussions with Keynes at Cambridge, 'We pressed him hard about his purpose in life – he spoke as tho' he only wanted a succession of agreeable moments, which of course is not really true. Lawrence likes him but can't get on with him; I get on with him, but dislike him. Lawrence has the same feeling against sodomy as I have; you had nearly made me believe there is no great harm in it, but I have reverted; and all the examples I know confirm me in thinking it sterlizing.' In writing to Lady Ottoline later, Lawrence did not indicate any liking for Keynes. 'There *is* a principle of evil. Let us acknowledge it once and for all. I saw it so plainly in K. at Cambridge, it made me sick. I am sick with the knowledge of the prevalence of evil, as if it were some insidious disease.'

The occasion on which Keynes read *My Early Beliefs* has been recalled by one of the younger members of the Memoir Club. Quentin Bell's recollection completes the setting for this famous essay and suggests further qualifications of its interpretation of Bloomsbury: 'It was in the summer of 1938, the summer before Munich; the audience consisted of the Memoir Club, that is to say a more or less Bloomsbury audience, and two persons who were not in any real sense Bloomsbury, Jane Bussy, a niece of Lytton Strachey, and myself. A certain part of the paper was addressed to, or at, us – the younger generation. Maynard knew that we, and indeed some of his contemporaries, considered that he had become very reactionary. His plea for the traditional values, his attacks on Marxism, his sympathy for Lawrence's attitude towards intuition as opposed to reason was meant to shock and irritate us; it succeeded in doing so. . .'

Garnett's edition of *My Early Beliefs* included the following list of identifications:

List of Persons Mentioned Otherwise Than by Their Full Names

Bunny: David Garnett

Bertie: Bertrand Russell (Earl Russell)
Ottoline: Lady Ottoline Morrell
Gertler: Mark Gertler, the painter
Carrington: Dorothy Carrington (Mrs R. Partridge)
Moore: Professor G.E. Moore
Strachey: Lytton Strachey
Woolf: Leonard Woolf
Sheppard: J.T. Sheppard, now Provost of King's College, Cambridge
Hawtrey: R.G. Hawtrey, C.B., Assistant Secretary, H.M. Treasury
MacCarthy: Desmond MacCarthy
Ainsworth: A.R. Ainsworth, C.B.
Forster: E.M. Forster
McTaggart: J.M.E. McTaggart, the philosopher and Trinity College
    lecturer in moral sciences from 1897 to 1923
Dickinson: Goldsworthy Lowes Dickinson
Russell: Bertrand Russel (Earl Russell)
Sidgwick: Henry Sidgwick, the philosopher
Bob Trevy: R.C. Trevelyan, the poet
Ludwig: Ludwig Wittgenstein, the philosopher.]

I can visualize very clearly the scene of my meeting with D.H. Lawrence in 1914 (Bunny seems to suggest 1915, but my memory suggests that it may have been earlier than that) of which he speaks in the letter from which Bunny quoted at the last meeting of the Club. But unfortunately I cannot remember any fragment of what was said, though I retain some faint remains of what was felt.

It was at a breakfast party given by Bertie Russell in his rooms in Neville's Court. There were only the three of us there. I fancy that Lawrence had been staying with Bertie and that there had been some meeting or party the night before, at which Lawrence had been facing Cambridge. Probably he had not enjoyed it.[1] My memory is that he was morose from the outset and said very little, apart from indefinite expressions of irritable dissent, all the morning. Most of the talk was between Bertie and me, and I haven't the faintest recollection of what it was about. But it was not the sort of conversation we should have had if we had been alone. It was *at* Lawrence and with the intention, largely unsuccessful, of getting him to participate. We sat round the fireplace with the sofa drawn across. Lawrence sat on the right-hand side in rather a crouching position with his head down. Bertie stood up by the fireplace, as I think I did, too, from time to time. I came away feeling that the party had been a failure and that we had failed to establish contact, but with no other particular impression. You know the sort of situation when two familiar friends talk *at* a visitor. I had never seen him before, and I never saw him again. Many years later he recorded in a letter, which is printed in his published correspondence, that I was the only member of Bloomsbury who had supported him by subscribing for *Lady Chatterley*.

That is all I *remember*. But Bunny's story suggests some inferences to me. In the passage of his life which Bunny had described I think that Lawrence was influenced by two causes of emotional disturbance. One of them centred round Ottoline. As always, Ottoline was keeping more than one world. Except for Bertie, the Cambridge and Bloomsbury world was only just beginning to hold her. Lawrence, Gertler, Carrington were a different strand in her furbelows. Lawrence was jealous of the other lot; and Cambridge rationalism and cynicism, then at their height, were, of course, repulsive to him. Bertie gave him what must have been, I think, his first glimpse of Cambridge. It overwhelmed, attracted and repulsed him – which was the other emotional disturbance. It was obviously a civilisation, and not less obviously uncomfortable and unattainable for him – very repulsive and very attractive. Now Bunny had come into his life quite independently, neither through Ottoline nor from Cambridge and Bloomsbury; he was evidently very fond of Bunny; and when he saw *him* being seduced by Cambridge, he was yet more jealous, just as he was jealous of Ottoline's new leanings that way. And jealousy apart, it is impossible to imagine moods more antagonistic than those of Lawrence and of pre-war Cambridge.

But when all that has been said, was there something true and right in what Lawrence felt? There generally was. His reactions were incomplete and unfair, but they were not usually baseless. I have said that I have forgotten what the conversation was about. But I expect it was pretty brittle stuff – not so brittle as Frankie Birrell's – but pretty brittle all the same. And although it was silly to take it, or to estimate it, at its face value, did the way of responding to life which lay behind it lack something important? Lawrence was oblivious of anything valuable it may have offered – it was a *lack* that he was violently apprehending. So Bunny's memoir has thrown my mind back to reflections about our mental history in the dozen years before the war; and if it will not shock the club too much, I should like in this contribution to its proceedings to introduce for once, mental or spiritual, instead of sexual, adventures, to try and recall the principal impacts on one's virgin mind and to wonder how it has all turned out, and whether one still holds by that youthful religion.

I went up to Cambridge at Michaelmas 1902, and Moore's *Principia Ethica* came out at the end of my first year. I have never heard of the present generation having read it. But, of course, its effect on *us*, and the talk which preceded and followed it, dominated, and perhaps still dominate, everything else. We were at an age when our beliefs influenced our behaviour, a characteristic of the young which it is easy for the middle-aged to forget, and the habits of feeling formed then still persist in a recognisable degree. It is those habits of feeling, influencing the majority of us, which make this Club a collectivity and separate us from the rest. They overlaid, somehow, our otherwise extremely different characters – Moore himself was a puritan and precisian, Strachey (for that was his name at that time) a Voltairean, Woolf a rabbi, myself a nonconformist, Sheppard a conformist and (as it now turns out) an ecclesiastic, Clive a gay and amiable dog, Sydney-Turner a quietist, Hawtrey a dogmatist and so on. Of those who had come just before, only MacCarthy and Ainsworth, who were much influenced by their personal feelings for Moore, came under his full influence. We did not see much of Forster at that time; who was already the elusive colt of a dark horse. It was only for us, those who were active in 1903, that Moore completely ousted McTaggart, Dickinson, Russell. The influence was not only overwhelming; but it was the extreme opposite of what Strachey used to call *funeste*; it was exciting, exhilarating, the beginning of a renaissance, the opening of a new heaven on a new earth, we were the forerunners of a new dispensation, we were not afraid of anything. Perhaps it was because we were so brought up that even at our gloomiest and worst we have never lost a certain resilience which the younger generation seem never to have had. They have enjoyed, at most, only a pale reflection of something, not altogether superseded, but faded and without illusions.

Now what we got from Moore was by no means entirely what he offered us. He had one foot on the threshold of the new heaven, but the other foot in Sidgwick and the Benthamite calculus and the general rules of correct behaviour. There was one chapter in the *Principia* of which we took not the slightest notice. We accepted Moore's religion, so to speak, and discarded his morals. Indeed, in our opinion, one of the greatest advantages of his religion, was that it made morals unnecessary – meaning by 'religion' one's attitude towards oneself and the ultimate and by 'morals' one's attitude towards the outside world and the intermediate. To the consequences of having a religion and no morals I return later.

Even if the new members of the Club know what the religion was (do they?), it will not do any of us any harm to try and recall the crude outlines. Nothing mattered except states of mind, our own and other people's of course, but chiefly our own. These states of mind were not associated with action or achievement or with consequences. They consisted in timeless, passionate states of contemplation and communion, largely unattached to 'before' and 'after'. Their value depended, in accordance with the principle of organic unity, on the state of affairs as a whole which could not be usefully analysed into parts. For example, the value of the state of mind of being in love did not depend merely on the nature of one's own emotions, but also on the worth of their object and on the reciprocity and nature of the object's emotions; but it did not depend, if I remember rightly, or did not depend much, on what happened, or how one felt about it, a year later, though I myself was always an advocate of a principle of organic unity through time, which still seems to me only sensible. The appropriate subjects of passionate contemplation and communion were a beloved person, beauty and truth, and one's prime objects in life were love, the creation and enjoyment of aesthetic experience and the pursuit of knowledge. Of these love came a long way first. But in the early days under Moore's influence the public treatment of this and its associated acts was, on the whole, austere and platonic. Some of us might argue that physical enjoyment could spoil and detract from the state of mind as a whole. I do not remember at what date Strachey issued his edict that certain Latin technical terms of sex were the correct words to use, that to avoid them was a grave error, and, even in mixed company, a weakness, and the use of other synonyms a vulgarity. But I should certainly say that this was later. In 1903 those words were not even esoteric terms of common discourse.

Our religion closely followed the English puritan tradition of being chiefly concerned with the salvation of our own souls. The divine resided within a closed circle. There was not a very intimate connection between 'being good' and 'doing good'; and we had a feeling that there was some risk that in practice the latter might interfere with the former. But religions proper, as distinct from modern 'social service' pseudo-religions, have always been of that character; and perhaps it was a sufficient offset that our religion was altogether unworldly – with wealth, power, popularity or success it had no concern whatever, they were thoroughly despised.

How did we know what states of mind were good? This was a matter

of direct inspection, of direct unanalysable intuition about which it was
useless and impossible to argue. In that case who was right when there
was a difference of opinion? There were two possible explanations. It
might be that the two parties were not really talking about the same
thing, that they were not bringing their intuitions to bear on precisely
the same object, and, by virtue of the principle of organic unity, a very
small difference in the object might make a very big difference in the
result. Or it might be that some people had an acuter sense of
judgment, just as some people can judge a vintage port and others
cannot. On the whole, so far as I remember, this explanation prevailed.
In practice, victory was with those who could speak with the greatest
appearance of clear, undoubting conviction and could best use the
accents of infallibility. Moore at this time was a master of this
method – greeting one's remarks with a gasp of incredulity – *Do* you
really think *that*, an expression of face as if to hear such a thing said
reduced him to a state of wonder verging on imbecility, with his mouth
wide open and wagging his head in the negative so violently that his hair
shook. *Oh!* he would say, goggling at you as if either you or he must be
mad; and no reply was possible. Strachey's methods were different;
grim silence as if such a dreadful observation was beyond comment and
the less said about it the better, but almost as effective for disposing of
what he called death-packets. Woolf was fairly good at indicating a
negative, but he was better at producing the effect that it was useless to
argue with *him* than at crushing *you*. Dickinson knew how to shrug his
shoulders and retreat unconvinced, but it was retreat all the same. As
for Sheppard and me we could only turn like worms, but worms who
could be eventually goaded into voluble claims that worms have at least
the *right* to turn. Yet after all the differences were about details.
Broadly speaking we all knew for certain what were good states of mind
and that they consisted in communion with objects of love, beauty, and
truth.

I have called this faith a religion, and some sort of relation of
neo-platonism it surely was. But we should have been very angry at the
time with such a suggestion. We regarded all this as entirely rational and
scientific in character. Like any other branch of science, it was nothing
more than the application of logic and rational analysis to the material
presented as sense-data. Our apprehension of good was exactly the same
as our apprehension of green, and we purported to handle it with the
same logical and analytical technique which was appropriate to the
latter. Indeed we combined a dogmatic treatment as to the nature of
experience with a method of handling it which was extravagantly

scholastic. Russell's *Principles of Mathematics* came out in the same year as *Principia Ethica*; and the former, in spirit, furnished a method for handling the material provided by the latter. Let me give you a few examples of the sort of things we used to discuss.

If A was in love with B and believed that B reciprocated his feelings, whereas in fact B did not, but was in love with C, the state of affairs was certainly not so good as it would have been if A had been right, but was it worse or better than it would become if A discovered his mistake? If A was in love with B under a misapprehension as to B's qualities, was this better or worse than A's not being in love at all? If A was in love with B because A's spectacles were not strong enough to see B's complexion, did this altogether, or partly, destroy the value of A's state of mind? Suppose we were to live our lives backwards, having our experiences in the reverse order, would this affect the value of our successive states of mind? If the states of mind enjoyed by each of us were pooled and then redistributed, would this affect their value? How did one compare the value of a good state of mind which had bad consequences with a bad state of mind which had good consequences? In valuing the consequences did one assess them at their actual value as it turned out eventually to be, or their probable value at the time? If at their probable value, how much evidence as to possible consequences was it one's duty to collect before applying the calculus? Was there a separate objective standard of beauty? Was a beautiful thing, that is to say, by definition that which it was good to contemplate? Or was there an actual objective quality 'beauty', just like 'green' and 'good'? And knowledge, too, presented a problem. Were all truths equally good to pursue and contemplate? — as for example the number of grains in a given tract of sea-sand. We were disposed to repudiate very strongly the idea that useful knowledge could be preferable to useless knowledge. But we flirted with the idea that there might be some intrinsic quality — though not, perhaps, quite on a par with 'green' and 'good' and 'beautiful' — which one could call 'interesting', and we were prepared to think it just possible that 'interesting' knowledge might be better to pursue than 'uninteresting' knowledge. Another competing adjective was 'important', provided it was quite clear that 'important' did not mean 'useful'. Or to return again to our favourite subject, was a violent love affair which lasted a short time better than a more tepid one which endured longer? We were inclined to think it was. But I have said enough by now to make it clear that the problems of mensuration, in which we had involved ourselves, were somewhat formidable.

It was all under the influence of Moore's method, according to which you could hope to make essentially vague notions clear by using precise language about them and asking exact questions. It was a method of discovery by the instrument of impeccable grammar and an unambiguous dictionary. 'What *exactly* do you mean?' was the phrase most frequently on our lips. If it appeared under cross-examination that you did not mean *exactly* anything, you lay under a strong suspicion of meaning nothing whatever. It was a stringent education in dialectic; but in practice it was a kind of combat in which strength of character was really much more valuable than subtlety of mind. In the preface to his great work, bespattered with the numerous italics through which the reader who knew him could actually hear, as with Queen Victoria, the vehemence of his utterance, Moore begins by saying that error is chiefly 'the attempt to answer questions, without first discovering precisely *what* question it is which you desire to answer. . . . Once we recognize the exact meaning of the two questions, I think it also becomes plain exactly what kind of reasons are relevant as arguments for or against any particular answer to them'. So we spent our time trying to discover *precisely what* questions we were asking, confident in the faith that, if only we could ask precise questions, everyone would know the answer. Indeed Moore expressly claimed as much. In his famous chapter on 'The Ideal' he wrote:

Indeed, once the meaning of the question is clearly understood, the answer to it, in its main outlines, appears to be so obvious, that it runs the risk of seeming to be a platitude. By far the most valuable things, which we know or can imagine, are certain states of consciousness, which may be roughly described as the pleasures of human intercourse and the enjoyment of beautiful objects. No one, probably, who has asked himself the question, has ever doubted that personal affection and the appreciation of what is beautiful in Art or Nature, are good in themselves; nor if we consider strictly what things are worth having *purely for their own sakes*, does it appear probable that any one will think that anything else has *nearly* so great a value as the things which are included under these two heads.

And then there was the question of pleasure. As time wore on towards the nineteen-tens, I fancy we weakened a bit about pleasure. But, in our prime, pleasure was nowhere. I would faintly urge that if two states of mind were similar in all other respects except that one was pleasurable and the other was painful there *might* be a little to be said for the former, but the principle of organic unities was against me. It was the general view (though not quite borne out by the *Principia*) that pleasure had nothing to do with the case and, on the whole, a pleasant state of mind lay under grave suspicion of lacking intensity and passion.

In those days X. had not taken up women, nor Woolf monkeys, and they were not their present blithe selves. The two of them, sunk deep in silence and in basket chairs on opposite sides of the fireplace in a room which was at all times pitch dark, would stop sucking their pipes only to murmur that all good states of mind were extremely painful and to imply that all painful states of mind were extremely good. Strachey seconded them – it was only in his second childhood that Lytton took up pleasure – though his sorrow was more fitful than their settled gloom. But with Sheppard and myself cheerfulness could not but break through, and we were in great disgrace about it. There was a terrible scene one evening when we turned insubordinate and reckless and maintained that there was nothing wrong in itself in being cheerful. It was decided that such low habits were particularly characteristic of King's as opposed to the austerity of Trinity.

Socrates had persuaded Protarchus that pure hedonism was absurd. Moore himself was only prepared to accept pleasure as an enhancement of a state of affairs otherwise good. But Moore hated evil and he found a place in his religion for vindictive punishment.

Not only is the pleasantness of state *not* in proportion to its intrinsic worth; it may even add positively to its vileness... The infliction of pain on a person whose state of mind is bad may, if the pain be not too intense, create a state of things that is better *on the whole* than if the evil state of mind had existed unpunished. Whether such a state of affairs can ever constitute a *positive* good is another question.

I call attention to the qualification 'if the pain be not too intense'. Our Ideal was a merciful God.

Thus we were brought up – with Plato's absorption in the good in itself, with a scholasticism which outdid St Thomas, in calvinistic withdrawal from the pleasures and successes of Vanity Fair, and oppressed with all the sorrows of Werther. It did not prevent us from laughing most of the time and we enjoyed supreme self-confidence, superiority and contempt towards all the rest of the unconverted world. But it was hardly a state of mind which a grown-up person in his senses could sustain literally. When MacCarthy came down for a week-end, he would smile affectionately, persuade Moore to sing his German Lieder at the piano, to hear which we all agreed was a very good state of mind indeed, or incite Bob Trevy to deliver a broken oration which was a frantic travesty of the whole method, the charm of it lying in the impossibility of deciding whether Bob himself meant it, half at least, seriously or not.

It seems to me looking back, that this religion of ours was a very good one to grow up under. It remains nearer the truth than any other that I know, with less irrelevant extraneous matter and nothing to be ashamed of; though it is a comfort to-day to be able to discard with a good conscience the calculus and the mensuration and the duty to know *exactly* what one means and feels. It was a purer, sweeter air by far than Freud cum Marx. It is still my religion under the surface. I read again last week Moore's famous chapter on 'The Ideal'. It is remarkable how wholly oblivious he managed to be of the qualities of the life of action and also of the pattern of life as a whole. He was existing in a timeless ecstasy. His way of translating his own particular emotions of the moment into the language of generalised abstraction is a charming and beautiful comedy. Do you remember the passage in which he discusses whether, granting that it is mental qualities which one should chiefly love, it is important that the beloved person should also be good-looking? In the upshot good looks win a modest victory over 'mental qualities'. I cannot forbear to quote this sweet and lovely passage, so sincere and passionate and careful:

I think it may be admitted that wherever the affection is most valuable, the appreciation of mental qualities must form a large part of it, and that the presence of this part makes the whole far more valuable than it could have been without it. But it seems very doubtful whether this appreciation, by itself, can possess as much value as the whole in which it is combined with an appreciation of the appropriate *corporeal* expression of the mental qualities in question. It is certain that in all actual cases of valuable affection, the bodily expressions of character, whether by looks, by words, or by actions, do form a part of the object towards which the affection is felt, and that the fact of their inclusion appears to heighten the value of the whole state. It is, indeed, very difficult to imagine what the cognition of mental qualities *alone*, unaccompanied by *any* corporeal expression, would be like; and, in so far as we succeed in making this abstraction, the whole considered certainly appears to have less value. I therefore conclude that the importance of an admiration of admirable mental qualities lies chiefly in the immense superiority of a whole, in which it forms a part, to one in which it is absent, and not in any high degree of intrinsic value which it possesses by itself. It even appears to be doubtful, whether, in itself, it possesses so much value as the appreciation of mere corporeal beauty undoubtedly does possess; that is to say, whether the appreciation of what has great intrinsic value is so valuable as the appreciation of what is merely beautiful.

But further if we consider the nature of admirable mental qualities, by themselves, it appears that a proper appreciation of them involves a reference to purely material beauty in yet another way. Admirable mental qualities do, if our previous conclusions are correct, consist very largely in an emotional contemplation of beautiful objects; and hence the appreciation of them will consist essentially in the contemplation of such contemplation. It is true that the most valuable appreciation of persons appears to be that which consists in the appreciation of their appreciation of other persons: but even here a reference to material beauty appears to be involved, *both* in respect of the fact that what is appreciated in the last instance may be the contemplation of what is merely beautiful, *and* in respect of the fact that the most valuable appreciation of a person appears to *include* an appreciation of his corporeal expression. Though, therefore, we may admit that the appreciation of a person's attitude towards other persons, or, to take one instance, the love of love, is far the most valuable good we know, and far more valuable than the mere love of beauty, yet we can only admit this if the first be understood to *include* the latter, in various degrees of directness.

The New Testament is a handbook for politicians compared with the unworldliness of Moore's chapter on 'The Ideal'. I know no equal to it in literature since Plato. And it is better than Plato because it is quite free from *fancy*. It conveys the beauty of the literalness of Moore's mind, the pure and passionate intensity of his vision, *un*fanciful and *un*dressed-up. Moore had a nightmare once in which he could not distinguish propositions from tables. But even when he was awake, he could not distinguish love and beauty and truth from the furniture. They took on the same definition of outline, the same stable, solid, objective qualities and common-sense reality.

I see no reason to shift from the fundamental intuitions of *Principia Ethica*; though they are much too few and too narrow to fit actual experience which provides a richer and more various content. That they furnish a justification of experience wholly independent of outside events has become an added comfort, even though one cannot live to-day secure in the undisturbed individualism which was the extra-ordinary achievement of the early Edwardian days, not for our little lot only, but for everyone else, too.

I am still a long way off from D.H. Lawrence and what he might have been justified in meaning when he said that we were 'done for'. And even now I am not quite ready to approach that theme. First of all I must explain the other facet of our faith. So far it has been a question of our attitude to ourselves and one another. What was our under-standing of the outside world and our relation to it?

It was an important object of Moore's book to distinguish between goodness as an attribute of states of mind and rightness as an attribute of actions. He also has a section on the justification of general rules of conduct. The large part played by considerations of probability in his theory of right conduct was, indeed, an important contributory cause to my spending all the leisure of many years on the study of that subject: I was writing under the joint influence of Moore's *Principia Ethica* and Russell's *Principia Mathematica*. But for the most part, as I have said, we did not pay attention to this aspect of the book or bother much about it. We were living in the specious present, nor had begun to play the game of consequences. We existed in the world of Plato's *Dialogues*; we had not reached the *Republic*, let alone the *Laws*.

This brought us one big advantage. As we had thrown hedonism out of the window and, discarding Moore's so highly problematical calculus, lived entirely in present experience, since social action as an end in itself and not merely as a lugubrious duty had dropped out of our Ideal, and, not only social action, but the life of action generally, power, politics, success, wealth, ambition, with the economic motive and the economic criterion less prominent in our philosophy than with St Francis of Assisi, who at least made collections for the birds, it follows that we were amongst the first of our generation, perhaps alone amongst our generation, to escape from the Benthamite tradition. In practice, of course, at least so far as I was concerned, the outside world was not forgotten or forsworn. But I am recalling what our Ideal was in those early days when the life of passionate contemplation and communion was supposed to oust all other purposes whatever. It can be no part of this memoir for me to try to explain why it was such a big advantage for us to have escaped from the Benthamite tradition. But I do now regard that as the worm which has been gnawing at the insides of modern civilisation and is responsible for its present moral decay. We used to regard the Christians as the enemy, because they appeared as the representatives of tradition, convention and hocus-pocus. In truth it was the Benthamite calculus, based on an over-valuation of the economic criterion, which was destroying the quality of the popular Ideal.

Moreover, it was this escape from Bentham, joined with the unsurpassable individualism of our philosophy, which has served to protect the whole lot of us from the final *reductio ad absurdum* of Benthamism known as Marxism. We have completely failed, indeed, to provide a substitute for these economic bogus-faiths capable of protecting or satisfying our successors. But we ourselves have remained – am I not right in saying *all* of us? – altogether immune from the virus, as safe in the citadel of our ultimate faith as the Pope of Rome in his.

This is what we gained. But we set on one side, not only that part of Moore's fifth chapter on 'Ethics in relation to Conduct' which dealt with the obligation so to act as to produce by causal connection the most probable maximum of eventual good through the whole procession of future ages (a discussion which was indeed riddled with fallacies), but also the part which discussed the duty of the individual to obey general rules. We entirely repudiated a personal liability on us to obey general rules. We claimed the right to judge every individual case on its merits, and the wisdom, experience and self-control to do so successfully. This was a very important part of our faith, violently and aggressively held, and for the outer world it was our most obvious and dangerous characteristic. We repudiated entirely customary morals, conventions and traditional wisdom. We were, that is to say, in the strict sense of the term, immoralists. The consequences of being found out had, of course, to be considered for what they were worth. But we recognised no moral obligation on us, no inner sanction, to conform or to obey. Before heaven we claimed to be our own judge in our own case. I have come to think that this is, perhaps, rather a Russian characteristic. It is certainly not an English one. It resulted in a general, widespread, though partly covert, suspicion affecting ourselves, our motives and our behaviour. This suspicion still persists to a certain extent, and it always will. It has deeply coloured the course of our lives in relation to the outside world. It is, I now think, a justifiable suspicion. Yet so far as I am concerned, it is too late to change. I remain, and always will remain, an immoralist.

I am not now concerned, however, with the fact that this aspect of our code was shocking. It would have been not less so, even if we had been perfectly right. What matters a great deal more is the fact that it was flimsily based, as I now think, on an *a priori* view of what human nature is like, both other people's and our own, which was disastrously mistaken.

I have said that we were amongst the first to escape from Benthamism. But of another eighteenth-century heresy we were the unrepentant heirs and last upholders. We were among the last of the Utopians, or meliorists as they are sometimes called, who believe in a continuing moral progress by virtue of which the human race already consists of reliable, rational, decent people, influenced by truth and objective standards, who can be safely released from the outward restraints of convention and traditional standards and inflexible rules of conduct, and left, from now onwards, to their own sensible devices, pure motives and reliable intuitions of the good. The view that human nature is reasonable had in 1903 quite a long history behind it. It underlay the ethics of self-interest – rational self-interest as it was called – just as much as the universal ethics of Kant or Bentham which aimed at the general good; and it was because self-interest was *rational* that the egoistic and altruistic systems were supposed to work out in practice to the same conclusions.

In short, we repudiated all versions of the doctrine of original sin, of there being insane and irrational springs of wickedness in most men. We were not aware that civilisation was a thin and precarious crust erected by the personality and the will of a very few, and only maintained by rules and conventions skilfully put across and guilefully preserved. We had no respect for traditional wisdom or the restraints of custom. We lacked reverence, as Lawrence observed and as Ludwig with justice also used to say – for everything and everyone. It did not occur to us to respect the extraordinary accomplishment of our predecessors in the ordering of life (as it now seems to me to have been) or the elaborate framework which they had devised to protect this order. Plato said in his *Laws* that one of the best of a set of good laws would be a law forbidding any young man to enquire which of them are right or wrong, though an old man remarking any defect in the laws might communicate this observation to a ruler or to an equal in years when no young man was present. That was a *dictum* in which we should have been unable to discover any point or significance whatever. As cause and consequence of our general state of mind we completely misunderstood human nature, including our own. The rationality which we attributed to it led to a superficiality, not only of judgment, but also of feeling. It was not only that intellectually we were pre-Freudian, but we had lost something which our predecessors had without replacing it. I still suffer incurably from attributing an unreal rationality to other people's feelings and behaviour (and doubtless to my own, too). There is one small but extraordinarily silly manifestation of this absurd idea of what is 'normal', namely the impulse to *protest* — to write a letter to *The Times*, call a meeting in the Guildhall, subscribe to some fund when my presuppositions as to what is 'normal' are not fulfilled. I behave as if there really existed some authority or standard to which I can successfully appeal if I shout loud enough — perhaps it is some hereditary vestige of a belief in the efficacy of prayer.

I have said that this pseudo-rational view of human nature led to a thinness, a superficiality, not only of judgment, but also of feeling. It seems to me that Moore's chapter on 'The Ideal' left out altogether some whole categories of valuable emotion. The attribution of rationality to human nature, instead of enriching it, now seems to me to have impoverished it. It ignored certain powerful and valuable springs of feeling. Some of the spontaneous, irrational outbursts of human nature can have a sort of value from which our schematism was cut off. Even some of the feelings associated with wickedness can have value. And in addition to the values arising out of spontaneous, volcanic and even wicked impulses, there are many objects of valuable contemplation and communion beyond those we knew of — those concerned with the order and pattern of life amongst communities and the emotions which they can inspire. Though one must ever remember Paley's *dictum* that 'although we speak of communities as of sentient beings and ascribe to them happiness and misery, desires, interests and passions, nothing really exists or feels but *individuals*', yet we carried the individualism of our individuals too far.

And as the years wore on towards 1914, the thinness and superficiality, as well as the falsity, of our view of man's heart became, as it now seems to me, more obvious; and there was, too, some falling away from the purity of the original doctrine. Concentration on moments of communion between a pair of lovers got thoroughly mixed up with the, once rejected, pleasure. The pattern of life would sometimes become no better than a succession of permutations of short sharp superficial 'intrigues', as we called them. Our comments on life and affairs were bright and amusing, but brittle — as I said of the conversation of Russell and myself with Lawrence — because there was no solid diagnosis of human nature underlying them. Bertie in particular sustained simultaneously a pair of opinions ludicrously incompatible. He held that in fact human affairs were carried on after a most irrational fashion, but that the remedy was quite simple and easy, since all we had to do was to carry them on rationally. A discussion of practical affairs on these lines was really very boring. And a discussion of the human heart which ignored so many of its deeper and blinder passions, both good and bad, was scarcely more interesting. Indeed it is only states of mind that matter, provided we agree to take account of the pattern of life through time and give up regarding it as a series of independent, instantaneous flashes, but the ways in which states of mind can be valuable, and the objects of them, are more various, and also much richer, than we allowed for. I fancy we used in old days to get round the rich variety of experience by expanding illegitimately the field of aesthetic appreciation (we would deal, for example, with all branches of the tragic emotion under this head), classifying as aesthetic experience what is really human experience and somehow sterilizing it by this mis-classification.

If, therefore, I altogether ignore our merits – our charm, our intelligence, our unworldliness, our affection – I can see us as water-spiders, gracefully skimming, as light and reasonable as air, the surface of the stream without any contact at all with the eddies and currents underneath. And if I imagine us as coming under the observation of Lawrence's ignorant, jealous, irritable, hostile eyes, what a combination of qualities we offered to arouse his passionate distaste; this thin rationalism skipping on the crust of the lava, ignoring both the reality and the value of the vulgar passions, joined to libertinism and comprehensive irreverence, too clever by half for such an earthy character as Bunny, seducing with its intellectual *chic* such a portent as Ottoline, a regular skin-poison. All this was very unfair to poor, silly, well-meaning us. But that is why I say that there may have been just a grain of truth when Lawrence said in 1914 that we were 'done for'.

9th September 1938

Note

1. Professor G.E. Moore tells me that he sat next Lawrence in Hall that night and found nothing to say to him, but that afterwards Lawrence was introduced to Professor Hardy, the mathematician, with whom he had a long and friendly discussion. From the moment of Lawrence's introduction to Hardy, the evening was a success. [David Garnett's note.]

Duncan Grant: Virginia Woolf

Reprinted from Horizon, *III (June, 1941), 402–6, by permission of the author and Cyril Connolly.*

[Duncan Grant's reminiscences of Virginia Woolf, written after her death in 1941, are as much a recollection of the beginnings of Bloomsbury by one of its original members. The most distinguished painter of the Bloomsbury Group, Grant has written very little, but his brief description of the Thursday evenings in Fitzroy Square is among the most interesting of Bloomsbury memoirs.]

I first knew Virginia Stephen when she and her brother Adrian took No 29 Fitzroy Square, soon after her sister Vanessa married Clive Bell. It was a house on the south-west corner of the square with a view of the two fine Adams' façades. It was a derelict square. The houses of the great had gradually decayed and were taken as offices, lodgings, nursing homes and small artisans' workshops.

I had taken for a studio two rooms on the second floor of a house on the same side of the square. There was certainly not much gentility left in the district; the only relic of grandeur was a beadle to march round the square and keep order among the children, in a top-hat and a tail-coat piped with red and brass buttons. The Stephens were the only people I remember who had a complete house there; complete with their cook Sophie Farrell, their maid Maud, a front-door bell and a dog, Hans. A close friendship sprang up between Adrian Stephen and myself, and I had only to tap at the window of the ground-floor room to be let in. 'That Mr Grant gets in everywhere,' Maud once remarked to Virginia. But irregular as my visits were, in a sense they soon became frequent enough to escape notice.

The house was conveniently divided to suit the inhabitants. On the ground floor was Adrian's study lined with books. Behind was the dining room. The first floor was entirely a drawing room – the room least used in the house. It was a pleasantly proportioned room, with long windows overlooking the square. It had a green carpet, red brocade curtains; a Dutch Portrait of a Lady and Watts' portrait of Sir Leslie Stephen were the only pictures on the walls. In the back part of the room there was an instrument called a Pianola, into which one put rolls of paper punctured by small holes. You bellowed with your feet and Beethoven or Wagner would appear.

Anyone coming into the room might have thought that Adrian was a

Paderewski — the effort on the bellows gave him a swaying movement very like that of a great performer, and his hands were hidden.

I do not remember that Virginia ever performed on this instrument, but it must have played a part in her life, for Adrian on coming home from work would play in the empty room by the hour. Entirely empty it nearly always was and kept spotlessly clean.

It was here that Virginia sometimes saw her less intimate friends and it was here that the dog Hans made mess on the hearthrug when Lady Strachey was paying her first visit, and no mention was made of the fact by either lady.

The more lively rooms were Virginia's own workroom above this, and Adrian's downstairs. Her room was full of books untidily arranged and a high table at which she would write standing. The windows on this floor were double. She was very sensitive to sound, and the noise from the mews and street was severe. The time she gave to her writing was two and a half hours in the morning. She never, I believe, wrote for more than this time, but very regularly.

The study on the ground floor had the air of being much lived in. It was to this room that their friends came on Thursday evenings — a continuation of those evenings which began in Gordon Square before Thoby Stephen died and before Vanessa married. It was there that what has since been called 'Bloomsbury' for good or ill came into being.

About ten o'clock in the evening people used to appear and continue to come at intervals till twelve o'clock at night, and it was seldom that the last guest left before two or three in the morning. Whisky, buns and cocoa were the diet, and people talked to each other. If someone had lit a pipe he would sometimes hold out the lighted match to Hans the dog, who would snap at it and put it out. Conversation; that was all. Yet many people made a habit of coming, and few who did so will forget those evenings.

Among those who constantly came in early days were Charles Sanger, Theodore Llewelyn Davies, Desmond MacCarthy, Charles Tennyson, Hilton Young (now Lord Kennet), Lytton Strachey.

It was certainly not a 'salon'. Virginia Stephen in those days was not at all the sort of hostess required for such a thing. She appeared very shy and probably was so, and never addressed the company. She would listen to general arguments and occasionally speak, but her conversation was mainly directed to someone next to her. Her brother's Cambridge friends she knew well by this time, but I think there was always something a little aloof and even a little fierce in her manner to most men at the time I am speaking of. To her women friends, especially older women like Miss Pater and Miss Janet Case, who had taught her Greek, she was more open and less reserved. They were alive to her, by remembrance as well as presence, and had already their place in her imagination as belonging to the world she knew and had left — that life with her parents and her half-brothers at Hyde Park Gate. Henceforward she and her brother and sister had tacitly agreed to face life on their own terms.

I do not think that her new existence had 'become alive' to Virginia's imagination in those first years. She gave the impression of being so intensely receptive to any experience new to her, and so intensely interested in facts that she had not come across before, that time was necessary to give it a meaning as a whole. It took the years to complete her vision of it.

It is very difficult for one who is no writer to attempt to describe so subtle a thing as the 'feeling' of long ago. But I must make the attempt to explain why it was that the effect of these young people on a contemporary was so remarkable. To begin with they were not Bohemians. The people I had come across before who had cut themselves off from respectable existence had been mainly painters and Bohemians. If the Stephens defied the conventions of their particular class, it was from being intellectually honest.

They had suffered much, had struggled and finally arrived at an attitude of mind which I think had a great influence on their friends.

If it was an influence Virginia Stephen and her sister were unconscious of the fact.

The impression generally given must have been that these two young women were absorbing the ideas of their new Cambridge friends. And of course this was true up to a point. Saxon Sydney-Turner, Clive Bell, Lytton Strachey, Maynard Keynes, were willing to discuss anything and everything with them or before them. It was a gain all round. What the Cambridge of that time needed was a little feminine society. It was a little arid, and if it took almost everything seriously it had mostly left the Arts out of account. It took some things religiously. 'This is my Bible' was said by one, pointing to the *Principia Ethica*, by G. Moore. This eminent philosopher was certainly the overwhelming influence on these young men. Conversations on the 'Good' and the value of certain states of mind were a frequent subject of discussion; and these Apostolic young men found to their amazement that they could be shocked by the boldness and scepticism of two young women.

To be intimate with Virginia Stephen in those days was not to be on easy terms. Indeed the greater the intimacy the greater the danger — the

danger of sudden outbursts of scathing criticism. I have the impression
that no one had much encouragement for anything they produced. Nor
was it looked for. Nothing was expected save complete frankness (of
criticism) and a mutual respect for the point of view of each. To work
for immediate success never entered anyone's head, perhaps partly
because it seemed out of the question. Virginia Stephen was working on
her first novel, *The Voyage Out*. It took seven years to finish. But I do
not remember that this was thought to be an out of the way length of
time in which to produce a novel.

The inner fierceness of her attitude to which I have already alluded
is worth remembering, and will possibly surprise those who only knew
her in later life when it seemed to have entirely disappeared or to have
found expression in quite other ways.

It then expressed itself sometimes, as I have said, by an appearance
of acute shyness. Upon an unforeseen introduction, for instance, there
was an expression of blazing defiance, a few carefully chosen banalities,
and a feeling of awkwardness. It came from a sort of variant of
Cézanne's *grappin dessous*, which made her literally turn tail from
misadventure. As when she saw Mrs Humphry Ward advancing along a
narrow passage in the Louvre and hid herself behind a totally
inadequate post.

No one so beautiful and so fierce could give offence except to the
very stupid. But she was capable of inspiring feelings of respect in the
most philistine.

This shyness or fierceness was a necessary self-defence in her war
with the world. The world must, she surmised, accept her on her own
terms or not at all.

If these notes have any interest it is because they may to some revive
the memory, to others suggest the existence, of that seemingly very
different Virginia Woolf known to a variety of people in later years.

Marriage and possibly a growing appreciation of her work had the
effect of seeming to make her very much more at ease in the world.

Desmond MacCarthy: The Post-Impressionist Exhibition of 1910

Reprinted from Memories *(London, MacGibbon and Kee, 1953),
178–183, by permission of Granada Publishing Ltd.*

[Post-impressionist painting was in certain ways the justification for the aesthetics of Bloomsbury's two art critics, Roger Fry and Clive Bell. But the violent public reaction to the exhibition that Fry organized in 1910 was almost as interesting to Bloomsbury as the paintings themselves. Desmond MacCarthy was the secretary for the first exhibition (Leonard Woolf was the secretary for the second – see his account, pp.115–17), and in 1945 he recalled the experience.]

When Roger Fry proposed that I should go abroad and help assemble a respresentative exhibition of pictures by Cézanne, Matisse, Van Gogh, Gauguin, Seurat, Picasso and other now familiar French painters (incidentally he promised me a few days' bicycling in France) I don't think he chose me because he had special trust in my judgment. Of course he knew I was fond of pictures and that if confronted with one I could look at it with interest for more than two minutes – a faculty not so common as you might suppose. (Next time you are in a gallery you can verify this by timing people as they go round.) And then, though I could not generalize about artists, I did occasionally say something about a picture which would interest him, though it might be only 'I'm almost sure that cow is too near the tree' or 'that crimson blob next her nose – of course, I see something of the kind is necessary and I didn't notice it at all at first, but now I have – it bothers me'. But what really influenced him in choosing me was that we were happy together. My failings were not the sort which annoyed him, nor (equally important) were my virtues. Masterful men often prefer a rather incompetent colleague to an over-confident one. Fry was capable of making muddles himself; he would not have been quite comfortable with anyone implacably efficient. And here I must mention that he was also a most persuasive man.

Hearing that the Grafton Galleries had no show for the months between their usual London Season exhibition and the new year's, he proceeded to convince them that they might do worse than hold a stop-gap exhibition of modern foreign artists – also that Desmond MacCarthy was an excellent man of business which indeed, in my opinion (but of this you must judge for yourselves) he did turn out to be. It was all settled in a tremendous hurry. I had just time to interview the director of the Galleries. He apologized for the smallness of my fee (a hundred pounds). But if – he added, with a pitying smile – if there were profits, I might have half of them. Neither the committee of the Grafton Galleries nor Roger Fry thought for one moment that the show could be a financial success.

Then I was stricken down with an influenza. However, Roger wasn't a man to be put out by a little thing like that. He made me rise from bed, drink a bottle of champagne and catch the boat for Calais with him. I arrived in Paris feeling as though my head were about the size and weight of an apple.

Of course, the first people we went to see in Paris were dealers who had modern pictures. If they could be persuaded to lend, then the London show would be representative. We spent day after day looking at the pictures, and nearly all those which Roger preferred were at our disposal. I remember his raptures. He would sit in front of them with his hands on his knees groaning repeatedly 'Wonderful! wonderful!' I don't think at that date anybody in England possessed any specimens of these artists' works, except Sutro, the playwright, who had a small Van Gogh. At these interviews with dealers I used to pose as M. le Publique, and on one point my verdict was final: Was there, or was there not, anything in some nude which might create an outcry in London?

Then off we went for our little tour, after which Roger returned to London and I was sent on to Munich and Holland to get other pictures. In Amsterdam Van Gogh's sister, Madame Gosschalk Bonger, had, of course, many of her late brother's, and they were still admirably cheap. When we came to price them she was asking a hundred and twenty pounds or less for some admirable examples of his art. Then I returned to Paris to settle the business side.

Now, though I was supposed to be a man of affairs, when the biggest dealer asked me what percentage the Galleries wanted on sales, I confess I was floored. It was a point on which I had neglected to inform myself before starting. At a venture I murmured, 'twenty per cent', and he replied, '*Parfaitement, Monsieur.*' Then he went on, 'If you get an offer for a picture, do not communicate at once with the artist, but with me first. He may accept less and then we can share the difference.' Now the success of the exhibition largely depended on keeping on good terms with him. How would you have behaved? Well, I summoned up all the tact for which an aunt of mine had been famous, and replied: 'I don't think I can agree to anything not down in black and white, but if you write to me. . .'. He looked a little hard at me and then repeated, '*Parfaitement, Monsieur.*' Of course, I never received that letter. We remained on excellent terms, and all was well.

On my return to London I reported that several hundred interesting pictures were available (transit insurance probably £150). I was told that expenses had to be kept down as the venture was a certain loss;

still, one hundred pounds might be spent on advertising; *that* was satisfactory. I was about to leave when the director casually remarked: 'I suppose you secured our usual percentage on sales?' Feebly, I murmured: 'You never told me what it was.' There was an oppressive pause. 'Do you mean to say you didn't ask if you didn't know? What *did* you get?' 'Twenty per cent.' 'Twenty? Why, we've *never* got more than eleven!' For several days after that I was convinced that I was cut out for a business career.

What was the exhibition to be called? That was the next question. Roger and I and a young journalist who was to help us with publicity, met to consider this; and it was at that meeting that a word which is now safely embedded in the English language — 'post-impressionism' — was invented. Roger first suggested various terms like 'expressionism', which aimed at distinguishing these artists from the impressionists; but the journalist wouldn't have that or any other of his alternatives. At last Roger, losing patience, said: 'Oh, let's just call them post-impressionists; at any rate, they came after the impressionists.' Later he handed over to me, with a few notes, the ticklish job of writing the preface to the catalogue — the unsigned preface. This work of mine was far more widely quoted than anything I was ever destined to write, and phrases from it like 'A good rocking-horse is more like a horse than the snapshot of a Derby winner' were quoted and re-quoted with laughter.

The hurried agonies of that picture-hanging are still vivid to me. Roger was entirely absorbed in deciding which picture would look best next another, while it lay with me to number them. As he was continually shifting them about when I was elsewhere, I was terrified that the numbers and titles wouldn't always correspond, with the effect of increasing the mockery, which I now felt certain the exhibition would excite. It was four AM. before I got to bed the night before Press day, and then I couldn't sleep for worrying. When the newspaper was brought to me with coffee in bed, although it happened to contain a long and laudatory review of a book I had just published, I couldn't even read that. The prospect of public ridicule owing to having, say, catalogued a nude girl as 'Station-master at Arles', made my walk to the gallery more like a walk to the gallows. Soon after ten, the Press began to arrive. Now anything new in art is apt to provoke the same kind of indignation as immoral conduct, and vice is detected in perfectly innocent pictures. Perhaps any mental shock is apt to remind people of moral shocks they have received, and the sensations being similar, they attribute this to the same cause. Anyhow, as I walked about among the tittering newspaper critics busily taking notes (they saw at once that

the whole thing was splendid copy) I kept overhearing such remarks as
'Pure pornography', 'Admirably indecent'. Not a word of truth, of
course, in this. As M. le Publique I had been careful to exclude too
frankly physiological nudes and, indeed, at the last moment, instead of
hanging two of the pictures, I told Roger they had better be kept, for a
time, in my sanctum downstairs.

The Press notices were certainly calculated to rouse curiosity. And
from the opening day the public flocked, and the big rooms echoed
with explosions of laughter and indignation. Sometimes I hovered
about trying to explain what I thought was the point of a picture,
drawing attention to colour or arrangement, and here and there, now
and then, I did find a receptive listener. One young lady seemed to
come nearly every day for a lecture and presently proposed to me,
which was almost a fault in the opposite direction. I hit on a device for
calming those of the furious who stormed down in a rage to my
sanctum beneath the galleries. To these I would first explain that I was,
after all, only the secretary, so I could not very well close the
exhibition on my own initiative that very evening. But I would add,
'Your point of view is most interesting, and if you will write it down
and sign it, I shall be most happy to pin it up in the entrance for all to
read.' This suggestion acted as a sedative. The indignant one would
reply, 'Oh, I don't know that I want to put anything on paper; only I
did feel that what I have said ought to be said.' Occasionally I did get a
document to pin up. I wish I had kept them.

The people who annoyed me most were, I think, cultivated women
who went deliberately into trills of silvery laughter in front of pictures.
With those who were genuinely amused I had some sympathy. I
remember, for instance, a stout, elderly man of a good appearance, led
in by a young woman, who went into such convulsions of laughter on
catching sight of Cézanne's portrait of his wife in the first little room
that his companion had to take him out and walk him up and down in
the fresh air. When they re-entered, I watched him going round the
other rooms, where there really were some startling pictures. He did so
without a smile. Now when one has laughed oneself weak, one can't
laugh again even at something far funnier. This man's amusement had
been genuine, not wilful, or superior, or offensive, and I forgave it.

Presently we actually began to sell pictures. The Art Gallery at
Helsinki bought a very find Cézanne for £800, I remember; and when
we closed, my share of the profits amounted to – what do you
think? – over £460 – such a lump sum as I had never earned before,
and would never earn again! Not only had the exhibition been the

theme of non-stop correspondence in the papers and of pamphlet wars – all the best known painters were, alas, against us – but it, also provoked lectures from mental specialists. Fry himself did not make one penny out of the exhibition, nor did he out of the Omega workshops, which he started seven years later. Indeed, by introducing the works of Cézanne, Matisse, Seurat, Van Gogh, Gauguin and Picasso to the British public, he smashed for a long time his reputation as an art critic. Kind people called him mad, and reminded others that his wife was in an asylum. The majority declared him to be a subverter of morals and art, and a blatant self-advertiser . . .

Vanessa Bell: Notes on Bloomsbury

[Bloomsbury has occasionally been described by critics and biographers as a matriarchy, the matriarch being Vanessa Bell. As the eldest child of Leslie and Julia Stephen (who died when Vanessa was sixteen), and as the first to have children, she was certainly the most maternal figure at the centre of Bloomsbury. The fact that she painted rather than wrote may have added to the slightly mysterious aura that apparently surrounded her. Vanessa did write several papers on Bloomsbury for the Memoir Club, however, and they are among the most delightful and revealing accounts of the Group.

Vanessa Bell's most extended recollections of Bloomsbury, entitled 'Notes on Bloomsbury', is published here for the first time with the kind permission of her daughter, Mrs Angelica Garnett. It shows that, painter though she was, she could write like a Stephen. In addition to detailing the London beginnings of Bloomsbury, her memoir argues for an interpretation of the Group that would equate it with what she calls Old Bloomsbury. According to Vanessa Bell's view, Bloomsbury ceased really to exist with the First World War – before any of the major works of Lytton Strachey, Virginia Woolf, J.M. Keynes, and others had been published. The continuity in the Memoir Club itself for which she wrote her paper is denied by her in reaction, it seems, to the loose and pejorative way that the term 'Bloomsbury' had come to be used by the time she wrote this memoir in 1951.

In editing the memoir I have spelled out a number of abbreviations and ignored various cancellations; several alternative sheets attached to the memoir have been omitted as they develop, in slightly different ways, points that are already treated in the main body of the memoir.]

It is lucky perhaps that Bloomsbury has a pleasant reverberating sound, suggesting old fashioned gardens and out of the way walks, and squares; otherwise how could one bear it? If every review, every talk on the radio, every biography, every memoir of the last fifty years, were to talk instead incessantly of Hoxton or Brixton, surely one's nerves would be unbearably frayed. Perhaps they are even as it is, yet here am I proposing to add to the chaos. What excuse have I? Simply that of having been one of the original members of Old Bloomsbury, and so thinking that I may possibly know more of the relevant facts than do later-comers.

Yet I know very well, having always lived among them, that I am no writer and that all I can hope to do is to jot down notes for others to use. They will be as true as I can make them and at least I shall not claim distinguished writers like T.S. Eliot or W.B. Yeats as members of Bloomsbury. Perhaps some other original member (for not all of us are dead yet) will be induced to write his or her account, and though no doubt we should see the whole from different angles yet possibly with luck each might paint one true facet of the whole. I may be told that just as Mrs Thrale considered Boswell to be a most inaccurate biographer of her friend Dr Johnson so would any two members of Bloomsbury disagree violently about the character of a third – yet each view may throw light and make the subject alive. The two portraits of Chocquet by Cézanne and Renoir give very different views of the same man. That only adds to one's knowledge of the original, but what should we learn from one of those posthumous portraits done from a photograph and advertised as the work of 'an exhibitor at the R.A.'? It would have much the same effect on me as do those brightly written descriptions of a dead society which the author never knew, but to which I happened to belong.

What is to be done then? Perhaps historians should wait till the last survivors have gone and no one lives to say 'Oh no: it wasn't like that.'

If this is too much to ask, at least let us try for accuracy of dates, places and persons. I look in the first account I come across and learn that my sister, Virginia Woolf, was born in Cornwall, instead of being a pure-bred Cockney as I had always believed: that all members of Bloomsbury were rich and independent – unfortunately far from being true; in another I learn that a house on the north side of Gordon Square was one of the homes of Bloomsbury. Do these things matter? Perhaps not very much, but why get them all wrong? And when it comes to painting a picture with many of the figures in it such as never could have been there then I think it does matter. A quite false atmosphere

results and it might as well be called by any name other than
Bloomsbury.

To begin with then. This is how it all arose.

My father was Leslie Stephen. Anyone who wishes to can find out all
they need about the Stephen family from the DNB and I shall leave it
at that. He lived with his four children and two stepsons at 22 Hyde
Park Gate a pleasant quiet cul-de-sac, then as now, with Kensington
Gardens just across the main road at the top. No 22 was near the
bottom of the sac and hardly any traffic came past it. It was a tall
house, having been added on to at the top by my parents and was very
spacious in its own way, with a large double room on the ground floor a
dining room built out in the back garden and a large light study for my
father at the very top. Yet many of the rooms were pitch dark,
Virginian Creeper hung down in a thick curtain over the back drawing
room window, the kitchen and other basement rooms could only be
seen by candle or lamp light and most of the paint was black. Not until
quite a short time before my father's death did we have electric light
and even then not everywhere.

The atmosphere of the house was melancholy in every way during
those last years. There had been tragedy following on tragedy and now
my father was old and dying. The two stepsons, George and Gerald
Duckworth (the publisher) and we four younger ones made up the
household. When my father died in the spring of 1904 and the house
was evidently too large for us we had to decide where to live. It was
then that Bloomsbury came into our lives and that after various
inspections of other districts we finally took 46 Gordon Square. When I
say 'we' I mean the Stephen members of the household only, consisting
of myself, my brother Julian Thoby, my sister Virginia and my brother
Adrian Leslie. We were very near each other in age. I the eldest 25 and
Adrian 21. George Duckworth married at about that time and Gerald
was glad to live a bachelor life in rooms.

We knew no one living in Bloomsbury then and that I think was one
of its attractions. True, people did live there whom we might easily
have known, but they were of the older generation, such as the George
Protheros in Bedford Square with whom I had actually once dined.
Then there was the Slade in Gower Street to which I went as an art
student for a short time; but to me Professor Tonks, then in control,
was a most depressing master, I made no friends there and soon left. It
seemed as if in every way we were making a new beginning in the tall
clean rather frigid rooms, heated only by coal fires in the old fashioned

open fireplaces. It *was* a bit cold perhaps, but it was exhilarating to
have left the house in which had been so much gloom and depression,
to have come to these white walls, large windows opening on to trees
and lawns, to have one's own rooms, be master of one's own time, have
all the things in fact which come as a matter of course to many of the
young today but so seldom then to young women at least. The only
thing really lacking to make all easy was money. As my father, like
most Victorians, was mad on the subject, never happy unless he had an
enormous balance at the Bank and constantly telling us we were rapidly
heading for 'The Workhouse' we had learnt not to take the subject very
seriously. I don't think we ever knew how much we had nor at what
rate we were living but just went on gaily as long as we could. No doubt
the Workhouse *would* have been our fate if other things had not
intervened. For the time being it did not seem important.

Soon after this beginning in Gordon Square, I think in the summer
of 1905, Thoby, not long down from Cambridge and now reading for
the Bar, began to gather round him such of his Cambridge friends as
were also starting life in London. It seemed to him a good plan to be at
home one evening a week and though I do not think it had at first
occurred to him to include his sisters in the arrangement, still there
they were. So it happened that one or two of his Cambridge friends
began to drift in on Thursday evenings after dinner. The entertainment
was frugal. I believe there was generally some whisky to be had but
most of us were content with cocoa and biscuits. In fact as everyone
had had something to eat and perhaps even to drink at about 8 o'clock
it didn't seem to occur to them to want more at 9 or at any time
between then and midnight. Then, perhaps, exhausted by conversation,
serious or frivolous, they welcomed some nourishment. It was one of
the things which made entertaining cheap in those days.

Among those who first came fairly often were Saxon Sydney-
Turner, then living in rooms in Great Ormond Street, Lytton Strachey
living when in London with his family in Hampstead, Clive Bell from
his lovely rooms in the Temple, Charles Tennyson, Hilton Young,
Desmond MacCarthy, Theodore Llewelyn Davies, Robin Mayor. Plenty
of odd creatures came too who would I suppose hardly be called
'Bloomsbury' who would in fact have been horrified by the idea of such
a thing. A few old family friends or the younger ones of our generation
sometimes looked in, even our half-brothers the Duckworths
occasionally honoured us. But they did not altogether approve of our
way of life and I remember Gerald Duckworth's disdain when Thoby
tried to persuade him that it might be profitable to publish the works

of Lytton Strachey, Clive Bell and others. (For all Thoby's friends were geniuses in his view.) It was not only the Duckworths who disapproved. It seemed as if, as soon as our very innocent society got under way and began to have some life in it, hostility was aroused. Perhaps this always happens. Any kind of clique is sneered at by those outside it as a matter of course and no doubt our ways of behaviour in our own surroundings were sufficiently odd, according to the customs of the day, to stir criticism. Certainly I remember being questioned curiously by a group of young and older people at an ordinary conventional party as to whether we really sat up talking to young men till all hours of the night? What did we talk about? – Who were these young men?, etc. They laughed, even then there was a tone of disapproval.

What *did* we talk about? The only true answer can be anything that came into our heads. Of course the young men from Cambridge were full of the 'meaning of good'. I had never read their prophet G.E. Moore, nor I think had Virginia, but that didn't prevent one from trying to find out what one thought about good or anything else. The young men were perhaps not clear enough in their own heads to mind trying to get clearer by discussion with young women who might possibly see things from a different angle. At any rate talk we all did, it's true, till all hours of the night. Not always, of course about the meaning of good – sometimes about books or painting or anything that occurred to one – or told the company of one's daily doings and adventures. There was nothing at all unusual about it perhaps, except that for some reason we seemed to be a company of the young, all free, all beginning life in new surroundings, without elders to whom we had to account in any way for our doings or behaviour, and this was not then common in a mixed company of our class: for classes still existed. Naturally it made a difference that the company included people like Lytton Strachey and Virginia, but I think we were hardly aware of this. Virginia in fact in those days was apt to be very silent nor could Lytton be relied on to take any trouble in the way of conversation. He might suddenly place some remark in his high voice which was incredibly amusing or shattering – but then again he might not. It all depended upon how he was feeling and too often he was not feeling well. But somehow Thoby's beauty and geniality, Clive Bell's power of starting good subjects and encouraging everyone to pursue them and the feeling that acute intelligence was present even if unexpressed, made a curious atmosphere. That this was real and meant some unusual bond between us is proved I think by the fact that all those who were then young together and are still alive have in spite of violent quarrels and differences of opinions of all kinds, yet kept a certain feeling about members of Bloomsbury.*

Not that Bloomsbury was called so by anyone then, not even I think by its enemies. I believe it was first called Bloomsbury by Mrs Desmond MacCarthy, to distinguish it from Chelsea — where at least as many of the 'high-brows' lived and always have lived. The MacCarthys in spite of living in Chelsea themselves were and are a most important ingredient of Bloomsbury. Her slightly mocking attitude had great uses and he naturally knew all the Cambridge people and had also known and admired my father, so he was perhaps the one link with the past. Not that one could or can ever think of him as a 'link' — or is that one of his great gifts? Certainly he seems to be always in touch with more people of more different kinds than anyone else in the world and so he can choose, when it suits him, whether or not to be a 'link'.

Besides these there were other members of the Strachey family, James, Lytton's brother and Marjorie, his sister, whose astonishing gifts as a music-hall artiste were perhaps appreciated only in Bloomsbury. Visitors from other districts were apt to be shocked by her renderings of innocent nursery rhymes. Another elusive visitor was E.M. Forster, completely at home when with us but vanishing as completely to a world of his own.

Holidays in the country interrupted Thursday evenings and made a change from Bloombsury. Its earliest chapter was very short — from the summer of 1905 to the autumn of 1906. Then after a holiday in Greece social evenings and our small circle generally seemed crushed by the tragedy of Thoby's death of typhoid fever at the age of twenty-six. He had seemed essential to the life and structure of our circle, but in youth, I suppose, no one is essential. The young mercifully recover from any blow and though it was true that life was changed for us yet something began to revive.

Then Clive Bell and I were married in the spring of 1907; that and the fact that in those terrible weeks such friends as Lytton and Saxon had become closer and more intimate helped a new life to begin. So when Virginia and Adrian moved from Gordon Square to Fitzroy Square in the spring of 1907 leaving us, a newly married couple, in Gordon Square they began fairly soon to have Thursday evenings again.

*Note. This does not mean that one did not later come to have most intimate friends who were definitely not of Bloomsbury. Even at the time some, for one reason or another, were quite outside it and later, of course, people who probably would have belonged to it could not be members of a circle which no longer existed.

They were different from the old ones of course. Virginia was now hostess and this made her, I think, much less silent. She also asked what seemed to the rest of us some peculiar guests. I wonder what those who imagine a rarefied atmosphere of wit, intelligence, criticism, self-conscious brilliance and never any tolerance of ordinary dullness, would have thought of the rather stiff young ladies to whom it never occurred not to talk about the weather, or of Adrian's dog Hans who insisted on entertaining the company by blowing out matches, of a great many rather childish doings and discussions. When it is said that we did not hesitate to talk of anything, it must be understood that this was literally true. If you could say what you liked about art, sex, or religion you could also talk freely and very likely dully about the ordinary doings of daily life. There was very little self-consciousness I think in those early gatherings; but life was exciting, terrible and amusing and we had to explore it, thankful that one could do so freely.

Perhaps it made a difference that no one (at least if you discount the young ladies and a few other curious relics from the past such as Clara Pater, Walter Pater's sister, and Janet Case, both of whom had taught Virginia Greek in Kensington days) had any feelings to be considered. None of us had the slightest respect, for instance, for religion or religious emotions. If we wanted to mock some doctrine which seemed to us laughable we could do so as freely as if we were mocking some ludicrous happening in daily life. I suppose my experience of religion, or something like it had happened to many of us. Having been brought up to believe nothing in particular I was converted to Christianity (of a rather vague kind I admit) when I was about twelve by some well brought up children of the same age. It lasted two or three years, then one day walking through Kensington Gardens and enjoying the sight of the trees, suddenly I knew quite certainly that religion meant nothing to me and that never again need I bother about it. It was a great relief. Possibly others of us had had some experience of the kind, or perhaps had had even less 'bother' than I had had. Anyhow it was a help to ease and intimacy not to have to consider in conversation such 'feelings' as might have existed either about religion or anything else.

This freedom was I believe largely owing to Lytton Strachey. Every one knows his qualities as a writer, his wit and brilliance. But only those just getting to know him well in the days when complete freedom of mind and expression were almost unknown, at least among men and women together, can understand what an exciting world of explorations of thought and feeling he seemed to reveal. His great honesty of mind and remorseless poking fun at any sham forced others to be honest too and

showed a world in which one need no longer be afraid of saying what
one thought, surely the first step to anything that could be of interest
or value.

Some of those who were to become most intimate members of
Bloomsbury were still hardly known to the others. When I talk of
members I do not mean that there was any sort of club or society. Yet
people were definitely 'Bloomsbury' or not and this is a convenient way
of classifying them. One of these was Duncan Grant, who was of course
already intimate with his Strachey cousins. When after a year as an art
student in Paris he settled down in London, I think in 1908(?) he very
soon knew us all. He was living with his family in Hampstead but he
also shared rooms in Fitzroy Square with Maynard Keynes and through
him and Lytton and James Strachey had known all the Cambridge
friends or nearly all. He was penniless but seemed unaware of the fact.
If he wanted to go from one place to another he would borrow the
exact sum 2½d perhaps, which any of us could afford. If he wanted a
meal he appeared, and contributions from each plate were willingly
made. So he solved the problem of living on air with satisfaction to
everyone, and soon of course selling his pictures solved it even further.
As he had a studio of kinds in Fitzroy Square it was easy for him to see
a lot of Adrian and Virginia of whom he has published his own account.
It was natural too that Maynard Keynes should become one of the
circle and I think he very quickly felt at home in it.

Yet one more was to come, perhaps the most important of
all – Roger Fry. Older than any of us, though that never seemed of the
least importance, he had the advantage of greater experience of life and
of art. But how one laughed at him and how ready he was to see the
joke, how ready to discuss anything with the most ignorant of us. It is
impossible and unnecessary for me to describe him for this has been
done by Virginia in her Life. She knew him of course very intimately
and he was one of her warmest and greatest admirers. Even now
seventeen years after his death one is constantly surprised by the way in
which those who knew him speak of him. English and French, both
writers and painters, even those who were hardly grown up when he
died, all seem to have been stirred by a deep affection and admiration
and tell one how they still miss him. 'How honest he was – He never
minded admitting that he had been quite wrong and changing his mind
if only he could come a little nearer the truth.' So someone who knew
him well but who had never been a member of Bloomsbury said to me
the other day. Not only did he bring himself to our circle, he knew
many people both French and English who were strangers to us and he

seemed to draw them to Bloomsbury, not as members necessarily but as delightful and sympathetic visitors. Such were Jacques Copeau, Charles Vildrac, a tiny and charming painter called Doucet (later killed in the War) Auguste Bréal and others. When we went for jaunts to Paris with him he took us to see various painters, among them Picasso then quite young and little known, Matisse, and even to rather stiff and alarming luncheon parties with a dealer like Vollard, made worth while by the Cézannes and Renoirs mysteriously produced from cellars. When Roger Fry had been buyer for the Metropolitan Museum of New York of course every dealer had besieged him and was only too ready to grant him (and his friends) the great favour of the most private of views, hoping even then that something to their advantage might result. They were right, as they always are in matters of business, for no doubt the great boom in modern French art to follow a little later was largely owing to Roger Fry's interest and enthusiasm.

During the years 1908 or 09 to 1911, two more, Leonard Woolf who had been one of Thoby's greatest friends at Cambridge and Oliver Strachey, Lytton's brother, returned from Ceylon and from India. It was inevitable that they should be as they have been ever since members of the innermost circle.

In 1911 Virginia and Adrian decided to give up the house in Fitzroy Square and move to a large house in Brunswick Square which they proposed to share with friends of whom Leonard Woolf was one. Each member of the household was to have their own room, carrying up their own meals to it and so living completely separate existences, with the advantages of shared expenses. The other inhabitants, besides Leonard Woolf, were Maynard Keynes, Duncan Grant and Gerald Shove. This meant that Thursday evenings were given up, but members of Bloomsbury met as often or oftener than before. Brunswick Square was a little nearer Gordon Square than was Fitzroy Square and all sorts of parties at all hours of the day or night happened constantly. Rooms were decorated, people made to sit for their portraits, champagne was produced (rashly left unlocked up by Maynard Keynes who was half the time in Cambridge), to while away the morning sittings — all seemed a sizzle of excitement. Brunswick would come round to Gordon when tired of the tray system of meals and in those easy days the larder always held enough for two or three unexpected guests, and servants seemed to welcome them with delight. So it was natural to say 'stay to dinner' and to sit and talk as of old till all hours, either in the familiar room at No 46 or in the Square garden. Then (in 1912?) Leonard Woolf and Virginia were married and presently moved to another part of

London and later to Richmond.

It was in these years, from 1909 or −10 to 1914 that there came the great expansion and development of Bloomsbury, that life seemed fullest of interest and promise and expansion of all kinds. Most of the members were writers or civil servants, only two in the earlier part of this time, Duncan Grant and myself, were painters. But when Roger Fry came bringing in his train painters both English and French the general attention was more directed to painting and less perhaps to the meaning of good. Other painters such as Sickert, Spencer Gore, F. Etchells, Henry Lamb and Francis Dodd, who were often in our company and on the friendliest terms with everyone, without belonging to Bloomsbury, helped to encourage talk about the visual arts. And then came the great excitement of the Post-Impressionist exhibition in 1910−11 which caused even more dismay and disapproval than Bloomsbury itself. How full of life those days seemed. Everything was brim full of interest and ideas and it certainly was for many of us 'very heaven' to be alive.

It must now be almost incredible how unaware we were of the disaster so soon to come. I do not know how much the politicians then foresaw, but I think that we in Bloomsbury had only the haziest ideas as to what was going on in the rest of Europe. How could we be interested in such matters when first getting to know well the great artists of the immediate past and those following them, when beauty was springing up under one's feet so vividly that violent abuse was hurled at it and genius generally considered to be insanity, when the writers were pricking up their ears and raising their voices lest too much attention should be given to painting: when music joined in the general chorus with sounds which excited ecstasy rage and derision: a great new freedom seemed about to come and perhaps would have come, if it had not been for motives and ambitions of which we knew nothing. But surely such unawareness can never come again and it is difficult to explain it to those who cannot hope to feel it.

In 1913 the Omega Workshops were started by Roger Fry at the wrong time for success. It was a difficult venture, with not enough money or experience behind it and temperamental artists to be driven the way they should go by Roger. All the same his pottery, lovely and perfect in its own way, would not have existed without it and many of the textiles, rugs, screens and painted furniture had character and beauty, too soon to be imitated and vulgarized by other shops. Then when it seemed as if in spite of all difficulties the Omega might survive and succeed, came the War. It could struggle on only for another year or so. The difficulties were too great.

Bloomsbury was not destroyed as probably many other circles were destroyed by the departure of all its young men to the wars. Perhaps one reason for much of the later abuse was that many were Conscientious Objectors. For some time therefore they were let alone and quietly pursued their usual professions. Women of course were not conscripted during that war and could do as they liked. So for a time Bloomsbury still existed even if crushed and bored by the outer world. The excitement and joy had gone. The hostility of the general public was real now, no longer a ridiculous and even stimulating joke, and the dreariness of the universal Khaki seemed only too appropriate. There was not even fear to create sympathy in unlikely quarters as in the last war. All the world was hostile close round one and Bloomsbury had no changing atmosphere in which to move and expand and grow. So when the young men were finally forced to take some share in what was going on for the most part they chose to work on farms, and this meant a dispersal and general scattering.

Most went to the country: but some like Maynard Keynes and others from Cambridge came to London to do war work. He took our house, 46 Gordon Square, and lived there with three or four others during the War, eventually continuing to live there for the rest of his life. I was among those who left London in 1916 and when I came back three years later I realized very clearly how all had changed. Nothing happens twice and Bloomsbury had had its day. It dissolved in the newer world and the younger generation, now known as the Twenties. This contained of course many brilliant, possibly more brilliant, writers, than Bloomsbury had known, such as the Sitwells, Raymond Mortimer, Aldous Huxley, Francis Birrell, L.H. Myers, T.S. Eliot and many others. There was I think one figure, David Garnett, who was completely of Bloomsbury in its latest moments of disintegration and yet also outside it, for he had grown up in an entirely different circle.

When therefore the critics of today abuse Bloomsbury let them in the interests of accuracy distinguish it from all that came after the 1914—18 War. Abuse or criticism has never done it much harm that I know of, but why should Bloomsbury be singled out from all other districts? Why not Hampstead or Chelsea? Chelsea had always been the home of painters and writers and highbrows generally. There were George Moore and his circle, universally admired and respected, with Logan Pearsall Smith round the corner and painters of course by the hundred. Augustus John, Tonks, Steer, McEvoy and many others formed a bigger circle than Bloomsbury can ever have done. In

Hampstead too there must have been a group of the same kind, with Sir
William Rothenstein, D.S. MacColl and Sir Charles Aitken to make a
beginning. Yet one never heard a word against them and who now
would be understood if he talked sneeringly of Chelsea or Hampstead?

No: say what you like, but while there are still those who remember
take the trouble to get your facts right.   V.B. 1951

Clive Bell: Bloomsbury

Reprinted from Old Friends: Personal Recollections *(London, Chatto &
Windus, 1956), 126–137, by permission of Professor Quentin Bell and
Chatto & Windus.*

[Clive Bell's essay on Bloomsbury was originally published in 1954
under the title 'What was "Bloomsbury"?' It displays the same
irritation to be seen in his wife's memoir at the irresponsible way in
which the label 'Bloomsbury' was being used by journalists, academics,
and others. Bell's emphasis on the distinctions to be made inside
Bloomsbury is important, though his insistence that a definition of
Bloomsbury identify its common and peculiar characteristics is
questionable.

The reading society that Bell mentions discussing in another chapter
of *Old Friends* was the Midnight Society 'which met at midnight
because another – the X – of which some of us were members, met
earlier on Saturday evenings. . .and, having strengthened itself with
whisky or punch and one of those gloomy beef-steak pies which it was
the fashion to order for Sunday lunch, proceeded to read aloud some
such trifle as *Prometheus Unbound, The Cenci, The Return of the
Druses, Bartholomew Fair* or *Comus*.' It was in this society that Bell
felt the foundations of Bloomsbury were to be found.

Bell's essay was illustrated in *Old Friends* with a photograph of Mrs
St John Hutchinson, E.M. Forster, Duncan Grant, and himself in the
garden at Charleston. The first *Times Literary Supplement* article he
refers to was a review of J.K. Johnstone's *The Bloomsbury Group*; the
second, entitled ' "Bloomsbury" and Beyond', criticized Bloomsbury
for 'calling attention to its melancholy self by passionate rejection of
anything approaching enjoyment in art'. When queried by Oliver
Strachey in a letter, the *T. L. S.* replied that a distinction had to be
made between the distinguished artists and writers who lived in
Bloomsbury and the nonentities 'who, for nearly twenty years attracted

to themselves what reflected glory they might from the luminaries of
WC1'.]

There is mystery in the word, and money too perhaps. Or is it merely
for fun that grave historians and pompous leader-writers no less than
the riff-raff of Fleet Street and Portland Place chatter about the thing?
'The thing', I say, because that is the least committal substantive I can
think of, and it is not always clear whether what the chatterers are
chattering about is a point of view, a period, a gang of conspirators or
an infectious disease. Beyond meaning something nasty, what do they
mean by 'Bloomsbury'? Assuming, as seems reasonable, that they all
have in mind, amongst other things, a gang or group or clique (for
without human beings you cannot well have a point of view or a
doctrine, and even an epidemic needs 'carriers'), I invite them to name
the men and women of whom this gang or group or clique was
composed. Who were the members of Bloomsbury? Let them give the
names: then they may be able to tell us what were the tastes and
opinions held in common by and peculiar to the people to whom these
names belong, what, in fact, is or was the 'Bloomsbury doctrine'.[1]

But we must not ask too much — and it is much to think clearly and
state one's thought perspicuously — of columnists and broadcasters, so
to *The Times Literary Supplement* and a Fellow of All Souls I turn.
The *Supplement* has before now castigated Bloomsbury in reviews and
even in a leading article; while only the other day I caught one of the
most prominent fellows of the glorious foundation writing in *The
Times* of 'Bloomsbury historians'. From such high courts we may
expect clear judgments. I implore the *Supplement*, I implore Mr Rowse,
to give categorical answers to a couple of straight questions: (*a*) Who
are or were the members of Bloomsbury? (*b*) For what do they, or did
they, stand?

I have been stigmatized as 'Bloomsbury' myself, and the epithet has
been applied freely to most of those who are, or were — for many are
dead — my intimate friends, so, if it be true that something that can
fairly be called 'the Bloomsbury group' did exist, presumably I am
entitled to an opinion as to who were the members and what were their
thoughts and feelings. Of course I am aware that people born in recent
years and distant lands hold opinions clean contrary to mine. By all
means let them enjoy a Bloomsbury of their own invention; only,
should they chance to write on the subject, let them state clearly whom
and what they are writing about. Otherwise historians unborn will

flounder in a sea of doubt. Knowing that 'Bloomsbury' was the curse of a decade or two in the twentieth century, but unable to infer from a mass of woolly evidence who precisely were the malefactors and what precisely was the thing, some will be sure that it was a religious heresy, a political deviation or a conspiracy, while others, less confident, may suspect it was no more than a peculiar vice.

So, having appealed to the highest authorities for simple answers to simple questions, I now repeat my request to the smaller fry. Let everyone have his or her notion of 'Bloomsbury'; but let everyone who uses the name in public speech or writing do his or her best to say exactly what he or she intends by it. Thus, even should it turn out that in fact there never was such a thing, the word might come to have significance independent of the facts and acquire value as a label. I dare say Plato would have been at a loss to discover the connection between his philosophy and the epithet 'platonic' as used by lady-novelists and reviewers in the nineteenth and twentieth centuries; nevertheless in refined conversation the word now has a recognised meaning. 'Bloomsbury' may yet come to signify something definite, though as yet few people, so far as I can make out, understand by it anything more precise than 'the sort of thing we all dislike'. Wherefore I repeat, let publicists and broadcasters be explicit. That is my modest request: which made, I will give what help I can by telling all I know.

The name was first applied to a set of friends by Lady MacCarthy – Mrs Desmond MacCarthy as she then was – in a letter: she calls them 'the Bloomsberries'. The term, as she used it, had a purely topographical import; and the letter, which doubtless could be found at the bottom of one of five or six tin boxes, must have been written in 1910 or 1911. But the story begins earlier. It begins, as I have recorded in an earlier chapter, in October 1899 when five freshmen went up to Trinity – Cambridge, of course – and suddenly becoming intimate, as freshmen will, founded a society as freshmen almost invariably do. It was a 'reading society' which met in my rooms in the New Court on Saturdays at midnight, and here are the names of the five original members: Lytton Strachey, Sydney-Turner, Leonard Woolf, Thoby Stephen, Clive Bell.[2] After he had gone down, and after the death of his father, Thoby Stephen lived at 46 Gordon Square, Bloomsbury, with his brother Adrian and his two sisters Vanessa (later Vanessa Bell) and Virginia (later Virginia Woolf). These two beautiful, gifted and completely independent young women, with a house of their own, became the centre of a circle of which Thoby's Cambridge friends were what perhaps I may call the spokes. And when, in 1907, the elder married, the circle was not broken but enlarged; for Virginia, with her surviving brother Adrian, took a house in nearby Fitzroy Square: thus, instead of one *salon* — if that be the word — there were two *salons*. If ever such an entity as 'Bloomsbury' existed, these sisters, with their houses in Gordon and Fitzroy Squares, were at the heart of it. But did such an entity exist?

All one can say truthfully is this. A dozen friends — I will try to name them presently — between 1904 and 1914 saw a great deal of each other. They differed widely, as I shall tell, in opinions, tastes and preoccupations. But they liked, though they sharply criticized, each other, and they liked being together. I suppose one might say they were 'in sympathy'. Can a dozen individuals so loosely connected be called a group? It is not for me to decide. Anyhow the first World War disintegrated this group, if group it were, and when the friends came together again inevitably things had changed. Old friends brought with them new and younger acquaintances. Differences of opinion and taste, always wide, became wider. Close relationships with people quite outside the old circle sprang up. Sympathy remained. But whatever cohesion there may have been among those who saw so much of each other in Gordon Square and Fitzroy Square, among Lady MacCarthy's 'Bloomsberries' that is, by 1918 had been lost. That was the end of 'old Bloomsbury'.

Now I will try to name these friends. There were the surviving members of the Midnight Society. Thoby Stephen had died in the late autumn of 1906: Leonard Woolf was in Ceylon between 1904 and 1911: remained in Bloomsbury, Lytton Strachey (who, in fact, lived in Hampstead), Saxon Sydney-Turner, Clive Bell. There were the two ladies. Add to these Duncan Grant, Roger Fry, Maynard Keynes, H.T.J. Norton and perhaps Gerald Shove, and I believe you will have completed the list of those of the elder generation who have been called 'Bloomsbury'. Certainly Desmond and Molly MacCarthy and Morgan Forster were close and affectionate friends, but I doubt whether any one of them has yet been branded with the fatal name. So much for the old gang.

As I have said, after the war a few men of a younger generation became intimate with most of us. I will do my best to name these, too; but as the new association was even looser than the old, the classification will be even less precise. First and foremost come David Garnett and Francis Birrell, both of whom we — by 'we' I mean the old Bloomsberries — had known and liked before 1914. Immediately after the War, by a stroke of good luck, I made the acquaintance of

Raymond Mortimer[3]; and about the same time Lytton Strachey, lecturing at Oxford, met Ralph Partridge. I do not know who discovered Stephen Tomlin: but I remember well how Keynes brought Sebastian Sprott and F.L. Lucas from Cambridge to stay at a house in Sussex shared by him with my wife, myself and Duncan Grant. I think it may have been through Francis Birrell that we came to know a brilliant girl from Newnham, Frances Marshall (later Mrs Ralph Partridge).

Now whether all or most of the people I have named are the people publicists have in mind when they speak of 'Bloomsbury' is not clear. In fact that is one of the questions I am asking. But from words let fall in broadcasts and articles I infer a tendency to lump together the two generations and call the lump 'Bloomsbury'. We can be sure of nothing till the journalists and broadcasters and the high authorities too have favoured us with their lists. I have given mine; and so doing have given what help I can and set a good example. I have named the friends who were intimate before 1914 and have added the names of those, or at any rate most of those, who became friends of *all* these friends later. Naturally, with time and space at their familiar task, the bonds of sympathy loosened – though I think they seldom snapped – and so the friends of 'the Twenties' were even less like a group than the friends of the pre-War period. That, as I have said, has not prevented some critics lumping them all together, and calling the combination or compound, which it seems exhaled a mephitic influence over the twenties, 'Bloomsbury'. It is impossible, I repeat, to know whom, precisely, they have in mind; but, assuming their list to be something like mine, again I put the question: What had these friends in common that was peculiar to these friends?

Not much, I believe you will agree, if you will be so kind as to read my chapter to the end. For beyond mutual liking they had precious little in common, and in mutual liking there is nothing peculiar. Yes, they did like each other; also they shared a taste for discussion in pursuit of truth and a contempt for conventional ways of thinking and feeling – contempt for conventional morals if you will. Does it not strike you that as much could be said of many collections of young or youngish people in many ages and many lands? For my part, I find nothing distinctive here. Ah, say the pundits, but there was G.E. Moore the Cambridge philosopher; Moore was the all-pervading, the binding influence; 'Moorism' is the peculiarity the Bloomsberries have in common. I should think there was G.E. Moore; also the influence of his *Principia Ethica* on some of us was immense – on some but not on all,

nor perhaps on most. Four of us certainly were freed by Moore from
the spell of an ugly doctrine in which we had been reared: he delivered
us from Utilitarianism. What is more, you can discover easily enough
traces of Moorist ethics in the writings of Strachey and Keynes and, I
suppose, in mine. But not all these friends were Moorists. Roger Fry,
for instance, whose authority was quite as great as that of Lytton
Strachey was definitely anti-Moorist. So, in a later generation, was
Frances Marshall who, beside being a beauty and an accomplished
ballroom dancer, was a philosopher. Assuredly Raymond Mortimer,
Ralph Partridge and Stephen Tomlin – all three Oxford men – were
not devout believers in *Principia Ethica*; while F.L. Lucas, who in those
'Twenties' may well have heard himself called 'Bloomsbury', at that
time called himself a Hedonist. I doubt whether either of the Miss
Stephens gave much thought to the all important distinction between
'Good on the whole' and 'Good as a whole'. Also it must be
remembered that Bertrand Russell, though no one has ever called him
'Bloomsbury', appeared to be a friend and was certainly an influence.

Lytton Strachey, I have agreed, was a Moorist. Of him I have written
at some length elsewhere and have said that, being a great character,
amongst very young men he was inevitably a power. But at Cambridge,
and later among his cronies in London, his influence was literary for the
most part. He inclined our undergraduate taste away from
contemporary realism towards the Elizabethans and the eighteenth
century. But when, about 1910, Roger Fry and I became fascinated by
what was being written in France he did not share our enthusiasm.
Quite the contrary: and as for contemporary painting, Lytton, who had
a liking, a literary liking, for the visual arts, thought that we were
downright silly about Matisse and Picasso, and on occasions said so.[4] It
begins to look – does it not? – as though this thing called
'Bloomsbury' was not precisely homogeneous. Maynard Keynes, whose
effect on economic theory was, I understand, immense, bore no sway
whatever amongst his friends in the West Central district. They liked
him for his cleverness, his wit, the extraordinary ingenuity with which
he defended what they often considered absurd opinions, and his
affectionate nature. They disliked other things. He had very little
natural feeling for the arts; though he learnt to write admirably lucid
prose, and, under the spell of Duncan Grant, cultivated a taste for
pictures and made an interesting collection. Said Lytton once: 'What's
wrong with Pozzo' – a pet name for Maynard which Maynard
particularly disliked – 'is that he has no aesthetic sense'. Perhaps
Lytton was unjust; but with perfect justice he might have said the same

of Norton. On the other hand, Pozzo and Norton might have said of
some of their dearest friends that what was wrong with them was that
they were incapable of wrestling with abstractions. You see we were
not so much alike after all.

I have done my best to name those people who certainly were
friends and of whom some at any rate have often been called
'Bloomsbury'. I have suggested that the people in my list held few, if
any, opinions and preferences in common which were not held by
hundreds of their intelligent contemporaries: I emphasize the words 'in
common'. Wherefore, if my list be correct, it would seem to follow that
there can be no such thing as 'the Bloomsbury doctrine' or 'the
Bloomsbury point of view'. But is my list correct? It should be. And
yet I cannot help wondering sometimes whether the journalists and
broadcasters who write and talk about Bloomsbury have not in mind
some totally different set of people. There are critics and expositors,
for instance that leader-writer in *The Times Literary Supplement*, who
describe Bloomsbury as a little gang or clique which despises all that is
old and venerable and extols to the skies, without discrimination, the
latest thing whatever that thing may be — the latest in art or letters or
politics or morals. Also, according to this school of critics, the writers
of Bloomsbury delight in a private and cryptic language, unintelligible
to the common reader, while mocking at whatever is clear and
comprehensible. Now who are these crabbed and wilfully obscure
writers who despise all that is old? Surely not those reputed pillars of
Bloomsbury, Lytton Strachey, Roger Fry, Maynard Keynes, David
Garnett? I beseech the *Supplement* to give us the names.[5]

There are other critics, of whom I know as little as they appear to
know of the reputed pillars of Bloomsbury, who hold a clean contrary
opinion. I write from hearsay; but I am told there are brisk young
fellows, authorities on the 'Twenties', whose distressing accents are
sometimes heard on the wireless by those who can stand that sort of
thing, who explain that in 'the Twenties' there still existed in England a
gang or group which for years had devoted itself to stifling, or trying to
stifle, at birth every vital movement that came to life. Oddly enough
this gang, too, goes by the name of Bloomsbury. Now who can these
baby-killers have been? Obviously not Roger Fry who introduced the
modern movement in French painting to the British public, nor
Maynard Keynes, who, I understand, revolutionized economics. Nor
does it seem likely that the critics are thinking of Lytton Strachey who,
are from being reactionary, went out of his way to help the cause of
Women's Suffrage when that cause was reckoned a dangerous fad, or of

Leonard Woolf who was a Fabian long before British socialism had become what the Americans call a racket. Whom can these castigators of 'Bloomsbury' have in mind? Clearly not Virginia Woolf who invented what amounts almost to a new prose form; nor, I hope, certain critics who, long before 1920, had appreciated and defended the then disconcerting works of Picasso and T.S. Eliot.

Once more I cry aloud: Who were the members of Bloomsbury? For what did they stand? In the interests of history, if common decency means nothing to them, I beseech the Bloomsbury-baiters to answer my questions; for unless they speak out and speak quickly social historians will have to make what they can of wildly conflicting fancies and statement which contradict known facts. Thus, disheartened by the impossibility of discovering opinions and tastes common and peculiar to those people who by one authority or another have been described as 'Bloomsbury', the more acute may well be led to surmise that Bloomsbury was neither a chapel nor a clique but merely a collection of individuals each with his or her own views and likings. When to this perplexity is added the discovery that no two witnesses agree on a definition of the 'Bloomsbury doctrine', historians are bound to wonder whether there ever was such a thing. At last they may come to doubt whether 'Bloomsbury' ever existed. And did it?

Notes

1. *The Times Literary Supplement* (20th August 1954) published a long review of a book the name of which escapes me. This review, or essay rather, was entitled 'The air of Bloomsbury'; and is by far the most intelligent and penetrating piece that has been written on the subject. There were errors of fact to be sure, errors there must be in an appreciation by someone who is not himself a part of the society described, by someone who was neither an eye nor an ear witness. But the essay, admirably written, reveals a remarkable power of understanding complex characters and peculiar points of view. It has value much beyond that of most ephemeral, or rather hebdomadal, criticism. And it is to be hoped that it will soon be published in easily accessible and durable form.
2. I maintain that A.J. Robertson was also an original member, but he disclaims the honour – or dishonour.
3. Raymond Mortimer reminds me that, after the first war, he was brought to 46 Gordon Square by Aldous Huxley. That was our first meeting.
4. Well do I remember Lytton drawing me aside and saying: 'Cannot you or Vanessa persuade Duncan to make beautiful pictures instead of these coagulations of distressing oddments?' Duncan Grant at that

time was much under the influence of the Post-Impressionists and
had been touched by Cubism even.

5. A week or so after this leading article appeared Mr Oliver Strachey
made the same request, and received from the *Supplement* (31st
July 1948) what I can only consider a disingenuous reply.

Leonard Woolf: Cambridge Friends and Influences

Reprinted from Leonard Woolf, Sowing: An Autobiography of the
Years 1880–1904 *(London, the Hogarth Press, 1960) 102–7, 119–20,
123–4, 127–9, 130, 131–7, 144–54, 155–6, by permission of the
author's literary estate and the Hogarth Press;* © *1960 by Leonard
Woolf, reprinted by permission of Harcourt Brace Jovanovich, Inc.*

[The five volumes of Leonard Woolf's autobiography, all published in
the 1960s, contain the fullest and most reliable account of Bloomsbury's origins, developments, and achievements. In the group of
excerpts collected here from *Sowing*, the first volume, Woolf sets forth
the Cambridge backgrounds of Bloomsbury. Three of Woolf's Trinity
College/Bloomsbury friends, Saxon Sydney-Turner, Thoby Stephen,
and Clive Bell, are characterized; the fourth, Lytton Strachey, has been
omitted here because an earlier account of him by Woolf is given in the
second section of this collection. After the description of his friends
comes Woolf's eloquent exposition of G.E. Moore's deep influence on
him and his friends (and on Desmond MacCarthy, an older friend who
is also described by Woolf in the second section). For Leonard Woolf,
G.E. Moore was 'the only great man whom I have ever met or known in
the world of ordinary, real life'. And in explaining his importance
Woolf takes issue with Keynes's account in *My Early Beliefs* (see pp.
48–64).

... I must return to Cambridge in the autumn and winter of 1899.
I felt terribly lonely in my first few days at Trinity... But suddenly
everything changed and almost for the first time one felt that
to be young was very heaven. The reason was simple. Suddenly I
found to my astonishment that there were a number of people near
and about me with whom I could enjoy the exciting and at the same
time profound happiness of friendship. It began casually in what was
called the screens, the passage through the Hall from Trinity Great
Court to Neville's Court. I was looking at the notices on the board after
dining in Hall and said something to a man standing next to me. We

walked away together and he came back to my rooms. He was a scholar
from Westminster, Saxon Sydney-Turner. Saxon was a very strange
character with one of the strangest minds I have met with. He was
immensely intelligent and subtle, but had little creativeness. In one of
the university scholarship examinations they set us for Greek translation a piece from a rather obscure writer which had a riddle in it.
Saxon won one of the scholarships and it was said that he was the only
person to get the riddle bit right. It was characteristic of him. When,
years later, crossword puzzles were invented and became the rage, he
was a champion solver. And it was characteristic of him that he was a
champion solver, never an inventor, of crossword puzzles and other
mental gymnastics, including the art of writing. He had an immense
knowledge of literature, but he read books rather in the spirit in which
a man collects stamps. He would tell you casually that last night he had
read for the second time in three weeks Meister Eckhart's *Buch der
gottlicher Tröstung und von den edlen Menschen* much in the tone of
voice in which a great stamp collector might casually remark – to
épater his fellow collectors – that yesterday afternoon he had bought
for 2*s.* 6*d* in a shop in a back street of Soho two perfect specimens of a
very rare 1*d* Cape of Good Hope stamp. Later in life, when he was in
the Treasury and lived in Great Ormond Street, he was an inveterate
concert and opera goer in London and Bayreuth. He kept a record,
both on paper and in his head, of all the operas he had ever been to.
Normally with other people he was reserved, spoke little, and fell into
long and unobtrusive silences. But sometimes he would begin to talk
almost volubly about opera. He would tell you that last night he had
been at Covent Garden and heard *Siegfried* for the thirty-fifth time. X
had sung Brünnhilde; the great duet in the last act was quite good. X
sang well and reminded him of Y whom he had heard sing the same part
at Bayreuth, in 1908, Z being Siegfried, when he had been to *Siegfried*
for the seventh time. The best performance he had ever heard of the
opera was his twelfth, also at Bayreuth; Y was again Brünnhilde and
there was the greatest of all Siegfrieds, W. The fourteenth time he saw
the opera was . . . and so on.

The rooms which Saxon lived in for many years in Great Ormond
Street consisted of one big sitting-room and a small bedroom. On each
side of the sitting-room fireplace on the wall was an immense picture of
a farmyard scene. It was the same picture on each side and for over
thirty years Saxon lived with them ever before his eyes, while in his
bedroom there were some very good pictures by Duncan Grant and
other artists, but you could not possibly see them because there was no

light and no space to hang them on the walls. As time went on, Saxon acquired more and more books and, since he suffered from a variety of ailments, more and more medicine bottles. His bookcases filled up and soon a second and third row, one behind the other, became necessary, and then piles and piles of books covered the floor. There were books upon the tables and chairs, and everywhere there were empty medicine bottles on the books, and the same two pigs, the same two sheep, and the same two dogs looked down upon, one presumes, the unseeing Saxon from the same two pictures on either side of the mantelpiece.

I was up at Trinity for five years. The first two years I had rooms in New Court; in the last three years Saxon and I had a double set of rooms in Great Court. It had one very large room on the first floor and two small bedrooms on the second. Saxon was a short, thin man with a very pale face and straw-coloured hair. He seemed to glide, rather than walk, and noiselessly, so that one moment you were alone in a room and next moment you found him sitting in a chair near you though you had not heard the door open or him come in. We saw very little of each other except in the evenings for he used to get up very late as a rule whereas I was up at eight. We hardly ever had a meal together for he ate very little and at the most erratic hours.

Both physically and mentally Saxon was ghost-like, shadowy. He rarely committed himself to any positive opinion or even statement. His conversation – if it could rightly be called conversation – was extremely spasmodic, elusive, and allusive. You might be sitting reading a book and suddenly find him standing in front of you on one leg in front of the fire knocking out his pipe into the fireplace and he would say without looking up: 'Her name was Emily'; or perhaps: 'He was right.' After a considerable amount of cross-examination, you would find that the first remark applied to a conversation weeks ago in which he had tried unsuccessfully to remember the christian name of Miss Girouette in *Nightmare Abbey*, and the second remark applied to a dispute between Thoby Stephen and myself which I had completely forgotten because it had taken place in the previous term.

During the years we were at Trinity, Henry James was at the height of his powers, writing those strange, involved, elusive novels of his last period. We read *The Sacred Fount, The Wings of the Dove*, and *The Golden Bowl* as they came out. Lytton Strachey, Saxon, and I were fascinated by them – entranced and almost hypnotized. I don't know whether we thought that they were really great masterpieces. My enjoyment and admiration of them have always been and still are great, but always with a reservation. There is an element of ridiculousness, even of 'phoneyness' in them which makes it impossible to rank them with the greatest or even the great novels. But the strange, Jamesian, convoluted beauty and subtlety of them act upon those who yield to them like drink or drugs; for a time we became addicts, habitual drunkards — never, perhaps, quite serious, but playing at seeing the world of Trinity and Cambridge as a Jamesian phantasmagoria, writing and talking as if we had just walked out of *The Sacred Fount* into Trinity Great Court. The curious thing was that, whereas Lytton and I were always consciously playing a game in talking or writing like Mrs Brissenden and Mrs Server, Saxon quite naturally talked, looked, acted, *was* a character in an unwritten novel by Henry James . . .

Lytton Strachey, Thoby Stephen, and Clive Bell all came up to Trinity in the same year as Saxon and I did and we soon got to know them well. We were intimate friends — particularly Lytton, Saxon, and myself — but intimacy in 1900 among middle-class males was different from what it became in generations later than ours. Some of us were called by nicknames; for instance we always called Thoby Stephen 'The Goth', but we never used christian names. Lytton always called me Woolf and I always called him Strachey until I returned from Ceylon in 1911 and found that the wholesale revolution in society and manners which had taken place in the preceding seven years involved the use of christian names in place of surnames. The difference was — and is — not entirely unimportant. The shade of relationship between Woolf and Strachey is not exactly the same as that between Leonard and Lytton. The surname relationship was determined by and retained that curious formality and reticence which the nineteenth-century public school system insisted upon in certain matters. Now, of course, the use of christian names and their diminutives has become so universal that it may soon perhaps become necessary to indicate intimacy by using surnames. . .

The characters in *The Waves* are not drawn from life, but there is something of Lytton in Neville. There is no doubt that Percival in that book contains something of Thoby Stephen, Virginia's brother, who died of typhoid aged twenty-six in 1906. Thoby came up to Trinity from Clifton with an exhibition in the same year as Lytton, Saxon, and I. He gave one an impression of physical magnificence. He was six foot two, broad-shouldered and somewhat heavily made, with a small head set elegantly upon the broad shoulders so that it reminded one of the way in which the small head is set upon the neck of a well-bred Arab horse. His face was extraordinarily beautiful and his character was as beautiful as his face. In his monolithic character, his monolithic common-sense, his monumental judgments he continually reminded one of Dr Johnson, but a Samuel Johnson who had shed his neuroticism, his irritability, his fears. He had a perfect 'natural' style of writing, flexible, lucid, but rather formal, old-fashioned, almost Johnsonian or at any rate eighteenth century. And there was a streak of the same natural style in his talk. Any wild statement, speculative judgment, or Strachean exaggeration would be met with a 'Nonsense, my good fellow', from Thoby, and then a sentence of profound, but humorous, common-sense, and a delighted chuckle. Thoby had a good sense of humour, a fine, sound, but not brilliant mind. He had many of the characteristic qualities of the males of his family, of his father Leslie Stephen, his uncle James Fitzjames Stephen and his cousin J.K. Stephen. But what everyone who knew him remembers most vividly in him was his extraordinary charm. He had greater personal charm than anyone I have ever known, and, unlike all other great 'charmers', he seemed, and I believe was, entirely unconscious of it. It was, no doubt, partly physical, partly due to the unusual combination of sweetness of nature and affection with rugged intelligence and a complete lack of sentimentality, and partly to those personal flavours of the soul which are as unanalyzable and indescribable as the scents of flowers or the overtones in a line of great poetry.

Thoby was an intellectual; he liked an argument and had a great, though conservative and classical, appreciation and love of literature. But he also, though rather scornful of games and athletics, loved the open air – watching birds, walking, following the beagles. In these occupations, particularly in walking, I often joined him. Walking with him was by no means a tame business, for it was almost a Stephen principle in walking to avoid all roads and ignore the rights of property owners and the law of trespass. Owing to these principles we did not endear ourselves to the gamekeepers round Cambridge. Though fundamentally respectable, conservative, and a moralist, he was always ready in the country to leave the beaten track in more senses than one . . .

Clive Bell came up to Trinity the same year as we did, 1899, and when we first got to know him he was different in many ways from us and even from the Clive Bell whom I found married to Vanessa Stephen and living in Gordon Square when I returned from Ceylon in 1911. He came into our lives because he got to know Saxon, having rooms on the same staircase in New Court. Lytton, Saxon, Thoby, and I belonged, unconcealably and unashamedly, to that class of human beings which is regarded with deep suspicion in Britain, and particularly in public schools and universities, the intellectual. Clive, when he came up to Trinity from Marlborough, was not yet an intellectual. He was superficially a 'blood'. The first time I ever saw him he was walking through Great Court in full hunting rigout, including – unless this is wishful imagination – a hunting horn and the whip carried by the whipper-in. He was a great horseman and a first-rate shot, very well-off, and to be seen in the company of 'bloods', not the rowing, cricket, and rugger blues, but the rich young men who shot, and hunted, and rode in the point-to-point races. He had a very attractive face, particularly to women, boyish, goodhumoured, hair red and curly, and what in the eighteenth century was called, I think, a sanguine complexion.

Clive became great friends with Thoby, for they both were fond of riding and hunting. In those early days, and indeed for many years afterwards, intellectually Clive sat at the feet of Lytton and Thoby. He was one of those strange Englishmen who break away from their environment and become devoted to art and letters. His family of wealthy philistines, whose money came from coal, lived in a large house in Wiltshire. Somehow or other, Mr and Mrs Bell produced Clive's mind which was a contradiction in terms of theirs.[1] For his mind was eager, lively, intensely curious, and he quickly developed a passion for literature[2] and argument. We had started some reading societies for reading aloud plays, one of which met at midnight, and Clive became a member of them. In this way we came to see a good deal of him and his admiration for Lytton and Thoby began to flourish.

It is necessary here to say something about the Society – The Apostles – because of the immense importance it had for us, its influence upon our minds, our friendships, our lives. The Society was and still is 'secret', but, as it has existed for 130 years or more, in autobiographies and biographies of members its nature, influence, and membership have naturally from time to time been described. There is a good deal about it in the autobiography of Dean Merivale, who was elected in 1830, and in the memoir of Henry Sidgwick, who was elected in 1856, and information about its condition in the early years of the present century can be found in *The Life of John Maynard Keynes* by R.F. Harrod, who was not himself an Apostle. . .

. . .When Lytton, Saxon, and I were elected, the other active undergraduate members were A.R. Ainsworth, Ralph Hawtrey, and J.T. Sheppard.[3] When Maynard Keynes came up, we elected him in 1903.

Sidgwick says that the Society absorbed and dominated him, but that is
not quite the end of the story. Throughout its history, every now and
again an Apostle has dominated and left his impression, within its spirit
and tradition, upon the Society. Sidgwick himself was one of these, and
a century ago he dominated the Society, refertilizing and revivifying its
spirit and tradition. And what Sidgwick did in the fifties of last
century, G.E. Moore was doing when I was elected. . .

It was, I suppose, in 1902 that I got to know Moore well. He was seven
years my senior and already a Fellow of Trinity. His mind was an
extraordinarily powerful instrument; it was Socratic, analytic. But
unlike so many analytic philosophers, he never analyzed just for the
pleasure or sake of analysis. He never indulged in logic-chopping or
truth-chopping. He had a passion for truth, but not for all or any truth,
only for important truths. He had no use for truths which Browning
called 'dead from the waist down'. Towards the end of the nineteenth
century there was an extraordinary outburst of philosophical brilliance
in Cambridge. In 1902, among the Fellows of Trinity were four
philosophers, all of whom were Apostles: J.E. McTaggart, A.N.
Whitehead, Bertrand Russell, and G.E. Moore. McTaggart was one of
the strangest of men, an eccentric with a powerful mind which, when I
knew him, seemed to have entirely left the earth for the inextricably
complicated cobwebs and *O altitudos* of Hegelianism. He had the most
astonishing capacity for profound silence that I have ever known. He
lived out of college, but he had an 'evening' once a week on Thursdays
when, if invited or taken by an invitee, you could go and see him in his
rooms in Great Court. The chosen were very few, and Lytton, Saxon,
and I, who were among them, every now and again nerved ourselves to
the ordeal. McTaggart always seemed glad to see us, but, having said
good evening, he lay back on a sofa, his eyes fixed on the ceiling, in
profound silence. Every five minutes he would roll his head from side
to side, stare with his rather protuberant, rolling eyes round the circle
of visitors, and then relapse into immobility. One of us would
occasionally manage to think of something banal and halting to say, but
I doubt whether I ever heard McTaggart initiate a conversation, and
when he did say something it was usually calculated to bring to a
sudden end any conversation initiated by one of us. Yet he did not
seem to wish us not to be there; indeed, he appeared to be quite
content that we should come and see him and sit for an hour in silence.

In the early 1890s McTaggart's influence was great. He was six years
older than Russell and seven years older than Moore, and these two in

their early days at Trinity were first converted to Hegelianism by McTaggart. But Moore could never tolerate anything but truth, common-sense, and reality, and he very soon revolted against Hegel: Bertrand Russell describes the revolt in the following words:

> Moore, first, and I closely following him, climbed out of this mental prison and found ourselves again at liberty to breathe the free air of a universe restored to reality.

When I came up to Trinity, McTaggart, though regarded with respect and amused affection as an eccentric, had completely lost his intellectual and philosophical influence. The three other philosophers' reputation was great and growing, and they dominated the younger generation. In 1902 Whitehead was forty-one years old, Russell thirty, and Moore twenty-nine. It is a remarkable fact — a fine example of our inflexible irrationality and inveterate inconsistency — that, although no people has ever despised, distrusted and rejected the intellect and intellectuals more than the British, these three philosophers were each awarded the highest and rarest of official honours, the Order of Merit. 1903 was an *annus mirabilis* for Cambridge philosophy, for in that year were published Russell's *Principles of Mathematics* and Moore's *Principia Ethica*. Russell used to come to Moore's rooms sometimes in order to discuss some difficult problem that was holding him up. The contrast between the two men and the two minds was astonishing and fascinating. Russell has the quickest mind of anyone I have ever known; like the greatest of chess players he sees in a flash six moves ahead of the ordinary player and one move ahead of all the other Grand Masters. However serious he may be, his conversation scintillates with wit and a kind of puckish humour flickers through his thought. Like most people who possess this kind of mental brilliance, in an argument a slower and duller opponent may ruefully find that Russell is not always entirely scrupulous in taking advantage of his superior skill in the use of weapons. Moore was the exact opposite, and to listen to an argument between the two was like watching a race between the hare and the tortoise. Quite often the tortoise won — and that, of course, was why Russell's thought had been so deeply influenced by Moore and why he still came to Moore's rooms to discuss difficult problems.

Moore was not witty; I do not think that I ever heard him say a witty thing; there was no scintillation in his conversation or in his thought. But he had an extraordinary profundity and clarity of thought, and he pursued truth with the tenacity of a bulldog and the integrity of a saint. And he had two other very rare characteristics. He had a genius for seeing what was important and what was unimportant and irrelevant, in thought and in life and in persons, and in the most complicated argument or situation he pursued the relevant and ignored the irrelevant with amazing tenacity. He was able to do so because of the second characteristic, the passion for truth (and, as I shall show, for other things) which burned in him. The tortoise so often won the race because of this combination of clarity, integrity, tenacity, and passion.

The intensity of Moore's passion for truth was an integral part of his greatness, and purity of passion was an integral part of his whole character. On the surface and until you got to know him intimately he appeared to be a very shy, reserved man, and on all occasions and in any company he might fall into profound and protracted silence. When I first got to know him, the immensely high standards of thought and conduct which he seemed silently to demand of an intimate, the feeling that one should not say anything unless the thing was both true and worth saying, the silences which would certainly envelope him and you, tinged one's wish to see him with some anxiety, and I know that standing at the door of his room, before knocking and going in, I often took a deep breath just as one does on a cool day before one dives into the cold green sea. For a young man it was a formidable, an alarming experience, but, like the plunge into the cold sea, once one had nerved oneself to take it, extraordinarily exhilarating. This kind of tension relaxed under the influence of time, intimacy, and affection, but I do not think that it ever entirely disappeared — a proof, perhaps, of the quality of greatness which distinguished Moore from other people.

His reserve and silences covered deep feeling. When Moore said: 'I *simply* don't understand *what* he means,' the emphasis on the 'simply' and the 'what' and the shake of his head over each word gave one a glimpse of the passionate distress which muddled thinking aroused in him. We used to watch with amusement and admiration the signs of the same thing when he sat reading a book, pencil in hand, and continually scoring the poor wretch of a writer's muddled sentences with passionate underlinings and exclamation marks. I used to play fives with him at Cambridge, and he played the game with the same passion as that with which he pursued truth; after a few minutes in the court the sweat poured down his face in streams and soaked his clothes — it was excitement as well as exercise. It was the same with music. He played the piano and sang, often to Lytton Strachey and me in his rooms and on reading parties in Cornwall. He was not a highly skilful pianist or singer, but I have never been given greater pleasure from playing or singing. This was due partly to the quality of his voice, but principally to the intelligence of his understanding and to the subtlety and intensity of his feeling. He played the Waldstein sonata or sang 'Ich grolle nicht' with the same passion with which he pursued truth; when the last note died away, he would sit absolutely still, his hands resting on the keys, and the sweat streaming down his face.

Moore's mind was, as I said, Socratic. His character, too, and his influence upon us as young men at Cambridge were Socratic. It is clear from Plato and Xenophon that Socrates's strange simplicity and integrity were enormously attractive to the young Athenians who became his disciples, and he inspired great affection as well as admiration. So did Moore. Plato in the *Symposium* shows us a kind of cosmic absurdity in the monumental simplicity of Socrates; and such different people as Alcibiades, Aristophanes, and Agathon 'rag' him about it and laugh at him gently and affectionately. There was the same kind of divine absurdity in Moore. Socrates had the great advantage of combining a very beautiful soul with a very ugly face, and the Athenians of the fifth century B.C. were just the people to appreciate the joke of that. Moore had not that advantage. When I first knew him, his face was amazingly beautiful, almost ethereal, and, as Bertrand Russell has said, 'he had, what he retained throughout his life, an extraordinarily lovable smile'. But he resembled Socrates in possessing a profound simplicity, a simplicity which Tolstoy and some other Russian writers consider to produce the finest human beings. These human beings are 'simples' or even 'sillies'; they are absurd in ordinary life and by the standards of sensible and practical men. There is a superb description of a 'silly' in Tolstoy's autobiography and, of course, in Dostoevsky's *The Idiot*. In many ways Moore was one of these divine 'sillies'. It showed itself perhaps in such simple, unrestrained, passionate gestures as when, if told something particularly astonishing or confronted by some absurd statement at the crisis of an argument, his eyes would open wide, his eyebrows shoot up, and his tongue shoot out of his mouth. And Bertrand Russell has described the pleasure with which one used to watch Moore trying unsuccessfully to light his pipe when he was arguing an important point. He would light a match, hold it over the bowl of his pipe until it burnt his fingers and he had to throw it away, and go on doing this – talking the whole time or listening intently to the other man's argument – until the whole box of matches was exhausted . . .

I feel that I must now face the difficult task of saying something about Moore's influence upon my generation. There is no doubt that it was immense. Maynard Keynes in his *Two Memoirs* wrote a fascinating, an extremely amusing account or analysis of this influence of Moore upon us as young men. Much of what he says is, of course, true and biographically or autobiographically important. Maynard's mind was incredibly quick and supple, imaginative and restless; he was always thinking new and original thoughts, particularly in the field of events and human behaviour and in the reaction between events and men's actions. He had the very rare gift of being as brilliant and effective in practice as he was in theory, so that he could outwit a banker, business man, or Prime Minister as quickly and gracefully as he could demolish a philosopher or crush an economist. It was these gifts which enabled him to revolutionize economic theory and national economic and financial policy and practice, and to make a considerable fortune by speculation and a considerable figure in the City and in the world which is concerned with the patronage or production of the arts, and particularly the theatre and ballet. But most people who knew him intimately and his mind in shirtsleeves rather than public uniform would agree that there were in him some streaks of intellectual wilfulness and arrogance which often led him into surprisingly wrong and perverse judgments. To his friends he was a lovable character and these faults or idiosyncrasies were observed and discounted with affectionate amusement.

It is always dangerous to speak the truth about one's most intimate friends, because the truth and motives for telling it are almost invariably misunderstood. In all the years that I knew Maynard and in all the many relations, of intimacy and business which I had with him, I never had even the ghost of a quarrel or the shadow of unpleasantness, though we often disagreed about things, persons, or policies. He was essentially a lovable person. But to people who were not his friends, to subordinates and to fools in their infinite variety whom one has to deal with in business or just daily life, he could be anything but lovable; he might, at any moment and sometimes quite unjustifiably, annihilate some unfortunate with ruthless rudeness. I once heard him snap out to an auditor who was trying to explain to the Board of Directors of a company some item in the audited accounts: 'We all know, Mr X, that auditors consider that the object of accounts is to conceal the truth, but surely not even you can believe that their object is to conceal the truth from the Directors.'

It was this streak of impatience and wilfulness combined with a restless and almost fantastic imagination, which often induced Maynard to make absurdly wrong judgments. But once having committed himself to one of his opinions or judgments, theories or fantasies, he would without compunction use all the powers and brilliance of his mind, his devastating wit and quickness, to defend it, and in the end would often succeed in convincing not only his opponent, but himself. In several points in *Two Memoirs* his recollection and interpretation are quite wrong about Moore's influence, I think. His main point in the memoir is that Moore in *Principia Ethica* propounded both a religion and a system of morals and that we as young men accepted the religion, but discarded the morals. He defines 'religion' to mean one's attitude towards oneself and the ultimate, and 'morals' to mean one's attitude towards the outside world and the intermediate. Moore's religion which we accepted, according to Maynard, maintained that

> nothing mattered except states of mind, our own and other people's of course, but chiefly our own. These states of mind were not associated with action or achievement or with consequences. They consisted in timeless, passionate states of contemplation and communion, largely unattached to 'before' and 'after' . . . The appropriate objects of passionate contemplation and communion were a beloved person, beauty and truth, and one's prime objects in life were love, the creation and enjoyment of aesthetic experience and the pursuit of knowledge. Of these love came a long way first.

Although Maynard calls this doctrine which we accepted a 'faith' and a 'religion', he says that Moore's disciples and indeed Moore himself regarded it as entirely rational and scientific, and applied an extravagantly rationalistic, scholastic method of ascertaining what states of affairs were or were not good. The resulting beliefs were fantastically idealistic and remote from reality and 'real' life. The effect of this curious amalgam of extreme rationalism, unworldliness, and dogmatic belief was intensified by our complete neglect of Moore's 'morals'. We paid no attention at all to his doctrine of the importance of rightness and wrongness as an attribute of actions or to the whole question of the justification of general rules of conduct. The result was that we assumed that human beings were all rational, but we were complete 'immoralists', recognizing 'no moral obligation on us, no inner sanction, to conform or obey'.

In my recollection this is a distorted picture of Moore's beliefs and doctrine at the time of the publication of his *Principia Ethica* and of the influence of his philosophy and character upon us when we were young men up at Cambridge in the years 1901 to 1904. The tremendous influence of Moore and his book upon us came from the fact that they suddenly removed from our eyes an obscuring accumulation of scales, cobwebs, and curtains, revealing for the first time to us, so it seemed, the nature of truth and reality, of good and evil and character and conduct, substituting for the religious and philosophical nightmares, delusions, hallucinations, in which Jehovah, Christ, and St Paul, Plato, Kant, and Hegel had entangled us, the fresh air and pure light of plain common-sense.

It was this clarity, freshness, and common-sense which primarily appealed to us. Here was a profound philosopher who did not require us to accept any 'religious' faith or intricate, if not unintelligible, intellectual gymnastics of a Platonic, Aristotelian, Kantian, or Hegelian nature; all he asked us to do was to make quite certain that we knew what we meant when we made a statement and to analyze and examine our beliefs in the light of common-sense. Philosophically what, as intelligent young men, we wanted to know was the basis, if any, for our or any scale of values and rules of conduct, what justification there was for our belief that friendship or works of art for instance were good or for the belief that one ought to do some things and not do others. Moore's distinction between things good in themselves or as ends and things good merely as means, his passionate search for truth in his attempt in *Principia Ethica* to determine what things are good in themselves, answered our questions, not with the religious voice of Jehovah from Mount Sinai or Jesus with his sermon from the Mount, but with the more divine voice of plain common-sense.

On one side of us, we were in 1901 very serious young men. We were sceptics in search of truth and ethical truth. Moore, so we thought, gave us a scientific basis for believing that some things were good in themselves. But we were not 'immoralists'; it is not true that we recognized 'no moral obligation on us, no inner sanction, to conform or obey' or that we neglected all that Moore said about 'morals' and rules of conduct. It is true that younger generations, like their elders, were much less politically and socially conscious in the years before the 1914 War than they have been ever since. Bitter experience has taught the world, including the young, the importance of codes of conduct and morals and 'practical politics'. But Moore himself was continually exercised by the problems of goods and bads as means of morality and rules of conduct and therefore of the life of action as opposed to the life of contemplation. He and we were fascinated by questions of what was right and wrong, what one *ought* to do. We followed him closely in this as in other parts of his doctrine and argued interminably about the consequences of one's actions, both in actual and imaginary situations. Indeed one of the problems which worried us was what part Moore (and we, his disciples) *ought* to play in ordinary life, what, for instance, our attitude *ought* to be towards practical politics. I still possess a paper which I wrote for discussion in 1903 and which is explicitly concerned with these problems. It asks the question whether we ought to follow the example of George Trevelyan,[4] and take part in practical politics, going down into the gloomy Platonic cave, where 'men sit bound prisoners guessing at the shadows of reality and boasting that they have found truth', or whether we should imitate George Moore, who though 'he has no small knowledge of the cave dwellers, leaves alone their struggles and competitions'. I said that the main question I wanted to ask was: 'Can we and ought we to combine the two Georges in our own lives?' And was it rational that George Moore, the philosopher, should take no part in practical politics, or 'right that we should as we do so absolutely ignore their questions?' My answer in 1903 was perfectly definite that we *ought* to take part in practical politics and the last words of my paper are: 'While philosophers sit outside the cave, their philosophy will never reach politicians or people, so that after all, to put it plainly, I *do* want Moore to draft an Education Bill.'

I have said that we were very serious young men. We were, indeed, but superficially we often appeared to be the exact opposite and so enraged or even horrified a good many people. After all we were young once – we were young in 1903; and we were not nearly as serious and solemn as we appeared to some people. We were serious about what we considered to be serious in the universe or in man and his life, but we had a sense of humour and we felt that it was not necessary to be solemn, because one was serious, and that there are practically no questions or situations in which intelligent laughter may not be healthily catalytic. Henry Sidgwick, in his *Memoir*, looking back in old age to the year 1856 when he was elected an Apostle wrote:

No consistency was demanded with opinions previously held – truth as we saw it then and there was what we had to embrace and maintain, and there were no propositions so well established that an Apostle had not the right to deny or question, if he did so sincerely and not from mere love of paradox. The gravest subjects were continually debated, but gravity of treatment, as I have said, was not imposed, though sincerity was. In fact it was rather a point of the apostolic mind to understand how much suggestion and instruction may be derived from what is in form a jest – even in dealing with the gravest matters.

I am writing today just over a century after the year in which Sidgwick was elected an Apostle, and looking back to the year 1903 I can say that our beliefs, our discussions, our intellectual behaviour in 1903 were in every conceivable way exactly the same as those described by Sidgwick. The beliefs 'fantastically idealistic and remote from reality and real life', the absurd arguments, 'the extravagantly scholastic' method were not as simple or silly as they seemed. Lytton Strachey's mind was fundamentally and habitually ribald and he had developed a protective intellectual façade in which a highly personal and cynical wit and humour played an important part. It was very rarely safe to accept the face value of what he said; within he was intensely serious about what he thought important, but on the surface his method was to rely on 'suggestion and instruction derived from what is in form a jest – even in dealing with the gravest matters'. I think that in my case, too, there was a natural tendency to express myself ironically – and precisely in matters or over questions about which one felt deeply as being of great importance – for irony and the jest are used, particularly when one is young, as antidotes to pomposity. Of course we were young once; we were young in 1903, and we had the arrogance and the extravagance natural to the young.

The intellectual, when young, has always been in all ages enthusiastic and passionate and therefore he has tended to be intellectually arrogant and ruthless. Our youth, the years of my generation at Cambridge, coincided with the end and the beginning of a century which was also the end of one era and the beginning of another. When in the grim, grey, rainy January days of 1901 Queen Victoria lay dying, we already felt that we were living in an era of incipient revolt and that we ourselves were mortally involved in this revolt against a social system and code of conduct and morality which, for convenience sake, may be referred to as bourgeois Victorianism. We did not initiate this revolt. When we went up to Cambridge, its protagonists were Swinburne, Bernard Shaw, Samuel Butler in *The Way of All Flesh*, and to some extent Hardy and Wells. We were passionately on the side of these champions of freedom of speech and freedom of thought, of common-sense and reason. We felt that, with them as our leaders, we were struggling against a religious and moral code of cant and hypocrisy which produced and condoned such social crimes and judicial murders as the condemnation of Dreyfus. People of a younger generation who from birth have enjoyed the results of this struggle for social and intellectual emancipation cannot realize the stuffy intellectual and moral suffocation which a young man felt weighing down upon him in Church and State, in the 'rules and conventions' of the last days of Victorian civilization. Nor can those who have been born into the world of great wars, of communism and national socialism and fascism, of Hitler and Mussolini and Stalin, of the wholesale judicial murders of their own fellow-countrymen or massacres of peasants by Russian communists, and the slaughter of millions of Jews in gas-chambers by German nazis, these younger generations can have no notion of what the long-drawn out tragedy of the Dreyfus case meant to us. Over the body and fate of one obscure, Jewish captain in the French army a kind of cosmic conflict went on year after year between the establishment of Church, Army, and State on the one side and the small band of intellectuals who fought for truth, reason, and justice, on the other. Eventually the whole of Europe, almost the whole world, seemed to be watching breathlessly, ranged upon one side or other in the conflict. And no one who was not one of the watchers can understand the extraordinary sense of relief and release when at last the innocence of Dreyfus was vindicated and justice was done. I still think that we were right and that the Dreyfus case might, with a slight shift in the current of events, have been a turning point in European history and civilization. All that can really be said against us was that our hopes were disappointed.

It is true that in a sense 'we had no respect for traditional wisdom' and that, as Ludwig Wittgenstein complained, 'we lacked reverence for everything and everyone'. If 'to revere' means, as the dictionary says, 'to regard as sacred or exalted, to hold in religious respect', then we did not revere, we had no reverence for anything or anyone, and, so far as I am concerned, I think we were completely right; I remain of the same opinion still – I think it to be, not merely my right, but my duty to question the truth of everything and the authority of everyone, to regard nothing as sacred and to hold nothing in religious respect. That attitude was encouraged by the climate of scepticism and revolt into which we were born and by Moore's ingenuous passion for truth. The dictionary, however, gives an alternative meaning for the word 'revere'; it may mean 'to regard with deep respect and warm approbation'. It is not true that we lacked reverence for everything and everyone in that sense of the word. After questioning the truth and utility of everything and after refusing to accept or swallow anything or anyone on the mere 'authority' of anyone, in fact after exercising our own judgment, there were many things and persons regarded by us with 'deep respect and warm approbation': truth, beauty, works of art, some customs, friendship, love, many living men and women and many of the dead.

The young are not only ruthless; they are often perfectionist; if they are intelligent, they are inclined to react against the beliefs, which have hardened into the fossilized dogmas of the previous generation. To the middle-aged, who have forgotten their youth, the young naturally seem to be not only wrong, but wrong-headed (and indeed they naturally often are); to the middle-aged and the old, if they are also respectable, the young seem to be, not only wrong, but intellectually ill-mannered (and indeed they often are). In 1903 we were often absurd, wrong, wrong-headed, ill-mannered; but in 1903 we were right in refusing to regard as sacred and exalted, to hold in religious respect, the extraordinary accomplishment of our predecessors in the ordering of life or the elaborate framework which they had devised to protect this order. We were right to question the truth and authority of all this, of respectability and the establishment, and to give our deep respect and warm approbation only to what in the establishment (and outside it) stood the test and ordeal of such questioning.

It will be remembered that Maynard's *Memoir*, in which he analyses the state of our minds (and Moore's) when we were undergraduates, starts with an account of a breakfast party in Bertrand Russell's rooms in Cambridge, at which only Russell, Maynard, and D.H. Lawrence were present. . .

In the whole of the *Memoir*, Maynard confuses, I think, two periods of his and of our lives. When our Cambridge days were over, there grew up in London during the years 1907 to 1914 a society or group of people which became publicly known as Bloomsbury. Later in my autobiography I shall have to say a good deal about Bloomsbury, the private nature and the public picture. Here all I need say is that Bloomsbury grew directly out of Cambridge; it consisted of a number of intimate friends who had been at Trinity and King's and were now working in London, most of them living in Bloomsbury.

Lawrence's breakfast party took place in 1914 or 1915. The people to whom he refers are not the undergraduates of 1903, but Bloomsbury, and a great deal of what Maynard wrote in his *Memoir* is true of Bloomsbury in 1914, but not true of the undergraduates of 1903. In 1903 we had all the inexperience, virginity, seriousness, intellectual puritanism of youth. In 1914 we had all, in various ways or places, been knocking about the world for ten or eleven years. A good deal of the bloom of ignorance and other things had been brushed off us. *Principia Ethica* had passed into our unconscious and was now merely a part of our super-ego; we no longer argued about it as a guide to practical life. Some of us were 'men of the world' or even Don Juans, and all round us there was taking place the revolt (which we ourselves in our small way helped to start) against the Victorian morality and code of conduct. In 1914 little or no attention was paid to Moore's fifth chapter on 'Ethics in relation to Conduct', and pleasure, once rejected by us theoretically, had come to be accepted as a very considerable good in itself. But this was not the case in 1903 . . .

Notes

1. I do not think that I ever met either of Clive's parents, but I have heard so much about them from him and from others that I have no doubt about the truth of what I say here.
2. It is worth noting that in those days we set little or no store by pictures and painting. I never heard Clive talk about pictures at Cambridge, and it was only after he came down and lived for a time in Paris and got to know Roger Fry that his interest in art developed. Music already meant a good deal to Lytton, Saxon, and me and we went to chamber music concerts in Cambridge and orchestral concerts in London, but I do not think that it has ever meant much to Clive.
3. Ainsworth became a civil servant in the Education Office; Hawtrey, now Sir Ralph Hawtrey, a civil servant in the Treasury; Sheppard, now Sir J.T. Sheppard, Provost of King's College, Cambridge.
4. George Macaulay Trevelyan, OM, the historian and for many years Master of Trinity College. He was four years my senior at Trinity and, when I first knew him, had just become a Fellow of the college. He was a rather fiercely political young man.

Leonard Woolf: Old Bloomsbury

Reprinted from Beginning Again: An Autobiography of the Years 1911–1918 *(London, The Hogarth Press, 1964), 21–6, by permission of the author's literary estate and The Hogarth Press;* © *1963, 1964 by Leonard Woolf, reprinted by permission of Harcourt Brace Jovanovich, Inc.*

[Towards the end of his discussion of Cambridge in *Sowing*, Leonard Woolf wrote, 'By the time I left Cambridge I had become very intimate

with Thoby Stephen and Lytton Strachey and knew their families, and
so the foundations of what became known as Bloomsbury were laid.'
But during the early formation of the Group Woolf was absent. For six
and a half years he was a civil servant in Ceylon. He returned in 1911
and was welcomed into Bloomsbury by his old college friends. The
following excerpt reveals what he found Old Bloomsbury to be like. In
his later discussion of the Memoir Club (see pp.122–3), he decided,
however, that what he was describing here was a kind of
'ur-Bloomsbury'.

But the following excerpt was not Leonard Woolf's first description
of Bloomsbury, old or ur. In 1914 Leonard Woolf published his second
novel, *The Wise Virgins*, and in it he treated Bloomsbury, as he had just
come to know it, quite critically. His fictional account of Bloomsbury
is, I believe, the first published criticism of Bloomsbury, and it is
appropriate that it should have come from a member of Bloomsbury
itself. Some idea of the kind of criticism that Woolf directs against
some of the members of the Group (though not against all, for *The
Wise Virgins* is dedicated to Desmond MacCarthy) can be had from the
following passage; the 'epicures' referred to are characters who resemble
rather closely Clive and Vanessa Bell, Lytton Strachey, and Virginia
Woolf:

> These epicures in the art of emotions and the emotions of art had
> emancipated themselves from the convention that there are some
> things that men and women cannot talk about, and they had done
> this so successfully that a stranger might at first have been led to
> conclude from their practice that those are the only things that men
> and women of intelligence can talk about. Such a conclusion would
> have been hasty. It was perhaps from their weakness, at any rate
> intellectually, that they never did those things – but then they never
> did anything.

This attack is qualified in the novel by being from the point of view
of the young suburban Jewish outsider who is the central character of
The Wise Virgins. The passage nevertheless indicates, as do many of the
memoirs of Bloomsbury, that from its earliest days Bloomsbury was
never a mutual admiration society.

The paragraphs from *Beginning Again* in which Woolf returns to
Moore's influence on himself and his friends contain perhaps the
clearest statement of any piece in this collection of what the nature of
the Bloomsbury Group was, though the denial of 'a communal

connection' between their works is somewhat overstated.]

...On Monday, July 3rd, [1911] only three weeks after I had arrived in England, 1 went and dined with Vanessa and Clive Bell in Gordon Square. I was alone with them at dinner, but afterwards Virginia, Duncan Grant, and Walter Lamb came in. This was, I suppose, so far as I was concerned, the beginning of what came to be called Bloomsbury.

'What came to be called Bloomsbury' by the outside world never existed in the form given to it by the outside world. For 'Bloomsbury' was and is currently used as a term – usually of abuse – applied to a largely imaginary group of persons with largely imaginary objects and characteristics. I was a member of this group and I was also one of a small number of persons who did in fact eventually form a kind of group of friends living in or around that district of London legitimately called Bloomsbury. The term Bloomsbury can legitimately be applied to this group and will be so applied in these pages. Bloomsbury, in this sense, did not exist in 1911 when I returned from Ceylon; it came into existence in the three years 1912 to 1914. We did ourselves use the term of ourselves before it was used by the outside world, for in the 1920s and 1930s, when our own younger generation were growing up and marrying and some of our generation were already dying, we used to talk of 'Old Bloomsbury', meaning the original members of our group of friends who between 1911 and 1914 came to live in or around Bloomsbury.

Old Bloomsbury consisted of the following people: the three Stephens: Vanessa, married to Clive Bell, Virginia, who married Leonard Woolf, and Adrian, who married Karin Costello; Lytton Strachey; Clive Bell; Leonard Woolf; Maynard Keynes; Duncan Grant; E.M. Forster (who will be referred to in this book as Morgan Forster or Morgan); Saxon Sydney-Turner; Roger Fry. Desmond MacCarthy and his wife Molly, though they actually lived in Chelsea, were always regarded by us as members of Old Bloomsbury. In the 1920s and 1930s, when Old Bloomsbury narrowed and widened into a newer Bloomsbury, it lost through death Lytton and Roger and added to its numbers Julian, Quentin, and Angelica Bell, and David (Bunny) Garnett, who married Angelica.[1]

That Monday night of July 3, 1911, when I dined with Vanessa and Clive in Gordon Square, as I said, Bloomsbury had not yet actually come into existence. The reasons were geographical. At that moment only Vanessa and Clive and Saxon lived in Bloomsbury. Virginia and

Adrian lived in Fitzroy Square and Duncan in rooms nearby. Roger lived in a house outside Guildford; Lytton in Cambridge and Hampstead; Morgan Forster in Weybridge; Maynard Keynes, as a Fellow of King's College, in Cambridge. I was a visitor from Ceylon. Ten years later, when Old Bloomsbury had come into existence, Vanessa, Clive, Duncan Maynard, Adrian, and Lytton all lived in Gordon Square; Virginia and I were in Tavistock Square; Morgan in Brunswick Square; Saxon in Great Ormond Street; Roger in Bernard Street. Thus we all lived geographically in Bloomsbury within a few minutes walk of one another.

I am not, in this book, writing a history of Bloomsbury in any of its forms or manifestations, real or imaginary, and I shall have, after these first pages, very little to say about it. I am trying to write my autobiography, a true account of my life in relation to the times and the society in which I have lived, to the work I have done, and to people, whether intimates, acquaintances, or public persons. The twelve included by me in the previous paragraphs as members of Old Bloomsbury had a great influence upon my life. The account of what happened to me during the ten or twelve years after my return from Ceylon will necessarily show how we came to congregate in those nostalgic London squares and the real nature of our congregation. Here there are one or two facts about us which I want to insist upon before going on with my narrative. We were and always remained primarily and fundamentally a group of friends. Our roots and the roots of our friendship were in the University of Cambridge. Of the thirteen persons mentioned above three are women and ten men; of the ten men nine had been at Cambridge, and all of us, except Roger, had been more or less contemporaries at Trinity and King's and were intimate friends before I went to Ceylon.

There is another point. In the first volume of my autobiography, in dealing with my years at Cambridge, I said that it was 'necessary here to say something about the Society – The Apostles – because of the immense importance it had for us, its influence upon our minds, our friendships, our lives'. Of the ten men of Old Bloomsbury only Clive, Adrian and Duncan were not Apostles. Of the other seven of us, Desmond, Morgan, Lytton, Saxon, Maynard, and I, all overlapped more or less at Cambridge and had already grown into a peculiar intimacy there as active members of the Society. I tried in *Sowing* to give some idea of the character of G.E. Moore and of his tremendous intellectual (and also emotional) influence upon us and upon the Society of those days. The main things which Moore instilled deep into our minds and characters were his peculiar passion for truth, for clarity and common sense, and a passionate belief in certain values. I have said that Moore's influence upon us was lifelong. How profound it was is shown by what Maynard Keynes wrote in his book *Two Memoirs*. What Moore and his *Principia Ethica* gave to us as young men and what we sixty years ago embraced with the violence and optimism of youth Maynard calls a religion and he is affectionately critical of its and our adolescent one-sidedness and absurdities. But as a final summing up he writes:

> It seems to me looking back that this religion of ours was a very good one to grow up under. It remains nearer the truth than any other that I know, with less irrelevant extraneous matter and nothing to be ashamed of; though it is a comfort today to be able to discard with a good conscience the calculus and the mensuration and the duty to know *exactly* what one means and feels. It was a purer, sweeter air by far than Freud cum Marx. It is still my religion under the surface.

That is the point: under the surface all six of us, Desmond, Lytton, Saxon, Morgan, Maynard, and I, had been permanently inoculated with Moore and Moorism; and even Roger, who was seven years older than Moore and highly critical of his philosophy, continually proved by his criticism of Moorism that he was 'under the surface' a Moorist. Through us and through *Principia Ethica* the four others, Vanessa and Virginia, Clive and Duncan, were deeply affected by the astringent influence of Moore and the purification of that divinely cathartic question which echoed through the Cambridge Courts of my youth as it had 2,300 years before echoed through the streets of Socratic Athens: 'What do you mean by that?' Artistically the purification can, I think, be traced in the clarity, light, absence of humbug in Virginia's literary style and perhaps in Vanessa's painting. They have the quality noted by Maynard in Moorism, the getting rid of 'irrelevant extraneous matter'.

There have often been groups of people, writers and artists, who were not only friends, but were consciously united by a common doctrine and object, or purpose artistic or social. The utilitarians, the Lake poets, the French impressionists, the English Pre-Raphaelites were groups of this kind. Our group was quite different. Its basis was friendship, which in some cases developed into love and marriage. The colour of our minds and thought had been given to us by the climate of Cambridge and Moore's philosophy, much as the climate of England gives one colour to the face of an Englishman while the climate of India

gives a quite different colour to the face of a Tamil. But we had no
common theory, system, or principles which we wanted to convert the
world to; we were not proselytizers, missionaries, crusaders, or even
propagandists. It is true that Maynard produced the system or theory of
Keynesian economics which has had a great effort upon the theory and
practice of economics, finance, and politics; and that Roger, Vanessa,
Duncan, and Clive played important parts, as painters or critics, in what
came to be known as the Post-Impressionist Movement. But Maynard's
crusade for Keynesian economics against the orthodoxy of the Banks
and academic economists, and Roger's crusade for Post-Impressionism
and 'significant form' against the orthodoxy of academic 'representational' painters and aestheticians were just as purely individual as
Virginia's writing of *The Waves* – they had nothing to do with any
group. For there was no more a communal connection between Roger's
'Critical and Speculative Essays on Art', Maynard's *The General Theory
of Employment, Interest and Money*, and Virginia's *Orlando* than there
was between Bentham's *Theory of Legislation*, Hazlitt's *Principal
Picture Galleries in England*, and Byron's *Don Juan*.

I can now return to Monday night, July 3, 1911. In Cambridge
during my week-end there, as I have said, I had had the reassuring
pleasure of finding men and things, truths and values, to whom or to
which I had given the love or loyalty of youth, unchanged and
unchanging. In Gordon Square I re-entered a society which had
completely changed since I left it seven years before, but in which I
found myself immediately and completely at home. Nothing is more
silly than the principle, which too often fatally influences practice, that
you ought to be consistent in your feelings and your likes and dislikes.
Where taste is concerned there is no law of contradiction. It is absurd to
think, as many people do, that the love of cats or claret is a reason or
excuse for not loving dogs or burgundy. So I get as much pleasure from
the comfort of finding that nothing has changed as from the excitement
of finding that everything is new.

There had certainly been a profound revolution in Gordon Square. I
had dined in 46 Gordon Square with Thoby and his two sisters, the
Misses Stephens, in 1904 only a few days before I left England for
Ceylon. Now seven years later in the same rooms meeting again for the
first time Vanessa, Virginia, Clive, Duncan, and Walter Lamb I found
that almost the only things which had not changed were the furniture
and the extraordinary beauty of the two Miss Stephens. . .

Note

1. There is proof of this chronological classification. We had what we called a Memoir Club, *i.e.* we met from time to time and we each in turn read a chapter, as it were, of autobiography. The original thirteen members of the Memoir Club were the thirteen members of Old Bloomsbury given above. Twenty years later the four younger persons were members.

Leonard Woolf: The Second Post-Impressionist Exhibition

Reprinted from Beginning Again: An Autobiography of the Years 1911–1918 *(London, The Hogarth Press, 1964), 93–6, by permission of the author's literary estate and The Hogarth Press;* © *1963, 1964 by Leonard Woolf, reprinted by permission of Harcourt Brace Jovanovich, Inc.*

[Leonard Woolf was in Ceylon during the first Post-Impressionist exhibition. His experiences as secretary for the second one complement Desmond MacCarthy's account of the first one (see pp.68–73). Henry James did not care much for the pictures. For the sequel to Wyndham Lewis's troubles with Roger Fry, see pp.331–61.]

...The first job which I took was a curious one. The second Post-Impressionist Exhibition, organized by Roger Fry, opened in the Grafton Galleries in the autumn of 1912. In Spain on our honeymoon I got an urgent message from Roger asking me whether I would act as secretary of the show on our return. I agreed to do so until, I think, the end of the year. It was a strange and for me new experience. The first room was filled with Cézanne water-colours. The highlights in the second room were two enormous pictures of more than life-size figures by Matisse and three or four Picassos. There was also a Bonnard and a good picture by Marchand. Large numbers of people came to the exhibition, and nine out of ten of them either roared with laughter at the pictures or were enraged by them. The British middle class – and, as far as that goes, the aristocracy and working class – are incorrigibly philistine, and their taste is impeccably bad. Anything new in the arts, particularly if it is good, infuriates them and they condemn it as either immoral or ridiculous or both. As secretary I sat at my table in the large second room of the galleries prepared to deal with enquiries from

possible purchasers or answer any questions about the pictures. I was
kept busy all the time. The whole business gave me a lamentable view
of human nature, its rank stupidity and uncharitableness. I used to
think, as I sat there, how much nicer were the Tamil or Sinhalese
villagers who crowded into the veranda of my Ceylon kachcheri than
these smug, well dressed, ill-mannered, well-to-do Londoners. Hardly
any of them made the slightest attempt to look at, let alone
understand, the pictures, and the same inane questions or remarks were
repeated to me all day long. And every now and then some well
groomed, red faced gentlemen, oozing the undercut of the best beef
and the most succulent of chops, carrying his top hat and grey suede
gloves, would come up to my table and abuse the pictures and me with
the greatest rudeness.

There were, of course, consolations. Dealing with possible purchasers
was always amusing and sometimes exciting. Occasionally one had an
interesting conversation with a stranger. Sometimes it was amusing to
go round the rooms with Roger and a distinguished visitor. I have
described in *Sowing* Henry James's visit. Roger came to the gallery
every day and spent quite a lot of time there. We used to go down into
the bowels of the earth about 4 o'clock and have tea with Miss
Wotherston, the secretary, who inhabited the vast basement, and we
were often joined by Herbert Cook who owned Doughty House,
Richmond, and a superb collection of pictures. I saw so much of Roger
that at the end of my time at the Grafton Galleries I knew him much
better than when I first went there. His character was more full of
contradictions even than that of most human beings. He was one of the
most charming and gentle of men; born a double dyed Quaker, he had
in many respects revolted against the beliefs and morals of The Friends,
and yet deep down in his mind and character he remained profoundly,
and I think unconsciously, influenced by them. Like his six remarkable
sisters, he had a Quaker's uncompromising sense of public duty and
responsibility and, though he would have indignantly repudiated this,
ultimately the Quaker's ethical austerity. And yet there were elements
in his psychology which contradicted all these characteristics. I was
more than once surprised by his ruthlessness and what to me seemed to
be almost unscrupulousness in business. For instance, we discovered,
shortly after I took on the secretaryship, that when Roger had been
preparing the exhibition and asking people to exhibit, owing to a
mistake of his, they had been offered much too favourable terms – the
figure for the Exhibition's commission on sales was much too low.
When the time came to pay artists their share of the purchase amounts

of pictures sold, Roger insisted upon deducting a higher commission
without any explanation or apology to the painters. Most of them
meekly accepted what they were given, but Wyndham Lewis, at best of
times a bilious and cantankerous man, protested violently. Roger was
adamant in ignoring him and his demands; Lewis never forgave Roger,
and, as I was a kind of buffer between them, he also never forgave me...

Leonard Woolf: The Beginnings of The Hogarth Press

Reprinted from Leonard Woolf, Beginning Again: An Autobiography of
the Years 1911–1918 *(London, The Hogarth Press, 1964), 234–7,
240–42, by permission of the author's literary estate and the Hogarth
Press;* © *1963, 1964, by Leonard Woolf and reprinted by permission of
Harcourt Brace Jovanovich, Inc.*

[In 1915 Virginia and Leonard Woolf moved into an eighteenth-century
house in the Richmond district of London. The Hogarth Press that they
started there in 1917 took its name from the house. All of Virginia
Woolf's books, except her first two novels, and most of Leonard
Woolf's were subsequently published by the Hogarth Press. Many of the
members of Bloomsbury and their works were associated with the
Press, though it was not the principal publisher of E.M. Forster, Clive
Bell, or Lytton Strachey.

Leonard Woolf's story of the founding of the Hogarth Press (it was
started as a manual occupation to take Virginia's mind off her writing)
is an important part of the history of the Bloomsbury Group. The taste
of the Press was to a large degree the taste of Bloomsbury, and the
works it published reflect the wide spectrum of interests and ideas that
were current in Bloomsbury. The significance of the Hogarth Press
extends considerably beyond Bloomsbury; among its publications are
some of the most influential works of twentieth-century English
literature. It is worth pointing out, at least to those who believe that
the Bloomsbury Group was out of sympathy with the major English
writers of their time, that the Hogarth Press published T.S. Eliot's *The
Waste Land* in 1923 and almost succeeded in publishing James Joyce's
Ulysses. According to Woolf – and there are differing accounts of the
matter – he and Virginia definitely decided to publish it but were
advised by printers they approached that no respectable printer would
print the book for them.

In later volumes of his autobiography Leonard Woolf continues the

history of the Hogarth Press, recounting the different series of books
they started — the most important was the standard edition of Sigmund
Freud's works that Lytton Strachey's brother James translated — and
telling, in his words, of the 'succession of brilliant and not quite so
brilliant young men' who came to the Press as assistants and managers.
Noteworthy among them were Ralph Partridge, George Rylands, Angus
Davidson, and John Lehmann. (For a view of Bloomsbury from the
basement of the Hogarth Press, see the account by Lehmann, pp.
272–83).]

. . . On March 23, 1917, we were walking one afternoon up Farringdon
Street from Fleet Street to Holborn Viaduct when we passed the
Excelsior Printing Supply Co. It was not a very large firm, but it sold
every kind of printing machine and material, from a handpress and type
to a composing stick. Nearly all the implements of printing are
materially attractive and we stared through the window at them rather
like two hungry children gazing at buns and cakes in a baker shop
window. I do not know which of us first suggested that we should go
inside and see whether we could buy a machine and type and teach
ourselves. We went in and explained our desire and dilemma to a very
sympathetic man in a brown overall. He was extremely encouraging. He
could not only sell us a printing machine, type, chases, cases, and all the
necessary implements, but also a sixteen-page pamphlet which would
infallibly teach us how to print. There was no need to go to a school of
printing or to become an apprentice; if we read his pamphlet and
followed the instructions, we should soon find that we were competent
printers. Before we left the shop we had bought a small hand-press,
some Old Face type, and all the necessary implements and materials for
a sum of £19.5s 5d. The machine was small enough to stand on a
kitchen table; it was an ordinary platen design; you worked it by
pulling down the handle which brought the platen and paper up against
the type in its chase. You could print one demy octavo page on it, and,
I think, you could just squeeze in two crown octavo pages.

When the stuff was delivered to us in Richmond, we set it all up in
the dining-room and started to teach ourselves to print. The Excelsior
man proved to be right; by following the directions in the pamphlet we
found that we could pretty soon set the type, lock it up in the chase,
ink the rollers, and machine a fairly legible printed page. After a month
we thought we had become sufficiently proficient to print a page of a
book or pamphlet. We decided to print a paper-covered pamphlet

containing a story by each of us and to try to sell it by subscription to a limited number of people whom we would circularize. Our idea was that, if this succeeded, we might go on to print and publish in the same way poems or other short works which the commercial publisher would not look at.

We set to work and printed a thirty-two page pamphlet, demy octavo, with the following title page:

Publication No. 1.

TWO STORIES

WRITTEN AND PRINTED

BY

VIRGINIA WOOLF
AND
L. S. WOOLF

HOGARTH PRESS
RICHMOND
1917

Virginia's story was *The Mark on the Wall* and mine was *Three Jews*. We even had the temerity to print four woodcuts by Carrington. I must say, looking at a copy of this curious publication today, that the printing is rather creditable for two persons who had taught themselves for a month in a dining-room. The setting, inking, impression are really not bad. What is quite wrong is the backing, for I had not yet realized that a page on one side of the sheet must be printed so that it falls exactly on the back of the page on the other side of the sheet.

We began to print *Two Stories* on May 3 in an edition of about 150 copies. We bound it ourselves by stitching it into paper covers. We took a good deal of trouble to find some rather unusual, gay Japanese paper for the covers. For many years we gave much time and care to finding beautiful, uncommon, and sometimes cheerful paper for binding our books, and, as the first publishers to do this, I think we started a fashion which many of the regular, old established publishers followed. We got papers from all over the place, including some brilliantly patterned from Czechoslovakia, and we also had some marbled covers made for us by Roger Fry's daughter in Paris. I bought a small quantity of Caslon Old Face Titling type and used it for printing the covers.

We printed a circular offering Publication No 1 for 1s 6d net and explaining that we in The Hogarth Press proposed to print and publish in the same way from time to time paper-covered pamphlets or small books, printed entirely by our two selves, which would have little or no chance of being published by ordinary publishers. We invited people to become subscribers to the publications of The Hogarth Press, either A subscribers to whom all publications would automatically be sent, or B subscribers who would be notified of each publication as it appeared. We sent this notice to people whom we knew or who, we thought, might be interested in our publications. I do not know how many people we circularized, but we published in July and by the end of the month we had practically sold out the edition for we had sold 124 copies. (The total number finally sold was 134.) I still have a list of the 87 people who bought the 134 copies and all but five or six of them were friends or acquaintances. There are some rather unexpected names among them, *e.g.* Charles Trevelyan, MP, Arthur Ponsonby, MP, Mrs Sidney Webb, and Mrs Bernard Shaw. The total cost of production was £3. 7s 0d, which included the noble sum of 15s to Carrington for the wood-cuts, 12s 6d for paper, and 10s for the cover paper. The two authors were not paid any royalty. The total receipts wer £10. 8s 0d, so that the net profit was £7. 1s 0d. Eventually forty-five people became A subscribers and forty-three B subscribers. Among the A subscribers was one bookseller, James Bain of what was then King William Street, Strand, and except for him every copy of our first publications was sold to private persons at the full published price. By 1923 the Press had developed to such an extent that we had become more or less ordinary publishers, selling our books mainly to booksellers at the usual discount, and we therefore gave up the subscriber system altogether.

We so much enjoyed producing *Two Stories* and its sale had been so successful (134 copies!) that we were induced to go on to something more ambitious. Katherine Mansfield and Murry were extremely interested in what we were doing, and Katherine offered us for Publication No 2 a long short story which she had written, *Prelude*. When I look at my copy of *Prelude* today, I am astonished at our courage and energy in attempting it and producing it only a year after we had started to teach ourselves to print. For we printed only in the afternoon and even so not every afternoon; it is a sixty-eight-page book and we printed and bound it entirely with our own hands. The edition must have consisted of nearly 300 copies for, when it went out of print, we had sold 257 copies. Virginia did most of the setting and I did all the machining, though I did set when there was nothing to machine.

I did not machine *Prelude* on our small handpress; in fact, it would have taken much too long to do it page by page. I machined it on a large platen machine which printed four crown octavo pages at a time and which belonged to a jobbing printer called McDermott . . .

By having [Virginia Woolf's short stories] *Monday or Tuesday* printed for us [in 1921] by a commercial printer, we were, of course, abandoning the original idea of the Press, which was to print small books ourselves. In fact we had been already in 1919 forced fortuitously to take a similar step, the first step on the path which was to end in our becoming regular and professional publishers. In 1918 we printed two small books: *Poems* by T.S. Eliot and *Kew Gardens* by Virginia. Of Tom's *Poems* we printed rather fewer than 250 copies. We published it in May 1919 price 2*s* 6*d* and it went out of print in the middle of 1920. Of *Kew Gardens* we printed about 170 copies (the total sold of the first edition was 148). We published it on May 12, 1919, at 2*s*. When we started printing and publishing with our Publication No 1, we did not send out any review copies, but in the case of *Prelude*, Tom's *Poems*, and *Kew Gardens* we sent review copies to *The Times Literary Supplement*. By May 31 we had sold 49 copies of *Kew Gardens*. On Tuesday, May 27, we went to Asham and stayed there for a week, returning to Richmond on June 3rd. In the previous week a review of *Kew Gardens* had appeared in the *Literary Supplement* giving it tremendous praise. When we opened the front door of Hogarth House, we found the hall covered with envelopes and postcards containing orders from booksellers all over the country. It was impossible for us to start printing enough copies to meet these orders, so we went to a printer, Richard Madley, and got him to print a second edition of 500 copies, which cost us £8. 9*s* 6*d*. It was sold out by the end of 1920 and we did not reprint.

The expansion of the Press into something which we had never intended or originally envisaged can be seen in the following list of books published by us in the first four years of its existence:

1917 L. and V. Woolf. *Two Stories.* Printed and bound by us.
1918 K. Mansfield. *Prelude*. Printed and bound by us.
1919 V. Woolf. *Kew Gardens*. 1st ed. printed and bound by us.
 T.S. Eliot. *Poems*. Printed and bound by us.
 J. Middleton Murry. *Critic in Judgment*. Printed for us.
1920 E.M. Forster. *Story of the Siren*. Printed and bound by us.
 Hope Mirrlees. *Paris*. Printed and bound by us.
 L. Pearsall Smith. *Stories from the Old Testament*.

Printed for us.
Gorky. *Reminiscences of Tolstoi*. Printed for us.

Leonard Woolf: The Memoir Club

Reprinted from Downhill All the Way: An Autobiography of the Years
1919–1939 *(London, The Hogarth Press, 1967), 114–5, by permission
of the author's literary estate and The Hogarth Press;* © *1967 by
Leonard Woolf and reprinted by permission of Harcourt Brace
Jovanovich, Inc.*

[Although Leonard Woolf's recollection of the Memoir Club is not
completely correct in stating that its members were all the original ones
of Bloomsbury (see p.115), it is nevertheless of value in emphasizing
the continuity of Bloomsbury's development.

In an undated one-page fragment of a paper written for the Memoir
Club, Leonard Woolf expressed himself a little more directly about the
Club. After admitting that he had experienced considerable difficulty in
writing for the Club, Woolf went on to explain why:

The downfall – I use the word in the sense given to it by the servant
class – of Bloomsbury was its intolerance of every one and every
thing which was not all the time amusing. Perhaps that is an
exaggeration, but it is true that, just as one hesitated in Moore's
rooms at Cambridge to say anything amusing which was not also
profound and true, so in Bloomsbury one hesitated to say anything
true or profound unless it was also amusing. In my experience what
is amusing is very rarely true or profound, and what is true or
profound is hardly ever amusing.

Despite his caveats, and maybe even because of them, Leonard
Woolf became Bloomsbury's chief memoirist.]

. . . I find some difficulty in determining exactly when what is called
Bloomsbury came into existence. In *Beginning Again* [see pp.111–5]
I treated it as having come into existence in the three years 1912 to
1914. I should now prefer to say that in those three years a kind of
ur-Bloomsbury came into existence. Of the thirteen members of Old
Bloomsbury, as we came to call it, only eight at that time actually lived

in Bloomsbury: Clive and Vanessa in Gordon Square and Virginia, Adrian, Duncan Grant, Maynard Keynes, and myself in Brunswick Square, with Saxon Sydney-Turner in Great Ormond Street. It was not until Lytton Strachey, Roger Fry, and Morgan Forster came into the locality, so that we were all continually meeting one another, that our society became complete, and that did not happen until some years after the war. First the war scattered us completely and then Virginia's illness, by banishing us to the outer suburb of Richmond, made any return to our day-to-day intimacy impossible. But as Virginia's health improved and it became possible for us to go up to London more often to parties and other meetings, what archaeologists might call a second period of ur-Bloomsbury began. For instance, in March 1920 we started the Memoir Club and on March 6 we met in Gordon Square, dined together, and listened to or read our memoirs.

The original thirteen members of the Memoir Club, identical with the original thirteen members of old Bloomsbury, were all intimate friends, and it was agreed that we should be absolutely frank in what we wrote and read. Absolute frankness, even among the most intimate, tends to be relative frankness; I think that in our reminiscences what we said was absolutely true, but absolute truth was sometimes filtered through some discretion and reticence. At first the memoirs were fairly short; at the first meeting seven people read. But as time went on, what people read became longer and, in a sense, more serious, so that after a few years normally only two memoirs were read in an evening. They were usually very amusing, but they were sometimes something more. Two by Maynard were as brilliant and highly polished as anything he wrote — one describing his negotiations with the German delegates and, in particular, Dr Melchior, in the railway carriages at Tréves after the 1914 War, and the other about Moore's influence upon us and our early beliefs at Cambridge — and these were after his death published, exactly as they were originally read to us, under the title *Two Memoirs*. Some of Virginia's were also brilliant, and Vanessa developed a remarkable talent in a fantastic narrative of a labyrinthine domestic crisis. The years went by and the Club changed as the old inhabitants died and the younger generation were elected. The last meeting took place, I think, in 1956, thirty-six years after the first meeting. Only four of the original thirteen members were left, though in all ten members came to the meeting . . .

BLOOMSBERRIES

INTRODUCTION

The memoirs of the previous section reveal how the individual members experienced and regarded the Bloomsbury Group. In this section various writers – many of them also members of the Group – examine, sometimes directly and sometimes obliquely, the relations of the individual members to Bloomsbury. The differing nature of these relations can be illuminated by one of the central ideas of G.E. Moore's *Principia Ethica*. Moore argued that the worth of what he termed an organic whole 'bears no regular proportion to the sum of the values of its parts'. In particular, 'the value of a whole must not be assumed to be the same as the sum of the values of its parts'. Moore illustrated his conception of an organic whole by explaining how the value of a whole that is made up of a state of consciousness of a beautiful object is not simply the sum of the value of consciousness and of the object, neither of which has much value by itself. Moore's idea is useful in assessing not only the contribution that individual members of Bloomsbury made to the Group as a whole but also the effect that the Group had on its members. The importance of the individual or his work outside Bloomsbury bore no regular proportion to his value in the organic whole that the Bloomsbury Group was. That is why an examination of Bloomsbury should include a consideration of particular and even peculiar relations of the parts to the whole and the whole to the parts.

Perhaps the simplest way of distinguishing the parts of Bloomsbury from the whole is to use the term 'Bloomsberries' that, according to Clive Bell, Molly MacCarthy coined around 1910 or 1911 in order to arrange her friends topographically (see p.86). The Bloomsberries discussed here have been arranged by their age to bring out the nearly twenty-year difference between the eldest and youngest. Unlike the first section, which includes practically all the available memoirs on Bloomsbury by its original members, there is a considerable amount of writing to choose from about some of the Bloomsberries. In making selections I have tried to choose pieces that reflect the relation of the part and the whole.

Roger Fry by Virginia Woolf

Reprinted from Virginia Woolf: Roger Fry: A Biography *(London, The Hogarth Press, 1940), 261–8, 269–70, 278–9, 288–94, by permission of the author's literary estate and The Hogarth Press; © 1940c by Harcourt Brace Jovanovich, Inc.; © 1968 by Leonard Woolf; reprinted by permission of the publisher.*

[After Roger Fry's death in 1934 his sister asked Virginia Woolf to take up Fry's suggestion that she should 'put into practice your theories of the biographer's craft in a portrait of himself'. A previous suggestion for a full-length Bloomsbury biography had arisen after Lytton Strachey's death, but it was quickly realized that a true biography of him could not be a reticent one, and at that time no other kind of biography could have been written. Reticence remained one of the difficulties of Virginia Woolf's biography of Fry; pressures from his family as well as Virginia Woolf's own artistic impatience with the mass of biographical facts that had to be manipulated prevented *Roger Fry* from being as good as it might have been. Yet it is a beautifully written biography, and in the extracts presented here, which have to do mainly with his value as an art critic and as a friend, Fry's enormous importance for Bloomsbury can be seen. Except for her remarks about how a mutual admiration society 'if such things exist – and according to some observers they do – would have expelled Roger Fry at its first meeting', Virginia Woolf does not treat Fry's relation to Bloomsbury directly, though it is implicit in almost everything that is said here.]

But if Oxford rejected him [for the Slade Professorship in 1927], London accepted him. He found in these years to his amazement that he could fill the Queen's Hall when he lectured upon art. The winter exhibitions at Burlington House gave him the opportunity. He lectured on Flemish art, on French art, on Italian art; and the hall was filled. The audience, as one of them records, 'was enthusiastic and rapt'. It was an astonishing feat. There was the Queen's Hall, full those winter evenings of greenish mist, echoing with the sneezings and coughings of the afflicted flock. And to entertain them there was nothing but a gentleman in evening dress with a long stick in his hand in front of a cadaverous sheet. How could contact be established? How could the world of spiritual reality emerge in those uncongenial surroundings? At first by 'personality' – the attraction, as Mr Hannay says, 'of the whole man'. 'He had only to point to a passage in a picture . . . and to murmur

the word "plasticity" and a magical atmosphere was created.' The voice
in which he murmured was conciliatory, urbane, humorous. It
conveyed what was not so perceptible in his writing — the tolerance,
the wide experience, that lay behind the hob-goblin mask of the man
who had the reputation of being either a crack-brained theorist or the
irresponsible champion of impossible beliefs. But as he went on it was
clear that the beliefs were still there. Many listeners might have inferred
that the lecturer, who looked like a 'fasting friar with a rope round his
waist' in spite of his evening dress, was inviting them to the practice of
a new kind of religion. He was praising a new kind of saint — the artist
who leads his laborious life 'indifferent to the world's praise or blame';
who must be poor in spirit, humble, and doggedly true to his own
convictions. And the penalty for back-sliding was pronounced — if he
lies 'he is cut off from the chief source of his inspiration'. No Fry
among all the generations of Frys could have spoken with greater
fervour of the claims of the spirit, or invoked doom with more severity.
But then, 'Slide, please', he said. And there was the picture —
Rembrandt, Chardin, Poussin, Cézanne — in black and white upon the
screen. And the lecturer pointed. His long wand, trembling like the
antenna of some miraculously sensitive insect, settled upon some
'rhythmical phrase', some sequence; some diagonal. And then he went
on to make the audience see — 'the gem-like notes; the aquamarines;
and topazes that lie in the hollow of his satin gowns; bleaching the
lights to evanescent pallors'. Somehow the black-and-white slide on the
screen became radiant through the mist, and took on the grain and
texture of the actual canvas.

   All that he had done again and again in his books. But here there was
a difference. As the next slide over the sheet there was a pause. He
gazed afresh at the picture. And then in a flash he found the word he
wanted; he added on the spur of the moment what he had just seen as if
for the first time. That, perhaps, was the secret of his hold over his
audience. They could see the sensation strike and form; he could lay
bare the very moment of perception. So with pauses and spurts the
world of spiritual reality emerged in slide after slide — in Poussin, in
Chardin, in Rembrandt, in Cézanne — in its uplands and its lowlands, all
connected, all somehow made whole and entire, upon the great screen
in the Queen's Hall. And finally the lecturer, after looking long through
his spectacles, came to a pause. He was pointing to a late work by
Cézanne, and he was baffled. He shook his head; his stick rested on the
floor. It went, he said, far beyond any analysis of which he was capable.
And so instead of saying, 'Next slide', he bowed, and the audience

emptied itself into Langham Place.

For two hours they had been looking at pictures. But they had seen one of which the lecturer himself was unconscious – the outline of the man against the screen, an ascetic figure in evening dress who paused and pondered, and then raised his stick and pointed. That was a picture that would remain in memory together with the rest, a rough sketch that would serve many of the audience in years to come as the portrait of a great critic, a man of profound sensibility but of exacting honesty, who, when reason could penetrate no further, broke off; but was convinced, and convinced others, that what he saw was there.

The success of the lectures surprised him. Perhaps he had misjudged the British public. Perhaps in its queer way the public had more feeling for art than he allowed. At any rate there was the fact –

> under certain conditions the English public becomes interested in 'highbrow' stuff. . . . Roger Fry had the power of making other people feel the importance of art . . . In spite of a complete absence of purple passages or playing to the gallery he was able to keep his audience at a high pitch of interest and curiosity.

People, drawn from all classes and callings, would fill the Queen's Hall when he lectured. And not only would they fill the Queen's Hall – they threatened to fill Bernard Street into the bargain. 'I am as usual', he wrote after one of these lectures, 'swamped by telephone calls and people at me all the time. Miss – wishes to know if she may come and look at my Matisse. Mr – wants advice upon a lot of old masters. . . A. wants to borrow my Vlaminck. B. came to consult me about his son's education as an art student.' And there were the letters – the innumerable letters. One from a schoolgirl ran:

> Dear Mr Fry . . . Our art mistress from school took a party to the Persian art Exhibition and we were attracted in many pictures, to people with their first fingers held to their lips. Also in some designs animals are seen biting each other. If these mean anything, or are symbolical in any way, I should be very grateful if you could tell me. Another thing is, does our common cat originate from Persia?

He was delighted to answer schoolgirls' questions. He was delighted to give advice. He would show 'hordes of school marms from the USA armed with note-books seeking information', round his rooms; and then 'a very intelligent young man from Manchester' who was interested in Chinese pottery; and then go on to a committee meeting at Burlington House to arrange the Italian Exhibition; and from that to a committee meeting of the *Burlington Magazine*; and when he got home in the evening, there was somebody waiting to 'ask my advice about getting up a show of Russian ikons'. That was an ordinary day's work; and it was no wonder that at the end of a season of such days he would exclaim 'London's impossible!'

It was an exclamation that burst forth irrepressibly every year about February or March. It was necessary to escape from London and its attractions and distractions if he was to have any peace at all. And it was equally necessary if he was to continue lecturing. He must fill his cistern from the main source; he must see pictures again. And so he was off – to Berlin, to Tunis, to Sicily, to Rome, to Holland, to Spain and again and again to France. The old pictures must be seen once more; they must be seen afresh. 'I spent the afternoon in the Louvre. I tried to forget all my ideas and theories and to look at everything as though I'd never seen it before... It's only so that one can make discoveries... Each work must be a new and a nameless experience.'

His method was the same in his sixties as it had been in his thirties. He went to the gallery as soon as it was opened; for six hours he worked steadily round, looking at each picture in turn, and making rough notes in pencil. When lunch-time came he was always taken by surprise; and always, as in the old days, he compared his impressions with his companion's, and scribbled his theories down in letters to friends at home. 'I'm getting my aesthetic feeling absolutely exhausted with the amount I've looked at. I doubt if I've ever had such hard work in my life – one's absolutely driven to it by the wealth of these museums', he wrote to Vanessa Bell from Berlin in 1928. A long list of pictures seen and noted follows. There was Menzel; there was Liebermann; there was Trübner. There were 'magnificent Cézannes'; there were Manets. There was Egyptian art; there was the art of Central Asia. Berlin had ten galleries filled with paintings and sculptures and miniatures, whereas the British Museum had only a few cases. Stimulated by all these sights, theories began to form themselves; perhaps too rapidly – perhaps they might have to be scrapped. 'In fact I don't know what I'm getting at at all. All sorts of vague hints at new aesthetics seem to be simmering in my brain...'

It was thus, in front of the pictures themselves, that the material for the lectures was collected. It was from these new and nameless experiences that vague hints at new aesthetics came into being. Then the vagueness had to be expelled; the simmer had to be spun into a tough thread of argument that held the whole together. And after the lecture had been given the drudgery of re-writing the spoken word would begin. The obstinate, the elusive, word had to be found, had to be coined, had to be 'curled round' the sensation. And so at last the books came out one after another – the books on French art, and Flemish art and British art; the books on separate painters; the books on whole periods of art; the essays upon Persian art and Chinese art and Russian art; the pamphlets upon Architecture; upon Art and Psychology – all those books and essays and articles upon which his claim to be called the greatest critic of his time depends.

But if, in order to write and lecture, it was necessary to see pictures 'as if for the first time', it was almost equally necessary to see friends. Ideas must be sketched on other people's minds. Theories must be discussed, preferably with someone, like Charles Mauron, who could demolish them. But even if the friend was incapable of demolishing them, they must be shared. 'He was so sociable that he could never enjoy anything without at once feeling the need to share it with those around him', as M. Mauron says. It was the desire to share, to have two pairs of eyes to see with, and somebody at hand, or at least within reach of the pen, to argue with that made him scribble those letters which it is impossible to quote in full, for they have neither beginning, middle nor end, and are often illustrated with a sketch of a landscape, or with the profile of a sausage-maker's wife at Royat, or with a few notes to indicate what he was 'getting at' in his own picture. But if the letters cannot be quoted in full, here is a complete post-card:

> In the train going to Edinburgh. I wonder whether you could send me to Edinburgh 1. my béret which is very nice for travelling. 2. Slides of Picasso's sculptures, those queer birds. They're in the Vitality series upstairs I think and still all together and on the bureau. 3. A negro head [sketch] the very blank one with no features. It's in the negro lecture which I left on the old French chest of drawers in my sitting-room. The carriage is scarcely warmed. Damn the English.

'Damn the English' – the words ceased to apply to the English – was not England the only country where free speech was allowed? But they may serve as a hint that he was not one of those characters who have, as we are told by their biographers, an instinctive love of their kind. His kind often amazed him and shocked him. His eyes, shining beneath the bushy black eyebrows, would fix themselves suddenly, and, looking as formidable as his father the Judge, he would pronounce judgment. 'You are bolstering people up in their natural beastliness', his words to Sir Charles Holmes who had given him, innocently, a book on fishing recall some awkward moments in his company. But if not gregarious he was sociable — 'incurably sociable' he called himself. His friends meant so much to him that he would give up the delights of wandering from village to village, from gallery to gallery, in order to be with them. Spring after spring he would exclaim, 'I feel very much inclined never to come back to England, just to wander on into Spain and Morocco . . .', but the sentence would end, 'if you wretches will live in London, then to London I must be dragged back'.

A list of those friends would be a long one. It would include many famous names — the names of painters, writers, men of science, art experts, politicians. But it would include many names that are quite unknown — people met in trains, people met in inns, mad poets and melancholy undergraduates. Often he had forgotten their names; names mattered less and less to him. He went out into society sometimes, but he came back disillusioned. 'Your old friend', he wrote (to Virginia Woolf), 'went to that charming Princess . . . and came back with another illusion gone — he now knows that *all* aristocrats are virtuous but incredibly boring and refuses to suffer them any more . . . the said Princess having been his last desperate throw of the net on that barren shore.' After the war his old dream of a society in which people of all kinds met together in congenial surroundings, and talked about everything under the sun, had to be given up. People were too poor, their time was too occupied, and the English moreover had little gift for discussing general ideas in public. Perhaps the best substitute for this society was at Pontigny. . .

But in London he was less ambitious. The attraction of London to him was that it was easy to get together little parties where old friends met new ones even if their names had slipped his memory. For if names mattered less and less, people mattered more and more. How much they mattered, how from one end of his life to the other he lived in his friendships, how in letter after letter he broke into praise of his friends — all that is not to be conveyed by lists of names. If certain friends — Lowes Dickinson, Desmond MacCarthy, Vanessa Bell, Philippa Strachey, the Maurons, his sister Margery — stand out, they are surrounded by so many others from so many different worlds, talking so many different languages, that to choose from among them or to say what it was that he got from each of them is impossible. But to be with them was one of his chief pleasures. 'Do you realise what delightful little parties we shall be able to have?' he wrote when he moved to Bernard Street; and one of those little parties may stand as the type of many.

His guests found him writing. He had forgotten the time; he was trying to finish a lecture. But he was delighted to stop writing and to begin to talk. The room was as untidy as ever. Ink-bottles and coffee-cups, proof sheets and paint-brushes were piled on the tables and strewn on the floor. And there were the pictures — some framed, others stood against the wall. There was the Derain picture of a spectral dog in the snow; the blue Matisse picture of ships in harbour. And there were the negro masks and the Chinese statues, and all the plates — the rare Persian china and the cheap peasant pottery that he had picked up for a farthing at a fair. Always there was something new to look at — a new picture, or a little panel of wood perhaps with a dim face upon it — very possibly it was the portrait of Dante, painted by Giotto and carried in Dante's funeral procession. The room was crowded, and for all Roger Fry's acute sensibility, he was curiously indifferent to physical comfort. The chairs had passed their prime; the lifts in the tube station opposite clanged incessantly; a flare of light came in from the arc-lamp in the street outside; and what he called 'the hymnology of Bernard Street' brayed from a loud-speaker next door. But it did not matter. 'The dinner', he wrote of one of those little parties, 'was a great success. The wild ducks were a trifle tough, but our friends are not really critical. And after dinner', the letter goes on,

we settled in to a good old Cambridge Apostolic discussion about existence, whether good was absolute or not. Charles [Mauron] and I representing modern science managed to make it clear that Oliver [Strachey] and Leonard [Woolf] were mystics. They could not accept the complete relativity of everything to human nature and the impossibility of talking at all about things in themselves. It's curious how difficult it is to root out that mediaeval habit of thinking of 'substances' of things existing apart from all relations, and yet really they have no possible meanings. . . Poor Oliver was horribly shocked to think he was in that *galère*. . . It was a delightful talk. Philosophy was varied by some free criticisms of — to begin with. He was left a good deal damaged, but with some sympathy for him as a character — when Oliver said, 'But the really wicked man is — ' And then the hunt was up and a fine run across country. . .

Fortunately the younger generation, his own children and the children of his friends, was growing up and proved of great help in carrying on the business of living. 'They are entirely lacking in reverence,' he noted. They had greatly improved upon his own generation. When they were small he would teach them the rudiments of chemistry, making a beautiful blue-green solution of copper sulphate, or brewing coal gas in a clay pipe plugged with plasticine on the drawing-room fire. He would appear at a children's party glittering in chains and frying-pans bought at Woolworth's, a fancy dress which brought out, as fancy dress so often does, a spiritual likeness, in his case indisputably, to Don Quixote. Later he would arrive at their rooms in Cambridge and, remembering his own attitude to his elders, exclaim in delight, 'They talk about their own interests and their pleasure in life without troubling to recognize our presence'. But there he was wrong. They were well aware of his presence — of his humours, of his eccentricities; of his 'immense seriousness', and of his equally immense powers of enjoyment. He would plunge at once into his own interests and his own problems. He would make them help to translate Mallarmé, he would argue for hours on end with 'terrific Quaker scrupulosity and intellectual honesty'; and he would play chess, and through playing chess bring them to understand his views on aesthetics. 'He was extraordinarily good at gaining one's confidence,' one of those undergraduates, Julian Bell, wrote,

> principally because he always took one's ideas seriously enough to discuss them, and contradicted them if he disagreed. . . He made one share his pleasure in thinking. . . He had a power of analyzing poetry, of showing what was happening, that was extraordinarily useful. . . I've never known anyone so good at making one share his enjoyments . . . He always seemed ready to enjoy whatever was going on, food, drink, people, love affairs. I was never once bored in his company. He never grew old and cursed.

And Roger Fry returned the compliment. For Julian Bell himself he had a deep affection — 'the most magnificent human being I have known since Jem Stephen', he called him. Fresh from talk with him and his friends, he went on to reflect how much more at his ease he felt with the young than with his own generation. They made him realize 'how curiously far I have travelled from the standpoint of my own generation... Not that I didn't enjoy seeing [an old friend] very much, but it just showed me how much I'd joined the younger generation'.

... He was beginning, he sometimes complained, to feel old – 'you begin to feel your whole body creaking, that's what it is . . . Don't tell people this – I'd rather they didn't know it.' It was difficult to know it; the more work he had on hand the greater his energy became. It was difficult even to know that he was working, for he carried on so many other activities simultaneously. A specimen day is described in a letter written at that time by Clive Bell:

> Up and on the motive before breakfast; after breakfast just slips over to Tilton to see Sam Courtauld, and arrange about lectures, and telephone to Hindley Smith; painting in Vanessa's studio till lunch; at lunch moans and groans about not being allowed to eat anything; has Lottie put on to cook special invalid dishes but meanwhile makes a hearty meal off roast beef and plum-tart; hurries over to Seaford to inspect Hindley Smith's collection; back in time for an early tea so that he can drag Vanessa and Duncan to Wilmington to paint landscape; after dinner just runs through a few of Mallarmé's poems, which he is translating word for word into what he is pleased to consider blank verse; bedtime – 'Oh just time for a game of chess, Julian'. I look out of window at half-past one and see the old object, lying like a tomb, in bed on the terrace, reading by the light of a candle. He had to start early this morning in order to lunch with Lady Colefax. But, while I am dressing, I hear him shouting to Julian through the ground-floor window – 'I think before I go we've just time to run through *L'Après-Midi d'un faune*'.

It was in the midst of such distractions, playing chess with one hand, correcting Mallarmé with another, that the inaugural lecture was written. Whether it was a day's work or a day's pleasure – and it was difficult to say where work ended and pleasure began – it was a full day at any rate. If in his company, as Sir Kenneth Clark has said, 'one felt sometimes that the proper answer to Tolstoy's "What is art?" was the counter question "What isn't?" ' so in his company the proper answer to the question 'What is life?' seemed to be 'What isn't?' Everything was drawn in, assimilated, investigated. The body might creak, but the mind seemed to work with more sweep, with less friction than ever. It reached out and laid hold of every trifle – a new stitch, a zip-fastener, a shadow on the ceiling. Each must be investigated, each must be examined, as if by rescuing such trifles from mystery he could grasp life tighter and make it yield one more drop of rational and civilised enjoyment. And here fittingly, since he was no lover of vague statements, may follow his own definition 'of what I mean by life ... I mean the general and instinctive reaction to their surroundings of those men of any period whose lives rise to complete self-consciousness, their view of the universe as a whole and their conception of their relation to their kind'. Could he but live five years longer, he wrote in 1933, 'life will have done all for me that I can expect'.

Only one subject seemed to escape his insatiable curiosity; and that was himself. Analysis seemed to stop short there. Perhaps human nature, until we have more knowledge of psychology, is inexplicable; we are only beginning, he would insist, to know anything about this very queer animal man. He was delighted, of course, to hazard theories – about the effect of a puritan upbringing, about the origin of the inferiority complex which he observed cropping up in him from time to time. And if pressed, though very little interested in the past compared with the present, he would try to set down what he could remember. 'The first thing', one such fragment of autobiography begins, 'is the play of light on the leaves of the elm trees outside the nursery window at Highgate...' He could remember many sights, and here and there an amusing incident or character – his father skating, for example, or Pierpont Morgan, with his strawberry nose and his little red eyes, buying pictures in Italy. But the central figure remained vague. '... I don't pretend to know much on the subject. It so rarely interests me', he wrote when asked to explain himself. 'You say I'm wild and want to know if I'm impulsive', he went on (to Helen Anrep).

> Why I should have thought, but of course I don't know, that I was impulsive (which I don't like and suspect you don't) but not wild. No, surely not wild – infinitely sane, cautious, reasonable – what makes me look wild is that I don't happen to accept any of the world's *idées reçues* and values but have my own and stick to them... But I should have said impulsive, *i.e.* moved rather jerkily and suddenly by what appeals to me, and I think it implies something wasteful and incoherent in me which I also lament and would like you to forgive – oh, and cure, perhaps.

This lack of interest in the central figure – that central figure which was so increasingly interested in everything outside itself – had its charm. It made him unconscious, a perfect butt for the irreverent laughter, in which he delighted, of the young; unaware too of the astonishment that his appearance, clasping *le diable* in his arms, created among the respectable residents in middle-class hotels. But it had its drawbacks, for if he ignored himself, he sometimes ignored other people also. Thus it would be quite possible to collect from different sources a number of unflattering portraits of Roger Fry. They would be contradictory, of course. To some people he seemed insincere – he changed his opinions so quickly. His enthusiasm made the first sight so exciting; then his critical sense came into play and made the second sight so disappointing. The swan of yesterday would become the goose of to-day – a transformation naturally, and often volubly, resented by the bird itself. To others he seemed on the contrary only too ruthless, too dictatorial – a Hitler, a Mussolini, a Stalin. Absorbed in some idea, set upon some cause, he ignored feelings, he overrode objections. Everybody he assumed must share his views and have the same ardour in carrying them out. Fickle and impulsive, obstinate and over-bearing – the unflattering portraits would be drawn on those lines.

And he was the first to realize that there was some truth in them. He was impulsive, he knew; he was obstinate; he was, he feared, egotistical. 'I suddenly see,' he wrote, 'the curious twisted egotism that there is somewhere in me that used to come out when I was little in my indignation against "the twinges", as I used to call Isabel and Agnes, for wanting to play with my things.' Also he was 'cross, fussy, stingy, pernickety and other things'. Perhaps psycho-analysis might help; or perhaps human nature in general and his own in particular was too irrational, too instinctive, either to be analyzed or to be cured. And he would go on to deplore the natural imperviousness of the human mind to reason; to gird at the extraordinary morality with which human beings torture themselves, and to speculate whether in time to come they may not accept the simple gospel 'that all decency and good come from peoples gradually determining to enjoy themselves a little, especially to enjoy their intellectual curiosity and their love of art'. In such speculations about the race in general, Roger Fry lost sight of himself in particular. Certainly he would have refused to sit for the portrait of a finished, complete or in any way perfect human being. He detested fixed attitudes; he suspected poses; he was quick to point out the fatal effect of reverence. And yet whether he liked it or not he would have had to sit for the portrait of a man who was greatly loved by his friends. Truth seems to compel the admission that he created the warmest feeling of affection and admiration in the minds of those who knew him. It was Roger Fry, to sum up many phrases from many letters, who set me on my feet again, and gave me a fresh start in life. It was he who was the most actively, the most inaginatively helpful of all my friends. And they go on to speak of his considerateness, of his humanity, and of his profound humility. So though he made some enemies and shed some acquaintances, he bound his friends to him all the more for the queer strains of impulsiveness and ruthlessness that lay on the surface of that very deep understanding.

But there was the other life – the artist's. He felt no need to apologize for his conduct there. A work of art was a work of art, and nothing else: personal considerations counted for nothing there. He was a difficult man, it is easy to believe, on committees. He gave his opinion uncompromisingly; he gave it wittily and pungently, or sometimes he gave it sufficiently with one deep groan. He had no respect for authority. 'If you said to him, "This must be right, all the experts say so, Hitler says so, Marx says so, Christ says so, *The Times* says so", he would reply in effect, "Well, I wonder. Let's see" . . . You would come away realizing that an opinion may be influentially backed and yet be tripe.' Naturally, artists and art critics being what they are, he was bitterly attacked. He was accused of caring only for the Old Masters or only for the latest fashions. He was always changing his mind and he was obstinately prejudiced in favour of his friends' work. In spite of failings that should have made his opinion worthless, it had weight – for some reason or other Roger Fry had influence, more influence, it was agreed, than any critic since Ruskin at the height of his fame.

How, without any post to back it he came to have such influence, is a question for the painters themselves to decide. The effect of it is shown in their works, and whether it is good or bad, no one, it is safe to say, will hold that it was negligible. To the outsider at any rate, the secret of his influence seemed based, in one word, upon his disinterestedness. He was among the priests, to use his own definition, not among the prophets, or the purveyors. By ignoring personalities and politics, success and failure, he seemed to penetrate beyond any other critic into the picture itself. To this the outsider could also add from direct observation another characteristic – he did not indulge in flattery. Friends he had – he cannot be acquitted of liking some people better than others. But a mutual admiration society, if such things exist – and according to some observers they do – would have expelled Roger Fry at the first meeting. He was as honest with his friends' work as with his enemies'. He would look long and searchingly, and if he liked what he saw, he would praise generously, dispassionately. But if he did not like what he saw, he was silent; or his one word of condemnation was enough. But his detachment, his disinterestedness was shown most impressively by his own attitude to his own work. His painting was beyond comparison more important to him than his criticism. He never lost hope that he had à little sensation', as he called it, or that he had at last been able to express it. He would set his own canvas on the easel and await the verdict. It was often adverse; those whose praise he would have valued most highly were often unable to give it. How keenly he minded that silence is shown again and again in his letters. But it made no difference. His own picture would be set with its face to the wall, and he would turn to the work of those who had been unable to praise his own. He would consider it with perfect single-mindedness, and if he liked it, he praised it, not because it was a friend's work, but because he admired it. 'One thing I can say for myself', he wrote. 'There are no pangs of jealousy or envy when I see someone else doing good work. It gives me pure delight.' There perhaps lay the secret of his influence as a critic.

But his influence as a human being – his own words, 'We know too little of the rhythms of man's spiritual life', remind us of the perils of trying to guess the secret that lay behind that. He did not believe with all his knowledge that he could guess the secret of a work of art. And human beings are not works of art. They are not consciously creating a book that can be read, or a picture that can be hung upon the wall. The critic of Roger Fry as a man has a far harder task than any that was set him by the pictures of Cézanne. Yet his character was strongly marked; each transformation left something positive behind it. He stood for something rare in the general life of his time – 'Roger Fry's death is a definite loss to civilization', wrote E.M. Forster. 'There is no one now living – no one, that is to say, of his calibre – who stands exactly where he stood.' He changed the taste of his time by his writing, altered the current of English painting by his championship of the Post-Impressionists, and increased immeasurably the love of art by his lectures. He left too upon the minds of those who knew him a very rich, complex and definite impression . . .

Roger Fry by Clive Bell

Reprinted from Clive Bell, Old Friends: Personal Recollections *(London, Chatto & Windus, 1956), 62–91, by permission of Professor*

Quentin Bell and Chatto & Windus.

[The art criticism of Roger Fry and Clive Bell are more closely
associated than any other work in Bloomsbury except maybe the
painting of Duncan Grant and Vanessa Bell. Clive Bell's tribute to Fry,
first published in 1952, allows an unusual view of a Bloomsbury
relationship. The recently published letters of Roger Fry show that
there were more than enough causes for bad feeling between Fry and
Bell in personal as well as professional matters, yet the friendship
endured and the following estimate of Fry was possible. Like Virginia
Woolf's biography, Bell's recollections only obliquely indicate Fry's
place in Bloomsbury by describing his qualities as a friend and a critic.

Bell's essay also brings out one of the most important ideas of most
of the members of Bloomsbury: their formalistic aesthetics. The idea
appears clearly in Bell's re-definition of his famous term 'significant
form'. The closeness of Bell and Fry, in the eyes of one observer, at any
rate, is represented in the Max Beerbohm cartoon that Bell used as the
frontispiece to *Old Friends*. The cartoon shows Bell talking with Fry,
and the dialogue, appropriately entitled 'Significant Form' is as follows:

Mr Clive Bell: I always think that when one feels one's been carrying
     a theory too far, *then*'s the time to carry it a little further.
Mr Roger Fry: A little? Good heavens, man! Are you growing old?

Two passages from Bell's essay have been omitted — a digression on
the Courtauld Collection and another anecdote of Fry's gullibility.]

'You knew him well, why don't you give us your picture of him?' said
an American friend with whom I was talking about Roger Fry. Because,
said I, Virginia Woolf wrote a biography which, besides being as
complete an account of Fry's life as for the present it would be seemly
to publish, happens to be a masterpiece: I have no notion of entering
into competition with one of the great writers of my age. Of course I
knew well enough that what my friend had in mind was something
utterly unlike Mrs Woolf's biography; what he expected of me was an
appetising lecture, fifty-five minutes of lively gossip, a chapter from my
unpublished memoirs. But here again a lion was in the way: for though,
as a matter of fact, I did jot down soon after Fry's death, for the
amusement of my friends and his, a handful of anecdotes intended to
illustrate just one facet of his nature — the lovably absurd — I felt that
to enjoy these fantastic tales it was necessary to have known the hero

and to have known him well. Now Virginia Woolf made us know him so well that she was able to avail herself of my collection — which was of course at her service — dropping delicately here an absurdity there an extravagance with telling effect: but I am not Virginia Woolf. I cannot bring the dead to life, and so I cannot effectively retell my own stories. All I can do is to give, or try to give, the impression made on me by the man, the critic and the painter, drawing more on my recollection of what he said and did than on what he published, which is after all accessible to all and I hope familiar to most. For his ideas I must go sometimes to his books; but of his character and gifts I will try to give an account based on what I remember of his sayings and doings.

'How did Roger Fry strike you?' That, I suppose, is the question. It is not easily answered. That fine, old sport of analyzing characters and reducing them to their component qualities or humours is out of fashion, and was, I admit, as a method, unsubtle. Still, no one who knew Roger is likely to quarrel with me if I say that some of the things that come first to mind when one thinks of him are intelligence, sweetness, ardour and sensibility; nor I believe will it be denied that one of the first things to catch the attention of anyone who was coming acquainted with him was likely to be his prodigious and varied knowledge. To be sure, the very first thing that struck me was his appearance. He was tall — about six foot I dare say; but did not look his height. Maybe he stooped a little; he was well made, by no means lanky, anyhow he certainly did not give the impression of a very tall man. What one noticed were his eyes which were both round and penetrating — an uncommon combination — and were made to appear rounder by large circular goggles. One noticed his hair too — once black, I believe, but greyish when I met him — which, long, rebellious and silky, somehow accentuated his features which, in profile at all events, were very sharply defined. He was clean shaven. There was something the air of a judge about him, but still more the air of one who is perpetually surprised by life — as indeed he was. At moments he reminded me of a highly sagacious rocking-horse. He wore good clothes badly. Obviously they had been made by the right tailor, but there was always something wrong with them. It might be a too decorative tie fashioned out of some unlikely material, or a pair of yellow brown sandals worn when black shoes would have been appropriate. His hats were peculiar; broad-brimmed, round, Quakerish and becoming. Only in full evening dress — white tie, white waistcoat, boiled shirt and collar — did he appear smart. Then, with his silvery hair carefully brushed, he looked infinitely distinguished.

So much for the impression made at first meeting. Acquaintance ripening to friendship, you would probably note a restless activity of mind and body. Ardent he was, as I have said, intelligent, sensitive, sweet, cultivated and erudite: these qualities and attainments revealed themselves sooner or later, and soon rather than late, to everyone who came to know him, and of them I must speak first. But what charmed his intimate friends almost as much as his rare qualities was his boundless gullibility: of that I shall speak later.

I have said that his knowledge was what might well have struck you in the beginning. One was surprised by the amount he knew before one realized that it was a mere means to something far more precious – to culture in the best sense of the word. Roger Fry was what Bacon calls 'a full man'; but his various erudition was only a means to thought and feeling and the enrichment of life. Knowledge he knew added immensely to the fun of the fair, enabling one to make the most of any odd fact that comes one's way by seeing it in relation to other facts and to theories and so fitting it into the great jig-saw puzzle. But he never cared much to be given a result unless he could learn how that result had been obtained; and therein you will recognize one of the essential qualifications of a scholarly critic. At Cambridge his studies had been scientific: that is something to have in mind for it helps to an understanding of the man, his merits and some of his defects. He took a first in the Natural Science tripos. To do that, I am assured, requires more than smattering a little Botany and cutting up a few frogs: to have done it is, I suspect, to have given the mind a bent which the most varied and thrilling experiences of later life will hardly rectify.

I shall ask you to bear in mind, then, that Roger Fry was a man of science by training and to some extent by temper. I shall not ask you to bear in mind that he was intelligent and lovable, because intelligence and charm are the very oil and pigment in which the picture of his life is to be painted. These qualities, I hope, will make themselves felt without demonstration as my tale proceeds. His old friends will not be surprised if I do not insist on them; what may surprise some is that I did not put first among his qualities, Sensibility. That Fry had acquired exquisite sensibility was clear to all who knew him or read his writings or listened to his lectures, and clearer still to those who worked with him. To watch, or rather catch, him — for in such matters his methods were summary – disposing of a foolish attribution, was to realize just how convincing a decision based on trained sensibility and knowledge can be. I have seen a little dealer, with all due ceremony, reverence and precaution, produce from a triply locked safe what purported to be a

Raphael Madonna; I have seen Fry give it one glance or two and heard him say sweetly but firmly 'an eighteenth-century copy and a bad one at that'; and I have seen the dealer, himself for the moment convinced, fling the picture back into the safe without so much as bothering to lock the door. Such was the force of Fry's sensibility – trained sensibility supported by intelligence and knowledge. His possession of that has never been called in question so far as I know. What perhaps he did not possess, in such abundance at all events, was that innate sensibility, that hankering after beauty, that liking for art which resembles a liking for alcohol, that 'gusto' as Hazlitt would have called it, which is the best gift of many second- and third-rate painters and of some critics even – Théophile Gautier for instance. In a later chapter I shall try to recall the joy of wandering about Paris, a boy just down from Cambridge, with the Canadian, J.W. Morrice – a typical good second-rate painter (first-rate almost) – and of being made to feel beauty in the strangest places; not in cafés and music-halls only (in those days, about 1904, the classic haunts of beauty), but on hoardings and in shop-windows, in itinerant musicians singing sentimental romances, in smart frocks and race-meetings and arias by Gounod, in penny-steamers and sunsets and military uniforms, at the *Opéra comique* even, and even at the *Comédie française*. With Roger Fry I have been privileged to travel in many parts of Europe, and from him I have learnt to discover uncharted subtleties and distinguish between fine shades of expression; but I do not think he could have found beauty where Morrice found it. Perhaps Roger possessed in the highest degree sensibility of a methodical kind, what I have called 'trained sensibility'; whereas Morrice had the sensibility of an artist – innate. I do not know.

His first approach to art was so hampered by family tradition, lofty and puritan, that it was I dare say inevitable that he should make some false starts and fall into some pits from which a normal, barbarous upbringing might have saved him. Also the climate of Cambridge in the 'Eighties', and even later, was not altogether favourable to growth of the aesthetic sense. Also he was reading science. All this I take into account: and all this notwithstanding I do feel, re-reading the story of his early years, that his blunders of commission and omission, his baseless enthusiasms and blind spots, were not those of a very young artist but of an intellectual at any age. Assuredly the admirations and anathemas of the very young are never to be brought up against them; but in 1892 Fry was twenty-six and, what is more, had for some time been an art-student, which makes it hard to believe that, had sensibility been innate, he could have spent months in Paris – at Jullian's too – without feeling a thrill for the Impressionists and could have found in the Luxembourg nothing more exciting than Bastien Lepage.

I spoke of family tradition lofty and puritan: the puritan strain in Roger's character his friends might like but could not ignore. To his hours of abandon even it gave an air of revolt. His paganism was protestant – a protest against puritanism. Intellectually the freest of men, and almost indecently unprejudiced, he made one aware of a slight wrench, the ghost of a struggle, when he freed his mind to accept or condone what his forbears would have called 'vile pleasures'. It is on this streak of puritanism the devil's advocate will fasten when Roger comes up, as come up he will, for canonisation. He was open-minded, but he was not fair-minded. For though, as I have said, he was magnificently unprejudiced, he was not unprincipled; and he had a way of being sure that while all his own strong feelings were principles those of others, when they happened to cross his, were unworthy prejudices. Thanks to his puritanical upbringing he could sincerely regard his principles as in some sort the will of God. From which it followed that anyone who opposed them must have said, like Satan, 'Evil be thou my good'. People who happened not to agree with him found this annoying.

Few of us are all of a metal; most, as Dryden puts it, are 'dashed and brewed with lies'. The best founded even are flawed with some disharmony. The cup is just troubled with an 'aliquid amari', and the bitterness will now and then catch in the throat and spoil the flavour of life as it goes down. A tang of puritanism was in Roger's cup: it was barely appreciable, yet to it I believe can be traced most of his defects as man and critic. Not all: there are defects that can be traced to his scientific training and temper, but here there is gain to record as well as loss. The pure unscientific aesthete is a sensationalist. He feels first; only later, if he happens to be blest – or curst – with a restless intellect, will he condescend to reason about his feelings. It would be false and silly to suggest that Roger Fry's emotions were at the service of his theories; but he was too good a natural philosopher to enjoy seeing a theory pricked by a fact. Now the mere aesthete is for ever being bowled over by facts: the facts that upset him being as a rule works of art which according to current doctrine ought not to come off but which somehow or other do (e.g. the Houses of Parliament or the works of Kipling). The aesthete, sensationalist that he is, rather likes being knocked down by an outsider. He picks himself up and goes on his way rejoicing in an adventure. Roger Fry did not altogether like it.

He entered a gallery with a generalization in his head — a generalization which, up to that moment, was, or should be, a complete explanation of art. He was not the man to deny facts, and he was much too sensitive to overlook the sort I have in mind; but I do think he was inclined to give marks to pictures which, because they were right in intention, ought to have been right in achievement, and sometimes, I think, he was rather unwilling to recognize the patent but troublesome beauty of works that seemed to be sinning against the light. Nine times out of ten this tendency towards injustice was due to a puritanical aversion from charm, and to counter it the spirit of science had made him magnificently open-minded. He was the most open-minded man I ever met: the only one indeed who tried to practise that fundamental precept of science — that nothing should be assumed to be true or false until it has been put to the test. This made him willing to hear what anyone had to say even about questions on which he was a recognized authority, even though 'anyone' might be a schoolboy or a housemaid: this also made him a champion gull — but of that later. Had he fallen in with a schoolboy — a manifestly sincere and eager schoolboy — in the Arena Chapel at Padua, and had that boy confessed that he could see no merit in the frescos, Roger would have argued the question on the spot, panel by panel: and this he would have done in no spirit of amiable complacency. Always supposing the boy to be serious and ardent, the great critic would have been attentive to the arguments and objections of the small iconoclast: convinced, I suppose, he would have modified his judgment and, if necessary, recast his aesthetic.

About that aesthetic, which gave him so much trouble, I shall soon have a word to say. But first let me give an example of open-mindedness and integrity which will, I hope, make some amends for what I have said or shall say concerning his slightly biased approach to works of art. Always he had disliked Indian art: it offended his sense of reasonableness and his taste. Late in life, having enjoyed opportunities of studying more and better examples may be, or perhaps merely having studied more happily and freely examples that were always within his reach, he changed his mind. That done, the next thing to do was to 'own up'. And 'own up' he did in a discriminating lecture. When you remember that at the time of writing this palinode Roger Fry was getting on for seventy and was the foremost critic in Europe, I think you will agree that he gave proof of considerable open-mindedness and a lesson to us all. The scientific spirit is not without its uses in the appreciation of the fine arts: neither is character.

Indeed he was open-minded; which is not to say, as jealous fools were at one time fond of saying, that he was a weather-cock, slave to every gust of enthusiasm. It is a memorable fact, to which Sir Kenneth Clark sorrowfully calls attention in his preface to *Last Lectures*, that, try as he would, Fry could never bring himself greatly to admire Greek sculpture. He would have been glad to admire it: for Greek civilization, for the Greek view and way of life, for Greek prose and verse, philosophy and science, he felt what all intelligent and well educated people must feel. He realized that Athens was man's masterpiece. And so, towards the end of his life, he went with three friends – one an accomplished Hellenist and all highly intelligent -- to see whether he could not prove himself wrong. The will to admire was there: but honesty, but fidelity to his personal reaction, proved the stronger. He found Greek sculpture, whether archaic or of what is called 'the great age', comparatively dull. And he said so.

Roger Fry was troubled by aesthetics; anyone who cares for art yet cannot keep his intellect quiet must be. Roger cared passionately, and positively enjoyed analysing his emotions: also he did it better, I think, than anyone had done it before. Having analyzed he went on to account for his feelings, and got into that fix which everyone gets into who makes the attempt: *experto credite*. Art is almost as wide as life; and to invent a hypothesis which shall comprehend it may be as difficult, just as it may appear as simple, as to explain the universe. The place where Roger stuck is where we all stick. There is a constant in art just as, once upon a time, there was supposed to be a constant in life. I have a notion they called it 'C': anyhow that was a long time ago. But I feel pretty sure that in those far off days the difference between Organic and Inorganic was determined by the presence or absence of a definable somewhat; and still it is permissible to say that a work of art cannot exist unless there be present what I used to call 'significant form', and you may call by any name you please – provided that what you mean by your name is a combination of lines and colours, or of notes, or of words, in itself moving, *i.e.* moving without reference to the outside world. Only, to say that, is no more to answer the question 'What is art?' than to chatter about what 'C' is, or ever was, or to answer the question 'What is life?' Renoir, painting pictures of girls and fruit, concentrated his attention exclusively on their forms and colours. But implicit in those forms and colours, for Renoir inseparable from them, was appetizingness – the feeling that girls are good to kiss and peaches to eat. Easy enough to see that when a painter sets out to make you feel that his girls would be nice to kiss he ceases to be an artist and becomes a pornographer or a sentimentalist. Renoir never dreams of trying to make you feel anything of that sort; he is concerned only with saying what he feels about forms and colours. Nevertheless, he does feel, consciously or subconsciously, embedded in those forms and colours, deliciousness. All that he feels he expresses. Now all that an artist expresses is part of his work of art. The problem is turning nasty, you perceive; complicate it, multiply instances and diversify them, and you will be near where Roger stuck. He never quite swallowed my impetuous doctrine — Significant Form first and last, alone and all the time; he knew too much, and such raw morsels stuck in his scientific throat. He came near swallowing it once; but always he was trying to extend his theory to cover new difficulties — difficulties presented, not only by an acute and restless intellect, but by highly trained sensibility playing on vast experience. Need I say that his difficulties were always ahead of his explanations? In wrestling with them he raised a number of interesting questions; better still — far better — he threw a flood of brilliant light on art in general and on particular works. Read again that masterly chapter in *Transformations* called 'Some Questions in Aesthetics', a matter of fifty pages, in which he goes deeper into the subject than anyone had gone before or has gone since — I am not forgetting Max Eastman whom I greatly admire. You will find the destructive criticism entirely satisfying; you will be enlightened by the analysis of aesthetic experience; you will enjoy seeing the finest mince-meat made of Mr Richards's simple-minded psychological explanations, which boil down to the absurd conclusion that our responses to works of art are the same as our responses to life; and when it comes to justification let Fry speak for himself:

> As to the value of the aesthetic emotion — it is clearly infinitely removed from those ethical values to which Tolstoy would have confined it. It seems to be as remote from actual life and its practical utilities as the most useless mathematical theorem. One can say only that those who experience it feel it to have a peculiar quality of 'reality' which makes it a matter of infinite importance in their lives. Any attempt I might make to explain this would probably land me in the depths of mysticism. On the edge of that gulf I stop. (*Vision and Design*, p. 199)

Certainly his wrestlings helped to give muscle to the body of Fry's criticism; but to the building of that body went many rare aliments — trained sensibility, intellect, peculiar knowledge, wide general culture, the scientific spirit and honour. Virginia Woolf speaks of 'his power of

making pictures real and art important'. Words could not give better a
sense of just what it was Roger Fry did for my generation and the next.
Having learnt to feel intensely the beauty and glory and wonder of a
work of visual art he could, so to speak, unhook his emotion and hold
it under, I will not say a microscope, but an uncommonly powerful pair
of spectacles. That done, he could find, and sometimes invent, words to
convey feelings and analyses of feelings into the apprehension of the
reader – or listener: it was even better to be a listener than a reader. I
am not thinking of those unforgettable conversations and discussions
before particular works of art in churches and galleries, but of his
lectures. Roger Fry's lectures were his best critical performances: he
was the perfect lecturer almost. And the lecture with slides is the
perfect medium for pictorial exegesis, permitting, as it does, the
lecturer to bring before the eyes of his audience images of the objects
about which he is speaking, thinking and feeling. To hear a lecture by
Roger Fry was the next best thing to sight-seeing in his company. He
stuck but loosely to his text, allowing himself to be inspired by
whatever was on the screen. It was from a sensation to a word. Almost
one could watch him thinking and feeling.

To say the excruciatingly difficult things Fry set himself to say he
was obliged to work language pretty hard. In my opinion he worked it
well. His prose was lucid and lively, and on occasions he could be
delightfully witty and verbally felicitous. His biographer glances,
critically but affectionately, at his habit of repeating favourite phrases.
The fault is unavoidable in the prose of an art-critic since there is no
vocabulary of art-criticism. If such terms as 'plastic sequence', 'plastic
unity', 'inner life', 'structural planes' keep cropping up, that is because
they are the only symbols available for subtle and complex things
which themselves keep cropping up. It is essential to understanding that
readers or listeners should know precisely what the critic is referring to;
and only by repeatedly describing in the same terms the same concepts
can he hope to give these terms anything like generally accepted
significance. To some extent the art-critic must create his own
vocabulary.

Writing, as a fine art, was Roger's foible. Of prose and verse rhythms
he was indistinctly aware; but he liked spinning theories about them. Of
his translations of Mallarmé the less said the better: the one significant
thing about them is that he believed them to be adequate. They have
made me think of Bentley editing Milton; for, after all, Bentley was a
great, a very great critic, and in some ways understood Greek poetry as
it never had been understood by a modern. Having named Milton I find

myself thinking of some gibberish Roger once wrote – for the benefit
of intimate friends only – gibberish which did possess recognizable
similarity of sound with the *Ode on the Nativity* but did not possess
what he firmly believed it to possess, *i.e.* all, or almost all, the merits of
the original. The gibberish was, of course, deliberate gibberish – a
collection of sounds so far as possible without meaning. It was highly
ingenious, and I am bound to reckon the theory behind it pretty, seeing
that it was much the same as one I had myself propounded years earlier
as an explanation of visual art. Only, at the time Roger's experiment
was made we were deep in the Twenties and the fine frenzy of
Post-Impressionism was a thing of the past. There was now no
controversial axe to grind. Simply, Roger liked the theory because he
felt it was one in the eye for 'magic'. It came from the heart rather than
the head and he wanted to believe it. Now it was this gibberish, and his
opinion of it, and the passion with which he defended his opinion, that
finally opened my eyes to a truth which had, I suppose, always been
plain to those who did not love him: Roger's feeling for poetry was
puritanical. The charm, the romance, the imagery, the glamour, the
magic offended the quaker that was in him; wherefore he was very
willing to believe that all that signified could be reduced to clean, dry
bones.

Having said so much about writing and lecturing, I must say
something, I suppose, about painting. It is an unenviable taks; for,
preposterous as it must seem to those who know him only by his
achievement, Roger Fry took his painting more seriously than he took
his criticism. It was the most important thing in his life, or at any rate
he thought it was. He said so and his friends were bound to believe him;
yet some of them wondered: surely he knew that he was the best critic
alive, and, at the bottom of his heart, can he have believed that he was a
very good painter? He knew that those whose opinion he valued did not
think so. To me it seems that his early work, especially his
water-colours and paintings on silk, are his happiest productions. They
are frankly eclectic; the influence of some master, of some English
water-colourist as a rule, being acknowledged at every turn. But in most
of these works – things done before 1910 shall we say? – there are
pleasing qualities which later I seek in vain. Unashamed, in those
unregenerate days, he could utilize his knowledge, and exploit his taste,
the delicacy of his perceptions, his sleight of hand. All these assets
contributed to a tentative style which did in some sort express a part of
his nature. The Post-Impressionist revolution which set free so many of
his latent capacities overwhelmed these modest virtues. It set free his

capacity for living and enjoying, but it did no good to his painting. On the contrary, that movement which was to liberate the creative powers of all those young and youngish artists who possessed any powers worth liberating, that movement of which in this country he was the animator, did Fry's painting harm, driving it into uncongenial ways. He tried to paint in a manner which he understood admirably and explained brilliantly but could not make his own. No longer decked in the rather antiquated finery which had fitted his temper on one side at any rate, his painting gift appeared naked, and we perceived to our dismay that it amounted to next to nothing. His very energy and quickness, qualities elsewhere profitable, here served him ill. He worked too fast. Neither had he that ruminating enjoyment which lingers over a subject till the last oozings of significance have been tasted, nor yet the patience which will elaborate a design to its last possibilities. I have seen him, out of sheer conscientiousness, or in some desperate hope of a miraculous revelation, work on at a picture to which he knew he could add nothing, for all the world like an examination candidate who has written all he knows and vainly strives to improve the appearance of his paper by writing it all over again. Roger knew that he had added nothing. Maybe he knew too much.

Roger Fry was a good, though impatient, craftsman, proper of his hands and quick to learn a trade. His best productions in this sort are the white pots and plates he made for the Omega; and it is to be hoped that a few will be preserved in some public collection, for they grow rare. But no sooner did he think it necessary to embellish a chair or a table or a chest of drawers, to beautify a curtain, a lamp-shade or a frock, then something went wrong. There must have been a devil, I have sometimes fancied, a demon born of puritanism and pampered in young 'artistic' days, which lurked in his sub-consciousness and on favourable occasions poked up its nose. At any rate, in all that he did for the Omega, with the exception of those plain white pots and plates, I taste an unpleasant flavour – a flavour redolent of 'artistry'. That was the devil's revenge; and perhaps it was this same evil spirit that forbade Fry the paradise of creation. From that delectable country he was excluded; he could not reach the frontiers because where art begins some perverse sub-consciousness or self-consciousness arrested him. What was it precisely? I hardly know. Could he have believed – no, he could not have believed nor thought either – but could he have hoped, in some dark corner of his being inaccessible to reason, that style could be imposed? A horrid fancy: that way lie art guilds and gowns, sandals, homespun and welfare-work, and at the end yawns an old English

tea-room. If Roger had finished a picture before he had begun a work
of art, that may have been because he could not practise what he
preached so well – that in creating all the horses must be driven
abreast, that you cannot hitch on style or beauty as an ostler used to
hitch on a tracer. And if I am asked why Roger Fry's painting seems
dead, all I can say is what Renoir said when asked whether art comes
from the head or the heart: '*des couilles*' he replied.

But if Roger Fry was not an artist, he was one of the most
remarkable men of his age, besides being one of the most lovable. This
his biographer has established; his other friends can but bring a few
flowers to the monument and cherish the inscription. I first met him
appropriately enough in the morning train from Cambridge to King's
Cross. It was early in 1910, a moment at which Fry was in a sense
beginning a new life. The tragedy in which the old had ended, the
courage and devotion with which that tragedy had been fought and for
a while warded off, Mrs Woolf has most movingly recounted. In 1910
Roger Fry was in his forty-fifth year: one life was ending and a new,
and perhaps more exciting, about to begin. Indeed, it was a moment at
which everyone felt excitement in the air: had not I – even I – just sat
down to describe the general state of affairs in an *opus* to bear the
pregnant title *The New Renaissance*, an *opus* of which the bit I did
publish three years later, a book called *Art*, would have formed a mere
chapter. Certainly there was stir: in Paris and London at all events there
was a sense of things coming right, though whether what we thought
was coming could properly be described as a 'renaissance' now seems to
me doubtful. The question is academic: as usual the statesmen came to
the rescue, and Mr Asquith, Sir Edward Grey and M. Viviani declared
war on Germany. But in 1910 only statesmen dreamed of war, and
quite a number of wide-awake people imagined the good times were
just round the corner. Miracles seemed likely enough to happen; but
when Roger Fry told me that morning in the train that he proposed to
show the British public the work of the newest French painters, I told
him that I would be proud to help in any way I could but that his
scheme was fantastic. Not that there was any question of my being of
serious use – Roger never needed an *État-Major*; but as I had written in
praise of Cézanne and Gauguin and other 'revolutionaries' he thought I
might as well give a hand. Anyhow, I was put on a committee which did
nothing, and late that summer I joined Roger and Desmond MacCarthy
in Paris: in the autumn opened the first Post-Impressionist exhibition . . .

One result of the first Post-Impressionist exhibition was that Roger Fry became the animator and advocate of the younger British painters; but not the master. Few young painters mistook him for a master, though to him they looked for advice and encouragement and sometimes for material support. With his fine intellect, culture and persuasive ways he became spokesman for modern art – our representative in the councils of the great; for he could place his word where he would. *The Times* felt bound to print letters from him in large type on the leader page. Even fine ladies, even the Prime Ministress, had to pretend to listen. And, under the wand of the enchanter, with his looks, his voice, his infinite variety and palpable good faith, those who began to listen found themselves becoming converts. It was now, in these last years of peace, that France became for him what for the rest of his life she remained – his second country; and there he made friends, deep, affectionate and charming, who later were to do much to lighten the gloom of declining years. At home, too, between 1910 and 1914 he was making friends, some of whom were to grow into close companions and collaborators; and of these most, it is to be noted, were of a generation younger than his own. They were, I think, gayer, more ribald, more unshockable, more pleasure-loving and less easily impressed by grave airs and fine sentiments than the friends – whom, by the way, he never lost nor ceased to love – with whom he had grown to middle age. It was from these younger people that he learnt to enjoy shamelessly almost – yes, almost. Their blissful adiabolism helped him to ignore the nudgings of the old puritan Nick. And this I like to count some small return for all they learnt from him. He taught them much: amongst other things, by combining with an utterly disinterested and unaffected passion for art a passion for justice and hatred of cruelty, he made them aware of the beauty of goodness. That virtue could be agreeable came as a surprise to some of us. Like all satisfactory human relationships, these new friendships were matters of give and take; and I know who gave most. Nevertheless, between the first Post-Impressionist exhibition and the First War I have a notion that Roger Fry changed more than he had changed in all the years between Cambridge and that exhibition.

I have suggested that one reason why Roger was unable to elaborate a work of art and knocked off too many works of craft was that his boundless energy induced impatience. This energy, allied with prodigious strength of will, was terrifying; and it is not surprising that his enemies, and his friends too when they chanced to be his victims, called him ruthless and obstinate; for it is provoking to be driven straight into a field of standing corn because your driver cannot admit that his map may be out of date or that he may have misread it. Of this

energy and wilfulness an extract from my unpublished notes may
perhaps give some idea. So,

I recall a cold and drizzling Sunday in August: I cannot be sure of
the year. Roger is staying with us at Charleston, convalescent; for,
like many exceptionally robust and energetic men, Roger was a
valetudinarian. I remember hearing my wife say, probably at
breakfast, that she suspected him of intending to be motored some
time in the afternoon to Seaford, eight or nine miles away, where
dwelt his curious old friend, Hindley Smith; but that she, the
weather being vile, the road slippery, the car open and ill-humoured,
had no intention of obliging him. Just before lunch Frances Marshall
(Mrs Ralph Partridge) who also was staying with us, and possessed,
like my wife, what most would deem a will of iron, told me she had
a headache and meant, the moment lunch was over, to slip off to
bed, if that could be done without causing commotion. In any case
she was not going to play chess with Roger. For my part I never
cared about playing chess with Roger; if, by any chance, one
succeeded in some little plot for surprising his queen or rook – and
setting traps is what amuses all thoroughly bad players such as I – he
would dismiss the strategem as 'uninteresting', retract a series of
moves – generally to his own advantage – and so continue till on
scientific and avowable principles he had beaten one to his
satisfaction. Anyhow, on this dark and dismal Sunday, lunch
finished, Roger sprang to his feet – all invalid that he was he could
spring when the occasion seemed to demand action – exclaiming:
'Now Frances for a game.' And, as soon as Frances had been allowed
to lose in a way of which he could approve, again he sprang: 'Now,
Vanessa, we've just time to go and see Hindley Smith.' Vanessa went
like a lamb.

I have spoken of Roger's open-mindedness, of his readiness to listen to
anyone he thought sincere: that was fine. His aptitude for discovering
sincerity in unlikely places was fine, too, I suppose; but sometimes it
landed him in difficulties. Not to mince words, he was a champion gull:
gullibility was the laughable and lovable defect of a quality. Stories
illustrating this weakness abound; one or two, which, I am proud to
say, are drawn from my notes, appear in Virginia Woolf's biography . . .

Inevitably one so gullible and so often gulled grew suspicious – not of
the crooks, but of old friends and well meaning acquaintances. To make

matters worse, Roger had no turn for practical psychology. A poorer judge of men I have seldom met, and it goes without saying he piqued himself on penetration. He was as ready as Rousseau to believe in *conspirations holbachiques*, and was given to explaining plots which he supposed to have been woven against him, and had in truth been woven in his own imagination, by facts and motives which his friends knew to be non-existent. Does this sound sinister? It was not; for his attention could be diverted with the greatest ease from private grievances to general ideas or, better still, to particular events – in plain words to gossip. In both he delighted; also his mind was far too nimble, his capacity for enjoyment too keen, his taste too pure, his sense of fun too lively, for him to dwell long on petty troubles. He was not much like Rousseau after all. But suspicious he was, and in his fits of suspicion unjust. He could be as censorious as an ill-conditioned judge: possibly the trait was hereditary. Then it was that the puritan came out from hiding undisguised and made him believe that those who differed from him must be actuated by the foulest motives. In such moods it was that he suspected those who opposed him of having said, like Satan, 'evil be thou my good'; also, it seems to me, these moods grew more frequent with the years, bringing with them a perceptible loss of magnanimity. So it seems to me. Or was it that some of his old friends were growing touchy? That explanation is admissible too.

In this discursive chapter I hope to have given some idea of the qualities that made Roger Fry one of the most remarkable men of his age. A combination of intellect and sensibility, extensive culture not in the arts only but in history and science as well, dexterous manipulation of a fine instrument, and an unrivalled power of getting close in words to thoughts and feelings, made him indisputably our first critic. In fact he was more than the first critic of the age; so far as I can judge from my readings in three languages he was one of the best writers on visual art that ever lived. There may be Russians or Germans who have responded more delicately and analyzed their responses more acutely, who have contrived to come nearer the heart of the matter; if so, I shall be glad to study their works as soon as they have been translated. Add to these gifts, which were as one may say open to the public, those with which in private he charmed his friends, a playful intellect for instance, free fancy and a sense of fun, along with taste in food and wine, and you have beside a great critic a rare companion. Men I have known who possessed tempers to me more congenial, but none better equipped to please generally. His was, on the whole, a happy disposition, and a cause of happiness in others. One permanent anxiety beset him: it was

the child of his virtues. He dreaded, especially during the last years of
his life, the collapse of civilization. For civilization he cared nobly; and
the prevalence of its mortal enemies — fanaticism, superstition, dogmatism, unreasonableness, the cult of violence and stupidity, contempt
of truth and the ways of truth — dismayed him. In naming these vices I
have indicated his virtues, which were their contraries. He was a man of
many virtues; what is more, in practice he contrived to make them
amiable.

Desmond MacCarthy by E.M. Forster

Reprinted from 'Tributes to Sir Desmond MacCarthy, II,' The Listener
*(June 26, 1952), 1031, by permission of The Society of Authors on
behalf of the estate of E.M. Forster.*

['He had, I suspect, a good deal to do with the genial social climate of
Bloomsbury, with the reconciliation of difficult and angular characters
and with the general spirit of tolerance and compromise which
triumphed over the disputes and acerbities which were also a part of
that environment.' This evaluation of Desmond MacCarthy's role in
Bloomsbury by Quentin Bell is supported by E.M. Forster's tribute,
taken from a Memoir Club paper and published along with other
tributes in *The Listener* after MacCarthy's death in 1952.]

I have not many recollections of the early Desmond MacCarthy, but
fortunately I can clearly remember the first time we met. It was about
fifty years ago, in Cambridge, and at one of those little discussion
societies which are constantly being born and dying inside the
framework of the university. They still continue, I am glad to say, and I
know that he too would be glad.

This particular society was called the Apennines. Its invitation card
displayed a range of mountains, and there was also a pun involved,
upon which I will not expatiate. I had to read a paper to the Apennines,
then I was pulled to pieces, and among my critics was a quiet, dark
young man with a charming voice and manner, who sat rather far back
in the room, and who for all his gentleness knew exactly what he
wanted to say, and in the end how to say it. That was my first
impression of him, and I may say it is my last impression also. The
young man became an old one and a famous one, but he remained

charming and gentle, he always knew his own mind, and he always sat rather far back in the room. Compare him in this respect with that trenchant critic Mr So-and-So, or with that chatty columnist Sir Somebody Something, who always manage to sit well in front. I do not think it was modesty on Desmond's part that made him retiring. He just knew where he wanted to be. Some years after the Apennines, when he was doing literary journalism, he chose for a pseudonym the name 'Affable Hawk'. Nothing could have been more apt. He was affable to his fellow writers, whenever possible. But if a book was shallow or bumptious or brutal, then down pounced the hawk, and the victim's feathers flew.

He and I were always friendly and I stayed with him in Suffolk in those far-off days, and elsewhere later on, but all my vivid memories of him are in a group with other people. So let us now move from Cambridge to London. There, in the early years of this century, I remember a peculiar organization which had been formed for the purpose of making Desmond write his novel. He wanted to write his novel. He could talk his novel – character, plot, incidents, all were fascinating: I recall a green valley in Wales where a famous picture had got hidden. But he could not get his novel on to paper. So some of his friends thought that if a society was formed at which we all wrote novels and read a fresh chapter aloud at each meeting, Desmond would be reluctantly dragged down the path of creation. Needless to say, he eluded so crude a device. Other people wrote their novels – which usually began well and fell to bits in the second chapter. He – he had forgotten, he had mislaid the manuscript, he had not the time. And he did not write his novel. And after the First World War the group was reconstituted: not to write novels but to write reminiscences.

Here Desmond was supreme. 'Memory', he often said, 'is an excellent compositor'. And in the midst of a group which included Lytton Strachey, Virginia Woolf, and Maynard Keynes, he stood out in his command of the past, and in his power to rearrange it. I remember one paper of his in particular – if it can be called a paper. Perched away in a corner of Duncan Grant's studio, he had a suit-case open before him. The lid of the case, which he propped up, would be useful to rest his manuscript upon, he told us. On he read, delighting us as usual, with his brilliancy, and humanity, and wisdom, until – owing to a slight wave of his hand – the suit-case unfortunately fell over. Nothing was inside it. There was no paper. He had been improvising.

Desmond MacCarthy by Leonard Woolf

Reprinted from Leonard Woolf, Beginning Again: An Autobiography of
the Years 1911–1918 *(London, The Hogarth Press, 1964), 135–41,
142, 143, by permission of the author's literary estate and the Hogarth
Press;* © *1963, 1964, by Leonard Woolf and reprinted by permission of
Harcourt Brace Jovanovich, Inc.*

[Leonard Woolf's analysis of Desmond MacCarthy is taken from the
third volume of Woolf's autobiography. Along with the description of
MacCarthy in Virginia Woolf's diary that is included here, these
memories set forth MacCarthy's brilliant promise – he was 'the most
gifted of us all' according to Virginia Woolf – and disappointing
achievement.]

. . . It is true that Desmond did look like a dishevelled bird when he was
middle-aged, and he knew it himself – hence his characteristic pen
name Affable Hawk. But when I first saw Desmond – he was
twenty-six and just returned from a Grand Tour of Europe – there was
nothing of the dishevelled fledgling fallen from the nest about him; he
looked like a superb young eagle who with one sweep of his great wing
could soar to any height he chose. He not only looked it; the good
fairies had lavished upon him every possible gift and particularly those
gifts which every would-be writer and novelist would pray for. Why did
he never fulfil his promises? Why did the splendid eagle degenerate into
an affable hawk, a dishevelled fledgling? . . .

. . . The human being is psychologically so infuriatingly complex
that you can never explain his thoughts, actions, or character by
trotting out a single superficial cause. One of the difficulties is that in
the human mind the same element is at the same time both a cause
and an effect. Thus in the case of Desmond it is probably true to say
that 'his special gift of conversation' was a cause of his not writing
novels, but it is also true that (1) it was an *excuse* for his not writing
novels, and (2) his not writing novels was a cause of his special gift
for conversation. One summer Desmond came to stay for a few days
with us in the country at Asham House. He was slightly depressed
when he arrived and soon told us the reason. His friend A.F.
Wedgwood, the novelist, had recently died leaving a posthumous
novel and Desmond had promised the widow to write an introduction
and memoir of the author for the book. He had continually put off
doing this; the book had been printed, was ready for binding, and

was completely held up for Desmond's introduction; the publisher
was desperate and desperately bombarding Desmond with reply paid
telegrams. Desmond had sworn that he would write the thing over
the week-end and post it to the publisher on Monday morning. He
asked me to promise that next morning I would lock him up in a
room by himself and not let him out until he had finished the
introduction. And he told me then that he really suffered from a
disease: the moment he knew that he ought to do something, no
matter what that something was, he felt absolutely unable to do it
and would do anything else in order to prevent himself from doing it.
It did not matter what 'it' might be; it might be something which he
actually wanted to do, but if it was also something which he knew he
ought to do, he would find himself doing something which he did
not want to do in order to prevent himself doing something which he
ought to do and wanted to do.

Here for instance was a fairly common situation in Desmond's life:
he is engaged to dine at 7.30 with someone whom he likes very much in
Chelsea; he looks forward to the evening; at 7 he is sitting in a room at
the other end of London talking to two or three people whom he does
not very much like and who are in fact boring him; at 7.5 he begins to
feel that he ought to get up and leave for Chelsea; at 7.30 he is still
sitting with the people whom he does not much like and is
uncomfortably keeping them from their dinner; at 8 they insist that he
must stay and dine with them; at 8.5 he rings up his Chelsea friends,
apologizes, and says that he will be with them in 20 minutes.

I should add that that evening at Asham Desmond recovered his
spirits and was in fine form. After we had gone to bed, we heard him
for a short time walking up and down the corridor groaning: 'O God!
God!' Next morning he was quite cheerful when I locked him in the
sitting room. An hour later he thumped on the door and shouted: 'You
must let me out, Leonard, you must let me out.' He had run out of
cigarettes and I weakly let him out so that he could walk over to
Rodmell, a mile away, and buy some at the village shop. I cannot
remember whether when he left us on Monday or Tuesday morning, he
had finished the introduction. I rather think he had not.

Now one of the several reasons why Desmond never fulfilled his
youthful aquiline promise and never wrote that brilliant novel which in
1903 lay embryonically in his mind was that he thought that he *ought*
to write a novel and that the novel *ought* to be absolutely first class.
Desmond was in many ways Moore's favourite apostle and Desmond
loved and followed Moore with the purity and intensity of the disciple

devoted to the guru or sage. He, as an impressionable young man, like all of us in the Cambridge of those days, took *Principia Ethica* as a bible of conduct. In *Sowing*, [see pp.98–109] I tried to describe and define this influence of Moore and his book upon us. The book told us what we *ought* to do and what we ought not to do, and, when one thought of those words, it was impossible not to see and hear Moore himself, the impassioned shake of his head on the emphasized words as he said: 'I think one *ought* to do that,' or 'I think one ought *not* to do that.' So when Desmond sat down to write, an invisible Moore, with the 'oughts' and 'ought nots', stood behind his chair. But both as a man and a writer his gifts were of a lyrical kind; they had to be given a free hand; his imagination would not work and so he could not write on a tight, intellectual rein.

The best, said the Greeks, is the enemy of the good. The vision of the best, the ghostly echoes of *Principia Ethica*, the catechism which always begins with the terrifying words: 'What exactly do you *mean* by *that*?,' inhibited Desmond. When he wrote 'seriously', he began to labour, and the more he tinkered with what he wrote the more laboured and laborious it became. This brings me back to the point from which I started, the effect of journalism upon Desmond and writers like him. Journalism provided him with the easy way out of his difficult and complicated situation as regards writing a novel. He thought that he ought to write a novel – something serious – and as the habit grew upon him of not being able to do what he thought he ought to do, the habit of always doing something else in order to avoid doing what he ought to do, writing the weekly article for the *New Statesman* or *Sunday Times* became his refuge and shelter from his duty to be a great writer. (Of course, there was the further stage that, when the moment came at which he *ought* to begin writing the article, he had to find something else to prevent his doing so, and it was only a devoted and efficient secretary who managed somehow or other to get Affable Hawk's article, usually a few minutes after the very last moment, to an infuriated printer.)

But writing an article as a refuge for Desmond against doing what he thought he ought to do, *i.e.* writing a novel, was only part of the story. In literature he had tremendously high standards, and, if he had ever been inclined to lower them, the memories of Cambridge, Moore, and *Principia Ethica* would have warned him off. To write a book, say a novel, as a serious artist, requires a good many qualities, by no means common, besides the ability to write. However sensitive you may be to praise or blame, you have to be at some point ruthless and impervious — and ruthless to yourself. The moment comes when the writer must say to himself: 'I don't care what they say about it and me; I shall publish and be damned to them.' And he has to accept responsibility, the responsibility for what he has written; he must strip himself artistically naked before the public and take the icy plunge. People like Desmond, once they begin to doubt whether what they are writing is really any good — and such doubts occasionally torture practically all good writers — cannot stay the course. They cannot force themselves through those despairing moments of grind in the long distance race before you get your second wind and they cannot face responsibility. Here again journalism is the refuge. Even *Principia Ethica* would allow one to lower one's standards in the *Sunday Times* or *New Statesman*, where one is writing not *sub specie aeternitatis*, but for a short week-end. And in any case the responsibility is not so much yours as the editor's. Journalism is the opiate of the artist; eventually it poisons his mind and his art.

Off and on over the years I saw a good deal of Desmond, walking and talking with him at all hours of day and night, watching him try to write and even occasionally working with him. I am sure that his psychology as a writer was more or less that analyzed by me in the previous paragraphs. One can only add that the charm of the dead cannot be reproduced second-hand in words. One can only record the fact that Desmond was the most charming of men, the most amusing companion, and finally had about him in friendship the honesty and faithfulness which I associate with old sheep dogs.

When I had written this, I remembered that Virginia had once in her diaries, when after being ill she was for a time only able to write her novel for an hour a day, amused herself by writing short accounts of her friends' characters. I turned up what she had written about Desmond and this is what she said in January 1919:

How many friends have I got? There's Lytton, Desmond, Saxon: they belong to the Cambridge stage of life; very intellectual . . . I can't put them in order, for there are too many. Ka and Rupert and Duncan, for example, all come rather later . . . Desmond has *not* rung up. That is quite a good preface to the description of his character. The difficulty which faces one in writing of Desmond is that one is almost forced to describe an Irishman. How he misses trains, seems born without a rudder to drift wherever the current is strongest; how he keeps hoping and planning, and shuffles along,

paying his way by talking so enchantingly that editors forgive and
shopmen give him credit and at least one distinguished peer leaves
him a thousand in his will . . . Where was I? Desmond, and how I
find him sympathetic compared with Stracheys. It is true; I'm not
sure he hasn't the nicest nature of any of us – the nature one would
soonest have chosen for one's own. I don't think that he possesses
any faults as a friend, save that his friendship is so often sunk under
a cloud of vagueness, a sort of drifting vapour composed of times
and seasons separates us and effectively prevents us from meeting.
Perhaps such indolence implies a slackness of fibre in his affections
too – but I scarcely feel that. It arises rather from the consciousness
which I find imaginative and attractive that things don't altogether
matter. Somehow he is fundamentally sceptical. Yet which of us,
after all, takes more trouble to do the sort of kindness that comes
his way? Who is more tolerant, more appreciative, more understanding of human nature? It goes without saying that he is not an
heroic character. He finds pleasure too pleasant, cushions too soft,
dallying too seductive and then as I sometimes feel now, he has
ceased to be ambitious. His 'great work' (it may be philosophy or
biography now, and is certainly to be begun, after a series of long
walks, this very spring) only takes shape, I believe, in that hour
between tea and dinner, when so many things appear not only
possible, but achieved. Comes the daylight, and Desmond is
contented to begin his article; and plies his pen with a half humorous
half melancholy recognition that such is his appointed life. Yet it is
true, and no one can deny it, that he has the floating elements of
something brilliant, beautiful – some book of stories, reflection,
studies, scattered about in him, for they show themselves indisputably in his talk. I'm told he wants power; that these fragments
never combine into an argument; that the disconnection of talk is
kind to them; but in a book they would drift hopelessly apart.
Consciousness of this, no doubt, led him in his one finished book to
drudge and sweat until his fragments were clamped together in an
indissoluble stodge. I can see myself, however, going through his
desk one of these days, shaking out unfinished pages from between
sheets of blotting paper, and deposits of old bills, and making up a
short book of table talk, which shall appear as a proof to the
younger generation that Desmond was the most gifted of us all. But
why did he never do anything? they will ask.

. . . His wife Molly was . . . charming, amusing; hesitant, and unsure of herself . . . She was one of those people whose minds go blank the moment they are faced by the slightest crisis; her vagueness and fluttering indecision must have been perpetually nourished by a life-time of waiting for Desmond to return to dinner to which he had forgotten that he had invited several friends . . .

The last time I saw him, not long before he died, I walked away with him from the house in Gordon Square where we had had a Memoir Club meeting. It was 11 o'clock and a cold autumn night. He was suffering terribly from asthma and was racked by a sudden fit of it as we turned out of the Square. I made him wait while I ran off to find him a taxi. When I put him into the taxi, he looked, not like an affable hawk or even a dishevelled fledgling, but like a battered, shattered, dying rook. At the corner of Gordon Square I suddenly saw him again as a young man walking with me on the hills above Hunter's Inn in Devonshire when we were on an Easter 'reading party' with Moore and Lytton. There are few things more terrible than such sudden visions of one's friends in youth and vigour through the miseries of age and illness. I left Desmond sitting in the taxi, affectionate, dejected, unheroic, because so obviously broken and beaten by asthma and by life; but brave in not complaining and not pretending and in still, when he could, making his joke and his phrase . . .

E.M. Forster by David Garnett

*Reprinted from David Garnett, 'Forster and Bloomsbury', A*spects of E.M. Forster, *ed. Oliver Stallybrass (London, Edward Arnold, 1969), 29–35, by permission of Edward Arnold, Ltd.*

[David Garnett's essay 'Forster and Bloomsbury' first appeared in *Aspects of E.M. Forster*, an aptly titled collection presented to Forster on his ninetieth birthday. The aspect of Forster that Garnett sees in Bloomsbury should lay forever the ghost of the question as to whether or not Forster was a member of the Bloomsbury Group.]

'We did not see much of Forster at that time; who was already the elusive colt of a dark horse,' Lord Keynes wrote[1] of the years about 1902 when he was forming his early beliefs, based on the philosophy of G.E. Moore and the discussions in the Society, otherwise known as the

Apostles. Leonard Woolf lists the active Moorists as Maynard Keynes, Lytton Strachey, Saxon Sydney-Turner, Thoby Stephen and himself, 'and at varying distances from the centre Clive Bell, J.T. Sheppard, R.G. Hawtrey and A.R. Ainsworth orbiting at some distance beyond'. 'Forster and Desmond MacCarthy,' he adds, 'moved erratically in and out of this solar system of intellectual friendship, like comets.'[2]

The explanation of Morgan Forster's making only occasional appearances was the difference in age, which is never more important than at school or the university. He was four years older than Maynard Keynes and had gone down from Cambridge in 1901, two years before the Moorist revelation was most influential. (*Principia Ethica* was not published till 1903.) Forster would revisit Cambridge for a meeting of the Society, and, more important to him, to see Goldsworthy Lowes Dickinson, and then vanish.

Forster's friendships with Nathaniel Wedd and Dickinson were far more formative than those with any of the younger men. He must have met Moore occasionally, but he only got to know him well towards the end of Moore's life; and I have been told that Ainsworth, rather than Moore, is the model for Stewart Ansell, the young philosopher in *The Longest Journey*. Wilfred Stone has said that no one ever called Forster a Moorist, though Henry James got the two men mixed up.[3] Yet the two fundamental tenets of *Principia Ethica* underlie much of Forster's writing. By these I mean that what matter are states of mind, not necessarily associated with action, and that since it is impossible to calculate the final effects of any act one must only take into account the immediate result: thus a brutal or a barbarous action can never be justified because of its possible long-term results. Forster applies this not only to such acts as the bombing of a foreign country but to every form of unkindness.

Artists, in which term I include imaginative writers, reflect a climate of opinion rather than devote themselves to ethical propaganda; and it is the climate of opinion which Forster absorbed at Cambridge from Dickinson and his friends in the Society that one finds expressed with such subtlety in the novels.

No one has questioned that the Cambridge which produced that climate of opinion existed. But when the young men from Cambridge went to London, got married, or set up house there, did they form 'Bloomsbury'? Clive Bell denied that it ever existed. But whether he was right or wrong, it has been invented, worshipped by some and abominated by others. If there was a Bloomsbury, it certainly centred round No 46 Gordon Square, the house in which Clive Bell and Vanessa

Stephen went to live after their marriage. It is arguable that the factor which distinguished the group in Cambridge after they moved to London was not a matter of space and time but the presence of two women, the daughters of Sir Leslie Stephen, Vanessa and Virginia. There is truth in Cyril Connolly's recent description of Bloomsbury as a 'milieu which is more intense, more spacious and more loving [than our own]. Bloomsbury was such a society, matriarchal despite the brilliance of the courtiers, and at the centre of the maze sat the unwobbling pivot, Vanessa Bell.'[4]

Friendships formed at the university often fall apart as life brings new experiences and interests. Work absorbs and scatters groups of friends. This did not happen to the 'Bloomsburies', for several reasons. Most of them were heretics who did not accept conventional standards of art, literature, morals or ethics. They were men and women with strong intellectual interests and great originality. They were, moreover, attached to and interested in each other. These facts kept them together. And then Clive Bell was extremely hospitable.

Of the others, Virginia and her brother Adrian Stephen set up house together in Brunswick Square. Maynard Keynes, Duncan Grant and Gerald Shove took rooms in it. The whole group went to the opera, to the ballet, they gave parties and had play-readings and played poker far into the night. Naturally changes took place as the years went by. Virginia married Leonard Woolf and they had various homes, moving out to Richmond and back to Bloomsbury; Adrian Stephen married and came to live in No 51 Gordon Square; the Strachey family left Hampstead and took No 50 next door; James Strachey married and took No 41 Gordon Square. Maynard Keynes married and took over the lease of No 46. Clive took a flat at the top of Adrian's house and Vanessa took a lease of No 37. Roger Fry went to live in Bernard Street, and Morgan Forster had a *pied-à-terre* in my mother-in-law's house, No 27 Brunswick Square. It was of this period that Leonard Woolf writes: 'It was not until Lytton Strachey, Roger Fry and Morgan Forster came into the locality, so that we were all continually meeting one another, that our society became complete.'[5]

Yet Morgan Forster was on the periphery rather than at the heart of this circle. I would not describe his visits as sudden and comet-like, blazing through the solar system. He seemed to turn up when something interesting was occurring; and he himself was always interesting. The elusiveness that Maynard Keynes notes is very characteristic, and was made more noticeable by the fact that for many years, just as the party was warming up, he had to catch a train back to

Weybridge. He was more like the Cheshire Cat than a comet.

The friendship that originally brought him into Bloomsbury was that with Leonard Woolf. He had known Leonard before the latter went to Ceylon, and the friendship grew after his return. Forster had met Virginia before her marriage, but his friendship with her, based largely on their both being professional writers, only grew close because she and Leonard were a couple usually seen together. For Morgan Forster, Leonard Woolf was a practical man whose advice and help he was anxious to get in any difficulty.

When, at the beginning of 1921, he was invited to go out to India as temporary private secretary to the Maharajah of Dewas Senior, Forster thought that he ought to be able to ride a horse. He consulted Leonard and asked him to give him lessons. Leonard agreed and lessons took place at Richmond. Morgan shared the trust that so many people, particularly the young and the simple, and all animals feel for Leonard. But, if he sought Leonard's advice, Virginia came to respect and depend on his criticism and good opinion of her writing more than on that of Lytton Strachey or Clive Bell or Roger Fry. His importance to her is best described in the following passage from her diary, written after a visit by Forster to Hogarth House and a walk along the banks of the Thames:

> We talked very rarely, the proof being that we (I anyhow) did not mind silences. Morgan has the artist's mind; he says the simple things that clever people don't say; I find him the best of critics for that reason. Suddenly out comes the obvious thing that one has overlooked. He is in trouble with a novel of his own. . .[6]

It was not a one-way traffic: Morgan's value to Virginia was repaid by Leonard. After his return from India, he showed Leonard the unfinished manuscript of *A Passage to India* which he had abandoned in despair. Leonard pronounced it a great work and urged him to finish it. Moreover, his consciousness of the Bloomsbury audience consisting of his friends, Virginia and Leonard, Clive, Lytton, Maynard, and Roger had, I suspect, a restraining influence on his vein of fantasy. At the time of the early novels – 1905 to 1910, when Bloomsbury was only just coming into existence – Edward Garnett had influenced him far more than the Stracheys or Stephens ever did. In these novels and in the stories Pan, satyrs and dryads sometimes make their appearance and are always present in the wings. Even in *Howards End* there are pigs' teeth in the wych-elm. Edward Garnett had told him that these sublimations or symbolisations of sex were often out of key and unconvincing, and Bloomsbury later reinforced his judgement. Morgan Forster himself recalls that ' "The Point of It" was ill-liked when it came out by my Bloomsbury friends. "What *is* the point of it?" they queried thinly, nor did I know how to reply' *(Collected Short Stories,* vii). It is possible that without this restraining influence the immanent spirit in the Marabar caves might have become an overt presence, disastrous to the credibility of *A Passage to India.*

If Morgan Forster sought the aid of Leonard as a practical man, the situation was sometimes reversed in his relations with Lytton Strachey. In September 1915, at the end of Lytton's tenancy of Hilton Young's cottage in Wiltshire, Morgan not only helped him to pack up all his possessions, but undertook to see them safely delivered to the Strachey home in Belsize Park Gardens while Lytton went off on a round of visits. At the beginning of the friendship Morgan and Lytton had been rather shy of one another, but understanding and affection grew after the war and until Lytton's death. It was founded, not on admiration of each other's work, but on shared jokes and sympathetic appreciation of each other's attitude to life.

Another early acquaintance which grew into friendship with the years was that with Roger Fry. Their friendship was enhanced by their interest in Charles Mauron, the French writer on aesthetics who later translated *A Passage to India.*

The first time that I met Forster in Bloomsbury was at a party given by Lady Ottoline Morrell in Bedford Square. The next day, going to Duncan Grant's studio at the top of No 22 Fitzroy Street, I found Forster sitting there. Then the bell sounded and I ran down and admitted D.H. Lawrence and Frieda, who had also come to look at Duncan's pictures. Forster was, I think, interested to meet Lawrence again, but after one or two pictures had been set up on the easel Lawrence began a didactic harangue, and an expression of pain came into Morgan's face. I have often noticed him wince when someone has said something brutal or insensitive. Usually it is only for a moment as he braces himself to face the harshness of the outside world. But as Lawrence launched himself on a denunciation of the evil that he discovered in Duncan's paintings the look of pain was replaced by one of pure misery, and very soon he murmured something about a train to Weybridge and disappeared.

Though the wince of pain is one of my most vivid memories of Morgan Forster, the delighted appreciation of a remark which had pleased him is a more frequent memory. His broad, rather heart-shaped face would light up, the eyes would sparkle and a sort of suppressed sneeze which became a surreptitious laugh would reveal how greatly he had been pleased and amused. It was a pleasure that was almost anguish. I have most often witnessed this reaction at readings of the Memoir Club. Sometimes a preliminary look of pain would be followed by the little sneeze of joy when he listened to the inspired gossip which was characteristic of Bloomsbury – gossip which its chroniclers stigmatize as malicious, but which was actually the result of an almost gourmet-like love of the foibles of old and intimate friends. What would be malicious if told about a stranger or a slight acquaintance may be free of malice if told about a loved one. Such were the anecdotes at the expense of Vanessa and Duncan and Roger Fry. And rich and varied they were.

I myself saw most of Morgan Forster when I was a bookseller and he did more than anyone in Bloomsbury, or outside it, to help Francis Birrell and me make our shop pay its way.

He was not at that time the world-renowned author he has become. One of his introductions led to our supplying the state of Hyderabad with educational books, another to our equipping Palestine with terrestrial globes. A recommendation from him got me a job as a reviewer on the *Daily Herald* at a time when I was very hard up. After I became an author he recommended a book of mine to a Danish lady who translated it. For all these considerate and generous acts I have always been grateful. But the greatest gift was to feel that one was liked, and the greatest pleasure to watch his face light up with appreciation or approval of something one had said and to provoke the little sneeze of anguished, slightly surreptitious, laughter.

Laughter was omnipresent in Bloomsbury, but how different were its individual tones. Clive had a loud uncontrolled guffaw that did one's heart good, Virginia a sudden bird-like crow. Lytton's laughter took many forms to match the wide range of his feelings which it expressed. Leonard's and Vanessa's were often reluctant. But Morgan's appreciative, anguished, but always critical laughter is the most abiding memory I have of him among his friends in Bloomsbury.

Notes

1. *Two Memoirs* [see p.52].
2. *Sowing* (Hogarth Press, London, 1960), p. 171.
3. Wilfred Stone, *The Cave and the Mountain: A Study of E.M.*

Forster (1966) pp.65–6; and E.M. Forster, 'Henry James and the Young Men', *The Listener* LXII (1959) 103.

4. Review of *Lytton Strachey: a Critical Biography*, vol. 2, by Michael Holroyd, in *Sunday Times Weekly Review*, 25 Feb. 1968, p. 51.

5. *Downhill All the Way* [see p.123].

6. *A Writer's Diary* (Hogarth Press, London, 1953), p. 21.

Vanessa Bell by Virginia Woolf

Reprinted from Recent Paintings by Vanessa Bell, *with a Foreword by Virginia Woolf (The London Artists' Association), February 4th to March 8th, 1930, quoted by permission of Professor Quentin Bell.*

[Although she has been described as the unwobbling pivot at the centre of the Bloomsbury maze (see p.165), Vanessa remains among the more mysterious of the Bloomsberries. Her son Julian Bell described her as follows:

> And one, my best, with such a calm of mind,
> And, I have thought, with clear experience
> Of what is felt of waste, confusion, pain,
> Faced with a strong good sense, stubborn and plain;
> Patient and sensitive, cynic and kind.
>
> The sensuous mind within preoccupied
> By lucid vision of form and colour and space,
> The careful hand and eye, and where resides
> An intellectual landscape's living face,
> Oh certitude of mind and sense, and where
> Native I love, and feel accustomed air.

But Julian also said the lines could be applied to Roger Fry as well as to his mother.

In 1930 Virginia Woolf wrote a foreword to the catalogue of an exhibition of her sister's paintings. In her appreciation of Vanessa's work can be glimpsed also an appreciation of the sensibility and the stability on which Bloomsbury in general and Virginia in particular depended. (See also pp.173–7 for Angelica Garnett's comparison of Vanessa and Virginia.)]

That a woman should hold a show of pictures in Bond Street, I said, pausing upon the threshold of Messrs Cooling's gallery, is not usual, nor, perhaps, altogether to be commended. For it implies, I fancy, some study of the nude, and while for many ages it has been admitted that women are naked and bring nakedness to birth, it was held, until sixty years ago that for a woman to look upon nakedness with the eye of an artist, and not simply with the eye of mother, wife or mistress was corruptive of her innocency and destructive of her domesticity. Hence the extreme activity of women in philanthropy, society, religion and all pursuits requiring clothing.

Hence again the fact that every Victorian family has in its cupboard the skeleton of an aunt who was driven to convert the native because her father would have died rather than let her look upon a naked man. And so she went to Church; and so she went to China; and so she died unwed; and so there drop out of the cupboard with her bones half a dozen flower pieces done under the shade of a white umbrella in a Surrey garden when Queen Victoria was on the throne.

These reflections are only worth recording because they indicate the vacillations and prevarications (if one is not a painter or a critic of painting) with which one catches at any straw that will put off the evil moment when one must go into the gallery and make up one's mind about pictures. Were it not that Mrs Bell has a certain reputation and is sometimes the theme of argument at dinner tables, many no doubt would stroll up Bond Street, past Messrs Cooling's, thinking about morality or politics, about grandfathers or great aunts, about anything but pictures as is the way of the English.

But Mrs Bell has a certain reputation it cannot be denied. She is a woman, it is said, yet she has looked on nakedness with a brush in her hand. She is reported (one has read it in the newspapers) to be 'the most considerable painter of her own sex now alive'. Berthe Morisot, Marie Laurencin, Vanessa Bell — such is the stereotyped phrase which comes to mind when her name is mentioned and makes one's predicament in front of her pictures all the more exacting. For whatever the phrase may mean, it must mean that her pictures stand for something, are something and will be something which we shall disregard at our peril. As soon not go to see them as shut the window when the nightingale is singing.

But once inside and surrounded by canvases, this shillyshallying on the threshold seems superfluous. What is there here to intimidate or perplex? Are we not suffused, lit up, caught in a sunny glow? Does there not radiate from the walls a serene yet temperate warmth, comfortable in the extreme after the rigours of the streets? Are we not surrounded by vineyards and olive trees, by naked girls couched on crimson cushions, by naked boys ankle deep in the pale green sea? Even the puritans of the nineteenth century might grant us a moment's respite from the February murk, a moment's liberty in this serene and ordered world. But it is not the puritans who move us on. It is Mrs Bell. It is Mrs Bell who is determined that we shall not loll about juggling with pretty words or dallying with delicious sensations. There is something uncompromising about her art. Ninety-nine painters had nature given them her susceptibility, her sense of the lustre of grass and flower, of the glow of rock and tree, would have lured us on by one refinement and felicity after another to stay and look for ever. Ninety-nine painters again had they possessed that sense of satire which seems to flash its laughter for a moment at those women in Dieppe in the eighties, would have caricatured and illustrated; would have drawn our attention to the antics of parrots, the pathos of old umbrellas, the archness of ankles, the eccentricities of noses. Something would have been done to gratify the common, innocent and indeed very valuable gift which has produced in England so rich a library of fiction. But look round the room: the approach to these pictures is not by that means. No stories are told; no insinuations are made. The hill side is bare; the group of women is silent; the little boy stands in the sea saying nothing. If portraits there are, they are pictures of flesh which happens from its texture or its modelling to be aesthetically on an equality with the China pot or the chrysanthemum.

Checked at that point in our approach (and the snub is none the less baffling for the beauty with which it is conveyed) one can perhaps draw close from another angle. Let us see if we can come at some idea of Mrs Bell herself and by thus trespassing, crack the kernel of her art. Certainly it would hardly be possible to read as many novels as there are pictures here without feeling our way psychologically over the features of the writer; and the method, if illicit, has its value. But here, for a second time, we are rebuffed. One says, Anyhow Mrs Bell is a woman; and then half way round the room one says, But she may be a man. One says, She is interested in children; one has to add, But she is equally interested in rocks. One asks, Does she show any special knowledge of clothes? One replies, Stark nakedness seems to please her as well. Is she dainty then, or austere? Does she like riding? Is she red haired or brown eyed? Was she ever at a university? Does she prefer herrings or Brussels sprouts? Is she – for our patience is becoming exhausted – not a woman at all, but a mixture of Goddess and peasant, treading the clouds with her feet and with her hands shelling peas? Any writer so ardently questioned would have yielded something to our curiosity. One defies a novelist to keep his life through twenty-seven volumes of fiction safe from our scrutiny. But Mrs Bell says nothing. Mrs Bell is as silent as the grave. Her pictures do not betray her. Their reticence is inviolable. That is why they intrigue and draw us on; that is why, if it be true that they yield their full meaning only to those who can tunnel their way behind the canvas into masses and passages and relations and values of which we know nothing – if it be true that she is a painter's painter – still her pictures claim us and make us stop. They give us an emotion. They offer a puzzle.

And the puzzle is that while Mrs Bell's pictures are immensely expressive, their expressiveness has no truck with words. Her vision excites a strong emotion and yet when we have dramatised it or poetised it or translated it into all the blues and greens, and fines and exquisites and subtles of our vocabulary, the picture itself escapes. It goes on saying something of its own. A good example is to be found in the painting of the Foundling Hospital. Here one says, is the fine old building which has housed a million orphans; here Hogarth painted and kind hearted Thackeray shed a tear, here Dickens, who lived down the street on the left-hand side, must often have paused in his walk to watch the children at play. And it is all gone, all perished. House breakers have been at work, speculators have speculated. It is dust and ashes – but what has Mrs Bell got to say about it? Nothing. There is the picture, serene and sunny, and very still. It represents a fine eighteenth century house and an equally fine London plane tree. But there are no orphans, no Thackeray, no Dickens, no housebreakers, no speculators, no tears, no sense that this sunny day is perhaps the last. Our emotion has been given the slip.

And yet somehow our emotion has been returned to us. For emotion there is. The room is charged with it. There is emotion in that white urn; in that little girl painting a picture; in the flowers and the bust; in the olive trees; in the provençal vineyard; in the English hills against the sky. Here, we cannot doubt as we look is somebody to whom the visible world has given a shock of emotion every day of the week. And she transmits it and makes us share it; but it is always by her means, in her language, with her susceptibility, and not ours. That is why she is so tantalising, so original, and so satisfying as a painter. One feels that if a canvas of hers hung on the wall it would never lose its lustre. It would never mix itself up with the loquacities and trivialities of daily life. It would go on saying something of its own imperturbably.

And perhaps by degrees – who knows? – one would become an inmate of this strange painters' world, in which mortality does not enter, and psychology is held at bay, and there are no words. But is morality to be found there? That was the very question I was asking myself as I came in.

Vanessa Bell by Angelica Garnett

Reprinted from Recollections of Virginia Woolf, *ed. Joan Russell Noble (London, Peter Owen, 1972) 83–8, by permission of the publisher and the author; © 1972 by Joan Russell Noble and reprinted by permission of William Morrow & Co., New York.*

[In 1910 Sydney Waterlow wrote in his diary, 'Dined with the Clive Bells. . . No one else but Virginia S[tephen]. We had talk that begins to be really intimate. Vanessa very amusing on pederasty among their circle. I realize for the first time the difference between her and Virginia. Vanessa icy, cynical, artistic, Virginia much more emotional, and interested in life rather than beauty'. Angelica Garnett's recently written comparison of her mother and her aunt was originally done for a book of recollections about Virginia Woolf, but it is as much about Vanessa as Virginia and goes far beyond Waterlow's early, tentative observations. The complementarity of the sisters that is so evocatively set forth here by Mrs Garnett appears to have been an indispensable condition for the existence, survival, and success of the Group.]

Asked to write about Virginia, the best approach seems to be through my mother Vanessa. These two Vs, angular and ambiguous, undecided whether to symbolize V or U. Both sisters started life with the same initials, V.S., then one changed to V.W., a variant on the original, the other to V.B., a round and solid addition. When I see V.B. on the registration plate of a car it immediately causes me a tremor of recognition. V.W. never seems to occur in such places.

Vanessa was the more practical, the more solid, the earthier of the two sisters. Virginia always said so, and the difference must have been marked even when they were young. Vanessa was the elder, a social success, married first and had children. She could mix colours, stretch canvases, cook meals and deal with unpalatable situations. She had a feminine capacity for listening tolerantly to the arguments and ideas of

the men they both knew. This made a special place for her in the heart
of Bloomsbury. Men from college, used to the freedom of masculine
society or the polite and inconsequential chatter of their mothers and
sisters, found it delightful to be listened to by a madonna with a sense
of humour – a little wild perhaps and original, a little *sans façons* –
how piquant it was and, in the end, how restful to be surrounded by a
feminine atmosphere without the false obligations created by convention.

Virginia, on the contrary, was shy and awkward, often silent or, if in
the mood to talk, would leap into fantasy and folly and terrify the
innocent and unprepared. This combination of limpid beauty and
demon's tongue proved fatal to those who were too timid to respond
and who, ensnared while unconscious, woke like Bottom to find
themselves in a fairyland echoing with malicious laughter.

Virginia remained always capable of demolishing the unwary: it was
too easy for her, and it was a temptation that sometimes proved
irresistible. Like many people who make inordinate demands, Virginia
also had much to give; if she sometimes wounded her friends they
forgave her and came back to her for her quality, the purity of which
fascinated so many different people. It was like a diamond stream of
water, hard and scintillating, transparent, bubbling, austere and
life-giving.

When I knew her best, age and experience had softened her and lit
her with a more tender light. She always looked vulnerable – those
shadowy temples over which stretched a transparent skin showing
threads of blue; the wrinkled waves of her high, narrow forehead; the
taughtness of those sardonic lips pulled downwards at the corner; her
bladed nose, like the breastbone of a bird or the wing of a bat,
surmounted by deeply hooded melancholy grey-green eyes. She had the
worn beauty of a hare's paw.

Like all the Stephens she was sad in repose – it seemed their most
natural attitude – and yet the slightest ripple round her would cause a
lightning-flicker in her eye, a flare of sympathy and intelligence. She
was a great teaser and a shameless flatterer, avid for affection from
those she loved. She adored nicknames: calling Vanessa Dolphin, herself
Billy Goat or The Goat, I was Pixerina, Leonard was Leo – and so on.
Virginia invented an extra personality for us, a luxury which we
enjoyed but which half irritated, half amused, making us appear
wonderfully changed as in a fairground mirror.

Virginia's version of Vanessa tended to soar into the Olympic
regions, where she subconsciously felt that Nessa belonged. Like a

highly coloured transparency held over the original design, sometimes it corresponded, sometimes not. She magnified the importance of Vanessa's practical abilities out of all relation to reality. It was true that Virginia could not bring herself to mend her clothes and preferred to pin up her silk rags with a gold brooch; but she could cook, and bottle fruit – well do I remember the pride she took in her cupboard of jade-green gooseberries and sad-purple raspberries on the stairs at Monks House. She also had a gift for appearances: the interiors of her houses were cool and civilized, the colours muted but various. There was in them nothing planned or self-conscious, though she was discriminating in her choice of objects and furniture. Leonard said that she saw things in antique shops from the window of the car which were nearly always worth stopping for.

Vanessa's strength lay in her closeness to reality, to the everyday world. By comparison she was calm, like a pool on which the coloured leaves slowly change their pattern. She accepted, rather than protested; was passive, rather than avid. She did not care deeply about abstract ideas, and was led by her sensibilities rather than her intellect. In theory she supported rationalism, though her own acts were usually compulsive. She instinctively limited her life to the two things she cared for most: her painting and her family. The wider world seemed to her to threaten these two points, and she appeared to choose the limits of her affection and sympathies. Love, with her, was an exclusive rather than an inclusive emotion; there was a chosen circle round which was planted a high palisade that cast its shadow both on those without and those within.

To Virginia, I think, Vanessa seemed at times formidable, embodying the spirit of justice and authority inherited from her Stephen ancestors. Virginia danced round her like the dragon-fly round the water-lily, darting in to attack and soaring away before Vanessa could take action. Vanessa had a kind of stoical warmth about her, a monolithic quality that reminded one now of the implacable smile of primitive Aphrodite, now of the hollow wind-whistling statues of Erewhon. She sat and sewed or painted or listened; she was always sitting, sometimes at the head of the table, sometimes by the fire, sometimes under the apple tree. Even if she said little, there emanated from her an enormous power, a pungency like the smell of crushed sage. She presided, wise yet diffident, affectionate and a little remote, full of unquenchable spirit. Her feelings were strong, and words seemed to her inadequate. She was content to leave them to her sister and to continue painting. Virginia's attitude was far from sitting, it was

striding; long narrow thighs and shins in long tweed skirts, loping over
the Downs, across the water-meadows, beside the river, or through the
traffic in London, under the trees in the park and round the square. She
was never placid, never quite at rest. Even when, knees angular under
the lamp and cigarette in holder, she sat with a friend after tea, she
quivered with interest in the doings of other people.

Leonard kept Virginia on very short purse-strings, allowing her so
much pocket money a week. This she was free to spend as she chose,
though she referred to her dependence in teasing, bantering terms.
Since she had to count the shillings, she was more conscious of the
pleasure they could bring. She adored shopping as much as any child
and was ready to fall for the temptations of coloured string and
sealing-wax, notebooks and pencils. We would visit Kettle's shop in
New Oxford Street and supply ourselves with printed paper, glue and
paper-clips, and sniff the curious smell of dust and brown paper. It was
not unlike the smell of Virginia's writing-room in the basement of
Tavistock Square, where she sat by the gas fire, surrounded by parcels
of books and walls of paper. I did not go to see her there often. Usually
I went upstairs, where we amused ourselves by making paper dolls and
throwing lumps of sugar out of the window to the cart-horses.
Enormously generous, Virginia (when she became richer) would pile
presents on Vanessa and on me. As I grew older these took the form of
clothes, and the afternoons spent in this way were less happy. The shop
assistants made her feel shy and out of place, and she did not know
how to say that a dress did not suit me or what to do about it, so we
generally ended with some uneasy compromise relieved by the
knowledge that we would soon be going home to tea and Chelsea buns.

The two families, Bells and Woolfs, met frequently. In London they
saw each other on Sundays at Clive Bell's flat in Gordon Square; in the
summer there were week-end tea parties held either at Monks House or
at Charleston. There, if the weather was fine, tea was brought into the
garden. Nessa presided at a very low table, while Virginia and Clive
teased each other from the depths of Rorky chairs which squeaked
when they moved. Clive was relaxed and reflective, puffing his pipe
with pleasure, his clothes clean but old. Virginia often wore a hat, and
somehow combined elegance with angularity of movement. She seemed
more subdued, more observant at Charleston than at Monks House
where she herself was hostess. There we always had tea in the
dining-room which was sunk below the level of the garden, and dimly
green like a fish-pond. Indeed there was an aquarium in one corner
which I would stop to look at as Leonard's shaking hands scattered

ants' eggs for the fish to eat; they would swim lazily to the surface to swallow, reject and swallow again with apparent indifference. The plants on the window-sills cast a green light into the room, and through their interstices the legs and feet of late or unexpected visitors could be seen arriving. Here Virginia waved her cigarette with infectious excitement and embarked on fantasies which made us hilarious. We egged her on until Leonard punctured her sallies with a sardonic comment, or the flat statement that what she was saying was completely untrue. Then we would troop into the garden for the ritual game of bowls.

Apart from these family invasions the atmosphere of Monks House was concentrated, quiet and mysterious. Pen and ink replaced brushes and turpentine and there were no manual occupations, except for Leonard's gardening. Often when one arrived he would emerge from the bushes in shirt-sleeves, with clay on his boots and a pair of sécateurs in his hand. Then we would go together in search of Virginia, to be found reading in or near her garden-room under the chestnut trees by the churchyard. Their chief amusement was conversation, and many different kinds of people came and went; the house was like a sea-shell through which the water flows, leaving behind it a taste of salt.

There were many occasions when I went to see Virginia alone with Vanessa, and I amused myself while they enjoyed what they called a good old gossip. The intimacy of those occasions remains with me, and leads me to envy the relations between sisters. They understood each other perfectly and were probably at their best in each other's company. They were bound together by the past, and perhaps also by the feeling that they were opposite in temperament and that what one lacked she could find only in the other.

Lytton Strachey by Leonard Woolf

Reprinted from The New Statesman and Nation *(January 30, 1932), 118–9 by permission of* The New Statesman *and the author's literary estate.*

[The influence of Lytton Strachey on his contemporaries at Cambridge and in Edwardian Bloomsbury was considerable. According to Clive Bell, for example, it was Strachey who made history in Bloomsbury by writing to him on 25th November 1906, as 'Dear Clive'. 'It was at the time of my engagement to Vanessa Stephen that we took to Christian names, and it was entirely Lytton's doing. No question here of drifting into a habit, the proposal was made formally when he came to congratulate us. The practice became general. . . Henceforth between friends manners were to depend on feelings rather than conventions.' After the Bells and the Woolfs established themselves in Sussex and Lytton set up his own extraordinary Berkshire *ménage*, there was inevitably less interaction between Strachey and other Bloomsberries. It might almost be said that Strachey's influence on Bloomsbury was inversely proportional to his fame; the celebrated ironist of *Eminent Victorians* remained a close member of Bloomsbury, but a number of the Group felt that somehow he never completely fulfilled their high expectations.

If Leonard Woolf agreed with this criticism, there is no indication of it in his tribute to Strachey written just after his death. Woolf's account of Strachey, especially during their Cambridge years, should be compared with Bertrand Russell's much less favourable recollections (see pp.403—6).]

Many of those who have written about Lytton Strachey during the last week have said that as a writer he left a mark upon his age. No contemporary can be certain of his judgment as to the ultimate value in literature, biography, or history of *Eminent Victorians, Queen Victoria*, and *Elizabeth and Essex*, but the great effect and importance of these books during the last fourteen years are shown both by the admiration and the hostility which they have roused. I think that the most significant thing about Lytton Strachey both as a person and as a writer is that his writings came so directly from himself, from the very core of his character, that years before he had achieved anything or had become famous he was impinging (as he would have said himself) upon practically everyone with whom he came in contact in exactly the same way in which he impinged upon the reading public by his books. There were two reasons for this: first, the extreme individuality of his character, a character which united in a most fascinating way a whole series of pairs of contradictory qualities; secondly, an intellectual integrity which, when he was a young man, was extraordinarily violent and passionate.

When he came up to Trinity, Cambridge, in 1899, he knew and was known to none of his contemporaries. He had never been to a public school, and Walter Headlam, at King's, a fellow and much older than Strachey, must have been, I think, the only person in Cambridge who really knew anything about him. By the end of his first year he had already an intimate circle of friends and was recognized by many undergraduates and dons in Trinity and King's as a man of very remarkable character and powers. All through the time that he was in residence at Trinity his influence increased, and it is not an exaggeration to say that in the end it had become a dominating influence upon the intellectuals of his generation. And this domination did not end when technically he had 'gone down'. He still continued to spend a good deal of his time in Cambridge, and generations of undergraduates fell under his powerful spell. Its power extended even to the characteristic intonation of his voice, and when I visited Cambridge again after a long interval in 1911, it was amusing to find half the undergraduates at King's talking in what was called the Stracheyesque voice.

One reason for his immediate effect upon his generation was his astonishing maturity. When he arrived at Trinity in 1899 he already had intellectually the equipment which made it possible for him nineteen years later to write *Eminent Victorians* and combined with this intellectual maturity he had the fiery and violent intransigence of youth. With age and success he became extremely mellow and gentle; when a young man, his external demeanour was gentle and almost diffident, but was accompanied by an intellectual prickliness and ruthlessness which was extraordinarily impressive and at times devastating. The effect was increased by his peculiar method of conversation. When he was with those whom he liked, he would talk with animation, dropping every now and then into the general stream of conversation, casually and in his low staccato voice, some maliciously illuminating and extraordinarily witty phrase or comment. But in those days, though his conversation was fascinating and brilliant, it was often difficult, for he required much, including stimulus, from the person to whom he was talking. If the person or persons with whom he found himself in contact happened not to be congenial or their remarks unintelligent, the result would often be a social disaster, painful at the moment to a third party, though extremely amusing in retrospect. His legs inextricably intertwined, he would lie back in his chair, in black gloom and complete silence, and then quite suddenly drop, this time probably into the most uncomfortable moment of silence, a sardonically witty remark which stripped the last shred of self-control and intelligence from his victim.

These combinations of ruthlessness and gentleness, silence and wit, prickliness and affection only increased the charm of his personality for those whom he liked. It was this charm, when united with his extraordinary intellectual gifts, his highly individual outlook on life, and his very definite opinions, which made him the dominating influence upon three or four generations of Cambridge undergraduates. When he first came to Trinity it was clear that he would be a writer, and his contemporaries were convinced that he would be a great writer. In those days he wrote much more poetry than prose. I think that perhaps all through his life he would have preferred to achieve something in poetry or the drama than in any other sphere of literature. But he demanded of himself the same tremendous standards that he required in others, and it is significant that, though he wrote a great deal of poetry, he never published it. He became a prose writer partly because his verse never came up to the standard which he himself demanded of poetry, and partly because the immense influence which Professor G.E. Moore and *Principia Ethica* exercised upon him, as upon so many of his contemporaries, turned his mind in other directions.

As a matter of fact, prose was, I am sure, the right instrument for his thoughts, given the fact that he was living not in the eighteenth, but the twentieth century. His mind was fundamentally of the order of Swift's and Voltaire's, a critical and analytical mind which delighted to express itself with natural brilliance in satire and wit. Some of the most brilliant things which he ever wrote were Voltairian squibs and essays written when an undergraduate on subjects about which he felt deeply and violently. It was these writings which showed that, as I said, at nineteen he already possessed the intellectual equipment of the author of *Eminent Victorians* and *Queen Victoria*.

His published writings are the direct product of his character, which, by its curious combination of contradictory qualities, was always producing something rich and strange. He was an iconoclast who loved traditions, so that, for instance, on a subject like the French Revolution he could feel with Burke and think with Tom Paine. He combined extreme originality, and even eccentricity, with a true love of the elaborate manners, forms, and formalities of a highly civilised and sophisticated society. He was a realist and a cynic, and yet he was a romantic who loved the pageantry of life and history. Though the standards he set for himself and demanded of others were so high and though one of the most remarkable things about him was his intellectual integrity, he would display, on occasions, an almost contemptuous, if not unscrupulous, disregard of accuracy in detail. These qualities determined his choice of subject and moulded his biographical method and literary style. They account both for the enormous effect which the iconoclasm of *Eminent Victorians* had upon a generation and for the reaction against him as a biographer and historian which has been so marked in the last few years. His romanticism and disregard of detailed accuracy are fairly open to criticism, and it is arguable that his methods, used by others without his genius and wit, have done harm to both biography and history. But many of his critics merely convict themselves of the biographical sentimentality and the historical humbug against which much of his work was rightly and triumphantly directed. And in doing so they often showed themselves to be blind to what I have called his intellectual integrity. An example which would certainly have amused Lytton Strachey himself may be quoted. In the recent controversy on the question whether General Gordon drank too much brandy and soda, one of his critics was very angry with him. He was indignant that a mere writer should suggest that a distinguished soldier who read the Bible could drink too much brandy. And in order to clinch the argument, he asked what right Lytton Strachey had to criticize General Gordon – Lytton Strachey who had never been in the East, had never been out in the sun without an umbrella, had never been far from a cup of tea or glass of lemonade. At that moment Lytton Strachey was enduring a long, painful illness with extraordinary patience and fortitude, and, though without the consolations of either a Christian or a soldier, was facing the prospect of imminent death with courage and equanimity.

Lytton Strachey by Michael Holroyd

Reprinted from Michael Holroyd, Lytton Strachey, A Critical Bio-graphy *(London, Heinemann, 1967), I, 395–7, 408–410, by per-mission of the author and publishers;* © *1967 by Michael Holroyd, and by permission of Holt, Rinehart and Winston, Inc.*

[Some twenty years after Lytton Strachey's death Clive Bell observed, at the end of a portrait of him in *Old Friends*, that many years would have to pass before a biography that took into account Strachey's love and lust life could be attempted. It took, in fact, another twenty years. Michael Holroyd's biography of Strachey was the first frank, extended biography of a member of the Bloomsbury Group. What he revealed about the open heterosexual and homosexual ideas and habits of various individuals in and around Bloomsbury has made the Group appear very contemporary.

Holroyd's interpretation of Strachey's personality and character was criticized, however, first by James Strachey in a number of footnotes to the biography, and then by Leonard Woolf, who observed in a review that Holroyd 'takes Lytton too seriously and too literally... It is strange too that throughout Lytton is represented as outside and even hostile to what is called the Bloomsbury "group" or "gang". If the Bloomsbury group ever did exist, then one of its most esoteric and characteristic members was Giles Lytton Strachey'.

When Holroyd came to revise his biography for a paper-back edition, he divided it into a volume on Strachey's life and a volume on his work which he entitled *Lytton Strachey and the Bloomsbury Group: His Work, Their Influence.* In the excerpt that follows, Holroyd summarizes what he thinks Strachey's relationship to Bloomsbury was before Strachey became famous – and before he became involved in that 'complex molecule', as Holroyd calls it, of love relationships that contained Strachey and his lovers and Carrington and her lovers. Bloomsbury, at least in the strict sense of the word, was not directly involved very much in this molecule, except for Strachey himself of course; but Bloomsbury watched, gossiped, consoled the participants when necessary, and agreed at least in theory with the sexual freedom practised by Strachey and his friends.]

As we have seen, the five years immediately succeeding Lytton's time at Cambridge form the most unsettled and indeterminate period of his adult life. Everything was speculative, uncertain, fluctuating. He had plenty of plans, but they were all vague and impractical, so that he pursued them only with faint heart. After quitting the one society of which he had managed to become an integral part, he had been pitch-forked back to London, to his family, to nothing. His environment was still largely that of his childhood days, which he had partly outgrown and from which he alternately longed and feared to cut free. At the same time he felt his most urgent need was to merge with – perhaps to create – another congenial society where he could lay the foundations of a successful career; a society that would help to assuage his longing, and comfort his sense of fear. 'Oh dear me!' he had written to Maynard Keynes six months after coming down from Trinity,

when will my Heaven be realized? – My Castle in Spain? Rooms, you know, for you, Duncan and Swithin, as fixtures – Woolf of course, too, if we could lure him from Ceylon; and several suites for guests. Can you conceive anything more supreme! I should write tragedies; you would revolutionize political economy, Swithin would compose French poetry, Duncan would paint our portraits in every conceivable combination and permutation, and Woolf would criticize us and our works without remorse.

Such was the dream; and reality approximated to it only haphazardly. Three years later a substitute community for Cambridge, something along the lines which Lytton envisaged, had already taken shape in the purlieus of unfashionable Bloomsbury. It was not, of course, the ideal Castilian concourse of Lytton's quixotic yearnings, nor did he succeed in planting within it the seeds of his own propitious future. In a sense it held him back from realizing his ambitions sooner, for Bloomsbury took the edge off his discontent, making discomfort and obscurity almost endurable. It mitigated, too, a little the claustrophobia of family life. In a letter to his sister, Dorothy Bussy, (25th February 1909) he wished desperately that he had achieved something spectacular, but he confesses that

I seem to be as far off from even starting as ever. My condition is not encouraging. With this damned *Spectator* every week I see no hope of ever doing anything. It's pretty sickening. On Monday I shall be in my 30th year, and if I happened to die there'd be precious little to show for them all — perhaps one or two poems of highly doubtful taste, *et voilà tout*. It's sickening and occasionally I'm absolutely in despair. If I had decent health I should go into a garret and starve until I'd done something, but that's impossible. The only consolation is that as it is I lead a very tolerable life.

At the present moment, as usual, I take more interest in Duncan than in anyone else. He's a genius and charming, but I think he's still rather younger than his age, so that what he does seems to me immature. But I suppose there's no harm in that. Otherwise the people I see and like most are two women — viz. Vanessa and Virginia, with neither of whom I'm in love (and *vice versa*).

As Duncan Grant gradually faded from the forefront of Lytton's life, these two custodians and hostesses of the so-called Bloomsbury Group began to figure more prominently. While at Cambridge he had sometimes been invited by Thoby to 22 Hyde Park Gate, where the two girls lived and cared for their invalid father. Deaf, suffering from

internal cancer, almost completely helpless, Sir Leslie Stephen was
wholly dependent upon his daughters. On 22nd February 1904 he died,
and the four children, Vanessa and Virginia, Thoby and Adrian, left
their old home to set up house together at 46 Gordon Square.

Lytton's visits to the Stephens had now grown more frequent. 'On
Sunday I called at the Gothic mansion,' he wrote to Leonard Woolf
(21st December 1904) not long after they had moved into their new
home, 'and had tea with Vanessa and Virginia. The latter is rather
wonderful, quite witty, full of things to say, and absolutely out of
rapport with reality. The poor Vanessa has to keep her three mad
brothers and sister in control. She looks wan and sad.'

At this time, however, the two sisters existed in Lytton's mind as
little more than spectral adjuncts to the magnificent Goth, and he used
to refer to them collectively as the 'Visigoths'. After Thoby's tragic
death, they had not vanished from his life, but slowly asserted
themselves as separate individuals, full of their own interest and
fascination. When Clive Bell married Vanessa, Virginia and Adrian
moved to a nearby house previously occupied by Bernard Shaw, 29
Fitzroy Square, so as to allow the newly married couple to live alone in
Gordon Square. Their circle of friends, of which Thoby's Cambridge
contemporaries formed the nucleus, was not broken up by this move,
but enlarged . . .

Though the routine of his life, divided between his family and friends,
Hampstead and Bloomsbury, was less well arranged and homogeneous
than before, though perhaps he was less contented inwardly than as an
undergraduate, Lytton did not appear to languish in greater gloom and
despair. No longer, surrounded by kindred spirits, did his long,
emaciated form crouch in odd and angular shapes on sofas, tables,
basket-chairs, wrapped for hours in deep imponderable silence. For now
that he and his friends were less absurdly young, their methods of
communal conviviality, if still idiosyncratic, had grown more relaxed
and mature. The infiltration of feminine society into the circle also did
something to lighten the intensity of austere scholasticism that had so
resolutely typified their Cambridge dialectics. The Cambridge
garrison of Bloomsbury, a civilized fortress, as they saw themselves,
isolated amid the hostile, native population of London, was inevitably
less immune than the university itself from the vulgar assaults of
ignorant masses. Life was necessarily composed of less subdued and
even tones, less prim and exclusive conduct, less absolute free thinking,
less rigid informality, now that they were no longer sequestered from

everyday, human activity in the dingy, antiquarian charm of a few
literary back-waters. 'In exchange for the peace of Cambridge', J.K.
Johnstone acutely comments, 'the traffic of London clattered by on
the pavements just outside. The world was closer, and there was certain
to be a new awareness of it.'

What passing references there are in Lytton's essays to the boom and
bombast of twentieth-century living show his deeply ingrained dislike,
and even horror of it. 'He was quite definitely', wrote Max Beerbohm in
his Rede Lecture, 'and quite impenitently, what in current jargon is
called an escapist.' Bloomsbury society was for him a quiet but active
oasis in this desert of loud, claustrophobic loneliness. Yet he was always
conscious of those vast, unplanned areas of city life which began only a
few steps away and sprawled in all directions for so many hideous
miles. He dreamed of an ordered, reasonable, unrespectable, tidy,
refreshingly simple world, where happiness, beauty and companionship
were not stigmatized as immoral – the very antithesis of sophisticated
London. The seven consecutive years he spent there after coming down
from Trinity served to widen that fissure in his nature which he was
later to dramatize so successfully.

This peculiar dualism was at the same time echoed in his strange,
carefully modulated speech. He used two strikingly different types of
voice. One, high-pitched and tinny, was employed deliberately to
deflate pomposity; to express astonished disagreement with some
opinion (when it was often accompanied by a raising of the eyebrow);
to introduce either an element of clowning or baiting into the
conversation; or to tease someone he liked. 'Sometimes in this mood,'
recalled E.B.C. Lucas,[1]

> his splendid, architectural nose would appear larger than usual,
> presumably owing to an angle of the head. The high voice, then, was
> an affectation. Lytton would not have denied this. The comment on
> a friend's narrative: '*Too* ghastly, my dear', was an affectation so
> transparent that it constituted a sort of musical phrasing, part of a
> style. Like all 'Bloomsberries', he disliked pretension and silliness –
> the former much more than the latter, which after all could be a
> trait in youth, and so, forgivable; and in order to show up
> pretension, he would assume the high voice and the high brows, and
> so prick the bubble.

Occasionally, to parody or ridicule some attitude, he would chant
whole sentences in a feeble, monotonous falsetto. At other times – in

moments of intimacy or when reading out loud – he would employ a rather deep, bass voice, which with a strange inversion of stress might all at once rise to a reedy crescendo in emphatic termination of his sentence. As shown by his letters, he was much affected by the weather, and in rain and cold was apt to fall silent for long stretches. He did not often laugh. But an expression which was not exactly a smile would slip over his face, his eyes gleaming and fixed on whoever was speaking, and the mental climate grew warm and sunny. His two celebrated voices were, then, not entirely natural, but a contrived over-emphasis of a natural idiosyncrasy. In 1909, this dual voice was still something of a novelty, adopted to help establish for himself the *persona* which he wished others to accept and remember. But later in his life these voices, together with other distinctive appendages to his new Bloomsbury image – the beetroot-brown beard, the attenuated fingers, and a variety of runcible hats and cloaks – worked themselves into the recognized fabric of his highly stylized personality. They were no longer put on, but came as it were spontaneously to him, just as lines do to a good actor. In the opinion of Ralph Partridge, who knew Lytton only during the last twelve years of his life, 'these two voices of his were not an affectation but a natural gamut of expression – and the top notes were an echo of Voltaire's "high cackle" from the eighteenth century'.

In spite of his involuntary contact with a wider, more cosmopolitan world than Cambridge, Lytton's demeanour could still be as rigidly uncompromising as ever. When Clive Bell invited some French friends of his to Gordon Square, the francophil Lytton responded in a manner highly reminiscent of his grandfather, Edward Strachey. Resenting the intrusion of strangers, and uncomprehending foreigners at that, he stubbornly pretended to be incapable of speaking or understanding a word of the French language, and retreated into one of his grim spells of non-communication. Like Virginia Stephen he tended to distrust people whom he did not know well, and was supremely anxious not to fail in any attempt to impress them. But then again, if they were not handsome, or quick-witted, what, in any case, could possibly be the point in impressing them? They hardly existed. All the same he detested obscurity, and dreamt of being welcomed on his own terms by a society that he scorned. This feeling was shared by several of his friends, and it was on a superfine mixture of arrogance and diffidence, of ambitious talent and crippling shyness, that the Bloomsbury Group was largely founded. Such were some of its biographical and psychological origins; the various and conflicting myths which were erected round the group during later years were vaguer and vaster. But since the sociological and literary legends of Bloomsbury have, as the phrase is, 'caught the public imagination', and gained a wide acceptance despite only random approximation to the truth, they can no longer be corrected and set aside by a simple, qualified alternative statement, but call for some rather more detailed re-examination.

Note

1. E.B.C. Jones, the novelist, and first wife of F.L. Lucas of King's College, Cambridge. Known to her friends as 'Topsy', she had a rather arch way of referring to herself, in a deep voice, as 'Monkey' – 'Monkey doesn't read Shakespeare', etc. Living in Cambridge, she exerted a considerable influence on some of the most gifted undergraduates there. [Holroyd's note.]

Leonard Woolf by Noel Annan

Reprinted from Noel Annan, 'Leonard Woolf's Autobiography', The Political Quarterly, *41 (Jan.–March, 1970) 35–41, by permission of Lord Annan and* The Political Quarterly.

[In the final volume of his autobiography (which appeared after his death in 1969) as well as in the earlier ones, Leonard Woolf revealed in more detail than any other member of Bloomsbury had done what his life in and beyond Bloomsbury was like. Noel Annan's review of *The Journey Not the Arrival Matters* was published in *The Political Quarterly* which Woolf had helped to found forty years before. A dismissive review of Woolf's book in the *Times Literary Supplement* gave Lord Annan the opportunity to make clear how Woolf's political work and public service fitted into the Bloomsbury milieu.]

As he was writing the closing paragraphs of his biography of Lowes Dickinson, E.M. Forster suddenly found Mephistopheles at his elbow. Why have you written this book? asked the Devil. It really doesn't matter that your friend was beloved, affectionate, unselfish, intelligent, witty, inspiring. These influences will vanish when he, and you, and all his friends are dead. What then will survive? Nothing. He was not a great writer or thinker, and one only has to add that he worked before and after the First World War to establish the League of Nations to show that his efforts to make the world a more civilized place were futile. There was no need, therefore, to have written his biography.

The publication of the last volume of Leonard Woolf's auto-biography finds Mephistopheles in excellent spirits. This time he is to be found wearing a domino cloak of anonymity and writing in the *Times Literary Supplement*. Encouraged by a characteristic piece of calculation in which Woolf reckoned that in his eighty-eight years he had worked some 200,000 hours and achieved 'practically nothing', Mephistopheles cleverly questions our readiness to praise this discerning modesty. It was not modest, he says, but smug. Had Woolf been really honest and truthful he would have admitted that all his high-flown notions of truth and justice have been proved to be absurd. This preserver of the countryside, this lover of Sussex by the sea, this Fabian, was all the time propagating the politics of urbanization which speeded up the progress of industrializing England and, all too successfully, covering it with the hideous red brick villas which he himself detested. His own brand of political rationalism produced blue-prints for non-existent people. Hitler was the man who understood what human beings are like. The man who wrote *Principia Politica* was as much an ass about politics as a doctor would be in medicine if he denied the existence of bacteria. His life was one long delusion, and the greatest of all the delusions was his self-flattering belief that he and his friends stood out as an heroic minority against a Philistine world ruled by madmen or fools: whereas, in fact, he was always swimming strongly with the tide, the perfect apogee of conventional wisdom. *Beati sunt qui in domino moriuntur.*

But Mephistopheles really cannot have it both ways. Either he takes Woolf's assessment of his own value, or he must admit that so far from being in the swim, Woolf was way out on a limb. Not perhaps on the same limb of the tree as the one on which Bertrand Russell sat, but certainly on a branch on the same side of the tree. If British public opinion today is vastly more sceptical than it was of the necessity of hanging all murderers, enforcing monogamous sexual relations and imprisoning homosexuals, blasting colonial people with cordite, pro-claiming as offensively as possible the superiority of the white to all other races, and, therefore, its inalienable right to treat them as second-class citizens, some of the credit goes to Russell and Woolf and their friends. If in the ninth decade of their lives, they saw their own countrymen, at last accepting in principle the kind of behaviour they had urged them to adopt in the 1920s, they can hardly be said to have been lazily swimming with the tide all their lives. They were the men who helped to turn the tide.

Woolf heard as a child his father quoting from the prophet Micah, 'What doth the Lord require of thee but to do justly, and to love mercy, and to walk humbly with thy God'. This text was much beloved by Low Churchmen as a comfortable indication that one should not overburden oneself with conscience, or feel obliged to be ostentatiously pious or to be over-zealous and go around looking for trouble. But Woolf took it as a call to action. In this last volume of his autobiography, he recalls how the aged Gladstone transformed the headmistress of his sister's school into an apostrophe of indignation who descended upon her friends demanding them to render up or knit woollen socks and mittens for the survivors of the Armenian massacres. (Gladstone was, in fact, not eighty-five at the time, as Woolf asserts, but eighty-one, and the Government was not led by Disraeli but by Salisbury.) Shortly after this the Dreyfus affair began. These two events, the one a protest against inhuman treatment of a people, the other a protest on behalf of a single person against whom were ranged Church, State, and Army, gave Woolf his vision of what justice and mercy meant in this world.

Woolf tells us that, as with numbers of his class, the experience of social work, in his case with the Charity Organisation Society, converted him to socialism. To spend a quarter of an hour in Hoxton with a victim of the social system was to realize that nothing but a social revolution could cure the disease which could not be halted by paternalism or charitable good works. He next made a study of co-operative societies in England and Scotland and, seeing how the working clan in the north lived, joined the Labour Party and the ILP. This happened to him after he had left the Colonial Service in 1912. Two years later came the shattering experience of the First World War. Our own generation is apt to forget how traumatic that war was to the intelligentsia. Some of them, like H.G. Wells or Rupert Brooke, responded emotionally to it as a war against militarism and atrocities, only to be bitterly undeceived as the slaughter went on. Others were pacifists from the start and became ever more revolted by the propaganda and deception of governments as they tried to justify the war to their citizens. The only comparable trauma in the Second World War occurred after it: namely, the Bomb and the massacre of seven million Jews, a massacre of a dimension and of organized ruthlessness which seemed scarcely credible to those whose sensibility was formed in the days of the haphazard massacre of the Armenians. The shock of the First World War threw Woolf into the movement for the prevention of war and led him to write his book *International Government*. For the next twenty-seven years he was Secretary of the Labour Party's Advisory Committee on International Affairs which advised the Party Executive and the Parliamentary Party how the general principles which the Party supported could be applied to actual situations and problems as they arose.

He was also for the same length of time Secretary of the Labour Party's Advisory Committee for Imperial Questions. (As in the case of the International Committee he was also a member of the corresponding Fabian Society's bureau.) There he tried to explain to the rank-and-file supporters the facts and problems of Imperialism, to warn them what the movement for independence and self-government in the colonies would mean, and to suggest ways by which the colonial peoples could be educated for independence in those colonies where they were not already capable of taking over.

Woolf has no need to boast. He simply states as a fact that he was fairly good at this work. He could make the jump from the theoretical to the practical; Ceylon had taught him to take difficult decisions; he could manage to persuade a team of trade unionists and intellectuals to pull in harness; and he got to know the leaders of the Labour Party so that he was more than a back-room boy. By the end of the Second World War he was also a member of the Civil Service Arbitration Tribunal, a director of the *New Statesman*, and editor and director of this journal. He also positively revelled in work round the parish pump. For seventeen years he was Clerk of the Parish Council at Rodmell, and for twenty years delighted in being the President of the Horticultural Society.

Woolf has to admit that at times he and his committees may have faintly influenced somebody. The trade unionists of the inter-war period were understandably almost entirely ignorant of international or colonial affairs and were not likely to be made any wiser when MacDonald sent to the Colonial Office Jimmy Thomas 'an ignorant, frivolous, political buffoon'. Certainly he provided at that time the Labour Party with policies for the African Colonies which then appeared to be advanced and today would be accepted as platitudinous. But to Woolf at eighty-eight this work appeared to be a delusion and as phoney as MacDonald himself. There was never any hope that either party would make a go of the League, or when it failed, back collective security against Hitler. Just as Sidney Webb, when Colonial Secretary, refused to provide some grotesquely small sum for the education of black Kenyan children, so Attlee as Deputy Prime Minister in the War stonily refused to back the Labour Party's policy towards India. Could any work be more futile?

Why did he do it? And was it futile? He did it, so he says, because committee work amused him. He was amused by the sight and sound of the grinding of axes and the falls with no holds barred. He was susceptible to the ignoble pleasure of male importance which suffuses most committees, or of the faint whiff of power, which committees exhale. In Woolf's eyes there were a limited number of styles of life. You can try and be a 'great man' in politics. Or you can opt for the hum-drum life; family, friends, the everyday pleasures and trivialities which end with the final triviality of death. Or you can reject the life of public affairs and create your own world which has some eternal and 'real' meaning if you are a great artist. But you are merely eccentric and 'unreal' if you reject the world by spinning a cocoon around yourself as the friend of his undergraduate days, Saxon Sydney-Turner, did.

In his case he knew that he could never have succeeded in politics and, in a sense, he would have despised himself had he done so. Similarly, he was too fiercely honest to spin a cocoon. He knew he was not an artist. So his final defence is that he went on doing his thing aware that it was ineffective yet consoling himself that it was as important as the lifework of the vast majority of men and hoping occasionally through his personal life to add to the happiness of others, and to diminish ignorance, cruelty and injustice.

In this last volume Leonard Woolf, therefore, is still debating a dilemma which the Apostles had debated in his day as an undergraduate. Should those who care for truth, for the distinction between right and wrong, and for the private virtues exemplified by the communion between friends, distrust and despise the world of politics and the compromises of political action? The generation in the Society before Woolf were fiercely for commitment in politics. G.M. Trevelyan was then a fiery radical in action as well as by commitment, and the loathing which he felt later in life for Lytton Strachey, was not only born of Strachey's contempt for the sacredness of the past and the historical importance of eminent men, but also of the success which Strachey had in capturing the Society to his way of thinking. Strachey mocked those who seek salvation through politics. But in his first volume Woolf reminds us that Strachey did not have it all his own way, and the notion that Keynes put about – namely, that G.E. Moore's ethics were taken by the Society as a repudiation of the proposition that the consequences of one's actions are relevant to the question as to whether the actions are good or bad — was monstrously mistaken. In 1903 Woolf wrote a paper for the Society in which he urged that philosophers should also be kings; and that 'we should combine the two Georges in our life', *i.e.*, Moore and Trevelyan — or 'to put it plainly, I *do* want Moore to draft an Education Act'.

Many people write today as if the members of Old Bloomsbury (the group of friends who met together before 1914) were political innocents engaged purely in contemplation of the eternal verities and of their own genitals when excited by the behaviour of other members of the group. In fact, Keynes and Woolf were throughout their lives engaged in politics — Keynes's desire to saunter through the corridors of power was foretold in their Cambridge days by Strachey, who called him Pozzo di Borgo after a subtle Corsican diplomat. Gerald Shove was a Fabian economist, and far more of Forster's essays than is usually suspected deal obliquely with political problems. Woolf's middle stump Socialism was the most articulate political response, but it was not in itself unique. If, at this stage in time, Strachey or Virginia Woolf appear to have been rather too acutely aware of the fact that they were born into the class of ladies and gentlemen, Leonard Woolf and Morgan Forster, born at a time when England rocked with explosions of snobbery as the old class distinctions began to break up, behaved naturally and without affectation towards their working-class friends and acquaintances.

Someone should do for him what he would have laughed at doing: make an anthology of his political essays. Woolf was not a notable political philosopher. This pained him. Like Leslie Stephen, who remained convinced to the end that his *Science of Ethics* was his most enduring work (although it has rightly remained unread), so Woolf looked with regret at the reception given to his *Principia Politica*. He had not got an original mind and, despite his apprenticeship at Moore's feet, he had little aptitude for abstract analysis. But his strength lay in his ephemeral writings, particularly on colonial affairs.

It would be instructive to set these articles against the inflated volumes of Harold Macmillan's autobiography. Macmillan is out to obtain for himself a niche in history as the far-seeing, clever, adept pilot, who steered the Tory Party through the shoals of the last days of imperialism by recognizing that the Wind of Change was blowing. For thirty years and more Woolf and his political colleagues had forecast the change in the weather and had advocated the very policy of imperial divestment which Macmillan, with the blood of Suez and Cyprus on his hands, announced. Woolf does himself less than justice.

He remembered Attlee's stony silence when, as the prisoner of war-time coalition, he did not feel able to sponsor the Labour Party's policy towards India. But with the defeat of Churchill, Attlee did not hesitate. Once he had tested the bitterness of feeling in India, he decided for independence under any terms. Not so Macmillan. To him the decision 'seemed an abdication of duty as well as power'. This was the mistake that he and the Tories were to make again and again in the fifties. They wanted to make a tidy dignified exit from the colonies, all of whom were to have been given blue-print constitutions based on a party system of government. And so arose the ludicrous Federation of Rhodesia and other misbegotten schemes. Woolf knew that self-government for Asians and Africans is better than good government, and that the only way to get acceptable government was for the indigenous political leaders themselves to decide.

Indefatigable worker as Woolf was, politics came second in his life. His first loyalty was to Virginia, to keeping her well and her mental sickness at bay, to publishing her books, and in time of stress rationing the visits of her friends and their parties, so that she did not become exhausted. He judged she had genius and that originality which he did not possess. Mephistopheles of course is adept, as he always is, in detecting the chink in the armour. There is in Woolf's writing that tone of mild astonishment that mankind can be so irrational and intent on their own destruction, which is the hall-mark of so much of Bloomsbury's writing. It sets the nerves on edge today as we observe how group after group in society becomes converted to the view that strike action, or violent demonstration, is the most efficacious way to influence governments some of whom are unwilling to employ their citizen soldiers against civilians so that today we face the bizarre spectacle of policemen with shields, helmets and staves fighting students with shields, helmets and staves, the police barely holding their own by using tear-gas. It is as if the party of change in Western European countries had decided to taunt the party of order into counter-measures that they themselves would deplore. And yet, if there was one political belief that Woolf cherished, it was that once violence replaces reason, tyranny is round the corner.

The answer which Woolf made to Mephistopheles is contained in the title of this, the last volume of his autobiography. Which of us has the temerity as we await death in old age, to say that our ideals have been achieved? Only the foolish fail to understand that for every gain in one direction there has been a loss in another. 'You must always', writes Cavafy,

You must always have Ithaca in your mind
Arrival there is your predestination
But do not hurry the journey at all
Better that it should last many years.
Be quite old when you anchor at the island . . .
Poor though you find it, Ithaca has not deceived you.
You are now so wise, you have seen so much,
That by now you will understand the meaning of an Ithaca.

Clive Bell by David Garnett

Reprinted from David Garnett, The Flowers of the Forest *(London, Chatto & Windus, 1955), 21–4, by permission of the author and Chatto & Windus;* © *1955 by David Garnett and reprinted by permission of Harcourt Brace Jovanovich, Inc.*

[According to his son, Clive Bell 'helped to temper the austerities' of early Bloomsbury;

> he was different from the others in that he was better dressed, had a good seat on a horse and was an excellent wing shot; for while all the rest were pretty obviously intellectual, he came from a society which hunted birds, animals, and, in his case, girls . . . .At Cambridge he was, I think, underrated by his friends; they did not look in the one direction in which he was, intellectually, more alert than they. In his rooms hung a reproduction of a painting by Degas, someone of whom most of them had probably never heard, for Cambridge at the turn of the century was aesthetically blind.

The sketches of Clive Bell by David Garnett and John Russell that follow emphasize respectively his personal and professional roles in Bloomsbury. Garnett's picture begins with a party in 1915 in which he was first introduced to Bloomsbury.]

. . . Forty-six Gordon Square, where the Bells lived, is a large house in the middle of the East side of one of the most pleasant squares in Bloomsbury. There was already a large party when we arrived and were ushered into the dining-room on the ground floor. I immediately noticed a cubist painting by Picasso, which I had seen reproduced in

Clive's book *Art*. I also noticed a Vlaminck which I liked better. The pictures gave dignity to a room which was beautiful, although already crowded with people, among whom I recognized many old friends. James, Lytton and several other Stracheys were there. So were Karin and Ray Costello, who soon afterwards married Adrian Stephen and Oliver Strachey. Brynhild [Popham] had brought Harold Hobson's sister Mabel Scott. There was also the strikingly handsome figure of Lady Ottoline Morrell, whom I had admired from a distance two or three years before at a political dinner, given at the Savoy Hotel, to Mr Morgan Shuster, the American financial adviser of the Persian Government who had been driven out of his job by Russian intrigue backed by the policy of Sir Edward Grey. My parents felt passionately about the division of Persia into Anglo-Russian spheres of influence, and had taken me with them to attend the dinner. Here was Lady Ottoline again and soon I was introduced and she was purring out in a cajoling drawl: 'Do come to a party I am giving after dinner, next Thursday, Mr Garnett. Why do they call you Bunny?' Her words and instant invitation turned my head.

We sat down to listen to Mozart played by the three D'Aranyi sisters. Jelly, the youngest, was then in the first flower of her beauty. After the music we went upstairs to see a performance of the last scene of Racine's *Bérénice*, acted by three gigantic puppets, eight feet high, which had been made by Duncan. They were cut out of thick cardboard and were flat, but could move their jointed arms and legs.

At a crisis in the play, Bérénice, who had been seated up till then, rose to her feet, and the puppet in the centre moved his eyes to look at his companions as they spoke in turn. The scene acted was the tragic ending when Antiochus confesses his love for Bérénice to Titus and all three part for ever.

The words were spoken by members of the Strachey family whose excellent French accents and elocution were almost as impressive as the puppets. The size and artificiality of the figures made them perfect mouthpieces for Racine's heroic poetry.

The evening ended with Gerald Shove enthroned in the centre of the room, crowned with roses, which must have been taken from a vase of hot-house flowers. His charming good humour was the best possible tribute to Clive's hospitality and the excellent quality of the whisky. But I do not remember which lady saw that it was appropriate for Gerald to be wearing a wreath of roses, or set it round his Roman brow.

Soon after that party I found myself on terms of warm friendship not only with Duncan and Maynard, but with Clive and Vanessa.

Forty-six Gordon Square became for me a house where I felt sure of being welcome and Blanche, the thin tall housemaid who opened the door, and the children, Julian and Quentin aged six and four, soon began to greet me as a friend.

I do not think such a rapid friendship would have been possible but for Clive, whose character was in many ways complementary to Vanessa's, just as that of Jack Sprat was complementary to that of his lady who could eat no lean. Clive created the atmosphere of Number Forty-six more than Vanessa and I shall therefore attempt a superficial sketch of his character.

In one of Hans Andersen's fairy tales there is a Princess who is so sensitive that she cannot sleep if there is so much as a crumpled rose petal beneath the mattress of her bed. Clive is like the princess, he cannot be happy if he is aware of anyone feeling unhappy in the vicinity. Thus, perhaps for selfish reasons, he does everything to create happiness about him. He is an almost perfect example of James Mill's Utilitarian theory that a man cannot become rich without enriching his neighbours. If everyone were like Clive, the theory might be generally true.

At this time Clive was not in the slightest degree interested in me and would not have cared if he had never seen me again. But if I was going to haunt Gordon Square, it was essential for his comfort that I should be feeling happy when I did. He was therefore far kinder to me than an altruistic man would have been. When the door was opened, a warm stream of Clive's hospitality and love of the good things of life poured out, as ravishing as the smell of roasting coffee on a cold morning. Heaviness, dullness, coldness, the besetting sins of English people and of the English climate, were impossible in Clive's house and Clive's company. Such jolly hearty good-fellowship is traditionally associated with fox-hunters and shooting parties and it was, in fact, from that milieu that Clive inherited his temperament. His tastes had led him into the chillier world of philosophers, mathematicians, critics and artists where the spiritual virtues of the hunt breakfast were unknown. Clive therefore provided an essential element in the formation of Bloomsbury. He brought to what might otherwise have been a bleak intellectual world

> a beaker full of the warm South
> Full of the true, the blushful Hippocrene
> With beaded bubbles winking at the brim.

He saved Bloomsbury from being another Clapham Sect, devoted, in the same cold unworldly way, to aesthetics and the pursuit of abstract truth instead of to evangelical religion. This was by no means all of Clive's contribution, for though he gives the impression of an airy quick-witted talker, he has the habits of a scholar. He always spends a good many hours a day reading. Clive's wide reading, quick wit and common sense was an essential ingredient in the brilliant talk to be heard in Bloomsbury. The other most important elements in it were the talk of Lytton, Virginia, Maynard, Desmond MacCarthy and Harry Norton. Clive cannot endure illness and he is often an absentee at the sick-beds of his nearest and dearest. Yet in other ways he is not squeamish. A secret horror of 46 Gordon Square was that the basement kitchen was infested with cockroaches. When the pest became bad, Clive would put on his shooting boots and go down in the middle of the night to stamp on them. No one else in Bloomsbury (except myself) would have done that . . .

Clive Bell by John Russell

Reprinted from John Russell, 'Clive Bell', Encounter, 23 (December, 1964) 47–9, by permission of Encounter and the author.

[John Russell, art critic of the *Sunday Times*, stresses in his tribute to Clive Bell the significance of art in Bloomsbury. The influence of Bell's aesthetic interests on Bloomsbury predated Roger Fry's. But the particular accomplishment that Clive Bell came to take most pride in was a feat of literary criticism. He helped his sister-in-law with her first novel. Years later Virginia Woolf told him, 'you were the first person who ever thought I'd write well'; that, wrote Bell after her death, 'seems to me the finest feather I shall ever be able to stick in my cap . . .'.]

Clive Bell (who died in September, at the age of eighty-three), had been a part of English intellectual life since the day in October, 1899, when he went up to Trinity College, Cambridge, and found that his fellow-freshmen included Lytton Strachey, Leonard Woolf, and Thoby Stephen (brother of Virginia, who became Mrs Woolf, and Vanessa, who became Mrs Bell). Bloomsbury, as a group, was in being from that very day, although Clive himself dated its origin not so much from the

Cambridge reading society, which the four friends founded with Saxon Sydney-Turner, as from the time in 1904 onwards when the group met constantly in London and was enlarged to take in Duncan Grant, Roger Fry, John Maynard Keynes, and one or two others.

Even quite young people know the outline of his career: that he had worked with Roger Fry on the Post-Impressionist exhibitions of 1910 and 1912; that his books and ephemeral writings, and above all his concept of 'significant form', had had an immense influence in their day; that he was as much at home in France as in England, and that Picasso, Matisse, Derain, Segonzac, and others had prized his friendship and kept it in good repair. The uncompromising view of aesthetic experience which he put forward throughout his life sometimes led strangers to picture him as a wincing aesthete in full withdrawal from the hard realities of the day. ('To appreciate a work of art', he had written in perhaps the most famous of his polemical passages, 'we need bring with us nothing from life, no knowledge of its ideas and affairs, no familiarity with its emotions'.) But until his first and last illness made its cruel inroads upon him, Clive Bell looked what he was: a prosperous country gentleman who would be as good company in brushing-room and butts as he was in the National Gallery or the Tate. And he was a country gentleman such as Charles James Fox would have been happy to stay with: a scholar who had mastered the Greek and Latin classics in the original, and yet knew the world of power and privilege at first hand. He was ready to talk about anything: and however feebly the ball might be put up, he would always give of his best.

He had in a very rare degree the sense of occasion which makes even chance encounters memorable. Equally gifted as guest and as host, he had an Edwardian fondness for the full-scale anecdote and an Edwardian readiness to bring one out when the conversation seemed to demand it. But he never hogged the floor, and he contrived to make even the timid and the ineffective feel that they too had contributed something to the talk. His voice called for the open air: undeniably loud, it was never over-bearing, and its characteristic note was one of high expectation and shared enjoyment. He had an enormous amount of style in everyday life, and it was the style of someone who had never had to hurry; like all the founder-members of Bloomsbury, he had also a highly-developed sense of the ridiculous, and applied it to subjects and situations which it is traditional to take very seriously indeed. He had passed all his life among people who knew how to take care of themselves in conversation, and he never resented plain speaking. 'Yes'

he would say after some notorious *mauvaise langue* had been to see
him, 'He spoke a good deal of ill of all of us, but I must say I found him
very agreeable'.

Not much of this came out in his later writings, and his reminiscential
sketches, *Old Friends*, are too courtly and digressive in style to give the
full flavour of his company. Some idea of that flavour can, however, be
got from his essays of fifty and more years ago, for he perfected in his
twenties and thirties the robust and antithetical style which made him
famous. If he was outrageous, it was because only outrage would
penetrate at all deeply; and he used in his earlier writings the techniques
of calculated overstatement which he later reserved for conversation.
Here he is (again from the opening section of *Art*) at his most
characteristic:

> Most people who care much about art find that of the work that
> moves them the greater part is what scholars call 'Primitive'. Of
> course there are bad primitives. For instance, I remember going, full
> of enthusiasm, to see one of the earliest Romanesque churches in
> Poitiers and finding it ill-proportioned, over-decorated, coarse, fat,
> and heavy... But such exceptions are rare. As a rule primitive art is
> good, for, as a rule, it is free from descriptive qualities. In primitive
> art you will find no accurate representation; you will find only
> significant form. Yet no other art moves us so profoundly.

In *Art* (1914) he bit off more than could be chewed, even then, by any
one young man, and no doubt today's thin-lipped censors would find
much to mock at in that book's wilder and more panoramic allusions.
But the feat of demolition: that no one can deny. Clive Bell took the
agreed hierarchy of aesthetic values and destroyed it for ever. Any
first-year student at the Courtauld Institute can mug up arguments to
show that *Art* can be faulted. But the point is that all subsequent
writing on art in this country has benefited by the climate of freedom
which Clive Bell initiated. 'We are not yet clear,' he wrote in one
chapter of *Art*, 'of the Victorian slough. The spent dip stinks on into
the dawn.' That second sentence – and how many people now writing
on art would have been capable of it? – describes a state of affairs
which Clive Bell did more than anyone to destroy. What he did was to
carry over into the field of aesthetic speculation the concept of total
freedom in the discussion of human affairs which was common to all
members of Bloomsbury. *Anything*, however contrary to accepted

form, could be discussed, much as the great navigators of an earlier century would flout the hypotheses of their predecessors.

He was very good, too, at getting a situation down on paper in such a way that the reader says to himself, 'I wonder what happened next'. When he first wrote, in 1912, that 'the Romantics and the Realists were like people coming to cuffs about which is the more important thing in an orange — the history of Spain or the number of pips,' it really did tidy up a still-straggling discussion; and it seemed inevitable to the reader that something allied to neither point of view must come into being. (Ibsen was the subject of the essay, but it applied equally to Cézanne.) It is possible, of course, to fall into a habit of heavy emphasis, and in this way to give an impression of unvarying dogmatism. Clive Bell sometimes did this, both in writing and in conversation. There was nothing tentative about his opinions, and he felt it only fair to everyone that he should express them as forthrightly as he could. But it is worth saying that about the notion of 'significant form' he was a great deal more modest and diffident than legend suggests. The problem as he defined it was: 'Why are we so profoundly moved by certain combinations of forms?' and his answer had by no means the Sinaitical assurance which it acquired in the minds of people who had never read the original text. 'I suggested very cautiously. . . I was, and still am, extremely diffident. . .': these are the phrases which he used of the notion of significant form at a time when he might have been expected to lash out at the opposition.

He never allowed himself to get far away from the first-hand shock, the intimate and lasting disturbance, of actual contact with first-rate works of art. Nor did he allow that disturbance to lose the kindling element of sensuality. Abstract thought was one thing — and no one had a greater respect for it — but it was never allowed to take precedence over the senses. Bonnard, for instance, will be all the rage, this next year or two, with our local band-wagoners, but I doubt if anyone will get much nearer to the truth about Bonnard in a few lines than did Clive Bell in this passage, now nearly fifty years old:

> The first thing one gets from a picture by Bonnard is a sense of perplexed, delicious colour: tones of miraculous subtlety seem to be flowing into an enchanted pool and chasing one another there. From this pool emerge gradually forms which appear sometimes vaporous and sometimes tentative, but never vapid and never woolly. When we have realized that the pool of colour is, in fact, a design of extraordinary originality and perfect coherence, our

aesthetic appreciation is at its height. And not until this excitement begins to flag do we notice that the picture carries a delightful overtone — that it is witty, whimsical, fantastic.

The language dates a little? Yes, but how assuredly is authentic perception allied to a thought-out and consistent point of view! A reproach often levelled at Clive Bell was that in later years his perception was confined to a limited range of works of art; initially he argued that a knowledge of Kandinsky and the *Blaue Reiter*, of Brancusi, of the Italian Futurists, and of Larionov and Goncharova was indispensable to the critic of modern art; but he himself did not pursue the study of these artists very far. Parisian loyalties proved too strong, as did others bred within his own household, and with advancing age he inclined to settle for what he knew and liked already. Too little of a humbug to ape an enthusiasm which he did not feel, he did not go much beyond Victor Pasmore's landscapes of 1945, in English painting, or the friends of his own generation in France. I remember Ben Nicholson saying, 'He got so near to the point of what we were doing, and then he didn't carry it through . . .'. Well, perhaps he didn't — any more than he 'carried it through' to the newest in literature, preferring to re-read *Paradise Lost* and *Tristram Shandy*. But he was in the right at a great moment in the history of painting. He and Roger Fry (and he was more independent of Roger Fry than many people suppose) were right about Cézanne at a time when even Sickert thought Cézanne was '*un grand raté*'; right about cubism when Tonks said 'this talk of cubism . . . is killing me'; right about Matisse when intelligent people from the Art-Workers' Guild shouted 'Drink or drugs?' when Fry showed them one of his paintings. He helped to bring about a decisive shift in the history of taste: thanks to Fry and Bell, French painting of the period 1880–1914 became recognized as one of the greatest of human achievements in art. He had his shortcomings, even at that moment, but in the context of his own generosity and impetuosity of mind, and of the general thickness and dullness of the opposition, those shortcomings were remarkably few. He was the right man in the right place at the right moment, and there are not many art-critics of whom that can be said.

Virginia Woolf by T.S. Eliot

Reprinted from T.S. Eliot, 'Virginia Woolf', Horizon, III (May, 1941)
314–6, by permission of Faber and Faber Ltd.

[Because there were no major poets in Bloomsbury, because the
Bloomsberries did not unreservedly admire the work of D.H. Lawrence
or James Joyce, and because most of them had misgivings about the
value of the irrational in literature and in politics, the Bloomsbury
Group has been regarded by some literary critics as a backwater rather
than the main stream of modern English literature. Yet their early
recognition of and long friendship with T.S. Eliot is an inconvenient
feature for such a map of the literary waterways. Though he was never
a member of Bloomsbury, Eliot's poetry was published by the Hogarth
Press (his *Poems* was their fourth publication) and he was welcomed
and respected by the Woolfs, Clive Bell, Lytton Strachey, J.M. Keynes,
and others of the Group.

Eliot's observations on Virginia Woolf and Bloomsbury, taken from
a note he wrote for *Horizon* magazine shortly after her death, are
among the most interesting statements by a contemporary on the
nature and significance of the Group.]

. . . The future will arrive at a permanent estimate of the place of Virginia
Woolf's novels in the history of English literature, and it will also be
furnished with enough documents to understand what her work meant
to her contemporaries. It will also, through letters and memoirs, have
more than fugitive glimpses of her personality. Certainly, without her
eminence as a writer, and her eminence as the particular kind of writer
she was, she would not have occupied the personal position she held
among contemporaries; but she would not have held it by being a writer
alone – in the latter case it would only be the cessation of work which
would here give cause for lament. By attempting to enumerate the
qualities and conditions which contributed, one may give at first a false
impression of 'accidental advantages' concurring to reinforce the
imaginative genius and the sense of style which cannot be contested, to
turn her into the symbol, almost myth, which she became for those
who did not know her, and the social centre which she was for those
who did. Some of these advantages may have helped to smooth the
path to fame – though when a literary reputation is once established,
people quickly forget how long it was in growing – but that fame itself
is solidly enough built upon the writings. And these qualities of

personal charm and distinction, of kindness and wit, of curiosity about
human beings, and the particular advantage of a kind of hereditary
position in English letters (with the incidental benefits which that
position bestowed) do not, when enumerated, tell the whole story:
they combined to form a whole which is more than the sum of the
parts.

I am well aware that the literary-social importance which Virginia
Woolf enjoyed, had its nucleus in a society which those people whose
ideas about it were vague — vague even in connection with the
topography of London — were wont, not always disinterestedly perhaps, to deride. The sufficient answer *ad hoc* — though not the final
answer — would probably be that it was the only one there was: and as
I believe that without Virginia Woolf at the centre of it, it would have
remained formless or marginal, to call attention to its interest to the
sociologist is not irrelevant to my subject. Any group will appear more
uniform, and probably more intolerant and exclusive from the outside
than it really is; and here, certainly, no subscription of orthodoxy was
imposed. Had it, indeed, been a matter of limited membership and
exclusive doctrine, it would not have attracted the exasperated
attention of those who objected to it on these supposed grounds. It is
no part of my purpose here either to defend, criticize or appraise *élites*;
I only mention the matter in order to make the point that Virginia
Woolf was the centre, not merely of an esoteric group, but of the
literary life of London. Her position was due to a concurrence of
qualities and circumstances which never happened before, and which I
do not think will ever happen again. It maintained the dignified and
admirable tradition of Victorian upper middle-class culture — a
situation in which the artist was neither the servant of the exalted
patron, the parasite of the plutocrat, nor the entertainer of the mob — a
situation in which the producer and the consumer of art were on an
equal footing, and that neither the highest nor the lowest. With the
death of Virginia Woolf, a whole pattern of culture is broken: she may
be, from one point of view, only the symbol of it; but she would not be
the symbol if she had not been, more than anyone in her time, the
maintainer of it. Her work will remain; something of her personality
will be recorded, but how can her position in the life of her own time
be understood by those to whom her time will be so remote that they
will not even know how far they fail to understand it? As for us — *l'on
sait ce que l'on perd. On ne sait jamais ce que l'on rattrapera.*

Virginia Woolf by E.M. Forster

Reprinted from E.M. Forster, Virginia Woolf, The Red Lecture *(The Cambridge University Press, 1942) by permission of King's College, Cambridge, and The Society of Authors.*

[In trying to convey the effect of Virginia Woolf on her closest friends, Clive Bell wrote,

> I remember spending some dark, uneasy winter days during the first war in the depth of the country with Lytton Strachey. After lunch, as we watched the rain pour down and premature darkness roll up, he said, in his searching, personal way, 'Loves apart, whom would you most like to see coming up the drive?' I hesitated a moment, and he supplied the answer: 'Virginia of course.'

E.M. Forster's Rede lecture on Virginia Woolf, delivered at the beginning of the Second World War, is a public estimate of her work by the person whose professional judgement she most respected. Forster's essay is possibly the best introduction to her work and personality that had been written. Because he was a close friend as well as a novelist and critic, Forster gives us a view of Virginia Woolf from Bloomsbury that reveals her toughness, that evaluates her aestheticism and her feminism, that is not uncritical about her fiction or her snobbery, and that celebrates the values Forster shared with Virginia Woolf and their friends.

The lecture is dedicated to Leonard Woolf. (Two footnotes to the lecture have been omitted here.)]

When I was appointed to this lectureship the work of Virginia Woolf was much in my mind, and I asked to be allowed to speak on it. To speak on it, rather than to sum it up. There are two obstacles to a summing up. The first is the work's richness and complexity. As soon as we dismiss the legend of the Invalid Lady of Bloomsbury, so guilelessly accepted by Arnold Bennett, we find ourselves in a bewildering world where there are few headlines. We think of *The Waves* and say 'Yes – that is Virginia Woolf': then we think of *The Common Reader*, where she is different, of *A Room of One's Own* or the preface to *Life as we have known it*: different again. She is like a plant which is supposed to grow in a well-prepared garden bed – the bed of esoteric literature – and then pushes up suckers all over the place, through the gravel of the front drive, and even through the flagstones of the kitchen yard. She was full of interests, and their number increased as she grew older, she was curious about life, and she was tough, sensitive but tough. How can her achievement be summed up in an hour? A headline sometimes serves a lecturer as a life-line on these occasions, and brings him safely into the haven where he would be. Shall I find one to-day?

The second obstacle is that the present year is not a good date on which to sum up anything. Our judgments, to put it mildly, are not at their prime. We are all of us upon the Leaning Tower, as she called it, even those of us who date from the nineteenth century, when the earth was still horizontal and the buildings perpendicular. We cannot judge the landscape properly as we look down, for everything is tilted. Isolated objects are not so puzzling; a tree, a wave, a hat, a jewel, an old gentleman's bald head look much as they always did. But the relation between objects — that we cannot estimate, and that is why the verdict must be left to another generation. I have not the least faith that anything which we now value will survive historically (something which we should have valued may evolve, but that is a different proposition); and may be another generation will dismiss Virginia Woolf as worthless and tiresome. However this is not my opinion, nor I think yours; we still have the word, and when you conferred the Rede Lectureship on me — the greatest honour I have ever received — I wondered whether I could not transmit some honour to her from the university she so admired, and from the central building of that university. She would receive the homage a little mockingly, for she was somewhat astringent over the academic position of women. 'What? I in the Senate House?' she might say; 'Are you sure that is quite proper? And why, if you want to discuss my books, need you first disguise yourselves in caps and gowns?' But I think she would be pleased. She loved Cambridge. Indeed, I cherish a private fancy that she once took her degree here. She, who could disguise herself as a member of the suite of the Sultan of Zanzibar, or black her face to go aboard a Dreadnought as an Ethiopian — she could surely have hoaxed our innocent praelectors, and, kneeling in this very spot, have presented to the Vice-Chancellor the exquisite but dubious head of Orlando.

There is after all one little life-line to catch hold of: she liked writing.

These words, which usually mean so little, must be applied to her with all possible intensity. She liked receiving sensations — sights, sounds, tastes — passing them through her mind, where they encountered theories and memories, and then bringing them out again, through a pen, on to a bit of paper. Now began the higher delights of authorship. For these pen-marks on paper were only the prelude to writing, little more than marks on a wall. They had to be combined, arranged, emphasised here, eliminated there, new relationships had to be generated, new pen-marks born, until out of the interactions, something, one thing, one, arose. This one thing, whether it was a novel or an essay or a short story or a biography or a private paper to be read to her friends, was, if it was successful, itself analogous to a sensation. Although it was so complex and intellectual, although it might be large and heavy with facts, it was akin to the very simple things which had started it off, to the sights, sounds, tastes. It could be best described as we describe them. For it was not about something. It was something. This is obvious in 'aesthetic' works, like *Kew Gardens* and *Mrs Dalloway*; it is less obvious in a work of learning, like the *Roger Fry*, yet here too the analogy holds. We know, from an article by Mr R.C. Trevelyan, that she had, when writing it, a notion corresponding to the notion of a musical composition. In the first chapter she stated the themes, in the subsequent chapters she developed them separately, and she tried to bring them all in again at the end. The biography is duly about Fry. But it is something else too; it is one thing, one.

She liked writing with an intensity which few writers have attained, or even desired. Most of them write with half an eye on their royalties, half an eye on their critics, and a third half eye on improving the world, which leaves them with only half an eye for the task on which she concentrated her entire vision. She would not look elsewhere, and her circumstances combined with her temperament to focus her. Money she had not to consider, because she possessed a private income, and though financial independence is not always a safeguard against commercialism, it was in her case. Critics she never considered while she was writing, although she could be attentive to them and even humble afterwards. Improving the world she would not consider, on the ground that the world is man-made, and that she, a woman, had no responsibility for the mess. This last opinion is a curious one, and I shall be returning to it; still, she held it, it completed the circle of her defences, and neither the desire for money nor the desire for reputation nor philanthropy could influence her. She had a singleness of purpose which will not recur in this country for many years, and writers who have liked writing as she liked it have not indeed been common in any age.

Now the pitfall for such an author is obvious. It is the Palace of Art, it is that bottomless chasm of dullness which pretends to be a palace, all glorious with corridors and domes, but which is really a dreadful hole into which the unwary aesthete may tumble, to be seen no more. She has all the aesthete's characteristics: selects and manipulates her impressions; is not a great creator of character; enforces patterns on her books; has no great cause at heart. So how did she avoid her appropriate pitfall and remain up in the fresh air, where we can hear the sound of the stable boy's boots, or boats bumping, or Big Ben; where we can taste really new bread, and touch real dahlias?

She had a sense of humour, no doubt, but our answer must go a little deeper than that hoary nostrum. She escaped, I think, because she liked writing for fun. Her pen amused her, and in the midst of writing seriously this other delight would spurt through. A little essay, called *On Being Ill*, exemplifies this. It starts with the thesis that illness in literature is seldom handled properly (de Quincey and Proust were exceptional), that the body is treated by novelists as if it were a sheet of glass through which the soul gazes, and that this is contrary to experience. There are possibilities in the thesis, but she soon wearies of exploring them. Off she goes amusing herself, and after half a dozen pages she is writing entirely for fun, caricaturing the type of people who visit sick-rooms, insisting that Augustus Hare's *Two Noble Lives* is the book an invalid most demands, and so on. She could describe illness if she chose — for instance, in *The Voyage Out* — but she gaily forgets it in *On Being Ill*. The essay is slight, and was not offered for public sale, still it does neatly illustrate the habit of her mind. Literature was her merry-go-round as well as her study. This makes her amusing to read, and it also saves her from the Palace of Art. For you cannot enter the Palace of Art, therein to dwell, if you are tempted from time to time to play the fool. Lord Tennyson did not consider that. His remedy, you remember, was that the Palace would be purified when it was inhabited by all mankind, all behaving seriously at once. Virginia Woolf found a simpler and a sounder solution.

No doubt there is a danger here — there is danger everywhere. She might have become a glorified *diseuse*, who frittered away her broader effects by mischievousness, and she did give that impression to some who met her in the flesh; there were moments when she could scarcely see the busts for the moustaches she pencilled on them, and when the bust was a modern one, whether of a gentleman in a top hat or a youth on a pylon, it had no chance of remaining sublime. But in her writing, even in her light writing, central control entered. She was master of her complicated equipment, and though most of us like to write sometimes seriously and sometimes in fun, few of us can so manage the two impulses that they speed each other up, as hers did.

The above remarks are more or less introductory. It seems convenient now to recall what she did write, and to say a little about her development. She began back in 1915 with *The Voyage Out* – a strange tragic inspired novel about English tourists in an impossible South American hotel; her passion for truth is here already, mainly in the form of atheism, and her passion for wisdom is here in the form of music. The book made a deep impression upon the few people who read it. Its successor, *Night and Day*, disappointed them. This is an exercise in classical realism, and contains all that has characterized English fiction, for good and evil, during the last two hundred years: faith in personal relations, recourse to humorous side-shows, geographical exactitude, insistence on petty social differences: indeed most of the devices she so gaily derides in *Mr Bennett and Mrs Brown*. The style has been normalized and dulled. But at the same time she published two short stories, *Kew Gardens*, and *The Mark on the Wall*. These are neither dull nor normal; lovely little things; her style trails after her as she walks and talks, catching up dust and grass in its folds, and instead of the precision of the earlier writing we have something more elusive than had yet been achieved in English. Lovely little things, but they seemed to lead nowhere, they were all tiny dots and coloured blobs, they were an inspired breathlessness, they were a beautiful droning or gasping which trusted to luck. They were perfect as far as they went, but that was not far, and none of us guessed that out of the pollen of those flowers would come the trees of the future. Consequently when *Jacob's Room* appeared in 1922 we were tremendously surprised. The style and sensitiveness of *Kew Gardens* remained, but they were applied to human relationships, and to the structure of society. The blobs of colour continue to drift past, but in their midst, interrupting their course like a closely sealed jar, stands the solid figure of a young man. The improbable has occurred; a method essentially poetic and apparently trifling has been applied to fiction. She was still uncertain of the possibilities of the new technique, and *Jacob's Room* is an uneven little book, but it represents her great departure, and her abandonment of the false start of *Night and Day*. It leads on to her genius in its fullness; to *Mrs Dalloway* (1925), *To the Lighthouse* (1927), and *The Waves* (1931). These successful works are all suffused with poetry and enclosed in it. *Mrs Dalloway* has the framework of a London summer's day, down which go spiralling two fates: the fate of the sensitive worldly hostess, and the fate of the sensitive obscure maniac; though they never touch they are closely connected, and at the same moment we lose sight of them both. It is a civilized book, and it was written from personal experience. In her work, as in her private problems, she was always civilized and sane on the subject of madness. She pared the edges off this particular malady, she tied it down to being a malady, and robbed it of the evil magic it has acquired through timid or careless thinking; here is one of the gifts we have to thank her for. *To the Lighthouse* is, however, a much greater achievement, partly because the chief characters in it, Mr and Mrs Ramsay, are so interesting. They hold us, we think of them away from their surroundings, and yet they are in accord with those surroundings, with the poetic scheme. *To the Lighthouse* is in three movements. It has been called a novel in sonata form, and certainly the slow central section, conveying the passing of time, does demand a musical analogy. We have, when reading it, the rare pleasure of inhabiting two worlds at once, a pleasure only art can give: the world where a little boy wants to go to a lighthouse but never manages it until, with changed emotions, he goes there as a young man; and the world where there is pattern, and this world is emphasized by passing much of the observation through the mind of Lily Briscoe, who is a painter. Then comes *The Waves*. Pattern here is supreme – indeed it is italicized. And between the motions of the sun and the waters, which preface each section, stretch, without interruption, conversation, words in inverted commas. It is a strange conversation, for the six characters, Bernard, Neville, Louis, Susan, Jinny, Rhoda, seldom address one another, and it is even possible to regard them (like Mrs Dalloway and Septimus) as different facets of one single person. Yet they do not conduct internal monologues, they are in touch amongst themselves, and they all touch the character who never speaks, Percival. At the end, most perfectly balancing their scheme, Bernard, the would-be novelist, sums up, and the pattern fades out. *The Waves* is an extraordinary achievement, an immense extension of the possibilities of *Kew Gardens* and *Jacob's Room*. It is trembling on the edge. A little less – and it would lose its poetry. A little more – and it would be over into the abyss, and be dull and arty. It is her greatest book, though *To the Lighthouse* is my favourite.

It was followed by *The Years*. This is another experiment in the realistic tradition. It chronicles the fortunes of a family through a documented period. As in *Night and Day*, she deserts poetry, and again she fails. But in her posthumous novel *Between the Acts* (1941) she returns to the method she understood. Its theme is a village pageant, which presents the entire history of England, and into which, at the close, the audience is itself drawn, to continue that history; 'The curtain rose' is its concluding phrase. The conception is poetic, and the text of the pageant is mostly written in verse. She loved her country – her country that is 'the country', and emerges from the unfathomable past. She takes us back in this exquisite final tribute, and she points us on, and she shows us through her poetic vagueness something more solid than patriotic history, and something better worth dying for.

Amongst all this fiction, nourishing it and nourished by it, grow other works. Two volumes of *The Common Reader* show the breadth of her knowledge and the depth of her literary sympathy; let anyone who thinks her an exquisite recluse read what she says on Jack Mytton the foxhunter, for instance. As a critic she could enter into anything – anything lodged in the past, that is to say; with her contemporaries she sometimes had difficulties. Then there are the biographies, fanciful and actual. *Orlando* is, I need hardly say, an original book, and the first part of it is splendidly written: the description of the Great Frost is already received as a 'passage' in English literature, whatever a passage may be. After the transformation of sex things do not go so well; the authoress seems unconvinced by her own magic and somewhat fatigued by it, and the biography finishes competently rather than brilliantly; it has been a fancy on too large a scale, and we can see her getting bored. But *Flush* is a complete success, and exactly what it sets out to be; the material, the method, the length, accord perfectly, it is doggie without being silly, and it does give us, from the altitude of the carpet or the sofa-foot, a peep at high poetic personages, and a new angle on their ways. The biography of Roger Fry – one should not proceed direct from a spaniel to a Slade Professor, but Fry would not have minded and spaniels mind nothing – reveals a new aspect of her powers, the power to suppress herself. She indulges in a pattern, but she never intrudes her personality or over-handles her English; respect for her subject dominates her, and only occasionally – as in her description of the divinely ordered chaos of Fry's studio with its still-life of apples and eggs labelled 'please do not touch' – does she allow her fancy to play. Biographies are too often described as 'labours of love', but the *Roger Fry* really is in this class; one artist is writing with affection of another, so that he may be remembered and may be justified.

Finally, there are the feminist books – *A Room of One's Own* and *Three Guineas* – and several short essays, etc., some of them significant. It is as a novelist that she will be judged. But the rest of her work must be remembered, partly on its merits, partly because (as Mr William Plomer has pointed out) she is sometimes more of a novelist in it than in her novels.

After this survey, we can state her problem. Like most novelists worth reading, she strays from the fictional norm. She dreams, designs, jokes, invokes, observes details, but she does not tell a story or weave a plot, and — can she create character? That is her problem's centre. That is the point where she felt herself open to criticism — to the criticisms, for instance, of her friend Hugh Walpole. Plot and story could be set aside in favour of some other unity, but if one is writing about human beings, one does want them to seem alive. Did she get her people to live?

Now there seem to be two sorts of life in fiction, life on the page, and life eternal. Life on the page she could give; her characters never seem unreal, however slight or fantastic their lineaments, and they can be trusted to behave appropriately. Life eternal she could seldom give; she could seldom so portray a character that it was remembered afterwards on its own account, as Emma is remembered, for instance, or Dorothea Casaubon, or Sophia and Constance in *The Old Wives' Tale*. What wraiths, apart from their context, are the wind-sextet from *The Waves*, or Jacob away from *Jacob's Room*! They speak no more to us or to one another as soon as the page is turned. And this is her great difficulty. Holding on with one hand to poetry, she stretches and stretches to grasp things which are best gained by letting go of poetry. She would not let go, and I think she was quite right, though critics who like a novel to be a novel will disagree. She was quite right to cling to her specific gift, even if this entailed sacrificing something else vital to her art. And she did not always have to sacrifice; Mr and Mrs Ramsay do remain with the reader afterwards, and so perhaps do Rachel from *The Voyage Out*, and Clarissa Dalloway. For the rest — it is impossible to maintain that here is an immortal portrait gallery. Socially she is limited to the upper-middle professional classes, and she does not even employ many types. There is the bleakly honest intellectual (St John Hirst, Charles Tansley, Louis, William Dodge), the monumental majestic hero (Jacob, Percival), the pompous amorous pillar of society (Richard Dalloway as he appears in *The Voyage Out*, Hugh Whitbread), the scholar who cares only for young men (Bonamy, Neville), the pernickety independent (Mr Pepper, Mr Banks); even the Ramsays are tried out first as the Ambroses. As soon as we understand the nature of her equipment, we shall see that as regards human beings she did as well as she could. Belonging to the world of poetry, but fascinated by another world, she is always stretching out from her enchanted tree and snatching bits from the flux of daily life as they float past, and out of these bits she builds novels. She would not plunge. And she should not have plunged. She might have stayed folded up in her tree singing little songs like *Blue-Green* in the *Monday or Tuesday* volume, but fortunately for English literature she did not do this either.

So that is her problem. She is a poet, who wants to write something as near to a novel as possible.

I must pass on to say a little – it ought to be much – about her interests. I have emphasized her fondness for writing both seriously and in fun, and have tried to indicate how she wrote: how she gathered up her material and digested it without damaging its freshness, how she rearranged it to form unities, how she was a poet who wanted to write novels, how these novels bear upon them the marks of their strange gestation – some might say the scars. What concerns me now is the material itself, her interests, her opinions. And not to be too vague, I will begin with food.

It is always helpful, when reading her, to look out for the passages which describe eating. They are invariably good. They are a sharp reminder that here is a woman who is alert sensuously. She had an enlightened greediness which gentlemen themselves might envy, and which few masculine writers have expressed. There is a little too much lamp oil in George Meredith's wine, a little too much paper crackling on Charles Lamb's pork, and no savour whatever in any dish of Henry James's, but when Virginia Woolf mentions nice things they get right into our mouths, so far as the edibility of print permits. We taste their deliciousness. And when they are not nice, we taste them equally, our mouths awry now with laughter. I will not torture this great university of Oxbridge by reminding it of the exquisite lunch which she ate in a don's room here in the year 1929; such memories are now too painful. Nor will I insult the noble college of women in this same university – Fernham is its name – by reminding it of the deplorable dinner which she ate that same evening in its Hall – a dinner so lowering that she had to go to a cupboard afterwards and drink something out of a bottle; such memories may still be all too true to fact. But I may without offence refer to the great dish of Bœuf en Daube which forms the centre of the dinner of union in *To the Lighthouse*, the dinner round which all that section of the book coheres, the dinner which exhales affection and poetry and loveliness, so that all the characters see the best in one another at last and for a moment, and one of them, Lily Briscoe, carries away a recollection of reality. Such a dinner cannot be built on a statement beneath a dish-cover which the novelist is too indifferent or incompetent to remove. Real food is necessary, and this, in fiction as in her home, she knew how to provide. The Boeuf en Daube, which had taken the cook three days to make and had worried Mrs Ramsay as she did her hair, stands before us 'with its confusion of savoury brown and yellow meats and its bay leaves and its wine'; we peer down the shiny walls of the great casserole and get one of the best bits, and like William Banks, generally so hard to please, we are satisfied. Food with her was not a literary device put in to make the book seem real. She put it in because she tasted it, because she saw pictures, because she smelt flowers, because she heard Bach, because her senses were both exquisite and catholic, and were always bringing her first-hand news of the outside world. Our debt to her is in part this: she reminds us of the importance of sensation in an age which practises brutality and recommends ideals. I could have illustrated sensation more reputably by quoting the charming passage about the florists' shop in *Mrs Dalloway*, or the passage where Rachel plays upon the cabin piano. Flowers and music are conventional literary adjuncts. A good feed isn't, and that is why I preferred it and chose it to represent her reactions. Let me add that she smokes, and now let the Boeuf en Daube be carried away. It will never come back in our lifetime. It is not for us. But the power to appreciate it remains, and the power to appreciate all distinction.

After the senses, the intellect. She respected knowledge, she believed in wisdom. Though she could not be called an optimist, she had, very profoundly, the conviction that mind is in action against matter, and is winning new footholds in the void. That anything would be accomplished by her or in her generation, she did not suppose, but the noble blood from which she sprang encouraged her to hope. Mr Ramsay, standing by the geraniums and trying to think, is not a figure of fun. Nor is this university, despite its customs and costumes: 'So that if at night, far out at sea over the tumbling waves, one saw a haze on the waters, a city illuminated, a whiteness in the sky, such as that now over the hall of Trinity where they're still dining or washing up plates: that would be the light shining there – the light of Cambridge.'

No light shines now from Cambridge visibly, and this prompts the comment that her books were conditioned by her period. She could not assimilate this latest threat to our civilization. The submarine perhaps. But not the flying fortress or the land mine. The idea that all stone is like grass, and like all flesh may vanish in a twinkling, did not enter into her consciousness, and indeed it will be some time before it can be assimilated by literature. She belonged to an age which distinguished sharply between the impermanency of man and the durability of his monuments, and for whom the dome of the British Museum Reading Room was almost eternal. Decay she admitted: the delicate grey churches in the Strand would not stand for ever; but she supposed, as we all did, that decay would be gradual. The younger generation – the Auden-Isherwood generation as it is convenient to call it – saw more clearly here than could she, and she did not quite do justice to its vision, any more than she did justice to its experiments in technique – she who had been in her time such an experimenter. Still, to belong to one's period is a common failing, and she made the most of hers. She respected and acquired knowledge, she believed in wisdom. Intellectually, no one can do more; and since she was a poet, not a philosopher or a historian or a prophetess, she had not to consider whether wisdom will prevail and whether the square upon the oblong, which Rhoda built out of the music of Mozart, will ever stand firm upon this distracted earth. The square upon the oblong. Order. Justice. Truth. She cared for these abstractions, and tried to express them through symbols, as an artist must, though she realized the inadequacy of symbols.

> They come with their violins, said Rhoda; they wait; count; nod; down come their bows. And there is ripples and laughter like the dance of olive trees. . .
> 'Like' and 'like' and 'like' – but what is the thing that lies beneath the semblance of the thing? Now that lightning has gashed the tree and the flowering branch has fallen . . . let me see the thing. There is a square. There is an oblong. The players take the square and place it upon the oblong. They place it very accurately; they make a perfect dwelling-place. Very little is left outside. The structure is now visible; what is inchoate is here stated; we are not so various or so mean; we have made oblongs and stood them upon squares. This is our triumph; this is our consolation.

The consolation, that is to say, of catching sight of abstractions. They have to be symbolized, and 'the square upon the oblong' is as much a symbol as the dancing olive trees, but because of its starkness it comes nearer to conveying what she seeks. Seeking it, 'we are not so various or so mean'; we have added to the human heritage and re-affirmed wisdom.

The next of her interests which has to be considered is society. She was not confined to sensations and intellectualism. She was a social creature, with an outlook both warm and shrewd. But it was a peculiar outlook, and we can best get at it by looking at a very peculiar side of her: her Feminism.

Feminism inspired one of the most brilliant of her books — the charming and persuasive *A Room of One's Own*; it contains the Oxbridge lunch and the Fernham dinner, also the immortal encounter with the beadle when she tried to walk on the college grass, and the touching reconstruction of Shakespeare's sister — Shakespeare's equal in genius, but she perished because she had no position or money, and that has been the fate of women through the ages. But Feminism is also responsible for the worst of her books — the cantankerous *Three Guineas* — and for the less successful streaks in *Orlando*. There are spots of it all over her work, and it was constantly in her mind. She was convinced that society is man-made, that the chief occupations of men are the shedding of blood, the making of money, the giving of orders, and the wearing of uniforms, and that none of these occupations is admirable. Women dress up for fun or prettiness, men for pomposity, and she had no mercy on the judge in his wig, the general in his bits and bobs of ribbon, the bishop in his robes, or even on the harmless don in his gown. She felt that all these mummers were putting something across over which women had never been consulted, and which she at any rate disliked. She declined to co-operate, in theory, and sometimes in fact. She refused to sit on committees or to sign appeals, on the ground that women must not condone this tragic male-made mess, or accept the crumbs of power which men throw them occasionally from their hideous feast. Like Lysistrata, she withdrew.

In my judgment there is something old-fashioned about this extreme Feminism; it dates back to her suffragette youth of the 1910s, when men kissed girls to distract them from wanting the vote, and very properly provoked her wrath. By the 1930s she had much less to complain of, and seems to keep on grumbling from habit. She complained, and rightly, that though women today have won admission into the professions and trades they usually encounter a male conspiracy when they try to get to the top. But she did not appreciate that the conspiracy is weakening yearly, and that before long women will be quite as powerful for good or evil as men. She was sensible about the past; about the present she was sometimes unreasonable. However, I speak as a man here, and as an elderly one. The best judges of her Feminism are neither elderly men nor even elderly women, but young women. If they, if the students of Fernham, think that it expresses an existent grievance, they are right.

She felt herself to be not only a woman but a lady, and this gives a further twist to her social outlook. She made no bones about it. She was a lady, by birth and upbringing, and it was no use being cowardly about it, and pretending that her mother had turned a mangle, or that Sir Leslie had been a plasterer's mate. Working-class writers often mentioned their origins, and were respected for doing so. Very well; she would mention hers. And her snobbery – for she was a snob – has more courage in it than arrogance. It is connected with her insatiable honesty, and is not, like the snobbery of Clarissa Dalloway, bland and frilled and unconsciously sinking into the best armchair. It is more like the snobbery of Kitty when she goes to tea with the Robsons; it stands up like a target for anyone to aim at who wants to. In her introduction to *Life as we have known it* (a collection of biographies of working-class women edited by Margaret Llewelyn Davies) she faces the fire. 'One could not be Mrs Giles of Durham, because one's body had never stood at the wash-tub; one's hands had never wrung and scrubbed and chopped up whatever the meat is that makes a miner's supper.' This is not disarming, and it is not intended to disarm. And if one said to her that she could after all find out what meat a miner does have for his supper if she took a little trouble, she would retort that this wouldn't help her to chop it up, and that it is not by knowing things but by doing things that one enters into the lives of people who do things. And she was not going to chop up meat. She would chop it badly, and waste her time. She was not going to wring and scrub when what she liked doing and could do was write. To murmurs of 'Lucky lady you!' she replied, 'I am a lady', and went on writing. 'There aren't going to be no more ladies. 'Ear that?' She heard. Without rancour or surprise or alarm, she heard, and drove her pen the faster. For if, as seems probable, these particular creatures are to be extinguished, how important that the last of them should get down her impressions of the world and unify them into a book! If she didn't, no one else would. Mrs Giles of Durham wouldn't. Mrs Giles would write differently, and might write better, but she could not produce *The Waves*, or a life of Roger Fry.

There is an admirable hardness here, so far as hardness can be admirable. There is not much sympathy, and I do not think she was sympathetic. She could be charming to individuals, working-class and otherwise, but it was her curiosity and her honesty that motivated her. And we must remember that sympathy, for her, entailed a tremendous and exhausting process, not lightly to be entered on. It was not a half-crown or a kind word or a good deed or a philanthropic sermon or a godlike gesture; it was adding the sorrows of another to one's own.

Half fancifully, but wholly seriously, she writes:

> But sympathy we cannot have. Wisest Fate says no. If her children,
> weighted as they already are with sorrow, were to take on them that
> burden too, adding in imagination other pains to their own,
> buildings would cease to rise; roads would peter out into grassy
> tracks: there would be an end of music and of painting; one great
> sigh alone would rise to Heaven, and the only attitudes for men and
> women would be those of horror and despair.

Here perhaps is the reason why she cannot be warmer and more human
about Mrs Giles of Durham.

This detachment from the working-classes and Labour reinforces the
detachment caused by her Feminism, and her attitude to society was in
consequence aloof and angular. She was fascinated, she was unafraid,
but she detested mateyness, and she would make no concessions to
popular journalism, and the 'let's all be friendly together' stunt. To the
crowd – so far as such an entity exists – she was very jolly, but she
handed out no bouquets to the middlemen who have arrogated to
themselves the right of interpreting the crowd, and get paid for doing so
in the daily press and on the wireless. These middlemen form after all a
very small clique – larger than the Bloomsbury they so tirelessly
denounce, but a mere drop in the ocean of humanity. And since it was
a drop whose distinction was proportionate to its size, she saw no
reason to conciliate it.

'And now to sum up', says Bernard in the last section of *The Waves*.
That I cannot do, for reasons already given; the material is so rich and
contradictory, and ours is not a good vintage year for judgments. I
have gone from point to point as best I could, from her method of
writing to her books, from her problems as a poet-novelist to her
problems as a woman and as a lady. And I have tried to speak of her
with the directness which she would wish, and which could alone
honour her. But how are all the points to be combined? What is the
pattern resultant? The best I can do is to quote Bernard again. 'The
illusion is upon me', he says, 'that something adheres for a moment, has
roundness, weight, depth, is completed. This, for the moment, seems to
be her life.' Bernard puts it well. But, as Rhoda indicated in that earlier
quotation, these words are only similes, comparisons with physical
substances, and what one wants is the thing that lies beneath the
semblance of the thing; that alone satisfies, that alone makes the full
statement.

Whatever the final pattern, I am sure it will not be a depressing one. Like all her friends, I miss her greatly – I knew her ever since she started writing. But this is a personal matter, and I am sure that there is no case for lamentation here, or for the obituary note. Virginia Woolf got through an immense amount of work, she gave acute pleasure in new ways, she pushed the light of the English language a little further against darkness. Those are facts. The epitaph of such an artist cannot be written by the vulgar-minded or by the lugubrious. They will try, indeed they have already tried, but their words make no sense. It is wiser, it is safer, to regard her career as a triumphant one. She triumphed over what are primly called 'difficulties', and she also triumphed in the positive sense: she brought in the spoils. And sometimes it is as a row of little silver cups that I see her work gleaming. 'These trophies', the inscription runs, 'were won by the mind from matter, its enemy and its friend.'

John Maynard Keynes by R.F. Harrod.

Reprinted from R.F. Harrod, The Life of John Maynard Keynes *(London, Macmillan, 1951), 191–4, by permission of Macmillan, London and Basingstoke; © 1951 by R.F. Harrod, reprinted by permission of Harcourt Brace Jovanovich, Inc.*

[J.M. Keynes was the most influential member of Bloomsbury in the great world that they more or less scorned, and they influenced him in his patronage of the arts. He came to Bloomsbury a little later than some of the other members, and his work in the government and in King's College, Cambridge (he was the only don among the Bloomsberries) took him away from Bloomsbury frequently; yet he maintained residences both in Gordon Square and, after his marriage to Lydia Lopokova in 1925, at Tilton near Charleston.

R.F. Harrod's biography of Keynes, published in 1951, concentrates on his economic career rather than his personal life, about which Harrod is very reticent; in the excerpt given here Harrod summarizes Keynes's relation to Bloomsbury. J.T. Sheppard was a close friend of Keynes's, an Apostle, a classicist, and eventually provost of King's; Harvey Road is where Keynes's parents lived in Cambridge.]

. . . He profited much from the constant stimulus and affection of his

Bloomsbury friends. And of course he gave much. They on their side were stimulated by his delightful company, his vitality and the impact of his abounding interests. And they gained, too, from his resources of knowledge and worldly contact. He was their main pillar of strength, their sage, their financial adviser, their patron. He was always ready to help, in one way or another, to promote their material interests. They also drew intellectual sustenance from him. Was he not a logician, a mathematician, a philosopher, an economist and an expert on many aspects of public affairs? They valued his judgment on all these topics. They were not flimsy *littérateurs*, content to take up philosophical or scientific ideas by hearsay or from inferior sources. One and all, they wished their work to be well based, if only it were possible, on a sound philosophy. 'Is it right, Maynard?' 'Is it sound?' 'Is it logically tenable?' 'Are these really the facts?'

They were all people of strong individuality, and were strongly individualist in creed. And so was Maynard. He was an individualist to the finger-tips. For him those concerned with government were a lesser breed of men, whose rôle was essentially a subordinate one. The idea that a government, however popularly elected, should be entrusted to make certain value judgments on behalf of the community was anathema to him. He had no sympathy with the project of limiting consumers' freedom of choice for the sake of greater efficiency, mass production or standardization.

On the other hand, he was violently opposed to *laissez-faire*. Mr Sheppard recalls a speech which he made at a Liberal meeting when an undergraduate. He defined Conservatives and Liberals in this way: let there be a village whose inhabitants were living in conditions of penury and distress; the typical Conservative, when shown this village, said, 'It is very distressing, but, unfortunately, it cannot be helped'; the Liberal said, 'Something must be done about this'. That was why he was a Liberal. Sheppard was impressed with this simple statement of creed. Whether or not it can be regarded as an adequate and comprehensive definition of the philosophies of the two parties at that time, the view asserted to be Liberal was assuredly Maynard's throughout his life. He believed that distress in all its forms should not go unheeded. He believed that, by care and pains, all our social evils, distressed areas, unemployment and the rest, could be abolished. He believed in planning and contriving. A way could be found. That was his experience in his private life and in the affairs of his college, and the same maxim should be applied in public affairs. He always had a scheme. His mental energy and resources were limitless. If a thing could not be done in this way, it could be done in that.

How can one reconcile the adamant and uncompromising individualism which was at the centre of his being and his fervent belief in planning? Did he resolve what might seem on the surface to be a contradiction? – a question of no little interest, since its successful resolution may be the prerequisite for the maintenance of the kind of civilization we have known. In Keynes' economic writings is to be found his solution of this dilemma. It is one of the problems to which he applied his whole mind, a not inconsiderable one, and deep study of his conclusions will long remain worth while.

This problem is tied up with another, to which he gave less explicit thought. We have seen that he was strongly imbued with what I have called the presuppositions of Harvey Road. One of these presuppositions may perhaps be summarized in the idea that the government of Britain was and would continue to be in the hands of an intellectual aristocracy using the method of persuasion. If, owing to the needs of planning, the functions of government became very far-reaching and multifarious, would it be possible for the intellectual aristocracy to remain in essential control? Keynes tended till the end to think of the really important decisions being reached by a small group of intelligent people, like the group that fashioned the Bretton Woods plan. But would not a democratic government having a wide multiplicity of duties tend to get out of control and act in a way of which the intelligent would not approve? This is another dilemma – how to reconcile the functioning of a planning and interfering democracy with the requirement that in the last resort the best considered judgment should prevail. It may be that the presuppositions of Harvey Road were so much of a second nature to Keynes that he did not give this dilemma the full consideration which it deserves.

There is also the eternal question in economics of the relation of means to ends. Conscientious economists usually stress the point that their science is concerned with means only, and that it is for others to prescribe the ends. None the less it is hard to draw the line, especially when the economist concerns himself with practical issues. An idea as to what the appropriate ends are may lurk implicit in his recommendation. Some economists are felt to have had too narrow a view of the ends of society. Not so Keynes. His writings are instinct with broad and generous views. We need not attribute this to the influence of Bloomsbury; but we can associate it with his being the kind of man who would enjoy Bloomsbury society.

While he had his own inner vision, he was none the less aware that economists as such must not overstep the mark. He once defined his position in some words very carefully chosen. It was at the end of his speech at a dinner given him by the Council of the Royal Economic Society in 1945 on his retirement from the Editorship of the *Economic Journal* after thirty-three years. It had been a wonderful speech, easy, pleasantly flowing, mellow, full of amusing anecdotes and fascinating character sketches of Balfour, Haldane and other eminent people, with whom he had had contact as secretary of the Society. Finally he came to the toast. 'I give you the toast of the Royal Economic Society, of economics and economists, who are the trustees . . .' It would have been easy to say 'the trustees of civilization', and to have sat down amid appropriate applause, '. . . who are the trustees, not . . .' One could not help having the idea – 'Why this pedantic "not"?' Surely this was not the moment for academic qualifications, for ifs and buts. It was true that he was addressing the members of the Council of the Royal Economic Society, professors, men of learning. But still, we were also human. It was a golden hour; our hearts had been touched; we had drunk champagne. We had in fact each had one modest glass of champagne, but had arranged that Maynard should have champagne only, from the soup onwards through the evening. Really there was something intolerable about the donnish 'not' coming at this hour and place. It was so unlike Maynard not to say a thing simply and boldly. But he was choosing his words: '. . . and to economists, who are the trustees, not of civilization, but of the possibility of civilization.' He had said what he wanted to say.

And what he had said was true, not something slipshod, which might pass muster on such an occasion, but an accurate description, which would bear the test of close scrutiny in the clear light of day. And it did full justice to economics. When he came to the 'not', did there flit through his mind a vision of Lytton, of Duncan, of Virginia? They were the trustees of civilization. Economists had the humbler, but still quite indispensable, rôle; it was that to which he had devoted his own life.

John Maynard Keynes by David Garnett

Reprinted from David Garnett, The Flowers of the Forest *(Chatto & Windus, London, 1950), 145–51, by permission of the author and Chatto & Windus;* © *1955 by David Garnett and reprinted by permission of Harcourt Brace Jovanovich, Inc.*

[Clive Bell, who had a number of reservations about Keynes, called him 'the cleverest man I ever met' — and Bell had met some clever people, including Bertrand Russell. David Garnett's picture of Keynes in Bloomsbury during the First World War complements Harrod's discussion of Keynes and Bloomsbury, and suggests how Keynes could both delight and annoy his Bloomsbury friends.]

Degas, one of the last survivors of the great French Impressionists, died in 1917 leaving a wonderful collection of pictures. Early in 1918 the news came that it was to be sold in Paris, and Duncan wrote and obtained a catalogue of the sale. It seemed to him to be a wonderful opportunity for the National Gallery to acquire pictures by the great Impressionists and Maynard was persuaded to fall in with Duncan's scheme.

By a coincidence, the sale of the pictures occurred during the last week of March 1918, when Maynard had to attend an inter-Ally conference on finance in Paris. After his departure the news suddenly came of the German break-through south of the Somme and of the rout of the British Fifth Army under General Gough. The situation was obviously extremely grave and Paris itself appeared to be threatened. But at Charleston we were wondering how the news from the Front would affect the sale of the pictures. Clive came down on Thursday, the twenty-eighth of March, after a visit of several days to London. At dinner we had two bottles of claret and listened gaily to Clive's gossip. He had gone out to dinner with Cecil Taylor and Sheppard who declaimed first in Greek, then in Italian, reciting the opening of the Inferno, and finally in French, much to the astonishment of those dining at other tables in the restaurant.

Suddenly we heard the front door open and, a moment later, Maynard, whom we had thought in Paris, walked in. He had crossed the Channel that afternoon and Austen Chamberlain, who was staying the week-end at Five Ashes, had given him a lift from Folkestone, dropping him at Swingate.

'I've got a Cézanne in my suitcase. It was too heavy for me to carry, so I've left it in the ditch, behind the gate.'

Duncan and I jumped up and ran out. It was a clear moonlight night and we ran all the way down to Swingate and, breathless with excitement, retrieved the bag and carried it back in triumph between us.

Maynard had eaten little during the day and was very hungry. Dinner was brought back, another bottle was opened and while Maynard ate and we sat round, he told us the story of his adventures from the beginning.

In order to put through Duncan's scheme, Maynard had first won over one of the permanent officials at the Treasury, Mr Meiklejohn, whose opposition might have been dangerous. He had then gone to see the Director of the National Gallery, Charles Holmes, and drafted a letter which Holmes agreed to send Maynard. Holmes was naturally astonished and delighted at this roast pigeon unexpectedly flying into his mouth and agreed to see Lord Curzon, one of the Trustees, whom he successfully won over to the plan. Next morning Maynard went to see Bonar Law, showed him Holmes's letter, told him that Lord Curzon supported the proposal and that he favoured it himself. Bonar Law was much amused by Maynard's enthusiasm and said it was the first time Maynard had been in favour of expenditure of any sort. He thereupon initialled a draft for 550,000 francs. Maynard at once put it through and obtained a passport for Holmes. The British party consisted of Austen Chamberlain, Lord Buckmaster, then Governor of the Bank of England, Maynard, Geoffrey Fry, his assistant, and Holmes himself, who had shaved off his moustache and assumed a pair of spectacles so that he should not be recognized by any of the Paris dealers. The subject of the sale and Holmes in his disguise interested the other members of the party far more than the financial business – of arranging further credits for the French.

Bidding was done through Knoedlers who were outside the ring of Paris dealers. Duncan had indeed advised Maynard to 'be as professional as possible in the buying and get at the right people . . .' On the second day the auction was exciting as they had to bid against the Louvre for the *Baron de Schwiter* by Delacroix and were successful. But Holmes, in spite of Maynard's urging, had refused to buy any of the Cézannes and came away from the sale with £5000 unspent, which had to be returned to the Treasury. He could have bought two El Grecos with the money. However he had secured four pictures by Ingres, two by Delacroix, two by Manet, a small Gauguin and a number of drawings.

Maynard himself had spent less than £500 for which he bought a little still life of apples by Cézanne, a little picture of a horse by Delacroix, a lovely drawing by Ingres, and several large charcoal drawings by Degas. He gave a drawing for a decoration by Delacroix to Duncan. Prices at the sale had been low as the Germans were shelling Paris with a long-range gun, though Maynard had never heard any of the explosions. There had been the greatest excitement and apprehension during his visit and at one moment everything was being got ready for evacuation of the city by the Government. But the military news with which Maynard returned was good. The Germans, after having completely routed our Fifth Army, were being held owing to their utter exhaustion after three days of continuous fighting without food, or sleep. Their supply organization had broken down. But it seemed clear to us that if the Germans failed, so would any Allied offensive that might follow it.

We were all delighted by Maynard's having put through Duncan's plan so successfully and in a letter which I wrote to him I said: 'Nessa and Duncan are very proud of you. . . You have been given complete absolution and future crimes also forgiven.'

The explanation of this sentence is that among many of his friends, particularly Lytton, Clive, Norton and Sheppard, there was a fear that 'Pozzo', as Lytton and the Stracheys called Maynard, after Pozzo di Borgo, was going to the bad. By that they meant that he was sacrificing his principles to his ambition and that he would lend himself to carrying out the plans of the most unscrupulous politicians. His friends did not hesitate to tell Maynard what they thought and he was sometimes rude and irritable when they did so. With Vanessa, Duncan and me he was very seldom irritable, for I think he felt sure of our love and loved us without reserve.

Shortly after the purchase of the pictures, there was an extremely painful scene at 46 Gordon Square. One evening, when Vanessa was in London, they were sitting up late after dinner talking over the refusal of the Emperor Karl's Peace Overtures which had been published that day. Maynard came into the room, after working late at the Treasury, and hearing what they were talking about, treated their views with the utmost contempt. Later the conversation turned on conscientious objection and Maynard declared that he did not believe anyone had a genuine conscientious objection. If he said this to exasperate Vanessa and Norton he certainly succeeded. When they expostulated he said several times: 'Go to bed. Go to bed.' Sheppard became angry at this behaviour and said: 'Maynard, you will find it is a mistake to despise your old friends.'

When Maynard had gone to bed his friends discussed his character. Vanessa took a gloomy view. She thought that Maynard had reached a critical point in his life and that the strain of prolonged overwork might have injured the quality of his brain, or at least have made him disinclined to use it. Indeed he might be so far on the downhill path that nothing would save him. Harry Norton thought that Maynard's behaviour was due to complex psychological reasons. For example, he was sure that the reason for his bad table manners — Maynard would help himself from the nearest dish with his own knife and fork when dining with his friends, instead of passing his plate — was that it flattered him to believe that he was so much liked that they did not mind how he behaved in small ways. His schoolboy insolence to them that evening was another instance of the same thing.

Sheppard, who seems to have been the angriest, attributed it to Maynard's nonconformist ancestry. He believed also that Maynard had a touch of what the French call *folie de grandeur* — an overweening sense of his own importance. Later, when I visited London, Sheppard told me that he had overheard Maynard call Jessie the cook up the basement stairs and say to her: 'I'm going to dine with the Duke of Connaught. Isn't that grand?'

On hearing this anecdote I said that any one of us might have said the same. The remark was slightly ironical, at his own expense, and partly because it was a piece of news that would greatly interest Jessie who would certainly think it grand. Sheppard maintained that Maynard really did think it was grand. If he had not done so, he would have told Sheppard about it when he opened the invitation, instead of which he had left the room to boast of the grand event to Jessie, knowing that he could not do so to him. 'It's nonconformist snobbery. They are like bugs in a rug.'

It is easy to see now that these criticisms were partly the result of the intense strain of the war. Maynard was the object of attack because he was in a particularly difficult position. He had risen with rapidity to a post of great responsibility and importance, and he was aware of hundreds of secrets which he could not divulge in order to justify his opinions, when they were challenged by his friends. Impatience and irritability were the natural consequences. It is perhaps significant that Duncan, who knew Maynard better than anyone, never added a word to the chorus of criticism. I think he alone understood and made full allowance for the difficulty of Maynard's position.

This account of the war-time differences between Maynard and his closest friends may appear to some readers to be a superficial matter which I should have been better advised to allow to remain forgotten. I have included it because I think their critical attitude at this time was a factor of great importance in Maynard's career. One of the chief characteristics of his great intelligence was the capacity to see both sides of a question, and the criticisms and anxieties of his friends led him to a stricter examination of his own motives and of the policies which he had to advocate as a servant of the Government, than he would otherwise have made. It was because his friends kept him aware of the danger that he might, for the sake of a brilliant official career, be a party to bringing about terrible evils, that he finally took the course he did in resigning his post rather than accept the reparations clauses of the Peace Treaty. That resignation led to the writing of *The Economic Consequences of the Peace* which was the foundation of his subsequent fame.

The habit of going beneath surface appearances, of analyzing and detecting far-reaching consequences, was native to his mind. But the criticisms of his most intimate friends encouraged him to criticize and justify the work that he was doing during the war and made his ultimate resignation necessary for his own peace of mind.

And I am quite sure that even though Maynard was often acutely irritated by the criticisms of his friends, he looked upon Duncan, and to a lesser extent Vanessa, as the keepers of his conscience . . .

Duncan Grant by Roger Fry

Reprinted from Living Painters: Duncan Grant *(London, The Hogarth Press, 1923), v-ix, by permission of Mrs Pamela Diamand and the Hogarth Press.*

[Duncan Grant is the youngest and now the only surviving member of Bloomsbury's immediate family. In Roger Fry's introduction to a selection of his paintings Grant is related to Bloomsbury implicitly through the discussion of 'the personality of his work' — its naturalness, spontaneity and joyfulness. Grant's indifference to what the public might want in art and his own passion to follow where his art led him are thoroughly of a piece with Bloomsbury's convictions.

Fry's commentary on Grant's paintings is an example of the critical skills he brought to bear even on the work of a close friend. The whole enterprise of *Living Painters: Duncan Grant* — the introduction, the paintings, and the publication by the Hogarth Press — is a Bloomsbury production. To its enemies the book may have been an indication of a mutual admiration society's power, while to its friends the work demonstrated the diversity of Bloomsbury's talents.]

Duncan Grant may almost be called a popular artist. He has not, of course, a big popularity, nor is he likely ever to obtain it. But he has, for so pure and uncompromising an artist, a surprisingly large circle of genuine admirers. I hasten to add that he has never done a single stroke of work with a view to ingratiate himself. He pleases, but merely by the accident of being what he is, never because he has sought in any way to satisfy the possible demands of the public. He pleases because the personality his work reveals is so spontaneous, so unconstrained, so entirely natural and unaffected. And these happy dispositions of his nature reveal themselves in his work — in his drawings by a singularly melodious and rhythmic line, in his painting by a corresponding fluency and elegance of handling. His naturalness gives him his singular charm of manner. But more than this, he has a peculiar happiness of disposition. A certain lyrical joyousness of mood predominates in his work. And this leads him to affect and enjoy what is beautiful in nature, and to express that delight in beauty in his work. I use the words beautiful and beauty here in the ordinary sense. In the more strict sense of that which is aesthetically significant, all genuine artists love beauty and create beauty. But many artists — and among them some of the greatest — have built their aesthetically beautiful constructions out of material that would be called ugly. In their outlook on life they are attracted rather by what is sinister, ugly, or exaggeratedly characteristic than by what the layman would call beautiful. Artists in whom the dramatic sense of life is uppermost generally avoid what is ordinarily felt to be beautiful, whilst those in whom the lyrical sentiments are strong are likely to affect beauty in life.

Translated into more strictly aesthetic language, this amounts, I think, to saying that artists like Duncan Grant feel most naturally those harmonies which are easy to grasp, which are fluent, persuasive, and can be followed without effort. This is true not only of the quality of Duncan Grant's design, but also of his colour. In his earlier work particularly his colour had a peculiar pellucid clearness and gaiety. Even when he restricted himself, as he often did, to a limited palette of ochres, greys, and dull greens, he was able to make his tones extraordinarily resonant and gay. In his later work an effort to give more plastic density to his forms has led him to complicate his colour schemes, with the result of a more united effect with some loss of purity and resonance.

Although in developing his means of expression Duncan Grant has been very much influenced by the great modern French masters, his talent is peculiarly English. He has, what is comparatively rare in the French school, a great deal of invention. But I do not call him English merely because of the fact that he has invention, since one could, after all, cite a good many inventors among the French, but rather because of the quality of his invention — the peculiar playful, fantastic element in it, which reminds one occasionally of the conceits of Elizabethan poetry. This shows itself particularly in such pictures as the 'Tight-rope Walker' or the 'Woman in the Tub', with its odd and unexpectedly happy use of the accessories of the toilet as elements in the design.

The very idea of invention in painting implies a literary or representational element, since the painter who is entirely preoccupied with the manner of representation will not be likely to be at the pains to invent motives, but will accept more or less what Nature provides. The inventor is almost necessarily concerned to some extent with the significance of the objects his invention brings to his mind. Having once invented his theme, he may concern himself exclusively with the manner of presenting it, but *what* he invents is likely to retain a certain value in the total result. I have sometimes thought that Duncan Grant has never exploited as fully as he should his particular gift of invention.

It was perhaps inevitable that, coming at a time when the movement of creative artists was in favour of insisting almost exclusively upon the formal elements of design, he should have tended to suppress his natural inclination to fantastic and poetic invention. Fortunately, however, this has found an outlet from time to time in his decorative work.

Gifted as he is with a peculiarly delightful rhythmic sense and an exquisite taste in colour, he is peculiarly fitted to apply his talents to decoration. When he was working at the Omega workshops his fellow-artists all recognized the peculiar charm, the unexpected originality, and the rare distinction of his ideas, and I should be inclined to say that some of the designs which he then made for carpets, for marquetry, and for needlework represent the high-water mark of applied design in England. Later on he has occasionally decorated rooms, working in collaboration with Vanessa Bell, and he has, I think, always succeeded in creating a singularly delightful atmosphere in his interiors, by reason of the unexpectedness of his fancy, the gaiety and purity of his colour — which, however, never ceases to be essentially discrete and sober — and the perfect adaptation of even the oddest inventions to the decorative purposes of the work in hand.

He has occasionally designed costumes for the ballet and given designs for scenery. These, alas, have been all too rarely executed, thanks to the conventionalism and timidity of producers. One of these designs, a proposed backcloth for a Venetian ballet with eighteenth-

century costume, is reproduced. It illustrates well enough Duncan
Grant's peculiar aptitude for such work. The datum being 'Eighteenth-
Century Venice', he has made a composition essentially modern in
feeling, but with a witty allusion to Guardi. In all his costumes one
finds him singularly sensitive to this allusive element, which plays so
large a part in the art of dress. But his wit — for such in effect such
allusions undoubtedly are — is never hard or merely brilliant. It is
always tempered by that lyrical and poetic quality which characterizes
his work. Naturally, he keeps as far as possible from pedantic archaism,
though by a subtle hint he may let those who know into the secret of
how sensitive he himself is to the art of the past.

It is indeed greatly to be regretted that so rare a talent as Duncan
Grant shows for all kinds of decorative design can find so little outlet in
our modern life. And in Duncan Grant's case this is peculiarly
regrettable, since it is difficult to him to find scope within the limits of
the easel picture for his finest gifts. He is, I think, always more inspired
by having a problem of adaptation and a theme for development given
to him than when he is confronted with the unlimited possibilities of
canvas and oils. And, indeed, the tendency of art of the last few years
had been unfavourable to him. The effort to create complete and
solidly realized constructions in a logically coherent space, which has
succeeded of late to the more decorative conception that derived from
Gauguin, has, I think, hampered rather than helped his expression.
Duncan Grant co-ordinates form more fully on the flat surface than in
three dimensions. He is more plastic when he suggests relief by the
quality of his contour than when he tries to realize it in all its
complexity, and finally the attempt to realize a completely coherent
three-dimensional whole tends to inhibit invention, which can never
hope to attain quite the same completeness of realization as the
rendering of the thing seen.

In the slow process of the development of an artist Duncan Grant is
still young. It remains to be seen whether he will get the opportunities
to utilize fully his exceptional gifts as a decorative designer, or whether,
failing that, he will find — a difficult, but by no means impossible
task — just that pictorial formula which will give full play to all his
faculties, his charming poetic invention, his infallible tact in colour
oppositions, and his melodious rhythm.

Of one thing his past assures all those who know his work, and that
is, that no outward circumstances could ever make him deviate a
hair's-breadth from the direction which his passion for art points out.

Duncan Grant by Raymond Mortimer

Reprinted from Raymond Mortimer, Duncan Grant *(Penguin Modern Painters Series Harmondsworth, Middlesex, Penguin Books, 1944), 3–14, by permission of the author and Penguin Books Ltd.*

[Raymond Mortimer's introduction to Duncan Grant's paintings, written twenty-five years after Roger Fry's for another series on modern painters, places Grant clearly in the setting of Bloomsbury. Mortimer, a literary critic and close associate of members of the Group in the twenties and thirties, suggests how Duncan Grant's environment affected him as a painter. Mortimer's attempt to distinguish between the painting of Grant and Vanessa Bell is interesting, if not completely convincing, in what it shows about the closeness of the two artists' work.]

The year 1910 is of capital importance in the history of English painting. It was then that the first Post-Impressionist Exhibition at the Grafton Galleries enjoyed a success comparable to that of a knock-about farce. Rubicund clubmen in tall hats flocked to guffaw at the masterpieces of Cézanne; in front of paintings by Van Gogh and Matisse ladies in feather boas brandished angry parasols or broke into peals of carefully silvery laughter. Eminent physicians diagnosed the types of ophthalmia or insanity from which the painters must suffer; learned critics vied with ingenuous Academicians in the virulence of their abuse. But to a few young artists the show was a revelation, and among these was Duncan Grant. His age, his temperament, and the circle in which he lived combined to make him the most ready of converts.

Born in 1885 at Rothiemurchus, in Inverness-shire (of which his paternal ancestors had for centuries been lairds), he was the only child of a regular soldier. His mother was a McNeil from Kirkcudbrightshire, but both his grandmothers were English. His early years were spent in India – where his father's regiment was serving – with journeys home on leave every two years. Then came an English prep-school, and holidays spent, since his parents were still abroad, with his father's sister, Lady Strachey, a woman remarkable for character and culture. Like many others who in adult life are conspicuous for their powers of enjoyment, he was unhappy at school. His home, however, was now with a large family distinguished by intellectual brilliance and force of personality. There were five brothers and five sisters, all with the wit, fantasy and taste for learning which made one of them, Lytton

Strachey, so delightful a writer. The young Duncan Grant was destined for the Army; so when he left his prep-school to become a dayboy at St Paul's, he was placed in the Army class and obliged to concentrate on mathematics, of which he could understand nothing. Lady Strachey saw that her nephew was wasting his time at school, and that he had not the makings of a Major. She persuaded his parents to let him leave St Paul's, and go, in 1902, to the Westminster School of Art. Already at prep-school he had prayed that one day God would make him paint like Burne-Jones; and later he had received encouragement and advice from the French artist, Simon Bussy, who was engaged to one of his Strachey cousins. But at the Westminster School of Art he made no particular mark; moreover, he was found unworthy of admission to the Royal Academy School.

He made a journey to Italy, where he copied the Masaccios in the Carmine, and received an indelible impression from the paintings of Piero della Francesca. Then, in 1906, he spent a year in Paris as a pupil of Jacques-Emile Blanche, who proved an admirable teacher. He was now captivated by the Impressionists, and spent much of his time at the Luxembourg, where the Caillebotte collection was then housed. The Chardins in the Louvre were also subjects for repeated and delighted study. When he returned to London he tried the Slade School for half a term, and then took a studio in Fitzroy Square.

The next few years saw the formation of that circle of friends, often nicknamed 'Bloomsbury', some account of which is here relevant. It centred round the daughters of Sir Leslie Stephen, Vanessa and Virginia (who married respectively Clive Bell and Leonard Woolf). Their brothers brought their Cambridge friends to the House. Prominent among these was Lytton Strachey, who introduced Grant to the group. This now also included Roger Fry (who was older than the others), Maynard Keynes, E.M. Forster, and Desmond MacCarthy and his wife. Fry, already well known both as a painter and an expert authority on the Old Masters, was a fascinating and invaluable companion for Duncan Grant, but the whole Bloomsbury group gave him an environment different from that of most young painters. They were passionately interested in the arts, they had no respect for the conventions — their ways of talk and behaviour were often thought shocking — but they had a breadth of culture and, under all the wit, a seriousness that distinguished them from the general run of Bohemians.

Duncan Grant, like most painters, is fascinated by the vehement life of great cities, the jostle of crowds in pubs and *bistros*, the waterfronts of ports like Toulon and Marseilles. Listening to the endless and

animated arguments of the Bloomsbury intellectuals was a pleasure of a
different order. He was a few years younger, and one imagines him
unconsciously adopting their standards, and soon contributing himself
to the already very various flavour. For his slightly hesitant manner
could never conceal for long an uncommonly distinct and decided
personality. The Bloomsbury circle was intolerant of everything
mediocre, contemptuous of official standards, of easygoing worldliness
and of any compromise with the public taste. But there was none of the
priggishness often attributed to highbrows, and, above all, no mutual
adulation. Duncan Grant found himself with individuals who were
affectionate in their friendship but caustic in their criticism.

He travelled to Sicily, to Tunisia, to Greece. (*The Lemon Gatherers*,
now in the Tate, was painted in 1908 from Sicilian memories.) In Paris
he saw for the first time, in the Stein collection, works by Picasso and
Matisse. He showed pictures himself at the Friday Club, a Chelsea
studio in which the Bloomsbury group used to meet. Then in 1910
came the first Post-Impressionist Exhibition.

It was organized by Roger Fry; the Secretary was Desmond
MacCarthy, whose eyes had been opened by the Van Goghs in Munich
and Amsterdam. (He and Clive Bell were, I fancy, the first English
writers to cotton on to what is called 'modern' painting.) Fry had been
critical of the Impressionists, whose influence prevailed at the New
English Art Club and who in England were still considered alarmingly
'advanced'. Imbued with Italian Art, he deplored their insistence upon
realism and their frequent negligence of composition. In Cézanne,
Seurat, Van Gogh and Gauguin he recognized with delight a return to
the emphasis upon design that was traditional with the Old Masters. But
when he brought their works to London — and works by their
successors, Picasso, Matisse, Derain, Vlaminck, Friesz — very few of his
fellow *cognoscenti* could see, as he did, beneath the superficial
differences, a basic similarity to the great art of the past. Sargent, it
must be remembered, was then the painter most admired by the
cultivated English. Even those who genuinely cared for the Italian
Primitives and for the sculpture of Chartres were horrified when the
Post-Impressionists used analogous liberties. Taste had accommodated
itself to a lack of realism and to calculated distortion in the Old
Masters, but collectors of Sienese altar-pieces and of Japanese prints
complained as angrily as the Philistines that the pictures of Cézanne and
Van Gogh were not 'like life'. Now that reproductions of their works
are best-sellers, and their influence ubiquitous in posters and even in
chintzes, it may be difficult to see why they caused such agitation

thirty years ago. It was, of course, one more repetition of a familiar story. Ingres was condemned as an inaccurate draughtsman — in a sense justly, for he made ruthless distortions; Napoleon III slashed at a Courbet with a riding-whip; Manet's pictures excited howls of derision. But if in England in 1910 even the cultivated public laughed or became indignant, the new way of painting was spreading from Paris all over Europe, and giving young artists an exhilarating sense of liberation. The years between, say, 1908 and 1928 saw an extraordinary outburst of talent. Painters and sculptors flocked from every continent to Paris. A new and splendidly fertile territory had been discovered for the visual artist to explore. The young, ardent in imagination and eager to express themselves, gained a particular impetus from the new school. Painters like Derain and Vlaminck and Friesz produced brilliant works by the side of which their later performance is sadly disappointing. It may even be held that Picasso is the only painter of the time – except, perhaps, Rouault — whose imaginative powers have not slackened with the passing years. In excitement and fruitfulness the early period of Post-Impressionism can be compared with the period when the infectious example of Giorgione gave to a whole school of painters an effective inspiration.

Duncan Grant was just at the right age to get the most advantage from the new movement. For eight years he had been studying the Old Masters and improving his technique for depicting appearances so that now he could afford to take liberties. (Post-Impressionism has been a temptation and a trap to many apprentice painters: to try to distort before you can represent is like trying to dance before you can walk.) He began a series of paintings that are without a parallel in the history of the British School. A bunch of flowers, a woman in a bath-tub, a lamp on a table, a coster with a greyhound, a group of ballet-dancers, a friend sitting in a garden — anything, indeed, that caught his eye and memory provided a theme upon which he would elaborate a fantasia. The natural forms were wrested into arabesques; the colours were arbitrary or rather chosen merely for the felicity of their interaction; the concern with volume was hardly greater than in Chinese and Sienese painting. At the time these pictures were astonishing, and intensely delightful to the few who were able to accept them. They no longer look odd, but they still surprise one by their originality, and I find as much delight in them as ever. They are very various, some painted in closely allied tones, others depending on sharp contrasts. Almost all are vernal, gay and lyrical with a charming air of spontaneity. Here was a painter who could make a tune out of a stove-pipe or a towel-horse.

One could catch references to Byzantine mosaics, to Matisse, to African sculpture, to early Italians – and still specially to Piero della Francesca – but the pictures were conspicuously personal. It was clear, moreover, that they were the work of a born decorator.

In 1911 Duncan Grant collaborated with Roger Fry, Etchells, Adeney, Max Gill and Albert Rutherston in the decoration of a room, now destroyed, at the Borough Polytechnic. In 1913 Roger Fry, always indefatigable in enterprise, organized the Omega workshops for the production and sale of applied art. The designs were couched in the idiom of Post-Impressionism, and here for the first time cubism was applied to textiles, noble ancestors, as it were, of the degenerate 'modernist' stuffs that now proliferate. Fry had a particular distaste for the mechanical rigidity of pattern in machine-made goods – a rigidity prized by the 'functionalist' school of modern designers. He insisted, therefore, on the value of the slight irregularities that reveal the hand of the artist even in the repetitions of a formal design. Duncan Grant has a charming 'handwriting' whether he is defining a contour in a nude study or scribbling a border for a book-jacket or a carpet. He may be thought, however, to exaggerate sometimes the irregularities admired by Roger Fry, and also, as it were, to over-punctuate: the tendency to multiply criss-crosses and croquet-hoops round his decorations, to leave not an inch unadorned, is a legacy, I presume, from the Omega workshops. There he painted screens and tables and pottery, made designs for printed linens and carpets and marquetry trays. He used Omega textiles, Vanessa Bell's as well as his own, for the costumes of *Twelfth Night*, produced in Paris at the Vieux Colombier theatre by Copeau in 1914. The first appearances of the Russian Ballet in Western Europe were revealing to painters the alluring possibilities of designing for the stage. About the same time Grant made some decorative panels for the country house of Mr and Mrs St John Hutchinson, whose appreciation of his work has been constant. Lady Ottoline Morrell was another whose encouragement and hospitality – Bertrand Russell, D.H. Lawrence, Aldous Huxley and Mark Gertler were her frequent guests – stimulated Duncan Grant in these early years.

This period of artistic vitality in France and England was suddenly interrupted by the war of 1914. Grant worked on farms in Suffolk and Sussex, but managed also to do some painting, including a set of costumes for a Copeau production of *Pelléas and Mélisande*. After the war he took a studio in Hampstead, and then one that had been Whistler's, Sickert's and Augustus John's, in Fitzroy Street. During the next few years he saw a great deal of Sickert, who did not so much influence directly his painting as encourage him with appreciation and criticism. In 1920 he had his first one-man show at the Carfax Gallery. He continued to decorate rooms — for Mr Henry Harris, for Mr Peter Harrison, for Mr Maynard Keynes, for Mr and Mrs St John Hutchinson, for Miss Sands and Miss Hudson, for Mr and Mrs Woolf, for Lady Gerald Wellesley. He made some further theatrical designs – for Beatrice Mayor's *The Pleasure Garden*, and a Greek play at Cambridge. (The latter was one of the most beautiful *décors* of our time.) But already in the early 1920s he became increasingly pre-occupied with other ambitions.

It has been the fate of many among the best painters of the British School to begin with the display of extraordinary gifts; and then either they give way to the requirements of the public, like Gainsborough (though indeed he continued also to paint superbly for his own satisfaction), or else, like Conder and Wilson Steer, they surrender to the fluency of their hands and do what comes easiest. The first of these pitfalls can never have been a danger to so conscientious an artist as Duncan Grant; the second he has been careful to avoid. Indeed, it may be thought that in his later easel-pictures he too often is working against the grain of his temperament. 'The effort to create complete and solidly realized constructions in a logically coherent space has, I think, hampered rather than helped his expression. Duncan Grant co-ordinates more fully on the flat surface than in three dimensions.' This was Roger Fry's opinion in 1924. Since then Grant has persisted with unabated industry in painting realistically to create volumes in space. He uses colour to provide modelling, sacrificing his gift for decorative colour; or rather reserving it for specifically decorative works. These realistic pictures often contain passages that are lurid or morose. And even the texture becomes heavy. At the worst such works can be commended for their thoroughness: Grant pushes his pictures further, I think, than any of his contemporaries dare to do. And some of them seem to me entirely admirable: the full-length portrait of Mrs Bell, for instance, is a sumptuous harmony. It is arguable, moreover, that these painstaking works provide a necessary discipline, without which the decorative paintings would become merely fluent repetitions. Duncan Grant's decorative panels, pastels and water-colours reflect the man one meets — mercurial, full of humour, quick in response to sensuous beauty, delightful in the unexpectedness of his comments. Some of the easel-pictures must express an otherwise hidden side of his nature, perhaps a dourness inherited from a Covenanter among his ancestors. A poet often becomes clumsy when he argues in prose, and it

is unlikely that Veronese could have painted with success in the style of
Philippe de Champagne.

Duncan Grant's decorations in point of fact are, as a whole series of
sketches will prove, no less painstaking than his realistic works; but the
labour does not show. This goes to prove that they express the natural
bent of his genius. Unluckily he has not enjoyed much opportunity for
large-scale decoration. Grant, from the days of the Omega workshops,
has remained interested in applied art. The textiles he designed for the
firm of Allan Walton I consider the most beautiful printed stuffs I have
seen. He has also designed delightful dinner and tea services for Messrs
Brain; and he has painted on pots and plates made by Miss Phyllis
Keyes. Embroideries of his design, executed with consummate taste by
his mother, are masterpieces of contemporary applied art. But the
history of his most important commission is a cautionary tale. In 1935
he was engaged to decorate a large room in SS *Queen Mary*. The scheme
included three great painted panels; but when these were completed, Sir
Percy Bates, the chairman of the Cunard-White-Star Company, intervened, and refused to have them put up. I see good reasons for this
decision. They would have contrasted violently with the style of
decoration in which the rest of the ship was lavishly embellished.
Moreover, they would certainly not have appealed to the film-stars,
opera-singers, oil-magnates and other Big Business tycoons who before
the war were bound to be the most valuable patrons of a luxury liner. It
would perhaps have been better if the Company had thought of this
before commissioning so distinguished and so inappropriate an artist.
The panels have found an honourable home for the present in the
canteen of the National Gallery.

Unluckily a lot of Duncan Grant's decorative work has been
destroyed by German bombs. The houses of Miss Sands and Mr and Mrs
Woolf were demolished; so was the artist's own studio in Fitzroy Street,
with some of his works in it. He has now completed a large
wall-painting for the chancel-arch of the parish church of Berwick in
Sussex, near his country home, while Vanessa Bell has decorated the
sides of the chancel with an Annunciation and a Nativity. She has
collaborated with Grant in so many of his decorations that when
writing about his work the critic must also consider hers. It is
sometimes assumed that she is, as it were, his pupil. Certainly there are
conspicuous similarities between Vanèssa Bell's work and Duncan
Grant's, and often they have painted simultaneously from the same
model. Yet it seems to me clear that the influence has been not
one-sided but reciprocal. Careful comparison suggests moreover that,

though they share many tastes, they are quite unlike in temperament. Vanessa Bell is, I think, by nature a realist. (Unlike Grant she has a great gift for catching a likeness.) She is altogether a graver, less exuberant, artist; her landscapes and still-lifes bear the signs of careful consideration and are all the better for this. The resemblances between her work and his have, I think, prevented her gifts receiving the full appreciation that they merit. Their virtues seem to me markedly different in character, and each paints best when painting least like the other. The tempo natural to her is *andante*, while his is *allegro*.

Many of his happiest pictures have been inspired by classical mythology. Venus in her conch, Narcissus leaning over his watery looking-glass, Arion astride a dolphin, a satyr snatching the drapery from a sleeping nymph — such subjects come to him as naturally as to the Florentine painters or the Elizabethan song-writers. He is unversed in the Greek and Latin tongues, and there is evidently nothing antiquarian in his taste for classical themes. But no English painter has been more profoundly influenced by Italian art. As late as 1928 he made a full-size copy of the Piero di Cosimo *Death of Procris*; and when in London he was much at the National Gallery. Between 1927 and 1938 he spent part of each year at Cassis near Marseilles, where among the vineyards and olive-groves, with, in the distance, the white houses and red roofs clustering round the harbour and the fickle blues of the bay, he found the Mediterranean light that has made painters happy from Raphael and Claude to Renoir and Matisse. Some of the pastels in particular that derive from these sojourns are among Grant's most attractive works. The effect of the Southern scene, no less than of the Italian Masters, is powerful in almost all his decorative paintings.

Duncan Grant is a conspicuously accomplished draughtsman. The studies of the nude, on which he bases his decorative compositions, are exemplary in observation as well as in sensibility. But he draws in mass rather than in outline, and conveys the contours by overlapping strokes of his pencil or chalk; and the public prefers a tighter method. (Augustus John's drawings for this reason are more in demand than Sickert's.) Often, too, whether he is drawing in pencil or in oils, Grant is content to indicate a hand by a seemingly arbitrary scribble. He likes to emphasize the contrasts between the male and female forms, giving his women massively rounded torsos, arms and legs — even calumniously thickening the wrists and ankles. (Similarly it has, one notices, been the fashion among modern sculptors, such as Maillol and Henry Moore, to broaden the human figure. The Romanesque sculptors preferred to lengthen it. Both methods are justified by their results.) On the other hand, when Grant draws the male nude, which he does more often than most contemporary artists, he inclines to refine the forms, or at least to choose slender models.

His handling of paint, like his drawing, in his best work brims with vitality; and even in his less successful works there are always beautiful passages. His inventiveness in colour has from the first been remarkable. He is an exceptionally prolific painter, in the sense that each year he covers a great number of canvases. But he is apt to be dissatisfied with most of them, and he puts them aside in the hope of returning to them. His actual output is therefore small. He has had one-man shows at Agnew's; and pictures by him are sometimes to be seen also at the Leicester Galleries, the Lefevre, the Redfern and the Leger. He was an early member of the London Group, and he belonged to the London Artists' Association which used to have a room at the Cooling Gallery. He never sends to the Royal Academy, but one of his pictures was exhibited there in 1941, because it had been purchased by the Chantrey Bequest.

In this introduction I have made no attempt to conceal my own tastes and prejudices. A critic, as opposed to an historian of art, must write from his own eye, his personal responses. It is now accepted that the principal function of a picture is not to give information about the visible world, but to express the imagination of the painter and to infect the spectator with his emotion. The degree to which he chooses to represent phenomena varies with individuals and epochs. I usually prefer Duncan Grant in his more fanciful and less factual moods. But I am aware that I am prejudiced aesthetically in favour of elegance. (Consequently I am handicapped by a constitutional inability to feel enthusiasm for the Flemish Primitives.) Duncan Grant works in two such contrasting styles that perhaps full justice could be done to him only by two critics with similarly contrasting temperaments. This confession made – and I think critics should be more honest about their natural limitations – I can hope that readers will take more notice of the praise I have given than of the reserves I have made. I believe Grant to be conspicuous in the history of the British School alike for his gifts and for the energy and integrity with which these have been cultivated. I hope that after the war public bodies will prove more discriminating than rich men have shown themselves; and that the country of his birth, having at last produced a consummate decorator, will provide him with the opportunities he deserves, and posterity with a legacy of fine visual pleasure.

BLOOMSBURY OBSERVED

INTRODUCTION

The attention that Bloomsbury attracted from its contemporaries is shown in the last two parts of this collection. *Bloomsbury Observed* presents views of the Bloomsbury Group by individuals who, while not uncritical, were nevertheless friendly, at least to many of the members. A number of the observers represented here were well known social or literary figures, and many of them were quite close to Bloomsbury. Yet most of them write of Bloomsbury not as members but as outsiders watching and occasionally participating in some activity of Bloomsbury.

These eye-witness accounts were written between the twenties and the sixties; the periods of Bloomsbury they describe range all the way from before the First World War until after the Second. The pieces are arranged according to the date of their writing to indicate how the Group's increasing fame influenced some of the later views of Bloomsbury.

Raymond Mortimer: London Letter

Reprinted from Raymond Mortimer, 'London Letter', The Dial, LXXXIV (February, 1928), 238–40, by permission of the author.

[1928 saw the publication not only of Virginia Woolf's *Orlando* and Lytton Strachey's *Elizabeth and Essex* but also of the first accurate description of the Bloomsbury Group. Raymond Mortimer's 'London Letter' to the American *Dial* enumerates for the first time some of the members and convictions of Bloomsbury. His brief description is, of course, incomplete — yet it is more reliable than many of the accounts that have subsequently been published; the Americans needed to have Bloomsbury explained to them from the beginning. It was some time before anyone explained Bloomsbury as clearly and fairly to the English.

Raymond Mortimer succeeded Desmond MacCarthy as literary editor of *The New Statesman* and then as senior literary critic for the *Sunday Times*. He is frequently mentioned as one of the younger generation of Bloomsbury that flourished in the twenties and thirties. Mr Mortimer once commented on what Bloomsbury meant to him in a review of Carrington's letters and diaries; after mentioning that Strachey's biographer had failed to bring out the characteristic gaiety of the Group, he observed, 'They were the best company I ever had the luck to find'.

The following note was kindly supplied by Mr Mortimer as an introduction to the reprinting of his 1928 letter: 'In the years 1922 to 1929 I contributed to *The Dial* a series of London Letters. This one includes a joke that may now need explanation. I quote from an imaginary book published thirty-two years after the date on which I was writing.']

February 1928

> A small group of friends who were undergraduates at Cambridge at the beginning of the century came to have an influence on their time which can still hardly be gauged. Among these were the sons of Sir Leslie Stephen, the eminent Victorian biographer and agnostic. The Misses Vanessa and Virginia Stephen, their sisters, lived in London; and their house became the nucleus of the group, when the two brothers and their friends left Cambridge.

I am quoting from the seventh volume of Sir Raymond Mortimer's trustworthy if academic *Studies in Twentieth-Century Culture* (Hogarth Press 1960).

> The young ladies, who were as remarkable for their beauty as for their intellect, married two of their brothers' friends, Clive Bell and Leonard Woolf, who were to become celebrated, the one as an apostle of contemporary art, a vigorous pamphleteer, a poet, a historian of civilization, and a psychological biographer; the other as an editor, a publisher, and a politician. An important figure in this group was Edward Morgan Forster, novelist, critic, and historian. Perhaps the most influential was Giles Lytton Strachey, who later revolutionized the art of history: he is said to have shown from the first the almost fanatical intransigence in conduct and opinion which marks the leaders of important movements. But the group was always an oligarchy – fierce mutual criticism was the breath of its existence. Another dominating figure was John Maynard Keynes, the

economist and politician, who by his marriage years later with Mme Lopokova, the first dancer of her day, brought leadership in yet another of the arts into this astonishing circle. Duncan Grant, though not a member of the University, was an early intimate of the group, and so was Roger Fry, though of an older generation of Cambridge men. It thus appears that from one small band of friends have come the subtlest novelists, the most famous economist, the most influential painters, the most distinguished historian, and the liveliest critics of the post-war period in England.

I have preferred to quote from the veteran critic, because my relations with the persons concerned are too close for me to be able to speak of them easily without impertinence. But the name of Bloomsbury is becoming familiar in Berlin, Paris, and, I presume, New York as well as in London, and I think the time has come when a study of the genesis of the group and the character of those who compose it should be made public. I am certainly not the person to do this; but since I am writing a letter I may perhaps take a letter-writer's privileges and put down a few casual comments on what I see around me.

It is impossible to say where Bloomsbury begins, and where it ends. Are the painters, scholars, and journalists of a younger generation to be included? Arthur Waley? Francis Birrell? George Rylands? Douglas Davidson? Are old and intimate friends who have never become entirely imbued with the Bloomsbury spirit? And in fact what exactly is this spirit? I do not dare a definition. But I would place first a belief in Reason, and a conviction that the pursuit of Truth and a contemplation of Beauty are the most important of human activities. Obviously many of Bloomsbury's fiercest enemies might subscribe to this creed. The distinction of the leaders of the group is that they have acted upon it to an extraordinary extent. No subject of conversation has been taboo, no tradition accepted without examination, and no conclusion evaded. In a hypocritical society, they have been indecent; in a conservative society, curious; in a gentlemanly society, ruthless; and in a fighting society, pacifist. They have been passionate in their devotion to what they thought good, brutal in their rejection of what they thought second rate; resolute in their refusal to compromise. 'Narrow in their tastes, loose in their view of morals, irreverent, unpatriotic, remote, and superior,' their enemies say. And, I think, truly. For will not relentless reasoning and delicate discrimination make a man all these things?

Such vivid personalities as the leaders of the group could never of course commit themselves to any corporate doctrine of taste. But they have tended to exalt the classical in all the Arts: Racine, Milton, Poussin, Cézanne, Mozart, and Jane Austen have been their more cherished artists. Already the signs of a romantic revival are everywhere perceptible. The next generation is likely to react vigorously against the intellectualism of Bloomsbury. The younger French care as little for Voltaire as they do for Anatole France. Keyserling and Maurras, Chesterton and Lawrence, are united in their hatred of intellectualism. Indeed M. Julien Benda seems almost the only important figure on the Continent whose views are akin to Bloomsbury's. But here anti-intellectualism has not yet found a champion adequately armed.

Obviously there is a romantic poet in Mrs Woolf, a mystic in Mr E.M. Forster, whereas Mr Strachey, for all his appreciation of Blake and Beddoes, remains in his outlook almost a contemporary of Voltaire. But compare these three writers with any outside the group, great Edwardians like Wells and Bennett, for instance, and a certain consonance in the Bloomsbury artists becomes, I think, apparent. For one thing they remain singularly unspotted by the world; too disillusioned to expect that their scale of values can ever command general assent. (Perhaps the fact that they almost all possessed small independent incomes gave them an initial advantage over many of their rivals.) The east wind of Cambridge philosophy braces their nerves. Pragmatism, Bergsonism, Oxford idealism, wither beneath it. And the historian of Bloomsbury will have to discuss the enormous influence on the group of George Moore, the author not of *The Book Kerith* but of *Principia Ethica*.

Why Bloomsbury? someone who does not know London may ask. It was Mrs Desmond MacCarthy, the author of *A Nineteenth Century Childhood* (she and her husband have always been intimate with the group) who, I believe, first gave it this name from the quarter of London where most of its members lived. It is a quarter honeycombed with spacious squares, where houses built for the gentry in the eighteenth century declined later into boarding-houses for impoverished foreigners and students at the University of London. The houses are for the most part still too big to be inhabited by single families, but the quarter is replacing Chelsea as the home of painters and writers. On summer evenings there is tennis on the lawns, and the Vicar's daughters can be seen playing with the bigwigs, ignorant of the dangerous company they keep. Around are figures reading and talking, and as night falls, the mourning veils in which London soot has dressed the Georgian façades become unnoticeable, and in these gardens you may fancy yourself in the precincts of a college. The passing of a quarter of a century is forgotten, the quick exchanges and curious conjectures, the vehement arguments, remake the past; and the commercial traveller arriving late at St Pancras' from the north, catches a glimpse as he passes of an unfamiliar and unhurrying London, of

> groups under the dreaming garden-trees,
> And the full moon, and the white evening star.

Lady Ottoline Morrell: 'Artists Revels'

Reprinted from The Early Memoirs of Lady Ottoline Morrell, *ed.*
Robert Gathorne-Hardy (London, Faber and Faber, 1964), 178–81,
reprinted by permission of the publisher; © *1963 by Julian Vinogradoff*
and Robert Gathorne-Hardy; reprinted by permission of Alfred A.
Knopf, Inc.

[As the most celebrated and hospitable hostess and patron of the arts of her time, Lady Ottoline Morrell was intimately involved with at least one member of Bloomsbury and generously receptive to them all, especially during the First World War when her Oxfordshire manor Garsington became a refuge for conscientious objectors who were supposed to be doing agricultural work. She was aristocratic, eccentric, sentimental, extravagant – a figure of fun in Bloomsbury and else-where. Yet there was a genuine fondness and respect for her too, as is shown in *The Times* obituary of her, written by Virginia Woolf.

For her part, Lady Ottoline had reservations about Bloomsbury's behaviour and pretensions. Her observations of pre-war Bloomsbury printed here are taken from memoirs based on diaries that she kept at the time; the memoirs were written sometime between the mid-twenties and her death in 1938.]

. . . I was now beginning to see more of Virginia Stephen and her friends and to go to her Thursday evenings in Fitzroy Square, where long-legged young men would sit in long basket-chairs smoking pipes and talking almost inaudibly in breathless voices of subjects that seemed to me thrilling and exciting. When the pool that lay between us grew calm and overcast, Virginia's bell-like voice would be heard, swinging, swinging and resonant, awaking and scattering dull thought, and giving warning that a light would be thrown into the darkness, the rays of which would light up her own lovely face and our stagnant prosy minds. She would lead us swiftly along into the streets or the lives of any she may meet, and the world of poetry, showing her light into dull corners, and making them appear full of fantasy and beauty. This strange, lovely, furtive creature never has seemed to me to be made of common flesh and blood. She was rather like some Diana of the realm of the mind who, though she had forsaken forest and the chase of deer, now treads the ways of man still carrying hidden under her veil her crescent of light. She comes and goes, she folds her cloak around her and vanishes, having shot into her victim's heart a quiverful of teasing arrows.

She walks in London streets, she travels in an omnibus, and with her penetrating light searches the hearts of those she meets. She sees their thoughts and feels the tenderest and frailest vibrations of emotions traversing their beings. She hears the distant song of beauty or the sigh of despair.

To this visitant from another sphere our lives appear more strange, more vivid and fantastically exciting than they do to oneself.

As years have gone by, and her sojourning here has inured her to our ordinary life, she seems now to sit with almost familiar ease in my room, and I no longer feel the fear that this enchanting and bewildering goddess will sail away before I have recovered from her entry and before I had caught a glimpse of her crescent light. I feel I have made her see into my heart.

Since the days of Fitzroy Square, when she led her followers on to the *Dreadnought* dressed up as an Eastern princess, and out to Covent Garden at dawn to buy armfuls of flowers, she has known the love of many, she has married, she has written, and she is now recognized and admired. But I like to remember her in the old days with her little circle of companions: her brother Adrian, her sister Vanessa, Vanessa's husband, Clive Bell, that happy, flattering, good-tempered Autolycus holding out gay leaves for us to admire. Roger Fry, who had not yet set sail on the sea of modern French art; Lytton Strachey and Duncan Grant — what a delightful company they seemed!

Of Lytton Strachey I used to feel most shy, for he said so little and he seemed to live far away in an atmosphere of rarefied thought. His voice so small and faint, but with definite accentuations and stresses of tone, giving a sense of certainty and distinction, appeared to come from very far away, for his delicate body was raised on legs so immensely long that they seemed endless, and his fingers equally long, like antennae. It was not till I knew him better that I found how agile those long legs could be, and what passion and feeling lay in that delicate body, and how rapidly those long and beautiful antennae could find passages in Racine or Dryden, and the strength and vigour of his voice when he read these passages aloud to me. But at this time he seemed so melancholy and aloof that I hardly dared approach him, though he would come to see me now and then. Duncan Grant, too, was shy and vague and elusive, but always bewitching.

It was in this year that the first Russian dancers appeared in London, not the Diaghilev Ballet, which did not arrive here until a year or so later, but some forerunners who seemed to our unspoilt sight as winged fairies. How lovely, how gay, how enchanting they were, as if Conder's pictures had come to life. I was so enthusiastic about them that night after night I took friends to see them: John and Dorelia, and Desmond MacCarthy and Roger Fry, Virginia and Duncan Grant, were all led there. How anxiously I watched their faces to see if they were as thrilled as I was. I often lost whole precious moments of this all too short joy by scanning the faces of those I had taken to see the effects on them. Their appreciation never really satisfied me.

Then one day the Clive Bells asked us to go with them to Artists Revels at the Botanical Gardens. What a picture of gaiety the two words evoked, 'Artists Revels'. Philip and I dressed up, he in his black velvet court suit, I in a very full black taffeta dress, with black lace mantilla.

It was my first and only experience of a fancy dress ball and I visualized a Mozartian scene of lovely gaily-dressed youths and maidens flitting in and out of dark trees lit up by coloured lights – a ballet in real life. But even at the dinner in Gordon Square with the Bells a certain disillusionment began. I felt that our companions had not chosen very appropriate costumes. Vanessa's Madonna-like beauty surely could have found a happier alias than that of a Pierrot, and Virginia was hardly suited to pose as Cleopatra, whose qualities, as I had imagined them, were just those that Virginia did not possess. Adrian, her brother, too, was not very convincing as a young Cardinal, but I excused these little lapses as high-handed carelessness on the part of intellectuals.

On arriving at the Botanical Gardens, however, the scene that I had anticipated was nowhere to be found. I searched indoors and out. I recoiled from the jumble-tumble of awkward young men waving long, raw, red arms and legs, and young women equally crude and ungainly, pretentiously and unsuitably decked out in badly adjusted garments of all ages and periods. What a different scene to the one I had expected of ordered and exquisite beauty! Has the past indeed so literally vanished that no trace of its minor arts and finery remains in our instincts? Are our ancestors so completely buried under their monuments that no spark of their delicate taste and courtly grace remains in our blood? We still live in their homes and recite their poems, but to wear their clothes clearly is a vanished art. The buoyant, athletic bodies of these young people have grown sadly unsuited to the buckram of the past. Their minds have developed their bodies into a different mould.

From behind the dark trees I caught the sound of mocking laughter. Was it from these lords and ladies whose earthly garments were being so travestied by the ungainly young revellers? I seemed to hear them say, 'You think we looked like that, do you? Silly children, how blind you are not to see and understand us better than that. Go and put on your cricket flannels and tennis skirts, your football shorts and motor goggles, and play your hoydenish games which you understand. Leave ruffs and farthingales, embroidered stomachers and waistcoats, powdered wigs and minuets to us.'

I put my arm through Philip's and drew my black lace veil close round me hoping that no one would search my face that night to read the melancholy disappointment that I felt at the sight of English artists revelling!

Perhaps, after all, I belonged to the time of hoops and loops and billowing skirts – a rare survival – one of those who were laughing from behind the trees.

Vita Sackville-West: The Vitality of Bloomsbury

Reprinted from Harold Nicolson's Diaries and Letters, 1930–1939, *edited by Nigel Nicolson (London, 1966), 350–1. Harold Nicolson's Diaries and Letters © 1966 by William Collins Sons & Co. Ltd. V. Sackville-West's Letters © 1966 by Sir Harold Nicolson. Introduction and Notes to this volume © 1966 by Nigel Nicolson. Reprinted by permission of Collins Publishers, London, and Atheneum Publishers, USA.*

[Vita Sackville-West became acquainted with Bloomsbury through her intense friendship with Virginia Woolf – a friendship that led to the writing of *Orlando* among other things. Vita and Harold Nicolson were never much involved with the Group, though the Hogarth Press published her fiction and some of his work as well.

As Harold Nicolson put it in a diary entry written in 1940,

> Vita says that our mistake was that we remained Edwardian for too
> long, and that if in 1916 we had got in touch with Bloomsbury, we
> should have profited more than we did carrying on with Mrs George
> Keppel, Mrs Ronald Greville and the Edwardian relics. We are
> amused to confess that we had never even heard of Bloomsbury in
> 1916. But we agree that we have had the best of both the plutocratic
> and the Bohemian worlds, and that we have had a lovely life.

In 1938 Vita Sackville-West wrote to her husband the following
letter that describes her admiration for Bloomsbury, together with the
inevitable qualifications.]

3rd August 1938. Sissinghurst.
I went to Rodmell for last night, and very nice it was too. We sat out in
the garden watching the late sunlight making the corn all golden over
the Downs. Then I had a long talk this morning with Virginia, who was
in her most delightful mood. Tell your host [Somerset Maugham], if
you think it would please him, that Virginia much admired his
autobiography. She had liked the clarity of his style, and also the
honesty with which he tried to get at the truth. She liked the analysis
of his own methods of writing.

Oh my dear, what an enchanting person Virginia is! How she weaves
magic into life! Whenever I see her, she raises life to a higher level. How
cheap she makes people like — seem! And Leonard too: with his
schoolboyish love for pets and toys (gadgets), he is irresistibly young
and attractive. How wrong people are about Bloomsbury, saying that it
is devitalized and devitalizing. You couldn't find two people less
devitalized or devitalizing than the Wolves — or indeed people more
vitalizing than Roger Fry, for example. I think that where Bloomsbury
has suffered is in its hangers-on like — and equivalent young men, and
of course the drooping Lytton must have done its cause a great deal of
harm. I hated Lytton.

Osbert Sitwell: Armistice in Bloomsbury

Reprinted from Osbert Sitwell, Laughter in the Next Room *(London,*

Macmillan, 1949), 16–23, by permission of the author and the
publishers.

[The three. Sitwells are sometimes compared and even confused with
the Bloomsbury Group. Yet it appears from their autobiographies that
Osbert and Edith looked askance at the Group *qua* Group, though they
were friend with individual Bloomsberries.

Bloomsbury figures very briefly in Sir Osbert Sitwell's extended
autobiography. In the following excerpt, as in many accounts of
Bloomsbury, Sir Osbert's early recollections of Bloomsbury in 1918 are
merged with his later, rather more acidulous attitude towards
Bloomsbury.]

. . . It was not until we reached the far corner of the Mall that the full
degree of the general rejoicing became evident. We had found a
taxicab – by no means an easy feat at the end of the 1914–18
War – but we were obliged to crawl, so thick was the crowd, and so
numerous were the revellers who clambered round, and rode on, the
roof. Eventually we reached the Adelphi. The spacious Adam room,
covered with decoration as fine as a cobweb, was hung inappropriately
with a few large pictures by the Paris School – by Matisse, for
example – and by several of the Bloomsbury Group, its satellite and
English Correspondent. There were a number of paintings, for instance,
by Mark Gertler – at that moment an artist much patronized by the
cognoscenti: (heavy designs of Mile-End Road figures, very stiff but oily
of trees, fleshy in their aspect, under the solid shade of which trod
ape-like beings, or still-lives, apples and pears of an incomparable rosy
rotundity falling sideways off cardboard cloths – yet these possessed
some kind of quality). Here, in these rooms, was gathered the élite of
the intellectual and artistic world, the dark flower of Bloomsbury. And
since this name has occurred twice already in this paragraph – as it
surely must if one is to attempt to describe the achievements or
environment of the early post-war generation – a word or two is
necessary to indicate what it stood for before its so rapid decline.

The great figures were Roger Fry, Virginia Woolf, Clive Bell, Vanessa
Bell, Lytton Strachey and Duncan Grant. After them followed a
sub-rout of high-mathematicians and low-psychologists, a tangle of
lesser painters and writers. The outlook, natural in the grand exemplars,
and acquired by their followers, was one of great tolerance: surprise
was never shown at any human idiosyncrasy, though an amused wonder

might be expressed at the ordinary activities of mankind. The chief, most usual phrases one heard were 'ex-quisitely civilized', and 'How *simply too* extraordinary!', the first applying to some unusual human concatenation, the second to some quite common incident of burgess life, such as a man going to a railway station to meet his wife returning after a long absence from home. But, no less than by the sentiments themselves, the true citizens of Bloomsbury could be recognized by the voice to which they were expressed. The tones would convey with supreme efficacy the requisite degree of paradoxical interest, surprise, incredulity: in actual sound, analyzed, they were unemphatic, save when emphasis was not to be expected; then there would be a sudden sticky stress, high where you would have presumed low, and the whole spoken sentence would run, as it were, at different speeds and on different gears, and contain a deal of expert but apparently meaningless syncopation. Many sets of people in the past have developed their own manner of talking, almost their own language: the Court of Caroline of Ansbach, composed of such persons as Molly Lepell and Lord Hervey, possessed their own cant, and so later did Georgiana Duchess of Devonshire and her Whig friends, and, almost in our time, Mrs Hwfa Williams and her Edwardian circle. Most of these lingoes had their own voice, as well as phraseology and words, and arose, I believe, on a basis of clan. Thus the Bloomsbury voice, too – that characteristic regional way of speaking, as rare and ritualistic outside the bounds of West Central London as the state voice of the Emperor of China beyond his pleasances and palaces – originated, I believe, more in a family than in a flock. Experts maintain that it originated as an apanage of the Strachey family – of Lytton Strachey, that is to say, and of his brothers and sisters, in whom it was natural and delightful – and that from them it spread and took captive many, acclimatizing itself first in the *haute vie intellectuelle* of King's College, Cambridge: thence it had marched on London, prospering particularly in Gordon and Mecklenburgh Squares and in the neighbouring sooty piazzas, and possessing affiliations, too, in certain country districts – Firle in Sussex, for example, and Garsington in Oxfordshire. The adoption by an individual of the correct tones was equivalent, I apprehend, to an outward sign of conversion, a public declaration of faith, like giving the Hitler salute or wearing a green turban. Once, indeed, I was privileged to be present when one of the Lesser – but now Greater – Bloomsburys took the plunge. I had known him well before he joined up, and then, gently-spoken reader, he talked as you or I do – and so judge of my surprise when, in the middle of a dinner-party, I heard his tongue suddenly slide off sense, making for a few moments meaningless but emphatic sounds that somehow resembled words, and then, as quickly, creak into the Bloomsbury groove, like a tram proudly regaining its rails! . . . I wondered what initiation rites and tribal ceremonies had taken place in the local Berlitz School.

Tonight, at Monty Shearman's, the Bloomsbury Junta was in full session. In later years, towards the moment of its disintegration, Bloomsbury, under the genial viceroyalty of my friend Clive Bell, took a trend, hitherto unexpected, towards pleasure and fashionable life: but in these days it was still austere, with a degree of Quaker earnestness latent in it. (But then Roger Fry, its leading and most engaging aesthetic apostle, came of Quaker stock.) The women were of a type different from that to be seen elsewhere. Something of the Victorian past clung to them still, though they were so much more advanced than their sisters, both in views and intelligence. Virginia Woolf, for instance, notably beautiful with a beauty of bone and form and line that belonged to the stars rather than the sun, manifested in her appearance, in spite of the modernity that was also clearly hers, a Victorian distinction. She made little effort to bring out the quality of her looks, but she could not destroy it. It has often occurred to me, when I have seen Roman patrician busts of the fourth century, how greatly she resembled them, with her high forehead, fine, aquiline nose and deep-set, sculptural eye-sockets. Her beauty was certainly impersonal, but it was in no way cold, and her talk was full of ineffable fun and lightness of play and warmth. I have never known anyone with a more sensitive perception of the smallest shadows cast in the air round her: nor could I ever understand why people were – but certainly they *were* – frightened of her; because, though there was, and I am sure she would have admitted it, a human amount of malice in her composition (and how greatly the dull-minded would have complained if there had not been!), there was very much more, and most unusual, gentleness. To the young, to poets and painters, but not to dons, she was invariably kind; kind, moreover, to the extent that, in spite of the burden of her own work and correspondence, she would take trouble for them. She would, I am aware – for I have been present – lay traps for the boastful and the blunted, and greatly she enjoyed the snaring of them (I once had great difficulty in rescuing alive a popular American novelist, whose name was at that time written as a sky-sign round the roofs of Cambridge Circus): but for the most part they deserved their fate. She possessed, too, a beautiful, clear, gentle speaking voice. Though sometimes, when many people were present, she could be seen swaying

a little, preparing herself with nervous effort to say the words, to break
through the reserve that lay over her, yet I have heard her dare to make
a speech. It was at a dinner for the London Group of painters about a
year later than the party. Roger Fry, who was president or chairman,
had asked me to be present and to speak. When I arrived, I found to my
great pleasure that I was sitting next to Virginia. But she was pitiably
nervous that night because of the prospect of having to make a speech;
her distress was obvious. I felt miserable on her behalf and tried,
indeed, to comfort her: for after having just fought an election, oratory
held temporarily few terrors for me. I concluded – and it may have
been the case – that she was unused to the strain of these occasions,
and had only consented to speak because Roger was one of her oldest
friends. If so, what happened was the more astonishing. I spoke first,
and adequately, I hope, in a matter-of-fact sort of way. The audience
laughed at the jokes I made. Then I sat down, and the moment I had
dreaded for Virginia arrived. She stood up. The next quarter of an hour
was a superb display of art and, more remarkable, of feeling, reaching
heights of fantasy and beauty in the description of the Marriage of
Music to Poetry in the time of the Lutanists, and how, in the coming
age, Painting must be similarly united to the other arts. It was a speech
beautifully prepared, yet seemingly spontaneous, excellently delivered,
and as natural in its flow of poetic eloquence as is a peacock spreading
its tail and drumming. Somehow I had not foreseen this *bravura*; it was
a performance that none present will ever forget, and, as she sat down, I
almost regretted the sympathy I had wasted on her.

There were few women of a distinction equal to Virginia's in the
room tonight: but all, pretty or *fade* or plain, wore their own clothes,
either more fashionable than elsewhere, without fashion, or smacking
of Roger's Omega workshop, wholesome and home-made. Some of the
men were in uniform, but a proportion – equally courageous in their
way – had been conscientious objectors and so were able to appear in
ordinary clothes – if *ordinary* is not, perhaps, a misnomer for so much
shagginess (the suits, many of them, looked as if they had been woven
from the manes of Shetland ponies and the fringes of Highland cattle in
conjunction), and for such flaming ties as one saw. It was a singular
dispensation – though welcome to me, because I admired their moral
bravery, sympathized with the standard they upheld with a singular
toughness, and liked them personally – that in the next few years
several of the chief artistic and literary lions of the fashionable world,
itself in every country then invariably chauvinistic, had been
conscientious objectors: but the war, thank heaven, was over, and a

moratorium on patriotism set in for about fifteen years. Those present tonight included several, I recall, who had worked at farming in the Arcadian colony presided over by Lady Ottoline Morrell. At Garsington during the war some of the best brains of the country were obliged to apply themselves to digging and dunging, to the potato patch or the pig-sty. Lady Ottoline had thrown herself into the role of farmer only in order to help her friends – to her credit, ever to be found in the minority – in a time of affliction to them, when intellectuals discovered that mind was more than usually contemned by the majority of the nation. Among the ribald, however, it was rumoured that some employed by her came in the course of time to regard themselves as very able and competent farm-hands, shockingly underpaid, and that they were perpetually threatening to strike. Indeed it was alleged that some cantankerous if cultivated hinds had broken into the Manor House, shouting 'Down with capitalist exploitation' (as justly might the silken shepherds of the Petit Trianon have roughly demanded a living wage from Queen Marie-Antoinette!). If this be true, it must have been disturbing for Lady Ottoline, as she sat, quietly eating bull's-eye peppermints out of a paper bag, in her room of small, sixteenth-century panelling, painted green like that of her ancestral Bolsover, discussing sympathetically and seldom with more than one person – it might be D.H. Lawrence, the present Lord Russell, Aldous Huxley or Mark Gertler – the sufferings and foibles of mankind, thus to be reminded, too, of their perversity and ingratitude.

Some of the donnish farm-labourers who were supposed to have invaded her sanctum with their harsh cries for 'More' had gathered here tonight. All equally, soldiers, Bloomsbury beauties, and conscientious objectors – all except Diaghilev – danced. I remember the tall, flagging figure of my friend Lytton Strachey, with his rather narrow, angular beard, long, inquisitive nose, and air of someone pleasantly awaking from a trance, jigging about with an amiable debility. He was, I think, unused to dancing. Certainly he was both one of the most typical and one of the rarest persons in this assembly. His individual combination of kindness, selfishness, cleverness, shyness and sociability made him peculiarly unlike anyone else. As I watched him, I remember comparing him in my mind to a benevolent but rather irritable pelican. A man now of about forty, he had achieved no renown (though he had possessed a high reputation for wit, learning and personality among his own friends from Cambridge), nor had sought any until the publication of *Eminent Victorians* raised him to the zenith of fame and popularity with a generation no longer tolerant of either the pretensions or the achievements of the Victorian great. Some chapters of this book I had, in the autumn of 1917, been given the pleasure of hearing him read aloud — rather faintly, for he was recovering from an attack of shingles, and sat in an armchair in front of a large fire, with a Shetland shawl draped round his shoulders. I remember that our hostess, a cousin of Lytton's, pressed her lively young daughter of seven to allow him to see her imitation of him. While the precocious mimic showed off, Lytton watched the child with a look of the utmost distaste, and when asked by the mother what he thought of the performance — one of real virtuosity — remarked in a high, clear, decisive voice, 'I expect it's amusing, but it isn't at all *like*!' ... As I say, he was at this moment enjoying great celebrity: my father, however, as was his way, had never heard of his name (it could not, I suppose, penetrate the loopholes of an ivory tower of medieval construction). Thus one day, a few years later, when Lytton had come over to have luncheon with us at Montegufoni, and when the issuing of his *Queen Victoria* had carried his work to an even wider public, his host demanded angrily, after the visitor had left, 'Who is he?', and further initiated what remains a haunting mystery, by adding, 'I do wish you'd ask some really interesting people here. I don't know why you never invite the great novelist.' 'Who do you mean?' 'Mitchell, of course. You know quite well!'

But though my father, after this, often mentioned the Master, and held him up frequently to us as a pattern of style and content, neither Sacheverell nor I was ever able, though the problem fascinated us and we tried perseveringly to solve it, to gain any clue to his identity. Sometimes we thought that he was, perhaps, an idealized composite figure formed from the various celebrated novelists of the day, Hardy, Conrad, Wells, Bennett, including all their various excellencies in his books, and with this workmanlike name thrown in to give reality to a dummy. All that we could get from my father, when we presssed him for the name of one of Mitchell's masterpieces, was, 'You know quite well. I saw you reading one of his books only the other day! He's much the finest of them — a real genius, they say!' ... Certainly the elusive Mitchell was absent, again, tonight: but among those I recall as being there were, in addition to Diaghilev and Lytton Strachey, Clive Bell, Roger Fry, Mark Gertler, Lady Ottoline, D.H. Lawrence and his wife, Maynard Keynes, Duncan Grant, Lydia Lopokova and David Garnett . . .

Edith Sitwell: Bloomsbury Taken Care of

Reprinted from Edith Sitwell, Taken Care of: The Autobiography of
Edith Sitwell *(London, Hutchinson, 1965), 81–7, by permission of the
author and the publishers.*

[The ambivalence of Dame Edith Sitwell's comments on Bloomsbury are
characteristic of her own literary personality as well as being typical of
the observations of others who watched the growing fame of
Bloomsbury as a literary and social circle.

The excerpts given here from her posthumous autobiography were
published in part in an essay on 'Coming to London' for *The London
Magazine* in 1957.]

Intellectual society was, at that time, divided into several camps, and to
none of these did I, by nature, belong. On the one side was the
bottle-wielding school of thought to which I could not, owing to my
sex, upbringing, tastes, and lack of muscle, belong. On another side was
the society of Bloomsbury, the home of an echoing silence. This section
of society was described to me by Gertrude Stein as 'the Young Men's
Christian Association – with Christ left out, of course'.

Some of the more silent intellectuals, crouching under the umbrella-
like deceptive weight of their foreheads, lived their toadstool lives
sheltered by these. The appearance of others aroused the conjecture
that they were trying to be foetuses. But to what rebirth and
subsequent life they looked forward, I do not know. One intellectual
lighthouse, as an American admirer called him, was immensely tall, and
if he had not been so inert one would have supposed him to have been
involved in a death-struggle with a lamp-post. They seemed to be
inextricably intertwined. From the top of this edifice from time to time
a few dim sparks emerged, but they did not cast much light on
anything.

In this world of superior intellect there were several models. There
was, for instance, the amphibian model – with gaping mouth, glassy
eyes staring at nothing in particular, and with a general air of
slipperiness and, at the same time, scaliness.

There was, too, the village idiot model, drooling, and with a boastful
exhibition of mental deficiency – also the deliberately awkward and
blundering good sportsman and cricketer-model.

The ladies of this world were not, to my mind, attractive. For the
most part they had faces like fawn-coloured felt hats that had been

inadvertently sat upon. They spent their time in chronicling the doings of the unexciting female chatterboxes of previous centuries – passed over by history (that terrible mill in which sawdust rejoins sawdust), and remarkable only because of their inexhaustible enthusiasm for dossing down in every ditch with every little frog disguised as a bull.

On the borders of this society was a purely social agglomeration – one alien to the society in which I was brought up – a society which, using money as a battering ram and broadmindedness as a weapon, brought off invasions of a world hitherto unknown to them. All these beings lived in the shade of certain powerful and protective persons, eminent and accommodating divines, sleek and pouting, filling their coats and own spiritual needs as completely and fully as a neatly rounded potato fits its skin – and leaders of society, some with voices like the bellowing of the golden (or brazen) Calf, others like a tunicate, possessing, to quote the scientific description of this elementary form of life, a preference for dwelling amidst mud. A stomach and a mouth, but neither nerves nor a heart. To these were added some elderly peers and a few clean-shaven Americans, or pseudo-American business-women, possessed of large salaries and immense competence, who carried huge and expensive bags, with gold fittings, from which they would produce what appeared to be timetables, and whose voices, movements, and general habits gave the impression that they had portable homes situated on the platforms of Victoria Station.

I knew the painter and distinguished art critic, Roger Fry, well, for I sat to him for several portraits. For one of these I wore a green evening dress, the colour of the leaves of lilies, and my appearance in this, in the full glare of the midsummer light of midday, in Fitzroy Square, together with the appearance of Mr Fry, his bushy, long grey hair floating from under an enormous black sombrero, caused great joy to the children of the district as we crossed from Mr Fry's studio to his house for luncheon.

Imagining us to be strayed revellers, they enquired at moments (perhaps not unnaturally) if our mothers knew we were out. At other moments they referred to the fifth of November, when, according to them, our appearance would have been better timed.

Mr Fry was a most delightful companion, learned and courteous; he had a great gift for attracting and retaining friendship. Warm-hearted, generous-minded and kindly, he was always espousing some lost cause, championing some unfortunate person, rushing at some windmill with a lance. In other respects he was dreamy and vague, incapable of noticing any but a spiritual discomfort. I remember an incident when I was lunching at his house after a sitting. Mr Fry's slippers could not be found anywhere, and a game of hunt-the-slipper ensued. In the midst of the fun, a loud crash was heard, and a hoarse voice said 'Coal Sir!' 'Put it, my good man,' said Mr Fry, whirling round and round like a kitten chasing its tail, losing his spectacles, and speaking in a voice weak from fatigue — 'Oh, well, put it on the bed.'

At this point I found the slippers in the milk-jug, and the fun stopped . . .

Virginia Woolf had a moonlit transparent beauty. She was exquisitely carved, with large thoughtful eyes that held no fore-shadowing of that tragic end which was a grief to everyone who had ever known her. To be in her company was delightful. She enjoyed each butterfly aspect of the world and of the moment, and would chase the lovely creatures, but without damaging the coloured dust on their wings. Whenever anyone present said anything pregnant, she would clasp her long delicate hands together and laugh with pleasure. In her own talk she always went straight to the point. For instance, on the first occasion when I met her, at a dinner party given by Osbert and Sacheverell, she asked me 'Why do you live where you do?' 'Because I have not much money.' 'How much money a year have you?' I told her. 'Oh well, I think we can do better for you than that' she said thoughtfully.

However, nothing came of this project, and I remained in Bayswater.

That, I think, was as well. I do not think I should have 'fitted into' the closely serried company of Bloomsbury. I was not an unfriendly young woman, but I was shy, and yet, at unexpected moments, was not silent — and silence was much prized, sometimes to the embarrassment of persons outside the inner circle of Bloomsbury.

I suppose I was always rather odd to look at, from a conventional point of view — (and nothing was more unconventionally conventional than the company of Bloomsbury). Looking back on myself I can see that I had an untidy elegance like that of a tall thin bird — and was a being who appeared to have but a few friends, a few snowflakes, perhaps, as I have said, and a small bough of early flowering almond blossom.

The company of Bloomsbury were kind-hearted, and from time to time I entered it on sufferance.

Lytton Strachey was a major Bloomsbury idol of this time. I knew him but slightly, and don't like his work. Also his letters to Virginia Woolf, now published, make me blush from head to foot, with the exclamations of 'oh deary Mary me!' and the enumeration of Countesses known and dimly related to them.

Visually, he made the impression on me of having strayed from the companionship of the kindly demons in the Russian ballet 'Children's Tales', who existed only in profile, and had long beards of gardener's bass – (actually I think he saw the beings of whom he wrote, with the exception of Queen Victoria, in profile only, never full face). He seemed to have been cut out of very thin cardboard. He wasted no words in conversation. A young and robust friend of ours, Constant Lambert, meeting him at a party, said 'You don't remember, Mr Strachey? We met four years ago.'

'Quite a nice interval, I think, don't you?' remarked Mr Strachey pleasantly, and passed on . . .

Stephen Spender: Bloomsbury in the Thirties

Reprinted from Stephen Spender, World Within World *(London, Hamish Hamilton, 1951), 139–44 and 151–9, reprinted by permission of the Regents of the University of California and A.D. Peters and Company of London.*

[Stephen Spender's observations of Bloomsbury are from the point of view of a young poet in the thirties. The Hogarth Press (Spender's story of its being founded on winnings from the Calcutta Sweepstake is fanciful) published anthologies of poetry in the early thirties that first brought to public attention the work of Spender, W.H. Auden, C. Day Lewis, William Plomer, John Lehmann, William Empson, and others, including Julian Bell. Several of these socially conscious poets, as Spender calls them, were critical of the politics and snobbery of some members of Bloomsbury – and of course some Bloomsberries, Virginia Woolf in particular, were critical of the literary implications of these poets' social consciences. There was, nevertheless, a considerable sympathy between the older and younger generations, as is shown not just in Spender's recollections but in those of John Lehmann (see pp. 73–83) and William Plomer (pp.296–302).]

. . . In this century, generation succeeds generation with a rapidity which parallels the development of events. The Georgian poets were a pre-1914 generation. The War of 1914–18 produced a generation of

War Poets, many of whom were either killed by the War or unable to
develop beyond it. The 1920s were a generation to themselves. We were
the 1930s.

Rather apart from both the 1920s and the 1930s, was the group of
writers and artists labelled 'Bloomsbury'. Bloomsbury has been derided
by some people and has attracted the snobbish admiration of others:
but I think it was the most constructive and creative influence on
English taste between the two Wars.

The label 'Bloomsbury' was applied to people more by others than
by themselves. Nevertheless if one examines the reasons for regarding
Bloomsbury as a serious tendency, if not as a self-conscious movement,
the label is meaningful.

The names most usually associated with Bloomsbury are Virginia
Woolf, Roger Fry, Lytton Strachey, Clive Bell, Vanessa Bell, Duncan
Grant, Raymond Mortimer, and perhaps David Garnett. E.M. Forster
and T.S. Eliot are associated with it rather than 'belonging' to it, if
'belonging' may be said of a free association of people with similar
tastes and talents.

Bloomsbury represented a meeting of certain influences and an
adoption of certain attitudes which became almost a cult.

Not to regard the French impressionist and post-impressionist
painters as sacrosanct, not to be an agnostic and in politics a Liberal
with Socialist leanings, was to put oneself outside Bloomsbury. For this
reason Eliot was too dogmatic in religion and too Conservative in
politics to fit in. It is more difficult to say why Forster does not quite
fit. He was perhaps too impish, too mystical, too moralizing.

But the positive qualities of Bloomsbury were shared not only by
Forster and Eliot, but by nearly all the best talent of this period. Roger
Fry, Lytton Strachey and T.S. Eliot, in their different ways, introduced
the influences of French impressionism, French prose, and in poetry
the French symbolists. All these writers were pre-occupied with
re-examining and restating the principles and aims of art and criticism.
They were interested in experiment, and were amongst the first to
discuss and defend James Joyce and Proust. Their attitude towards an
easy-going conventionality masquerading as traditionalism was critical:
at the same time, they were deeply concerned with traditional values
which they studied and restated with a vigour which made the old often
have the force of the revolutionary. They insisted on the necessity of
expressing past values in the imagery and idiom of today.

Most of these writers had begun writing before 1914, though they
did not become widely known until after the War. They had

sympathized with pacifism. Leonard Woolf, an intellectual Socialist who was at heart a Liberal, Maynard Keynes, the economist who denounced the Treaty of Versailles, Bertrand Russell and Harold Nicolson, were amongst their friends and colleagues who discussed politics, economics, philosophy, history and literature with them. In this way Bloomsbury was like the last kick of an enlightened aristocratic tradition. Its purism was founded on a wide interest in ideas and knowledge of affairs. Reading the essays of Lytton Strachey, Virginia Woolf, Clive Bell, Raymond Mortimer, and even Forster, one sees how inevitably they interested themselves in the eighteenth-century French salons and the English Whig aristocrats.

Like a watered-down aristocracy they made moderate but distinct claims on society. They were individualists who asked for themselves (and usually by their own efforts, from themselves) the independence in which to do their best work, leisure for reading, and pleasure. In order to produce a few works which seem likely to live, and a great many witty, intelligent and graceful conversation pieces, they needed to nourish themselves on a diet of the arts, learning, amusement, travel, and good living. They certainly were not malicious exploiters of their fellow men, and they expected less reward than the bureaucratically favoured Soviet writer receives today. At the same time, their standard of 'five hundred pounds a year and a room of one's own' (Virginia Woolf's formula in a well-known essay) made them decidedly unwilling to sacrifice their independence to the cause of the working-class struggle. They were class-conscious, conscious even of a social gulf which divided them from one of their most talented contemporaries – D.H. Lawrence, the miner's son. Despite their Leftist sympathies the atmosphere of Bloomsbury was nevertheless snobbish. They were tolerant in their attitude towards sexual morals, scrupulous in their personal relationships with each other.

To them there was something barbarous about our generation. It seemed that with us the thin wall which surrounded their little situation of independence and which enabled them to retain their air of being the last of the Romans had broken down. A new generation had arisen which proclaimed that bourgeois civilization was at an end, and which assumed the certainty of revolution, which took sides and which was exposed even within its art to the flooding-in of outside public events, which cared but little for style and knew nothing of Paris.

... Strachey, with his long russet-brown beard and his high, squeaky voice, was certainly the most astonishing of the Bloomsbury group. He combined strikingly their gaiety with their intermittent chilliness. Sometimes he would play childish games such as 'Up Jenkins', which we played one Christmas. Often he would gossip brilliantly and maliciously. At times there was something insidious about his giggling manner; at times he would sit in his chair without saying a word. He was delicate and hypochondriacal. Wogan Philipps, who was given to Celtic exaggeration, told me once that Strachey had an arrangement by which the wires of his bed under the mattress were electrically heated: so that lying in bed he was agreeably grilled all night long.

Thus I began to enter into this civilized world of people who lived in country houses, pleasantly modernized, with walls covered with areas of pale green, egg-shell blue, or pale pink distempering, upon which were hung their paintings and drawings of the modern French school. and a Roger Fry, Vanessa Bell, or Duncan Grant. They had libraries and good food and wine. They discussed few topics outside literature, and they gossiped endlessly and entertainingly about their friends. In my mind these houses in the south and south-west of England, belonging to people who knew one another and who maintained approximately the same standards of living well, talking well, and believing passionately in their own kind of individualism, were connected by drives along roads which often went between hedges. At night the head-lamps would project a hundred yards in front of us an image of what looked like a luminous grotto made of crystal leaves, coloured agate or jade. This moved always in front of us on the leaves and branches. Delight in a vision familiar yet mysterious of this kind was the object of much of their painting, writing and conversation, so that when we drove in the country at night, and I watched that moving brilliant core of light, I felt often that I was looking into the eyes of their sensibility.

. . . Sometimes I dined with Leonard and Virginia Woolf at their house in Tavistock Square. They lived in the upper half of this, the lower half being occupied by the offices of their publishing firm, the Hogarth Press. Their drawing-room was large, tall, pleasant, square-shaped, with rather large and simple furniture, giving, as I recollect it now, an impression of greys and greens. Painted panels by Duncan Grant and Vanessa Bell represented mandolins, fruit, and perhaps a view of the Mediterranean through an open window or a curtain drawn aside. These were painted thickly and opaquely in browns and terracottas, reds and pale blue, with a hatch work effect in the foreground with shadows of the folds of a curtain. These decorations were almost a hall-mark of Bloomsbury. Similar ones were to be found in the house of Lytton

Strachey. They represented a fusion of Mediterranean release with a certain restraint and austerity. Looking at them, one recollected that Roger Fry was of a family of Quakers, and that Virginia Woolf was the daughter of Leslie Stephen.

When her guests arrived, Virginia Woolf would be perhaps nervous, preoccupied with serving out the drink. Her handshake and her smile of welcome would be a little distraught. Now when I recall her face it seems to me that there was something about the tension of the muscles over the fine bones of the skin which was like an instrument tautly strung. The greyish eyes had a sometimes limpid, sometimes wandering, sometimes laughing, concentration or distractedness.

When we had gone upstairs and had sat down to dinner, she would say to William Plomer (we were often invited together): 'If you and Stephen insist on talking about Bloomsbury, I shall label you "the Maida Vale group".' 'Really,' Plomer said, raising his eyebrows and laughing. 'I am not aware of having talked of Bloomsbury, but you know how much one has to write these days. . .' 'Well then, if it's not you, it's Stephen!' 'Oh, Stephen. How like him! But still, please don't include him with me; I can assure you we are very different kettles of fish! Still, I can imagine nothing more charming than an essay by you, Virginia, on the Maida Vale group.' Then the conversation wandered a little. Perhaps the name of a critic who ran a small literary magazine in which he had made a scurrilous attack on her would be mentioned, and she would say aciduously: 'Why do you mention that name? Surely we have more interesting things to discuss.' The uncomfortable moment passed and she answered, with a warmer interest, someone's question whether adverse criticism annoyed her: 'Of course it annoys me for the moment. It is as though someone broke a china vase I was fond of. But I forget about it afterwards.' Then another name was dropped into the conversation, that of a poet, later to become a supporter of General Franco, who had written a satire directed at two friends whose crime was that they had lent him for an indefinite period a small house in their garden where he might work. 'What ungrateful people writers are!' she said. 'They always bite the hand that feeds them'. She looked pensive. As I write this it suddenly occurs to me, by the kind of intuition which remembering things across a gulf of years brings in the very act of writing, what she may have been thinking at that moment. For the people who had been ungratefully attacked were the Nicolsons: and her novel *Orlando* is a fantastic meditation on a portrait of Vita Sackville-West; and in this novel there is an account of a poet who comes to stay with Orlando, accepting his/her hospitality and then writing a cruel satire on the visit.

Did she say that when she wrote *Orlando* she began writing the first sentences without at all knowing how she would continue? Or am I thinking of something else? How Julian Green told me that he wrote his novels without in the least knowing how the story would develop? Or how Vita Sackville-West, who owned the manuscript of *Orlando*, showed me, written across the first page, a brief note explaining the idea for a novel, whose hero-heroine should live for three hundred years of English history, experiencing half-way through this life a change of sex, from hero into heroine. The excitement with which she embarked straight from this note on to her voyage of three centuries of English history, is shown by the letter which she wrote to Vita Sackville-West the same day: 'I dipped my pen in the ink, and wrote these words, as if automatically, on a clean sheet: *Orlando: A Biography*. No sooner had I done this than my body was filled with rapture and my brain with ideas. I wrote rapidly till 12.'

In recalling Virginia Woolf there is something which causes my memory to become even more a kind of reverie than most of what I write here. It is necessary to remind myself that often she served the meal herself efficiently, and that she cooked it well. The dining-room was a lighter, perhaps more successful, room than the drawing-room. There was a pleasant table of painted wood, the work of her sister, Vanessa Bell, who also had designed the dishes. The pink blodges, small black dots, lines like brackets, characteristic of this style of decoration, were extremely successful on the creamy white surface of the china. Then Virginia described the beginning of the Hogarth Press, and at the age I then was, I listened like a child entranced. Her husband, Leonard Woolf, had won a prize in the Calcutta Sweepstake. With this they bought a printing press and some type, and in the house where they then lived at Richmond they had printed stories by Virginia herself and by Leonard Woolf, T.S. Eliot's *The Waste Land*, and several other small volumes. She described how they had done this with little thought except to please themselves, and then one book (I think it was her own *Kew Gardens*) had been well reviewed in the *Times Literary Supplement*. She described running downstairs and seeing the door-mat deep in letters bringing orders for more copies. They then had to farm out the printing of a second edition with a local printer: and hence they found that they had become, not amateur printers who sold their own work privately, but The Hogarth Press, a small but flourishing firm which even produced a few best-sellers.

From publishing the conversation turned to writing. She asked:

'How do you write, William?' 'How do I write?' 'Yes, what do you do when you write? Do you look out of the window? Do you write while you are walking in the street? Do you cross out a lot? Do you smoke when you are writing? Do you start by thinking of one phrase?'

When William and I had both been examined, we would ask her how she wrote. She came out with something like this:

I don't think there's any form in which the novel has to be written. My idea is to make use of every form and bring it within a unity which is that particular novel. There's no reason why a novel shouldn't be written partly in verse, partly in prose, and with scenes in it like those in a play. I would like to write a novel which is a fusion of poetry and dialogue as in a play. I would like to experiment with every form and bring it within the scope of the novel.

She said that no one should publish before he or she is thirty. 'Write till then, but scrap it or put it aside.' She herself had covered reams of paper with what she called 'just writing for the sake of writing', and she had scrapped it all. She said she believed that prose was more difficult to write than poetry.

Then after dinner we would go down to the drawing-room again, and Virginia would smoke a cheroot. There would be talk perhaps of politics, that is to say, of war. For Leonard and Virginia were among the very few people in England who had a profound understanding of the state of the world in the 1930s; Leonard, because he was a political thinker and historian with an almost fatalistic understanding of the consequences of actions. So that when, in 1934, I asked him whether he thought there would be a war he replied: 'Yes, of course. Because when the nations enter into an armaments race, as they are doing at present, no other end is possible. The arms have to be used before they become completely out of date.' Virginia had also a profound political insight, because the imaginative power which she shows in her novels, although·it is concentrated often on small things — the light on the branches of the tree, a mark upon a whitewashed wall — nevertheless held at bay vast waters, madness, wars, destructive forces.

While Leonard was talking about war, labour, League of Nations, Virginia would fall silent. There was often after dinner this kind of political intermezzo. She had a little the air of letting the men talk: still more that of listening to Leonard.

The conversation passed from politics to gossip about personalities, quite possibly to Hugh Walpole. Now some stories seem so familiar to me that they have become inseparable from this life of literary London, as though it were woven out of them. For example, the story of how Hugh Walpole sat up all of one night reading an advance copy of Somerset Maugham's *Cakes and Ale*, to recognize himself in the cruel analysis of the career of the best-selling novelist.

Virginia had a passionate social curiosity, about the 'upper', the 'middle', and the 'lower' (I think these distinctions of class were sharply present in her mind). The Royal Family was a topic of intense interest to her. This preoccupation could be embarrassing – if one is embarrassed by snobbishness. Yet her interest in royalty was largely due to the fact that royalty, surrounded by an atmosphere of radiant adoration as though bathed in a tank of lambent water, were peculiar and exotic in precisely the way in which people are strange and luminous in her writing. The little episode in *Mrs Dalloway* where a chauffeur extends a small disc to a policeman, and the car shoots on ahead of the stopped traffic, exactly expresses like a minute phrase in a descriptive symphony what fascinated her – the privileged special life sealed off in the limousine whose driver has a pass. Indeed, her Mrs Dalloways and Mrs Ramsays are by nature queens shut off from other people who gaze at them with wonder, as through a window. The wonder of life is a wonder of royal self-realization, which has something akin to a gaping crowd staring at a lady dressed in ermine. When she writes – in her essay in *The Common Reader* – of Dr Johnson, and Fanny Burney, and the Elizabethans – one is staring at exotic fish swimming in their tank.

'Why are we so interested in them – they aren't so different from us?' she would exclaim after the talk on the Royal Family had bordered almost on tedium. The answer was 'because they are held up to our gaze', or 'because they are like a living museum of flesh and blood dressed in the clothes of past history', or 'because after all, their heredity does make them extraordinary'.

There was a division between her and other people which she attempted – not quite satisfactorily perhaps – to bridge by questions. She enquired of everyone endlessly about his or her life: of writers how and why they wrote, of a newly married young woman how it felt to be a bride, of a bus conductor where he lived and when he went home, of a charwoman how it felt to scrub floors. Her strength and her limitations were that she didn't really know how it felt to be someone else. What she did know was how it felt to be alone, unique, isolated, and since to some extent this is part of universal experience, to express this was to express what many feel. But she was lacking in the sense of a solid communal life, divided arbitrarily into separate bodies, which all nevertheless share. What bound people together escaped her. What separated them was an object of wonder, delight and despair.

She seemed as detached from herself as from everyone else. Thus she would talk about herself with an objectivity which was unambiguous in her but which in others would have seemed uneasy. She was simply interested in the point she was making or the story she was telling, and the fact that she herself might be deeply involved in it seemed irrelevant. Once the conversation having turned to Rupert Brooke, she said: 'He was very keen on living "the free life". One day he said, "Let's go swimming, quite naked".' 'And did you, Virginia?' William asked. 'Of course,' she answered, and then she added: 'Lytton always said that Rupert had bandy legs. But I don't think that was so.' She said that Rupert Brooke was writing at this time his poem which begins 'These have I loved', in which he lists a catalogue of sensations which had given him pleasure. She said that he was quite external in his way of making this list and that he surprised her by asking what was the brightest thing in nature, as he needed a dazzling image for his poem. She looked up at the sky and saw a poplar tree with white underleaves rotating to shimmer against the light. She said: 'Bright leaves against the sky.'

She seemed to hate her dinner parties to come to an end. Sometimes they would go on until two AM. She gave her guests an impression of gaiety which could plunge at any moment into the deepest seriousness. She would tell stories of things which amused her until the tears ran down her cheeks. Usually these stories concerned one or two people who played a kind of jester's role in her life. There was a trace of cruelty in her feeling towards them. One of these was Hugh Walpole, concerning whom I have quoted one of her stories, and another, Dame Ethel Smyth. There was always some new item about Dame Ethel. Once, when Dame Ethel was already eighty-four, Virginia had just received a letter from her, announcing that she had become attached to a lady aged eighty who lived next door. 'And to think that we have been close neighbours for five years,' Dame Ethel's letter complained, 'and that we might have met when she was seventy-five and I only seventy-nine.' Dame Ethel was a highly eccentric character. On one occasion the Woolfs invited her to dine at their house at Rodmell near Lewes, Sussex. Dame Ethel bicycled the twenty miles from the village where she lived to Rodmell, dressed in rough tweeds. About two miles from her destination she decided that perhaps she was not suitably dressed for a dinner party. She thought that possibly corsets were required to smarten up her figure. Accordingly, she went into a village shop and asked for some corsets. There were none. Distressed, she looked round the shop and her eye lighted on a bird cage, which she purchased. About twenty minutes later, Virginia went into her garden to discover Dame Ethel in a state of undress in the shrubbery struggling with the bird cage, which she was wrenching into the shape of corsets and forcing under her tweeds.

Virginia Woolf was a most scrupulous artist who demanded high standards of artistic integrity from others. Once I submitted to The Hogarth Press a novel which was rejected. It interested her and she spent some part of an afternoon discussing it with me. As she made several favourable comments, I asked how I could re-write it. 'Scrap it!' she exclaimed with force. 'Scrap it, and write something completely different.' When she said 'Scrap it!' I had a glimpse of the years during which she had destroyed her own failures.

She composed, I imagine, like a poet. That is to say, her writing proceeds from the organic development of images growing out of her subject matter. These become symbols in a discussion which often takes her beyond the subject itself. I have in front of me an essay called *The Leaning Tower*, which is the written version of a lecture given in 1939. The essay develops from the apparently simple image of a writer sitting in a chair at his desk. This image proliferates into further ones of the pen, the paper, and the writer's chair even: and these all become symbols of the writer's high calling, expressed in terms of the simple machinery of his trade, scarcely altering through the ages, and joining him to past writers. Within this symbolism there is a further symbol of the hand holding a pen: and through the veins of the hand there flows the blood which is the whole life of the literary tradition joining the writer, sitting at his desk, with Shakespeare. Such writing, dependent for its truth on the inter-relation of ideas in the structure of thought, developed parallel with the inter-relation of the images: the chair, the desk, the pen, etc., can only 'grow' like a poem. And I have heard that there were as many drafts of some of Virginia Woolf's essays as most poets make of a poem.

But just as my lack of belief in Original Sin divided me from the views of Eliot, so my attitude to politics divided me from Virginia Woolf. Not that we disagreed about the political issues themselves: for she hated Fascism, sympathized with the Spanish Republicans, and held much the same political views as we did. But she objected to the way in which our writing was put to the service of our views, and she discerned that my generation were 'sold' to a public sometimes more on account of their views than for the merit of their writing. Indeed all of us irritated her in this respect, and she sometimes showed her irritation. It occurs first in the *Letter to a Young Poet*, where she quotes Auden, Day Lewis, John Lehmann and myself in order to criticize us for our impatience, our preoccupation with external social factors, and with our desire to set the world right. She returns to the assault, less directly, in *A Room of One's Own*, where she discerns in George Eliot and Charlotte Brontë a desire to preach (though she excuses this as being the result of the position of women in their time). At the beginning of the war, in the essay I have mentioned, *The Leaning Tower*, she returns to the attack more directly. She felt that though we were aware of the calamitous condition of the world, we reacted to it with our intellects and wills, before we had experienced it fully through our sensibilities. 'You have to be beaten and broken by things before you can write about them,' she once said to me. To hold strong views and feel deeply about what, however significant and important, was outside the range of one's experience, was not enough. I might have replied – though I did not – that, often passing Edith Cavell's monument near Charing Cross, with its inscription of *Patriotism is not enough*, I reflected that I would like to have *Sensibility is not enough* engraved on my tombstone.

She and her circle formed a group of friends who shared the same ideas and who, within a common appreciation of high values, had a deep loyalty for one another. Living in their small country houses, their London flats, full of taste, meeting at week-ends and at small parties, discussing history, painting, literature, gossiping greatly, and producing a few very good stories, they resembled those friends who at the time of the Plague in Florence withdrew into the countryside and told the stories of Boccaccio. Our generation, unable to withdraw into exquisite tale-telling and beautiful scenery, resembled rather the *Sturm und Drang* generation of Goethe's contemporaries, terribly involved in events and oppressed by them, reacting to them at first enthusiastically and violently, later with difficulty and disgust . . .

David Garnett: Bloomsbury Parties

Reprinted from David Garnett, The Familiar Faces, *Vol. III of* The Golden Echo *(London, Chatto & Windus, 1962), 62–5;* © *by David Garnett. Reprinted by permission of Harcourt Brace Jovanovich, Inc.*

[Though he was too young to belong to Old Bloomsbury, David Garnett became closely identified with the Group during the First World War; he became a widely read novelist with the publication of *Lady into Fox* (1922), and after the death of his first wife Ray Marshall, in 1940 he married Angelica Bell.

Garnett's discussions of Forster, Clive Bell, Keynes, and D.H. Lawrence (see pp.163–9, 194–7, 222–6, and 363–70) that have been used in this collection demonstrate how important a source for the study of Bloomsbury his writings are, especially his three-volume autobiography *The Golden Echo*. The particular party Garnett describes below took place in the early twenties. 'Tommy' is the sculptor Stephen Tomlin; the famous unnamed authoress Garnett refers to was Berta Ruck (Mrs Oliver Onions).]

Bloomsbury parties were of all sorts except the formal. Those which took place in Duncan's studio were really the best of them. These often included Clive and Vanessa Bell's children and were to celebrate one of their birthdays. If the Bells were still at Charleston, their house in Sussex, as they often were for Quentin's birthday in September, there was a traditional feast with grouse and fireworks sent up on the further side of the pond. But when they were in London, birthday parties would be in Duncan's studio, and on these occasions a dramatic performance was usually presented. One such was written by Virginia Woolf on the subject of the marriage of Ellen Terry as a young girl to the famous painter Watts. Angelica Bell took the part of Ellen Terry and Duncan was Watts. Angelica's school-friend Eve Younger was Queen Victoria and Julian Bell was Tennyson. Another year the play was Julian's work and was largely aimed at making fun of Virginia.

There were many much grander parties than those given in Duncan's studio – the grandest I suppose being given by Maynard and Lydia Keynes at 46 Gordon Square. At several of these parties Lydia sang, usually Victorian drawing-room ballads chosen for her by Duncan whose father Major Bartle Grant had written the music for a number of them. Putting her hands together and her exquisite little head on one side she would invite our compassion with such lines as:

> My earrings! Oh my earrings!
> I have dropped them in the well.
> And how to tell my Mirza,
> I cannot cannot tell.

These grand parties were by no means limited to the inhabitants of Bloomsbury. Anyone might be there, and the worlds of Society, Art, Politics and Finance mingled with those of Old Bloomsbury and Young Cambridge. At one such party, given I think by Clive and Vanessa, I remember seeing Picasso talking to Douglas Fairbanks senior. At another, given by Maynard and Lydia, the most striking figure was a famous writer of sentimental novelettes.

The servants had learned that the authoress of their favourite works of fiction was in the house and they stole upstairs on to the landing in order to peep through the half-opened door at the woman whom they worshipped. Unfortunately Walter Richard Sickert, who had been paying court to her, had discovered that she could sing and had an extensive repertoire of the old risqué music-hall songs which he adored. She was delighting us with:

Never trust a sailor an inch above your knee.

At its conclusion I noticed that the housemaid supported by the cook, was being led downstairs sobbing. Both were bitterly disillusioned by the lack of refinement of their idol.

Sometimes Lydia danced, being partnered by Duncan, who acquitted himself with character and originality. But at one party Maynard danced a delightful *pas-de-deux* with Lydia in which she showed an exquisitely graceful solcitude in supporting him and making his part easier for him. By a lucky chance the programme of this ambitious entertainment has survived and I reproduce it here. The topical references which need explanation are that Mr Hayley Morris, a wealthy gentleman who had retired from the trade with China, and lived at Pippingford Park near Uckfield, had received unwelcome notoriety in the gutter press while being convicted for an offence against *les mœurs* involving a young woman under the age of consent. He also kept a number of large dogs which featured in the case. 'Georgeston' is of course Charleston; Clarissa, Vanessa Bell who was impersonated by Molly MacCarthy who could not have looked less like, a fact which added to the audience's amusement. Before the performance Molly wrote to Vanessa asking whether she minded her playing the part. Vanessa grimly replied: 'How can I possibly tell until I have seen it?'

Tommy, who wrote most of the songs, played the part of Hayley Morris. Molly turned a deaf ear to his overtures until he offered her a Cézanne and a Giotto when she accepted and went off with him. I should add perhaps that the parts of Messrs Sickert, Grant and Fry were performed by these distinguished painters. In Act I the Beauty Chorus consisted of three ladies, each of them over six foot, whose parts were taken by Angus and Douglas Davidson and Dadie Rylands. They were partnered by three gentlemen, Barbara Bagenal, Frances Marshall and Bea Howe.

DON'T BE FRIGHTENED or PIPPINGTON PARK

Act 1   The Front at Brighton
  1. Beauty (Welcome to Brighton)
  2. Art (Abide with me)
  3. Truth (I simply should like to remark)
  4. Ensemble (Come, come, come to the Metropole)

Act II   The Drawing-Room at Georgeston
  1. The abduction
  2. The rescue party sets out (Is Clarissa still alive?)
  Ballet The London Group — Messrs Sickert, Fry and Grant disguised as dogs.

Act III   The Park at Pippington
  1. Clarissa settles down (Bloomsbury never gave me a bow-wow)
  2. The dogs arrive (Take her back to dear old Bloomsbury)

Interval

Act IV   Garden Square rejoices. Clarissa's friends arrive to a select entertainment 'A little bit of sea-weed'.
  Pas-de-deux   The Keynes-Keynes.
  A Veteran does her best (Taraboumtia)

John Lehmann: Working for the Hogarth Press

Reprinted from John Lehmann, The Whispering Gallery *(Longmans, Green & Co., London, 1955), 141–2, 148–9, 164– 71;* I Am My Brother *(Longmans, Green, London, 1960), 34–5, by permission of author and publishers.*

[There is a growing body of memoirs by those who spent some part of their lives as office boys, secretaries, salesmen, managers, or partners in the Hogarth Press. Of all those involved in the Press besides the Woolfs themselves, John Lehmann was the most important. He originally began to work for the Press as a young poet just down from Cambridge in 1931. Leonard Woolf later wrote: 'In the two years during which he was with us he helped us to bring into the Hogarth Press some of the best writers of his generation.' In 1938 Lehmann rejoined the Press as a partner, and this continued until 1945 when he tried to buy out Leonard Woolf, who sold out instead to Chatto and Windus. (Lehmann's version of this episode is given in *I Am My Brother* and Woolf's — subsequently disputed by Lehmann in the *Times Literary Supplement* — appears in *The Journey Not the Arrival Matters*.)

The main excerpt reprinted here from Lehmann's autobiographies consists of his early memories of the Hogarth Press; it is preceded by his recollections, first, of Julian Bell, through whom he was introduced to Bloomsbury, and then of life at Charleston, which Lehmann contrasts to his own family home at Fieldhead. The last excerpt is Lehmann's recollection of life with the Woolfs at Monk's House just before the Second World War in 1939. It is naturally a somewhat sober picture and needs to be supplemented with that of another visitor earlier in the thirties. Nigel Nicolson, son of Harold and Vita, recalled life at Monk's House as follows:

There was very little apparent order in Virginia and Leonard's way of life, and no positive attempt to surround themselves with beautiful objects. There were paintings by Duncan Grant mixed up with coloured postcards from friends in Italy. There was a mass of books upon the shelves, lying stacked upon the floor, upon the staircase. A lot of dogs and cats, a lot of coming and going of domestics (although I think there was only one), but it always seemed there was a great bustle about the place, succeeded by periods of intense calm and concentration.]

... In my second or third year, I came to know the young poet with whom I struck up the most intimate intellectual friendship of my Cambridge years. Julian Bell was the elder son of Clive and Vanessa Bell, a nephew of Virginia Woolf, and one of the most gifted of that fortunate second generation of the Bloomsbury giants who inherited the well-laid-out gardens of ideas their elders had created, and basked in the sunshine of their artistic achievements. Julian was a great, untidy, sprawling figure of a young man, awkward in manner and dressed always in dishevelled clothes with buttons rarely meeting button-holes at the neck and wrists.

He imposed, nevertheless, by charm of expression in the smiling, intelligent face under the curly tangled hair, by natural force of temperament and by an obstinate persistence of intellectual curiosity – to which was added a conviction that the arguments he defended had the authority of graven tablets of the law: the tablets of Bloomsbury. He had had a Quaker schooling, followed by a period in France, but Bloomsbury had been his real education. An instinctual power, as strongly growing as a wild thicket of hawthorn and briar rose, was at war in him and never completely tamed by the rationalist ideas that his father, Clive Bell, Roger Fry and their friends represented. To act from reasonable motives that were clear to oneself and to avoid confused irrational emotions; to treat chastity and the sense of sin in sexual matters as relics of the barbarous dark, as uncivilized as religious superstition or any of the fashionable mumbo-jumbo mysticisms; to be a pacifist because war was futile and absurd as well as painful and destructive of beauty – all these principles were already inscribed on his banner, which he waved demonstratively in one's face during his first year at King's. And yet he had a passion for nature at its wildest, and the poetry he was writing at that time was remarkable because it was an attempt to let the countryside, the moods of wind and weather and life outside the cultivated human pale, speak for themselves without any interference of the poet's own moralizing thoughts. 'We receive but what we give' – perhaps; but if so it was the non-rational intuitive side of his temperament that Julian was finding in nature. As time went on, the struggle in his mind was almost completely resolved in favour of the eighteenth century, in my opinion much to the detriment of his poetry; but I am convinced that if he had lived there would have been a new turn in the struggle and a new creative phrase. No one who knew him at all intimately could doubt that he was born to lead in some intellectual sphere: I remember that a French poet who stayed at Cambridge for some time was so struck by him that he exclaimed: 'Julian Bell is not a young man like other young men, he is a force of nature.'

... Julian and I used to carry on endless discussions whenever we were together as well as by letter: walking along the Backs, in his room at King's or in mine overlooking the Great Court of Trinity. I lured him during the vacation to Fieldhead, and I visited him in return at Charleston. Life at Fieldhead in those days was not very formal, but nevertheless a sense of the formality of big country houses in Edwardian times still lingered about the softly carpeted corridors and the dining-room with its silver candlesticks on polished tables and its ring of onlooking family portraits; even though the occasions were rare when we dressed for dinner, and old James with his serio-comic grand manner and jingling keys was no longer there to carve the joint on the sideboard. The contrast of Charleston's bohemian atmosphere was an agreeable stimulus to me. I have always enjoyed being able to be the citizen of several worlds at the same time, and found a special pleasure a few years later in being accepted intimately in the working-class life of Vienna and the literary life of London. It amused me at this time to move between Charleston and Fieldhead and the even more traditional atmosphere of my sister Helen's comfortable home in Northampton-shire, from where I wrote to Julian: 'I'm here in the middle of the hunting country,' when I would sometimes find myself, inexplicably, discussing the merits of the various Hunts in the Southern Midlands with one of the grooms. There were no grooms touching their caps on the porch at Charleston, nor pink coats hanging up in the cupboards, and the discussion was about *The Nature of Beauty, Vision and Design* and *The Ego and the Id* rather than the way in which the Grafton or the Bicester was run by the latest MFH or the impact of rich American horsey enthusiasts on the ancient pattern of country life. The half-finished canvases by Duncan Grant, or Julian's mother Vanessa, or his brother Quentin piled carelessly in the studios, and the doors and fireplaces of the old farm-house transformed by decorations of fruit and flowers and opulent nudes by the same hands, the low square tables made of tiles fired in Roger Fry's Omega workshops, and the harmony created all through the house by the free, brightly coloured post-impressionist style that one encountered in everything from the huge breakfast cup one drank one's coffee from to the bedroom curtains that were drawn in the morning, not by a silent-footed valet or housemaid buy by one's own hand to let in the Sussex sunshine, excited the suppressed painter that lurked in my breast. They seemed to suggest how easily life could be restored to a paradise of the senses if one simply ignored the conventions that still gripped one in the most absurd ways, clinging from a past that had been superseded in the minds of people of clear intelligence and unspoilt imagination.

. . . One morning I received a letter from Leonard, which informed me not only that he and Virginia liked my poems very much and wanted to publish them, but also that they had heard that I might be interested in working in the Hogarth Press, and would I come and discuss it with them? I wrote off triumphantly to Julian:

I have heard from the Woolfs, and they say they will be glad to publish my poems. Bless them. I'm cheered, I don't mind saying. It won't be till the autumn – I'd rather it were the spring – but it scarcely matters, will be an admirable experience in patience for myself, and I'm grateful to have them published at all. I gather they are now being inspected by Lady G. Whether, if she disapproves of them, they'll publish them on their own, I know not. But I suppose having said they'll publish them, they will. Bear with my selfish pleasure.

'Lady G.' – Dorothy Wellesley (now the Duchess of Wellington), to whose patronage the series of Hogarth Living Poets owed its existence – announced her approval in spite of my fears. Gone at once were the rather sobering visions of a lifetime dedicated to etching and aquatint in the dusty recesses of the British Museum, banished forever the idea of following my uncles and cousins into the service of His Britannic Majesty, as I rushed off to see the Woolfs in 52 Tavistock Square at the beginning of January. Immediately I sent a report to Julian:

> I would have written to you before about your poems, if the end of last week had not been so hectic – interviews – consultations – calculations. I expect you know substantially what the offer of the Woolves was going to be: I was surprised when they made it to me – on Friday, at tea, when I met them both for the first time, and thought them most charming, Virginia very beautiful – and not a little excited. I've not decided I'm going to make every effort to accept the offer... I really can't imagaine any work that would interest me more, and to be a partner with them, with a voice in what's to be published (and how) and what isn't – it seems an almost unbelievable stroke of luck.

The consultations and calculations continued intensively for the next few days. There were problems to be solved about raising the money, but I found my mother sympathetic in general and pleased to see me launched on something that I obviously cared about so much. Looking back on it now, it seems to me that everything was settled with astonishing speed, for only six days later I could announce to Julian:

> This week has been a fevered one – I emerge with an agreement in my pocket, by which I become Manager of the Hogarth Press in

October — if not fired after eight months of apprenticeship. And I have the option of becoming a partner in a year or two. And I start in on Wednesday as ever is! Your advice was just what I wanted — very welcome. As a matter of fact Leonard had lost confidence in his first proposition even before my Trustee turned a dubious eye on it, so I think both parties feel better under the present agreement that we argued out in a series of interviews. I pray that I shall be a success: hard work, but congenial . . . and Leonard is giving me good holidays, long enough to get some writing done, I hope. But there's so much I want to say, that I can't say it all in a letter, and must wait till I see you. I was charmed by both Leonard and Virginia, and hope they liked me.

The year before, I had been staying in London with my sister Beatrix in St George's Square. Now I moved into the house in Heathcote Street, just off the Gray's Inn Road, that was occupied by Douglas Davidson, the painter, and his brother Angus, skilled translator from the Italian and author of an excellent book on Edward Lear. There the room which had previously been occupied by Dadie was made over to me. The advantage of Heathcote Street was that it was only a few minutes' walk from Tavistock Square. Every morning I set out to reach the Woolf's house at 9.15 AM., passing through a disused graveyard filled with ancient tombestones of the seventeenth and eighteenth centuries, its half-effaced inscriptions and funeral ornaments dappled with moss and lichen. The Burial Ground of St George-the-Martyr had become a quiet garden, and some old people used to sit there all day when the sun was shining: I would see the same faces on my return after work as I had observed on my setting out.

At No 52 the Press occupied the basement, formerly the kitchen and servants' quarters; a friendly firm of solicitors were installed on the ground and first floors, while on the top two floors Leonard and Virginia had their own living quarters. The basement was cold and draughty and ramshackle. My own office, as apprentice manager, was a small back room that had once been a pantry and cupboard room — the cupboards were piled high with the dusty files of the activities of the Press ever since it had started in 1917. It was badly in need of redecorating, it had a jammed window that looked out on a narrow outside passage and a gloomy wall, and a decrepit gas-fire in front of which Leonard would attempt, without any striking success, to warm his hands when he came in to see me with the day's correspondence soon after my arrival. My mother was appalled when she first visited me there; but to me nevertheless it was sacred ground. I was at last part of a publishing firm; and the one that seemed to me the most glamorous of all; I was associated every day with the – to me – legendary Leonard and Virginia Woolf; in the former scullery up the passage an actual printing-machine was installed, with its trays of type beside it, and there on many an afternoon Leonard could be found rolling off the firm's stationery, writing paper, invoices, royalty forms and review slips; while every now and then Virginia herself could be glimpsed setting the type for one of the small books of poetry that the Press still produced at home – at that time it was, I think, Vita Sackville-West's *Sissinghurst* – in spite of the fact that it had grown into a large business dealing with many of the biggest printers and binders. All round me, in all the rooms and down the dark corridors, were the piled packages of finished books as delivered from the binders. It gave me a special pleasure to explore among them, noting on the labels the names of books that were already precious to me, such as Virginia's *Monday or Tuesday* (not many of these) and *To the Lighthouse* in their original editions, and occasionally coming across a single, opened package of some early publication that had long been famous, Ivan Bunin's *The Gentleman from San Francisco*, or E.M. Forster's *Pharos and Pharillon*, or *The Notebooks of Anton Chekhov*, though not, alas, Katherine Mansfield's *The Prelude* or T.S. Eliot's *The Waste Land*, long out of print but tantalizingly advertised at the back of some of the other books. And I persuaded Leonard to allow me to make a collection of the early hand-set volumes of poetry, all different shapes and sizes in their prettily decorated paper covers, John Crowe Ransom's *Grace After Meat*, Herbert Read's *Mutations of the Phoenix*, Robert Graves's *Mockbeggar Hall*, curiosities such as Clive Bell's *Poems* and Nancy Cunard's *Parallax*, and many others, of which I can think of one instance, Fredegond Shove's *Daybreak*, unjustly forgotten today. By far the largest piles were in the studio room at the back where (as I have described elsewhere) Virginia had her work-desk; and I would slip in, with carefully controlled eagerness and as silently as possible, to hunt out some books that were suddenly needed on the packing-table in the front room, feeling that I was entering the holiest part of the house, the inmost ark of its presiding deity. I was even allowed, later, to work at the desk when they were both away.

No one could have been a kinder or more sympathetic teacher than Leonard. There was no nonsense of formal 'business relations' in the Press, and he would explain to me how to prepare estimates and contracts (on his own highly individual patterns), how to design a

book-page and an advertisement and how to organize the flow of books
to the shops, with steady patience and an assumption of intimate
interest in everything we published. He described the authors, the
printers' and paper-makers' travellers and all the other people with
whom I was to have to deal, including the persistent and unsnubbable
bores, at length and with characteristically caustic comment. The
absurd conventions of the trade, the prejudices of certain important
booksellers and reviewers, the inexplicably chancy ups and downs of
success and failure in the fortunes of books, would rouse him at all
times to exasperated and withering wit; and it was due to his teaching
that I learnt early on to face with a certain detached philosophy the
irrational behaviour that almost everyone who has to do with books is
so frequently capable of. In fact I learnt the essentials of publishing in
the most agreeable way possible: from a man who had created his own
business, had never allowed it to grow so big that it fell into
departments sealed off from one another, and who saw it all as much
from the point of view of an author and amateur printer as of someone
who had to make his living by it. If Leonard had a fault, it was in
allowing detail to loom too large at times. A small item that could not
be accounted for in the books, a misunderstanding about a point of
production would, without apparent reason, irritate him suddenly to
the extreme, he would worry it like a dog worrying a rat, until indeed
he seemed to be the rat and the detail the dog; and betray, I felt after
one or two such experiences, the long nervous tension he had lived
under in caring so devotedly for the genius of his wife.

My relations with Virginia began with an ardent youthful hero-
worship; but gradually, as I got to know her better, this turned into a
feeling of real affection as well as respect. At first she was irradiated in
my eyes with the halo of having written *Jacob's Room, To the
Lighthouse* and *Mrs Dalloway*. No other books seemed to me to express
with anything like the same penetration and beauty the sensibility of
our age; it was not merely the conception that underlay those works, of
time and sorrow and human longing, but also the way she expressed it,
the paramount importance in her writing of technical change and
experiment; almost everything else seemed, after I had read them,
utterly wide of the target and inadequately aware of what was needed. I
was influenced, of course, as a poet, by the skill with which she
managed to transform the material of poetry into the prose-form of the
novel; but that in itself seemed to me one of the major artistic problems
of our time, arising out of the terror and tension, the phantasmagoria of
modern life. I devoured the three novels again and again, and always

with fresh delight, valuing them far higher than *The Common Reader,
A Room of One's Own, Orlando* and even *Flush*, which, much as I
enjoyed them and popular as they were, seemed to me of far less
significance. In those early days I revered Virginia as the sacred centre,
the most gifted and adored (and sometimes feared) of the Bloomsbury
circle. But, as time went on, the feeling she inspired in me was more
one of happy release than of reverence. I found her the most
enchanting of friends, full of sympathy and understanding for my own
personal problems and the problems I was up against in my job, with an
intense curiosity about my own life and the lives of my friends in my
generation (many of whom were, of course, known and even related to
her). She liked to hear all about what we wanted to do in poetry, in
painting, in novel-writing. She would stimulate me to talk, she had an
unique gift for encouraging one to be indiscreet, and would listen with
absorption and occasionally intersperse pointed and witty comments.
Some of the happiest times I can remember in those years were the
luncheons and teas I would be invited up to in the Woolfs' part of the
house, where the walls were painted with frescoes by Duncan Grant and
Virginia's sister Vanessa Bell, discussing the plans of the Press, the
books submitted to us, and all the histories and personalities involved.
She was always bubbling with ideas, longing to launch new schemes and
produce books that no one had thought of before, that would startle
the conventional business minds of the book world. She found an
all-too-ready response in me, and had sometimes quietly to be checked
on the rein by Leonard.

There were days, however, when she seemed withdrawn behind a
veil, and it was hard to draw out her interest in the activities of the
Press or ignite the gaiety which at other times was so characteristic of
her. Sometimes this veil concealed her preoccupation with the problems
of whatever she was writing at the moment; at other times it was darker
and more opaque, bringing an uneasy atmosphere of strain and misery
to the house. It is not for me to explain or explore the moods of
fathomless melancholy that overcame Virginia Woolf at various periods
during her life, and nearly always began with a series of acute
headaches; I can only record the anxiety and distress they caused me
for her own sake and for Leonard, who had fought them with her for so
long, and my wonder that she managed to achieve so much with that
perpetual threat hanging over her, always dropping nearer when she was
in the throes of her finest creative achievement.

One of the worst of these fits of melancholy attacked her in the last
stages of her work on *The Waves*, and Leonard decided that she must

abandon it altogether for a time. The crisis passed, and she was able to get the book, to me the most daring if not the most successful of all her experiments, ready for press in the late summer. I could hardly contain my impatience to read it; it was for me the great event of the year, even though my own first book of poems was coming out in September. At last, at the beginning of the month, the advance copies arrived, just after I had spent a week-end with her and Leonard at Rodmell, and in writing to thank her I mentioned that I was in the middle of reading it. She immediately sent me a note insisting that I should write down for her exactly what I thought about it. I was deeply stirred by the book, and wrote her a long letter in which I tried, no doubt naïvely, to describe the impression it had made on me. In the same letter I suggested that it was high time for her to define her views about modern poetry, which we had discussed so often together. I received the following letter in reply, dated 17th September:

Dear John,

I'm most grateful to you for your letter. It made me happy all yesterday. I had become firmly convinced that *The Waves* was a failure, in the sense that it wouldn't convey anything to anybody. And now you've been so perceptive, and gone so much further and deeper in understanding my drift than I thought possible that I'm immensely relieved. Not that I expect many such readers. And I'm rather dismayed to hear we've printed 7,000: for I'm sure 3,000 will feed all appetites; and then the other 4 will sit round me like decaying corpses for ever in the studio (I cleared up the table – for you, not the corpses). I agree that it's very difficult – bristling with horrors, though I've never worked so hard as I did here, to smooth them out. But it was, I think, a difficult attempt – I wanted to eliminate all detail; all fact; and analysis; and myself; and yet not be frigid and rhetorical; and not monotonous (which I am) and to keep the swiftness of prose and yet strike one or two sparks, and not write poetical, but pure-bred prose, and keep the elements of character; and yet that there should be many characters and only one; and also an infinity, a background behind – well, I admit I was biting off too much.

But enough, as the poets say. If I live another 50 years I think I shall put this method to some use, but as in 50 years I shall be under the pond, with the goldfish swimming over me, I daresay these vast ambitions are a little foolish, and will ruin the press. That reminds me – I think your idea of a Letter most brilliant – 'To a Young

Poet' — because I'm seething with immature and ill considered and wild and annoying ideas about prose and poetry. So lend me your name — (and let me sketch a character of you by way of frontispiece) — and then I'll pour forth all I can think of about you young, and we old, and novels — how damned they are — and poetry, how dead. But I must take a look into the subject, and you must reply, 'To an Old Novelist' — I must read Auden, whom I've not read, and Spender (his novel I swear I will tackle tonight). The whole subject is crying out for letters — flocks, volleys of them, from every side. Why not get Spender and Auden and Day Lewis to join? But you must go to Miss Belsher, and I must go to my luncheon.

This is only a scribble to say how grateful I am for your letter.

Yrs

Virginia Woolf.

. . . From time to time I went down to Rodmell, to discuss Hogarth affairs with her and Leonard. In theory, I had bought Virginia out of the Press, but in fact she continued to be as keenly interested in all its activities as ever before, and every evening we would settle down in the little sitting-room upstairs, where the shelves were filled with books in Virginia's own binding and the tables and window-sills covered with the begonias, gloxinias and rare giant lilies that Leonard raised in his greenhouses, and we would discuss books and authors and the opportunities that were open to us in the new situation. Leonard stretched out his feet towards the fire in his armchair on one side, and puffed at his pipe; Virginia on the other lit another home-rolled cigarette in her long holder. Occasional visitor though I was, I had come to be very fond of Monk's House, the old village cottage they had bought just after the First War and rebuilt to make an ideal home for two authors to live and work in: I loved the untidy, warm, informal atmosphere of the house, with books and magazines littered about the rooms, logs piled up by the fireplaces, painted furniture and low tables of tiles designed by the Bloomsbury artists, and writing done in sunny, flower-filled, messy studios. A smell of wood smoke and ripe apples lingered about it, mixed with the fainter under-perfume of old bindings and old paper. We ate our meals always at the stove end of the long kitchen-scullery. I remember one Autumn evening there, just after Leonard's book *Barbarians at the Gate* had come out: I had been moved by the persuasive force of the argument he developed, the lucidity of the style and the underlying warmth, and I told him so, and how important I felt his warning was at a time when people were all too easily allowing themselves to believe that any means were justified by the ends. Virginia was splashing gravy in large dollops over my plate as I talked, and joined in with her praise, 'You know, Leo, it's a wonderful book', while Leonard himself sat in modest silence, with lowered eyes, like a schoolboy praised by the headmaster at an end-of-term prize-giving.

During those months Virginia alternated between cautious confidence and weary depression about the Roger Fry biography, very much as she always did when at work on a new book; but sometimes the depression seemed so deep that both Leonard and I encouraged her to leave it for a while, to put down on paper her objections to my generation of writers, and to prepare a third *Common Reader* collection of essays; the idea of a change nearly always lightened her mood. When *Roger Fry* was finished, however, just before Christmas, she was transformed: radiant and buoyant, full of teasing malice and the keenest interest in what her friends were doing, and finding a startling new beauty in London – the squares and side-streets in the black-out on a clear night – a transfigured look in the faces of the men and women she passed – the smartness of uniforms of every sort.

Gerald Brenan: Bloomsbury in Spain

Reprinted from Gerald Brenan, South from Granada *(London, Hamish Hamilton, 1957), 27–37, 139–46, reprinted by permission of Hamish Hamilton Ltd.*

[After the First World War Gerald Brenan, an impecunious, heroic young English officer, settled in a primitive mountain village south of Granada called Yegen. Brenan, whose writings include several books on Spain, had known Ralph Partridge during the war and through him met various members of Bloomsbury. For a time he was intensely involved in Lytton Strachey's *ménage* through his love for Carrington.

In 1957 Brenan published a book on Yegen and his life there. Separate chapters mixing specific observations with general reflections on Bloomsbury are devoted to the visits paid to him in 1920 and in 1923, first by Lytton, Carrington, and Ralph, and then by Leonard and Virginia Woolf.]

I had not long been settled in my house when I learned that I was to have visitors. My friend Ralph Partridge wrote that he proposed to arrive early in April and that he would bring with him a young woman known as Carrington and also a writer who had recently leaped into fame called Lytton Strachey. This was the best possible news, for it was six months since I had seen any of my friends, and I was beginning to feel my isolation. But perhaps before describing their visit, I should explain how I had come to know them . . .

I cannot recollect now how I came to know Carrington, for we had other friends in common besides Ralph, but I remember very well going over to Tidmarsh for the first time and meeting Lytton Strachey. It was one of those heavily overcast English summer days. The trees and the grass were steeped in a vivid green, but the purplish clouds overhead shut out the light and made the interiors of the houses dark and gloomy. Carrington with her restless blue eyes and her golden-brown hair cut in a straight page-boy bob came to the door -- she suggested to me one of the lute-playing angels, the fourth from the left, in Piero della Francesca's *Nativity* -- and I was shown into the sitting-room. At the further end of it there was an extraordinary figure reclining in a deep armchair. At the first glance, before I had accustomed my eyes to the lack of light, I had the illusion -- or rather, I should say, the image came into my mind -- of a darkly bearded he-goat, glaring at me from the bottom of a cave. Then I saw that it was a man and took in gradually the long, relaxed figure, the Greco-ish face, the brown sensitive eyes hidden behind thick glasses, the large, coarse nose and ears, the fine, thin, blue-veined hands. Most extraordinary was the voice which was both very low and in certain syllables very high-pitched, and which faded out at the end of the sentence, sometimes even without finishing it. I never attuned my ears to taking in everything that he said.

Tea was laid in the dining-room -- farm butter, honey in the comb, home-made cakes and jam and currant loaf, served in a pink lustre tea-service. Carrington was a devotee of Cobbett, and her housekeeping and furnishing expressed not only the comfort but the poetry of cottage and farmhouse life. Her very English sensibility, in love with the country and with all country things, gave everything she touched a special and peculiar stamp. But what struck me more strongly about her than anything else was the attention she paid to Lytton. Never have I seen anyone who was so waited on hand and foot as he was by her, or whose every word and gesture was received with such reverence. In a young woman who in all other respects was fiercely jealous of her independence, this was extraordinary.

How is one to describe the first beginnings of a long friendship? Later impressions fuse with earlier ones and distort them. Besides, I have to keep within the framework of this book, which requires that I put down only what will be necessary to make Lytton Strachey's visit to my remote and primitive village come alive. Scouring my memory then, I seem to remember that as I sat at the tea-table on that dark summer's afternoon I was puzzled by the contrast presented by the three people in front of me and wondered whether their peculiar relation (adopted father and married children, as it came in time to be) could last. They were in every way so extremely different from one another: Ralph with his look of an Oxford hearty – dirty white shorts, nondescript shirt and then rather stylized way of speaking which contrasted with the Rabelaisian laugh, rolling blue eyes and baritone voice in which he sang a jazz song or a ballad: Carrington with her simple, pre-Raphaelite clothes and her coaxing voice and smile that concealed so many intense and usually conflicting feelings: Lytton, elegant in his dark suit, gravely remote and fantastic, with something of the polished and dilettante air of a sixteenth-century cardinal. It was not any similarity of temperament or upbringing that had brought these three together, and Lytton's London friends, who resented their week-ends at Tidmarsh being diluted by people whom they looked on as outsiders, could not understand it. 'Bloomsbury' was still a small, closely guarded set, united both by old friendships and by a private philosophy, and it showed a strong resistance to accepting on an intimate footing people whom it did not regard as suitable.

It was February when I learned of my friends' expected visit, and this at once produced a crisis in my arrangements. Only two rooms of my house were as yet furnished and I should need to buy more things of every sort and in particular more beds and bedding . . .

. . . When we had exhausted the first burst of mutual communication, the problem of transporting Lytton Strachey to Yegen came up. He sat there silent and bearded, showing no signs of enthusiasm. In the end we decided to engage a carriage for the following morning to convey us as far as Orgiva and to send on two mules to meet us there and take us the rest of the journey.

We picked up the mules and then the question arose as to which route we should take. The shortest – it saved an hour – required us to ford the Rio Grande instead of crossing the bridge. According to the muleteers this was feasible, but when we reached the ford and the mules went in almost to their girths in the racing water, Lytton drew back. There was nothing to be done but to eat our lunch under the olive trees and return to the hotel, arranging with the men to make a fresh start on the following day.

The evening passed in general low spirits. Everyone's nerves were on edge. Ralph and Carrington were having a lovers' quarrel and Lytton was gloomy because, though he had been eager to see Spain, he had been most unwilling to come on this expedition. His stomach was delicate, Spanish food had disagreed with him, and he was not feeling in the mood for adventures. But Ralph, who was very loyal to his friends, was determined to visit me, and Lytton had refused to be left behind at Granada even if Carrington, in whose capacities he had little confidence, remained with him. This clinging to male protection was characteristic. Under his self-possessed manner he was a timid man who had arranged his life so that he should never be obliged to do anything that he found difficult. Now one of the things that he could not do was to speak to people who were outside of his particular range of interests. Thus, though he had been toying for some time with a Spanish grammar, nothing would have induced him even to order a cup of coffee in that language. In France he refused to utter a word of French although, naturally, he knew it well and read it aloud with a fair accent. He could not even give an order to an English servant. When, in his own house, he wanted some tea, he told Carrington and she told the maid and, if he was by himself, he went without. To avoid the risk of being spoken to in trains he always, even when he was badly off, travelled first class. Such were the rules he had drawn up for himself. From an early age he had planned his life, his career, even his appearance, and this plan required that he should keep strictly within that small circle of people where he could fly under his own colours and make himself understood without effort. No doubt the peculiarities of his voice and intonation as well as his dislike of any sort of social pretence made communication with the world at large difficult for him.

That evening, then, at Lanjarón, was spoiled by recriminations. Did I really know the road? Ralph asked me. Were the muleteers to be trusted? Would there be beds and eatable food when we arrived? The conveyance of the great writer to my mountain village began to assume more and more the appearance of a difficult military operation. Carrington, caught between two fires, became clumsily appeasing and only Lytton said nothing. As for myself, I never doubted my powers to go anywhere or to do anything of a physical sort that I wished to, but under my friends' bombardment I felt my unfitness for assuming responsibility for other people.

It was in this harassed and ruffled frame of mind that we set off once more on the following morning. For the first hour or so everything went well. As the carriage rolled along, the sun lit up the silver leaves of the olive trees and the birds rose and sank like shuttles between them and the tall bean plants below. But no sooner had we left the carriage and descended into the river valley than our difficulties began. Lytton found that he could not ride on mule-back because he suffered from piles, so that every time the track crossed the river, which happened about every half a mile, he had laboriously to climb onto the animal and then dismount again. This delayed us. It was not till a little before sunset that we reached Cádiar and he then felt so exhausted that he declared that he could not go any further. We drew up at the *posada* and looked at its best bed, but one glance at it made him change his mind and decide to go on.

The day was coming to an end so rapidly that we did not dare to take the short and comparatively easy track through Yátor. There was nothing to be done but climb straight up the mountainside to hit the end of the main road some 2,500 feet above. It was a dramatic ascent by a steep path often bordered by precipices and no one could do it sitting side-saddle on a mule, as Lytton and Carrington had to, without an unpleasant feeling inside. Slowly, as we climbed, the light faded. A rosy band mounted in the sky behind us, and the chasms and pinnacles took on a shadowy depth and height. Then the stars came out just as we reached the road, and Carrington and I hurried on to give warning of our arrival and to get a meal prepared. The distance was still some six miles. When at length we reached the village and stood looking down in the starlight on its flat, greyish roofs, only the tiniest occasional glow from the smallest oil lamp in the glassless foot-square frame of a window showed that it was still awake.

I do not remember much about the next few days. Lytton was tired and therefore not in a mood for talking much. We went for a walk up the mountain-side and Carrington took some photographs. One of them, if I remember right, showed him sitting side-saddle on a mule, bearded, spectacled, very long and thin, with his coarse red nose, holding an open sunshade above him. Even in England he was a strange figure to meet on a country ramble: here he looked exotic, aristocratic, Oriental rather than English, and above all incongruous.

On his last evening, however, cheered by the thought that his visit was drawing to an end, he relaxed and became almost lively. When he was in the mood, his conversation had great charm. The delicacy and precision of his mind came out much better than they usually did in his books, because in these he subordinated sensitivity of language and spontaneity of phrase to a preconceived pattern. He was not, like Virginia Woolf, a natural writer, and even in his letters his pen never ran away with him. But in conversation he was himself. He needed more than most people an attuned and sympathetic audience, but, given this, he became the most easy of companions, listening as much as he talked, making whimsical or penetrating comments and creating around him a feeling of naturalness and intimacy. One remembered afterwards his doubts and hesitations, his refusals to dogmatize, his flights of fantasy, his high, whispering voice fading out in the middle of a sentence, and forgot the very definite and well-ordered mind that lay underneath. But it is beyond my power to give any real account of so complex a character who, through some thickness in the needle, perhaps some deliberate plan of writing down to his readers, records himself with too poor fidelity in his literary works. One observed a number of discordant features – a feminine sensibility, a delight in the absurd, a taste for exaggeration and melodrama, a very mature judgement and then some lack of human substance, some hereditary thinness in the blood that at times gave people who met him an odd feeling in the spine. He seemed almost indecently lacking in ordinariness.

However, what I remember best about Lytton Strachey – for though I was never on intimate or even on easy terms with him, I had opportunities for seeing him in his own house and elsewhere over many years – was the great gentleness of his tone and manner when he was with people whom he liked. As a young man he had, I understand, shown a bitter and satirical vein and when, as often happened, he was unwell, he could be peevish and irritable. But friendship drew out his best qualities. There was a good deal in his cautiously hedonistic attitude to life that recalled the teachings of Epicurus. His world, like the Garden of that valetudinarian philosopher, consisted of a small, carefully chosen set of people whose society he enjoyed. Some of these were young men of good looks and intellectual promise whom he drew out and encouraged, for there was something of the teacher in him. Others were literary figures, such as Virginia Woolf, Maynard Keynes, Desmond and Molly MacCarthy and E.M. Forster. Outside this he would make sallies into a wider field – luncheons with Lady Oxford or Lady Ottoline Morrell, dinner parties at Lady Colefax's and even at ducal houses – and return home full of mischievous and ironical comments. But within these limits he remained. Although, as a Strachey, he took a certain interest in public affairs and stood by his

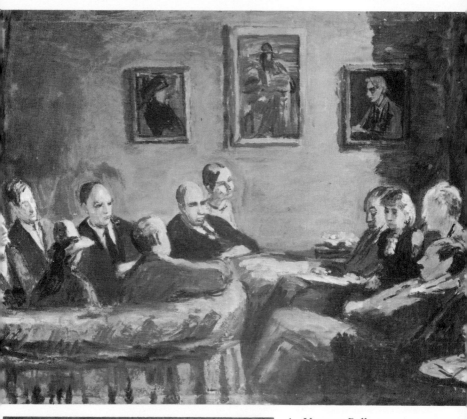

1 Vanessa Bell:
The Memoir Club c.1943
(Professor Quentin Bell)

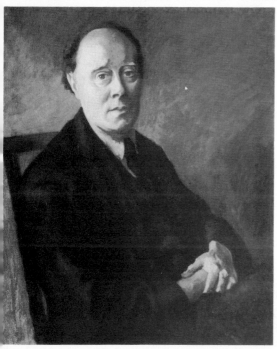

2 Roger Fry:
Clive Bell c.1924
(National Portrait Gallery)

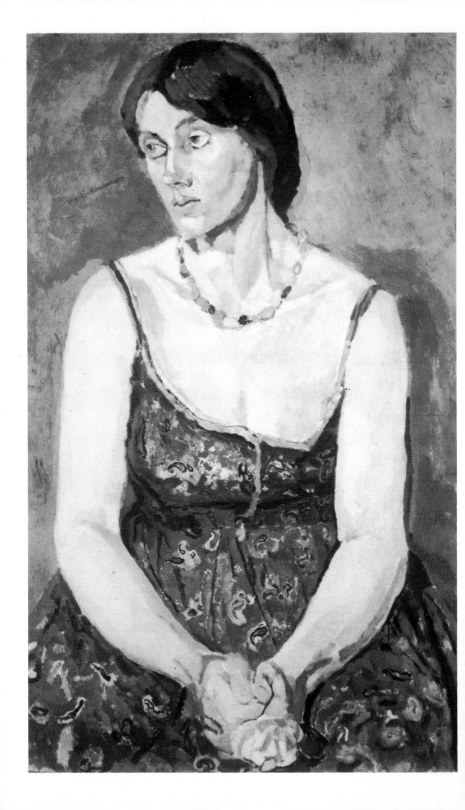

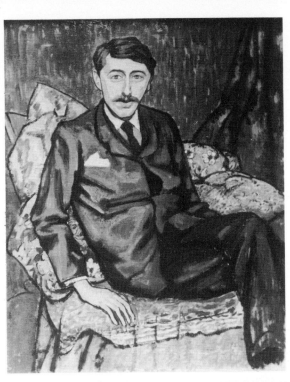

4 Roger Fry:
E.M. Forster 1911

3 *Facing page*: Duncan Grant:
Vanessa Bell c.1918
(National Portrait Gallery)

5 Vanessa Bell: *Roger Fry
and Julian Bell
Playing Chess* c. 1933
(King's College, Cambridge)

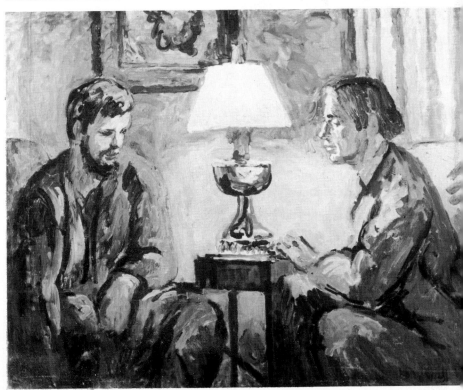

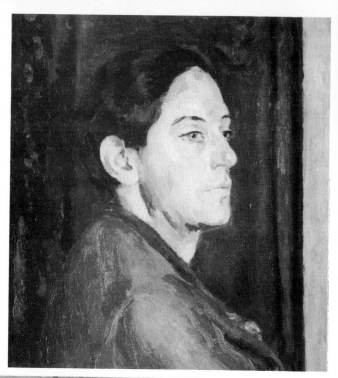

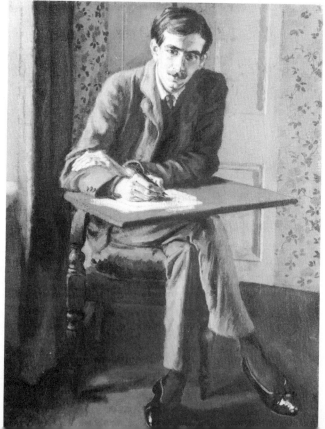

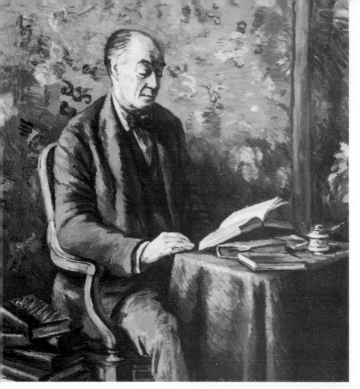

6 *Top left*: Vanessa Bell:
Duncan Grant 1930
(The Duke of Devonshire)

7 *Left:* Duncan Grant:
Maynard Keynes 1908
(King's College, Cambridge)

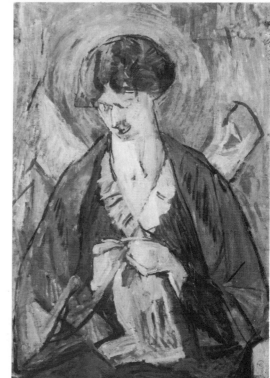

8 *Above*: Duncan Grant:
Desmond MacCarthy 1944
(National Portrait Gallery)

9 *Right*: Vanessa Bell:
Molly MacCarthy c.1912

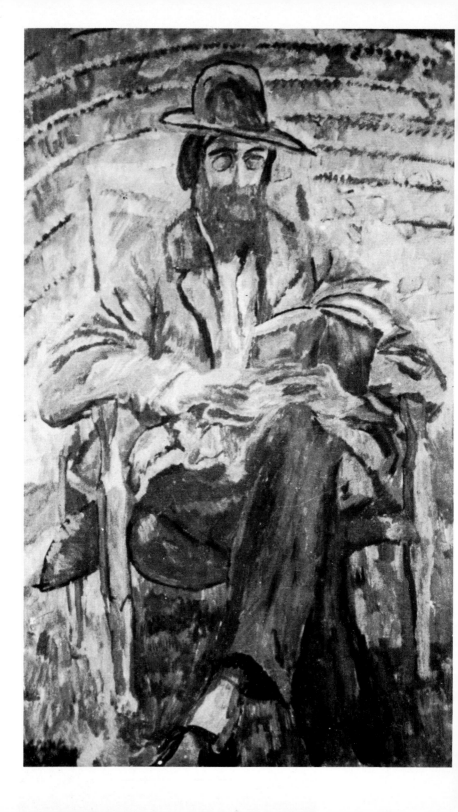

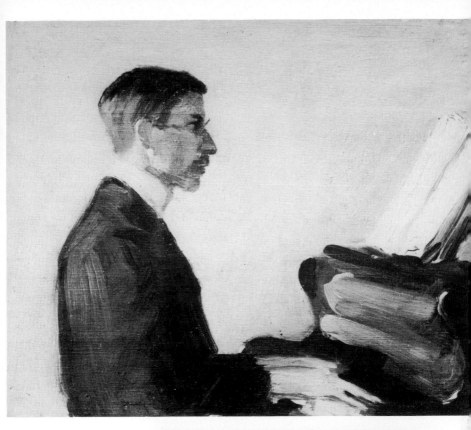

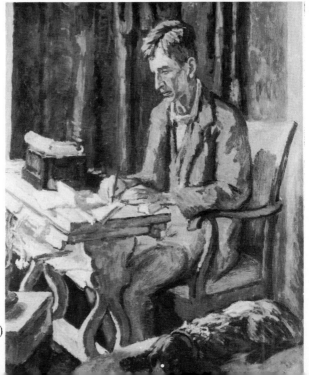

10 *Left:* Duncan Grant:
Lytton Strachey 1913

11 *Above:* Vanessa Bell:
Saxon Sydney-Turner
c. 1908
(Mrs Barbara Bagenal)

12 *Right:* Vanessa Bell:
Leonard Woolf c. 1938
(National Portrait Gallery)

13 Vanessa Bell:
Virginia Woolf c.1911–12
(Mrs Ian Parsons)

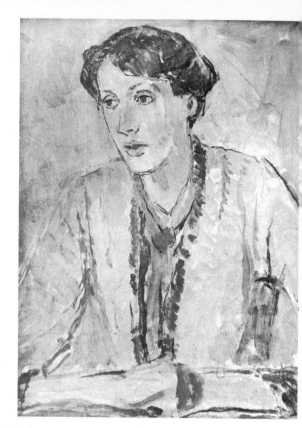

14 Duncan Grant:
Adrian Stephen c. 1910
(Mrs Ann Synge)

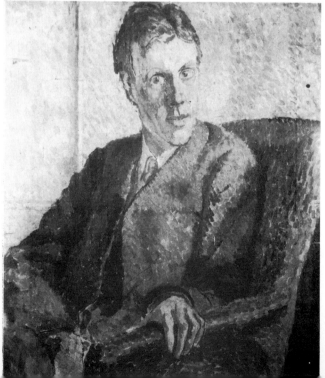

very moderate Liberal opinions, I got the impression that privately he thought of the world with its incomprehensible stupidity as something which it was best to keep at a distance. Unlike Voltaire, whom he admired so greatly, he regarded it as irreformable, and it was this attitude, I suspect, that angered Bertrand Russell and led him to speak harshly of him in a recent broadcast. The two men, who often met at Lady Ottoline's, were not made to like or understand one another, in spite of their sharing the same pacifist attitude to the War.

The day for my friends' departure came. A car arrived and took them to Almeria, where they caught the train for Madrid. The visit had been something of a strain for everyone. Much though I knew that I should miss Ralph and Carrington, whose presence in my house, in spite of all the difficulties, had given me the deepest pleasure, I breathed again at the thought that I should no longer be responsible for finding dishes that would suit Lytton's delicate digestion. The ruthless cuisine of Spanish villages, with its emphasis on potato omelettes, dried cod and unrefined olive oil, had made my task a difficult one. And he must have been even more relieved at making his escape. When, three years later, Leonard and Virginia Woolf were preparing to come out and stay with me, he advised them strongly against attempting it, declaring in his high-pitched voice that 'it was death':

It was in the spring of 1923 that Leonard and Virginia Woolf came out to see me. I met them at Granada at the house of some friends of mine, the Temples, who wished to discuss the African colonies with Leonard, and after a couple of nights there we came on by bus and mule to Yegen. This time the journey went smoothly, without any of the difficulties that had marked Lytton Strachey's passage three years before, and it was evident that they enjoyed it.

The first thing that comes to my mind when I think of Virginia as she was in those days, and particularly as I saw her in the quiet seclusion of my house, is her beauty. Although her face was too long for symmetry, its bones were thin and delicately made and her eyes were large, grey or greyish blue, and as clear as a hawk's. In conversation they would light up a little coldly while her mouth took an ironic and challenging fold, but in repose her expression was pensive and almost girlish. When in the evening we settled under the hooded chimney and the logs burned up and she stretched out her hands to the blaze, the whole cast of her face revealed her as a poet.

There are writers whose personality resembles their work, and there are others who, when one meets them, give no inkling of it. Virginia

Woolf belonged strikingly to the first category. When one had spent half an hour in a room with her one could easily believe that it was she who, as one was told, had scribbled quickly in purple ink in the summer house at Rodmell that fresh and sparkling article that had just appeared in *The Nation*, and when one saw her in a reflective or dreamy mood one recognized only a little less slowly the authoress of *To the Lighthouse*. One reason for this was that her conversation, especially when she had been primed up a little, was like her prose. She talked as she wrote and very nearly as well, and that is why I cannot read a page of *The Common Reader* today without her voice and intonation coming back to me forcibly. No writer that I know of has put his living presence into his books to the extent that she has done.

Not, however, that what she said was ever bookish. She talked easily and naturally in a pure and idiomatic English, often, like many of her friends, in a lightly ironical tone. Irony, it will be remembered, plays a great and important part in her writings. There it is of a gay and playful kind, sometimes verging on facetiousness, but in her conversation it became personal and took on a feminine, and one might almost say flirtatious, form. Leaning sideways and a little stiffly in her chair she would address her companion in a bantering tone, and she liked to be answered in the same manner. But whatever her vein, all the resources of her mind seemed to be at her immediate disposal at every moment. One felt a glass-like clarity, but it was not the clarity of a logician, but rather that of a kaleidoscope which throws out each time from the same set of pieces a different pattern. Much later, when she was, I think, working on *The Waves*, she told me that her difficulty lay in stopping the flow of her pen. She had been reading, she said, a life of Beethoven and envied his power of drawing up into his score by constant revision and correction themes which resisted being brought to the surface. I imagine that for her correction meant simply shaking the kaleidoscope and producing a new, more appropriate passage.

Perhaps because Virginia lacked the novelist's sense for the dramatic properties of character and was more interested in the texture of people's minds, she was much given to drawing them out and documenting herself upon them. She asked me a great many questions — why I had come to live here, what I felt about this and that, and what my ideas were about writing. I was conscious that I was being studied and even quizzed a little and also that she and Leonard were trying to decide whether I showed any signs of having literary talent. If so, I must publish with them. Yet it must not for a moment be thought that she was patronizing. On the contrary her deference to the views of the callow and rather arrogant youth with whom she was staying was quite surprising. She argued with me about literature, defended Scott, Thackeray and Conrad against my attacks, disagreed with my high opinion of *Ulysses* on the grounds that great works of art ought not to be so boring, and listened humbly to my criticisms of her own novels. That was the great thing about 'Bloomsbury' – they refused to stand on the pedestal of their own age and superiority. And her visit was followed by a succession of highly characteristic letters in which she continued the theme of our discussions.

I want to emphasize Virginia's real friendliness on this occasion and the trouble she took to advise and encourage me, because her recklessness in conversation – when she was overexcited she talked too much from the surface of her mind – made some people think that she lacked ordinary sympathies. I was young for my age, and rather earnest. The isolation in which I lived had made me self-centred, and like all people who are starved for conversation I was very talkative. She on the other hand was a writer of great distinction, approaching the height of her powers. Yet she and her husband not only concealed the impatience they must often have felt, but treated me as though I was their intellectual equal. Of course, one might say, they believed in encouraging young writers and spotting the winners among them. Virginia had a strong sense of the continuity of literary tradition and felt it a duty to hand on what she had received. She was also intensely and uneasily aware of the existence of a younger generation who would one day rise and sit in judgment on her. It may be, therefore, that she thought that my strange way of life and my passion for literature showed that I might have something to give. If so, however, both she and Leonard decided a few years later that they had been mistaken.

As I sit here, trying to collect my scattered memories of this fortnight, a few scenes come before me with vividness. I recall Virginia's face in the firelight, then the gaily bantering tone in which she spoke, and Leonard's easy, companionable one. Her manner at such times was vivaciously, though rather chillily, feminine, and her voice seemed to preen itself with self-confidence in its own powers. With a little encouragement it would throw off a cascade of words like the notes of a great pianist improvising, and without the affectation – born of delight in verbal mastery – that sometimes crept into the style of her novels. Leonard, on the other hand, was very steady, very masculine – a pipe-smoking, tweed-dressing man who could conduct an argument to a finish without losing the thread and who had what is called at Cambridge 'a good mind'. Moreover – and this impressed me more than anything – he could read Aeschylus without a crib.

Then, scrambling on the hillside among the fig trees and the olives, I see a rather different person. An English lady, country-bred and thin, her wide-open eyes scanning the distance, who has completely forgotten herself in her delight at the beauty of the landscape and at the novelty of finding herself in such a remote and Arcadian spot. She seemed, though quiet, as excited as a schoolgirl on a holiday, while her husband's serious, sardonic features had become almost boyish. On these walks they talked of themselves and of their life together with great frankness – to have no secrets from friends was another 'Bloomsbury' characteristic – and among other things I recall Virginia telling me how incomplete she felt in comparison to her sister Vanessa, who brought up a family, managed her house, and yet found plenty of time left in which to paint. Although I doubt if she ever lost this sense of her own inadequacy, of not being quite, in every sense of the word, a person of flesh and blood, she was practical and could cook and run a house better than most women, as well as lead a social life that often probably outran her strength.

It used to be said by those who were not invited to its parties that 'Bloomsbury' was a mutual admiration society who pushed one another's works. This charge, which has recently been repeated, is simply not true. Virginia Woolf greatly admired E.M. Forster's novels, which seemed to her to have the qualities of 'reality' which she perhaps felt hers lacked, and she also admired Roger Fry's writings on art as well as his marvellously eager and stimulating conversation. But she had a poor opinion of Lytton Strachey's biographies, though she was greatly attached to him personally, and praised the fineness and subtlety of his mind and his discrimination as a critic. One evening, I remember, while the Woolfs were at Yegen, the subject of his *Queen Victoria* came up. Both Leonard and Virginia pronounced decisively against it, declaring that it was unreadable. Although I did not care for its flat, spongy style, which gave me the sensation of walking on linoleum, this charge seemed to me absurd: readable was precisely what it was. Yet they maintained that they had been unable to finish it. Lytton, on the other hand, greatly admired most of Virginia's writings, but could not read Forster in spite of his strong personal friendship for him. I remember him saying, after looking through his little guide to Alexandria, *Pharos and Pharillon*, that it was a pity that he had taken to novel-writing when he was so much better at history. And he disliked both Roger Fry and his work.

Virginia had much to say of T.S. Eliot, of whom she was seeing a good deal at this time. She praised him warmly as a man, and spoke of his remarkable intelligence, but seemed a little half-hearted about *The Waste Land*, which the Hogarth Press was then publishing. Like myself, she had a poor opinion of D.H. Lawrence. The boring prophetic mantle he wore, the streams of slovenly and sentimental writing that poured from his pen obscured the sometimes extraordinary freshness of insight that showed itself in one or two of his novels and short stories. Nor had his admirers helped his reputation, for as usually happens in such cases, they had been more impressed by his bad books — those which contained his 'message' — than by his good ones. Yet she could change her mind, and when, some years later, she came across *Sons and Lovers*, she wrote an article on it which, though perhaps not very understanding, praised it highly. Has there ever been an age, one might ask, in which writers have admired more than one or two of their contemporaries?

To appreciate Virginia Woolf's brilliance as a talker one had to see her in her own circle of friends. It was a regular custom for five or six of these to meet every week after dinner either at her house or at her sister Vanessa's, and usually one or two of the younger generation would be invited to be present. In that capacity I went several times. The aces were Roger Fry, Duncan Grant, Vanessa Bell, Clive Bell, Lytton Strachey, Maynard Keynes, and occasionally one or two people such as Desmond MacCarthy and Morgan Forster who did not, I think, regard themselves as 'belonging to Bloomsbury', though they were accepted by the others on the same footing. The arrangements were informal, yet everyone was aware of the purpose of the meeting, which was to make good conversation. With this idea, for literary people at this time were very sober, no drinks except coffee were provided.

I very soon got the impression that these conversaziones were really of the nature of orchestral concerts. One might almost say that the score was provided, for the same themes always came up — the difference between the younger and the older generation, the difference between the painter and the writer, and so forth. The performers too were thoroughly practised, for they had been meeting every week or even more often over a space of many years to discuss the same not, one would have thought, very inspiring subjects. Thus they had each of them learned what part he must play to conduce to the best general effect and also how to stimulate and give the cue for the others. The solo instruments, one might say (both strings), were Virginia Woolf and Duncan Grant: they could be relied on to produce at the appropriate moment some piece of elaborate fantasy, contradicting the serious and persistent assertions of the other instruments. Roger Fry would drive forward on one of his provocative lines: Vanessa Bell, the most silent of the company, would drop one of her *mots*, while Clive Bell, fulfilling the role of the bassoon, would keep up a general roar of animation. His special function in the performance was to egg on and provoke Virginia to one of her famous sallies.

What one got from these evenings was, if my youthful judgment is to be relied on, conversation of a brilliance and (in spite of the rehearsals) spontaneity which, I imagine, has rarely been heard in England before. I have known other good talkers, one of them perhaps the equal of any of these, but they have always given solo performances. What 'Bloomsbury' evenings offered was the concert in which each talked to produce himself and to draw the best out of the others. I imagine that only continual practice by people who share the same general attitude to life and who are pleased by their friends' performance as by their own can provide anything like it.

For a young writer even a slight acquaintance with such a group of people was an education, though not perhaps a stimulus. They had standards — honesty, intelligence, taste, devotion to the arts, and social sophistication. They never, in their written judgments, let their vanity or their private friendships or their political or religious prejudices run away with them, and they were none of them out to compensate for their own weaknesses and deficiencies by attacking others. Yet it must, I think, be admitted that they lived — not singly, which would not have mattered, but collectively — in an ivory tower. Maynard Keynes and Leonard Woolf had roots outside it in the world of politics, and Roger Fry was too active and public spirited a man to let himself be confined. The others, however, were prisoners of their close web of mutual friendships and of their agreeable mode of life and also of their rather narrow and (as they held it) smug Cambridge philosophy. Virginia Woolf, it is true, was always aware of the typist queueing for her lunch in the cheap tea-shop and of the shabby old lady weeping in the third-class railway carriage, yet she too was tied to her set by her birth, her social proclivities, her craving for praise and flattery, and could only throw distant and uneasy glances outside it. Her sense of the precariousness of things, which gives her work its seriousness, came from her private life — from the shock of her brother Thoby's death and from her experience of madness. But the ethos of her group and indeed her whole cultured Victorian upbringing cut her off from the hard view of human nature that the novelist needs and drove her to develop her own poetic and mystical vision of things in what I at least feel was too subjective a way. Thus when one re-reads her novels now one feels again the ease and beauty of much of the writing and gets a certain muffled, Calderon-like impression of life being no more than a dream, yet one is left dissatisfied. For if one is to be convinced that life is a dream, one must first be shown, and pretty sharply, that what is set before one is life.

Looking back today it is not, I think, difficult to see that the weakness inherent in the splendid flower of English culture thrown up by 'Bloomsbury' lay in its being so closely attached to a class and mode of life that was dying. Already by 1930 it was pot-bound. Its members were too secure, too happy, too triumphant, too certain of the superiority of their Parnassian philosophy to be able to draw fresh energies from the new and disturbing era that was coming in. They had escaped the shock of the first German War either by being unfit for military service or by joining the ranks of the pacifists, and had not taken warning from the prophets who announced that the snug rationalist world they lived in was seriously threatened. When they should, therefore, have been in their prime, they were on their way to being an anachronism, even Virginia Woolf — the most open-minded of all except Maynard Keynes — being limited by some deep-seated doubt (connected possibly with her fits of madness) about the reality of almost everything except literature. Yet, I imagine, if the cobalt bomb does not obliterate everything, future ages will feel an interest in these people because they stand for something that the world always looks on with nostalgia — an *ancien régime*. They carried the arts of civilized life and friendship to a very high point, and their work reflects this civilization. Then, surely, two of them at least, Virginia Woolf and Maynard Keynes, possessed those rare imaginative gifts that are known as genius . . .

William Plomer: Evenings in Tavistock Square

Reprinted from William Plomer, At Home *(London, Jonathan Cape, 1958), 43–6, 50–6, by permission of the author, Jonathan Cape, and Farrar, Straus & Giroux, Inc. © 1958 by William Plomer.*

[The novelist, poet, and critic William Plomer came to England from South Africa. He shared none of his countryman Roy Campbell's animus towards Bloomsbury, however (see p.27); his memoir *At Home* provides various amusing glimpses of Bloomsbury, its inhabitants

and its neighbours. Plomer's description of E.M. Forster in *At Home* is
well known: 'Incurious fellow passengers in a train, seeing him in a
cheap cloth cap and a scruffy waterproof, and carrying the sort of little
bag that might have been carried in 1890 by the man who came to wind
the clocks, might have thought him a dim provincial of settled habits
and taken no more notice of him.' (When Forster showed this
description to his mother, she remarked, 'There! You see what Mr
Plomer says. How often have I told you Morgan dear, that you really
ought to brush your coat?')

Plomer's description of Virginia Woolf in Tavistock Square is from a
chapter in which he compares her home with that other famous literary
gathering place of the time, Lady Ottoline Morrell's in Bedford Square.]

. . . I was now just twenty-six, and several years had passed since the
publication in London of my first novel, the manuscript of which had
travelled some six thousand miles to the Hogarth Press. I had also
published two books of short stories. Like the novel they had been well
received – at least in some quarters – and I had therefore in some
respects more self-confidence than I should have had if I had not yet
published anything. To have known from the first that Leonard and
Virginia Woolf believed in me as a writer had been much; to have been
published by them was more still. The welcome they gave me when I
returned to England, and their subsequent friendship, I value as much
as anything in my life. Leonard Woolf used to send me books for review
in the *Nation*, of which he was then literary editor, and soon after my
return they had been good enough to invite me to the first of a long
series of evenings in Tavistock Square. Besides enjoying their beautiful
manners, incomparable conversation, and delicious food and wine, I
was enabled to meet there for the first time many persons of literary
distinction or unusual character. For a young writer, obscure, socially
and by experience and temperament rather isolated, poor, curious, and
both leisurely and energetic, these evenings were of such benefit and
pleasure, such an education in themselves, that I strongly hope there are
young writers today who find themselves half as delightfully and
fruitfully entertained.

In the upper room to which withdrawal was made after dinner the
lighting was fairly subdued, otherwise attention might have been
unduly distracted by the mural decorations from the hand of Virginia
Woolf's sister, Mrs Bell. In fact these rough trellises and wavy lines,
two-handled vases, guitars, fans, and sketchy floral motifs, made their

contribution to the unsolemn atmosphere of a room not quite like any other. Virginia Woolf, equally adept at entertaining and being entertained, unobtrusively kept those present as active, or attentive, as an orchestra, and unless some visitor was awkward, shy, or moody, the tempo was lively and the tone gay.

A card would have reached me, and her handwriting, sharp, delicate, and rhythmical as her prose, was pleasing in itself — the more so because it had formed an invitation; and there was often added, as if by way of an afterthought, 'X is coming.' X was almost always somebody eminent in the sphere of writing. . . . A card of invitation reached me. 'Lytton Strachey is coming,' it said.

Strachey was then still in his forties, but his beard and spectacles made him look older. Although he was lanky and Edward Lear was rotund, I imagine that Lear's beard and spectacles may also have seemed to create a certain distance between himself and others. About Strachey's eyelids, as he looked out through the windows of his spectacles over the quickset hedge of his beard, there was a suggestion of world-weariness: he had in fact just two more years to live. To me he did not seem like a man in early middle age, and although his beard made him look older than he was, I did not think of him in terms of a sum of years but as an intelligence alert and busy behind the appendage of hair and the glass outworks. A glint came into his eyes, the brain was on the move as swiftly as a bat, with something of the radar-like sensitivity of a bat, and when he spoke it was sometimes in the voice of a bat.

There was a story that in the First World War he had been summoned before some military tribunal, and had appeared before it tall, sad, spectacled, bearded, and carrying a tartan travelling rug and an air cushion. Applying the air cushion to the aperture in his beard he had slowly and gravely inflated it, had then put it on the seat, subsided gently upon it, and carefully and deliberately arranged the rug over his knees. A brisk military voice had then fired at him from the bench:

'We understand, Mr Strachey, that you are against *all* wars?'

'No,' came the piercing little voice of the pipistrel from the thicket. 'Only this one.'

I am glad to have set eyes upon this wit and revolutionary biographer, a master of English prose, so entertaining and such an influence. It happened that much later in my own life I was to have a particular reason for pondering over the workings of Strachey's mind in regard to certain historical characters. Benjamin Britten's opera *Gloriana*, which was produced at the time of Queen Elizabeth II's coronation, and for which I wrote the libretto, owed much to Strachey's *Elizabeth and Essex*.

Quite a different voice from Strachey's came crackling, dry and vibrant and precise, out of the intellectual head of Roger Fry, whose spectacles seemed to magnify both ways. To look him in the eyes was to look through twin lenses at two keen and magnified visual organs and simultaneously to be conscious of exposure to expert scrutiny. If one had been anywhere overpainted, or badly varnished, or if one had been wearing the exasperating label of a false attribution, one could hardly have gone on looking him in the face. His devotion to 'significant form' is pleasantly illustrated by the story that he was seen in the National Gallery lecturing about the composition of a large religious masterpiece to a docile squad of gaping self-improvers. Indicating with his long wooden pointer the presiding figure of God the Father, he was heard to say, 'Now, this important mass . . .'

Fry's own pictures have generally seemed to me saddish confections, like those of an amateur cook with sound training and well tried recipes but without the least spark of inspiration. He had been engaged by the Hogarth Press to design the dust jacket for my book of short stories on Japanese themes, *Paper Houses*. Though not at all Japanese in feeling, it was a pleasing design in blue and white, and aroused regret that dust jackets are such perishable things.

. . . Once when Virginia Woolf was sitting beside Lady Ottoline on a sofa their two profiles were suddenly to be seen, one in relief against the other, like two profiles on some Renaissance medal – two strange, queenly figures evolved in the leisured and ceremonious days of the nineteenth century. Each, by being herself, won an allegiance to herself in the twentieth. Both faces were aristocratic, but in that chance propinquity Virginia Woolf's appeared much the more fine and delicate. The two women admired one another, with reservations on one side at least; and they were affectionate in manner when together, though one appeared more affectionate than the other. They had a good deal in common. Both had what old-fashioned people used to call *presence* – a kind of stateliness, a kind of simple, unfussy dignity. Lady Ottoline Morrell, not always discriminating about people, recognized the uniqueness of Virginia Woolf. Virginia Woolf spoke admiringly of the independence and force of character which had enabled Lady Ottoline to emerge from the grand but narrow world into which she had been born (and of which she retained the panache) into a more varied world in which ideas and talent counted more than property or background.

Both had an insatiable curiosity about their fellow creatures, and both a love of gossip and the capacity to be amused or astonished which goes with that virtue. In the exercise of this curiosity the difference of approach was as striking as the difference in their profiles. Lady Ottoline would ask the most personal, direct questions, not in a hectoring way, but without the slightest compunction, and with the manner of a feudal grandee who had a right to be told what she wanted to know. Because most people like talking about themselves to a sympathetic listener she often got what she wanted, but not, as I have indicated, from me. Virginia Woolf's approach was less blunt and more ingenious. With a delicious and playful inventiveness she would often improvise an ironical fantasy about the life and habits of the person to whom she was talking, and this was likely to call forth protests, denials, and explanations which helped to make up something like a confession. Lady Ottoline, less tense and less discerning, was an easier mixer: Virginia Woolf sometimes frightened people by aloofness or asperity, for which they had sometimes their own clumsiness to blame. Yet she could show the most graceful restraint. In the course of several hours of the company of an individual who, she afterwards told me, caused her alternating emotions of anger, laughter, and utter boredom, she showed no sign of the first two and only a faint trace of the last — which is the most difficult of the three to hide.

The fact that Virginia Woolf did not make, either in social life or in her books, any concession to vulgarians, or offer any foothold to a banal understanding, or bait any traps for popularity, probably helped to create a legend about herself among the uninformed, the envious, and the ignorant, that she was some sort of precious and fragile being, ineffably superior and aloof, and quite out of touch with 'ordinary' life — whatever that may be. This legend has been completely dispersed. It is now understood that her life was rich in experience of people and places, and that her disposition, as is sometimes the case with those who are highly strung and have an inclination to melancholy, was genial. Her biographers, so far from having to chronicle the life of an etiolated recluse, may be embarrassed by the quantity and variety of their material. Clearly no adequate biography will be possible until her immense diary has been published in full. From her conversation I recall many interesting glimpses and facets of her earlier life — how, as a young girl, in an agony of shyness, she drove alone at night in a cab with straw on the floor to a ball at one of the great London houses, wearing no jewellery except a modest string of pearls ('but they were *real* pearls'); how she had Greek lessons with Clara, the sister of Walter

Pater, in Canning Place, in a setting of blue china, Persian cats, and
Morris wallpapers; how she took part in the *Dreadnought* hoax, one of
the world's great practical jokes and a superb piece of acting, a
demonstration that high-ranking hearts of oak at Portsmouth were
accompanied by heads of the same material, since they were unable to
see through a bogus Negus of Abyssinia and his preposterous 'suite';
how she went bathing with Rupert Brooke, whose profile was not quite
lived up to by his legs, those being perceptibly bowed; how she sat up
all night in a Balkan hotel reading the *Christian Science Monitor* to
cheat the bugs; and how there was a murder under her window in
Euboea.

Speaking of writing as a profession, she once remarked to me that
one is bound to upset oneself physically if one works for more than
two hours a day. She put so much of herself into her work that it must
have taken much out of her, and was in fact a prodigiously hard
worker. The volume of her published and unpublished writings,
including her letters and diary, is as impressive as the sustained high
level of all that has so far been printed. She was as energetic as her
father, to whom mountains were no obstacles, nor mountains of facts
either. To be so active, one's nature must be integrated. In each of us
there are two beings, one solitary and one social. There are persons who
cannot bear to be with others, and turn into hermits or something
worse; most cannot bear to be alone, and become common or shallow,
or both. In Virginia Woolf the two beings seemed to have an equal life
and so to make her into a complete person. She could be detached and
see things in perspective; and she could enter into things, into other
people's lives, until she became part of them. The two beings can be
perceived in her writings, sometimes distinct, sometimes merged. The
special genius of her rare and solitary spirit reached its purest
expression in *The Waves*, an exquisite, subjective book nearer to poetry
and music than to what is generally meant by 'the novel'. The social
being in Virginia Woolf, and (in my opinion) the novelist, can be seen
most clearly not in her fiction but in *The Common Reader*. Those
essays are full of shrewdness and knowledge of the world and of human
nature, qualities which, though discernible in her novels, are less
important to them than her own sensitivity, as an instrument to the
vibrations of the external world.

The old masters of fiction — Shakespeare, Balzac, Tolstoy — are such
because, besides all the other gifts, they are imaginative men of the
world with an exceptional robustness and gusto. They have also an
extreme preoccupation with sociology. This, when it goes more with

finesse than with animal spirits, produces novelists like Jane Austen, Flaubert, or Proust, and it was to such writers that Virginia Woolf was in some ways akin. It may be argued that her myth-making faculty was chiefly applied to sensations rather than to characters, and that her passion for sociology was in a sense scientific. Although she enjoyed embroidering facts about people, sometimes in a poetic or a fantastic or a censorious or an ironical way, she was really devoted to the facts themselves. The solitary being was a poet, the social being was a sort of scientist: the former discovered poetic truth, the latter anthropological truth.

During the last ten years of her life Virginia Woolf often told me how much more she enjoyed reading autobiographies than novels. She once said that she thought almost any autobiography more satisfying than a novel. When autobiographical memoirs were written by people she knew and found congenial — Lady Oxford, for instance (and what a sharp profile there!) or the bluff and breezy Dame Ethel Smyth — she not only had the pleasure of getting to know them better, but her appetite for social knowledge and reminiscence was much gratified. A passionate precision in collecting data about society (very strong in Flaubert and Proust) made her delight in anything that helped it.

At those evenings in Tavistock Square she was at her best with persons who, like herself, were not merely articulate but articulate in a new way. She had a gift for making the young and obscure feel that they were of value too. She admired physical as well as intellectual beauty. She could charm away diffidence, and, since she was something of a feminist, could be notably sympathetic with young women, in particular young women from Cambridge. A strong sense of the proper functions of literature and a highly and constantly cultivated taste gave her a proper pride (derived in part no doubt from her literary father and background) in her own gifts, but she was without arrogance, and wore her rare beauty without ostentation.

It is not enough to say that she was a hard-working writer, and that she always read a great deal. She also worked as a publisher, and even at times as a printer, with her husband. She examined a great number of typescripts and even of manuscripts for the Hogarth Press, books from which rightly bore the imprint of 'Leonard and Virginia Woolf'. No writer, known or unkown, could have wished for a more encouraging publisher's reader, or one with more openness to new ideas. She seemed unimpeded by prejudice and guided always by the knowledge that the true writer is a precision instrument with something unfamiliar to record. As early as 1930 she and her husband expressed some annoyance at the way the Hogarth Press was developing. They even seemed rather annoyed by the increasingly profitable sales of Hogarth Press books, and were seriously considering reducing the press to its original and remarkable dimensions – a hand press in a basement at Richmond, worked by themselves as amateurs. This was before John Lehmann was inducted into the business and began his long and conspicuous career as a publisher and editor. From the time I first saw him he showed an interest in my writings which has continued to this day, and I am only one of innumerable writers whom he has helped.

The nervous vitality of Virginia Woolf was greater than her physical strength. If it had not been so, she would not have gone on evoking such a response from the responsive in so many parts of the world. To write about her briefly is to be inadequate. She was complex. She looked for truth. She loved London and the country, her relations and friends; she loved her domestic surroundings; she loved the written word. She liked good talk, good food, and good coffee. I see her in a shady hat and summer sleeves, moving between the fig tree and the zinnias at Rodmell; I see her sitting over a fire and smoking one of her favourite cheroots; I see the nervous shoulders, the thin, creative wrists, the unprecedented sculpture of the temples and eye sockets. I see her grave and introspective, or in such a paroxysm of laughter that the tears came into her eyes. But her eyes are shut, and I shall never see her again.

Arthur Waley: Translating in Bloomsbury

Reprinted from Arthur Waley, 'Introduction' (1960), One Hundred and Seventy Chinese Poems, *translated by Arthur Waley (London, Constable, 1962), 5–6, quoted by permission of the publisher.*

[In the course of explaining more than forty years later how he came to study Chinese, Arthur Waley described Roger Fry's interest in having Waley's first book, the famous *One Hundred and Seventy Chinese Poems*, printed at the Omega workshops. Waley was closely associated with Bloomsbury for many years; the response to his celebrated translations was, like most things in Bloomsbury, varied.]

. . . I began to make rough translations of poems that I thought would go well in English, not at all with a view to publication, but because I wanted my friends to share in the pleasure that I was getting from reading Chinese poetry. Among people who were interested by these translations were Roger Fry, Lowes Dickinson and Logan Pearsall-Smith, the author of *Trivia*. Roger Fry was at that time interested in printing. He thought verse ought to be printed in lines that undulated in a way that reinforced the rhythms, and he asked if I objected to his printing some of my translations in this way, as an experiment. The idea of their being printed at all of course thrilled me, and spell-bound by Roger's enthusiasm (as everyone was) I had not the courage to say (what was in fact the case) that I could see no point at all in the 'undulations'. A meeting of the Omega workshops was called at which about a dozen people were present. Roger Fry asked each of them in turn how many copies of translations such as mine (irrespective of 'undulation') it would be possible to sell. The highest estimate was twenty. Saxon Turner, of the Treasury, answered inaudibly. He was asked to repeat what he had said and removing his pipe from his mouth, he answered with great firmness and clarity, 'None'. Roger had been collecting estimates (with or without undulation). It was clear that in order to cover costs he must sell at least two hundred copies, so as the result of the meeting he gave up the idea of printing my translations. But I, for the first time in my life, began in consequence of this meeting to have some vague idea about the cost of getting a small work printed. For a few pounds I had about forty short poems printed in a normal way by an ordinary printer, bound the sheets in some spare wall-paper and sent the resulting booklet to a number of friends, as a sort of Christmas card. It had a mixed reception. Professor Bateson, for example, wrote on a postcard: 'I am afraid I can't get much from your translations. I don't need a Chinese poet to tell me that rivers don't turn back in their courses.' He was evidently referring to the couplet:

> The hundred rivers eastward travel to the ocean;
> Never shall they turn back again to the West.

He was a cultivated and benevolent man and must, I think, to write such a postcard, have been very much irritated by the poems.

I had at that time a corporate admiration for the whole Strachey family, and longed for them to be interested in what I did. I was pained, then, when Lytton Strachey wrote ribald parodies of the poems, not intended of course for my eye; but Carrington (the paintress Dora Carrington who adored Lytton and looked after him for so long) took care that I should see them. I thought them very stupid, and Lytton fell off his pedestal . . .

Peter Stansky and William Abrahams: A Bloomsbury Childhood

Reprinted from Peter Stansky and William Abrahams, 'A Bloomsbury Childhood,' Journey to the Frontier: Julian Bell and John Cornford: Their Lives and the 1930's *(London, Constable, 1966), 5–7, 14–27, by permission of the authors; © 1966 by Peter Stansky and William Abrahams, with permission of the authors and Atlantic-Little Brown, Inc.*

[Though not observers of Bloomsbury in their own right, Peter Stansky and William Abrahams have provided a revealing view of Bloomsbury by basing their account of Julian Bell's childhood on the direct observations of those who knew Charleston. Stansky and Abrahams' description is from their dual biography of Julian Bell and John Cornford, both young English poets killed in the Spanish Civil War. In reviewing *Journey to the Frontier* Julian's brother noted how extraordinarily well the authors had been able to catch the brief lives of Bell and Cornford; he found only one fault with their treatment of Bloomsbury: 'It is a dangerous thing, and one of the few mistakes that these authors make, to treat Bloomsbury as a homogeneous entity. Indeed Clive Bell's *Civilization* is very nearly a summary of all that Julian Bell most detested.'

Stansky and Abrahams' discussion of Julian's schooling has been omitted here.]

Let us make a first approach to Bloomsbury — and to Julian — by way of an exchange of letters. It is April 1908. On Wednesday the 22nd, Virginia Stephen, who is on holiday in Cornwall, writes to Lytton Strachey in London. She has taken rooms at Trevose House, Draycot Terrace, St Ives, and she has been attempting to write a review for the *Cornhill Magazine* of a life of Delane, the editor of *The Times*. But the conditions are not favourable:

My landlady, though a woman of 50, has nine children, and once had 11; and the youngest is able to cry all day long. When you consider that the family sitting room is next mine, and we are parted

by folding doors only — what kind of sentence do you call
this? — you will understand that I find it hard to write of Delane
'the *Man*' . . .

I spend most of my time, however, alone with my God, on the
moors. I sat for an hour (perhaps it was 10 minutes) on a rock this
afternoon, and considered how I should describe the colour of the
Atlantic.

On Thursday the 23rd, Strachey replies:

I went away last Friday, partly to get rid of my cold, to the Green
Dragon, on Salisbury Plain, where James and Keynes and others
were for Easter. Of course it finally destroyed me — the coldest
winds you can imagine sweeping over the plain, and inferior food,
and not enough comfortable chairs. But on the whole I was amused.
The others were Bob Trevy . . . Moore, Hawtrey, and a young
undergraduate called Rupert Brooke — isn't it a romantic name? —
with pink cheeks and bright yellow hair — it sounds horrible, but it
wasn't. Moore is a colossal being, and he also sings and plays in a
wonderful way, so that the evenings passed pleasantly.

This letter leads us to the beginnings of Bloomsbury, but before we
follow it there, let us attend to Virginia's reply, written five days later.
It is Tuesday, April 28th, and she is still at Trevose House in St Ives.

Your letter was a great solace to me. I had begun to doubt my own
identity — and imagined I was part of a seagull, and dreamt at night
of deep pools of blue water, full of eels. However, Adrian came
suddenly that very day . . . Then Nessa and Clive and the Baby
[Julian, aged three months] and the Nurse all came, and we have
been so domestic that I have not read, or wrote. My article upon
Delane is left in the middle of a page thus — 'But what of the
Man?' — . . . A child is the very devil — calling out, as I believe, all
the worst and least explicable passions of the parents — and the
Aunts. When we talk of marriage, friendship or prose, we are
suddenly held up by Nessa, who has heard a cry, and then we must
all distinguish whether it is Julian's cry, or the cry of the 2 year
old — the landlady's youngest — who has an abcess, and uses
therefore a different scale . . .

We are going to a place called the Gurnard's Head this
afternoon — and now I look up and behold it pours! So we shall sit

over the fire instead, and I shall say some very sharp things, and
Clive and Nessa will treat me like a spoilt monkey, and the Baby will
cry. However, I daresay Hampstead is under snow. How is your
cold? I got a stiff neck on the rocks — but it went.[1]

A certain acerbity in this need not be taken seriously — in fact, Virginia
would prove to be the most affectionate of aunts, devoted to her
sister's three children, Julian, Quentin and Angelica, and they, as we
shall see, were devoted to her. But that is the future, to be looked at as
it happens . . .

'I stay myself — '
    These are the opening words of Julian Bell's poem, 'Autobiography',
which appeared in his second and, as it proved, his final volume, *Work
for the Winter* (1936). The remark is characteristic of his strong sense
of individuality: 'I stay myself — ' Yet at the same time he recognizes
that he is also

> . . . the product made
> By several hundred English years,
> Of harried labourers underpaid,
> Of Venns who plied the parson's trade,
> Of regicides, of Clapham sects,
> Of high Victorian intellects,
>   Leslie, FitzJames.

This, of course, is the Stephen inheritance. And it is equally
characteristic of Julian that he should acknowledge it with a kind of
sweeping inclusiveness: from the missionary austerities of the Clapham
Sect to the violence of the regicides. We are dealing with something
very different here from 'the enlightenment of Bloomsbury'. His
mother and his aunt might accept as just the praise accorded their
father, Sir Leslie; they would be less likely to respond to praise for their
uncle, Sir James Fitzjames Stephen, who, as a conservative Utilitarian,
had a decidedly more authoritarian cast of mind. Bloomsbury, with
Lytton Strachey in the forefront, had attempted to discredit at least
the immediate past, while Julian, one might almost say, revels in it,
revels in it all. 'I stay myself, the product made . . .' On the one hand
there are 'high Victorian intellects'; on the other, 'not among such
honoured, marble names'

> That cavalry ruffian, Hodson of Hodson's Horse,

> Who helped take Delhi, murdered the Moguls . . .

He was 'At least a soldiering brigand' — a category for which Julian would always entertain a certain fondness. 'There were worse,' he goes on to say,

> Who built a country house from iron and coal:
> Hard-bitten capitalists, if on the whole
> They kept the general average of their class.

This, of course, is the Bell inheritance, his father's side, very different from the Stephenses, representing a family which had made its money in coal, and at whose large, ugly, Victorian country house, at Seend in Wiltshire, the Clive Bells and their children spent some vacations and Christmases. To his parents, Clive appeared a wild radical and a dangerous advocate of a new aestheticism: thus they interpreted the fame he had won as the author of such books as *Art* and *Civilization*, as an exponent of the idea of 'significant form', and as a sponsor of the notorious exhibitions of Post-Impressionist painting which introduced Cézanne, Matisse and Picasso to England in the years before the First World War. But if he seemed a black sheep to his own family, to the Stephen side he seemed almost a little too conventional — in his 'huntin, shootin, fishin' interests, some of which he conveyed to his son, and in his comparatively conservative political views. Virginia Woolf, in a memoir of Julian written for Vanessa immediately after his death, felt he owed a great deal to the Bell inheritance. This differentiated him from her beloved Thoby, whose death, thirty years earlier, had had such a profound and lasting effect upon her. 'In fact Julian was much rougher, more impulsive, more vigorous than Thoby. He had a strong element of the Bell in him. What do I mean? I think I mean that he was practical and caustic and shrewd . . . He had much higher spirits. He was much more adapted to life. He was much less regularly beautiful to look at. But then he had a warmth, an impetuosity that the Stephens don't have.'

This is to give the Bell inheritance its due. But it must be said that Julian's family, in its loyalties and intimacies, almost seemed to exclude the non-Stephen part of it. Clive did not completely fit into the Stephen inheritance of 'Clapham sects/Of high Victorian intellects', nor did Leonard Woolf. Clive and Leonard were certainly original progenitors of Bloomsbury, of undoubted brilliance and importance; nevertheless one feels the slightest sense of unease in their relationships with their wives, the Stephen sisters, who were, whatever its Cambridge intellectual masculine origins, the heart of Bloomsbury. If Clive was a little too much to the right in his political thinking, perhaps Leonard went a little too far in his interests in the practice of radical socialism. And if Clive's squire background did not exactly fit with the Stephen inheritance, neither did the London professional and mercantile background of the Woolfs. In her memoir of Julian, Mrs Woolf speaks of 'L's family complex which made him eager, no, on the alert, to criticize [the Bell] children because he thought I admired them more than his family'. But it seems not to have occurred to her that this preference of hers was almost certainly the case, and, more importantly, that there was a Stephen 'family complex', of mutual affection and admiration, that must have appeared formidable (as well as enviable) to an outsider.

The most important person in Julian's life, from its very beginning to its very end, was his mother, the gifted and beautiful Vanessa Bell. Theirs was a relationship without a break and without concealment: in it the full implications of Bloomsbury candour were taken to their limits, and the connection between mother and son never weakened. It was an extraordinary rapport which one cannot but admire, and impressive testimony to Bloomsbury's belief in personal relations. Yet in some ways the relationship was so perfect that it may have truncated others, provided a standard impossible to achieve elsewhere. The possibility will have to be considered in its place, many years later, in the history of Julian's grand and casual ˋpassions; here it can be disregarded.

From the first his mother took great pains with his upbringing, intending it to be as 'natural' and undogmatic as possible: he was not to be Victorianized, a miniature grown-up, seen but not heard, in a spotless pinafore. Yet for all their intellectual adventuresomeness, the Bells were still a well-to-do upper-middle-class family in the comfortable years before the First World War. There were maids, and a series of governesses — one of whom Julian got rid of by pushing into a ditch. And whatever they might think of religion 'upstairs', Julian found it impossible to escape completely the religion of his country 'downstairs' — although it would leave no permanent mark upon him. In a fragment of autobiography written shortly before going out to Spain, he remarks: 'I remember as independent ideas — more or less — a Darwinian argument with Mabel and Flossie — our nurses — which must have been very early — pre-war Gordon Square.' In other words, this

memory dates from before Julian was six. 'Though obdurate I was
secretly frightened of Jehovah, and even asked to be taught prayers.
(Later, learning the Lord's Prayer, I used it as a magic defence against
ghosts, and still do: or as a soporific.)' But religion was hardly very
significant in Julian's life. Far more important was the education he
received from his mother. He writes of this same pre-war time, 'The
great liberating influence was the reading aloud by Nessa of elementary
children's astronomies and geologies'. And there was a similar
intellectual excitement when she read aloud to him a shortened
translation of the *Odyssey*. Before he was able to read himself, he made
Flossie read to him a school textbook of history. History, like
astronomy, was a passion. 'There was also the famous occasion when
Roger [Fry] demonstrated a home chemistry box, and brewed coal gas;
Mabel was sent out and bought a clay pipe from a pub; it was tamped
with plasticine, and, being cooked over the fire, eventually produced a
jet of flame.' In 1916, when he was eight years old, he had what he
called his 'first, definite, independent idea. It was a solution of the
desire for immorality. I worked out a possible cycle by which a human
body would return through grass and sheep, into another human
body.'[2] But it would be very misleading to give a picture of a male
blue-stocking pondering his science, classics and history at a tender age.
Rather, it would be more accurate to see him as an extremely
adventurous, reckless child bounding from activity to activity, with his
parents anxious to introduce him, through explanations and
discussions, to the Bloomsbury dictum of rationality, which held that
even irrational behaviour should be understood.

David Garnett, in a memoir of Julian, describes him as

a wilful child, swift and erratic in his movements; he looked at one
from large eyes and planned devilment... Julian was shrill,
sometimes noisy, always rather catlike and quick. My first row with
him was when I found him standing, unconscious of evil-doing, on
some vegetable marrow plants that he had trampled to pieces... He
had in those days often to be exhorted to reason, often to listen to
tedious explanations about the consequences of his violent
experiments. He flung newly-hatched ducklings into the pond and
after they had raced ashore flung them in again and again until one
or two were drowned. He was not punished as a child, but reasoned
with: one saw on his face the lovely sulky look of a half-tame
creature.[3]

And Mrs Woolf had a similar memory of about the same time – or
when Julian was slightly older:

> We were packing up the tea things. He took a bottle of water and
> smashed it. He stood there in his knickerbockers with long naked
> legs looking defiant and triumphant. He smashed the bottle
> completely. The water or milk spread over the path . . . He stood
> quite still smiling. I thought, This is the victorious male; now he feels
> himself the conqueror. It was a determined bold gesture, as though
> he wanted to express his own force and smiled at the consternation
> of the maids.

One should not make too much either of the enthusiasm for astronomy
and history, or of the mischief and high spirits, of a little boy, although
it is of some interest that Julian himself should remember the former,
and those of his parents' generation the latter. Still, it does not seem
too fanciful to read into the division the first hints of a theme that was
to figure importantly in Julian's life, and in the lives of many of his
contemporaries: how to reconcile the conflicting demands of the life of
the mind and the life of action.

The Bells made their home in Bloomsbury, but they were often in the
country, and Julian, in his attachment to the land, grew up much more
a child of the country than of the city – there would always be
something equivocal about his feelings for London; certainly they did
not go very deep. Whatever the attractiveness of Bloomsbury for the
grown-ups, the children found life more exciting and memorable in the
country: at Seend, the house of their Bell grandparents, and at a variety
of rented houses – Asheham, near Lewes in Sussex, rented by the
Woolfs from 1912 to 1918; Wissett in Suffolk, rented briefly in 1916
by Duncan Grant; and finally, Charleston, a short distance from
Asheham, which the Bells began to rent in the autumn of 1916, and
was thereafter their place in the country. For Julian, as for his brother
Quentin, two years younger than he, and his sister Angelica, born in
1918, Charleston meant childhood.

In his poem 'Autobiography', he recalls 'the passage of those
country years'. England was at war; and his, as he acknowledged, was 'a
war-time boyhood'; but apart from this reference, the details he chose
to record (in the poem) were timeless, of

> . . . orchard trees run wild,

> West wind and rain, winters of holding mud,
> Wood fires in blue-bright frost and tingling blood,
> All brought to the sharp senses of a child.

These are the simplicities of a child's (and a poet's) world. For his parents and their friends the War brought a more complex experience: a true crisis of conscience. On the whole, Bloomsburyans, as we have earlier suggested, tended to live at a certain aloof distance from the world. (This attitude is not to be mistaken for unworldliness. If they had little desire for luxury, or even the creature comforts, they did not scorn the world in its more amiable, civilized aspect: civilization, as they defined it, taking in the pleasures of food and wine and conversation. And Clive Bell was a great believer in *savoir vivre* and *savoir faire*, with an English Francophile's conviction that living and doing were done better across the Channel.) Apart from Keynes and Leonard Woolf, they were indifferent to the day-to-day or even the month-to-month practice of politics: the demands of the private life left one no time for that sort of public interest; one lived *au dessus de la mêlée*. The war changed all that – at least for the duration. After 1914, an attitude of aloofness became increasingly difficult to maintain, even untenable.

Maynard Keynes, Bloomsbury's authority on the subject, predicted a short war brought to an end by economic causes. This must have been some consolation in the beginning, for Bloomsbury was opposed to war in general ('the worst of the epidemic diseases which afflict mankind and the great genetrix of many of the others'[4]) and to this war in particular. But Keynes's optimism was confounded by events. The war was prolonged from one year to the next, and it required increasing tough-mindedness to withstand popular pressure to conform to the war enthusiasm. Not unexpectedly, Bloomsbury, with its belief in the importance of the private life and private convictions, proved extremely good at this. But in 1916, for the first time in British history, conscription was introduced, and thereafter the men of Bloomsbury were compelled to make public their consciences: that is, to declare themselves Conscientious Objectors to military service.

As such they came to public attention. At Trinity College, Cambridge, for example, Bertrand Russell's lectureship was not renewed, and it is hard to avoid the impression that his unpopular pacifist opinions had something to do with the College's action. Lytton Strachey, called before the Hampstead Tribunal to prove his conscientious objections, made in passing his celebrated reply to the

Military Representative ('What would you do, Mr Strachey, if you saw an Uhlan attempting to rape your sister?' 'I should try to interpose my own body'), and he, like various other members of Bloomsbury, was ordered to do work of National Importance. He and Russell both sought refuge at the farm attached to Garsington Manor, the home of their friends Philip and Lady Ottoline Morrell, outside Oxford. Clive Bell was at Garsington also. A pacifist, who had argued in his pamphlet *Peace at Once* (1915) that 'the war ought to be brought to an end as quickly as possible by a negotiated peace', he was working on the land, under the provisions of the Military Service Act. And Duncan Grant and David Garnett (who earlier had been with a Friends' Ambulance Unit in France) rented Wissett Lodge, outside a remote little village in Suffolk, where they meant to become fruit-farmers.

That summer (1916) Vanessa, with Julian, Quentin and the maid Blanche, came down from London to Wissett to keep house for Duncan and Bunny. The Lodge was 'a little early Victorian house with numerous small, exceptionally dark, rooms',[5] shadowed by an enormous ilex, which Julian and Quentin called 'the safety tree', for there, in its branches, they were safe from the grown-ups. Life went cheerfully at Wissett. Vanessa painted; the men worked hard in the orchard, kept bees, kept fowls — a large flock of white Leghorns: there were frequent visitors: Oliver and Lytton Strachey, Saxon Sydney-Turner, Lady Ottoline Morrell. For Julian it was a memorable time: 'orchard trees run wild, West wind and rain . . .' Long afterwards, with astonishing vividness, he recalled his first evening's fishing at Wissett,

> when I must have caught a couple of dozen roach . . . Bunny was fishing also: Clive advised me. They started to bite hard in the evening: that pond had never been fished before. I think my second was a big one — perhaps an eighth of a pound; impressive enough to a child. We filled a bucket, slimy, fishy smelling; there is something extraordinarily sensual and thrilling about a fish's body in one's hand: the cold, the vigour and convulsive thumping, the odd smell, the gasping open mouth you jag the hook out of.

It was at Wissett too that he read Gardiner's *History of England from Henry VIII to the Corn Laws* ('God knows how much I understood'), and it was there that he first developed 'a passion for war and war games'.[6] The irony of this, a war-minded child in a conscientiously objecting household, needn't be insisted upon: Julian himself saw it as 'a reaction'. He knew, of course, that his family and their friends were

COs: it explained 'the isolation, and later, at Charleston, the expectation of hostility'. The war game, which grew increasingly complex and took a variety of forms over the years, originated with Quentin, with Julian as an enthusiastic and inventive collaborator. In one version it was played on a board, moving counters about; in another, it was played 'life-size'. Perhaps its very beginning can be traced back to an afternoon when Bunny Garnett mounted fire-crackers on shingles and sailed them across the pond. There was the normal desire of little boys to play soldiers, to re-enact historical battles ('the Armada . . . the Roman wall with oak-apple armies'), although, out of deference to the household, contemporary history was not drawn upon: the opposing sides were never English and German. What is remarkable about the war game is that the interest in it should have continued well beyond childhood, and that war and military strategy fascinated Julian until the day of his death.

The fruit-farming at Wissett proved unsatisfactory: it had been entered upon, at Keynes's suggestion, to ensure the two men exemption from military service. But the Appeals Tribunal, to which their cases were referred, 'declared that though the Wissett Lodge holding might qualify as work of national importance, it was out of the question for us' – we are quoting from Garnett – 'to be our own employers'. The solution appeared simple enough: to continue doing work of National Importance, that is, to continue farming, but on someone else's farm. So Wissett was abandoned. It was thought 'preferable', Garnett explains, 'to go back to the neighbourhood of Asheham, where Leonard and Virginia were living, and where Vanessa had pre-war acquaintances among the Sussex farmers, rather than to seek work in Suffolk'.[7]

Thus it was that the Bells came to Charleston.

Charleston was rented by the Bells in the autumn of 1916. Until 1918 they lived there without interruption, having given up Gordon Square; thereafter they divided their time between Charleston and London, and in the later 1920s, a house in France, at Cassis on the Mediterranean. But for Julian, Charleston came to represent childhood, holidays from school as he grew older, the long summers: it was the place in which he was most happy, the most loved of his homes.

Charleston, which is owned by Lord Gage of Firle Place, is at the end of a dirt road off the main Lewes-Eastbourne road, right beneath the looming green eminence of Firle Beacon, the highest point on the Sussex downs. At the turn of the century the house had been a simple country hotel, and many of the small, low-ceilinged rooms still retain porcelain number plates on their doors. There was an orchard, a walled garden, and, across the patch of lawn from the front door, a small pond – large enough, however, for naval engagements. There was also, fulfilling the immediate needs of the household, a farm near by, and there the conscientious objectors loyally carried on work of National Importance until 11 o'clock on the morning of 11th November, 1918.

In the first decade of the post-war period, Charleston became the centre of what Quentin Bell calls 'Bloomsbury-by-the-Sea'. It was a triangular outpost, populated by the Charlestonians (the Bells and their frequent visitors, such as Duncan Grant and Roger Fry), the Tiltonians (Maynard and Lydia Keynes, who took up residence at Tilton on a branch of the dirt road leading to Charleston) and the Rodmellians (Leonard and Virginia Woolf, who moved from Asheham to Monk's House at Rodmell, on the other side of Lewes). The house, rambling in its construction and haphazard-seeming in its additions and out-buildings, was full of many oddly placed and sized rooms (not a disadvantage) and provided (apart from the usual bedrooms, sitting-rooms and a dining-room with an immense fireplace) a library for Clive Bell, and studios for Vanessa Bell and Duncan Grant, who, when they were not busy painting canvases, were busy painting walls, bedsteads, cupboards, tables, chairs, plates and almost any other flat surface they could find. The result of their industry was to give the house a colour and a magic (in its unexpectedness) that is unlike anything else: one has no sense, nor is one meant to have, of the self-conscious work of art, as in the Peacock Room of Whistler, or even, perhaps, in the rooms at Kelmscott. The children found the house, its grounds, and the surrounding countryside a perfect place for endless activity: for adventures, walks, war games, butterfly hunting, capture of animals – when older, shooting of birds – and noise: so much noise that poor Clive Bell, in desperation, built himself a little study apart from the house, in which he hoped to gain some quiet.

The children, along with the grown-ups, were at the centre of life at Charleston: that is its immediately distinguishing quality. They were not put to one side, categorized, or patronized, taken up enthusiastically and unceremoniously let down. That this did not happen is a tribute in part to their own charm, which appears to have been considerable, and even more to the character of the grown-ups, who had not only the ability to love children, but also, which is rarer, the ability to respect and to sympathize with them, to educate and to entertain them. Of all the grown-ups, it was Vanessa, naturally, who came first in their affections; and after her, Aunt Virginia. Mrs Woolf's arrivals 'were a signal for rejoicing on the part of Julian and Quentin who had secrets to share with her. Thus she was always led aside and from the corner of the walled garden where they were ensconced came her clear hoot of laughter – like the mellow hoot of an owl – and Julian's loud explosions of merriment, protests and explanations.[8] There were relationships of rare closeness, too, with Clive, Bunny, Duncan and Roger Fry. (Indeed, all that seems to have been lacking in this childhood was the presence of other children. When the Desmond MacCarthys came to visit, they would bring their daughter Rachel; one hears also, when Julian was eleven, of the daughter of a woman who was at Charleston to help in the house: with her, the daughter, Julian fenced and wrestled. But such encounters were the exception not the rule. On the whole, the children depended on each other, and the grown-ups, for company.)

Something of the spirit of Charleston can be glimpsed in the daily newspaper that Julian, the Editor, and Quentin, the Illustrator, put out quite regularly whenever they were in residence throughout the twenties, although one feels that in its later period it was carried on with more devotion by Quentin than by his elder brother. Only one copy was printed – *i.e.,* typewritten – and it was handed round for the enjoyment and edification of its readers, usually at the lunch table. There were weather reports, nature notes, news of arrivals and departures ('Today Mr Raymond Mortimer arrived to the great joy of the family'), accounts of Duncan's difficulties in building an ornamental pool ('Grant's Folly'), Clive's search for peace, the foibles and adventures of the servants, with particular emphasis on the attraction of Grace, the housekeeper, for most of the male population of Lewes and the surrounding countryside. Mortality was not neglected ('We regret greatly the death of Marmaduke, the perroquet, who expired suddenly through unknown causes this afternoon. We fear he will be much missed'), daily events were chronicled ('Angelica triumphed again yesterday, she succeeded without difficulty to persuade Nessa to cut her hair short. Afterwards, she danced a triumphal "black-bottom" to celebrate her victory.') and there was even an occasional advertisement:

The Life and Adventures of J. Bell by

VIRGINIA WOOLF

profusely illustrated by Quentin Bell, Esq.

Some press notices.

. . . a profound and moving piece of work
. . . psychological insight.
WESTERN DAILY NEWS

. . . superb illustrations . . . unwavering truth . . . worthy of royal
academy
. . . clearly the work of a pupil of Professor Tonks
ARTIST AND CRAFTSMAN

The paper, which began as the *Charleston Bulletin*, changed its name quite early in its history to the *New Bulletin*. It did not, however, until a later issue, state its credo: ' "The Bulletin" is unique among daily papers in being controlled by no millionaire or political party. It is not perhaps unique in having no principles.'

The *New Bulletin* did not confine itself to the activities of the residents of Charleston and their visitors, but spread the circulation, and coverage, of its single copy to Tilton and Rodmell:

> The local countryside is now menaced by a new peril. Following Nessa's sensational purchase of a Renault the Woolves have purchased a Singer. And the denizens of Tilton are now the proud owners of a secondhand Morris Cowley. Whatever we may think of the problem of pedestrian traffic and the missuse [*sic*] of motorcars, we must all agree that the car will be a great asset to the house and a permanent source of instruction and amusement to the rats in the duck shed [at Charleston, which was being used as a garage].

Towards Tilton, where the style of life was somewhat grander than at Charleston and Rodmell, the young Editor and Illustrator maintained an attitude of amused tolerance: 'We learn that Mr and Mrs Keynes are putting their chauffeur in livery. We remind our more absentminded readers that the Keynes arms are as follows: Innumerable £s rampant, numberless $$$ sinister in concentric circles *or*; Field black. Crest St

George Killing the Dragon.' Julian and Quentin were quite aware of Keynes's importance in the world: hence the references to Economic Consequences and Conferences that are slyly introduced into accounts not only of the 'Squire and his lady', but of the major-domo of the household, Harland, who assumes mythological proportions in the paper as a drunkard, bore and unsuccessful suitor for the favours of the alluring Grace. In 1925, while at Charleston for Christmas, they recorded a pheasant shoot in Tilton wood:

> We have heard from certain sources that Mr Maynard Keynes and some of his business friends formed the party. From the same source we learn that the bag consisted of: 2 pheasants, 4 rabbits, a blackbird, a cow, 7 beaters, 19 members of the party (including leaders, onlookers, etc.) and 1 dog (shot by mistake for a fox).

In the next number, along with the familiar teasing, there is a clear reflection of Keynes's bitter and justified opposition to the return of Britain to the Gold Standard:

> We learn that the story that the Keynes are at Tilton has now been fully authenticated. The reason they are not flying a flag to indicate that they are in residence (as, we believe, they intend to in future) is that the price of Union Jacks has risen owing to the introduction of the Gold standard, and only red flags are obtainable.

Towards the Rodmellians, Leonard and Virginia Woolf, the *New Bulletin* was more benign, although it entertained a somewhat equivocal attitude towards their dog Grizel. (Tiltonian dogs, too, were looked at askance: 'A stray mongrel, possibly the property of the Keynes's, appeared in the orchard this evening. If seen again it is to be shot at sight and the remains returned to its presumed owners.') Perhaps Mrs Woolf appears most memorably in these pages as: 'The Disappearing Aunt.' On 15th August 1925, the *New Bulletin* reported

> On Sunday the Woolves paid a visit to the Squire. Virginia, unable to face a Tilton tea with Harland in the offing, decided to walk over to Charleston. She was seen on the road by Angelica and Louie, and her voice is thought to have been heard by Duncan. She failed to appear at tea, however, and did not afterwards return to Tilton. The most widely accredited theory is that she had a sudden inspiration and sat down on the way to compose a new novel.

The next day a sequel was given:

> Nessa and the Illustrator visited the Woolves this afternoon and
> found the disappearing aunt safe and sound. It appears that for some
> whim she decided to eat her tea under a hay stack instead of in
> Charleston dining room. The difference, however, is not great, and it
> is even possible that she mistook the one for the other.

Let this stand for what, in fact, it was: the charming world of the
private joke, the private reference, the intimacy and reassurance within
a closely-knit family, the glorious private world of childhood; and let it
also stand for the *badinage*, the chaffing, yet the deep sense of
intellectual and emotional community that existed among the
Bloomsbury family and friends – and most particularly at the very
nucleus, Virginia, Vanessa and the Bell children. It was in precisely this
spirit of playfulness and affection that Mrs Woolf, in the splendidly
ironic Preface to *Orlando* (1928), acknowledged, along with a galaxy of
famous names, 'the singularly penetrating, if severe, criticism of my
nephew Mr Julian Bell ... my nephew Mr Quentin Bell (an old and
valued collaborator in fiction) ... Miss Angelica Bell, for a service
which none but she could have rendered'.

Notes
1. Virginia Woolf and Lytton Strachey, *Letters* (London, 1956), pp.
   9–14
2. Julian Bell, *Essays, Poems and Letters,* (London, 1938) pp.10–12.
3. *Ibid.*, p. 3
4. David Garnett, *The Flowers of the Forest* (London, 1955), p. 1
5. *Ibid.*, p. 112
6. Julian Bell, *Essays, Poems and Letters*, pp. 11–13
7. David Garnett, *Flowers of the Forest*, p. 124
8. *Ibid.*, p. 161

Quentin Bell: The Character of Bloomsbury

Reprinted from Quentin Bell, Bloomsbury *(London, Weidenfeld and
Nicholson, 1968), 103–18, by permission of the publishers; © 1968 by
Quentin Bell and reprinted with permission of Basic Books, Inc.,
Publishers, New York.*

['A filial tribute is, of all literary forms, the most difficult and the most perilous – censure is out of place and praise is discounted; impersonality is absurd and intimacy is embarrassing.' These words by Professor Quentin Bell describe the perils he has well avoided in his invaluable work on Bloomsbury. His heritage as the son of Vanessa and Clive Bell, and his achievements as an art critic, a social historian, and a biographer have made him Bloomsbury's best authority.

Bell's short *Bloomsbury*, the last chapter of which – minus the illustrations – is given here, is an excellent account in words and pictures of what Bloomsbury was. But it is also an account that has something of a thesis. For Bell the character of Bloomsbury is to be seen most clearly in those rational and especially pacific ideals that its members sought to maintain in a world that was becoming increasingly irrational and violent.]

I imagine that I have said enough to give the reader a fair idea of what I believe to be Bloomsbury's main characteristics. Before attempting to tie my arguments together in what I hope may be a reasonably tidy knot I would like once more to emphasize the fact that I am writing about something almost impalpable, almost indefinable.

Imagine a great highway up which walks a heterogeneous crowd – the British Intellectuals. There is in that great concourse a little group of people who talk eagerly together, it is but one of many similar groups and sometimes groups seem to merge. Figures move in towards the centre and move away again to walk elsewhere; some are silent, some are loquacious. When the great ambling procession begins to march in time to a military band, the part to which we devote our attention falls out of step; this makes it, for a time, conspicuous, and yet even so it is not perfectly definable. There are other groups which also become noticeably civilian; moreover, martial music is an infectious thing, and it is hard to say who is and who is not walking to its rhythms. Then, at a later stage, the group suddenly becomes enlarged. Everyone seems to be joining it, so that it is no longer a group, it has become a crowd. It dissolves, the original members disappear, and it is gone.

The image is sufficiently banal but I can find none better to convey the amorphous character of my subject.

What then had this group in common apart from the fact that it was talking? Perhaps this in itself may be a distinction, for there are groups that do not talk, they shout and yell and come to blows. Bloomsbury did none of these things. Despite tremendous differences of opinion, it

talked. Indeed it did more, it talked on the whole reasonably, it talked
as friends may talk together, with all the licence and all the affection of
friendship. It believed, in fact, in pacific and rational discussion.

Now there is nothing remarkable about this; most of us behave
quietly and carry on rational conversations. But we also do other
things: we create works of art and perform acts of worship, we make
love and we make war, we yell and we come to blows.

Bloomsbury sometimes did these things, too, and in fact we all live
our lives upon two contradictory principles, that of reason and that of
unreason. We come, as best we may, to a synthesis of opposites; the
peculiar thing about Bloomsbury was the nature of its dialectic.

A creative artist in modern society can hardly be unaware of the
charms of unreason. He is, by the nature of his employment, so very
much more dependent upon intuition than upon ratiocination. Art in
our time – I am thinking of the visual arts in particular – has broken
free from any pretence of utility. The artist is bound by no rational
programme, no reasonable dependence upon mimesis; his images are
made in accordance with unbiddable inner necessities, they are such
stuff as dreams are made on and are judged in accordance with an
aesthetic which is of its nature dogmatic and impervious to reason.
While this is obviously true of the musical and visual arts, in literature,
where a certain tincture of thought may be apprehended, the sway of
the unreasoning emotions, the 'thinking in the blood' that makes for
heroism, passion, chastity, and nearly all the strong emotions that are
the very stuff of tragedy, can be overwhelmingly powerful.

The irrational has an even stronger pull, in that it is so often a
communal phenomenon. He who thinks much is perforce a lonely man,
whereas the great unreasoning emotions of mankind bring us into a
glorious brotherhood with our kind. We feel (I quote from Wyndham
Lewis) 'the love and understanding of blood brothers, of one culture,
children of the same traditions, whose deepest social interests, when all
is said and done, are one: that is the only sane and realistic journey in
the midst of a disintegrating world. That, as I interpret it, is the
national socialist doctrine of *Blutsgefühl*.' [1]

These words were written at a time when it was still possible for a
partial observer to ignore the uglier side of National Socialism. They
may serve to remind us that the Janus-face of Social Love is Social
Hatred; it is hard to create a God without also creating a Devil.

In the year 1900 the world had not seen what a modern nation
could do when it puts its trust in *Blutsgefühl*, but it was obvious
enough that if men were to surrender to the voice of authority, to yield

to the strong irrational demands of religion, or nationalism, or sexual superstition, hatred no less than love would be the result. The hatred of Christian for Christian, of nation for nation, the blind unreasoning hatred that had hounded Oscar Wile or killed Socrates, these were all communal emotions that resulted from irrationality. The sleep of reason engenders monsters, the monsters of violence. It was therefore absolutely necessary, if charity were to survive in the world, that reason should be continually awake.

This I think was the assumption that determined Bloomsbury's attitude and gave a distinctive tone to its art and to its conversation.

No one today could for one moment suppose that the irrational forces in life, the love of death and of violence, were not present in the world, or that they do not lie somewhere within each of us, but whereas to some of us they are not merely immanent but something to be embraced and accepted with joy, connected as they are with so many great spiritual experiences, for Bloomsbury they were something to be chained, muzzled and as far as possible suppressed. The great interest of Bloomsbury lies in the consistency, the thoroughness and, despite almost impossible difficulties, the success with which this was done.

The first great step was to transfer nineteenth-century scepticism from the cosmic to the personal field. The rejection of dogmatic morality meant that the traditional sanctions of social hatred were removed. G.E. Moore's limpid intellectual honesty remained and with it a morality which excluded, or very nearly excluded, aggressive violence. As Maynard Keynes says:

> The New Testament is a handbook for politicians compared with the unworldliness of Moore's chapter on the 'Ideal'. Indeed there is, in *Principia Ethica*, a certain remoteness from the hurly-burly of everyday life, which, I suspect, results from the extraordinarily sheltered and optimistic society that was to be found in Cambridge at the beginning of the century, and this mild emotional climate was, I apprehend, an indispensable prerequisite for a society which attempted to lead a completely non-aggressive existence.

'We repudiated' — I am again quoting from Maynard Keynes — 'all versions of the doctrine of original sin, of there being insane and irrational springs of wickedness in most men.' Now this may be true, but if it is true it is surprising. It may be true, because the human mind is capable of such extraordinary feats of inconsistency, but if one considers the novels of E.M. Forster, which are deeply involved in this very question, I find it hard to believe that his contemporaries completely ignored the menace of the irrational.

Death and violence walk hand in hand through these novels; the goblins walk over the universe and although they are driven away, we know that they are still there; children are killed, young men are struck down with swords, blind hatred and blind prejudice are never far away. Where Forster differs from his friends and is not, to my mind, altogether Bloomsbury, is in his essentially reverent and optimistic attitude. His reverence is, to be sure, evasive and half veiled. But it is there all right, in the woods of Hertfordshire or the caves of Marabar; there is something that escapes his reasoning and I can just imagine him buying a rather small dim candle to burn before the altar of some rather unpopular saint – something that Lytton Strachey, for instance, could never have done.

Ethically however he seems to me altogether on the same side as Bloomsbury: conscious, deeply conscious of the dark irrational side of life but absolutely convinced of the necessity of holding fast to reason, charity and good sense.

Bloomsbury may or may not have appreciated the role of 'the insane and irrational springs of wickedness' that seem so close to the surface of life in *Howards End*, but must it not have seen them gushing forth in cascades of derisive laughter or in torrents of abuse in the Grafton Gallery Exhibition?

The public reaction to Gauguin, Cézanne and van Gogh was not founded upon any process of reasoning. The public laughed or was angry because it did not understand, and also, I think, because it *did* understand. People could hardly have been so angry, would hardly have reiterated, again and again, the charge of indecency (this hardly seems credible when we think of Cézanne's still lives) or of anarchism, unless they had become aware of some profoundly disturbing, some quite positive emotion in that which they so much hated and were later, with equal unreason, so greatly to love.

Now at first sight it would appear that when faced by such obstinate and furious aesthetic convictions reason would be powerless, and indeed speechless. Speechless she was not. Both Clive Bell and Roger Fry had plenty to say about art between 1910 and 1914. They would most willingly argue with anyone who would listen to them, and while Clive Bell elaborated his theory of significant form, Roger Fry was explaining, persuading, reasoning in talk and conversation, and in letters to the press. Here, Fry seems to be arguing a purely intellectual case.

His method is to find common ground and then proceed by a process of enquiry: We both agree in liking A but you do not like B. What then is the difference between A and B? It turns out of course to be something very insubstantial and the opponent is in a perfectly nice and entirely rational way flattered. Such is the method of his argument: he refuses to be dogmatic and he refuses to be angry. He appeals continually to reason.

There was a certain element of deception here, not, I think, of conscious deception. Up to a point Roger Fry's arguments were fair enough, but at a certain point a mixture of charm and what, for lack of a better word I would call 'overwhelmingness' would clinch the victory. His friends knew this to their cost, for when Roger started some really March hare, some business of black boxes, dark stars, thaumaturgic parascientific nonsense for which he had a strong though inconsistent affection, his force of character, his air of sweet reasonableness and scientific integrity, was such that he could convince himself and his friends of the truth of whatever chimerical bee might for the moment have flown into his bonnet.

The excellence of Seurat, Cézanne and Poussin were not, in my opinion at all events, chimerical nonsense, but Fry made his hearers believe in those excellencies, made them feel them by means of a method of argument which had the purest air of scientific objectivity, in a field which, ultimately, science has no authority. Roger Fry is concerned not only to present a 'fair argument' but to argue about fair things. By this I mean that he does not readily allude to the esoteric or mysterious side of art but talks rather about sensual and easily demonstrable characteristics. His attitude to primitive art is revealing: confronted by Negro sculpture he is amazed by its plastic freedom, its 'three-dimensionalness', the intelligence with which the negro translates the forms of nature, his exquisite taste in the handling of material. Only in one brief allusive phrase does he touch on the magical purposes of these articles. Compare this with the attitude of Emil Nolde, as reported by his latest biographer:

He saw in this art, with its abstract and rhythmic sense of ornament and color and its mystic power, an affirmation of his own anti-classical art. He was one of the first artists to protest against the relegation of primitive art objects to anthropological museums, where they were still exhibited as scientific specimens. His own 'blood and soil' mystique made him an early proponent of the indigenous art of all peoples. [2]

In fact, of course, the tendency of the Bloomsbury art critics was to look away from content altogether. It is a tendency better exemplified by Clive Bell than by Roger Fry; neither of them in fact held it with complete consistency. But undoubtedly the main tendency of their writings between, say, 1910 and 1925 is in the direction of a purely formalist attitude. The aesthetic emotion is, or at least can be and probably should be, something of almost virgin purity, a matter of harmonious relationships, of calculated patterning, entirely removed from the emotive feelings; and these, when they do occur in works of art, are not only irrelevant and 'literary' but productive of that vulgarity, sentimentality and rhetoric which is the besetting sin of nineteenth-century art. Indeed it is the existence of that kind of 'Salon Art' which, I fancy, prompted these rather hazardous generalizations. The sentimentality of Raphael and Correggio, the violence of Goya and Breughel, are not reproved but dismissed as irrelevant, or at least inessential.

Something of the same attitude may, I think, be traced in the actual paintings of the group. Bloomsbury finds its masters amongst the Apollonian rather than the Dionysiac painters, turning to Piero della Francesca rather than Michelangelo, Poussin rather than Bernini, Constable rather than Turner. Amongst the Post-Impressionists it looks to van Gogh and to Gauguin but above all to Cézanne.

Cézanne, whose genius is large enough to be interpreted in many ways, is used as a guide to architectonic solidity, to the careful ordering and redisposition of nature. He is not used as the Vorticists and the Germans use him, as a provider of anguished angularities, violent, emphatic, exclamatory drawing and dynamic chaos.

The insistence that art be removed from life, that painting should aspire to the condition of music, which may certainly be deduced from the writings of Clive Bell and Roger Fry, would, one might have thought, have been translated in practice into pure abstraction, but apart from a few brief essays made before 1914 Bloomsbury painting remains anchored to the visible world. For this there was an important psychological reason: the Bloomsbury painters were, I think, intensely interested in content.

Vanessa Bell continued to the last to paint landscapes and still lives, girls, children and flowers, which to me at all events seem to be replete with psychological interest, while at the same time firmly denying that the story of a picture had any importance whatsoever. Duncan Grant has always been rather less positive in his statements; his lyrical inventions are equally if not more suggestive of a highly literary mood.

And the mood, which may also be observed in the work of Roger Fry, is again one of passion firmly controlled by reason, sensual enjoyment regulated by the needs of serenity.

Looking at Duncan Grant's *Lemon Gatherers* in the Tate and considering its quietly lyrical quality, the calm precision of its design, its tacit sensuality, who could doubt that in 1914 he would be a conscientious objector? The answer of course is that anyone could doubt it and that paintings do not have such clear diagnostic value as that, but I let the sentence stand because, overstatement though it is, it conveys a certain measure of truth. Bloomsbury painting, like Bloomsbury writing and Bloomsbury politics, is pacific even when it is not pacifist. It is by no means unconscious of violence, but it reacts against it either by deliberately avoiding it, or by criticism and mockery, or by trying to find a formula to contain it.

On the whole the painters shrink from violence. Roger Fry attempts to explain art in other terms; for him violence was something stupid and irrational, a means to pain when clearly pleasure is the end of life. Lytton Strachey and Maynard Keynes both fight it with ridicule, Clive Bell veers between ridicule and evasion, Virginia Woolf finds its origin in the relationship of the sexes and seeks its cure in their fusion. All turn to reason as the one possible guide in human affairs precisely because the forces of violence lie within even the best-intentioned men. As Clive Bell wrote, 'those were not naturally cruel men who burnt heretics for not agreeing with them, and witches for being vaguely disquieting, they were simply men who refused to submit prejudice to reason.'[3]

Even those who would declare that faith is in some sort a higher thing than reason would, probably, agree that there is a good deal to be said for this view – in theory. The difficulty, as anyone who surveys the world from Birmingham, Alabama to Salisbury, Rhodesia, and back again by way of Saigon, will know is that when it comes to a struggle between reason and violence reason nearly always takes a beating.

And yet this is not the whole picture. Reason does win victories and Bloomsbury has helped to win them. This paradoxically is one of the things that makes us undervalue its achievements. It would be quite easy to compile an anthology of Bloomsbury's pronouncements on prudery, sexual persecution and censorship, which would command the assent of nearly all literate people at the present day and would, for that reason, be rather dull; the audacities of one age become the platitudes of the next.

But in its larger effort, the effort to live a life of rational and pacific freedom, to sacrifice the heroic virtues in order to avoid the heroic vices, Bloomsbury was attempting something which, to the next generation, seemed unthinkable. It could only have been thought of by people in a favoured social position at a particularly favourable moment in the history of England. It could be maintained, but only just maintained, between the years 1914 and 1918 because in that War it was still possible for an intelligent man or woman to be neutral. The advocates of reason, tolerance and scepticism frequently found themselves confronted by individuals who were partly or wholly on the other side. I have mentioned Fitzjames Stephen and his generation, D.H. Lawrence, Wyndham Lewis and Rupert Brooke — a very heterogeneous collection of talents, but all united in their belief that at a certain point emotion, not reason, must be our guide, and that heroic violence is more desirable than unheroic calm. But with all of these, as also with a belligerent England, some kind of parley, some kind of communication was possible; between them and Bloomsbury there was not a complete polarity of views. With the advent of Fascism, Bloomsbury was confronted by a quarrel in which, believing what they believed, neutrality was impossible. The old pacifism had become irrelevant and the group as a group ceased to exist.

Notes

1. Wyndham Lewis, *Hitler*, 1931. p. 109
2. Roger Fry, *Negro Sculpture*, 1920; repr. in *Vision and Design*, 1920; and Peter Selz, *Emil Nolde*, 1963. p. 33.
3. Clive Bell, *On British Freedom*, 1923. p. 47

BLOOMSBURY CRITICISMS AND CONTROVERSIES

INTRODUCTION

A conspicuous feature of the Bloomsbury Group's history is the criticism that it provoked among its contemporaries. Included in this section are many of the well known critics of Bloomsbury as well as some of the representative kinds of criticism made of it. Certain criticisms of Bloomsbury are represented here in the form of controversies – some of which are presented directly and others through interpretive accounts – that, while they may not fairly represent both sides, do clearly display the issues and arguments involved.

Before presenting a selection of the criticism of Bloomsbury it may be worthwhile to attempt a short summary of the kinds of criticism that were made of the Group. The disinterested reader should be warned, however, that the animosities stirred up by Bloomsbury still smoulder, and doubtless some partisans will find the general purpose of this collection, to say nothing of the selected criticism, to be controversial.

As a number of the earlier selections in the collection have shown, the criticism of Bloomsbury from within Bloomsbury itself began almost with the inception of the Group and continued throughout its development. In addition to the inevitable personal frictions among Bloomsberries, there were disagreements about the value of one another's work. Leonard Woolf was very critical of Clive Bell's books, Clive Bell did not care for Roger Fry's paintings, Lytton Strachey was bored by E.M. Forster's novels, Virginia Woolf had misgivings about Strachey's biographies and Forster's theories of the novel, etc. If Bloomsbury was – as many of its critics insisted – a mutual admiration society, this did not prevent it from being a mutual criticism society as well.

The internal appreciation and criticism was part of the vital stimulation that the members of Bloomsbury gave one another. The criticism of Bloomsbury from without the Group that is represented in this section had a quite different significance. The scope of the external criticism was naturally much wider than that given from within. It included attacks on the ethical assumptions of the Group, which were found to be too hedonistic, atheistic, and rationalistic. The aesthetics of

Bloomsbury was criticized for its formalistic theories and the Post-Impressionistic painting that most of the members valued so highly. Certain individual Bloomsberries together with the Group as a whole were repeatedly castigated for the powerful influences they were said to exercise in publishing, journalism, the art galleries, the universities – influences, it was maintained, that excluded genuine critics, painters, and writers who happened to disagree with Bloomsbury's ideas and tastes. Bloomsbury's politics were assailed from the left as well as the right for their liberalism and Fabian socialism. Bloomsbury was attacked as part of a leisured class that cultivated its sensibilities while living on unearned income. The Group was damned as an exclusive clique of mocking snobs who denigrated seriousness – especially moral seriousness – in any endeavour. And finally, Bloomsbury was condemned for its sexual promiscuities and perversions.

Some of this criticism is valuable for the understanding of the limitations as well as the achievements of the individual members of Bloomsbury. At least as interesting, however, is the significance of the criticism itself as a reaction to the Group. Rupert Brooke, whose background was very close to Bloomsbury's, complained as early as 1912 about 'the subtle degradation of the collective atmosphere of the people in those regions – people I find pleasant and remarkable as individuals'. 'Spit at Bloomsbury from me', he concluded in another letter. In the minds of many of its later critics 'the collective atmosphere' of Bloomsbury came to surround practically the entire establishment of the arts in London. The nature of the Bloomsbury Group – as explained in the introduction and illustrated in the memoirs of the first part of this collection – made it difficult to define the Group very precisely, and this allowed Bloomsbury to become an easy target for those who wished to attack one aspect or another of modern English culture. There is more than a whiff of paranoia in some of these battles, but more important is the difficulty of determining just what the term 'Bloomsbury' refers to in some of these criticisms. A surprising illustration of how loosely the term came to be used is to be found in an unpublished piece of Wyndham Lewis's entitled 'Say It with Leaves'; Lewis included within the precincts of his Bloomsbury F.R. and Q.D. Leavis – two of the most outspoken critics of Bloomsbury.

There is one type of criticism made of Bloomsbury by Wyndham Lewis and others than cannot be adequately represented by selection. In a number of novels, and in an occasional poem or play, various individuals in Bloomsbury, or the Group itself, have been depicted.

Within Bloomsbury, Leonard Woolf's *The Wise Virgins* (see p.110)
E.M. Forster's *Howards End* and *Maurice*, and Virginia Woolf's *The
Voyage Out*, *Night and Day*, *Jacob's Room*, and especially *The Waves*
all contain fictional representations of Bloomsberries that are both
critical and affectionate. Outside of Bloomsbury the fictional treat-
ments have been more directly satirical. Several novels of Lewis,
particularly *The Apes of God*, satirize certain members of Bloomsbury,
their friends and their ideas, along with other people and ideas that had
little or nothing to do with Bloomsbury. L.H. Myers's *The Root and
the Flower* is said to contain a satire on Bloomsbury in the
sixteenth-century Indian Prince Daniyal's 'Pleasance of the Arts'. In
both Lewis and Myers the phoneyness and the homosexuality of the art
world is ridiculed. Certain characters in D.H. Lawrence's fiction are,
according to some critics also hostile to Bloomsbury, representative of
'the Bloomsbury ethos', though the only member of Old Bloomsbury
actually to serve as a model for Lawrence was Duncan Grant, who
somewhat resembles the painter Duncan Forbes in *Lady Chatterley's
Lover*. And there are a number of now forgotten novels – W.J. Turner's
The Duchess of Popocatapetl is one – that allude to Bloomsbury in one
way or another.

More recently Bloomsbury seems to be re-entering fiction as a
historical phenemenon. One final example will serve to illustrate how
the use of Bloomsbury in fiction is beginning to turn from satire into
legend. In Anthony Powell's *Books Do Furnish a Room*, a character
muses after the Second World War on what Bloomsbury (the district
and the Group) must have been like in its prime: 'Every house stuffed
with Moderns from cellar to garret. High-pitched voices adumbrating
absolute values, rational states of mind, intellectual integrity, civilized
personal relationships, significant form . . . the Fitzroy Street Barbera is
uncorked. *Le Sacre du Printemps* turned on, a hand slides up a
leg . . . All are at one now, values and lovers.'

Wyndham Lewis

Quentin Bell and Stephen Chaplin, *The Ideal Home Rumpus*
Excerpt from Walter Michel, *Rumpus Replied To*
Quentin Bell, Stephen Chaplin, and Walter Michel, *Rumpus Revived*

Reprinted from Apollo *80 (October, 1964), 284–91; 82 (August,
1965), 130–3; 83 (January, 1966), 75, by permission of* Apollo *and
the authors.*

[An illustrated history of Wyndham Lewis's war with Bloomsbury would take up more space than all the criticisms of Bloomsbury brought together in this section. Lewis had both a professional contempt and personal antipathy for the members of Bloomsbury and their work. As 'The Enemy' – a persona he developed in one of his magazines – Lewis expressed his reactions to Bloomsbury in a variety of works written over a period of three decades.

The first concerted public attack to be launched at Bloomsbury was organized by Lewis in 1913. In the following article, reply, and rebuttals, Lewis's criticism is set forth, evaluated and defended. The personal bitterness of the original dispute, its mixture of personalities and aesthetics, and the longevity of the controversy (more than half a century after it started in the Omega workshops it was being continued in the columns of *Apollo* magazine) all combine to make it one of the most interesting Bloomsbury controversies.

As a painter and writer Lewis was well equipped to respond to Bloomsbury. After the explosion in what Lewis called 'Mr Fry's curtain and pincushion factory', Lewis proceeded to attack Bloomsbury in his criticism and his fiction. In his magazine *Tyro* in 1921, Lewis described Fry in such a way as to involve all of Bloomsbury in his condemnation:

> One of the anomalies in the more experimental section of English painting, is that a small group of people which is of almost purely eminent Victorian origin, saturated with William Morris's prettiness and fervour, 'Art for Art's Sake', late Victorianism, the direct descendants of Victorian England – I refer to the Bloomsbury painters – are those who are apt to act most as mediators between people working here and the Continent, especially Paris. And Paris gets most of its notions on the subject of English painting through this medium.
>
> Mr Roger Fry, the publicist and painter, is their honoured leader; Mr Duncan Grant their darling star-performer. Mr Clive Bell, second in command, grows almost *too* articulate with emotion whenever he refers to either of these figures.

(The year before Lewis wrote this, Bell – who was Bloomsbury's most effective polemicist – had provoked Lewis into a dispute in the *Atheneum*. The tone of that dispute may be gauged from Bell's reply to Lewis's reply to Bell's criticism of Lewis's painting; Bell began his reply, 'I should be sorry to quarrel with Mr Wyndham Lewis about anything so insignificant as his art or my character. . .'.)

The Apes of God (1930) is the best known of Wyndham Lewis's fictional incursions into Bloomsbury. In this novel he satirized what he called the new bohemian classes of London whose idly rich members ape the artist's life and thus confuse the public who identifies them with true art and intelligence. The worst species of these apes are the apes of God — those bohemians who, instead of merely patronizing bad art, produce a little of it themselves. Here is Lewis on the Bloomsbury apes of God:

> In England for a very long time this sort of *societification* of art has been in progress. It is even possible that the English were the first in the field with the *Ape* art-type. The notorious *amateurism* of the anglo-saxon mind makes this doubly likely. In *Bloomsbury* it takes the form of a select and snobbish club. Its foundation-members consisted of monied middle class descendants of victorian literary splendour. Where they approximate to the citizens of this new cosmopolitan Bohemia is in their substitution of money for talent as a qualification for membership. Private means is the almost invariable rule. In their discouragement of too much unconservative originality they are very strong. The tone of 'society' (of a spurious donnish social elegance) prevails among them. Where they have always *differed* has been in their *all* without exception being Apes of God. . . But altogether too many Apes and wealthy 'intelligentsia' have come on the scene for them to have maintained their unique position. I think you can disregard them. *Bloomsbury* is really only what is called 'old Bloomsbury', which is very moribund — the bloom is gone.

Lytton Strachey is the only member of Old Bloomsbury who is satirized to any extent in *The Apes of God*, but shortly afterwards Lewis put Virginia Woolf into his short satirical novel *The Roaring Queen*. Then in 1934 Lewis devoted a chapter to Virginia Woolf in his critique of modern literature, *Men Without Art*. For Lewis, Virginia Woolf was the queen of Bloomsbury (he once sent a New Year's card to David Garnett with a photograph of her in place of a stamp) but as a writer he found her 'extremely insignificant . . . purely a feminist phenomenon. . .'. Her experimental ideas about fiction, as expressed in her criticism of Wells, Bennett, and others demonstrated to Lewis the insignificance of Bloomsbury. And again the attack is on the ape-artist:

Those most influential in the literary world, as far as the 'highbrow'

side of the racket was concerned, have mostly. been minor
personalities, who were impelled to arrange a sort of bogus 'time' to
take the place of real 'time' – to bring into being an imaginary
'time,' small enough and 'pale' enough to accomodate their not very
robust talents. That has, consistently, been the so-called
'Bloomsbury' technique, both in the field of writing and of painting,
as I think is now becoming generally recognized. And, needless to
say, it has been very much to the disadvantage of any vigorous
manifestation in the arts; for anything above the *salon* scale is what
this sort of person most dislikes and is at some pains to stifle. And
also, necessarily, it brings into being a quite false picture of the true
aspect of our scene.

Even E.M. Forster came in for Lewis's ridicule. In his autobiographical
Blasting and Bombadiering (1937) Lewis recalled meeting Forster at
Lady Ottoline's after the war: 'I met Forster there as a fellow guest, the
"Bloomsbury novelist". A quiet little chap, of whom no one could be
jealous, so he hit off with the "Bloomsburies", and was appointed male
opposite number to Virginia Woolfe. [*sic*] Since then he has written
nothing. But the less you write, in a ticklish position of that sort, the
better.'

Shortly before Lewis's death Sir John Rothenstein reported him as
saying that 'Roger Fry and his "Bloomsbury" circle had ruined his life
and that had he known how much he would have suffered, in his own
words, "by a sneer of hatred or by a shy Bloomsbury *sniff*" he would
never have attacked Roger Fry.' Rothenstein, in discussing Lewis in
Modern English Painters, accused Bloomsbury of sustained malevolence
(see p.359); but when he issued a second edition of his book,
Rothenstein partially retracted some of his accusations, explaining that
the evidence for them was 'essentially not documentary, but what
painters have themselves described to me as being the effect that
Bloomsbury activities had on their lives. . .'. The apparent gap here
between cause and effect is one that will reapear in other criticisms of
Bloomsbury.

The illustrations accompanying Bell, Chaplin, and Michel's articles in
Apollo have been omitted here.]

Quentin Bell and Stephen Chaplin: *The Ideal Home Rumpus*

FOREWORD

Public interest in the scandalous rupture between Roger Fry and Wyndham Lewis in the autumn of 1913 has been revived by the publication of Lewis's letters in a scholarly edition.[1] This, therefore, seems the appropriate time to produce evidence which shows the affair in an entirely new light. At the outset, it must be said that this light is not all-pervading. Some aspects of the Ideal Home affair are, and are likely to remain, mysterious; there is much which becomes not less but more perplexing on an examination of the evidence which is now available.

The authors of this study decided to join forces when they discovered that they were engaged on parallel lines of research. They believe that their partnership has enabled them to write impartially, for, whereas one of them is bound by ties of family and friendship to some of the principal actors in this drama, the other has no such connexions and has been, throughout this research, the champion of objectivity. With the exception of the letters from Roger Fry to Spencer Gore, all the original documents have been examined by both authors. They accept joint responsibility for the text of the book.

They would like to thank Mrs Spencer Gore, Mr Duncan Grant, Miss Winifred Gill, Mrs Diamand, Mrs David Garnett, Sir John Rothenstein, the *Daily Mail* and the Librarian of King's College, Cambridge, for their help and for allowing them to use unpublished letters.

I

The opening of the Omega Workshops at 33 Fitzroy Square, London, in July 1913 was an event in art history hardly less important than the two Post-Impressionist exhibitions of 1910 and 1912. Here, for the first time, an astonished public could see tables and chairs, pottery, carpets and curtains in which the then outrageous principles of Cézanne and Gauguin and the still more outrageous idiom of the *avant-garde* were translated into terms of applied art. Among the artists employed were Duncan Grant and Vanessa Bell, Nina Hamnett, John Turnbull, Winifred Gill, Frederick Etchells, Wyndham Lewis, C.J. Hamilton and Edward Wadsworth. The business, which had as its primary object the maintenance of young artists who would receive a minimum weekly payment and sell anonymously, was conceived and organized by Roger Fry.

At the very outset, during the summer and autumn of 1913, the Omega was shaken by public quarrels in which Roger Fry was accused by Wyndham Lewis and three other artists of scandalous malpractices. There are two published accounts of the matter, one by Virginia Woolf in her life of Roger Fry, the other by Sir John Rothenstein in the second volume of *Modern English Painters*. It will be best to begin with the version of the affair supplied by Wyndham Lewis, C.J. Hamilton, Frederick Etchells and E. Wadsworth. This was a document addressed to all those interested in the Omega; it was referred to by Wyndham Lewis as the 'Round Robin'.

1 Brecknock Studios,
Brecknock Road, N.

Dear Sir,

Understanding that you are interested in the Omega Workshops, we beg to lay before you the following discreditable facts.

(1) That the Direction of the Omega Workshops secured the decoration of the 'Post-Impressionist' room at the Ideal Home Exhibition by a shabby trick, and at the expense of one of their members — Mr Wyndham Lewis, and an outside artist — Mr Spencer Gore. The facts are as follows.

Mr Spencer Gore was approached last July by the Agent of the *Daily Mail*, and, in an interview at Carmelite House was invited, in conjunction with Mr Wyndham Lewis and Mr Roger Fry, to do a room for the Ideal Home Exhibition. It was the idea of those who recommended these artists to the *Daily Mail* authorities that a room should be decorated on the lines of their joint decorations in the Cabaret Theatre Club[2]; Mr Fry, as head of the Omega Workshops, should supply the furniture.

Mr Gore was asked to arrange a meeting between the Agent of the *Daily Mail* and his colleagues. Immediately on leaving Carmelite House, he went to the Omega Workshops, there seeing a director of the Company, and leaving word to the above effect; neither Mr Fry nor Mr Lewis being there at the time. Mr Lewis, then working at the Omega Workshops, would, he naturally thought, be at once communicated with. After that Mr Gore heard nothing further of the matter.

Not only was this visit not mentioned to Mr Lewis, but the Direction at the Omega Workshops appropriated the commission, with the results at present visible to anyone visiting Olympia. As an example of the detailed working of this sordid game the following manoeuvre may be cited. When it was announced in the Workshop that the Ideal Home room had been secured by the 'Omega', and it came to apportioning the work, Mr Lewis was told by Mr Roger Fry that no decorations of any sort were to be placed on the walls, and was asked if he would carve a mantelpiece. Shortly after this, Mr Lewis went away on his holidays, and on his return in September, found large mural decorations, destined for the Olympia exhibition, around the walls of the workroom.

(2) A second unpleasant fact is the suppression of information in order to prevent a member from exhibiting in a Show of Pictures *not* organized by the Direction of the Omega. Mr Rutter, the Curator of the Leeds Art Gallery, in organizing a Post-Impressionist Exhibition in Bond Street, wrote to Mr Fry some weeks ago. In this letter he asked for Mr Etchells' address, wanting some of his work for the Exhibition. He was given to understand that Mr Etchells had no pictures ready and would have none till 1914. This statement of Mr Fry's was not only unauthorized but untrue. It is curious that a letter from Mr Rutter to Mr Lewis on the same subject, and addressed to the Omega Workshops, should never have reached him.

This mean and ludicrous policy of restraining artists might, perhaps, be justified if the Direction at all fulfilled its function of impresario: but its own Shows are badly organized, unfairly managed, closed to much good work for petty and personal reasons, and flooded with the work of well-intentioned friends of the Direction.

More incidents of the above nature could be alleged, but these two can be taken as diagnostics of the general tone of the place.

As to its tendencies in Art, they alone would be sufficient to make it very difficult for any vigorous art-instinct to long remain under that roof. The Idol is still Prettiness, with its mid-Victorian languish of the neck, and its skin is 'greenery-yallery', despite the Post-What-Not fashionableness of its draperies. This family party of strayed and Dissenting Aesthetes, however, were compelled to call in as much modern talent as they could find, to do the rough and masculine work without which they knew their efforts would not rise above the level of a pleasant tea-party, or command more attention.

The reiterated assurances of generosity of dealing and care for art, cleverly used to stimulate outside interest, have then, we think, been conspicuously absent in the interior working of the Omega Workshops. This enterprise seemed to promise, in the opportunities afforded it by support from the most intellectual quarters, emancipation from the middleman-shark. But a new form of fish in the troubled waters of Art has been revealed in the meantime, the Pecksniff-shark, a timid but voracious journalistic monster, unscrupulous, smooth-tongued and, owing chiefly to its weakness, mischievous.

No longer willing, to form part of this unfortunate institution, we the undersigned have given up our work there.

(Sgd.) Frederick Etchells
C.J. Hamilton
Wyndham Lewis
E. Wadsworth.

Of the two published accounts, that by Virginia Woolf comes closer to the facts alleged by this document. She summarizes the charges and quotes the concluding passages of the document. According to her (and she was a witness of these events, although not perhaps a very reliable one) Roger Fry was not very perturbed by the letter and although some of his friends urged him to bring an action he refused to take any notice of the accusation.

'No legal Verdict', as he observed:

would clear his character or vindicate the Omega. Publishing correspondence would only advertize the gentlemen, who, he sometimes suspected, rather enjoyed advertizement. He was quite content to abide by the verdict of time – *le seule classificateur impeccable*, as *The Times* critic has observed in another connexion. But the young artists themselves anticipated the verdict of time. They gave him then and there the most practical and emphatic proof of their confidence. They were quite ready to go on working for him; and, what was perhaps more remarkable, he was quite ready to go on working for them. The storm in a tea-cup blew over; though he noted bubbles from time to time – 'The Lewis group have got hold of the *New Age* critic and he's written an amusing thing which I send you – please send it back... The Lewis group do nothing even now [March 1914] but abuse me. Brzeska who sees them says he's never seen such a display of vindictive jealousy among artists'. (To Duncan Grant.)[3]

The classifications of time are perhaps less impeccable than one might desire. Virginia Woolf, writing nearly thirty years after the event, clearly believed that Lewis was a liar; Sir John Rothenstein writing in 1956 takes the opposite view:

'When Lewis came in one day he was told by Fry that the Omega had been given a "wonderful commission" by the *Daily Mail* to design and carry out the furnishing and decoration of a Post-Impressionist room at the Ideal Home Exhibition, and that the principal tasks were already allocated. "But you, Lewis," Fry said after a moment's reflection, "might carve an overmantel". Carving in the round is not one of Lewis's many talents, and he addressed himself gloomily to the task. A few days later he happened to meet P.G. Konody, art critic of the *Daily Mail* and art adviser to Lord Rothermere, its proprietor. Konody asked him how the Post-Impressionist room was shaping, and Lewis told him that, apart from his languishing overmantel, he knew little about it. "As the designer I think you *ought* to know," Konody complained. "The *designer*?" Lewis asked. Then Konody told him that he had called to see him at the Omega Workshops, been told he was out, that Fry had offered to take a message, and he had asked him to convey to Lewis and Spencer Gore an invitation from the *Daily Mail* to design the Post-Impressionist room.

'Talking with me years later about the episode, Lewis said that if he had known what protest would cost him he would have kept silent. But he did not know: so there was an angry interview, followed by the trailing of a coat, in the form of a letter that may one day find place in the anthologies of invective.'[4]

This account, as will be seen, does not tally with that given by Lewis and his friends in their 'Round Robin'. Spencer Gore is eliminated from the story, his rôle being replaced by that of P.G. Konody. This account is taken in perfect good faith from Wyndham Lewis, who at that distance of time not unnaturally made mistakes, but it is rather surprising that Sir John should have used two contradictory sources without realizing it.

II

There can be no doubt that the lead in the faction against Roger Fry was taken by Wyndham Lewis.

Any kind of collaboration between the two men was bound to be difficult. Roger Fry valued integrity, intelligence and humility; for him the legacy of Cézanne was the most precious thing in Post-Impressionism and he found in it the continuation of a great European style; he distrusted any form of bravura, stunt or rhetoric; he had little sympathy with the exclamatory art of Marinetti and the Futurists. But it was precisely to this development of twentieth-century art that Wyndham Lewis was most drawn. What *he* had to say had to be said with éclat: nothing less than a shout would do for what he proclaimed. With very considerable gifts as a writer, caustic, truculent and at times brutal, he was also, one may suppose, a very vulnerable character, easily wounded and naturally suspicious.

If Lewis was, in a sense, one of nature's *fascisti* and as such almost profesionally exasperating, Fry kept something of the maddeningly angelic quality of the Quakers whence he sprang, that implacable placability, that intolerable fairness with which the Society of Friends has for centuries confronted and outwitted powerful adversaries, an innocent guile which convinces us in the end that it is indeed the meek who inherit the earth. To those who knew him well and were in sympathy with his aims there could be no doubt concerning Fry's transparent honesty, but it is not hard to see how irritating that stern candour might be, particularly to a person of Lewis's temperament. With the hindsight of the historian, it is easy to see that Fry was mad to have anything to do with Lewis or Lewis with Fry.

The commission for the Post-Impressionist room at the Ideal Home Exhibition was presumably given soon after the opening of the Omega Workshops, that is to say, in the summer of 1913, and from the first it would seem that Lewis was dissatisfied and communicated his dissatisfaction to others. The 'angry interview' between Lewis and Fry mentioned by Rothenstein probably took place on 5 October; there was, it would seem, a dispute on the stairs at the end of which the four malcontents left in a body.

'*Ça c'est trop fort*', remarked Fry as they clattered downstairs and out, slamming the door.[5]

There is little doubt that if Wyndham Lewis and his three friends had been the only persons concerned in the business Fry would have left it at that. But a main agent and, as it appeared, one of the chief sufferers, had been Spencer Gore, a person whose integrity could by all accounts hardly be questioned and who, of all others, was least likely to assist in any ill-natured plot. The following letters tell their own story:

The Omega,
5th Oct. 1913

My dear Gore,

Lewis tells me that you said you left a letter here from the Ideal Home Exhibition people asking Lewis to to decorations and asking the Omega to do the furniture. I told him that the *Daily Mail* people had approached me directly and that they had never mentioned his name. He thereupon doubted my word and said that I accused you of telling a lie. I wish to let you know in case he carries this to you that I repeatedly told him that I did not doubt your word but had no knowledge of any request that he should do the decorations as separate from the Omega. We should scarcely have thought of undertaking it if that had been the condition as the Omega produces its work anonymously and would not expect to have the work distributed beforehand by outsiders amongst the various artists.

I have tried to treat Lewis with every consideration but I fear nothing I can do comes up to his ideal of what is due to him. He has left saying he will never come back which I knew must happen sooner or later.

Yours sincerely,

Roger Fry[6]

6 Cambrian Rd.,
Richmond,
Surrey.
7th Oct. 1913

Dear Fry,

Lewis misunderstood me when I said I had left a letter at 33 Fitzroy Street. But all the same I must back his grievance. The facts are as follows. About the middle of July the Ideal Home exhibition wrote to me asking me to meet their agent. I went up to see him at the office a day or two later. He said they wanted a room at the Ideal Home exhibition in the advanced style and, reffering [*sic*] to a note on a piece of paper, that I, Mr Fry and Mr Wyndham Lewis had been recommended to them, would I arrange a meeting between him and the three of us and fix it up. I said it would be quite easy as you and Lewis were usually at Fitzroy Square and the Omega Workshops would provide all the necessary fittings. I then took a book with photographs of last year's rooms and came straight up to Fitzroy Square. Unfortunately Lewis and you were both away. But I saw Duncan Grant, explained the offer to him, asked him to ask you to communicate with the agent, left the aforementioned booklet, and have since been rather surprised to have heard nothing from you whether or not you were going to do it, and still more surprised when I saw Lewis the other day and he told me the room was being done and found he did not know he was one of the people who had been asked to do it. As to the anonymity of the Omega I see no reason why Dicksee and Poynter should not arrange a room with materials supplied by Ω, that in a case of that kind the men in charge would stand outside the firm, and I think you owe us both some explanation. Of course the Ideal Home doesn't care as long as it gets the room.

Yours sincerely,
Spencer F. Gore[7]

Durbins,
Guildford.
9th Oct. 1913.

Dear Gore,

Do please come round to the Omega and see me tomorrow, Friday afternoon. I can explain it easier than in writing and really I assure you Lewis has no grounds for complaint as far as I can see. Your analogy of Poynter doesn't hold while Lewis was one of the Omega artists. But in no case could the Omega share a job like that. As a matter of fact Lewis wanted to do carving for it. It was his own suggestion and I considered it the most interesting and important job in the whole work. However he never carried it out in spite of constantly repeated assurances that he would and finally left me to substitute somebody else on the last day. Really he has behaved very ill to me but I don't want to make complaints, only to assure you that I haven't injured him in any way. But please come and discuss it if you can.

Yours sincerely,
Roger Fry[8]

Presumably Spencer Gore never did have an interview with Fry – it may well have been difficult; Fry left for a holiday in France soon afterwards. But Gore wrote a letter to Fry, which we have been unable to find, and in it, clearly, he stuck to his first opinion. Fry replied as follows:

Au Printemps,
Villeneuve les Avignon.
18th Oct. 1913

Dear Gore,

Thanks for your letter. I appreciate your frankness in telling me that you uphold Lewis. I don't of course know why you believe him rather than me, but I can't help it if I am less persuasive. I can only repeat to you that everything I said is true, that Lewis did express himself to me as delighted to do the carving. If he really was not I can only say that he was not frank with me. I shouldn't have had the slightest reason to make him do it, in fact I was perfectly willing to let him off at any time. I didn't tell him there would be no decoration. It is I fear useless to me to ask you to take my word for it but I must in self-defence tell you that this is so. The *Daily Mail* have fully confirmed my statement about the commission for the room and as you very unfortunately did not deliver the message yourself I think you must take my word for it that I never got it with sufficient clearness to make me consider it as compared with what I thought the quite authoritative full statement of the *Daily Mail*. Of course if you really believe the fantastic and gross nonsense that Lewis and Co. have written about me you will not believe a word of this. But ask yourself honestly which theory is more likely, that I am an almost incredible monster not only of iniquity but of folly (for what the Devil have I to gain by it), or that there has been a quite absurd misunderstanding produced by Lewis's predisposition to believe himself the object of subtle antagonistic plots.

Really I am far too busy to dream of these elaborate intrigues. The thing's so silly that I have barely patience to disown it. Naturally you who don't know me well are perfectly at liberty to believe the worst of me, but I think on reflection you'll see that the theory of Lewis and Co. won't wash.

Anyhow, until you assure me that you regard me as a 'Pecksniff shark', etc., etc. I shall prefer to remain

Yours sincerely,

Roger Fry.[9]

During the interval between Fry's departure and the posting of this letter the quarrel had developed in a new way. Wyndham Lewis and his friends had decided to publish their accusations; they sent the 'Round Robin' to shareholders of the Omega. At the same time, Lewis and Spencer Gore sent a letter to the press in which they repeated the main accusations of the 'Round Robin' and concluded:

The artists signing this letter wish to repudiate the pallid Charivari of what they should have done to be found among other Idealities at Olympia, and in defence of their own work, wish to publicly state that they had no hand in the decoration of this room.[10]

As far as we can discover this letter was not published. But it was the 'Round Robin' which engaged the attention of Roger Fry's friends.

Vanessa Bell had been left in charge of the Omega during Fry's absence. Naturally she had to decide what should be done, if anything, and, equally clearly she had to apply to Roger Fry himself.

Vanessa Bell to Roger Fry

46, Gordon Square,
Bloomsbury.
Sunday [12th Oct. 1913?]

My Dear Roger,

We have had a day of it! This morning Molly [MacCarthy] telephoned to say that they had had the enclosed circular letter from Lewis, Etchells and Co. which you had better read at this point as it will explain matters. It is so absurd that perhaps you'll think it unnecessary to do anything but laugh at it. On the other hand Molly evidently thought you must somehow, have given them cause to be very angry and Desmond [MacCarthy] thought that *your* enemies would be only too glad to get hold of any story against you and would be delighted at a split in the Omega and that you ought to defend yourself. Duncan [Grant] and Adrian [Stephen] came round here and D[uncan] and I decided that we had better see Etchells and try to get him to see that whether they were right or not they had behaved monstrously in writing this letter without first accusing you to your face. We went to see him this afternoon and talked for nearly two hours. He . . . could hardly be made to see our point at all. When he did see it he simply said that he didn't agree. He brought up a long tale of grievances of how he had gradually become convinced against his will of your meanness. Evidently he had been storing up small things which had at last been brought to a point by this. It is all such a muddle that one couldn't convince him of anything. But I don't think either he or the others will give in at all, or that there is any use in trying to get them to.

Desmond has been here for some hours and he and Clive [Bell] have concocted these letters which are the sort of thing they think you might say in reply. Etchells had written to Rutter to ask him for your letter, which I only hope *didn't* say that Etchells had no paintings! Apparently he had several and both he and Lewis are sending to the Doré, so anyhow they have taken no harm. Then Desmond thought that I – as I am supposed to be in charge at the O., had better see the *Daily Mail* man tomorrow and get him to say what happened at your interview with him. After I have seen him and got his statement which I will send on to you, you could write your letter if you think it all right. We have been discussing this all at great length today and now Leonard [Woolf] who is here is rather against your taking any notice of it. I think it rather depends on whether Rutter and the *Daily Mail* produce clear evidence. If they do, there are at any rate those two questions of fact about which they can be shown to be quite mistaken, and perhaps it would be better to leave out the rest. I have put alternative suggestions in the letter suggested. However it may of course be better not to answer in any case. You will have to settle this as you think best. Its the most awful nuisance. . . Etchells was going to send you a list of the people to whom they had sent their circular. Oh God — what utter idiots they are. It seems almost incredible. I have no other news as our day has been spent discussing this affair which I hope will seem to you happily remote and unreal. You can imagine how we enjoyed ourselves over it!

Addition by Clive Bell

It seems to me just possible that we have all rather lost our heads over this area row. I wonder whether it wouldn't be best to let the whole thing slide — for a time at any rate. We could then see what was happening. . . The whole thing's a matter of character and surely yours is good enough to stand a little scurrilous rhetoric. Everyone who knows what's what will draw his own conclusions from the style of the circular. The rest will be unaffected, won't they, by any reply that you can make. What about saying nothing, or at any rate about waiting before you say anything?

yrs.

Clive.

Addition by V.B.

Here is my first letter which has now returned. Just back from dinner with the Trevys [Trevelyans], where we met Melian [Stowell] who was very much upset about this affair and rather nice. I must go to bed but I'll write tomorrow, I don't enclose the letter [*i.e.* the Round Robin] again as I know you have it.[11]

Vanessa Bell to Roger Fry

46, Gordon Square,
Bloomsbury.
Oct. 13 [1913]

My Dear Roger,

    It was very difficult to write to you yesterday for as I expect you saw I was in a crowd and they all wanted to know what I was saying and to add remarks of their own. Well now I must tell you what has happened today about this silly affair. Clive had a letter from Lewis this morning written to explain *his* position.[12] He said the facts were beyond dispute, then he abused you and then he said he hoped Clive would not be alienated from him. Clive went out this afternoon and in Bond Street whom should he run into but Lewis, who came forward and said 'I hope you're not very much upset!' 'Oh no', said Clive, 'not in the least'. They then had a long talk walking about Bond Street and Piccadilly. Lewis explained that he had had to use politics to defend himself, that he had his way to make, etc. Clive pointed out that their letter had been a silly 'and surburban' affair which would convince no one of anything but the folly of the writers. Lewis then tried to put all the blame of the letter on the others and said it wasn't the sort of thing he liked doing. 'I hope my colleagues were not hurt by any remarks about Prettiness' he said. *He* had not wished to put in that sort of thing. Clive seems to have made him feel rather foolish and found out that they are all longing for you to reply. Lewis was very much disappointed that you had not rushed back from France at once! What they would really like would be an action for libel. It seems quite clear now that the best thing is to do nothing. It is quite evident that no one will believe anything they say and that they will be crushed more by silence than any reply. Clive met Clifden[13] who had heard about it from Gore and said evidently there had been some muddle but of course it was ridiculous to suppose you had ever tried to do harm to Etchells and the others. But I have made arrangements to see the *Daily Mail* man, Mr Craston, tomorrow at Olympia, as there is no harm in getting his evidence even if you don't use it. It might conceivably be worth while, if Rutter produces your letter and that *doesn't* say what he said it did about Etchell's having no pictures, to produce these two pieces of clear evidence that their only definite charges are untrue. But I daresay even that isn't worth doing. . .

Clive wants me to say that you mustn't think that Lewis was really in at all conciliatory mood to start with. His admissions were only made as he saw that he might have made himself rather foolish over this letter and so tended to make light of his share in it. But of course you won't take my report of their conversation as pretending to be accurate — Good God you're not likely to! I only put in these cautions in case by any chance you felt inclined to take action because of my account of the affair. But as you will know at this

distance it's not safe to rely on anything at 3rd or 4th hand. . .[14]
[Vanessa Bell went to Olympia on 14th October and saw an official:]
He was very friendly and entirely upheld your statement of course.
In fact he said he couldn't understand how the people at Carmelite
House could have given any commission for he wasn't at Carmelite
House but had offices elsewhere and knew nothing about them.[15]
He said the names of Lewis and Gore hadn't been mentioned in his
interview with you and that the commission had been given directly
to the Omega. He was delighted to come forward and say this, so I
gave him definite questions written out to be answered and he is
going to send me a letter saying this.[16]

This letter, it seems, went astray and a copy had to be applied for; this,
however, has been preserved.

F.G. Bussy to Vanessa Bell

Exhibition Offices,
Olympia,
Kensington.
22nd Oct. 1913

Mrs Bell,
46 Gordon Square,
London W.C.
Dear Madam,
    The commission to furnish and decorate a room at Olympia was
given by the *Daily Mail* to Mr Roger Fry without any condition as
to the artists he would employ.
    In the conversation between our representative and Mr Roger
Fry, there was no question of collaboration between the Omega
Workshops and any other artist or artists. The names of Mr Spencer
Gore and Mr Wynham [*sic*] Lewis were not mentioned by our
representative to Mr Roger Fry so far as he can remember, neither
do we recollect having any interview with either of the latter
gentlemen.
Yours faithfully,
F.G. Bussy, Secretary.

With this letter in his hands, Fry could almost certainly have brought an
action against the signatories of the 'Round Robin' and have won it. His
friends in London advised him to do nothing; Sickert and Lytton

Strachey thought the thing too silly to be noticed. The latter wrote to Etchells saying he 'sympathized deeply and it must indeed be terrible for Lewis to have lost the chance of making an Ideal Home'.[17] Duncan Grant wrote voicing what seems to have been a fairly general opinion:

Duncan Grant to Roger Fry

38 Brunswick Square,
W.C.
20th Oct. 1913.

My Dear Roger,

I think that the grand circular of which you have now heard has fallen rather flat, which of course does not excuse these people's abominable conduct to you, but should make you easy I think about not coming home on purpose to do anything.

I had a letter from Maynard [Keynes] who had been sent a circular and who knew nothing about the whole concern at all, and he at once saw that the whole thing was written from quite other motives to those given, and as far as I can find out everyone else that has had one has come to the same conclusion.

I think the whole thing is sickening, but it all seems explained to me by Lewis's conversation with Clive about it.

I'm perfectly sure the whole thing was engineered by Lewis simply to advertise himself and that he made use of the dissatisfaction of the others to bring about a general strike. It would have been fatal to his plans to try to get any evidence, so he simply impelled the others to believe his account of it, which I believe they did. I don't believe for a minute Lewis really believed it or he would have taken some trouble to get some evidence, and I suppose the others thought his was enough.

In a way I think it very bad luck on Etchells especially, who though he has behaved perfectly monstrously, has all along thought that he has been behaving from the purest motives. I mean I think it is bad luck because I think it quite likely that Lewis will quarrel with him quite soon.

Meanwhile the 'Omega' continues to exist, and Miles interviews young clergymen about ladies' dresses, and insults the insulters at the Ideal Home when they get rowdy in the evening. Please give my *amitiés* to Doucet.

yrs.

Duncan Grant.[18]

Clive Bell wrote reinforcing his first remarks and giving what he considered to be the general verdict: 'Everyone, I find, takes it for what it is, a piece of bloody foolery.'[19]

Augustus John, almost echoing these words, told Lewis that he had been 'a bloody fool'.[20]

By the end of October the first impact of the quarrel had died away so far as Fry and his friends were concerned and by the time that Fry had returned from Avignon it seemed to be generally agreed that no action should be taken.

The Omega continued for another six years and we have found no further mention of the Wyndham Lewis affair after 1913 in the voluminous correspondence which continued between Roger Fry and Vanessa Bell for the next twenty years. She and her friends almost forgot it; they forgot that Spencer Gore had been involved in the business, they forgot that the *Daily Mail* had been applied to or had produced written evidence; for them the thing had ceased to be important.

For Wyndham Lewis it was different; he believed that the quarrel had cost him dear. Fry did not bring him into the courts, but 'he had other means of visiting his rancour on the principal challenger. Of these he did not neglect to make unremitting use'. Thus Sir John – and he is, surely, quoting Lewis.

But what were the means? We are not told and it is doubtful whether Lewis himself could have described them in such a way as to carry conviction. But perhaps it was necessary for him to believe that he was the victim of a conspiracy. He believed that his complaints were justified and that Roger Fry was a monster of iniquity. It followed that he would, in one way or another, seek revenge. What more natural than to see in every misfortune, in every fancied slight or omission, the cruel workings of an implacable foe? If his fame as an artist was less than he deserved, might it not be that the hidden hand of Roger Fry was at work? Whether the subsequent persecution was real, or, as we think, imaginary, the affair was a tragedy for Wyndham Lewis.

III

The two chief witnesses in this affair, Spencer Gore and the *Daily Mail* official, contradict each other; and yet it is hard to believe that anyone is lying.

The officials at Olympia had no reason to lie and every reason to tell the truth. If Fry *had* appropriated the commission, then it was certainly not to *their* interest to appear as his accomplices; their good name was

at stake in a matter which might well be taken into court and it would
have been sheer lunacy in them to have said – still more to have
written – anything that could not be substantiated up to the hilt. 'It
would be absurd', wrote Lewis, 'for the *Daily Mail* people to say that
Gore had never seen their representative',[21] and yet this was precisely
what they did say.

In the same paragraph he adds: 'Gore . . . is not a man whose word
can be doubted', and here he was on much safer ground; Gore's
character as a man was by all accounts admirable. Nor is this all; we
have documentary evidence which shows that he was telling the truth.
Mme Strindberg, the widow of the dramatist and the owner of the
Cabaret Club -- the walls of which had been decorated by Gore, Lewis
and Ginner – wrote thus:

Mme Strindberg to Spencer Gore.
　　Dear Gore,
　　　　The Ideal Home Exhibition asked Konody for an eminent
　　Futurist painter, to decorate a room for them –
　　　　I told Konody to give them your name and address. He has done
　　so.
　　　　For God's sake don't recommend another man *but make the
　　money YOURSELF.*[22]

We know from a letter sent to him by Lewis[23] that Konody's part in
the business was not large. He gave Gore's name, also perhaps that of
Lewis and the Omega, to some person or persons in the *Daily Mail*. He
may perhaps have been guilty of some initial confusion, of setting two
officials to work who acted independently. We cannot tell, for the
archives of the *Daily Mail* were destroyed in 1940; but that some
confusion and reduplication of effort occurred would seem to be an
inescapable conclusion. On these terms we may believe that, while one
official approached the Omega, another approached Gore and that Gore
did indeed visit the Omega and leave a message and a book with Duncan
Grant. Mr Grant, who fifty years after the event was amazed to hear
that Spencer Gore was in any way involved in the business, supposes
that he might well have received and forgotten such a message.

If the conflicting testimony of Spencer Gore and the *Daily Mail* can
be reconciled by supposing some kind of administrative muddle, what
are we to say of the conduct of the two principal actors in this drama?

The case of Roger Fry is clarified by the evidence of Spencer Gore.
An attentive reading of his letter to Fry of 7th October shows that Fry

must be acquitted of all malicious intentions.

It was 'about the middle of July' that Gore was approached by the *Daily Mail* people, offered a valuable commission and asked to 'arrange a meeting'. He left a message at the Omega and nothing happened. He was, he says, 'rather surprised', but clearly he took no steps to find out what had gone wrong. Nor, and this is still inexplicable, did the representative of the *Daily Mail*; Lewis, also, was silent. Two months passed. By the middle of September it must have been perfectly clear that, if the decorations were to be ready for the opening of the exhibition in October, he would have to act at once. Still he did nothing. He was not, we are told, an absent-minded man and yet he would almost appear to have forgotten about the Ideal Home commission.

Now, if we are to suppose that Fry acted maliciously and with the definite intention of excluding Gore, we have to suppose also that Fry knew *in July* that Gore would take no further action until October, that the *Daily Mail* would have no further communications with Gore or with Lewis and that Gore and Lewis would never meet and correspond. Unless he had foreknowledge of these very improbable circumstances he would have known that his duplicity would at once have been revealed. In other words he was accused of committing a crime which was almost certain to miscarry and quite certain to be detected; of being, as he put it himself: 'an almost incredible monster not only of iniquity but of folly.' If to this we add the evidence of the officials at Olympia, the accusation collapses entirely. The gravest charge that can be made against Fry is that he may have misunderstood a message.

The case of Lewis is different: he was already angry with Fry and he could hardly be expected to scrutinize Gore's account of the matter very severely. He knew that Gore was an honest man; he believed Fry to be a rogue. And, yet, it is impossible not to contrast the behaviour of Fry's partisans with that of Lewis: the former went unhesitatingly to the offices at Olympia (which could, obviously, confirm or destroy the accusations) and, being assured that they were in the right, were silent. Lewis might have done likewise; he preferred to believe and at once to publish that which he wanted to believe. Had he attempted to verify his story he, and many other people, would have been spared a great deal of misery and there would have been no 'Ideal Home Rumpus'.

Notes

1. *The Letters of Wyndham Lewis*, ed. Professor W.K. Rose, 1963.
2. Sometimes referred to as 'The Cave of the Golden Calf'. Its proprietor, Mme Strindberg employed Wyndham Lewis, Spencer Gore and Charles Ginner as decorators.
3. *Roger Fry*, 1940, pp. 192—4.
4. *Modern English Painters*, II, 'Lewis to Moore', 956, pp. 26, 27.
5. Evidence of Miss Winifred Gill recorded by Stephen Chaplin.
6. Mrs. Spencer Gore.
7. Fry MSS., King's College, Cambridge.
8. Mrs. Spencer Gore.
9. Mrs. Spencer Gore.
10. Fry MSS., King's College, Cambridge.
11. Mrs. David Garnett.
12. This letter is published by Professor Rose (No. 50, p. 53) and can now be dated 12 October, 1913.
13. Perhaps Mr. Clifton, proprietor of the Carfax Gallery.
14. Mrs. David Garnett.
15. Gore declared later that 'he did not go to Carmelite House but to the *offices of the Ideal Home Exhibition*, which are, he believes, in Fleet Street'.
16. Mrs. David Garnett.
17. Vanessa Bell to Roger Fry, 16 October, 1913 (Mrs. David Garnett).
18. Mr. Duncan Grant.
19. Clive Bell to Roger Fry, dated 'Monday' (Clive Bell).
20. Vanessa Bell to Roger Fry, 22 October, 1913 (Mrs. David Garnett).
21. Lewis to Konody, Rose, *op. cit.*, letter 49, p. 52.
22. Mrs. Spencer Gore.
23. Lewis to Konody, Rose, *op. cit.*, letter 49, p. 52.

Walter Michel: *Rumpus Replied to*

... After the first draft of this article was written, the October 1964, issue of *Apollo*, containing a contribution by Professor Quentin Bell and Mr Stephen Chaplin on the Ideal Home Exhibition, and an essay on Roger Fry as the Editorial came to my notice. The latter of these pieces is not directly related to my subject. However, since it presents a recent, over-all re-consideration of Fry, it seems appropriate for me to define my own small area of interest with respect to this much broader context. My concern here is with that which even his closest friends and defenders have admitted existed, the 'bad' side of Fry, and with certain aspects of Fry's taste which would be likely to enter into any consideration by him of the kind of painting Lewis stood for. These aspects of Fry's activities are important for our discussion, because it is to them that Lewis was exposed.

The article by Professor Bell and Mr Chaplin impinges on my subject directly only in that it discusses the effect of Fry's hostility on Lewis's career, or, rather, asks how anyone could think that such an effect could possibly have existed. I believe this article will suggest to the authors some answers to the question. It remains for me to select for comment two general statements in their article, bearing on Lewis's stature as a whole.

Let us note, to begin with, two sentences which are weighty by virtue of being practically the opening ones of the section in which the authors give their own view of the underlying reasons for the Fry-Lewis antagonism: 'Any kind of collaboration between the two men was bound to be difficult. Roger Fry valued integrity, intelligence and humility; for him the legacy of Cézanne . . .'

In the context as quoted, the second sentence must be taken to mean that Lewis lacked the qualities enumerated, or had them to an insufficient degree. If witnesses be needed, there are many of considerable reputation who would differ from this opinion, which, most obviously in the case of the second-mentioned quality, is ludicrous. As for humility, it is ticklish to accuse another of not having it, for fear of appearing to lack it oneself. In any case, it is a question of humility before what, or whom, and of how much you have to be humble about. Finally, Lewis's integrity as a person is sufficiently revealed in the recent edition of his Letters (1963), although, as Lewis wrote in the preface to *The Enemy* (1927): 'Circumstances do not allow the editor of *The Enemy* to hope that he can live up to the business-like standards usually expected by the more irascible type of contributor.' As for Lewis's integrity as an artist, this is the one thing which almost all his critics agree in crediting him with.

The other passage which I should like to examine for a moment stands at the beginning of the second paragraph of the authors' expression of opinion: 'If Lewis was, in a sense, one of nature's *fascisti* and as such almost professionally exasperating, Fry kept something of the maddeningly angelic quality of the Quakers whence he sprang. . .'

The introductory 'if' allows of two interpretations: either Lewis is called a fascist, which is a meaningless insult, unless further qualified; or the intention is to allow that both Lewis and Fry had faults and that, to the extent that Lewis was fascist (with which goes the earlier 'at times brutal') Fry was maddeningly angelic. If one wished, one might, I suppose, argue that the emphasis is on the 'professionally exasperating' and not on the *fascisti*. Nevertheless, *fascisti* is there, 'if' only 'in a sense'.

As a general reaction to the passages quoted one may feel that an attack on the whole basis of a man and artist should not be made in a half-sentence or an 'if' sentence. More specifically, to reproach Fry in terms as mild, almost flattering, as the above, is inadequate. In a scholarly treatment of the Fry-Lewis controversy, the reader has a right to expect references to such criticisms as have been made of Fry bearing on the issues involved in that controversy. There was a 'ruthless' and 'obstinate' side to Fry: the terms are used by both Clive Bell[1] and Leonard Woolf.[2] Mr Woolf writes that he was 'more than once surprised by [Fry's] ruthlessness and what to me seemed to be almost unscrupulousness in business'. As an example, he tells how Fry, 'without any explanation or apology to the painters', deducted a higher commission than had been agreed on from artists whose pictures had been sold at the Post-Impressionist Exhibition of 1912.

Another criticism relevant to the subject of Professor Bell and Mr Chaplin's article is advanced by the American scholar Solomon Fishman.[3] Professor Fishman, who is on the whole extremely respectful towards Fry, makes the reservation that 'Fry now appears to have been excessively cautious, excessively limited by his traditionalism'. Professor Fishman continues: 'One could compose a long list of his deficiencies – his indifference to the linear tradition of Northern art, . . . his lack of interest in technical experiment, . . . ' The relevance of these statements to the Fry-Lewis controversy is obvious. Fry's occasional *acharnement* in business would naturally have been of concern to Lewis, who worked for him, as would also his disdain of linearity and technical experiment, the two outstanding characteristics of Lewis's style. A mention of the fact that Fry could be considered ruthless and unscrupulous even by his friends might have led some readers to accept more readily than the authors appear willing to do Lewis's assertion that the quarrel had cost him dear.

In general, the authors are correct in stating that it was madness for two such people as Lewis and Fry to attempt to work together. The kind of exasperation and irreconcilable opposition that must have been felt by both parties is illustrated in an unpublished note by Lewis, dating from January 1914. In this he objects to Fry's not being an impresario or manager, but a participant, 'just another artist', and to the tendency to suggest that 'his personal friends – Duncan Grant and Mrs Bell – were very rare spirits and peculiarly fine artists'.

With Roger Fry representing *the* modern movement in England, artists much closer, in fact, than he to the vital centres of twentieth-century art had a difficult time of it. I nearly said, earlier, to explain

Fry's preponderance, that 'there was no one else'. But Fry, as the swarm of letters quoted by Bell and Chaplin shows, may be said to have been quite the reverse of alone. There was, in fact, another critic, also a member of that circle, and the husband of Vanessa Bell, the late Mr Clive Bell. His association with Fry lent considerable weight to whatever Bell said. What he said, during and shortly after the war, about modern artists in England constituted a consistent, brash running down of the efforts of most of them, the most notable exceptions being Duncan Grant, who was extravagantly praised, Vanessa Bell, Mark Gertler and Richard Sickert.

In *The Burlington Magazine* of 1917, Clive Bell took nine columns to call contemporary British painting 'hopelessly provincial', allowing only, in the last column, that Grant, Lewis and Epstein

> have all seen the sun rise and warmed themselves in its rays; it is particularly to be regretted, therefore, that Mr Lewis should have lent his powers to the canalizing (for the old metaphor was the better) of the new spirit in a little backwater, called English Vorticism, which already gives signs of becoming as insipid as any other puddle of provincialism.

'The sun' was Paris. Two years later, reviewing an exhibition of modern French art at the Mansard Gallery, Paris, Roger Fry found 'even the general level of the work' in it (that is, quite apart from the big names) about 'ten times as good' as 'even' in the London Group. This was for Fry a somewhat heroic admission to make; for he and his friends had joined the London Group in 1917, and by 1920 they were setting its tone. The names of the artists whose 'general level' is referred to do not detract from the modesty of the statement. Fry lists them as follows: Mlle Halicka, Solà, Fournier, Darcy and Ramsey. Although, of the five, only the first (Mme Marcoussis) sustained a reputation, Fry's opinion at the time was that 'any one of these would make something of a sensation in an English exhibition'. One may assume that certain reservations were understood, or else an astonishing development became visible in Duncan Grant within the year; for in 1920, Clive Bell, who was 'so close [to Fry] that they may be regarded as collaborators' — I quote Professor Fishman — introduced a review of an exhibition of the painting of Duncan Grant as follows: 'at last we have in England a painter whom Europe may take seriously. Nothing of the sort has happened since the time of Constable; so naturally one is excited.'

It is by omission or implication that certain artists were most effectively dealt with. The same essay sees the modern movement as taking two directions — Naturalist and Cubist:

> The complete break [with naturalism, of the Cubist branch] allowed the possibility of a new kind of literary painting. Ideas, symbolized by forms, could be juxtaposed ... almost as they can be by words on a page, and Futurism came into being. That this idea was seized on, perhaps originated, by a group of rather crude Italian journalists, and in all countries appealed to painters of a journalistic turn, has stigmatized this off-shoot of Cubism.

One may note how effectively Vorticism, the home movement, is demolished, not even being found worthy of mention by name.

In 1920, Clive Bell, returning from France, found himself irritated by the exhibition of Imperial War Pictures at Burlington House. He took several columns in *The Athenaeum*, just before the X-Group Exhibition, to expand once more on the second-rateness of the current English painters compared to the Frenchmen he admired. What length these utterances could go to is seen in the concluding sentence of Bell's piece, faint praise followed by the *coup de grâce*:

> Let us admire, for instance, the admirable, though somewhat negative qualities in the work of Mr Lewis; the absence of vulgarity and false sentiment, the sobriety of colour, the painstaking search for design — without forgetting that in the Salon d'Automne or the Salon des Indépendants a picture by him would neither merit nor obtain from the most generous critic more than a passing word of perfunctory encouragement.

It should not be assumed that the innovating artists, and Lewis in particular, entirely lacked supporters, or that these supporters found the art columns completely closed to their point of view. John Middleton Murry, who wrote on the visual arts for *The Nation* from 1919 on, was not unfriendly towards Lewis and, in October 1920, characterized the London Group show as being composed of 'elderly amateurs'. Gertler and Grant, who were not represented in the exhibition, he exempted from this label. Having criticized Fry's book *Vision and Design* a few months earlier, Murry was able, in *The Nation* and *The Athenaeum* of August 1921, to praise Lewis's book *The Caliph's Design or Architects Where is Your Vortex?* over a slightly later book of Fry's entitled *Some Architectural Heresies of a Painter*. *The Nation*, in 1919, accepted regular exhibition reviews from ORD (Drey), who wrote for *The Tyro*, and RHW (Wilenski), both admirers of Lewis. It must be said, however, that the friendly notices were on a small scale in both space and weight, compared with the portentous and prominently displayed pronouncements of Roger Fry and Clive Bell.

It is also true that a general criticism of the British painting of the time was quite justified, and no one knew this better than some of the innovating painters. Fry and Bell's 'blasting' of these painters accomplished nothing except to make it difficult for those who depended on selling pictures for a livelihood to survive. These critics' disdain for contemporary British work would be particularly exasperating if one inclined to the view that it was precisely their influence which was undermining the chances of effective support for experimental painting in England. We have seen in what terms Bell, in 1917 and 1920, dealt with Vorticism, the one basis on which, in 1920, a notable English school of twentieth-century painting might have been established. Lewis observed in 1937 that if people somewhat more like Pound and Yeats (he refers to the 'Vienna Café *habitués* of those days') could have pushed themselves into power, instead of the 'really malefic "Bloomsburies", the writing and painting of London might have been less like the afternoon tea-party of a perverse spinster'.

In summary, it seems clear that the stand which Roger Fry and Clive Bell took against the innovating painters at home is too violent, too unnatural to be construed as merely a preference for the more traditional French artists. I believe that Sir John Rothenstein is not foolishly addicted, as he is on occasion made out to be, to spreading gossip supposedly poured into his ear by the blind and vindictive Lewis and that his account of Bloomsbury, as given in the second volume of his *Modern English Painters*, is a sound one. It is quite true, on the other hand, that, whatever the facts of the case, the second-last paragraph of the 'Round Robin' of 1913 (quoted in full by Bell and Chaplin) was unnecessarily provocative; that, as on a few later occasions, Lewis warmed too much to his subject. In taking stock of the hostility of Bloomsbury to the group of innovating painters it is useful to remember that at least three of the four signatories of this document were outstanding members of that group. Of the four who signed the 'Round Robin', Lewis remained the challenge most to be reckoned with, as artist, vital force and personality. As late as 1937, in a letter to a gallery planning an exhibition of his work, Lewis felt it advisable to point out that he thought the hostility of Fry could, at this date, no longer harm him. In one way, he may have been wrong, at that. Lewis's stand against the leftist sentiment of the thirties antagonized a circle much wider than Bloomsbury. This new hostility might have harmed him less if his reputation as a painter had been as secure as it deserved to be. As it was, only one painting was sold during the first week of the 1937 exhibition, the most considerable of Lewis's career. The unusual step was taken of drawing attention to the merits of this exhibition by a letter to *The Times*, signed by twenty-two artists and writers.

Notes

1. Clive Bell, *Old Friends*, 1956, p. 85.
2. Leonard Woolf, *Beginning Again*, 1964, p. 95.
3. Solomon Fishman, *The Interpretation of Art* (essay on Roger Fry), University of California Press, 1963.

Quentin Bell, Stephen Chaplin, and Walter Michel: *Rumpus Revived*
Sir,

May we, authors referred to by Mr Walter Michel in his extremely interesting and important contribution to your August issue, make a few observations?

When Mr Michel takes exception to remarks which we made concerning Wyndham Lewis, he states his arguments fairly and openly and your readers may form their own opinions. But his major purpose is to defend propositions the precise nature of which he does not explain, and here a commentary is needed.

For this purpose it is necessary to begin by looking at Mr Michel's explicit aim: he wants to prove that, after their quarrel in 1913, Wyndham Lewis was persecuted by Roger Fry. Now in order to prove that a critic has persecuted an artist it is not sufficient to show that the critic does not like that artist's work or that the two were on different sides in an aesthetic dispute. Persecution implies animus, and to convict a critic on this charge it is necessary to prove that animus existed.

We must confess that when we began to read Mr Michel's article we supposed that such a thorough and patient scholar with so excellent an understanding of the period would find a number of harsh remarks by Fry about Lewis which could, perhaps, be construed as being malicious. We were not prepared for the astonishing result of his researches: Mr Michel has produced nothing of the kind. During the 1920s Lewis attacked Fry, but Fry, it would seem, never said a word about Lewis.

Those of us who value Fry's reputation must always be grateful to Mr Michel for having thus disposed of the myth of persecution, and it would seem base ingratitude to comment upon the methods by which he attempts, so bravely, to stick to his guns; nevertheless, it must be observed that one cannot really support a charge of persecution against Fry by quoting from Clive Bell (even if one could show that Clive Bell displayed animus); nor can one justify such a proceeding by means of a rather light-hearted misquotation from Professor Fishman. Above all one cannot conclude that the 'account of Bloomsbury, as given [by Sir John Rothenstein] in the second volume of his *Modern English Painters*, is a sound one'.

Let us quote a few words of that account:

> ... there was nothing in the way of slander and intrigue to which certain of the 'Bloomsburys' would not descend. I rarely knew hatreds pursued with so much malevolence over so many years, against them neither age nor misfortune offered the slightest protection.[1]

Does Mr Michel really believe that this virulent philippic could fairly be addressed to Clive Bell and to Roger Fry? Despite his words we doubt it. We doubt whether this would be his considered opinion even if he could find a scrap of evidence with which to support it. What he surely does believe is that they did not value Lewis at his true merits and were on the wrong side in an aesthetic dispute. It would do Mr Michel's reputation no harm if he were to adopt this position.

May we end by offering an unpublished letter which we have recently found, and which sheds some light on the character of Clive Bell and of Roger Fry? It is a draft for a reply to the letter which Lewis wrote after the 'Omega Rumpus', a letter which ends by expressing the hope that 'this rather rough episode will not have entirely alienated you'.[2]

46 Gordon Square,
Bloomsbury.
[*October 1913*]

Dear Wyndham Lewis,

There will, be no 'alienation' unless you're prepared to do all the work.

I feel nothing but charity. Of course. One's always sorry to see a good artist and a man of intelligence making a bloody fool of himself; but one gets used to it. Your 'colleagues' are easily forgiven; they don't know any better: but I suspect you do. For instance, you're not so silly as to suppose that facts can ever prove much that's worth proving. It's the interpretation one puts on them that matters. The facts we're talking about you interpret in the light of your views of Fry's character. That's right enough. It's your view of his character that's completely wrong. After all, you hardly know him and I know him very well. I know that he's about as likely to try to put a spoke in your wheel as you are to go down on your knees and beg his pardon. There may be plenty that's irritating, or at any rate vexatious in Roger Fry, but he's not that sort: you're wrong. And anyway, whatever you think of him and his doing you ought not to bombard the town with pages of suburban rhetoric. The vulgarity of the thing! And the provincialism! That's what I mind. You don't belong to the suburbs, so what the devil are you doing there?

Yours ever,

Clive Bell

A maddening, teasing and exasperating letter; but one which hardly confirms the view that Fry was unscrupulous – an opinion which Mr Michel mistakenly ascribes to Bell – or that the writer was hateful, malevolent and vindictive.

'. . . he's not that sort: you're wrong'. The words may never have reached Wyndham Lewis, but perhaps his apologists may be persuaded to hear them.

Yours faithfully,

Quentin Bell

Stephen Chaplin

Sir,

Professor Bell and Mr. Chaplin's letter is of an astonishing simplicity. To refute a criticism of Fry and Bell, who were collaborators and close friends, they quote the latter saying the former is a nice fellow. To establish that Fry did not harm Lewis, they point out that he did not use 'harsh words' about him in print. I thought I had indicated in my article some of the other, more effective, means at the disposal of a man in Fry's position for enforcing his will upon an artist whose livelihood depended on the sales of his books and pictures.

Having said this much, I have to add that your correspondents reduce my argument unduly to a matter of personalities. There was, after all, a considerable *issue* of art involved. Of all people in Europe Fry was in the best position to further the new painting. Had he done so — as his very position of power may be thought to have obligated him to do — instead of putting his great weight against it, England might not have had to await the end of another war to produce an art of stature.

The following errors of fact in Bell and Chaplin's letter may be corrected: I did not give a 'light-hearted misquotation', but a *quotation* of Professor Fishman. The view that Fry could be unscrupulous I ascribed not to Mr Bell but to Mr Woolf. Mr Bell I quoted as stating that Fry could appear ruthless even to his friends. In both cases I gave the reference where the remark may be found, which should have obviated discussion. Finally, Lewis's letter, which elicited Clive Bell's pompous answer, did not 'end', as your correspondents state, with the sentence they quote, but continued as follows: 'Anyhow, I thought I would send you a personal word on my side of the matter', which leaves a rather different impression.

Yours faithfully,
Walter Michel

Notes

1. Rothenstein, *Modern English Painters*, 1962, p. 278.
2. W.K. Rose in *The Letters of Wyndham Lewis*, 1963 (letter 50, p. 53), publishes what is presumably a draft of the final version; this also was discovered among the papers of the late Mr. Clive Bell. There are only a few verbal differences between the two texts.

D.H. Lawrence
David Garnett, *Lawrence and Bloomsbury*

Reprinted from David Garnett, The Flowers of the Forest *(London, Chatto & Windus, 1955), 34–7, 50–5, by permission of the author and Chatto & Windus;* © *1955 by David Garnett and reprinted with permission of Harcourt Brace Jovanovich, Inc.*

[D.H. Lawrence's relations with Bloomsbury were brief, but his criticism of certain members of the Group has taken on almost mythic significance. J.M. Keynes was the first to call attention to Lawrence's

insight into Bloomsbury (see pp.48–64) and F.R. Leavis has developed
the importance of the encounter in his own criticism of Bloomsbury
(see pp.387–95). Lawrence's criticism of Bloomsbury is to be found
mainly in his letters, the most interesting of which are given by David
Gernett in his account of Lawerence's behaviour toward Garnett's
friends. (Additional letters have recently been published in *Ottoline at
Garsington*, the second volume of Lady Ottoline Morrell's memoirs, and
they make it clear that homosexuality in Bloomsbury was one of the
causes of Lawrence's dislike of the Group, especially of Keynes. See
p.49.

Apart from his letters, the only other criticism that Lawrence made
of Bloomsbury outside his fiction is contained in a late essay on
painting in which Lawrence ridiculed the idea of significant form. In
preparing to write the essay Lawrence read Clive Bell's *Art* – 'What a
fool Clive Bell is!' he wrote to a friend – and Roger Fry's *Cézanne*.
Lawrence agreed with Bell and Fry about the genius of Cézanne, but
for quite different reasons. Lawrence felt that significant form and
aesthetic experience were essentially attempts to evade the power of
the physical in art. He makes this clear in a passage which mocks the
evangelical aestheticians that he took Bell and Fry to be:

> But let scoffers scoff, the aesthetic ecstasy was vouchsafed only to
> the few, the elect, and even then only when they had freed their
> minds of false doctrine. They had renounced the mammon of
> 'subject' in pictures, they went whoring no more after the Babylon
> of painted 'interest', nor did they hanker after the flesh-pots of
> artistic 'representation'. Oh, purify yourselves, ye who would know
> the aesthetic ecstasy, and be lifted up to the 'white peaks of artistic
> inspiration'. Purify yourselves of all base hankering for a tale that is
> told, and of all low lust for likenesses. Purify yourselves, and know
> the one supreme way, the way of Significant Form. I am the
> revelation and the way! I am Significant Form, and my unutterable
> name is Reality. Lo, I am Form and I am Pure, behold, I am Pure
> Form. I am the revelation of Spiritual Life, moving behind the veil. I
> come forth and make myself known, and I am Pure Form, behold, I
> am Significant Form.

It has often been claimed that Bloomsbury was hostile or at least
indifferent to Lawrence's work. The truth is that, as with so many
things, it is difficult to make simple generalizations cover Bloomsbury's
attitudes towards Lawrence's genius. Indeed it is this very individualism

in Bloomsbury — the 'little swarming selves' [see p.368] — that Lawrence so detested in the Group. Virginia Woolf was not especially favourable to Lawrence in her published criticism, though she admired *Sons and Lovers*; in her diary and her unpublished correspondence, there is unmistakable evidence of her respect for his art. Clive Bell and Lytton Strachey publicly opposed the suppression of *The Rainbow*. And E.M. Forster stated flatly that Lawerence was 'the greatest imaginative novelist of our generation'. (After he read *A Passage to India*, Lawrence wrote to Forster that his was the only voice that had anything to say to him from England.) And Desmond MacCarthy, to Bloomsbury's enemies its representative spokesman in literary criticism, was described in print by Lawrence as 'one of my most sympathetic critics'.

David Garnett first met Lawrence as a protégé of his farther, the editor Edward Garnett who gave Lawrence crucial encouragement at the beginning of his career. David Garnett thus knew Lawrence apart from Bloomsbury and before Lady Ottoline had introduced Lawrence and his wife Frieda to various members of the Group. In the first excerpt that follows, Garnett describes Lawrence's reaction to Duncan Grant's art. In the second excerpt, Garnett describes a visit to the Lawrences with Francis Birrell, a close associate of Bloomsbury at this time. The Meynell family visited by the Lawrences, Garnett, and Birrell include Wilfred, Alice, and their son Francis.]

Ottoline had talked to Lawrence about Duncan's pictures and, as Lawrence asked to see some of them, Duncan invited him and Frieda and E.M. Forster to tea in his studio the following afternoon. Morgan was the first to arrive. I came next, a woeful spectacle, as I had a very bad black eye. Then came the Lawrences. While we drank a cup of tea, Duncan brought out his pictures. On one very large canvas there was a green giant kneeling and overshadowing St Paul's Cathedral. The green giant was the spiritual form of Sir Christopher Wren. Then came an astonishingly good portrait of Ottoline — a three-quarter view of her head. Round the neck Duncan had pinned a string of Woolworth pearls. Lawrence had done a little painting himself and had his own ideas about the art. He was, indeed, to take up painting again and have his rather washy indefinite nudes seized by the police and destroyed by the order of a London magistrate. But Mr Mead, on the bench in Marlborough Street, was not much stupider than Lawrence himself that afternoon. We all sat in silence as Duncan brought out one picture after another. Then Lawrence rose to his feet — a bad sign — and walking up and down the studio, began to explain to Duncan what was wrong with his painting. It was not simply that the pictures themselves were bad — hopelessly bad — but they were worthless because Duncan was full of the wrong ideas. He was barking up the wrong tree and would have to learn to approach his subjects in a completely different frame of mind if he wanted ever to become an artist.

Soon after Lawrence's first words, Morgan made some gentle remark about catching the train to Weybridge and faded out of the studio. Lawrence warmed to his subject and went on speaking with absolute frankness, having decided that it was better to open Duncan's eyes and tell him the truth. But as he talked he held his head on one side, as though in pain, and looked more at the floor than at the pictures. Frieda, unfortunately, was aware both of Duncan's feelings and of mine. Each time that Duncan rose in silence and brought out another picture, she exclaimed: 'Ah, Lorenzo! I like this one so much better! It is beautiful!' Her interventions were ignored by both sides. Lawrence would give a wincing glance at the new picture and discover in it new material for his argument. Finally, in despair, Duncan brought out a long band of green cotton on two rollers. I stood and held one roller vertically and unwound while, standing a couple of yards away, Duncan wound up the other, and a series of supposedly related, abstract shapes was displayed before our disgusted visitors. That was the worst of all.

Before Lawrence had reached his peroration, there was a ring at the bell and the lecture was held up while Duncan went down and returned with an uninvited figure — a dark Russian Jew called Koteliansky — who had come to pick up Lawrence and Frieda with whom he had arranged to spend the evening. He sat down and the lecture was resumed. Lawrence paced uneasily up and down looking at the floor. Koteliansky sat black and silent; Frieda occasionally burst out: 'But no, Lorenzo! We liked that portrait so much!'

Duncan himself appeared to have developed toothache and sat with his hands on his knees, rocking himself gently in his chair, not attempting a word in defence of his works. Everything, however, has an end, and at last Lawrence, feeling he had done his good deed for the day, said that they must be going. Frieda and Koteliansky rose and followed and Duncan showed them down the dimly lit stairs and ushered them politely out into the foggy night. I stayed in the studio. The blast of Lawrence's attack had been directed at Duncan, who no doubt felt that he had suffered an unexpected assault, but he had lost nothing. I knew that the hope I had nursed of happy hours with them both was vain. My two friends would never understand each other.

When Duncan came back, I did not make any attempt to console him in the style of Frieda. We stacked the canvasses back against the walls and washed up the cups and saucers in silence. Next day Lawrence who was living in Sussex at a cottage lent him by Alice Meynell, wrote:

27th Jan. 1915, Greatham, Pulborough, Sussex.
Dear Lady Ottoline,
    We liked Duncan Grant very much. I really liked him. Tell him not to make silly experiments in the futuristic line with bits of colour on moving paper. Other Johnnies can do that. Neither to bother making marionettes — even titanic ones. But to seek out the terms in which he shall state his whole. He is after stating the Absolute — like Fra Angelico in *The Last Judgment* — a whole conception of the existence of man — creation, good, evil, life, death, resurrection, the separating of the stream of good and evil and its return to the eternal source. It is an Absolute we are all after, a statement of the whole scheme — the issue the progress through Time — and the return, making unchangeable eternity. In a geometric figure one has the abstractions ready stated ○ so, or △ so. But one cannot build a complete abstraction, or absolute, out of a number of small abstractions, or absolutes. Therefore one cannot make a picture out of geometric figures. One can only build a great abstraction out of concrete units. Painting is not architecture. It is puerile to try to achieve architecture — third dimension — on a flat surface, by means of 'lines of force'. The architecture comes in painting, only with the conception of some whole, some conception which conveys in its own manner, the whole universe. Most puerile is that clabbing geometric figures behind one another, just to prove that the artist is being abstract, that he is not attempting representation of the object. The way to express the abstract whole is to reduce the object to a unit, a term, and then out of these units and terms to make a whole statement. *Do* rub this in to Duncan Grant and save him his foolish waste. Rembrandt, Corot, Goya, Manet have been preparing us our instances — now for the great hand which can collect all the instances into an absolute statement of the whole. I hope you aren't bored, but do tell this to Duncan Grant.

From that spate of verbiage one might think that Lawrence was refuting ideas that Duncan had put forward. But I was a witness to the fact that Duncan had behaved like Tar-Baby while Lawrence had worked himself up into a passion like Brer Rabbit. In his letter, Lawrence was belabouring a figment of his imagination, as well as pouring out a lot of nonsense. What would an abstract statement of the instances of Rembrandt, Corot, Goya and Manet look like?

It seems certain that a memory of the visit to Duncan's studio inspired the passage at the end of Chapter XVIII of *Lady Chatterley's Lover*. Mellors, the gamekeeper hero (Lawrence) is taken to the studio of Duncan Forbes, 'a dark-skinned taciturn Hamlet of a fellow with straight black hair and weird Celtic conceit of himself'. 'His art was all tubes and valves and spirals and strange colours, ultra-modern, yet with a certain power, even a certain purity of form and tone: only Mellors thought it cruel and repellent.'

Lawrence's letter did not influence Ottoline as regards Duncan's pictures: indeed, at that time, she bought several: a most lovely one of a vase of hot-house tulips, which she had given him, I remember particularly as it was painted while I was writing in the studio, and though I was glad that Duncan should get ten or fifteen pounds, I was sorry to see it go . . .

In the middle of April, Frankie and I accepted an invitation to visit Lawrence and Frieda and spend a night in the cottage which the Meynells had lent them at Greatham in Sussex. We took a train packed with young soldiers. Their complexions, burned by sun and wind, were clear bright red; their uniforms new and they themselves as soft and amiable as young foxhounds, with the same good-tempered doggish interest in each other's movements. If one lifted his pack from the rack, or searched his tunic pocket for a packet of Woodbines, it caused a stir in the whole carriage. Frankie and I got out at Steyning, and walked up the Downs to Chanctonbury Ring, then down to the Washington Inn and, from there, by Storrington to Greatham which we reached in plenty of time for supper. Frankie, as usual on our walks, did not stop talking and had no idea of the direction in which we were going. I, alone, found the way, looked at the trees, the short turf, the stray flints, the view over the weald, and listened to the larks singing and Frankie talking as effortlessly as the birds sang. Once or twice I may have broken in to defend my views on literature. At that time Frankie dismissed all contemporary writers with contempt and had not embarked on either French or Russian literature. He thought I was uneducated because I had not read Gibbon and the names of Lord Acton and Goldwin Smith meant nothing to me. I thought him hidebound, but our bickerings were always blown away in gales of laughter.

After supper, Lawrence and Frieda took us round to pay our respects to the Meynells and Saleebies. They seemed as remote to me as so many dark-eyed, dark-skinned South Sea Islanders. Some aura, their mother's poetry, or their Catholicism, separated them from the world in which I lived. When we left the big room, with its Italian bric-à-brac and Morris patterns and the glowing hearth with the young people grouped about the Poetess and the Patriarch, we went to bed early for we were very tired.

We have been invited to breakfast by the Meynells. The Patriarch was rustling the pages of *The Observer*; the room was filled with dark madonna-like girls and women; the Poetess was stretched upon a couch, and there was the question, to which I instinctively felt that a painful answer was expected: 'Where is Francis?' No one could say, but, just before we had finished our eggs and bacon, a tall handsome young man with a rapt expression came eagerly into the room. It was Francis Meynell who had run three miles across the marsh to mass with the Holy Fathers (or maybe Brothers) at Amberley. With what benign and holy joy did his parents look upon him then! And how like to a Blake engraving was the whole family at that moment!

Lawrence had disappeared to work after breakfast and Frankie and I were joined by Bertie Farjeon, his wife Joan, and his sister Eleanor and Margaret Radford and we all sat happily gossiping and roasting in the sun. It was only the 17th of April but it was as hot as midsummer. We were happy and little suspected that trouble might be brewing as we first talked, and then played, with a gnome-like Saleeby child. Our high spirits lasted all day. After the Farjeons and Margaret had departed for London Frankie talked, and I talked and I think Frieda laughed a lot at supper and looked as though she would have kissed us for being so noisy. But slowly I became aware that Lawrence was silent and that something dreadful was going on inside him. He was in the throes of some dark religious crisis and seemed to shrink in size with the effort of summoning up all his powers, all his spiritual strength. The muscles knotted and he became smaller — but he said nothing. Frieda, however, had observed what was going on. I said we were tired and that I had a long day's walk in front of me. Then Frankie and I took our candles and retired to our little rooms.

I was, actually, rather tired but I was kept awake by angry and incessant whispering in the next room which sounded most sinister. At last, however, Lawrence stopped and I soon dropped off. Suddenly, in the middle of the night, I was woken by a series of bangs and tumbles and strangulated sounds. I sat up and realized that someone was blundering about outside the door of my room. I lit a candle and investigated. Frankie was standing, swathed in a pair of thick flannel pyjamas, in the passage, dumb and obviously in great distress. He pointed to his mouth and in the light of the candle I saw it was open and choked with a large object. His tongue had swollen to an enormous size. I shoved the handle of my toothbrush into his mouth and he winced and gave nasal moans. Then Frieda, followed by Lawrence, came in and stared at us in astonishment. I explained matters and discussed doctors, poultices and fomentations with Frieda. There was a quiet, triumphant certainty in Lawrence's manner. He had prayed for deliverance to his Dark Gods and they had sent this mysterious sign, blasting his enemy in what had hitherto seemed his strongest organ. For a little while, Frieda and I tortured Frankie, one of us holding the candle, while the other tried to insert teaspoonfuls of almost boiling water into his mouth. Finally we pushed him off to bed and he was glad to escape from us. I had discovered by that time that his temperature was normal and went off to sleep encouraged to hope that he would last till next day, when I could take him to a doctor.

Morning came at last and, to the astonishment of us all, Frankie's tongue had resumed its normal size and functions. It was neither larger nor smaller than usual. Frieda and I contented ourselves with giving him a big dose of salts.

On the way to the station Frankie was more silent than usual. He went to London and I to Eleanor's. After our visit Lawrence wrote to Ottoline:

We had David Garnett and Francis Birrell here for the week-end. When Birrell comes, tired and bit lost and wandering — I love him. But, my God, to hear him talk sends me mad. To hear these young people talk really fills me with black fury: they talk endlessly, but endlessly — and never, never a good thing said. They are cased each in a hard little shell of his own and out of this they talk words. There is never, for one second, any outgoing of feeling and no reverence, not a crumb or grain of reverence. I cannot stand it. I will not have people like this — I had rather be alone. They made me dream of a beetle that bites a scorpion. But I killed it — a very large beetle. I scotched it and it ran off — but I came on it again, and killed it. It is this horror of little swarming selves I can't stand.

On the same day, the 19th of April 1915, Lawrence wrote to me:

Never bring Birrell to see me any more. There is something nasty about him like black beetles. He is horrible and unclean. I feel I should go mad when I think of your set, Duncan Grant and Keynes and Birrell. It makes me dream of beetles. In Cambridge I had a similar dream. I had felt it slightly before in the Stracheys.* But it came full upon me in Keynes and in Duncan Grant. And yesterday I knew it again in Birrell — you must leave these friends, these beetles. Birrell and Duncan Grant are done for forever. Keynes I am not sure — when I saw Keynes that morning in Cambridge it was one of the crises of my life. It sent me mad with misery and hostility and rage. The Oliviers and such girls are wrong. I could sit and howl in a corner like a child. I feel so bad about it all.

Enclosed was a letter from Frieda:

You always admire other people too much, you are really more than Birrell and the others. I *know*, but you daren't trust yourself, I think that Anna whom you loved, but there was something hopeless in it from the beginning, that has left such a lot of unbelief in you. But you do really want so much and much will come if you will only let it. Anyhow you are my dear friend. Frieda.

In a postscript after Frieda's letter, Lawrence had added: 'You have always known the wrong people. Harolds and Olivier girls. Love. D.H. Lawrence.' Lawrence's letter made me angry. He seemed to me to be mad and determined to interfere in my life. I therefore decided not to see him again. It was a great loss, for I loved both Lawrence and Frieda — especially Frieda — and I took the greatest interest in his work. Already it had begun to seem to me that he had taken a wrong turning, for how could the author of *The White Peacock* and *Sons and Lovers* write such turgid nonsense as *The Lion and the Crown* in Murry's *The Signature*? At Edward's request I had been responsible, eighteen months before, for choosing the selection published in *Love Poems and Others*, Lawrence's first volume of poems. I knew that, at his best, Lawrence was a very fine and very original poet. *Snapdragon*, which was not among those from which I could choose in 1913, was, I was certain, a very great poem and *Red Moonrise*, which I thought the

---

* It would be interesting to know which members of the family had produced this quasi-coleopterous impression. Oliver was still in India and Lawrence had not met Lytton. It must have been one of the Miss Stracheys and James

best of those in *Love Poems and Others*, an extraordinarily original and
exciting one. Lawrence had really forced me to break with him because
of his dislike, and perhaps jealousy, of my friends. He hated their
respect for reason and contempt for intuition and instinct. But angry as
I was, I was deeply unhappy that Lawrence should have forced me to
break with him. Frieda's letter made me love her more than ever. In
retrospect the most astonishing thing was Lawrence's dislike of
Frankie . . .

George Bernard Shaw

Clive Bell, *The Creed of an Aesthete*

George Bernard Shaw, *Reply to Clive Bell*

Affable Hawk, *Clive Bell and Bernard Shaw*

Clive Bell and Affable Hawk, *Good Words*

Reprinted from The New Republic *29 (25th January 1922), 241–2 and
29 (22nd February 1922), 361–2; reprinted from the* New Statesman
*18 (25th March 1922), 703 and 18 (1st April 1922), 729, by per-
mission of the* New Statesman, *Professor Quentin Bell, and The Society
of Authors on behalf of the Bernard Shaw estate.*

[In 1922 Clive Bell criticized George Bernard Shaw's *Back to Methuselah*
in *The New Republic*, and he did it in such a way as to emphasize pro-
vocatively the differences between Shaw's philosophy of life and his
own. Bell and Shaw had amiably disagreed about art nearly ten years
before in the correspondence columns of the *Nation*. The creed that
Bell set forth in *The New Republic*, especially the picture he draws of
what the good life ought to be, was not shared by other members of
Bloomsbury; Leonard Woolf, as a Fabian socialist, may have been closer
to Shaw's point of view than Bell's. Yet Bell's criticism of Shaw's
ignoring ends for means is rooted in Moore's *Principia Ethica* and
fundamental to Bloomsbury's ethics. Shaw's reply to Bell's criticism of
Back to Methuselah makes very clear the differences between his well
known ideas about the purpose of life and Bell's.

Desmond MacCarthy had by this time written some of the best
dramatic criticism of Shaw that had been done. He entered the dispute
under his pseudonym 'Affable Hawk'. In supporting Bell's ideas but not
his illustrations, MacCarthy again brings out the differences between
Shaw's ideas and what might be called Bloomsbury's – and 'got a
peace-maker's black eye for my pains' from Clive Bell. The dispute is

hardly edifying at the end, yet it does indicate once again that Bloomsbury's mutual admiration did not exclude the public exchange of some hard verbal blows.

There is another characteristic Bloomsbury aspect to Bell's dispute with Shaw. Lytton Strachey's friend Carrington felt that Bell was unjustified in his attack on Shaw's play, so she forged a letter from Shaw to Bell. The hoax took Bell in completely; he wrote to Shaw, receiving in return a postcard saying Shaw had never written to him. Here is Carrington's letter:

10 Adelphi Terrace, London

Dear Clive Bell,

Thank you for the numerous compliments you have paid me in this week's *New Republic*. I am sorry I cannot return the compliment that I think you, or your prose, 'Perfectly respectable'.

In my young days a 'taxicab' was a name given only to aged whores, ugly as Shaftesbury Avenue.

You would not, it would apear, lead a very enviable aesthetic life; to me it seems dull.

Yours,

Bernard Shaw]

Clive Bell: *The Creed of an Aesthete*

Mr Bernard Shaw is an admirable writer and a wit; he is one of the dozen living Englishmen whose prose is perfectly respectable; to compare him with Swift though unkind is not absurd; but he is not an artist, much less an aesthete. The difference between an artist and an aesthete is, I suppose, the difference between one who can create and one who can appreciate beauty: most artists are aesthetes as well – but not all. However, the difference does not concern me here because I am going to deal exclusively with appreciation, and, confining myself to the term 'aesthete' – under which may be ranged most artists – modestly draw attention to the fact that there are in the world quite a number of people to whom it may be applied, though apparently Mr Shaw is unaware of their existence.

Mr Shaw is a didactic; and one of the differences between didactics and aesthetes is that, whereas the latter rejoice in the knowledge that it takes all sorts to make a world, didactics are unable to believe that there are people who, without malice or stupidity, are fundamentally different from themselves. Thus Mr Shaw, one of the cleverest men alive, comes out, on the fortieth page of his new book *Back to Methuselah,* with a statement so astonishingly false that I read it through four times before I would accept its obvious import. After stating quite fairly, so far as I can judge, the Darwinian theory of Natural Selection and Survival – a theory as to the validity of which I have no opinion, not being deep in science – Mr Shaw rejects it on the ground that it makes nonsense of 'Beauty, Intelligence, Honour', etc. 'When its whole significance dawns on you,' says he, 'your heart sinks into a heap of sand within you': and he is quite sure that 'this hideous fatalism,' as he calls it, will never be accepted by people who care for Beauty, Truth, Love, Honour, etc., etc., because, by depriving these things of their divine origin and purpose, it deprives them of their value. If Life be a mere purposeless accident, the finest things in it must appear to everyone worthless. That is what Mr Shaw thinks, and the sooner he knows that it is not so the better. Whatever he may feel, the people who really care for beauty do not care for it because it comes from God or leads to anything. They care for it in itself; what is more, that is how they care for all the fine things in life.

The advantage of being an aesthete is that one is able to apreciate the significance of all that comes to one through the senses: one feels things as ends instead of worrying about them as means. And this intrinsic significance of external reality is so intensely moving and so various that it completely satisfies those who can apprehend it. Mr Shaw may be right and the neo-Darwinians wrong; life may be Heaven-sent and Heaven-directed towards some inconceivably glorious future: but, whether this be so or not, always life will be worth living by those who find in it things which make them feel to the limit of their capacity. Whatever its origin, beauty exists and so does the sensibility which reacts to it. A rose is a development of a briar which is a development of God-knows-what – and, incidentally, it grows out of manure; its beauties of form and color and smell appeal to a sense in me which may have grown out of primal lusts and appetites; but when I contemplate a rose I am not enjoying a chapter of natural history and I am using my sense of beauty and not my palate. Odd as it must seem to Mr Shaw, I at this moment, am enjoying a yellow rose, my contemporary; and though men of science assure me that both the rose and the I of this moment are the products of all preceding moments, our disgraceful past no more destroys my present pleasure than does my conviction that before long both the rose and I must perish.

Whatever is precious and beautiful in life is precious and beautiful irrespective of beginning and end. I have no patience with the snobbery that is forever deploring or denying our disreputable ancestry in a fortuitous concourse of atoms, or with the sentimentality that cannot do without a happy ending. Not long ago, one of that nasty brood of pseudo-scientists who nestle like woodlice in the decaying doctrine of Freud, produced a theory with an unprintable name from which it seemed to follow that our romantic and passionate feelings were merely developments of a disgusting habit which, if really common amongst German children, is probably the symptom of some mental disorder induced by under-feeding. Would you believe it, the sentimentalists who happened to come across this theory were up in arms against it, not on account of its manifest improbability, but because, if true, it would make nonsense of their emotions? As if every amorous experience, from the grandest passion to the flutteringest flirtation, were not a real and complete thing as distinct from its origins as a glass of champagne is distinct from the chalk hills of the Tardenois. Long before the neo-Freudians came pestering us with their ill-founded generalizations, men of science had demonstrated the probability that all that is most rare and complex in our spiritual make-up can be traced back to the most elementary animal desires. What difference does that make? The pleasure I take in listening to the music of Mozart may, possibly, be derived from the anticipatory orgasms of a cave-dweller listening to the bird he hopes to catch and eat. Mozart is not a pigeon on that account, neither are my feelings esurient. The antecedents of Mozarts's music and of my feelings have nothing to do with the present value of either. And though it should be proved up to the hilt that the world in which we live was created by a fluke and by a fluke will be destroyed, that would detract nothing from its aesthetic significance.

The great good fortune of aesthetes is their capacity for seeing things as ends whereby alone is one able to taste this significance. To Mr Shaw their capacity for enjoying life seems childish, and aesthetes, I fancy, will accept the epithet as complimentary and not inexact. Certainly children have a direct sense of things; and that is why gutter-snipes playing on a dust-heap appear to people like Mr Shaw unreasonably and irritatingly happy. Certainly about the happiness of those who appreciate the beauty, romance and fun of life there is a tipsy light-heartedness which reminds me of the irresponsible gaiety of schoolboys. These are merry because they have something to be merry about — the fullness of life and the glory thereof: whereas those unfortunate people who can never feel things in themselves but only can take an interest in their causes and effects are naturally worried, seeing that of ultimate causes and effects we can really know nothing at all. We can comprehend – embrace, that means – only the present; the rest is shadowy and unsure: wherefore, I am sorry to say, those who cannot live in the moment but must worry about the past and future are obliged to 'make up'. My grandmother did it: she made up a nice old gentleman with a long white beard who caused all, directed all, and would in the end make us all happy. Mr Shaw does not like him, and has made up instead a, to my taste, less attractive figure, called 'The Life-Force', of whom he knows precisely as much as old Mrs Bell did of Jehovah. When Mr Shaw's 'grown-ups' are asked what they want, they reply, 'Immortality'; and when Mr Shaw, who has ruled out as 'childish' Love and Art, is asked how they will spend their immortality, he replies 'in thought'; and when we pull a wry face at the prospect of endless and unmitigated cogitation, he sternly gives us to understand that we shall like it when we get there: my grandmother did the same when we, sceptical brats, protested that we should weary of playing on harps and casting our golden crowns upon the glassy sea.

It is only natural, I suppose, that those who cannot find happiness in the present because they want the power of appreciation should clamor for immortality – need I say that it is not for personal immortality but for the immortality of the race, the endless continuity of life, that Mr Shaw clamors? Yet it seems to me that even this betrays a lack of courage. If we can enjoy our individual lives, knowing them finite, surely it should not be impossible to face the fact of universal death. Men of science, whom of course Mr Shaw cannot allow himself to trust, assure us that Life, as we understand it, can exist only in conditions which have not always existed and will not exist always; that Man is doomed as inevitably as Everyman. It may be so. Meanwhile I am finishing this article and I have finished *Back to Methuselah*. The sun is blazing into the square, but into my cool room it comes pleasantly filtered through blinds. It is lunch time, and after lunch I shall light a pipe and sit reading, not Mr Shaw's admirable treatise, but the penultimate volume of Proust – an artist if ever there was one. I shall dine with a charming companion and go to the ballet where they give *Petrouschka, Sacre du Printemps* and *Carnaval*: Lopokova will dance. Later to a gay supper, with a dozen delightful people in a house full of beautiful objects: if Arthur Rubinstein is in good humor surely he will play the piano. And so home under stars, smoking a cheroot in the warm stillness of the sleeping streets and squares, sauntering up all the long loneliness of Piccadilly, and only at the beginning of ugly Shaftesbury Avenue picking up a 'taxi-cab'. The fruit and flowers go rumbling into Covent Garden. It is dawn almost. 'And tomorrow we die"? So be it.

George Bernard Shaw: *Reply to Clive Bell*

As will be seen in the above article, my friend Clive Bell is a fathead and a voluptuary. This a very comfortable sort of person to be, and very friendly and easy and pleasant to talk to. Bell is a brainy man out of training. So much the better for his friends; for men in training are irritable, dangerous, and apt to hit harder than they know. No fear of that from Clive. The layer of fat on his brain makes him incapable of following up his own meaning; but it makes him good company.

A man out of condition muscularly not only dislikes rowing or boxing, but cannot conceive anyone liking them. A man out of condition mentally not only dislikes hard thinking, but cannot conceive anyone enjoying it. To Falstaff, Carpentier is an object of pity. To Clive, Einstein is the most miserable of mortals. So am I.

He is mistaken as to both of us. Intellect is a passion; and its activity and satisfaction, which can be maintained from seven years old to 107 if you can manage to live so long, are keenly pleasurable if the brain is strong enough for the exercise. Descartes must have got far more pleasure out of life than Casanova. Hamlet had more fun than Des Grieux, who tried to live on his love for Manon Lescaut, relieved by cheating at cards. Clive tells us how he poisons the clear night air of London with his cheroots after an evening of wine, woman and song; and he is contemptuously certain that he has enjoyed himself far more than a handful of old gentlemen in a society of chemists, mathematicians, biologists or what not, discussing the latest thing in quantums of energy, or electrons, or hormones. It is the interest of the tobacconist, the restaurateur, the theatrical manager, the wine merchant and distiller, to suggest that delusion to him. And what a silly delusion it is! No pleasure of the first order is compatible with tobacco and alcohol, which are useful only for killing time and drowning care. For real pleasure men keep their senses and wits clear: they do not deliberately dull and muddle themselves. I have not the smallest doubt that when the human mind is as fully developed as the human reproductive processes now are, men will, like the ancients in *Back to Methuselah*, experience a sustained ecstacy of thought that will make our sexual ecstacies seem child's play.

Clive is troubled — you know it when he cries Who cares? — because a rose grows out of manure. This comes of taking hold of things by the wrong end. Why not rejoice because manure grows into a rose? The most valuable lesson in *Back to Methuselah* is that things are conditioned not by their origins but by their ends. What makes the Ancient wise is not the life he has lived and done with but the life that is before him. Clive says why not live in the present? Because we don't, and won't, and can't. Because there is no such thing as the present: there is only the gate that we are always reaching and never passing through: the gate that leads from the past into the future. Clive, meaning to insist on static sensation, slips inevitably into talking of '*the significance* of all that comes to one through the senses'. What then becomes of his figment of sense without significance? 'Whatever is precious and beautiful in life,' he says, 'is precious and beautiful irrespective of beginning and end.' Bosh! The only sensations intense enough to be called precious or beautiful are the sensations of irrestible movement to an all-important end: the only perceptions that deserve such epithets are perceptions of some artistic expression of such sensation or pre-figured ideal of its possibilities. The pain with which a child cuts its teeth, though felt, is not suffered because the child feels it as Clive pretends to feel his pleasures: that is, it cannot anticipate the next moment of it nor remember the last; and so, fretful as it may seem, it does not suffer at all. If Clive ever gets his pleasures down to the point at which he also does not anticipate the future or remember the past, he will not enjoy it in the least. In short, his imaginary present and its all sufficing delight is unconsidered tosh.

The reason Clive enjoys his suppers is that he first works hard enough to need relaxation — at least I presume and hope he does. If he did not he would be miserable, and would probably have to take to drugs to enable him to bear his pleasant evenings at the Russian Ballet. Even now he cannot get through them without the aid of cheroots. I never eat supper; I never smoke; I drink water; and I can sit out *Petrouchka* and enjoy the starlight in Piccadilly all the same. But clearly, if I could be persuaded that *Petrouchka*, instead of being a relaxation, is as creative as the Piccadilly starlight is recreative, I should enjoy it a thousand times more. So would anybody.

No, my Clive: in vain do you sing

> Sun, stand thou still upon Gibeon,
> And thou, Moon, in the valley of Ajalon.

They will not stop for you. Lopokova will dance, as you say; but when you stretch your arms to her and cry

Verweile doch, du bist so schön

you cannot stop, either of you, any more than Paolo and Francesca could stop in the whirlwind. You delight in the music of Mozart; but does it ever stop? It ends; but your delight ends with it. You are a destinate creature, and must hurry along helter skelter; so what is the use of waving your cheroots at us and assuring us that you are motionless and meaningless? There is nothing in the world more ridiculous than a man running at full speed, and shouting to everyone that he is in no hurry, and does not care two straws where he is going to.

Affable Hawk: *Clive Bell and Bernard Shaw*

In the columns of *The New Republic*, USA, which has many English readers, a controversy is being conducted between Bernard Shaw and Mr Clive Bell. Mr Clive Bell began it with an article called 'The Creed of an Aesthete'; it was a comment on *Back to Methuselah*. Mr Shaw had asserted in his preface that if the mechanical theory of the universe were true and life an accident, having neither divine origin nor a purpose with which man could identify himself, the finest things in life must appear to everyone worthless. And the play itself had been written to show that the things 'grown-ups' desire are not childish things, like Love and Art, but, for the race, an immortality of 'thought'. This, Mr Clive Bell replied, is the mistake of a man who has nothing of the aesthete in his composition. To the aesthetic sense the origin or consequences of things make no difference to their value; Love and Art are worth having, and if worth having, remain so, whatever their causes and even if they lead to nothing further. Mr Shaw now calls Mr Clive Bell 'a voluptuary and a fathead'.

It is indeed an old controversy, but what makes it interesting is that in this case both antagonists are not pitting arguments against each other so much as their respective temperaments; that is why they have come to blows: 'Voluptuary and fathead' are blows. Neither of them argued the intricate question as to how far the values of Love and Art or anything else are affected by the absence of religion; Mr Shaw asserted they were, Mr Bell that they were not, and as example of good things left unaffected, whether there is or is not such a thing as the Life Force, Mr Bell drew a little picture of himself and the incidents he found made each day worth living as it came along . . .

I admit there is a certain blooming, balmy fatuity in this picture, a rather irritating suggestion of repletion, of the shirt front open to the summer air, and one thumb in the arm hole of the waistcoat – and – it needs a lot of money. On the other hand, Mr Shaw's answer does not excite my sympathies. Oddly enough, I feel in it precisely the same kind of irritating complacency; only this time it is that of a man who has risen at seven and done Swedish exercises and is now going to sit down, after eating some proteids, to write an entirely misleading pamphlet, say, on the Capital Levy.

It seems that I was born to be moderator between them both. When Mr Shaw called Mr Bell 'a voluptuary and a fathead' the blow fell on my shoulders too, for candour compels me to say that I am one of the many who, on the whole, bear a stronger resemblance to Mr Pepys than to John Bunyan. But, on the other hand, the point Mr Bell makes against Mr Shaw is a sound one. Mr Shaw has all his life neglected as an artist the value which experiences may have in themselves. The consequence of a lifelong habit of judging things as means to something else is that when, as he does in *Methuselah*, he attempts to adumbrate a state of perfection, having first dismissed all emotions which men have valued most, the result is a perfect and absolute blank; he has no imaginative conception of the contemplative state. That is what is the matter with his 'ancients'. Years ago my colleague, Mr Desmond MacCarthy, writing about Mr Shaw's Heaven and Hell in *Man and Superman*, said:

> What are the qualities most extolled in his plays? Vitality, pugnacity, political and intellectual honesty, fearlessness and universal benevolence: these are clearly useful. What are the qualities and emotions which on the whole are depreciated or pointedly ignored? Personal affections, admiration, and sensitiveness to beauty: these cannot be shown to be such powerful means of bringing about a better state of society; but are they not essential elements in that better state itself? . . . What chills us in his Heaven is the misgiving that the phrase 'masters of reality' (so the heavenly inhabitants are described) is a euphemism for a society of people all devoted to making each other and everybody else more virtuous. Now, we can imagine [how mildly Mr MacCarthy puts it – what an infernal millennium that would be!] something better than that; and even Mr Shaw's Hell, if he had not been so grossly unfair to it, seems to offer a better foundation for its construction.

Methuselah is a decided step forward from this, but the hand of habit is heavy upon Mr Shaw and, instead of getting hints as to what 'contemplation' is from saints, sages and mystics (often drinkers, I fear), he has suggested that perfect joys are rather those of a number of Professor Einsteins, who differ from the Professor in that they can grow five heads if they wish, and certainly would see nothing in the works of Dostoevsky, even with one of them, though the actual Professor Einstein confesses he has got more satisfaction from those works than from the mathematics of Gauss. But 'Clive' did not, as far as I could see, deny in his article the value of intellectual joys.

Mr Shaw's quotation from *Faust* is not happy. It was not the transitoriness of satisfactions which tortured Faust, but the fact that he could not experience anything to which he could say, 'Stay, then, still, thou art so beautiful'. The Devil betted he would — and lost. Faust's last hope was establishing an ideal community, but that failed to satisfy him. I regret to say he was saved by angels.

There comes a time to some who follow perfection in Art or in Life in which all possible forms of beauty or goodness are, as it were, discerned at once; it is not beautiful or good things but Beauty and Goodness themselves which are perceived. The light of a faint aurora of this vision lies on a few pages of literature. It dims, no doubt, particular beauties (aesthetic pleasures), but it is not to be reflected by one who has asked persistently and scornfully what these were good for and why they did not last for ever: the vision itself, too, does not last.

Clive Bell and Affable Hawk: *'Good Words'*, to the Editor of *The New Statesman*.

Sir,

Maybe your Affable Hawk was, as he says, 'born to be moderator between them both' (Mr Shaw and Mr Bell) — the very phrase suggests a mind overflowing with good intentions — but he would stand a better chance of success were he to mend his manners. It is useless to insinuate that Mr Shaw may be a little overstepping the bounds of old-world courtesy in calling me 'a voluptuary and a fathead', if he, himself, a few lines lower down is going to call me 'blooming, balmy and fatuous'. I resent none of these pretty familiarities; one could no more mind being called fatuous by a man with such a style, than one could mind being called voluptuary by a gentleman in jaeger. Only I would point out that

Mr Shaw, your Hawk, and other periodic apostles of sweet reasonableness are bringing controversy and criticism to such a pass that,
before long, instead of discussing what a writer says, we shall be
concerned only with what he eats. The injunction 'Be personal' is
construed by our modern masters in a sense that would have astonished
the school of 1880: so Affable Hawk must not be surprised if, when
next 'his colleague', Mr Desmond MacCarthy, publishes a volume of
essays, the reviewer, instead of observing merely that 'these papers are
written in a style which reminds us of a greasy old retriever-dog making
himself a hole wherein he will ultimately lie down', should, not content
with these critical observations, go on to remark that this is all one can
expect of a seedy intellect debilitated by a plethora of food, drink and
tobacco and unsupported by habits of scrupulous personal cleanliness.
Should it come to this the Hawk must not be surprised — though I shall
be distressed, and shall very likely write to the papers about it. For to
say such things of our friend, Mr MacCarthy, would not be more
offensive than calling me 'voluptuary and fathead, a blooming, balmy,
fatuous, irritating, replete, thumb-in-the-armhole, open shirt-front
young man', and certainly not less inexact. At least, that is how it
strikes me; but then I may be prejudiced. — Yours, etc.

                                                              Clive Bell

The Affable Hawk writes: 'Mr Clive Bell invited personal comment by
inserting, as an example of wise living and an object-lesson to
philosophers, an imaginary picture of himself engaged in that pursuit.
However impeccable the style in which this picture was drawn, it was
open, not only to criticism inevitably personal, but, as now appears and
I am most ready to believe, to the grave objection of conveying a wrong
impression. I have shown Mr Bell's letter to Mr Desmond MacCarthy,
who sighed and said: "I envy you your pseudonym, for in criticizing
you he would doubtless have referred to the wheeling of a hawk before
it swoops; I must be content with an old retriever, turning round and
round before it settles down. However, I accept the simile in the spirit
in which it was meant; only the word 'greasy' gives me pain." '

Dmitri Mirsky
The Bloomsbury Intelligentsia

Reprinted from Dmitri Mirsky, The Intelligensia of Great Britain,

translated by Alec Brown (London, Victor Gollancz, Ltd. 1935), 77–9,
111–20, by permission of the publishers and Mrs Ana Brown.

['I have had three severe swingeings lately: Wyndham Lewis; Mirsky, and
now Swinnerton. Bloomsbury is ridiculed; and I am dismissed with it. I
didn't read W.L.: and Swinnerton only affected me as a robin affects a
rhinoceros – except in the depths of the night.' Virginia Woolf's diary
entry for 16th March 1935, reveals not only her sensitivity to criticism
but also the increasing attacks on Bloomsbury in the thirties. Wyndham
Lewis's criticism is described on p.333–4. Frank Swinnerton's swingeing
appeared in his *The Georgian Literary Scene*. There he discussed
Bloomsbury in general, and Clive Bell, Roger Fry, Lytton Strachey, and
Virginia Woolf in particular. Swinnerton's purpose is mainly expository,
but he admits writing harshly of Bloomsbury 'from sheer malice'. The
'ill-mannered and pretentious *dilettanti*' of Bloomsbury irritated
Swinnerton – who was himself a novelist and critic – because their
presumption was incongruous with their performance. Swinnerton
exempts Desmond MacCarthy from this charge and has little actual
criticism to make of either Fry or Bell. Almost in spite of himself
Swinnerton finds Lytton Strachey's work enthralling. As a reader for
Chatto and Windus he enthusiastically recommended *Eminent
Victorians* for publication, yet Swinnerton also damns Strachey as a
bookish *dilettante*, 'a male bluestocking'. In the debate between Arnold
Bennett and Virginia Woolf over the nature of the novel, Swinnerton is
firmly on Bennett's side; in reaction to her criticism of the Georgian
novelists' materialism, Swinnerton finds in Virginia Woolf's work a
'tottering pursuit of the will-o'-the-whisp' that signifies her lack of
interest in objective reality.

Swinnerton's criticism of Bloomsbury is fairly mild. In later editions
of *The Georgian Literary Scene* he made it even milder by rephrasing or
deleting a number of malicious remarks or anecdotes; he even stopped
calling them 'ill-mannered and pretentious *delettanti*'. Yet Swinnerton's
attitude towards Bloomsbury is typical of a kind of criticism that
Bloomsbury found to be basically anti-intellectual. Though he does not
use the term, Swinnerton's position is that of a middlebrow criticizing
highbrows. This was a kind of criticism that Bloomsbury did respond
to, as can be seen in such essays as Leonard Woolf's 'Hunting the
Highbrow' and Virginia Woolf's 'Middlebrow'.

Dmitri Mirsky's critique of Bloomsbury is largely contained in a
chapter of his *The Intelligentsia of Great Britain* entitled 'Highbrows'.
His point of view is completely different from Swinnerton's however.

Mirsky's Marxist analysis of British intellectuals is predictable in its generalizations yet shrewdly perceptive in its identification of certain literary sympathies of the Bloomsbury Group. Prince Mirsky was, in Leonard Woolf's words, 'an unusually courteous and even gentle man, highly intelligent, cultivated, devoted to the arts, and a good literary critic', who nevertheless reminded Woolf of 'one of those unpredictable nineteenth-century Russian aristocrats whom one meets in Aksakov, Tolstoy, and Turgenev'. Woolf knew Mirsky in the early thirties, before Mirsky returned to Russia where he eventually perished in a prison camp.

Mirsky's thesis on Bloomsbury is that it came into being after the First World War as a synthesis of pessimistic, sceptical individualists and optimistic progressives. In the first short excerpt from *The Intelligentsia of Great Britain* Mirsky discusses Keynes; in the second longer one he considers the Group as a whole, especially Forster, Virginia Woolf, and Strachey. (For an earlier attitude towards Roger Fry's ideas, see the dialogue with Mirsky printed in Denys Sutton's introduction to the *Letters of Roger Fry*.)]

. . . Only two of the prominent progressives have preserved any typical intelligentsia traits since the war. These are John Maynard Keynes and Bertrand Russell. By tradition they belong to two different branches of the progressive movement. Keynes is a bourgeois radical, and an opponent of socialism. Russell is a 'socialist', even a 'left' socialist.

But in spite of this difference between them there is also a great similarity. Both are far from the contented optimism of the pre-war progressives, and in both the progressive and social habit of thought is complicated by a highbrow aestheticism. Keynes views the post-Versailles world with the cynical eye of a man to whom it is quite clear that the whole thing is going to the devil, but who thinks it will last his time anyway. Bertrand Russell views it with the philosophic melancholy of a man to whom it is quite clear that history is inevitably developing in a direction opposed to his tastes and his aspirations.

Keynes has chosen the role of Cassandra — a prophet of misfortune whom nobody believes. Russell has invented a new *genre* — that of pessimistic utopias, and no *genre* could better suit an epoch in which all former ideals metamorphose into their opposites. Keynes is an amateur of French painting, a patron of the ballet, and one of the central figures of Bloomsbury, which is the citadel of British aestheticism. Russell is the most thoroughgoing and the most competent exponent of the 'philosophy of values', which provides the theoretic basis of that aestheticism.

Keynes is the most brilliant and witty of contemporary bourgeois economists, and often tells his class the bitter truths. He has won himself an honourable place in literature by his little book on the Versailles conference. The satiric portrait, in this brilliant pamphlet, of that great swindler, President Wilson, who helped the representatives of the *entente* to fool the whole world, and was himself fooled by them, is unforgettable. In his role of economist and publicist, Keynes from time to time makes biting witty exposures of 'stupidities' with which capitalism is constantly obliged to entangle and complicate its own postion. But his positive advice is utopian and quite impracticable, though he is saved from proof of that impracticability by the circumstance that the bourgeoisie cannot avoid committing those very stupidities which exclude all possibility of trying the Keynesian recipes.

Keynes hates Marx no less than Wells does. But being one of the most self-satisfied men in the world, he finds no need to lower himself to the wounded malice shown by Wells, and is content to refer to Marx with the same air of superiority he applies to everything else in the world . . .

With all this distinction between the old and the new emancipation, the 'progressive' and the aesthetic, they have not remained two distinct and separate currents, but have mingled their waters, and the turbid patch where those waters meet has become one of the most striking features of the intelligentsia of Great Britain. Indeed, it is the very group which first used the word *intelligentsia* and was first dubbed *highbrow*.

This group is specially connected with Cambridge, the university which by long tradition, from Newton to Rutherford, and from Spenser right down the line, has been the university of great pioneers of the exact sciences and of the greatest English poets. Particularly at the commencement of the twentieth century, Cambridge contained a brilliant group of young men who combined a political radicalism with an interest in the most 'intriguing' abstract problems, and further an extremely refined taste produced by study of English poetry and French painting. One of these was Bertrand Russell, another J.M. Keynes. It was in their time that the student society, known as 'The Heretics', was founded for the purpose of discussing and spreading unorthodox ideas in all fields of culture.

This Cambridge circle produced a group of intellectuals bound together by personal ties and resident in the district of London known as Bloomsbury – the same district contains the British Museum and the oldest college of London University, founded in 1827 by pupils of Bentham – and the group has become famous under the same name, *Bloomsbury*. The principal figures of this group were the above-mentioned Keynes, the biographer and essayist Lytton Strachey, the novelist Virginia Woolf, and two art critics, Roger Fry and Clive Bell. This group established its own weekly, *The Nation*, financed by Keynes, and a publishing-house, the Hogarth Press, founded by Virginia Woolf and her husband.

The basic trait of Bloomsbury is a mixture of philosophic rationalism, political rationalism, aestheticism, and a cult of the individuality. Their radicalism is definitely bourgeois, a product not even of Shaw's new progressivism or the Fabians, but of the old bourgeois radicalism and utilitarianism. Thus the weekly *Nation* (now dead) did not support the labourist movement, but the liberal left wing. Bloomsbury liberalism can be defined as a thin-skinned humanism for enlightened and sensitive members of the capitalist class who do not desire the outer world to be such as might be prone to cause them any displeasing impression.

The atmosphere of Bloomsbury is extremely atistocratic, the atmosphere of gentlemen in well-furnished studies. Bloomsburians live amid books, 'great minds' of the past (as assessed according to their outlook, of course), and move in the best intellectual and aesthetic circles (as assessed, etc.) of the day. They avoid all extremes and abnormalities, though they treat everything which is original and 'inspired' with great respect.

Their rationalism and liberalism mark them off very sharply from the common or garden aesthetic bohemians of modern times, and also very sharply from the Russian modernism of the opening of the century. Being theoreticians of the passive, dividend-drawing and consuming section of the bourgeoisie, they are extremely intrigued by their own minutest inner experiences, and count them an inexhaustible treasure store of further more minutious inner experiences. They have a high opinion of Dostoievsky and of Freud.

But even these writers are taken by them without any trace of common bohemian gluttony. They are agile-minded, and of Freudian concepts they make a very special kind of mental discipline; I may say that a prominent Bloomsburian once told me how he had trained himself, every time he wakes in the night, be it only for a single minute, immediately to take up his pencil and record all dreams experienced up to that point.

Yet the interest these people show in Dostoevsky and Freud is quite equalled by their interest in Voltaire and Spinoza. They believe (or should I say, they hope?) that reason plus education will some day bring an age in which people will be enlightened ladies and gentlemen much like themselves, and there will be no more wars or revolutions. But it must not be thought that they are in the least degree democrats. They see civilization as the privilege of people who are well brought up and enjoy leisure. Having 'one's own room' in which one can escape from the outer world and its racket is, so we are informed by a book written by Virginia Woolf on the emancipation of women, the first condition of civilized creative work. And Clive Bell has written a book which constitutes a kind of manifesto. It deals with 'Civilization'. He informs us that the only civilized epochs in history have been the age of Pericles in Athens, the Italian Renaissance, and the Eighteenth Century in France (*les salons!*). He lays it down that the indispensable condition of this civilization (in the given periods), was that there was an 'enlightened class' which was relieved of earthly cares by having an income for which it did not have to work.

The favourite, one might almost say the national, authors of Bloomsbury are — Proust and Chekhov. It goes without saying that the first would satisfy them. His passive but so persistent and well-disciplined introspection, free from any wild fantasy, is a perfect expression of the psychology of the 'enlightened' dividend-drawer. The cult of Chekhov is a little more unexpected. Chekhov reached Great Britain as the last word in Russian literature, and was judged against a background of Tolstoy and Dostoevsky. This explains it. Bloomsbury had found a Russian writer who was completely bourgeois, completely devoid of those distressing rough corners in which, as a result of serfdom, Russian writers used to abound, and when they read him they felt quite at home.

Moreover, what was especially attractive in Chekhov was his technical perfection, the discreet lyricism of his art, and the way in which he built up his story from passive experiences and kept action outside. Finally, in Chekhov they discovered an ethical system which was just like that gentleman ethical system of Samuel Butler, only expressed with far more discretion and finesse.

The influence of Bloomsbury has passed far beyond its confines. The chief propagandist of Bloomsbury, Middleton Murry, is a person in many respects the very opposite of all that Bloomsbury holds dear. The creative influence of Chekhov was particularly marked in Middleton Murry's short-lived wife, the talented New Zealand writer, Katherine

Mansfield. But we should say that in the real Bloomsburians we do not find so much an influence of Chekhov as a spiritual identity. The study of Chekhov did not begin till after the War, but the pre-war novels of two exemplary bloomsburians, Virginia Woolf and E.M. Forster, are completely Chekhovian in spirit.

Of these two Forster is the less true to type. He first published in the 1900s, in the period of the social-realistic novel, and the construction of his novels is more reminiscent of Turgenev than of Chekhov. The liberalistic individualistic chekhovian psychology appears in them in rather a naive form. Forster is a modest, direct writer who has not soaked himself in Proust and does not care a damn about aestheticism. But that element of psychological hair-splitting runs like a thread through all his work. Everything is reduced to a matter of personal relationships, of human kindliness and delicacy.

The most interesting of his novels is the latest one, *A Passage to India* (1924), a typical colonial novel of a bourgeois intellectual, in which the relationships between the colonizers and the natives is brought down to a question of personal decency in the treatment of others. The principal figure in the book is an Indian intellectual, a character sketched with real goodwill, but yet all the time from the lofty standpoint of European greatness.

But Virginia Woolf may be described as the principal literary expression of Bloomsbury. She is unquestionably a great artist. She has created her own method, a lyrical kind of exposition of her leading characters – what might be described as an aesthetisation of the method used by Chekhov in *The Three Sisters*. Virginia Woolf is even more thin-skinned than Forster is, and she experiences the suffering of others acutely. But the sufferings with which she deals are limited to purely physiological suffering, as that of a woman growing old, and to individual psychological sufferings caused by the breakdown of personal bonds. Wherever they do appear as socially conditioned sufferings, they are, as in Proust, without exception the sufferings of the parasitic cream of the bourgeoisie. One of the lyrically most powerful passages in her work is one describing the inward experiences of a society woman who accompanies her husband to a lunch with another society woman – to which lunch she is not invited.

But what is most striking in Virginia Woolf is the purpose of her lyric method. This is devised in order to master the particular suffering and dissolve it away. The suffering is wrapped up in self-contained rhythms and sublimated from the world of reality to a world of aesthetics. Her lulling rhythms are a fine example of the narcotic function which art takes on in the hands of liberal aesthetes, who turn it into a new and more perfect form of dope, though of course one not intended for the people.

We have a much smaller artist, though no less typical of Bloomsbury, in Lytton Strachey, author of 'artistic' biographies (*Victorian Portraits* and *Queen Victoria*). Strachey's method is simply the irony of an aesthete looking down with amusement from his highbrow eminence on the marionettes of history. Strachey is full of respect for poets and dreamers, but scornfully condescending to all practical activity, especially political. The irony with which he represented Victoria did for a time do somewhat to diminish the public estimation of that lady, though it did not contain a trace of a revolutionary spirit, nor even of a democrat's attempt to indicate the truth. And in his orgy of irony at the cost of political men who take themselves seriously Strachey falls easy prey to a charm he finds in political cynics and charlatans clever enough to supply the grinning sneer themselves. Thus in his *Queen Victoria* he makes the most attractive character none other than the cynical father of British imperialism – Benjamin Disraeli. After these experiments in the aesthetics of irony Strachey proceeded to artistic aesthetics, and, in his *Elizabeth and Essex*, attempted to serve up to the British public a queen more in keeping with their imperial hearts than one who was completely wrapped up in her world of industrial capitalism.

Thus did the liberal aestheticism of Bloomsbury reach the season of moulting; its ironical feathers disappeared and the world beheld it in a banal senile coat of imperialist worship of 'greatness' and 'grandeur' and 'the picturesque'. But then, that end was only to be expected, since the cultured leisure of those enlightened children of the bourgeoisie is ensured them by what shekels come in from colonial and other dependent lands.

F.R. Leavis

F.R. Leavis, 'Keynes, Lawrence and Cambridge', reprinted from The Common Pursuit *(Chatto & Windus, 1953), 255–60, by permission of the author and Chatto & Windus;* © *1952 by F.R. Leavis and reprinted by permission of New York University Press.*
F.R. Leavis, Keynes and Currency Values, *reprinted from 'Keynes, Spender and Currency Values,'* Scrutiny *XVIII (June, 1951), 50–6. By*

Permission of Dr Leavis and The Cambridge University Press.

[The most persistent and perhaps the most influential criticism of Bloomsbury has come, not unsurprisingly, from Cambridge. Dr F.R. Leavis, his wife Q.D. Leavis, and a number of contributors to their quarterly *Scrutiny* have vigorously criticized Bloomsbury, its books and its influence, for more than twenty years.

Although the Leavises and their followers have attacked the entire 'Bloomsbury ethos', they have also discriminated between the significance of various members. Leavis, for example, finds a 'real and very fine distinction' in E.M. Forster's fiction, but Forster's criticism is marred by the impact of Bloomsbury. Lytton Strachey is clearly the vilest of the Bloomsberries for the Leavises and *Scrutiny*. Virginia Woolf also comes off rather badly, except in *To the Lighthouse*, which Q.D. Leavis once called 'a beautifully constructed work of art' and which F.R. Leavis designated as her only good novel. In the very first issue of *Scrutiny* Virginia Woolf was censured for 'some cerebral etiolation' in her novels; ten years later Leavis reviewed her career, and said this about her relation to Bloomsbury:

> She belonged, of course, to the original Bloomsbury, the Bloomsbury of Clive Bell's *Civilization* and Lytton Strachey's wit (some of her essays are in his cheapest manner, and one can seldom feel quite safe from the communal note). A *milieu* that so often reminds us of its potency in the work of as distinguished a writer as E.M. Forster must be held accountable for a great deal in the development – or failure to develop – of Virginia Woolf.

But the most ferocious attack on Virginia Woolf is to be found in Q.D. Leavis's 'Caterpillars of the Commonwealth Unite!' – a review of the feminist polemic *Three Guineas*. Virginia Woolf's class assumptions about educated women and her scepticism about the use of teaching literature enraged Mrs Leavis, a professional teacher of literature and an educated woman whose class experience was different from Virginia Woolf's. In addition to its personal bitterness (Virginia Woolf is mocked for being childless), Mrs Leavis's response is also surprisingly conservative in its conclusion that for more female emancipation, 'the onus is on women to prove that they are going to be able to justify it, and that it will not vitally dislocate ... the framework of our culture'.

Q.D. Leavis's reaction to a 1937 lecture that Desmond MacCarthy gave in Cambridge on Leslie Stephen is almost as fierce as her review of

Three Guineas. MacCarthy had praised Stephen's moral strengths as a literary critic but had criticized his aesthetic limitations; life was more important than art in Stephen's judgment of literature. Mrs Leavis believed this was as it should be, and she called MacCarthy's lecture 'an insolent performance'. A Sunday reviewer, a modern representative of the decadent nineties' aesthetes, had presumed to pass judgment on a great Victorian critic. There is an important disagreement about the function of criticism here, but it is nearly obscured by the polemical form of Mrs Leavis's review. What is clear from much of the Leavises's criticism of Bloomsbury, however, is that they wished to save Leslie Stephen and the Cambridge intellectual tradition he represented from his descendants and admirers. Thus F.R. Leavis finds *To the Lighthouse* interesting not because of Virginia Woolf's art but because of its autobiographical depiction of Leslie Stephen's family life.

In Q.D. Leavis's attacks on Virginia Woolf and Desmond MacCarthy, Bloomsbury is only implicitly damned. In the best known of F.R. Leavis's criticisms of Bloomsbury, however, the brunt is born by the Group itself. Leavis's most interesting criticism of Bloomsbury is directed not against a novelist or a critic but an economist who was also a Cambridge don. In the two pieces that follow Leavis discusses J.M. Keynes as an example of what is wrong about Bloomsbury. As with Q.D. Leavis's attacks, there is a marked class-consciousness in the criticism that reinforces the fundamentally moral objection that the Leavises had against Bloomsbury. In their view, the lives and works of the members of the Bloomsbury Group lacked an essential moral seriousness. Leavis's first article is a review of Keynes's *My Early Beliefs* (see pp.48–64); Leavis argues here for the importance of D.H. Lawrence's criticism of Cambridge and Bloomsbury – an importance that Keynes for all his intelligence did not understand. The second piece is a discussion of R.F. Harrod's biography of Keynes, which Leavis reviewed in *Scrutiny* along with Stephen Spender's auto-biography. After commenting on the uncritical reviews of Spender's book, Leavis generalizes on the state of criticism and reviewing that has resulted from Bloomsbury's 'coterie power', and this leads on to a discussion of Keynes's and Bloomsbury's values.]

Keynes, Lawrence and Cambridge

For the repugnance felt by Lawrence towards Mr David Garnett's friends, and the Cambridge-Bloomsbury milieu in general, Mr Garnett

has a simple explanation: jealousy. 'He was a prophet who hated all
those whose creeds protected them from ever becoming his disciples.'
That Lawrence had gifts, Mr Garnett readily perceived. In fact, he has
'never met a writer who appeared to have such genius. I greatly
admired, and still admire, his short stories, his poems and several of his
novels, particularly his first novel, *The White Peacock*'. (So, by way of
paying one's tribute to James, one might say: 'Yes, tremendous! I
particularly admire *The American*.' Or, a greater genius being in
question: 'I particularly admire *Two Gentlemen of Verona*'). 'But', Mr
Garnett continues,

> I was a rationalist and a scientist, and I was repelled by his intuitive
> and dogmatic philosophy, whereas the ideas of my friends from
> Cambridge interested and attracted me.
>   It was thus inevitable that sooner or later Lawrence would spew
> me out of his mouth, since I could never take his philosophy
> seriously.

Keynes too, attempting his own explanation, invokes jealousy. But he
feels that more is needed. His Memoir (the second of the pair that Mr
Garnett introduces) is a piece of retrospective self-searching in which he
asks whether he and his friends may not have provided Lawrence with
some valid grounds for judging them adversely. Keynes, no one will
question, was a distinguished mind, and the distinction is there,
perhaps, in the very effort at self-criticism and a due humility. But the
significance of what he offers is not what he is conscious of; it lies in
the inadequacy of the effort, and in the justification he brings
Lawrence when he least intends it, or suspects it.
    The virtually intact complacency he exposes to our view gives us, at
the outset, the assumptions on which the inquiry is to proceed: 'But
when all that has been said, was there something true and right in what
Lawrence felt?' The 'but' leaves the assumptions with us as implicitly
granted, following as it does on this:

> Lawrence was jealous of the other lot; and Cambridge rationalism
> and cynicism, then at their height, were, of course, repulsive to him.
> Bertie gave him what must have been, I think, his first glimpse of
> Cambridge. It overwhelmed, attracted and repulsed him – which was
> the other emotional disturbance. It was obviously a civilization, and
> not less obviously uncomfortable and unattainable for him – very
> repulsive and very attractive.

'It was obviously a civilization' – shocked as the provincial and puritanical Lawrence must inevitably have been, he 'obviously' can't but have admired and envied. That Lawrence, judging out of his experience of something incomparably more worthy to be called a 'civilization', loathed and despised what was in front of him merely because he saw just what it was, is inconceivable to Keynes.

The Memoir is devoted to explaining the serious substance underlying the 'brittle stuff' of the conversation in which Lawrence couldn't be brought to join. Such 'brittle stuff' continued, even in the maturer years of the *élite*, to be a large part of the 'civilization' – at least one gathers so from the way in which Keynes (it is 1938) announces his theme:

> if it will not shock the Club too much, I should like in this contribution to its proceedings to introduce for once mental or spiritual, instead of sexual, adventures, to try and recall the principal impacts on one's virgin mind and to wonder how it has all turned out, and whether one still holds by that youthful religion.

The 'religion' was derived from G.E. Moore, and the Memoir is largely taken up with describing his influence. 'Influence' here, of course, means what was made of him, not in any field of disciplined study, but at the level of undergraduate 'civilization'. That Moore himself deserves the high terms in which Keynes speaks of him no one will wish to question. But the 'influence' – I well remember the exasperated despair with which its manifestations (in mild forms, I now see) filled me when I met them, just after the 1914 war, in friendly seniors who had been formed in that climate at the beginning of the century. Keynes, looking back, describes the intellectualities of the coterie and its religion with a certain amused irony; but it is not the detached irony of a mature valuation. Still in 1938 he takes them seriously; he sees them, not as illustrating a familiar undergraduate phase which should in any case be left behind as soon as possible, and which the most intelligent men should escape, but as serious and admirable – even, it would seem, when cultivated well beyond undergraduate years. And that is what seems to me most significant in the Memoir, and most revelatory of the Cambridge-Bloomsbury ethos.

Of course, Keynes criticizes the 'religion' for deficiencies and errors. But he can't see that, 'seriously' as it took itself, to be inimical to the development of any real seriousness was its essence. Articulateness and unreality cultivated together; callowness disguised from itself in

articulateness; conceit casing itself safely in a confirmed sense of high
sophistication; the uncertainty as to whether one is serious or not
taking itself for ironic poise: who has not at some time observed the
process?

It did not prevent us from laughing most of the time and we enjoyed
supreme self-confidence, superiority and contempt towards all the
rest of the unconverted world.

Broadly speaking we all knew for certain what were good states
of mind and that they consisted in communion with objects of love,
beauty and truth.

And Keynes describes the dialectical play ('It was a stringent
education in dialectic', he tells us) that was to merge into, and, one
gathers, was ultimately superseded by, the more 'brittle
stuff' — describes it whimsically, but without in the least realizing that
what he and his friends were illustrating was the power of an ancient
university, in some of its climatic pockets, to arrest development, and
that what they were finding in their intellectual performances was
sanction and reinforcement for an undergraduate immaturity: the more
confident they grew in their sophistication, the less chance had they of
discovering what seriousness was like.

The more worldly sophistication that Lawrence encountered in 1914
was not a more genuine maturity. One can readily imagine how the
incontinently flippant talk and the shiny complacency, snub-proof in
its obtuse completeness, infuriated him. He loathed the flippancy, not
because he was an inexperienced prude, but for quite opposite reasons.
He had been formed in a working-class culture, in which intellectual
interests were bound up with the social life of home and chapel, and
never out of touch with the daily business of ensuring the supply of the
daily bread. The intellectual interests were not the less real for that:
E.T.'s *D.H. Lawrence*, taken together with *Sons and Lovers*, shows
what an intense cultivation they had enjoyed during the formative years
at Eastwood and Nottingham. Nothing could be more ludicrously wide
of the mark than the assumption that Lawrence must have felt inferior
and ill-educated when introduced in Russell's rooms to the dazzling
civilization of Cambridge. But the thing to stress is his enormous
advantage in experience. The young ex-elementary school-teacher was
in a position to judge of the most distinguished intellectual among his
friends, as he does in a letter of a year or so later: 'What ails Russel is,

in matters of life and emotion, the inexperience of youth . . . It isn't
that life has been too much for him, but too little.' Keynes, looking
back, does of course criticize the 'religion' for certain defects that fall
under inexperience. He says that, in its account of human nature, it
ignored the formidable part of the irrational forces, and ignored at the
same time 'certain powerful and valuable springs of feeling'. But his
criticisms have a way of not being able to realize the weight they ought
to carry and the depth to which they ought to strike. 'We lacked
reverence, as Lawrence observed . . .' Keynes endorses, as he thinks, this
radical criticism. But what it means to him is just this and no more
(damaging enough by itself, of course):

> We had no respect for traditional wisdom or the restraints of
> custom . . . It did not occur to any of us to respect the extraordinary
> accomplishment of our predecessors in the ordering of life (as it now
> seems to me to have been) or the elaborate framework they had
> devised to protect this order.

How little Keynes can understand the full force of Lawrence's criticism
he shows when he explains what he calls the 'individualism of our
philosophy'.

> Now what we got from Moore was by no means entirely what he
> offered us. He had one foot on the threshold of the new heaven, but
> the other foot in Sidgwick and the Benthamite calculus and the
> general rules of correct behaviour. We accepted Moore's religion, so
> to speak, and discarded his morals.

> . . . we were amongst the first of our generation, perhaps alone
> amongst our generation, to escape from the Benthamite tradition. In
> practice, of course . . . the outside world was not forgotten or
> forsworn.

> Moreover, it was this escape from Bentham, joined with the
> unsurpassable individualism of our philosophy, which has served to
> protect the whole lot of us from the final *reductio ad absurdum* of
> Benthamism known as Marxism . . . But we ourselves have remained
> . . . altogether immune from the virus, as safe in the citadel of our
> ultimate faith as the Pope of Rome in his.

These extracts illustrate how seriously Keynes takes the 'civilization'

that must, he is sure, have impressed the 'ignorant, jealous, irritable'
Lawrence. The 'unsurpassable individualism of our philosophy' — call
the ethos evoked in the Memoir *that*, while granting that the
'philosophy' had weaknesses, and it becomes possible for Keynes to
conclude that 'this religion of ours was a very good one to grow up
under'. And it becomes possible for him to suggest that the Club-
members would have been more subject to the infection of Marxism if
they had been at all seriously affected by the spirit of Sidgwick. But
what Lawrence heard was the levity of so many petty egos, each primed
with conscious cleverness and hardened in self-approval: 'they talk
endlessly, but endlessly — and never, never a good thing said. They are
cased each in a hard little shell of his own and out of this they talk
words. There is never for one second any outgoing of feeling and no
reverence, not a crumb or grain of reverence: I cannot stand it.'

The kind of triviality that Lawrence describes here is indeed a worse
thing than Keynes was able to conceive it. And the significant fact that
emerges unmistakably from the Memoir is that he couldn't really grasp
the intention of the criticism he was considering. It is a fact that would
seem substantially to confirm Lawrence.

If this judgment seems too severe, let it be remembered that the
'civilization' celebrated by Keynes produced Lytton Strachey, and that
the literary world dominated by that 'civilization' made Lytton
Strachey a living Master and a prevailing influence. And if I should seem
to be making too much here of facts belonging to the history of taste
and literary fashion, I suggest a pondering of these comments which I
take from a review by Sir Charles Webster (he is dealing at the moment
with the other of the two memoirs in Keynes's book):

> Keynes let me read it in 1943, and its facts were then checked
> against the documents which record — in very different prose — the
> public incidents which it relates. They were accurate enough, as I
> told him at the time. But the details were of course selected and
> distorted to suit his purpose.

> These characterizations are of course caricatures. Keynes put
> down what suited his purpose at the moment. In this ruthless
> sacrifice of truth to literary purpose he was obviously much
> influenced by Lytton Strachey, whose popular books depended on
> little else. The political caricatures of the *Economic Consequences*
> did as much harm as the economic insight did good.

Keynes was a great representative Cambridge man of his time. Cambridge produced him, as it produced the 'civilization' with which he associated himself and which exercised so strong a sway over the metropolitan centres of taste and fashion. Can we imagine Sidgwick or Leslie Stephen or Maitland being influenced by, or interested in, the equivalent of Lytton Strachey? By what steps, and by the operation of what causes, did so great a change come over Cambridge in so comparatively short a time? These are the questions that we find ourselves once more asking as we put down Keynes's little book. The inquiry into which the second would lead, if seriously pursued, would tell us about a great deal more than Cambridge. That is a reason for thinking it very much worth undertaking.

Keynes and Currency Values

. . . The process of mass civilization that, by 1930, had so drastically reduced the number of critical organs and thus virtually abrogated the standards of criticism (for standards of criticism can have their effective existence only in an educated public that can make itself felt, as none can if there are not a considerable number of reviews, maintaining a large corps of intelligent and disinterested critics) – these reductive processes need not be discussed here. (Consider how different from what we have to contemplate now was that past state of affairs which we can deduce from R.G. Cox's article in the present (Vol. XVIII, No 1) *Scrutiny*. But it may still be wondered that there should have been, apparently, so little sense of what was happening, no protest, no note of scandal; certainly no resistance in places where one might have expected to find it. Can, for instance, so distinguished an intellectual as the Editor of *The Criterion*, assisting at the stultification of his work as poet and critic, have been as unaware as all that? Was it unawareness, or a sense that resistance was vain, and acquiescence a natural and inevitable course? In such a state of things the distinction is not a sharp one.

And about the 'state of things' it has to be said further at this point that, in the literary world, there was already an established tradition of coterie power, and of coterie power as a dazzling, creditable and proper thing. It was a tradition that, in ways more and less subtle, tended to countenance the intrusion of social and personal values into the field of criticism. In fact, not only conscience, but consciousness, in these matters had been gravely weakened. For an editor to attempt, in his review, to vindicate the function of criticism would have been to deserve the odium due to a gratuitous and most offensive moral heroism.

It is here that a consideration of the second book given at the head of this review becomes immediately relevant. Keynes, as Mr Harrod shows us, had a major share in the formation of 'Bloomsbury', belonged to it throughout his life, and was a main source of its strength. In fact, Mr Harrod shows us a Keynes who was the most formidable promoter of the coterie spirit that modern England has know. To say this of Keynes is to pay tribute to the great gifts that made him formidable. These are not in question – his gifts as economist, logician and financial speculator. But Mr Harrod credits him also with an all-round distinction; with gifts that qualified him to be a shaping and determining influence in the field of the humanities, and to be trusted, as a supreme intelligence, judging confidently and authoritatively, with the responsibilities of an enormously powerful patron. In this Mr Harrod pays an unconscious and revealing tribute to the power of the coterie influence, to which, as he tells us in his Preface, he enjoyed an early exposure: 'By good luck . . . I was brought into touch with a number of members of the "Bloomsbury" circle when I was a young man in the twenties. They made a sharp and indelible impression on my mind.'

He is – and in the very arts he practises in his book – an artless and admirable witness to what 'Bloomsbury' essentially was. He tells us, for instance (and it is an interesting minor contribution to English cultural history), that Lytton Strachey went before going to Cambridge to Liverpool University, drawn by the presence of Sir Walter Raleigh,

> whose influence was important. It is pleasant to think that Raleigh's beautiful dry humour was not lost upon Strachey. Raleigh was in the van of a shift of critical values [he asserted, we recall, Shakespeare's moral neutrality]. Cultivated persons of the late-Victorian period were no doubt well-read in our earlier masterpieces, but they were inclined to be over-zealous in their admiration of the Victorian pontiffs . . .

– it is plain that Raleigh's notion of style, too, was not lost upon Strachey.

But the point to be made is that Keynes's distinction was confined to the field in which he was a professional. Where he was an amateur, though he took with him his characteristic high confidence, he was a mere amateur; as critic, man of taste and humanist he reflected the taste, idiom and assumptions of the very inferior coterie *milieu* to which he belonged. 'And they gained, too, from his resources of knowledge and worldly contact. He was their main pillar of strength, their financial adviser, their patron. He was always ready to help, in one way or another, to promote their material interests.' That so distinguished and influential a man should have been formed by such a *milieu*, and should have used his power and his prestige to confirm its dominance and propagate its ethos, is a fact of some historical importance in relation to the matters discussed in the first part of this review.

We can see it to have been a significant moment in the history, not only of Cambridge, but of modern English culture, when, at the turn of the century, at the time of Keynes's going up to King's from Eton, the coterie had its start, and the character of the *milieu* began to define itself. It might be asked why the coterie should have been so inferior. Without offering to explain in any ultimate sense, one may say something about the nature and conditions of the inferiority. The group of young men, mainly King's and Trinity, that Mr Harrod describes, a group having in its connection with the famous 'Society', intimate contacts at more senior levels, and a continuity with an illustrious intellectual tradition, obviously contained some real distinction as well as a good deal of academic — and academic-social — brilliance. But there is something about the constitutive ethos of the *milieu* that the intellectual distinction and the continuity from the past make the more ominous. We have it here, in Keynes's attitude to a representative great Cambridge man of the immediate past (the letter is dated 1906)·

Have you read Sidgwick's Life? Very interesting and depressing . . . He never did anything but wonder whether Christianity was true and prove that it wasn't and hope that it was . . .

I wonder what he would have thought of us; and I wonder what we think of him. And then his conscience — incredible. There is no doubt about his moral goodness. And yet it is all so dreadfully depressing — no intimacy, no clear-cut boldness.

We can guess well enough what Sidgwick would have thought of Lytton Strachey. And an *élite* of young Cambridge minds that could find the ethos of Lytton Strachey more congenial than that of Henry Sidgwick was certainly a significantly new thing. But of course the name to be set

over against Sidgwick's is that of G.E. Moore (the following was also
written in 1906):

> It is *impossible* to exaggerate the wonder and *originality* of Moore;
> people are already beginning to talk as if he were only a kind of
> logic-chopping eclectic. Oh why can't they see!
>   How amazing to think that we and only we know the rudiments
> of a true theory of ethic; for nothing can be more certain than that
> the broad outline is true . . . I even begin to agree with Moore about
> Sidgwick — that he was a wicked edifactious person.

That Moore was, in his very limited way, a disinterested mind and
innocent spirit made him the more irresistibly the very sanction they
needed. 'The supreme values of life', writes Mr Harrod, summarizing
Moore's teaching, 'were the states of consciousness involved in human
relations and in the appreciation of beauty.' This congenial doctrine
(Keynes himself in the late 'Memoir'[1] notes what it left out) was
enforced in an austere logic which lent itself to deployment in a kind of
coterie dialectic. Thus the apostles were able to take a fixed and
complacent immaturity in themselves for something very different; to
associate an inveterate triviality with a suggestion of intellectual
distinction and moral idealism — with, in fact, a kind of unction.

Their devotion to their 'specific image of what is meant by the idea
of the good life' was 'sustained, no doubt,' says Mr Harrod, 'by certain
elements of unearned income'. The immediate point to be made is that
it was sustained by other 'unearned elements'; by an unrecognized
legacy of other than money-values (essentially unrecognized, as comes
out in the attitude to Sidgwick). It is all in the natural course of things
that a 'civilization' of this kind ('it was certainly a civilization,' says
Keynes in that late 'Memoir'), conscious of a high distinction of
refinement, should run not only to thinness and 'brittleness' (Keynes's
word for a characteristic kind of coterie talk), but to pretentious
cheapness and to something one can only call vulgarity (consider, in
their different ways, Lytton Strachey and Rupert Brooke).

As for the 'elements of unearned income', they need not, we know,
of themselves have involved the Bloomsbury idea of the good life. Quite
different moral, intellectual and practical habits ('civilizations') have
been sustained by 'elements of unearned income'. And a glance may be
given here at Mrs Keynes's recent very interesting account of Maynard's
education.[2] When he went to Eton, it was arranged, she tells us, that he
should be supplied with white ties by the gross, so that he should be

able to wear a new one every day, and when he was elected to College Pop, an order was placed with a local florist to deliver daily a fresh button-hole. A small matter, perhaps, but highly significant. It tells us a great deal about one aspect, at least, of what may be called his ethical education. The significance becomes the more apparent when we recall that Mrs Keynes's father was the minister of the Bunyan chapel (and the descent on the other side was in the same religious tradition). With such a background, an education in the belief that one belongs to a highly privileged oligarchy, and has a natural right to the best of everything ('best' being interpreted as it is in Vanity Fair), inevitably tended to produce in Keynes the result that we actually see.

Explaining why Keynes devoted his genius to financial speculation, and 'went deeply in' ('on a narrow margin of cover'), Mr Harrod tells us:

He was determined not to relapse into salaried drudgery. He must be financially independent. He felt that he had that in him which would justify such independence. He had many things to tell the nation. And he wanted a sufficiency. He must be able to take stalls at the Russian ballet whenever he wished – and entertain the dancers, if that struck his fancy. He must be able to buy his friends' pictures – and pay them handsomely. These other dealers in money merely squandered their earnings on banal conventional luxuries. He must use his brains to put some of their money into his pocket, where it would fructify not only financially, but in supporting the people who really mattered, and in giving his own powers scope.

The rejected 'salaried drudgery' was university teaching. Ah! but with the harvest of speculation he supported the arts, bought his friends' pictures, and bought other pictures too – with great acuteness for (though Mr Harrod reports the suspicion that he 'was never deeply moved by visual art') he left what turned out to be an extremely valuable private collection. And here what is to-day widely known as the Puritanic note has to be struck (a note of simple matter-of-fact moral observation to the minister of the Bunyan chapel). It regards an inevitable relation between the use for 'good' of the resources so amassed and the spirit of the amassing, the conception of the good life that encouraged it and throve on it.

'This exclusive Cambridge circle', writes Mr R.H.S. Crossman, reviewing the book in the *Universities Quarterly* for May, 'gave him the poise of an intellectual oligarch, who could afford to be condemned as inconsistent and irresponsible by the vulgar, so long as his peers recognized that he was acting according to their esoteric code.' That is an admirable way of describing Keynes's peculiar formidableness as a promoter of the coterie spirit. Even in the field of economics, where Keynes's relevant authority and his informed concern for standards are unquestioned, this spirit had, as Mr Harrod recognizes, some unfortunate consequences. 'The formation of a coterie', Mr Harrod ventures, 'may be valuable to sustain the courage of those whose work is in the realm of the imagination. But [he adds] Keynes may have tended to apply a helpful expedient in a sphere where it was inappropriate.' The evidence that Mr Harrod gives is of a spirit that has to be resisted as mischievous anywhere; that it should have got even into the sphere where Keynes was a specialist has a sinister significance for the present inquiry: ' "But there isn't anyone else," they said.' Mr Harrod intimates, deferentially, that this conviction was ill founded, and worked harm for economics.

'Really, you know, there isn't anyone else': a good deal earlier in the book he has reported this as the note of 'Bloomsbury' ('outsiders were neglected'). How could something of that spirit, and of the stultifying confusion of values that, at best, it must involve, *not* manifest itself in the patronage and the influence, the use of financial resources for 'good', made possible by Keynes's addiction to speculation?

'He maintained', says Mr Harrod of the (then) Bursar of King's, 'his interest in the quest for choice spirits in each new generation, for young men of intellect and sensibility who would carry on the traditions of his own undergraduate days ... and he gave them an *entrée* into Bloomsbury.' Though we are left in no doubt that the recruitment referred to here is not to be understood as having been merely of economists, we are not forbidden to suppose that it may have entailed academic status: in this region Mr Harrod sees no need to insist on distinctions, and the completeness with which he assumes that the criteria of 'Bloomsbury' are the unquestioned criteria of 'intellect and sensibility' reflects the completeness of the identification he found in the milieu on which Keynes conferred such power and influence. (If only one might quote – but no! one mustn't – Mr Harrod's account of his own introduction at Keynes's college! But there is much amusing and eloquent evidence of that kind in the book.)

To revert now to the questions provoked by the consideration of Mr Spender's book: How could there be such an absence of protest, of apparent resistance and sense of scandal, when the Fellow-travellers of the Poetical Renascence, in the early thirties, took possession of the organs of criticism? How could the illustriously edited *Criterion* lend itself so easily (it would appear) and so incongruously?

Considering these questions we can see what there is to be said with immediate relevance about Keynes's place in history. It is not (at least, it is not there the stress falls at the moment) that he promoted, in the cultural realm, the 'Bloomsbury' idea of the good life, or the ethos of any particular milieu, but that he promoted in enormously influential ways the habit of substituting the social-personal values for the relevant ones. If, on the one hand, belonging to a highly dominant intellectual and social milieu, you use your power and prestige to slight the essential intellectual standards and to discredit the notion of critical conscience, and, on the other, to give respectability and sanction to the natural human weakness for replacing the real standards by personal and coterie considerations, then you may be fairly credited with having helped substantially to bring about the state of things revealed in Mr Spender's autobiography. And it has to be remembered that the literary-intellectual 'world' was a small one, and that the parts of it not dominated from the axis Eton-King's-Bloomsbury-and-the-relevant-weekly couldn't matter much.

Today the triumph of the social-personal (or 'club', we may now call it) principle is complete. The club is not narrowly exclusive, but you must belong (and keep the rules) if you are to be recognized to exist. And if the club is not narrowly exclusive, the system of relations by which it controls the organs and institutions through which the currency-values are established and circulated is comprehensive and complete. The completeness with which the notions of criticism, critical principle and critical standard have been superseded was demonstrated when, a year or so ago, a note was printed in this journal pointing out the lack of obvious suitability in the judges for the Festival of Britain Poetry Prizes: there was genuine scandalized indignation in many quarters, including some that couldn't be thought of as being anything but disinterested. *That* kind of thing is inexcusable and unpardonable.

Yet now the prizes have been awarded, we find as respectable a newspaper as the *Manchester Guardian* reporting discouragement and dismay, and asking whether, with such a lack of obvious felicity in the appointment of judges, awards more calculated to promote life in English Poetry could have been expected. But the question that should be asked is whether, when things have got into the state in which they are now, the kind of encouragement of the arts from which Keynes hoped so much, that represented by the Arts Council, can really, in sum, do anything but encourage and strengthen the system referred to above – the system that, in literature at any rate, makes the restoring of the critical function (and so the recovery of a public) impossible.

Notes

1. *Two Memoirs by J.M. Keynes*, reviewed in *Scrutiny* Vol. XVI, No. 3, under the title *Keynes, Lawrence and Cambridge*. [see pp.389–95]
2. *Gathering up the Threads*, by Florence Ada Keynes (Heffer).

Bertrand Russell

Bertrand Russell, *Portraits from Memory: Keynes and Strachey*
E.M. Forster, *Reply to Russell*

Reprinted from The Listener *48 (17th July, 1952), 97–8 and 48 (24th July, 1952), 142, with permission of George Allen & Unwin Ltd., the Atlantic Monthly Press, and The Society of Authors on behalf of the estate of E.M. Forster.*

[Bertrand Russell is sometimes loosely grouped with Bloomsbury. His Cambridge education brought him close to a number of the members of the Group, particularly those who were Apostles. Russell's criticisms of J.M. Keynes and Lytton Strachey are therefore especially interesting. In criticizing Keynes, Russell accepts the interpretation of Moore's influence given in *My Early Beliefs* (see pp.48–64) and qualified by another Apostle, Leonard Woolf (see p.101 ff). Russell's severe judgment of Strachey is one of the few serious criticisms of him by a contemporary who knew him fairly well – and that is why E.M. Forster's rejoinder is so relevant.

Russell's recollections of Keynes and Strachey were the second of a series of 'portraits from memory' that he did for the BBC and then collected into a book in 1956. Curiously, the portrait of Keynes and Strachey was the only broadcast omitted from the collection – perhaps because of Forster's objections. But when Russell published the first volume of his autobiography in 1967, however, he included the portrait almost unchanged and went on to suggest that after his time The Apostles 'changed in one respect. There was a long drawn out battle between George Trevelyan and Lytton Strachey, both members, in which Lytton Strachey was on the whole victorious. Since his time, homosexual relations among the members were for a time common, but in my day they were unknown.' (For a different version of this battle, see p.191.) A recently published letter of Russell's to Lady Ottoline

Morrell (see p.49) indicates that 'sodomy' was one of the issues that Russell differed from Keynes and Strachey over.

Russell received the Order of Merit in 1950, and his talk was published in *The Listner* under the by-line 'Bertrand Russell, OM'.]

Bertrand Russell: *Portraits from Memory: Keynes and Strachey*

Keynes and Lytton Strachey both belonged to the Cambridge generation about ten years junior to my own. It is surprising how great a change in the mental climate those ten years had brought. We were still Victorian; they were Edwardian. We believed in ordered progress by means of politics and free discussion; the more self-confident among us may have hoped to be leaders of the multitude, but none of us wished to be divorced from it. The generation of Keynes and Lytton did not seek to preserve any kinship with the Philistine. They aimed rather at a life of retirement among fine shades and nice feelings, and conceived of the good as consisting in the passionate mutual admirations of a clique of the *élite*. This doctrine, quite unfairly, they fathered upon the philosopher G.E. Moore, whose disciples they professed to be. Keynes, in his memoir *Early Beliefs*, has told of their admiration for Moore and also, of their practice of ignoring large parts of Moore's doctrine. Moore gave due weight to morals and by the part of his doctrine that treated of organic unities avoided the view that the good consists of a series of isolated passionate moments, but those who considered themselves his disciples ignored this aspect of his teaching and degraded his ethics into advocacy of a stuffy girls'-school sentimentalizing.

From this atmosphere Keynes escaped into the great world, but Strachey never escaped. Keynes' escape, however, was not complete. He went about the world carrying with him everywhere a feeling of the bishop *in partibus*. True salvation was elsewhere, among the faithful at Cambridge. When he concerned himself with politics and economics he left his soul at home. This is the reason for a certain hard, glittering, inhuman quality in most of his writing. There was one great exception, *The Economic Consequences of the Peace*, of which I shall have more to say in a moment.

I first knew Keynes through his father, and Lytton Strachey through his mother. When I was young, Keynes' father taught old-fashioned formal logic in Cambridge. I do not know how far the new developments in that subject altered his teaching. He was an earnest non-conformist who put morality first and logic second. Something of

the non-conformist spirit remained in his son, but it was overlaid by the
realization that facts and arguments may lead to conclusions somewhat
shocking to many people, and a strain of intellectual arrogance in his
character made him find it not unpleasant to *épater les bourgeois*. In his
Economic Consequences of the Peace this strain was in abeyance. The
profound conviction that the Treaty of Versailles spelt disaster so
roused the earnest moralist in him that he forgot to be clever —
without, however, ceasing to be so.

I had no contact with him in his economic and political work, but I
was considerably concerned in his *Treatise on Probability*, many parts
of which I discussed with him in detail. It was nearly finished in 1914,
but had to be put aside for the duration. He was always inclined to
overwork, in fact it was overwork that caused his death. Once, in the
year 1904, when I was living in an isolated cottage on a vast moor
without roads, he wrote and asked if I could promise him a restful
week-end. I replied confidently in the affirmative, and he came. Within
five minutes of his arrival the Vice-Chancellor turned up full of
University business. Other people came unexpectedly to every meal,
including six to Sunday breakfast. By Monday morning we had had
twenty-six unexpected guests, and Keynes, I fear, went away more tired
than he came. On Sunday, 2nd August 1914, I met him hurrying across
the Great Court of Trinity. I asked him what the hurry was and he said
he wanted to borrow his brother-in-law's motor-cycle to go to London.
'Why don't you go by train?' I said. 'Because there isn't time', he
replied. I did not know what his business might be, but within a few
days the bank rate, which panic-mongers had put up to ten per cent,
was reduced to five per cent. This was his doing.

I do not know enough economics to have an expert opinion on
Keynes' theories, but so far as I am able to judge it seems to me to be
owing to him that Britain has not suffered from large-scale unemployment in recent years. I would go further and say that if his theories had
been adopted by financial authorities throughout the world the great
depression would not have occurred. There are still many people in
America who regard depressions as acts of God. I think Keynes proved
that the responsibility for these occurrences does not rest with
Providence.

The last time that I saw him was in the House of Lords when he
returned from negotiating a loan in America and made a masterly
speech recommending it to their Lordships. Many of them had been
doubtful beforehand, but when he had finished there remained hardly
any doubters except Lord Beaverbrook and two cousins of mine with a

passion for being in the minority. Having only just landed from the Atlantic, the effort he made must have been terrific, and it proved too much for him.

Keynes' intellect was the sharpest and clearest that I have ever known. Annihilating arguments darted out of him with the swiftness of an adder's tongue. When I argued with him, I felt that I took my life in my hands, and I seldom emerged without feeling something of a fool. I was sometimes inclined to think that so much cleverness must be incompatible with depth, but I do not think this feeling was justified.

Lytton Strachey, as mentioned before, I first got to know through his mother. She and I were fellow members of a committee designed to secure votes for women. After some months she invited me to dinner. Her husband, Sir Richard Strachey, was a retired Indian official, and the British Raj was very much in the air. My first dinner with the family was a rather upsetting experience. The number of sons and daughters was almost beyond computation, and all the children were to my unpractised eyes exactly alike except in the somewhat superficial point that some were male and some were female. The family were not all assembled when I arrived, but dropped in one by one at intervals of twenty minutes. (One of them, I afterwards discovered, was Lytton.) I had to look round the room carefully to make sure that it was a new one that had appeared and not merely one of the previous ones that had changed his or her place. Towards the end of the evening I began to doubt my sanity, but kind friends afterwards assured me that things had really been as they seemed.

Lady Strachey was a woman of immense vigour, with a great desire that some at least of her children should distinguish themselves. She had an admirable sense of prose and used to read South's sermons aloud to her children, not for the matter (she was a freethinker), but to give them a sense of rhythm in the writing of English. Lytton, who was too delicate to be long at school, was seen by his mother to be brilliant and was brought up to the career of a writer in an atmosphere of dedication. His writing appeared to me in those days hilariously amusing. I heard him read *Eminent Victorians* before it was published, and I read it again to myself in prison. It caused me to laugh so loud that the officer came round to my cell, saying I must remember that prison is a place of punishment.

Lytton was always eccentric and became gradually more so. When he was growing a beard he gave out that he had measles so as not to be seen by his friends until the hairs had reached a respectable length. He dressed very oddly. I knew a farmer's wife who let lodgings and she told me that Lytton had come to ask her if she could take him in. 'At first, sir', she said, 'I thought he was a tramp, and then I looked again and saw he was a gentleman, but a very queer one.' He talked always in a squeaky voice which sometimes contrasted ludicrously with the matter of what he was saying. One time when I was talking with him he objected first to one thing and then to another as not being what literature should aim at. At last I said, 'Well, Lytton, what should it aim at?' And he replied in one word — 'Passion'. Nevertheless, he liked to appear lordly in his attitude towards human affairs. I heard someone maintain in his presence that young people are apt to think about life. He objected, 'I can't believe people think about life. There's nothing in it'. Perhaps it was this attitude which made him not a great man.

His style is unduly rhetorical, and sometimes, in malicious moments, I have thought it not unlike Macaulay's. He was indifferent to historical truth and would always touch up the picture to make the lights and shades more glaring and the folly or wickedness of famous people more obvious. These are grave charges, but I make them in all seriousness.

E.M. Forster: *Reply to Russell*

Sir,
    I am more or less of Lord Russell's generation. I too am a Victorian. All the same I wish to protest against his ungenerous account of Lytton Strachey in his 'Portraits from Memory'. That he should find Strachey's personality uncongenial and his books unsatisfactory is understandable, but why ever does he want to reminisce about him? Could he find no one else? Surely it is better to forget a man whom one dislikes and thinks unimportant rather than to pursue him with unfriendliness twenty years after his death.
    It is true that Strachey was clever, although not as clever as Lord Russell, and it is also true that cleverness alone cannot make a man great. But there was more than cleverness in his case. There was the passion which shone through his work and made it vivid. There was his admirable style — it never reminded me of Macaulay's though I should not have sneered at it if it had. There was a certain historical power; the accuracy of *Queen Victoria* has, I believe, not been seriously impugned; *Elizabeth and Essex* is inaccurate but is in other ways his greatest work. There was, of course, his sense of humour, and, equally important but frequently forgotten, there was his fondness for fun. He liked playing about, and if people discussed

such a vast subject as Life not genuinely but in terms of hot air he would instantly play the fool. There was indeed a natural gaiety in him — a gaiety which supported Lord Russell as a prisoner but is evidently of no use to him as an OM.

If the tone of Lord Russell's remarks had been consistently frivolous, one could have regarded them as an amusing display of sniping, but in his concluding sentence he claims for them the importance of a frontal attack, and consequently they necessitate a reply.

Yours, etc.,

Aldeburgh   E.M. Forster

NOTES

Principa Ethica, Cambridge, 1903, p.189.   **p.1**

'no Bloomby', Complaints of Clive . . . ' *Lytton Strachey by Himself: A Self-Portrait*, edited by Michael Holroyd (London, 1971), p.120

                                                       p.4

'the life of Monday . . . ' *The Common Reader* (London, 1925), 189–90   **p.4**

'the most important woman . . . ' *Virginia Woolf: A Biography* (London, 1972), II, 59   **p.19**

'the greatest British painter . . . ' *Old Friends: Personal Recollections* (London, 1956), p.20   **p.19**

'He was an eccentric . . . ' *The Times* (13th November 1962), p.14 **p.20**

E.M. Forster stated, K.W. Gransden, 'E.M. Forster at Eighty', *Encounter*, XII (January 1959), 77   **p.24**

'He nibbles' *A Writer's Diary* (London, 1953), p.241   **p.25**

The Ascent of Humanity (London, 1929), pp.207–9   **p.25**

'It had seemed to me . . . ' *The Dreadnought' Hoax* (London, 1936), p.10   **p.33**

'I am glad to think . . . ', Yes, I'm sorry . . . ' Quentin Bell, *Virginia Woolf*, I, 215, 216   **p.33**

It had been said, Quentin Bell, *Virgini Woolf*, I, 113   **p.43**

'In those twilight days . . . ' Quentin Bell 'Brief Lives', *New Statesman*, LXXI (13th May 1966), 698   **p.43**

'We pressed him . . . ' 'There *is* a principle . . . ' *Ottoline at Garsington: Memoirs of Lady Ottoline Morrell, 1915–1918*, edited by Robert Gathorne-Hardy (London, 1974), pp.56, 60   **p.49**

'It was in the summer . . . ' Quentin Bell, *Bloomsbury* (London, 1968), p.74   **p.49**

'which met at midnight . . . ' *Old Friends*, p.26   **p.84**

'calling attention to . . . ', 'who, for nearly twenty . . . ' *Times Literary Supplement* (17th July 1948) p.401, and (July 31, 1948), p.429

                                                       p.84

'the only great man . . . ' *Sowing: An Autobiography of the Years 1880–1904* (London, 1960), p.131   **p.92**

'By the time I left . . . ' *Sowing*, p.180   **pp.109–110**

'These epicures . . . ' *The Wise Virgins* (London, 1914), p.114   **p.110**

'The downfall – I use . . . ' This fragment, preserved in Leonard Woolf's
   papers at the library of the University of Sussex, is quoted by
   permission of Mrs Ian Parsons   p.122
'bears no regular proportion . . . ' *Principa Ethica*, pp.27, 28   p127
'put into practice . . . ' 'Foreword', Virginia Woolf, *Roger Fry* (London,
   1940)   p.128
'He had, I suspect . . . ' Quentin Bell, *Virginia Woolf*, I, 103   p.156
'And one, my best . . . ' *Essays, Poems and Letters*, edited by Quentin
   Bell (London, 1938), pp.228–9   p.169
'Dined with the . . . ' Quentin Bell, *Virginia Woolf* I, 176   p.173
'It was at the time . . . ' Clive Bell, *Old Friends*, p.31   p.177
'takes Lytton too . . . ' 'Ménage à Cinq', *New Statesman*, 75 (23rd
   February 1968), 241   p.182
'helped to temper . . . ' *Virginia Woolf*, I, 103   p.194
'you were the first . . . ', 'seems to me . . . ' Quentin Bell, *Virginia
   Woolf*, I, 212   p.197
'I remember spending . . . ' *Old Friends*, p.118   p.204
'the cleverest man . . . ' *Old Friends*, p.52   p.222
'They were the best . . . ' *Sunday Times* (8th November 1970), p.27
                                                                     p.242
'Vita says that our . . . ' *Diaries and Letters* (London, 1967), II, 110
                                                                     p.249
'In the two years . . . ' *Downhill All the Way: An Autobiography of
   the Years 1919–1939* (London, 1967), p.174   p.273
Lehmann's account appears in a letter in the *Times Literary
   Supplement*, 30th October 1969   p.273
'There was very little apparent . . . ' *Recollections of Virginia Woolf*, ed.
   Joan Russell Noble (London, 1972), pp.128–9   p.273
'Incurious fellow passengers . . . ' *At Home* (London, 1958), pp.107–8
                                                                     p.296
'It is a dangerous . . . ' Quentin Bell, 'Brief Lives,' P.698   p.304
'A filial tribute . . . ' 'Bloomsbury and the Arts in the Early Twentieth
   Century,' *Leeds Art Calendar*, 55 (1964), 18   pp.318–9
'the subtle degradation . . . ', 'Spit at Bloomsbury . . . ' *The Letters of
   Rupert Brooke*, ed. Geoffrey Keynes (London, 1968), pp.380 and
   440   p.330
Lewis's 'Say It with Leaves' is preserved with his papers at Cornell
   University   p.330
Books Do Furnish a Room (London, 1971), p.119   p.331
'Mr Fry's curtain . . . ' *Wyndham Lewis on Art: Collected Writings ,
   1913–1956*, ed. Walter Michel and C.J. Fox (New York, 1969),

p.66   p.332
'One of the anomalies . . . ' *Wyndham Lewis on Art*, pp.198–9   p.332
'I should be sorry . . . ' *Atheneum*, 19th March 1920, p.379   p.332
'In England for a very . . . ' *Apes of God* (London, 1955), pp.123–4
                                                                   p.333
Lewis's card is reproduced in *The Letters of Wyndham Lewis*, ed. W.K.
   Rose (Norfolk, Connecticut, 1963), plate 12   p.333
'extremely insignificant . . . ' *Men Without Art* (London, 1934), p.159
                                                                   p.333
'Those most influential . . . ' *Men Without Art*, pp.167–8   p.333–4
'I met Forster . . . ' *Blasting and Bombardiering* (London, 1967),
   pp.235–6   p.334
'Roger Fry and his "Bloomsbury" . . . ' *Summer's Lease:
   Autobiography, 1901–1938* (London, 1965), p.129   p.334
'essentially not documentary . . . ' 'Preface to the Readers Union
   Edition', *Modern Painters* (London, 1957), p.xi   p.334
'What a fool Clive . . . ' *The Collected Letters of D.H. Lawrence*, ed.
   Harry T. Moore (New York, 1962), II, 1118   p.362
'But let scoffers . . . ' 'Introduction to These Paintings,' *Phoenix: The
   Posthumous Papers of D.H. Lawrence*, ed. Edward D. McDonald
   (London, 1936), pp.565–6   p.362
'the greatest imaginative novelist . . . ' *Nation and Atheneum* 46 (29
   March 1930), 888   p.363
'one of my most sympathetic . . . ' Pornography and Obscenity,'
   Phoenix, p.180, and Desmond MacCarthy, 'D.H. Lawerence,'
   Criticism (London, 1932), p.254   p.363
'got a peace-maker's' *New Statesman*, 19 (6th May 1922), p.124   p.370
'Dear Clive Bell . . . ' *Carrington: Letters and Extracts from Her Diaries*,
   ed. David Garnett (London, 1970), p.202   p.371
'I have had three . . . ' *A Writer's Diary*, p.240   p.381
'from sheer malice.', 'ill-mannered and pretentious . . . ', 'a male
   bluestocking.', 'tottering pursuit . . . ' *The Georgian Literary Scene*
   (New York, 1934), pp.339–40, 364, 374   p.381
'an unusually courteous . . . ' *Downhill All the Way*, pp.23–4   p.382
'real and very fine' *The Common Pursuit* (London, 1953), p.261   p.388
'a beautifully constructed . . . ' *Fiction and the Reading Public*
   (London, 1932), p.223   p.388
'some cerebral . . . ' M.C. Bradbrook, 'Notes on the Style of Mrs. Woolf'
   Scrutiny, I (May 1932), 38   p.388
'She belonged, of course . . . ' *Scrutiny*, X (January 1942), 298 p.388
'the onus is on . . . ' *Scrutiny* VII (September 1938), 212   p.388

'an insolent performance,' *Scrutiny*, VII (March 1939), 406   p.389
'changed in one respect . . .', *The Autobiography of Bertrand Russell,*
     1872–1914 (London, 1967), p.74   **p.402**

BIBLIOGRAPHIES

The following bibliographies are selective rather than exhaustive. For the most part books rather than articles or pamphlets have been listed. With E.M. Forster, J.M. Keynes, Lytton Strachey, and Virginia Woolf it has been necessary to be severely selective in choosing from the enormous body of commentary that has accumulated about them. There are no bibliographies for Saxon Sydney-Turner, whose only published writings are a series of contributions to *Euphrosyne*, or for Adrian Stephen, whose publications consist of seven articles and four reviews in psychoanalytic journals – and *The 'Dreadnought' Hoax*.

Unless otherwise indicated, the place of publication for all books is London.

ADDITIONAL WORKS ON BLOOMSBURY

This bibliography does not include works from which excerpts have been given in this collection.

Frank Swinnerton, 'Bloomsbury', *The Georgian Literary Scene* pp. 337–77, (New York) 1934.

Julian Bell, *Essays, Poems and Letters*, ed. Quentin Bell, 1938.

J.K. Johnstone, *The Bloomsbury Group: A Study of E.M. Forster, Lytton Strachey, Virginia Woolf, and Their Circle*, 1954.

'The Air of Bloomsbury', *Times Literary Supplement*, 20th August 1954, pp. 521–3; letter from Clive Bell, 27th August, p. 543.

Geoffrey Moore, 'The Significance of Bloomsbury', *The Kenyon Review*, 17 (Winter 1955), 119–29.

Noel Annan, 'The Intellectual Aristocracy', *Studies in Social History*, ed. J.H. Plumb, pp. 243–87, 1955.

William Van O'Connor, 'Toward a History of Bloomsbury', *Southern Review*, XL (Winter 1955), 36–52.

Sir Arthur Lunn, 'Bloomsbury and Other Inter-War Trends', *Memory to Memory*, pp. 101–13, 1956.

Irène Simon, 'Bloomsbury and Its Critics', *Revue des Langues Vivantes*, 23 (1957), 385–414.

G.H. Bantock, 'L.H. Myers and Bloomsbury', *The Pelican Guide to English Literature: The Modern Age*, ed. Boris Ford, pp.270–9. 1961.

Quentin Bell, 'Bloomsbury and the Arts in the Early Twentieth Century', *Leeds Art Calendar*, 55 (1964), 18–28.

Berel Lang, 'Intuition in Bloomsbury', *Journal of the History of Ideas*, 25 (1964), 295–302.

Christophe Campos, 'The Salon', *The View of France from Arnold to Bloomsbury*, pp. 208–237, 1965.

W. W. Robson, 'Liberal Humanists: The "Bloomsbury" Group', *Modern English Literature*, pp.93–102 1970.

Michael Holroyd, 'Rediscovery: The Bloomsbury Painters', *Art in America*, 58 (July 1970), 116–23.

Carolyn G. Heilbrun, 'The Bloomsbury Group', *Toward a Recognition of Androgyny*, pp.113–67, (New York) 1973.

David Gadd, *The Loving Friends: A Portrait of Bloomsbury*, 1974.

CLIVE BELL

BOOKS BY BELL

Criticism
Art, 1914
Pot-Boilers, 1918
Since Cézanne, 1922
Landmarks in Nineteenth-Century Painting, 1927
Proust, 1928
An Account of French Painting, 1931
Enjoying Pictures: Meditations in the National Gallery and Elsewhere, 1934

Social and Political Writings
Peace At Once, Manchester, [1915]
On British Freedom, 1923
Civilization: An Essay, 1928
Warmongers, [1938]

Poetry
Editor and contributor, *Euphrosyne: A Collection of Verse*, Cambridge, 1905
Ad Familiares, privately printed, 1917
Poems, Richmond, Surrey, 1921
The Legend of Monte della Sibilla or Le Paradis de la Reine Sibille, Richmond, Surrey, 1923

Autobiography
Old Friends: Personal Recollections, 1956

WORKS ON BELL

Bibliography
'Arthur Clive Heward Bell'. *The New Cambridge Bibliography of English Literature*. ed. I. R. Willison. Vol. IV: 1900–1950, 1003–4 Cambridge, 1972.
D.A. Laing, 'A Checklist of the Published Writings of Clive Bell', in William G. Baywater Jr's *Clive Bell's Eye*, Detroit, forthcoming.

Criticism
I.A. Richards, *Principles of Literary Criticism*, 1924.
Morris Weitz, 'Aesthetic Formalism' and 'The Critique of Formalism', *Philosophy of the Arts*, 1–34, Cambridge, Mass. 1950.
Beryl Lake, 'A Study of the Irrefutability of Two Aesthetic Theories', *Aesthetics and Language*, ed. William Elton, 100–113, Oxford, 1954.
Solomon Fishman, 'Clive Bell', *The Interpretation of Art*, 73–99, Berkeley, 1963.
Teddy Brunius, 'An Excursion to Bloomsbury', *G.E. Moore's Analysis of Beauty* 51–8, Uppsala, 1964.
Herbert Read, 'Clive Bell', R.K. Elliott, 'Bell's Aesthetic Theory and Critical Practice', R. Meager, 'Clive Bell and Aesthetic Emotion', H. Osborne, 'Alison and Bell on Appreciation', George T. Dickie, 'Clive Bell and the Method of *Principia Ethica*', *The British Journal of Aesthetics*, 5 (April 1965), 107–110, 111–22, 123–31, 132–8, 139–43.
Rosalind Ekman, 'The Paradoxes of Formalism', *The British Journal of Aesthetics* 10 (October 1970), 350–8.
William G. Bywater Jr, *Clive Bell's Eye*, Detroit, forthcoming.

VANESSA BELL

Recent Paintings by Vanessa Bell, foreword by Virginia Woolf (4th February—8th March 1930), London Artists' Association, The Cooling Galleries.

Catalogue of Recent Paintings by Vanessa Bell, foreword by Virginia Woolf (March 1934), The Lefevre Galleries.

Alan Clutton-Brock, 'Vanessa Bell and her Circle', *The Listener*, LXV (4th May 1961), 790.

Exhibition of Paintings by Vanessa Bell foreword by A. Dunoyer de Segonzac (6—27th October 1961), The Adams Gallery.

Vanessa Bell: A Memorial Exhibition of Paintings, introduction by Ronald Pickvance, Arts Council, 1964.

Vanessa Bell: Paintings and Drawings, introduction by Richard Morphet (20th November—12th December 1973), Anthony d'Offay Gallery.

E.M. FORSTER

BOOKS BY FORSTER

Collected Edition

The Abinger Edition of E.M. Forster, ed. Oliver Stallybrass: Vol. 8: *The Life to Come and Other Stories*; Vol. 11: *Two Cheers for Democracy*; Vol. 13: *Goldsworthy Lowes Dickinson and Related Writings*; Vol. 4: *Howards End*; Vol. 4a: *The Manuscripts of Howards End*. 1972—.

Fiction

Where Angels Fear to Tread, Edinburgh, 1905
The Longest Journey, Edinburgh 1907
A Room With A View, 1908
Howards End, 1910
The Celestial Omnibus and Other Stories, 1911
The Story of the Siren, Richmond, Surrey, 1920
A Passage to India, 1924
The Eternal Moment and Other Stories, 1928
Maurice, 1971
The Life to Come and Other Stories, 1972

Essays and Criticism
Pharos and Pharillon, Richmond, Surrey, 1923
Anonymity, 1925
Aspects of the Novel, 1927
Letter to Madan Blanchard, 1931
Abinger Harvest, 1936
What I Believe, 1939
Virginia Woolf, Cambridge, 1942
Two Cheers for Democracy, 1951
Albergo Empedocle and Other Writings, ed. George H. Thompson, New
    York, 1971

Biography and Autobiography
Goldsworthy Lowes Dickinson, 1934
The Hill of Devi, Being Letters from Dewas State Senior, 1953
Marianne Thornton: A Domestic Biography, 1956

Other Writing
Alexandria, Alexandria, 1922
England's Pleasant Land: A Pageant Play, 1940

WORKS ON FORSTER

Bibliography
B.J. Kirkpatrick, *A Bibliography of E.M. Forster*, 1965 (revised 1968).
Frederick P.W. McDowell, *E.M. Forster: An Annotated Bibliography of
    Writings About Him*, forthcoming.

Biography
P.N. Furbank, 'The Personality of E.M. Forster', *Encounter* XXXX
    (November 1970), 61–8.
J.R. Ackerley, *E.M. Forster: A Portrait*, 1970.

Criticism
Virginia Woolf, 'The Novels of E.M. Forster', [1927] *Collected Essays*,
    I, 342–351, 1966.
Lionel Trilling, *E.M. Forster* (Norfolk, Connecticut) 1943, revised
    1967.
E.K. Brown, 'Rhythm in E.M. Forster's *A Passage to India*', *Rhythm in
    the Novel*, 89–115, Toronto, 1950.
James McConkey, *The Novels of E.M. Forster*, Ithaca, New York, 1957.
    1957.

Frederick C. Crews, *E.M. Forster: The Perils of Humanism*, Princeton, 1962.

K.W. Gransden, *E.M. Forster*, Edinburgh, 1962.

Wilfred Stone, *The Cave and the Mountain: A Study of E.M. Forster*, Stanford, 1966.

Aspects of E.M. Forster: Essays and Recollections Written for his Ninetieth Birthday, ed. Oliver Stallybrass, 1969.

George H. Thompson, 'E.M. Forster, Gerald Heard, and Bloomsbury', *English Literature in Transition* 12 (1969) 87–91.

June Perry Levine, *Creation and Criticism: A Passage to India*, Lincoln, Nebraska, 1971.

E.M. Forster: The Critical Heritage, edited by Philip Gardner, 1973.

ROGER FRY

BOOKS BY FRY

Criticism

Giovanni Bellini, 1899

Sir Joshua Reynolds, *Discourses*, introduction and notes by Roger Fry, 1905

Vision and Design, 1920 (Revised 1923)

The Artist and Psycho-analysis, 1924

Art and Commerce, 1926

Transformations: Critical and Speculative Essays on Art, 1926

Cézanne: A Study of His Development, 1927

Flemish Art: A Critical Survey, 1927

Characteristics of French Art, 1932

Henri-Matisse, Paris, 1930

Reflections on British Painting, 1934

Last Lectures, Cambridge, 1939

Other Works

Twelve Original Woodcuts, Richmond, Surrey, 1921

A Sampler of Castile, Richmond, Surrey, 1923

(Translator) Stéphane Mallarmé, *Poems* with commentaries by Charles Mauron, 1936

Letters

Letters of Roger Fry, ed. Denys Sutton, 2 Vols. 1972

WORKS ON FRY

Bibliography
'Roger Eliot Fry', *The New Cambridge Bibliography of English Literature*, ed. I.R. Willison. IV: 1900–1950, 1042–4, Cambridge, 1972.

Biography
Virginia Woolf, *Roger Fry: A Biography*, 1940.
Denys Sutton, 'Introduction' and 'Chronology', *Letters of Roger Fry* I, 1–102, 1972.
Diamand, Pamela Fry, 'Recollections of Roger Fry and the Omega Workshops', *Virginia Woolf Quarterly* I (Summer 1973) 47–52.

Criticism
I.A. Richards, *Principles of Literary Criticism*, 1924.
E.M. Forster 'Roger Fry: An Obituary Note', *Abinger Harvest* 1936, pp. 39–41.
Kenneth Clark, 'Introduction', Roger Fry, *Last Lectures* ix–xxix, Cambridge, 1939.
Nikolaus Pevsner, 'Omega', *The Architectural Review*, XC (July 1941), 45–8.
William Gaunt, 'Threshold of a New Age', *The Aesthetic Adventure*, 1945 pp.198–214.
Morris Weitz, 'Aesthetic Formalism' and 'The Critique of Formalism', *Philosophy of the Arts*, 1–34, Cambridge, Mass., 1950.
Solomon Fishman, 'Roger Fry', *The Interpretation of Art*, 101–142, Berkeley, 1963.
Quentin Bell, *Roger Fry*, Leeds, 1964.
Quentin Bell, 'Roger Fry', Philip Troutman, 'Roger Fry–Painter', *Vision and Design: The Life, Work, and Influence of Roger Fry*. (An exhibition arranged by the Arts Council and the University of Nottingham), 6–10, 11–15, 1966.

DUNCAN GRANT

WORKS ON DUNCAN GRANT

Articles and Books
Clive Bell, 'Duncan Grant', [1920] *Since Cézanne*, 105–112, 1922.

Living Painters: Duncan Grant with an introduction by Roger Fry, Richmond, Surrey, 1923.

Duncan Grant, preface by W.G. Constable (British Artists of To-Day, Number VI), 1927.

John Rowdon, *Duncan Grant*, with a letter from Duncan Grant (Revaluation No. 1) 1934.

Raymond Mortimer, *Duncan Grant*, Penguin Modern Painters, Harmondsworth, Middlesex, 1948.

Catalogues

Duncan Grant: A Retrospective Exhibition introduction by Alan Clutton-Brock (12th May–20th June 1959).

Duncan Grant and His World introduction by Denys Sutton (November 1964) Wildenstein Gallery.

Portraits by Duncan Grant introduction by Richard Shone, Arts Council, 1969–70.

Duncan Grant: Watercolours and Drawings with a note by Stephen Spender (25th April–19th May 1972), d'Offay Couper Gallery.

JOHN MAYNARD KEYNES

BOOKS BY KEYNES

Collected Edition

The Collected Writings of John Maynard Keynes, 25 volumes: Vol. I: Indian Currency and Finance; II: The Economic Consequences of the Peace; III: A Revision of the Treaty; IV: A Tract on Monetary Reform; V and VI: A Treatise on Money; VII: The General Theory; VIII: Treatise on Probability; IX: Essays in Persuasion (with additions); Essays in Biography (with additions); XIII and XIV: The General Theory and After; XV: Activities: India and Cambridge; XVI: Activities: The Treasury and Versailles 1971–.

Economic Writings

Indian Currency and Finance, 1913

The Economic Consequences of the Peace, 1919

A Revision of the Treaty, 1922

A Tract on Monetary Reform, 1923

The Economic Consequences of Mr Churchill, 1925

A Treatise on Money, 2 vols. 1930
Essays in Persuasion, 1931
The General Theory of Employment, Interest and Money, 1936

Biography and Autobiography
Essays in Biography, 1933
Two Memoirs, 1949

Other Writings
A Treatise on Probability, 1921
A Short View of Russia, 1925
(Editor with P. Saffra): *David Hume. An Abstract of A Treatise of
    Human Nature, 1740*, Cambridge, 1938
The Arts Council: Its Policy and Hopes, [1945] 1951

WORKS ON KEYNES

Bibliography
Seymour E. Harris and Marganita Wilfort, 'Bibliography of Keynes's
    Writings', *The New Economics*, ed. Harris 665–86, New York,
    1947.
'John Maynard Keynes', *The New Cambridge Bibliography of English
    Literature*, ed. I.R. Willison. Vol.IV: 1900–1950, 1175–7,
    Cambridge, 1972.
The Collected Writings of John Maynard Keynes, Vol. 25, forthcoming.

Biography
John Maynard Keynes, 1883–1946 A Memoir prepared by the
    direction of the Council of King's College Cambridge, 1949.
R.F. Harrod, *The Life of John Maynard Keynes*, 1951.
F.A. Keynes, *Gathering Up the Threads: A Study in Family Biography*,
    1951.
Clive Bell, 'Maynard Keynes', *Old Friends* pp. 42–61, 1956

Criticism
Etienne Mantoux, *La paix calomniée, ou les consequences économiques
    de Keynes*, Paris, 1946.
The New Economics: Keynes's Influence on Theory and Public Policy,
    ed. Seymour E. Harris, New York, 1947.
Alvin Hansen, *A Guide to Keynes*, New York, 1953.
Kingsley Martin, 'Arguing with Keynes', *Encounter* 24 (February

1965), 75–87.

Robert Lekachman, *The Age of Keynes*, New York, 1966.

Michael Stewart, *Keynes and After* Harmondsworth, Middlesex, 1967.

Keynes: Aspects of the Man and His Work, ed. D.E. Moggridge, 1974.

DESMOND MACCARTHY

BOOKS BY MACCARTHY

Criticism

The Court Theatre, 1904–7: A Commentary and Criticism 1907 (with
     additions, ed. Stanley Weintraub, Coral Gables, Florida, 1966.

Remnants, 1918

Portraits I, (no further volumes issued) 1931

Criticism, 1932

Experience, 1935

Leslie Stephen, Cambridge, 1937

Drama, 1940

Shaw, 1951

Humanities, 1953

Memories, 1953

Theatre, 1954

Editing

*Lady John Russell: A Memoir with a Selection from Her Diaries and
     Correspondence* (with Agatha Russell) 1910

H.H.A.: Letters of the Earl of Oxford and Asquith to a Friend, 2 vols.,
     1933–4.

WORKS ON MACCARTHY

Bibliography

'Sir Desmond MacCarthy', *The New Cambridge Bibliography of English
     Literature*, I.R. Willison. Vol.IV: 1900–1950, 1084–5, Cambridge,
     1972.

Biography

James MacGibbon, 'MacCarthy, Sir (Charles Otto) Desmond', *Diction-
     ary of National Biography 1951–1960*, ed. E.T. Williams and
     Helen M. Palmer, 1971.

Criticism

Q.D. Leavis, 'Leslie Stephen: Cambridge Critic', *Scrutiny*, VII, (1939) 404–15.

Max Beerbohm, E.M. Forster, V.S. Pritchett, P. Hope-Wallace, C.V. Wedgwood, 'Tributes to Sir Desmond MacCarthy', *The Listener* 47 (26th June 1952), 1031–2.

Lord David Cecil, 'Preface' Desmond MacCarthy *Humanities*, vi–xii, 1953.

Raymond Mortimer, 'Foreword', Cyril Connolly, 'A Portrait', Desmond MacCarthy, *Memories*, pp 5–8, 9–15, 1953.

John Gross, *The Rise and Fall of the Man of Letters: Aspects of English Literary Life Since 1800*, pp. 242–5, 1969.

MARY MACCARTHY

Fiction
A Pier and a Band, 1918 (reprinted 'With an Introductory Appreciation by David Garnett') 1931.

Autobiography
A Nineteenth-Century Childhood, 1924

Essays
Fighting Fitzgerald and Other Papers, 1930
Handicaps: Six Studies, 1936
The Festival, Etc., 1937

LYTTON STRACHEY

BOOKS BY LYTTON STRACHEY

Collected Edition
The Collected Works of Lytton Strachey, ed. James Strachey. 6 vols. 1948 (*Books and Characters, Portraits in Miniature*, and *Characters and Commentaries*, minus six essays, were combined into two volumes entitled *Literary Essays* and *Biographical Essays*; one new essay was added.)

Biography and Criticism
Landmarks in French Literature, 1912
Eminent Victorians: Cardinal Manning, Florence Nightingale, Dr. Arnold, General Gordon, 1918
Queen Victoria, 1921
Books and Characters, French and English, 1922
Elizabeth and Essex: A Tragic History, 1928
Portraits in Miniature and Other Essays, 1931
Characters and Commentaries, ed. James Strachey, 1933
Spectatorial Essays, ed. James Strachey, 1964

Verse, Fiction and Other Writings
Contributor, *Euphrosyne: A Collection of Verse* Cambridge, 1905
Ermyntrude and Esmeralda, 1969
The Really Interesting Question and Other Papers, ed. Paul Levy, 1972

Letters and Autobiography
Virginia Woolf and Lytton Strachey: Letters, ed. Leonard Woolf and James Strachey, 1956.
Lytton Strachey by Himself: A Self-Portrait, ed. Michael Holroyd, 1971.

Editing
The Greville Memoirs with Roger Fulford, 8 vols., 1938.

WORKS ON LYTTON STRACHEY

Bibliography
Charles Richard Sanders, 'A Chronological Check List of Lytton Strachey's Writings', *Lytton Strachey: His Mind and Art*, 355–66, New Haven, Connecticut, 1957.
Martin Kallich, 'Lytton Strachey: An Annotated Bibliography of Writings About Him', *English Literature in Transition* 5 (1962) 1–77.

Biography
Michael Holroyd, *Lytton Strachey: A Critical Biography* 2 vols. 1967–8 (revised as *Lytton Strachey: A Biography* and *Lytton Strachey and the Bloomsbury Group* 2 vols., Harmondsworth, Middlesex, 1971).
Carrington: Letters and Extracts from her Diaries, ed. David Garnett, 1970.

Criticism

Harold Nicolson, *The Development of English Biography*, 148–154, 1928.

Vincent Sheean, 'Lytton Strachey: Cambridge and Bloomsbury', *The New Republic*, LXX (17th Feb. 1932), 19–20.

Wallace Stevens, 'Lytton Strachey, Also, Enters Heaven', [1935] *Opus Posthumous*, ed. S.F. Morse, pp. 38–9, New York, 1957.

Raymond Mortimer, 'Lytton Strachey', *Channel Packet*, 179–184, 1942.

Desmond MacCarthy, 'Lytton Strachey and the Art of Biography', [1934] *Memories*, 31–49, 1953.

K.R. Srinivasa Iyengar, *Lytton Strachey: A Critical Study*, 1938.

Virginia Woolf, 'The Art of Biography', [1939] *Collected Essays*, 4, 221–8, 1967.

Max Beerbohm, *Lytton Strachey*, Cambridge, 1943.

F.A. Simpson, 'Max Beerbohm on Lytton Strachey', *The Cambridge Review*, (9th December 1943) pp. 120–2.

Charles Richard Sanders, *Lytton Strachey: His Mind and Art*, New Haven, Connecticut, 1957.

Hugh Trevor-Roper, 'Lytton Strachey as Historian', *Historical Essays*, 279–284, 1957.

John Raymond, 'Strachey's Eminent Victorians', *The New Statesman and Nation*, (16th April 1955) 545–6.

Martin Kallich, *The Psycological Milieu of Lytton Strachey*, New York, 1961.

Noel Annan, 'Introduction', Lytton Strachey *Eminent Victorians*, 1959, 9–17.

Goronwy Rees, 'A Case for Treatment: The World of Lytton Strachey', *Encounter* XXX (March 1968), 71–83. (Reply by Leonard Woolf, *Encounter* (May 1968), 91.)

Noel Annan, 'A Very Queer Gentleman', *The New York Review*, (6th June 1968), 8–12.

LEONARD WOOLF

BOOKS BY WOOLF

Social, Political, Historical, and Literary Writings
International Government: Two Reports, 1916

The Future of Constantinople, 1917
Co-operation and the Future of Industry, 1918
Economic Imperialism, 1920
Empire and Commerce in Africa: A Study in Economic Imperialism, 1920
Socialism and Co-operation, 1921
Fear and Politics: A Debate at the Zoo, 1925
Essays on Literature, History, Politics, Etc., 1927
Hunting the Highbrow, 1927
Imperialism and Civilization, 1928
After the Deluge: A Study of Communal Psychology, 2 vols. 1931, 1939 (See also *Principia Politica*)
Quack, Quack!, 1935
Barbarians at the Gate (*Barbarians Within and Without* – the American title), 1939
The War for Peace, 1940
Principia Politica: A Study of Communal Psychology (Volume 3 of *After the Deluge*), 1953

Verse, Fiction and Drama

Contributor, *Euphrosyne: A Collection of Verse*, Cambridge, 1905
The Village in the Jungle, 1913
The Wise Virgins: A Story of Words, Opinions and a Few Emotions, 1914
'Three Jews,' Virginia and L.S. Woolf, *Two Stories*, Richmond Surrey, 1917
Stories from the East, Richmond, Surrey, 1921
The Hotel, 1939

Autobiography and Diaries

Sowing: An Autobiography of the Years 1880–1904, 1960
Growing: An Autobiography of the Years 1904–1911, 1961
Diaries in Ceylon, 1908–1911: Records of a Colonial Administrator (including *Stories from the East*), Dehiwala, Ceylon, 1962; London, 1963
Beginning Again: An Autobiography of the Years 1911–1918, 1964
Downhill All the Way: An Autobiography of the Years 1919–1939, 1967
The Journey Not the Arrival Matters: An Autobiography of the Years 1939–1969, 1970

Editing

The Framework of a Lasting Peace, 1917

Fabian Essays on Co-operation, 1923

The Hogarth Essays (with Virginia Woolf) First series, 1924–6; Second series, 1926–8; Third series, 1947. Selected essays from the first and second series were published as *The Hogarth Essays*, Garden City, New York, 1928

Hogarth Lectures on Literature (with George Rylands), 1927–1952

The Intelligent Man's Way to Prevent War, 1933

A Writer's Diary, Being Extracts from the Diary of Viginia Woolf, 1953

Virginia Woolf and Lytton Strachey: Letters, (with James Strachey), 1956

Virginia Woolf, *Collected Essays*, 4 vols., 1966–7

Translations

Maxim Gorky, *Reminiscences of Leo Nicolayevitch Tolstoi*, with S.S. Koteliansky, Richmond, Surrey, 1920.

The Notebooks of Anton Tchekhov (with S.S. Koteliansky), Richmond, Surrey, 1921.

The Autobiography of Countess Sophie Tolstoi (with S.S. Koteliansky), preface and notes by Vasilii Spiridonov, Richmond, Surrey, 1922.

Ivan Bunin, *The Gentleman from San Francisco and Other Stories* (with D.H. Lawrence and S.S. Koteliansky), Richmond, Surrey, 1922.

Maxim Gorky, *Reminiscences of Tolstoy, Chekhov and Andreev* (with Katherine Mansfield and S.S. Koteliansky), 1934.

Bibliography

Leila M.J. Luedeking, 'Bibliography of Works bt Leonard Sidney Woolf', *Virginia Woolf Quarterly* I (Fall 1972), 120–140.

Criticism

Noel Annan, 'Leonard Woolf's Autobiographies', *The Political Quarterly* 41 (Jan.–March 1970), 35–41.

Stephen Spender, 'The Perfectly Candid Man', *The New York Review* (23rd April 1970), 24–30.

Angus Davidson, *Recollections of Virginia Woolf by Her Contemporaries*, ed. Joan Russell Noble, 53–61, 1972.

Richard Kennedy, *A Boy at the Hogarth Press* 1972.

David H. Flood, 'Leonard Woolf's *The Village in the Jungle*: A Modern Version of Pastoral', *Virginia Woolf Quarterly*, I (Summer 1973), 78–84.

VIRGINIA WOOLF

BOOKS BY VIRGINIA WOOLF

Collected Writings
Uniform Edition of the Works of Virginia Woolf 17 vols., 1929–1955
Collected Essays, ed. Leonard Woolf, 4 vols., 1966–7

Fiction
The Voyage Out, 1915
'The Mark on The Wall', Virginia and L.S. Woolf, *Two Stories*, Richmond, Surrey, 1917
Night and Day, 1919
Kew Gardens, Richmond, Surrey, 1919
Monday or Tuesday, Richmond, Surrey, 1921
Jacob's Room, Richmond, Surrey, 1922
Mrs Dalloway, 1925
To the Lighthouse, 1927
Orlando: A Biography, 1928
The Waves, 1931
The Years, 1937
Between the Acts, 1941
A Haunted House and Other Short Stories (includes all of *Monday or Tuesday* except for two stories and adds twelve more), 1943
Mrs. Dalloway's Party: A Short Story Sequence, edited by Stella McNichol (includes four stories from *A Haunted House*, one uncollected story and two unpublished ones), 1973
Mrs Dalloway: A First Draft Version, ed. Stella McNichol, forthcoming.
The Waves: Two Holograph Drafts, ed. J.W. Graham, forthcoming.

Essays
Mr. Bennett and Mrs. Brown, Richmond, Surrey, 1924
The Common Reader, 1925
The Common Reader: Second Series, 1932
A Letter to a Young Poet, 1932
The Death of the Moth and Other Essays, 1942
The Moment and Other Essays, 1947
The Captain's Death Bed and Other Essays, 1950
Granite and Rainbow: Essays, 1958
Contemporary Writers, 1965

Feminist Books
A Room of One's Own, 1929
Three Guineas, 1938

Biography
Flush: A Biography, 1933
Roger Fry: A Biography, 1940

Diaries and Letters
A Writer's Diary: Being Extracts from the Diary of Virginia Woolf, ed.
Leonard Woolf, 1953.
Aileen Pippett, *The Moth and the Star: A Biography of Virginia Woolf*
(letters to Vita Sackville-West *passim*), Boston, 1955.
Virginia Woolf and Lytton Strachey: *Letters*, ed. Leonard Woolf and
James Strachey, 1956.

Translations
F.M. Dostoevsky, *Stavrogin's Confession and The Plan of the Life of a
Great Sinner* (with S.S. Koteliansky), Richmond, Surrey, 1922.
*Tolstoi's Love Letters with a Study on the Autobiographical Elements
in Tolstoi's Work* by Paul Biryukov (with S.S. Koteliansky),
Richmond, Surrey, 1923.
Talks with Tolstoi by A.B. Goldenveizer (with S.S. Koteliansky),
Richmond, Surrey, 1923.

WORKS ON VIRGINIA WOOLF

Bibliography
Maurice Beebe, 'Criticism of Virginia Woolf: A Selected Checklist',
Modern Fiction Studies 2 (February 1956) 36–45.
B.J. Kirkpatrick, *A Bibliography of Virginia Woolf*, 1957 (revised
edition, 1967).
Barbara Weiser, 'Criticism of Virginia Woolf from 1956 to the Present:
A Selected Checklist', *Modern Fiction Studies* 18 (Autumn 1972),
477–86.

Biography
Quentin Bell, *Virginia Woolf: A Biography*. Vol. 1: *Virginia Stephen*;
Vol. II: *Mrs. Woolf*, 1972.
Recollections of Virginia Woolf by her Contemporaries ed. Joan Russell
Noble, 1972.

Criticism

Winifred Holtby, *Virginia Woolf*, 1932.

T.S. Eliot, Rose Macaulay, Vita Sackville-West, William Plomer, Duncan Grant, 'Notes on Virginia Woolf', *Horizon*, III (May, June 1941), 313–327 402–6.

David Daiches, *Virginia Woolf*, 1942 (revised 1963).

Joan Bennett, *Virginia Woolf: Her Art as a Novelist*, Cambridge, 1945 (revised 1964).

Bernard Blackstone, *Virginia Woolf: A Commentary*, 1949.

Irma Rantavaara, *Virginia Woolf and Bloomsbury*, Helsinki, 1953.

Clive Bell, 'Virginia Woolf', *Old Friends* 92–118, 1956.

Monique Nathan, *Virginia Woolf par elle-même*, Paris, 1956.

Jean Guiguet, *Virginia Woolf et son oeuvre*, Paris, 1962.

Ralph Freedman, *The Lyrical Novel: Studies in Hermann Hesse, André Gide and Virginia Woolf*, Princeton, 1963.

A.D. Moody, *Virginia Woolf*, Edinburgh, 1963.

Herbert Marder, *Feminism and Art: A Study of Virginia Woolf* (Chicago) 1968

John Graham, 'Point of View in *The Waves*: Some Services of the Style', *University of Toronto Quarterly* XXXIX (April 1970) 193–211.

Harvena Richter, *Virginia Woolf: The Inward Voyage*, Princeton, 1970.

S.P. Rosenbaum, 'The Philosophical Realism of Virginia Woolf', *English Literature and British Philosophy*, ed. S.P. Rosenbaum, 316–356, Chicago, 1971.

Virginia Woolf: A Collection of Critical Essays, ed. Claire Sprague, Englewood Cliffs, New Jersey, 1971.

Alice van Buren Kelley, *The Novels of Virginia Woolf: Fact and Vision*, Chicago, 1973.

IDENTIFICATIONS

The following brief descriptions and cross-references are confined to the more important people and places mentioned in the text.

Affable Hawk: *see* MacCarthy, Desmond.

Anrep, Helen: *née* Maitland, 1885–1965, wife of Boris Anrep, companion of Roger Fry.

Apostles, The: The Cambridge Conversazione Society, known also simply as The Society – a secret Cambridge undergraduate discussion club founded in the early nineteenth century.

Asham (or Asheham) House: Woolfs' country home near Lewes, Sussex, 1912–19.

Bagenal, Barbara: *née* Hiles, 1892 – , wife of Nicholas Bagenal.

Barbara: *see* Bagenal, Barbara.

Bedford Square: Bloomsbury square in which Lady Ottoline Morrell's London home was located.

Bell, Angelica: *see* Garnett, Angelica.

Bell, Clive: Arthur Clive Heward Bell, 1881–1964, art critic, husband of Vanessa Stephen, father of Julian and Quentin Bell.

Bell, Julian: 1908–1937, poet, son of Vanessa and Clive Bell.

Bell, Quentin: 1910 – , art historian, biographer, artist, son of Clive and Vanessa Bell.

Bell, Vanessa: *née* Stephen, known as Nessa, 1879–1961, painter, daughter of Leslie and Julia Stephen, sister of Virginia Woolf and Adrian Stephen, wife of Clive Bell, companion of Duncan Grant, mother of Julian, Quentin, and Angelica Bell.

Belsize Park Gardens: Hampstead location of the Strachey family home, 1907–1920.

Bernard Street: Bloomsbury location of Roger Fry's London home.

Bertie: *see* Russell, Bertrand.

Birrell, Francis: Known as Frankie, 1889–1935, critic son of Augustine Birrell.

Bob Trevy: *see* Trevelyan, R.C.

Brenan, Gerald: 1894 – , writer.

Brooke, Rupert: 1887–1915, poet.

Brunswick Square: Bloomsbury square, location of the home at one time or another of Virginia and Adrian Stephen, J.M. Keynes, Leonard Woolf, Duncan Grant, E.M. Forster, and others.

Bunny: *see* Garnett, David.

Bussy, Dorothy: *née* Strachey, 1866–1960, author and translator, wife of Simon Bussy, sister of Lytton Strachey.

Bussy, Jane-Simone: painter, daughter of Simon and Dorothy Bussy.

Bussy, Simon-Albert: 1870–1954, painter, husband of Dorothy Strachey.

Cambridge Conversazione Society, The: *see* The Apostles.

Carrington, Dora: known as Carrington, 1893–1932, artist, companion of Lytton Strachey, wife of Ralph Partridge.

Cassis-sur-mer: village near Marseilles where the Bells, Duncan Grant and sometimes the Woolfs stayed from 1927 onwards.

Cecil, Lord David: 1902 – , critic, biographer, professor of English literature, husband of Rachel MacCarthy.

Charleston: country home near Firle, Sussex, of the Bells and Duncan Grant from 1916 onwards.

Clive: *see* Bell, Clive.

Costelloe, Karin: *see* Stephen, Karin.

Costelloe, Ray: *see* Strachey, Ray.

Cox, Katherine: known as Ka, died in 1934, married William Arnold-Foster.

Dadie: *see* Rylands, George.

Davidson, Angus: 1893 – , translator and critic.

Desmond: *see* MacCarthy, Desmond.

Dickinson, Goldsworthy Lowes: 1862–1932, teacher and author.

Duckworth, George: 1868–1934, half-brother of Vanessa Bell, Virginia Woolf, and Adrian Stephen.

Duckworth, Gerald: 1870–1937, publisher, half-brother of Vanessa Bell, Virginia Woolf, and Adrian Stephen.

Duncan: *see* Grant, Duncan.

Eliot, T.S.: 1888–1965, poet and critic.

Firle: Sussex village near Charleston.

Fitzroy Square: Bloomsbury square where Virginia and Adrian Stephen lived, 1907–1911 and where the Omega workshops were located, 1913–18.

Fitzroy Street: Bloomsbury street where Duncan Grant had a studio.

Forster, E.M.: Edward Morgan Forster, OM, known as Morgan, 1879–1970, novelist, essayist, critic, and biographer.

Frankie: *see* Birrell, Francis.

Fry, Pamela: 1902, daughter of Roger and Helen Fry, married Micu

Diamand.

Fry, Roger: Roger Eliot Fry, 1866–1934, art critic and painter, son of Sir Edward Fry, brother of Agnes, Isabel, and Margery Fry, married to Helen Coombe, father of Julian and Pamela Fry, companion of Helen Anrep.

Garnett, Angelica: *née* Bell, 1918 – , daughter of Vanessa Bell and Duncan Grant, married to David Garnett.

Garnett, David: known as Bunny, 1892 – , author, editor, son of Constance and Edward Garnett, married (1) Ray Marshall, (2) Angelica Bell.

Garsington: Oxfordshire country home of Lady Ottoline Morrell.

Gertler, Mark: 1891–1939, painter.

Goat, The: *see* Woolf, Virginia.

Gordon Square: Bloomsbury square where the Stephens, Stracheys, Bells, Woolfs, and Keyneses all lived at various times and addresses.

Goth, The: *see* Stephen, Thoby.

Grant, Duncan: Duncan James Corrowr Grant, 1885 – , painter, companion of Vanessa Bell, father of Angelica Garnett.

Great Ormond Street: Bloomsbury location of Saxon Sydney-Turner's home.

Guildford: Surrey location of Roger Fry's house Durbins.

Ham Spray House: Lytton Strachey's country home near Hungerford, Berkshire, from 1924 onwards.

Harvey Road: location of Keynes's parents' home in Cambridge.

Hawtrey, Sir Ralph G.: 1879 – , economist and treasury official.

Heretics, The: Cambridge discussion society.

Hiles, Barbara: *see* Bagenal, Barbara.

Hogarth House: Woolfs' home in Richmond, Surrey, 1915–1924.

Hope, Lottie: servant of the Woolfs and Bells.

Hutchinson, Mary: *née* Barnes, writer, cousin of Lytton Strachey, married to St John Hutchinson.

Huxley, Aldous: 1894–1963, novelist, critic, essayist.

Huxley, Maria: *née* Nys, wife of Aldous Huxley.

Hyde Park Gate: location of the family home of the Stephens in London, near Kensington Gardens.

James: *see* Strachey, James.

Julian: *see* Bell, Julian.

Jumbo: *see* Strachey, Marjorie.

Ka: *see* Cox, Ka.

Keynes, John Maynard, Baron: nick-named Pozzo, 1883–1946,

economist, treasury official, husband of Lydia Lopokova.

Keynes, Lydia Lopokova: 1892 – , ballerina, wife of Maynard Keynes.

Lacket, The: Lytton Strachey's cottage in Wiltshire, 1913–15.

Lamb, Henry: 1883–1960, painter, brother of Walter Lamb.

Lamb, Sir Walter: 1882–1961, classicist, secretary of the Royal Academy, brother of Henry Lamb.

Lawrence, D.H.: 1885–1930, novelist, poet, critic, essayist, husband of Frieda von Richthofen.

Lawrence, Frieda: *née* Baroness von Richthofen, 1879–1956, wife of D.H. Lawrence.

Leavis, Dr F.R.: 1895 – , critic and teacher, husband of Q.D. Leavis.

Leavis, Queenie D.: *née* Roth, critic and teacher, wife of F.R. Leavis.

Lehmann, John: 1907 – , writer and publisher.

Leonard: *see* Woolf, Leonard.

Lewis, Wyndham: 1882–1957, artist, novelist, critic, polemicist.

Lopokova, Lydia: *see* Keynes, Lydia Lopokova.

Lottie: *see* Hope, Lottie.

Louie: *see* Everest, Louie.

Ludwig: *see* Wittgenstein, Ludwig.

Lydia: *see* Keynes, Lydia Lopokova.

Lytton: *see* Strachey, Lytton.

MacCarthy, Desmond: Sir Charles Otto Desmond MacCarthy, pen-name Affable Hawk, 1877–1952, critic, husband of Mary Warre-Cornish.

MacCarthy, Mary Josefa: *née* Warre-Cornish, known as Molly, 1882–1953, writer, wife of Desmond MacCarthy.

MacCarthy, Rachel: daughter of Mary and Desmond MacCarthy, wife of Lord David Cecil.

McTaggart, John McTaggart Ellis: 1866–1925, philosopher.

Mansfield, Katherine: *née* Beauchamp, short-story writer, wife of Middleton Murry.

Maria: *see* Huxley, Maria.

Marshall, Frances: 1900 – , translator, wife of Ralph Partridge, sister of Ray Marshall.

Marshall, Rachel: known as Ray, 1891–1940, illustrator, wife of David Garnett, sister of Frances Marshall.

Mary: *see* Hutchinson, Mary.

Mauron, Charles: 1899–1966, French critic.

Maynard: *see* Keynes, John Maynard.

Mecklenburgh Square: Bloomsbury square where the Woolfs lived, 1939–40.

Memoir Club, The: club formed in 1920 by members of the

Bloomsbury Group to read one another their memoirs, last meeting in 1956.

Midnight Society, The: Cambridge undergraduate reading society, *c*1900.

Mill House: Lytton Strachey's country home at Tidmarsh, Berkshire, 1917–24.

Mirsky, Prince Dmitri: 1890–*c*1940, Russian literary historian and critic.

Molly: *see* MacCarthy, Mary.

Monk's House: Woolf's country home in Rodmell, near Lewes, Sussex, from 1919 onwards.

Moore, G.E.: 1873–1958, philosopher.

Morgan: *see* Forster, E.M.

Morrell, Lady Ottoline: nicknamed Ott, *née* Cavendish-Bentinck, 1873–1938, hostess, patroness of the arts, sister of the Duke of Portland, wife of Philip Morrell.

Morrell, Philip: 1870–1943, barrister, member of Parliament, husband of Lady Ottoline Cavendish-Bentinck.

Mortimer, Raymond: 1895 – , critic.

Murry, John Middleton: 1889–1957, writer, husband of Katherine Mansfield.

Myers, L.H.: 1881–1944, novelist.

Nessa: *see* Bell, Vanessa.

Nicolson, Sir Harold: 1886–1968, diplomat and author, husband of Vita Sackville-West.

Nicolson, Mrs Harold: *see* Sackville-West, Vita.

Norton, Harry T.J.: 1886–1937, mathematician.

Omega workshops, The: founded by Roger Fry to produce works of interior decoration, 1913–20.

Partridge, Ralph: died 1960, husband of (1) Dora Carrington, (2) Frances Marshall.

Pernel: *see* Strachey, Pernel.

Pippa: *see* Strachey, Pippa.

Plomer, William: 1903–1973, author, editor.

Pozzo: *see* Keynes, John Maynard.

Quentin: *see* Bell, Quentin.

Rodmell: Sussex village near Lewes where the Woolfs lived from 1919 onwards.

Roger: *see* Fry, Roger.

Rupert: *see* Brooke, Rupert.

Russell, Bertrand: third Earl Russell, known as Bertie, 1872–1970, philosopher.

Rylands, George: nicknamed Dadie, 1902 – , lecturer in English literature.

Sackville-West, Hon. Vita: 1892–1962, novelist, poet, wife of Harold Nicolson.

Sargant-Florence, Alix: *see* Strachey, Alix.

Saxon: *see* Sydney-Turner, Saxon.

Seend: Wiltshire country home of Clive Bell's parents.

Shaw, George Bernard: 1856–1950, playwright, critic.

Sheppard, Sir John: 1881–1968, classicist, Provost of King's College, Cambridge.

Shove, Fredegond: *née* Maitland, 1889–1949, poet, wife of Gerald Shove.

Shove, Gerald: 1887–1947, economist, husband of Fredegond Maitland.

Sickert, Walter: 1860–1942, painter.

Sidgwick, Henry: 1838–1900, philosopher and educator.

Sitwell, Dame Edith: 1887–1964, poet, biographer, critic, sister of Osbert and Sacheverell Sitwell.

Sitwell, Sir Osbert: 1892–1969, poet, autobiographer, essayist.

Sitwell, Sir Sacheverell: 1897 – , poet, essayist, travel-writer.

Smyth, Dame Ethel: 1858–1944, composer, author, feminist.

Society, The: *see* Apostles, The.

Spender, Stephen: 1909–, poet and critic.

Sprott, W.J.H.: known as Sebastian, 1897–1971, psychologist.

Stephen, Adrian: Adrian Leslie Stephen, 1883–1948, psychoanalyst, son of Leslie Stephen, brother of Vanessa Bell and Virginia Woolf, husband of Karin Costelloe.

Stephen, J.K.: known as Jem, 1859–1892, poet, cousin of Vanessa Bell, Virginia Woolf, and Adrian Stephen.

Stephen, Sir James Fitzjames: 1829–1894, government official, judge, essayist, brother of Leslie Stephen, father of J.K. Stephen.

Stephen, Jem: *see* Stephen, J.K.

Stephen, Julia: *née* Jackson, 1846–1895, wife of (1) Herbert Duckworth, (2) Leslie Stephen, mother of Vanessa Bell, Virginia Woolf, and Adrian Stephen.

Stephen, Karin: *née* Costelloe, 1889–1953, psychoanalyst, wife of Adrian Stephen.

Stephen, Sir Leslie: 1832–1904, biographer, critic, historian of ideas, father of Vanessa Bell, Virginia Woolf, Adrian Stephen.

Stephen, Thoby: Julian Thoby Stephen, nicknamed The Goth,

1880–1906, son of Leslie and Julia Stephen, brother of Vanessa Bell, Virginia Woolf, and Adrian Stephen.

Stephen, Vanessa: *see* Bell, Vanessa.

Stephen, Virginia: *see* Woolf, Virginia.

Strachey, Alix: *née* Sargant-Florence, 1892 – , psychoanalyst, wife of James Strachey.

Strachey, James: 1887–1967, psychoanalyst, translator of Freud, brother of Lytton Strachey, husband of Alix Sargant-Florence.

Strachey, Jane Maria: *née* Grant, 1840–1928, Lytton Strachey's mother.

Strachey, Lytton: Giles Lytton Strachey, 1880–1932, biographer, critic, son of General Sir Richard and Lady Jane Strachey, brother of Dorothy, Philippa, Oliver, Pernel, Marjorie, and James Strachey.

Strachey, Marjorie: nicknamed Jumbo, 1882–1964, teacher and writer, sister of Lytton Strachey.

Strachey, Oliver: 1874–1960, civil servant, brother of Lytton Strachey, husband of Ray Costelloe, father of Julia Strachey.

Strachey, Pernel: 1876–1951, Principal of Newnham College, Cambridge, sister of Lytton Strachey.

Strachey, Philippa: known as Pippa, 1872–1968, suffragist, sister of Lytton Strachey.

Strachey, Ray: *née* Rachel Costelloe, 1887–1940, author, feminist, wife of Oliver Strachey.

Strachey, General Sir Richard: 1817–1908, government official and geographer, husband of Jane Maria Grant, father of Lytton Strachey.

Swinnerton, Frank: 1884 – , critic.

Swithin: *see* Swithinbank, B.W.

Swithinbank, B.W.: 1884–1958, government official.

Sydney-Turner, Saxon: Saxon Arnoll Sydney-Turner, 1880–1962, treasury official.

Tavistock Square: Bloomsbury square in which the Woolfs' home was located, 1924–39.

Thoby: *see* Stephen, Thoby.

Tidmarsh: *see* Mill House.

Tilton: Keynes's Sussex country home near Charleston and Firle.

Tomlin, Stephen: known as Tommy, 1901–1937, sculptor, husband of Julia Strachey.

Tommy: *see* Tomlin Stephen.

Tonks, Professor Henry: 1862–1937, artist and teacher.

Trevelyan, George Macaulay: 1876–1962, historian, Master of Trinity

College, Cambridge, brother of R.C. Trevelyan.

Trevelyan, R.C.: 1872–1951, poet, brother of G.M. Trevelyan.

Turner, Saxon: *see* Sydney-Turner, Saxon.

Vanessa: *see* Bell, Vanessa.

Virginia: *see* Woolf, Virginia.

Waley, Arthur: 1889–1966, translator, poet, orientalist.

Waterlow, Sydney: 1878–1944, diplomat.

Weybridge: Surrey town where E.M. Forster lived.

Wissett Lodge: Suffolk farmhouse where David Garnett, Duncan Grant, Vanessa Bell and others lived in 1916.

Wittgenstein, Ludwig: 1889–1951, philosopher.

Woolf, Leonard: Leonard Sidney Woolf, 1880–1969, political theorist, critic, editor, publisher, author, husband of Virginia Stephen.

Woolf, Virginia: Adeline Virginia Woolf, *née* Stephen, nicknamed The Goat, 1882–1941, novelist, essayist, critic, daughter of Leslie and Julia Stephen, sister of Vanessa Bell and Adrian Stephen, wife of Leonard Woolf.

X Society: Cambridge undergraduate discussion society, *c*1900.

Yegen: Spanish town where Gerald Brenan lived.

Young, Hilton: Baron Kennet, 1879–1960, politician and writer.